ENFORCING CORPORATE SOCIAL RESPONSIBILITY CODES

Corporate social responsibility codes are guidelines that companies voluntarily develop and publish with the objective of showing the public their commitment to respect human rights, to improve fundamental workplace standards worldwide and to protect the natural environment. These corporate codes have become a crucial element in the regulatory architecture for globally operating companies. By focusing on the characteristics of the codes, their effects on society and their legal consequences, this book seeks to provide a comprehensive analysis of corporate codes and the law. *Enforcing Corporate Social Responsibility Codes* develops proposals on the relationship between global corporate self-regulation and the national private law systems. It uses methods of comparative law and sociological jurisprudence to argue that national private law can, and in fact should, enforce these codes as genuine legal obligations. The author formulates legal policy recommendations for English and German private law that indicate how the proposed legal enforcement could be realised in practice.

International Studies in the Theory of Private Law: Volume 12

International Studies in the Theory of Private Law

This series of books edited by a distinguished international team of legal scholars aims to investigate the normative and theoretical foundations of the law governing relations between citizens. The context for such investigations of private law systems is set by important modern tendencies in systems of governance. The advent of the regulatory state marks the withdrawal of the state from direct control and management of social and economic activity, and the adoption instead of procedural regulation and co-regulatory strategies that promote the use of private law techniques of ordering and self-regulation in social and economic interactions between citizens. The tendency known as globalisation and the corresponding increases in cross-border trade produce the responses of transnational regulation of commerce and private governance regimes, and these new systems of governance challenge the hegemony of traditional national private law systems. Furthermore, these tendencies towards transnational governance regimes compel an interaction between different national legal traditions, with their differences in culture and philosophy as well as their differences based upon variations in market systems, which provokes questions not only about competing policy frameworks but also about the nature and adequacy of different kinds of legal reasoning.

The series encompasses a diverse range of theoretical approaches in the examination of these issues including approaches using socio-legal methods, economics, critical theory, systems theory, regulation theory, and moral and political theory. With the aim of stimulating an international discussion of these issues, volumes will be published in Germany, France and the United Kingdom in one of the three languages.

Volumes published with Hart Publishing, Oxford
1. David Campbell, Hugh Collins und John Wightman (eds), *Implicit Dimensions of Contract: Discrete, Relational and Network Contracts* (2003)
2. Christian Joerges, Inger-Johanne Sand and Gunther Teubner (eds), *Transnational Governance and Constitutionalism* (2004)
3. Oren Perez, *Ecological Sensitivity and Global Legal Pluralism: Rethinking the Trade and Environment Debate* (2004)
4. Harm Schepel, *The Constitution of Private Governance* (2004)
5. Nili Cohen and Ewan McKendrick, *Comparative Remedies for Breach of Contract* (2005)
6. Marc Amstutz and Gunther Teubner (eds), *Networks: Legal Issues of Multilateral Co-operation* (2010)
7. Gunther Teubner (edited and with an Introduction by Hugh Collins), *Networks as Connected Contracts* (2010)

8. Christian Joerges and Josef Falke (eds), *Karl Polanyi, Globalisation and the Potential of Law in Transnational Markets* (2011)
9. Poul F Kjaer, Gunther Teubner and Alberto Febbrajo (eds), *The Financial Crisis in Constitutional Perspective: The Dark Side of Functional Differentiation* (2011)
10. Jean Braucher, John Kidwell and William C Whitford (eds), *Revisiting the Contracts Scholarship of Stewart Macaulay: On the Empirical and the Lyrical* (2013)
11. Thomas Dietz, *Global Order Beyond Law: How Information and Communication Technologies Facilitate Relational Contracting in International Trade* (2014)
12. Anna Beckers, *Enforcing Corporate Social Responsibility Codes: On Global Self-Regulation and National Private Law* (2015)

Volumes published in German by Nomos Verlagsgesellschaft, Baden-Baden
1. Peer Zumbansen, *Ordnungsmuster im modern Wohlfahrtsstaat: Lernerfahrungen zwischen Staat, Geseelschaft und Vertrag* (2000)
2. Dan Wielsch, *Freiheit und Funktion: Zur Struktur- und Theoriegeschichte des Rechts der Wirtschaftsgesellschaft* (2001)
3. Marc Amstutz, *Evolutorisches Wirtschaftsrecht: Vorstudien zum Recht und seiner Methode in den Diskurskollisionen der Marktgesellschaft* (2001)
4. Christian Joerges and Gunther Teubner, Gunther (eds), *Rechtsverfassungsrecht: Recht-Fertigungen zwischen Sozialtheorie und Privatrechtsdogmatik* (2003)
5. Gunther Teubner, *Netzwerk als Vertragsverbund: Virtuelle Unternehmen, Franchising, Just in Time in sozialwissenschaftlicher und juristischer Sicht (2004)*
6. Daniel Dédeyan, *Macht durch Zeichen: Rechtsprobleme der Kennzeichnung und Zertifikation* (2004)
7. Dietrich Claus Becker, *Von Namen und Nummern: Kollisionen unverträglicher Rechtsmassen im Interent* (2005)
8. Vagias Karavas, *Digitale Grundrechte: Elemente einer Verfassung des Informationsflusses im Intenet* (2007)
9. Peter Korth, *Dritthaftung von Ratingagenturen* (2009)
10. Cordula Heldt, *Baukooperation und Franchising als multilaterale Sonderverbindung. Vertragsnetzwerke - Parallelschuldverhältnisse - Personengesellschaften* (2010)
11. Jan Lüsing, *Die Pflichten aus culpa in contrahendo und positiver Vertragsverletzung (§ 241 II BGB): Über den hybriden Charakter der Schutzpflichten und zur Selbstbindung ohne Vertrag* (2010)
12. Moritz Renner, *Zwingendes transnationales Recht: Elemente einer Wirtschaftsverfassung jenseits des Staates* (2011)
13. Christoph Lüscher, *Zur Konzeptualisierung von Verbrauchervertragsrecht unter besonderer Berücksichtigung des schweizerischen und europäischen Verbrauchervertragsrechts. Eine Untersuchung im Schnittfeld von Vertragsrecht, Systemtheorie und Ökonomie* (2011)
14. Daniel Klösel, *Compliance-Richtlinien. Zum Funktionswandel des Zivilrechts im Gewährleistungsstaat* (2012)
15. Chunyi Qi, *Rechtstransfer in Chinas Produktionsregime? Zur Kontrolle der Allgemeinen Geschäftsbedingungen im deutschen und chinesischen Recht* (2013)

Enforcing Corporate Social Responsibility Codes

On Global Self-Regulation and National Private Law

Anna Beckers

·HART·
PUBLISHING
OXFORD AND PORTLAND, OREGON
2018

Hart Publishing
An imprint of Bloomsbury Publishing Plc

Hart Publishing Ltd
Kemp House
Chawley Park
Cumnor Hill
Oxford OX2 9PH
UK

Bloomsbury Publishing Plc
50 Bedford Square
London
WC1B 3DP
UK

www.hartpub.co.uk
www.bloomsbury.com

Published in North America (US and Canada) by
Hart Publishing
c/o International Specialized Book Services
920 NE 58th Avenue, Suite 300
Portland, OR 97213-3786
USA

www.isbs.com

HART PUBLISHING, the Hart/Stag logo, BLOOMSBURY and the Diana logo are trademarks of Bloomsbury Publishing Plc

First published in hardback, 2015
Paperback edition, 2018

British Library Cataloguing-in-Publication Data
A catalogue record for this book is available from the British Library.

ISBN: PB: 978-1-50992-007-5
HB: 978-1-84946-899-2

Typeset by Compuscript Ltd, Shannon

Preface

This book is a revised and updated version of my doctoral thesis which I defended at Maastricht University in 2014. Developments in legislation, case law and the relevant academic debates have been taken into consideration insofar as they took place before December 2014.

The ideas and arguments that are presented in this book grew with the help of many people who provided inspiration, critique and encouragement within the excellent academic environment that I found at Maastricht University, the European University Institute in Florence and Frankfurt University.

The most influential people were certainly Gunther Teubner and Nicole Kornet. They accompanied me throughout the entire process of writing the book and encouraged me on many occasions to continue with this impossible though necessary project of comparative sociological jurisprudence. Larry Catá Backer, Jan Eijsbouts, Christian Joerges, Hans Micklitz, Mieke Olaerts, Jan Smits and Bruno de Witte provided immensely helpful comments on the manuscript. I would also like to thank Damla Cavusoglu, Mark Dawson, Catalina Goanta, Malte Gruber, Mark Kawakami, Willem Loof, Elise Muir, Maddalena Neglia, Pierre Thielbörger and Sascha Ziemann for the many enlightening discussions that I had with them on the topic.

I would like to thank the editors of the series 'International Studies in the Theory of Private Law' for agreeing to the book appearing in the series and I owe the team at Hart Publishing a large debt of gratitude for working hard to prepare the book for publication.

On a more personal note, I would like to thank my family and my twin sisters of choice Julia and Maria von Oettingen for their support in the process of writing the book. The deepest gratitude is owed to Bert to whom this book is dedicated. His endless patience and encouragement have been much more important for the completion of this book than this dedication could ever express.

Contents

List of Abbreviations and Symbols

§	Paragraph (German symbol to indicate a section in an act)
§§	Paragraphen (sections)
AC	Appeal Cases Official Law Reports
AG	Amtsgericht
ALJR	Australian Law Journal Reports
All ER	All England Law Reports
AK-BGB	Alternativ-Kommentar zum Bürgerlichen Gesetzbuch
AktG	Aktiengesetz
ArbG	Arbeitsgericht
Art	Article
ASA	UK Advertising Standards Authority
ATS	Alien Tort Statute
BB	Betriebsberater
BCC	British Company Law Cases
BGB	Bürgerliches Gesetzbuch
BGH	Bundesgerichtshof
BGHZ	Entscheidungen des Bundesgerichtshofs in Zivilsachen, Amtliche Sammlung
BIT	Bilateral Investment Treaty
BKR	Zeitschrift für Bank- und Kapitalmarktrecht
BörsG	Börsengesetz
BSCI	Business Social Compliance Initiative
BT-Drucks.	Bundestagsdrucksachen
BVerfG	Bundesverfassungsgericht
BVerfGE	Entscheidungen des Bundesverfassungsgerichts, Amtliche Sammlung
BVerwG	Bundesverwaltungsgericht
CAP	UK Committee of Advertising Practice
CB (NS)	Common Bench Reports, New Series
Ch	Chancery Official Law Reports
ch	Chapter
CISG	Vienna Convention on the International Sale of Goods
CLC	Commercial Law Cases
CME	Coordinated market economy
CSR	Corporate social responsibility
DIN	Deutsches Institut für Normung
Dir	Directive
ECJ	European Court of Justice
ECR	European Court Reporter

EMLR	Entertainment and Media Law Reports
EuZW	Europäische Zeitschrift für Wirtschaftsrecht
EWCA Civ	England and Wales Court of Appeal Civil Division
f	Following (one more page)
ff	Following (two or more pages)
GRUR	Gewerblicher Rechtsschutz und Urheberrecht
HRC	United Nations Human Rights Council
HGB	Handelsgesetzbuch
ICANN	Internet Corporation for Assigned Names and Numbers
IGO	Intergovernmental Organisation
ILM	International Legal Materials
ILO	International Labour Organization
ISO	International Organization for Standardization
JZ	Juristenzeitung
KB	King's Bench Official Law Reports
LAG	Landesarbeitsgericht
LG	Landgericht
Lloyd's Rep	Lloyd's Law Reports
LME	Liberal Market Economy
LT	Law Times Report
MS	Manuscript
MüKo	Münchener Kommentar
NCP	National Contract Point
NGO	Non-governmental organisation
NJ	Nederlands Juristenblad
NJW	Neue Juristische Wochenschrift
NJW-RR	Neue Juristische Wochenschrift, Rechtssprechungsreport
NVwZ	Neue Zeitschrift für Verwaltungsrecht
NZA-RR	Neue Zeitschrift für Arbeitsrecht, Rechtssprechungsreport
OECD	Organisation for Economic Co-operation and Development
OLG	Oberlandesgericht
para	Paragraph
PIQR	Personal Injuries and Quantum Reports
PR	Public Relations
QB	Queen's Bench Official Law Reports
Reg	Regulation
RG	Reichsgericht
RGZ	Entscheidungen des Reichsgerichts in Zivilsachen, Amtliche Sammlung
s	Section
SGA	Sale of Goods Act
StGB	Strafgesetzbuch
S.Ct.	Supreme Court (US)
TLR	Times Law Reports
TNC	Transnational Corporation

UCPD	Unfair Commercial Practices Directive
UKHL	United Kingdom House of Lords, Official Law Reports
UKlG	Unterlassensklagegesetz
UN	United Nations
UNIDROIT	International Institute for the Unification of Private Law
UWG	Gesetz gegen den unlauteren Wettbewerb
VermAnlG	Vermögensanlagegesetz
Vol	Volume
WL	Westlaw Cases
WLR	Weekly Law Reports
WRC	Worker Rights Consortium
WRP	Wettbewerb in Recht und Praxis
WM	Wertpapiermitteilungen
WTO	World Trade Organization
ZIP	Zeitschrift für Wirtschaftsrecht

1

Introduction

1.1. FROM NEW YORK TO BANGLADESH: THE CHANGING SOCIETAL ROLE OF COMPANIES

THE SOCIAL ROLE of companies has changed profoundly over the past centuries. To illustrate this, let me contrast two events that proved to have a significant influence on the societal debate on the regulation of workplace standards.

In March 1911, a disastrous fire occurred in the Triangle Shirtwaist Factory in New York that caused the death of almost 150 garment workers. It became known as one of the deadliest industrial events in US history at that time.[1] The fire was caused not only by grave problems in the fire safety of the building, but also by the fact that easily inflammable material was stored at the premises. Another important reason for the high death rate was the bad working conditions in the garment factory, such as locked doors and stairwells that aimed to prevent workers, mostly migrant women working for low wages on a 72-hour week working schedule, from taking unauthorised breaks or leaving the building freely.[2] Jumping ahead in time to March 2013, the media across the world spread the news that an accident had occurred when a building in Savar, Bangladesh collapsed, causing the deaths of a still-unknown number of people who worked in the clothing factories that the building accommodated. The death toll eventually exceeded 1,100, with more than 2,500 people being injured. The catastrophe was equally described as 'Bangladesh's worst industrial disaster'.[3] Only a few days after the tragedy, one major cause of the collapse was identified in the substandard construction and safety of the building; a couple of days later, it was added that the high number of deaths was presumably also caused by inadequate working conditions, including the attitude of factory managers to pressure people to come to work in the building despite observed and reported cracks in the days before the collapse.[4]

Comparing these two events, it is not only the actual event and the scale of the catastrophe in its respective historical setting that is remarkably similar—the events also share as a common ground the following debate. After both catastrophes, a wider debate took place about what is colloquially described as 'sweatshops',

[1] Greenwald (2005) 127.

[2] Greenwald (2005) 129ff.

[3] See BBC News, 3 May 2013, www.bbc.co.uk/news/world-asia-22394094.

[4] The facts of this catastrophe have been reconstructed with the material available at the Business and Human Rights Resource Centre, available at: http://business-humanrights.org/Documents/Bangladeshbuildingcollapse.

where claims were made about the necessity of improving the building safety of garment factories. Yet, both tragedies also triggered a general debate on labour rights, covering issues of child labour as well as minimum wages, and helped the trade unions movement to become organised. Back in 1911, the fire resulted in a growing influence of the International Ladies' Garment Workers' Union, which in part pushed the development of safety laws, but the recent accident also triggered organised protests among factory workers who campaigned for fixed minimum wages and better working conditions in Bangladesh.

Based on this comparison, one could interpret both accidents simply as tragic events for countries while they climb the ladder of economic prosperity. The US climbed this ladder in the last century and it is now in developing countries that such events inevitably occur as part of their industrial development.[5] However, history does never repeat itself entirely. The many parallels of these two events notwithstanding, there is one crucial aspect in which the 1911 disaster differs from the recent tragedy in Savar: the societal discourse about the responsible actors and who is in charge to prevent future accidents differed for each tragedy. One of the main reactions to the factory fire in New York was that a state commission was set up and given the task of investigating the safety of buildings in other garment factories.[6] The reports of this commission, which indicated that a similar fire could as easily occur in other factories, eventually resulted in the adoption of different labour laws that dealt not only with fire safety requirements but also with other labour standards, such as maximum hours of work and the conditions under which children might be employed. As an observer put it, 'The real meaning of the fire rested … in the view of "innocent" victims needing a strong state to protect them' and had the result that 'the state remade itself … with the creation of new policies and laws'.[7] Hence, retrospectively, the fire can be read as a tipping point that eventually resulted in stricter statutory regulation of workplace standards and a stronger role of the state. The building collapse in Bangladesh, in contrast, also focused on a different actor. Although appeals were made to the government to improve domestic regulation concerning workplace standards and building safety, and the government equally set up a commission to further investigate the tragedy, claims were also made against private actors to take over responsibility for the building collapse and help to improve workplace standards.[8] The discussions on the disaster in particular addressed the role of large companies that sourced their garments from Bangladesh. In the immediate aftermath of the tragedy, consumers accused retailers of having tolerated these conditions[9] and non-governmental organisations (NGOs) demanded that large retailers take over responsibility and contribute to the long-term compensation

[5] See especially for this argument in the debate on sweatshops Norberg (2003) 192ff.

[6] Greenwald (2005) 154ff.

[7] ibid 153.

[8] See also on this perspective Nolan (2014) 11, text and note 20.

[9] Emily Jane Fox, 'Shoppers Lash Out at Stores over Bangladesh', CNN Money online, 2 May 2013, www.money.cnn.com/2013/05/01/news/companies/bangladesh-factory-shoppers/index.html.

of the victims and their families.[10] Interestingly, companies were not pressured into abandoning their production in this country; instead, they were called upon to take over responsibility proactively by helping to prevent such failures in the future.[11] It became one of the short-term successes that resulted from the tragedy that several, mainly European, clothing retailers and textile brands signed an agreement with international trade unions that contains concrete minimum fire and safety standards and a commitment by companies to continue sourcing from this country and, while doing so, to take an active organisational and financial role in improving working conditions in garment factories in Bangladesh.[12]

In short, while the 1911 fire can retrospectively be interpreted as an event that gave rise to a stronger role of the state in developing mandatory standards of social protection and in intensifying regulatory intervention, the building collapse in 2013 introduced companies as additional actors that should play an active role in the improvement of fundamental workplace standards. It is the current attempts of the companies to fulfil this role in the form of voluntary codes of conduct and the interaction of such codes with the legal system that will be the focus of this study.

1.2. CORPORATE SOCIAL RESPONSIBILITY AND THE LAW

The decision to focus on the voluntary initiatives of companies and their relevance in the law in the first place raises the question why such contributions have become so prominent. Why do these calls for companies to take a proactive role towards other members of society occur so frequently and why are they mentioned simultaneously with the obligation of states to enact mandatory laws? And why do the evolving voluntary corporate social responsibility initiatives also begin to interest legal researchers and practitioners? In the following, I seek to develop an answer to these questions by means of explaining the current emphasis on voluntary initiatives with the changes in the legal debate on the corporate social responsibilities.[13] In so doing, I seek to show that the shift from the state to corporations did not

[10] See, eg, the joint call for compensation from the Clean Clothes Campaign and the International Labour Rights Forum, 'Still Waiting: Six Months after History's Deadliest Apparel Industry Disaster, Workers Continue to Fight for Compensation', www.cleanclothes.org/resources/publications/still-waiting/view.

[11] See prominently Statement by the National Contact Points for the OECD Guidelines on Multinational Enterprises, Paris, 25 June 2013, www.mneguidelines.oecd.org/NCPStatementBangladesh-25June2013.pdf.

[12] Accord on Fire and Building Safety in Bangladesh, www.bangladeshaccord.org. In this context, it is important to also mention the Alliance for Bangladesh Worker Safety (www.bangladeshworker-safety.org), a rival plan of mainly US American retailers that was, however, criticised for being less strict than the Accord and for failing to sufficiently address the issue of financial assistance from the side of retailers for necessary improvements in the building safety that suppliers are expected to make. In addition, the catastrophe has resulted in efforts by the ILO to help improving the safety at garment factories through government funds and capacity-building. For a detailed overview of all these three initiatives, see also Nolan (2014) 11.

[13] Corporate *social* responsibilities are pursuant to the prevailing understanding in the corporate social responsibility literature substantively understood here as covering the Triple-P Bottom Line: People, Planet and Profit. See fundamentally on this distinction Elkington (1997).

appear out of nowhere. On the contrary, the current attention given to voluntary efforts follows a general change of the social role of companies that proved in the past to be mainly dealt with by the legal system in the form of mandatory laws, in particular corporate law (section 1.2.1). It is in this context particularly due to globalisation and the changing organisation of the corporate entity that the role of the state proves to become less strong and new regulatory initiatives come to the fore (section 1.2.2). This applies in particular to public and private codes of conduct that currently represent viable candidates to fill the regulatory gap (section 1.2.3).

1.2.1. The Past: Corporate Social Responsibility and Legal Obligations

Although the notion of corporate social responsibility is, particularly in economics and business ethics as well as in parts in the legal debate, deemed an entirely voluntary undertaking of companies beyond the law, this study perceives corporate social responsibility in line with the position of several legal and sociological scholars as consisting of legal and non-legal elements.[14] Pursuant to this understanding, the social responsibilities of companies are not understood as a purely ethical or philanthropic responsibility of companies beyond the law; corporate social responsibility can also take the form of genuine legal obligations. In fact, the legal system proved in the past to be a core instance that determined whether a broader social role for companies was obligatory or remained voluntary, and it did so by constituting and regulating the company as a legal actor with a separate legal personality.

This strong role of the law in shaping the corporate actor and its responsibilities can be traced back to the early understandings of corporate personality that deemed the corporate entity merely as a fiction that, in order to exist and have personality, was entirely dependent on the legal system.[15] It was then the strong role

[14] See, eg, McBarnet (2007), who describes CSR as 'beyond the law' as well as 'through the law', and Gunningham (2007), who defines corporate environmental responsibilities as the 'multi-faceted license to operate' consisting of economic, legal and social licenses. See also Kerr, Janda and Pitts (2009) 103, who hold that the debate on whether social responsibilities are mandatory or voluntary is 'futile' and suggest treating voluntary and mandatory elements as having a 'complementary role to play'; Eijsbouts (2011) 26ff; Mares (2010), who suggests an 'interactive regulatory perspective' on CSR. See also in this context the recent shift in the European Commission's definition of CSR from 'a concept whereby companies integrate social and environmental concerns in their business operations and in their interaction with their stakeholders on a voluntary basis' (Green Paper, Promoting a European Framework for Corporate Social Responsibility COM (2001) 366 final 6) to 'the responsibility of enterprises for their impacts on society' that consist of voluntary and regulatory elements (Communication, A Renewed EU Strategy 2011–14 for Corporate Social Responsibility, COM (2011) 681 final 6).

[15] The strong link between corporate personality and the law can be identified in the early decisions and debates on corporate legal personality. For the US, see *Trustees of Dartmouth College v Woodward* (1819) 17 US (4 Wheat) 518, at 636: 'a corporation is an artificial being, invisible, intangible and existing only in contemplation of law'; for England, see *Salomon v Salomon* [1897] AC 22, 51 (per Lord Macnaghten): 'the company is at law a different person altogether from the subscribers to the memorandum'. In the German debate, this understanding can be traced to fiction theory developed by Savigny (1840) vol II, at 277: ‚Der einzelne Mensch trägt seinen Anspruch auf Rechtsfähigkeit schon in seiner leiblichen Erscheinung in sich; … Wird nun die natürlich Rechtsfähigkeit des einzelnen Menschen durch Fiction auf ein ideales Subjekt übertragen, so fehlt jene natürliche Beglaubigung gänzlich; nur der Wille der höchsten Gewalt kann dieselbe ersetzen.'

of the legal system to create corporations that rendered the decision about its social obligations a matter of the law. The importance of the law to specify the social role of companies did not even diminish when the understanding of the corporate entity shifted towards an emphasis on the 'real' rather than the legal elements of the corporate entity. One could have predicted a move away from the legal components against the background of evolving approaches that emphasised the limits of the law in regulating corporations, such as Gierke's approach on the real personality of the collective that the law is not capable of regulating,[16] or the shift in the US from treating the company as a legally created entity towards viewing it as a 'natural entity' that consisted merely of an accumulation of capital.[17] If the law was able to create legal personality, but had a limited position in influencing the real elements of collective human organisation and the accumulation of capital that underlies classifying corporations as legal actors, it could have equally been a consequence that the law's influence on creating the corporate actor and its social role would also diminish. Yet the emphasis on the real elements of corporate personality turned out not to result in a diminishing role for the law; instead, a change in the legal focus occurred. The legal regulation of companies and their social role transformed from a question of the legal personality and the act of incorporation into how to regulate the underlying essence of companies, eg, the owners of the capital. It was now the discussion on the social obligations of economic capital, the underlying 'collective interest' of shareholders and, with the rise of large companies that were characterised by a separation of ownership and control,[18] the obligations of managers in their decision making where the legal debate on the social role of companies remained vital. These debates took different directions in the national political economies and resulted in what later became known as the ideal typical distinction between *shareholder* and *stakeholder* approaches within corporate law.

In the US context, which is taken here as the prime example for a shareholder-oriented corporate model, the debate on the social responsibilities was strongly influenced by the perception of companies as an accumulation of private property.[19] Being essentially private property, companies were considered to receive primarily constitutional protection and not to have obligations towards society. This understanding became particularly apparent in the prominent legal controversy between Berle and Dodd that dealt specifically with the obligations of managers and, more concretely, with whether managers were trustees of the owners only or also of other

16 Gierke (1887) 22: ‚Hat nun aber das Recht die Macht, die Eigenschaft der Rechtssubjektivität zu erzeugen, so ist es doch schlechthin nicht im Stande, die thatsächliche Unterlage dieser Eigenschaft zu erschaffen. Mag es in seinem Bereiche allmächtig sein: hier liegen die Grenzen seines Bereichs.'

17 See generally on this development Millon (1990) 211ff.

18 Berle and Means (1933) 47ff.

19 See fundamentally *The Railroad Tax Cases* 13 F 772 (CCD 1882) at 748: 'The courts will look through the ideal entity and name of the corporation to the person who compose it, and protect them, though the process be in its name … All the guarantees and safeguards of the constitution for the protection of property by individual may, therefore, be invoked for the protection of the property of corporations.' See also pointedly Millon (1990) 214: 'In other words, the fact that private individuals had chosen to do business as a corporation should not be a basis for subjecting their financial interests to regulation that otherwise would not apply.'

social groups.[20] Berle put forth the understanding of managers as trustees of the private capital of owners and saw the role of the law mainly in restricting the power of managers in order to protect the property of the owners. Dodd, in contrast, advocated that managers ought to be viewed as trustees of other social groups. Challenging the very understanding of the company as solely private property, he proposed an alternative legal approach that focuses on the corporate entity essentially as an institution with distinct social responsibilities.[21] In responding to Dodd, it was again Berle who emphasised that, although such a wider responsibility might be a desirable development, it would require a constitutional law reform that allowed restricting private property,[22] and it is this perspective on corporations upon which further developments in corporate law were built. Departing from the perspective of companies as private property, corporate theory culminated in the legal understanding of the company not as an entity in its own right, but rather as a nexus of contracts,[23] and the core social obligations of managers became translated into a contractual obligation to act profitably in the interest of the members. Or, to quote the famous claim of Milton Friedman that was made at that time, it became a prevailing understanding that 'the social responsibility of companies is to increase its profits'.[24] Thus, the specific legal understanding of the company as merely an accumulation of capital gave rise within corporate law to the understanding that a broader social role beyond the interest of capital must remain merely philanthropic and subordinated under the shareholder value.

Notwithstanding important socio-economic differences, a similar development towards a shareholder-oriented role of companies can be observed in the UK.[25] Also based on an understanding of the corporate entity as private capital, the focus in corporate law was equally set on the duties of managers to protect the property of the owners and maximise profits in their interest.[26] Although framed as a duty that is owed to the corporate entity, the traditional understanding was that 'the corporate entity is a vehicle for benefiting the interests of a specified group', namely the interests of shareholders.[27] In particular in the UK, one can, however, also identify a recent shift in corporate law away from strict shareholder primacy towards a stronger emphasis on the interests of other social groups.[28] It was here again the concept of the legal duties that managers owed to the corporation that became particularly important for this development, resulting most prominently

20 Berle (1931); Berle (1932); Dodd (1932).

21 Dodd (1932) 1160: 'But we are not bound to treat the corporation as a mere aggregate of stockholders.'

22 Berle (1932) 1371f.

23 For this theoretical approach, see Coase (1937); Jensen and Meckling (1976) 310f.

24 Milton Friedman, 'The Social Responsibility of Companies is to Increase its Profits', *New York Times Magazine*, 13 September 1970.

25 For an emphasis on the similarities between the US and the UK understanding of corporate law leading to their conceptualisation as the 'Anglo-American model ... that is distinguishable from models prevalent in Continental Europe', *cf* Campbell and Vick (2007) 241ff (quote at 242, note 5).

26 Parry (2005) 75.

27 Parkinson (1993) 76ff (quote at 77).

28 For this development with further references, see, eg, Campbell and Vick (2007) 249ff; Kerr, Janda and Pitts (2009) 130f.

in the 2006 reform of the Companies Act that made the interests of employees, business partners and the environment relevant factors that managers had to take into account.[29]

This specific perspective of conceptualising the social role of companies as voluntary and permissive with only recently introduced obligatory elements can be contrasted with developments in a different national context. As an indicative example, one can refer here to the development of corporate law in the Rhineland capitalism, where a different understanding of the social role of companies evolved. Within the national context of Germany, already at the beginning of the twentieth century, it became an important element in the debate that the rise of large companies would need to be accompanied by strong social obligations.[30] Thus, with the increasing power of large companies, the calls became stronger to assign companies a special role in society that encompassed not only rights, but also obligations. In addition, the development of corporate law was strongly influenced by a conceptually different understanding of the underlying 'essence' of the company. While it was clear that the company was ultimately based on shareholders and their capital investment, in the debate on the managerial duties, an important starting point represented the distinction between the financial interests of individual shareholders and the interests of the shareholders as a collective.[31] Based on the perception that these two interests could also collide, the debate became directed towards introducing legal regulation that ensured that the collective interest of all shareholders was appropriately protected. In the course of the debate, this focus on the collective interests of the shareholder transformed gradually into an understanding of the collective interest of the corporation, resulting in 1937 with the legal reform of the Corporate Stock Act. In the reformed Act, a provision was introduced that obliged corporate managers to act in the interests of the corporation. The period during which the legislative process took place already indicates that this particular provision was also influenced by the Nazi ideology and consequently contained connotations, such as *Volk* and *Reich*, that became later controversially debated. This influence had the result that the provision was removed from the Corporate Stock Act in 1965. Yet, notwithstanding the elimination of this codified provision, the underlying idea of a legal obligation for managers to act in the interests of the company and explicitly not only the interests of shareholders prevailed and continued to shape the debate in corporate law and corporate theory. It, in turn, gave rise to the prominent legal debate on

[29] UK Companies Act 2006, s 172. *cf* also on this aspect its predecessor, s 309 of the UK Companies Act 1985: 'The matter to which the directors of a company are to have regard in the performance of their functions include the interests of the company's employees in general, as well as the interests of its members.' For a slightly different and less strict development in the US towards recognising social interests as relevant for managerial decision making, one can in particular mention the development of Constituency Statutes that were enacted in several states. These statutes generally permit (not oblige) managers to take into consideration non-shareholder interests; see on this development more in detail Kerr, Janda and Pitts (2009) 138ff.

[30] See especially Rathenau (1922).

[31] The participants of this debate were Netter, Landsberger and Geisler. See generally on this debate Gelter (2011) 686ff, who also discusses the related developments in the case law.

the 'interest of the enterprise' that was deemed to be constituted by the different societal interests and explicitly not exclusively the interest of shareholders.[32] An influential participant of the debate put it as follows: 'If we remove the influence of national socialist ideology from this formula, we see in it nothing less than the separation of ownership and control and the public responsibility of the enterprise management vis-a-vis employees, state, and society.'[33] However, in the legal debate on the underlying 'corporate interest' and its influence on the legal regulation of the company, the target was not only the duties of managers; the debate on the company interest became a broader debate that also focused on the legally required structure of the company and the representation of interest groups. The most prominent and important development here certainly represents the debate on co-determination in companies and the Co-determination Act that gave the interest group of employees a strong role to control managers by constituting an obligation to have them represented on the supervisory board.[34] The embedding of employee interests in the company structure had the result that the company policy was not solely oriented on short-term profitability, but was also taking into consideration the objective of long-term prosperity with a view to the security of employment.[35] Interestingly, when deciding whether the Co-determination Act was a constitutional restriction of the private property of shareholders, the Constitutional Court once again emphasised the difference between private property and capital in shares. The latter was considered a specific form of indirectly awarded property that differs from ordinary private property and could be subject to higher restrictions.[36] Hence, based on an initial perspective between shareholder interest and the interest of the collective as fundamentally different, a legal approach evolved in this stakeholder-oriented corporate law that not only made it an obligation to conduct companies in the interest of shareholders, but also to consider the interests of society.[37] As a result, within this national corporate law development, companies were assigned a wider social role that differed from serving solely the interest of owners.

To conclude, when determining the social role of companies, in the past it was also the legal system, in particular the field of corporate law, that proved to be important. By means of specifying the duties of corporate managers and setting rules as to the legally required company structure, corporate law effectively decided to a large extent the social role that companies would have. In national socio-political contexts that derived from a shareholder-oriented understanding of the company, this legally codified social role was generally narrowly defined as a legal obligation to protect the capital interests of owners and, even in light of recent

[32] *cf* further on this debate with extensive references Raiser (1988) 122ff.
[33] Raiser (1988) 117.
[34] See instructively on this debate Wiethölter (1968) 263ff.
[35] Hoffmann (2004) 990.
[36] BVerfGE 50, 290, at 339ff.
[37] See pointedly Calliess and Zumbansen (2010) 189: 'The … "stakeholder"-oriented approach considers the actors in and around the firm and its business with regard to their vested interests in the firm. It sees the firm as *embedded* in a specific legal, economic and political culture, in which it occupies a place as a societal actor' (emphasis in original).

changes, to treat other social interests as merely subordinate to this shareholder value. Conversely, as could be observed on the basis of Germany, there are also different national evolutionary patterns in corporate law where a broader social role and respect for the interests of several societal groups evolved as a mandatory obligation.

1.2.2. Recent Transformations: Globalisation and the Rise of Transnational Corporations

The strong role played in the past by the legal system in defining the social role of companies is currently challenged by two important developments. First, the national corporate law models are confronted with the current transformation of society from territorial to global organisation. This challenges corporate law insofar as this area of law remains, in major parts, based on the ideal of a corporate entity that operates within a particular national territory. Second, the regulatory field of corporate law is currently also confronted with transformations of the corporate entity as the regulatory object. In particular, the character of large companies changed quite significantly from a hierarchical unit into a complex heterarchically structured fragmented structure with subsidiaries and networks of distributors and suppliers. It is in particular these two developments that brought to the fore different voluntary initiatives developed by actors other than states, which began to deal specifically with global standards of societally expected corporate conduct with regard to the specifics of such complex corporate structures.

To start with the first aspect, the regulation of companies by corporate law is quite significantly influenced by what is broadly framed as globalisation, ie, the general development in society that is characterised by an intensification and increasing relevance of cross-border social relations caused by, amongst others, the deregulation tendencies of politics, rapid technological developments, increase in cross-border migration, intensification of cross-border trade and foreign investment, and the emergence of genuine global risks.[38] In corporate law and theory, a controversial debate has already taken place as to whether the increasing cross-border transactions and investment, and thus the freedom of companies to choose their preferred legal system, would eventually put sufficiently strong pressure on stakeholder-oriented legal systems to make them converge with the more liberal and less regulatory shareholder model.[39] Yet even if one considers the prediction

[38] Scherer and Palazzo (2008) 415ff.

[39] This is of course a matter of controversy. A further development in corporate law towards the shareholder model due to regulatory competition is in the legal debate advocated by, eg, Hansmann and Kraakman (2001). A sceptical position on the survival of the Rhineland capitalism and its corporatist company structure under globalisation is also partly taken in the sociological debate, without, however, equalising this with a necessary adaption to the shareholder model; *cf* prominently Streeck (2009) 260ff. For observations towards hybridisation of corporate governance rules, eg, a transformation with remaining influence of national socio-economic institutions, but significant influence of global elements, see from the perspective of sociology Höpner (2003); Hoffmann (2004) 999ff and from the perspective of law Calliess and Zumbansen (2010) 194ff. For a more critical perspective on the adaption of the corporatist stakeholder model to the shareholder model, see, eg, Abelshauser (2003) 188ff.

of convergence to be not very likely, globalisation has nonetheless affected the regulation of companies quite profoundly. Due to globalisation, a comprehensive additional regulatory layer is required. Under the new premise of globally operating companies, the social role of companies would not only need to be specified for the national operations, and thus by national corporate laws, but also for global operations, in particular cross-border trade and foreign investment. However, the cumbersome law-making processes on an international level, the current lack of political feasibility of creating binding obligations for companies by an international treaty and the many practical and legal obstacles to enforcing any envisaged international obligations have effectively resulted in a situation in which the global operations of companies remain to a large extent unregulated today. According to the orthodox and so far still-prevailing understanding, international law does not lay down general obligations of companies towards society. In fact, today it still remains a fundamental principle in international law that it is states and individuals but not companies that are the subjects of international law.[40] The few international legally binding documents that provide for a specific legal position of companies equip them, leaving aside the few exceptions in the field of environmental protection,[41] primarily with rights, but they do not impose obligations on them. The prime examples in this context are the rights in bilateral investment treaties to fair, equal and most-favoured-nation treatment.[42] The United Nations Draft Norms on the Responsibilities of Transnational Corporations can be mentioned here as the most prominent attempt to change this situation. In the form of obliging 'transnational corporations and other business enterprises, as organs of society' to protect human rights,[43] the Norms pursued the ambitious project to assign to companies on an international level a position almost akin to states and to oblige them to protect human rights. The result of this attempt is very well known: the strong resistance of influential states and the business community, but also problems related to the legal concepts used in the Norms, in particular the notion of the spheres of influence and the open questions about an effective enforcement of the norms, led this effort eventually to fail. The Norms were never adopted. Instead, what remained from this attempt, at least in the first place, was a tense atmosphere in the United Nations among the actors involved that rendered comparable regulatory efforts a utopian vision rather than a practically viable option

Evidence in support of the survival and success of, in particular, the German model in light of the recent global economic crisis can also be found at, eg, Dustmann et al (2014).

40 Brownlie (2008) 66ff.

41 In the field of environmental protection, some noteworthy conventions exist on civil (including corporate) liability for environmental pollution, such as the civil liability conventions concerning nuclear energy (1960, the so-called Paris Convention), oil pollution (the 1969 International Convention) and transboundary movements of hazardous substances (1989, the so-called Basel Convention); see generally on these conventions and their narrowly confined role in establishing international corporate environmental obligations Zerk (2006) 284ff; Ratner (2008).

42 See generally on BITs and the rights of investors Muchlinski (2007b) 682ff.

43 UN Economic and Social Council, Sub-Committee on the Promotion and Protection of Human Rights, Economic, Social and Cultural Rights: Draft Norms on the Responsibilities of Transnational Corporations and Other Business Enterprises with regard to Human Rights, UN Doc E/CN.4/Sub.2/2003/12, quote taken from the preamble.

for the years to come.[44] Instead, the lacking political feasibility of developing a regulatory framework for cross-border activities resulted in a focus on alternative, more informal forms of regulation and it is here that codes of conduct, both from the public and the private side, evolved as important elements that specified the social role of globally operating companies.

In addition to the difficulty of setting up a regulatory framework for globally operating companies, the national legal frameworks that regulated companies were also challenged by the transformation of the company as the regulatory object. Naturally, a legal system that lays down legal obligations for the corporate entity reaches its limits when having to deal with the increasing complex organisation of companies, in particular the rise of transnational corporations. So far, no clear-cut definition exists of what would qualify as a transnational corporation, but it seems at least to be a common thread in the debate that these entities are understood as broader than their legal personality under corporate law. From the different definitions of transnational corporations,[45] one can identify at least two essential components that characterise these organisations. Next to their operation in more than one country, these entities are understood as having a specific organisational structure. Transnational corporations normally consist of several units with separate legal personality within different jurisdictions, where one entity in the group can exercise economic, managerial, factual or other influence over the other; however, there is still a remaining autonomy of each of the entities in the group.[46] Under the umbrella of this broad definition fall a variety of different forms of corporate structures, such as companies that invest directly in foreign countries by means of establishing subsidiaries that are separately incorporated and the company holds the majority or even 100 per cent of the shares in the subsidiary. Furthermore, it is equally possible that no such strong direct shareholder influence is present, but a dominant position of one company can be identified on the managerial level or where the financial means are to a major extent provided by the parent making the subsidiary economically dependent from the parent.[47] Yet, even where the parent company exercises influence in one way or another, the degree of influence can

[44] Instructively on the discussion surrounding the Norms and the fundamental conflicts between the business community and NGOs, see Ruggie (2013) 37ff. See also Kinley, Nolan and Zerial (2007).

[45] A detailed analysis and evaluation of the various attempts on the international level to give the transnational corporation a legal meaning has been conducted by Nowrot (2006) 52ff.

[46] See especially the definition in the 2011 OECD Guidelines for Multinational Enterprises, I, para 4: 'They usually comprise companies or other entities established in more than one country and *so linked that they may co-ordinate their operations* in various ways. While one or more of these entities may be able to exercise a *significant influence* over the activities of others, *their degree of autonomy within the enterprise may vary widely* from one multinational enterprise to another.' See also the definition in the 1990 UN Draft Code of Conduct on Transnational Corporations, No 1(a): 'enterprises ... which operate under a system of decision-making, *permitting coherent policies and a common strategy through one or more decision-making centres*, in which the entities are *so linked, by ownership or otherwise, that one or more of them may be able to exercise a significant influence over the activities of others* and, in particular, to share knowledge, resources and responsibilities with the others' (emphases added).

[47] See extensively on these different forms Muchlinski (2007b) 56ff, who also emphasises the differences between corporate groups from different countries. Interestingly, he demonstrates how, for instance, US companies seem to favour control in the form of a shareholder position, whereas this formal voting power is less important in Japanese companies where influence is created by strong managerial coordination of different entities.

also differ depending on the particular area in which the managerial decisions are taken. While there are aspects that are directly decided at the top-management level of the parent and are literally imposed on the subsidiary, there are equally areas in which the latter is given a high degree of autonomy. However, it is these flexible corporate group structures that directly challenge corporate law. This new form of corporate organisation requires expanding the regulatory scope of corporate law from the singular legally incorporated entity to the complex corporate group structure, with elements of hierarchical organisation as well as a remaining degree of autonomy. Certainly, the legal system has already developed some strategies to extend the regulatory focus of corporate law to corporate groups. Here one can mention the evolution of specific corporate group laws and the developments in several legal fields towards lifting the corporate veil and holding one entity within a corporate group liable for the behaviour of another entity.[48] Yet, in spite of these different efforts, the responsibilities of corporate groups, in particular the parent companies, towards outsiders are so far mainly accepted when the corporate group relation is characterised by a strong degree of control of one entity over the other.[49] With respect to more flexible forms, the fundamental legal principle of separate legal personality still prevails and thus prevents more flexible legal rules on legal responsibility towards outsiders of the different entities within corporate groups.

An additional development that currently challenges the legal system represents the increasing reliance of companies on the contract rather than incorporation as the organising paradigm. Increasingly, companies not only operate in different countries in the form of subsidiaries, but they are also beginning to outsource production to independent trading partners and, on the distribution side, to contract with retailers or independent distributors when seeking to place their products on foreign markets. In economics and sociology, these new forms of contracting on the supply and distribution side have already received some attention as new forms of network organisations.[50] Pursuant to this understanding, the network describes a social relation that is organised as a contract, but where

[48] In this context, one may first and foremost refer to the corporate law doctrine of 'piercing the corporate veil' that under exceptional circumstances recognises shareholder liability. In relation to parent–subsidiary constellations, this aims at holding the parent company liable for the wrongdoing of its subsidiary in its capacity as a shareholder. See on this concept of liability with a view to different legal systems Joseph (2004) 128ff; Glinski (2011) 310ff; Enneking (2012) 182ff. A development towards parent company liability in its capacity as a shareholder can also be identified in other areas, such as European anti-trust law, where a rebuttable presumption exists for liability of the parent companies for competition law infringements of the subsidiary in case of a 100 per cent shareholder position: European Court of Justice C-97/08 P *Akzo Nobel NV and others v Commission* [2009] ECR I-8237; and Case C-90/09 *General Quimica v Commission* [2011] ECR I-0000. See for this form of liability Cauffman and Olaerts (2011). An evolving model towards liability in corporate groups based on control is also discussed in tort law; for the different approaches, see, eg, Zerk (2006) 215ff; Enneking (2012) 176ff. Since this form of liability can also be influenced by corporate codes of conduct, aspects of this liability form will be discussed more in detail in section 4.1.2.2. (p 167) in text and accompanying footnotes. Finally, there are other theories of parent company liability that are discussed on occasion, in particular liability based on agency, vicarious liability or even a new concept of enterprise liability; see, eg, on these forms of liability Joseph (2004) 132ff; Zerk (2006) 223ff, 228ff.

[49] Zerk (2006) 235; Enneking (2012) 175.

[50] *Cf*, fundamentally, Williamson (1985) for economics and Powell (1990) for sociology.

elements, such as mutual cooperation, exchange of technological expertise or tailored manufacturing processes between the trading partners, render the contract different from the orthodox contractual relation based on arm's-length negotiation. It is only recently that these new forms of contractual networks have also received attention in the legal debate.[51] However, the current legal debate seems so far to be primarily concerned with the internal structure of these networks and the rights and obligations of different members of the network. Conversely, so far, less attention has been paid to the obligations of these new network relations towards third parties and their external liability.[52] One of the core hindrances for developing a regulatory framework that also deals with the social responsibilities of these networks relates to the fact that these evolving forms of economic organisation do not fall within the ambit of corporate law and the mandatory obligations specified therein. These contractual networks rely on the contract as their organising paradigm, which, as a result, means that constituting principles in contract law rather than corporate law become applicable. The privity of contracts prevents parties external to the network from holding liable members other than those that they have contractual affiliations with and, conversely, the general autonomy of the parties to a contract prevents the establishment of a general responsibility of the lead firm for the socially irresponsible behaviour in the network. It is again specifically this responsibility of contractual networks that public as well as private codes of conduct address and where they can consequently be of value.

To conclude, the identified national mandatory regulation of the corporate responsibilities towards society currently leaves specific gaps, particularly with regard to the obligations of companies towards society in the specific constellations of foreign investment and cross-border trade, and insofar as responsibilities of companies for their subsidiaries and business partners are concerned.

1.2.3. Evolving Global Regulation: Public and Private Codes of Conduct

For these constellations, voluntary public and private codes represent important instances that seek to fill the regulatory gap. These codes of conduct specify responsibilities of companies towards society, with a particular focus on the worldwide operation of companies and, in so doing, also address the responsibilities of entities in corporate groups and in distribution or supplier networks. When looking in more detail on the contribution of these codes of conduct, a first distinction needs to be made between the two different types of codes. There are, on the one hand,

[51] However, see with differences as to the proposed legal consequences for networks Grundmann (2007); Amstutz and Teubner (2008); Cafaggi (2008); Teubner and Collins (2011).

[52] So far, the main attempts to conceptualise a 'social responsibility' of contractual networks are made by Collins (1990); and Teubner and Collins (2011) ch 6, 235ff. *cf* also the analysis of Cafaggi, who observes a tendency in national law towards using non-contractual liability to deal with the negative external effects of bilateral contracts: Cafaggi (2008) 40ff. A first very recent attempt to conceptualise network liability for the case of human rights violations by transnational supply chains has been made by Osieka (2014) (with a view to the specifics of German law).

the codes of conduct that have been developed in international organisations as recommendations and guidelines of the international community for transnational corporations. On the other hand, companies and other private actors, such as business organisations and civil society actors, increasingly develop their own benchmark standards for decent and socially responsible business conduct. Both types of codes have also become important in legal scholarship where debates prominently surround their respective potential to become genuine legal obligations.

1.2.3.1. Public Codes of Conduct

1.2.3.1.1. Introducing Core Public Codes of Conduct

An important element in the current debate concerns the initiatives of international political institutions that, rather than regulating companies by developing international legally binding norms, have begun to develop recommendations that specify guidelines on socially responsible corporate conduct. The most prominent initiatives are, in this regard, the recently developed UN Guiding Principles on Business and Human Rights, the Organisation for Economic Co-operation and Development (OECD) Guidelines for Multinational Enterprises and the different declarations of the International Labour Organization (ILO), all of which will be introduced briefly.

The UN Guiding Principles on Business and Human Rights occupy, in this enumeration, the most prominent position. It is certainly not an exaggeration to declare them so far to be the most important document of the UN that deals with the relations between companies and human rights. The Guiding Principles are the result of a long-standing process at the UN that began after the failure of the UN Draft Norms with the appointment of John Ruggie as Special Representative for Business and Human Rights. After a phase of consultations and research, Ruggie developed and presented to the Human Rights Council the 'Protect, Respect, and Remedy' framework.[53] Described as a result of what Ruggie himself declared 'principled pragmatism', the framework was envisaged as an attempt to re-state the status quo on an international level concerning the human rights responsibilities of corporations that were presented as resting on three well-known core elements: the international hard law duty of states to protect human rights; the corporate responsibility to respect human rights understood as a social expectation towards companies to avoid infringing upon the rights of others and to address adverse impacts of their own activities and the activities that are linked to them through business relationships; and, finally, the necessity of greater access to effective judicial and non-judicial remedies for victims of human rights abuses. The three pillars of this framework provided the basis for further corporate-related human rights discourse in the UN, which was eventually operationalised in the form of the UN

[53] Human Rights Council, Eighth Session: Protect, Respect and Remedy: A Framework for Business and Human Rights, Report of the Special Representative of the Secretary-General on the issue of human rights and transnational corporations and other businesses, John Ruggie, A/HRC/8/5, 7 April 2008.

Guiding Principles that the UN Human Rights Council unanimously endorsed in 2011. In the UN Guiding Principles, a direct responsibility of companies to respect human rights is laid down in the form of a 'global standard of expected conduct to all businesses wherever they operate'.[54] The International Bill of Human Rights and the ILO's Declaration on Fundamental Principles and Rights at Work are mentioned as the baseline of internationally recognised human rights that companies have to respect.[55] Hence, the UN Guiding Principles re-state that the absence of an internationally mandatory framework concerning human rights obligations for companies cannot have the result that no responsibilities of corporations exist whatsoever. On the contrary, what remains is a global social expectation towards companies to respect fundamental human rights that are independent of the country in which they operate and whether the respective state fulfils its obligation to protect human rights. In addition, the Guiding Principles also contain rules that specify what this social expectation entails. Companies are expected to avoid causing and contributing to adverse human rights impacts, but they are also expected to mitigate such impacts if the impact is directly linked to their operations, products and services in the form of a business relationship.[56] Thus, the Principles not only specify a global standard concerning the human rights responsibilities of companies, they also set out rules on the responsibilities of large and complex multinational companies, including the responsibility for the human rights impact of business partners.[57] In order to fulfil the responsibility to respect human rights, the UN Guiding Principles concretely require companies to have in place a policy commitment on human rights compliance, carry out a process to assess their adverse impacts, integrate these findings in their business operations, communicate the findings and provide effective grievance mechanisms for victims.[58] Thus, the UN Guiding Principles have at least provided a first step towards filling the regulatory gap for globally operating multinational corporations by means of specifying concrete expectations as to the human rights responsibilities of companies on a global level, with a view not only to the responsibility of the corporate entity but also the responsibilities within corporate groups should they cause or contribute to adverse impacts or even should they solely be linked to it in the form of a business relationship.

The second important public code of conduct is the OECD Guidelines, which, in contrast to the UN Guiding Principles, have a significantly longer history and a broader scope. These guidelines not only deal with the human rights responsibilities of companies, but also address several issues that are relevant aspects for socially responsible corporate conduct. In fact, the Guidelines represent the

[54] UN Guiding Principles on Business and Human Rights, Principle 11, Commentary: 'The responsibility to respect human rights is a global standard of expected conduct for all business. It exists independently of States' abilities and/or willingness to fulfil their own human rights obligations, and does not diminish those obligations. And it exists over and above compliance with national laws and regulations protecting human rights.'

[55] UN Guiding Principles on Business and Human Rights, Principle 12.

[56] ibid, Principle 13.

[57] See especially Ruggie (2014) 13f.

[58] This is the so-called due diligence process that is laid down in Principles 16–22.

most comprehensive attempt so far to codify the global responsibilities of companies towards society and, following the latest update in 2011 that incorporated the standards laid down in the UN Guiding Principles, comprise standards on transparency, human rights, employment and industrial relations, the environment, combating bribery, consumer interests, science and technology, competition and taxation.[59] When it comes to the addressees of the standards, it should be emphasised that the Guidelines not only deal with the role of companies in their cross-border relations, but that they also place particular emphasis on the responsibility of the above-described complex forms of corporate organisation. In so doing, they determine the responsibility to safeguard adherence to the Guidelines within corporate groups by deeming each and every entity in the group responsible for adherence of the standards and, on top of that, require the entities in a group to 'co-operate and to assist one another to facilitate observance of the guidelines'.[60] Moreover, the Guidelines also pay attention to the responsibility of companies for their supply chain by means of expecting companies to mitigate the adverse impacts on the matters covered by the Guidelines 'where they have not contributed to this impact, when this impact is nevertheless directly linked to their operations, products or services by a business relationship'.[61] The Guidelines have been explicitly adopted as 'recommendations jointly addressed by governments to multinational enterprises'[62] that consist of principles and standards of good business practice.

Finally, in an enumeration of the most important public initiatives on corporate social responsibility, one also needs to mention the declarations of the ILO that, in addition to being integrated into other frameworks, also have to be read as a separate and self-standing framework that provides recommendations to companies. Although the ILO conventions primarily address the ratifying Member States by obliging their governments to transpose the conventions into national law, they also have a role to play as guidelines that are addressed to companies. This already became visible in the Tripartite Declaration of Principles on Multinationals and Social Policy that was adopted in 1976 in the form of a codified consensus among the different representatives in the ILO that was also directed towards companies. The Tripartite Declaration emphasised that companies should pursue social policies that promote adherence to national law and a variety of ILO conventions in their global operations.[63] The idea of deeming the existing ILO conventions the core international guidance for companies in relation to social policy continued in the 1998 Declaration on Fundamental Principles and Rights at Work, which

59 OECD Guidelines for Multinational Enterprises 2011, chs III–XI.

60 ibid, ch II, Part A, No 4.

61 ibid, ch II, Part A, No 12. In fact, the exact phrasing of this recommendation is equally a result of the incorporation of the UN Guiding Principles. One can in this context also refer to other elements of supply-chain responsibility in the Guidelines, in particular ch II, Part A, No 13 (encourage business partners to apply principles of responsible business conduct) and ch II, Part B, No 2 (engage in or support initiatives on responsible supply-chain management) and following the incorporation of the UN Guiding Principles, ch IV, No 3 (mitigate adverse human rights impacts of business partners).

62 ibid, ch I, No 1.

63 17 ILM 422 (1978), adopted 16 November 1977.

contained as a minimum standard the 'core' principles on employment relations. The principles laid down in the Declaration were promoted as expressing the universal global consensus on fundamental and globally accepted labour standards, which amounted specifically to the freedom from forced labour, the prohibition of child labour, the right to non-discrimination in employment, and the freedom of association and collective bargaining.[64] Although the strategy of promoting specific labour rights as general principles rather than legal rights was a matter of controversy,[65] the approach to promote the ILO conventions as a global consensus that also aims to provide authoritative guidance for companies prevailed. The declaration of the ILO to treat particular labour rights as the core of what is expected from companies in their global operation remains one of the most important documents that specify minimum expectations towards globally operating companies with a particular emphasis on workplace standards. Yet, in contrast to the UN Guiding Principles and the OECD Guidelines, it has to be clear that these ILO instruments primarily fulfil the role of constituting substantive standards for multinational corporations, but do not provide specific guidance on the responsibilities of members within corporate groups or concerning suppliers.

In order to complete this overview on public codes of conduct, it is necessary to at least mention the UN Global Compact, which is a forum initiated by the UN in which companies can participate by signing up and committing themselves to adhere to the 10 principles on human rights protection, fundamental workplace standards, environmental protection and anti-bribery.[66]

It is these frameworks that the European Commission describes in its recent strategy on corporate social responsibility as the core of internationally recognised principles and guidelines that specify rules on the responsibilities of companies towards society.[67]

1.2.3.1.2. A Transformation into Hard Law?

The interest of legal scholars in public codes of conduct currently surrounds, in particular, the question whether these guidelines are capable of truly filling the regulatory void on a global level by means of serving as new forms of legal obligations for globally operating corporations. While it seems to be quite uncontroversial to describe these codes of conduct as a form of international 'soft law',[68]

64 ILO Declaration on Fundamental Principles and Rights at Work, 37 ILM 1233 (1998), 86th Session, Geneva, June 1998.

65 *cf* in particular the debate between Alston (2004), Langille (2004) and Alston (2005).

66 www.unglobalcompact.org. See generally on the functioning of this particular framework the concise overview of Murphy (2005) 411ff.

67 European Commission, A Renewed EU Strategy 2011–14 for Corporate Social Responsibility COM (2011) 681 final, at 6, where, in addition to the aforementioned frameworks, the ISO 26000 Standard on Social Responsibility is mentioned.

68 The term 'soft law' is used here in a colloquially rather than a strictly legal or technical sense. It is of course recognised that the question whether all of the presented public codes would qualify as soft law remains a matter of controversy and depends highly on what concept of law one follows. The use of the term 'soft law' here should not be understood as taking a clear position in the debate that is characterised by so manifold qualifications. In particular, for the UN Guiding Principles, a variety of descriptions are offered, ranging from the endorsed Principles as already an 'authoritative instrument

their potential to be transformed into hard law obligations for companies is still a matter of controversy. In this context, one can identify two main directions in the legal debate concerning the potential of the codes.

In this context, it is necessary first to mention the debates that discuss the potential of public codes to partake in the development of a self-standing system of global law that is furthered by an autonomous application and interpretation of the standards in the autonomous conflict-solving instances that are part of these codes. From this perspective, the transformation of the public codes into hard law is viewed as conceptually similar to the understanding of *lex mercatoria*, *lex digitalis* or *lex sportiva* as a global law. Specific attention in this respect is given to the procedure that is in place to solve conflicts under the OECD Guidelines, eg, the National Contact Points (NCP) that governments have to set up in order to further the effectiveness of the Guidelines and to provide a form in which to resolve disputes between different actors about whether companies have in fact adhered to the guidelines.[69] With a view to this dispute-solving role of the so-called specific instance procedure, it is argued that, with the increase of cases brought before the NCPs, the likelihood increases that these procedures also gradually transform into quasi-judicial procedures that assist in transforming the Guidelines into an autonomous system of customary international law.[70] It should be noted that even proponents of this approach admit that this process, in the current form of the NCPs, is still far from a fully juridified system on international legal responsibilities.[71] Yet, this perspective on the public codes as an autonomous legal system can nonetheless be read as signposting the potential future direction of these public codes where 'under the guise of soft law, the OECD may be able to construct a system of customary law and practice as binding as any hard law system'.[72]

A different approach towards a transformation of these public codes of conduct into binding hard law is to focus on the potential reference of these public codes by national courts and their potential recognition as legally relevant standards.[73] In this regard, general tort law is viewed as a promising angle for this undertaking, but the discussions also surround the area of law relating to unfair commercial practices. Of particular importance in this discussion is the Alien Tort Statute,

of soft law' (Nolan (2013) 158), as a 'non-legal universal baseline expectation' that 'has become soft law' by means of its adoption by the OECD (Eijsbouts (2011) 46) or even as 'law in force but without legal sanctions' (Teubner (2011) 34).

[69] OECD Guidelines for Multinational Enterprises 2011, Part B, Procedural Guidance.

[70] Backer (2009); Calliess and Renner (2009) 274f; Eijsbouts (2011) 46.

[71] Backer (2009) 305; Calliess and Renner (2009) 275, who contrast this nascent form of juridification with the more advanced systems of the Internet Corporation for Assigned Names and Numbers (ICANN) and commercial arbitration.

[72] Backer (2009) 284.

[73] See (with conceptual differences as to the potential angles in national and international hard law) Genugten and Bijsterveld (1998) 170ff; Kocher (2005); Muchlinski (2007a) (pointedly at 433: 'emerging consensus on the social obligations of companies'); Jäger and Heijden (2008) 857ff; Calliess and Renner (2009) 274; Eijsbouts (2011) 19; Spießhofer (2014). *cf* also the extensive references provided by Backer (2009) 259f, notes 5, 6.

a unique provision in the US that provides jurisdiction for foreigners to remedy the violations of a small set of customary international laws.[74] This provision also proved important in relation to corporate liability and the potential use of public codes in this respect.[75] Such transformations of public codes of conduct into binding obligations are certainly considered a conceivable option; yet, based on the current developments, this option currently seems rather limited. In particular, it must be taken into consideration that the proposal that public codes of conduct can be transformed into hard law when judges use open-ended concepts departs from a particular understanding on how courts can interpret such open-ended norms. In this context, one must also take into consideration the fact that there are equally restrictions for courts on how to use international documents in order to interpret open norms.[76] In relation to the public codes, two core arguments in fact suggest that a more reluctant attitude on the side of the courts is likely to be taken. First, in the course of discussing the character of public codes of conduct, it still needs to be taken into consideration that they have explicitly been adopted as guidelines and recommendations, and not as documents that should be read as binding treaties or resolutions. To use an explicitly non-binding document in the court to justify a legal obligation seems against this background to be, at the very least, difficult to justify. Second, it must still be taken into consideration that corporations are not subjects of international law and thus it is difficult to hold them liable for violations of customary international law in general.[77] The prediction that the transformation of public codes of conduct into hard law with the help of domestic courts remains a cumbersome process is particularly evidenced in the recent development in relation to the Alien Tort Statute. In issuing the judgment in *Kiobel v Shell*, the US Supreme Court delivered a long-expected decision on the future possibility of corporate liability concerning violations of international law under US law and, in doing so, narrowed down the scope of potential corporate

[74] 28 United States Code, § 1350. For the evolution of the Alien Tort Statute as a provision that provides jurisdiction to remedy violations of a small set of customary international laws (including violations committed by private actors), see *Filartiga v Penala-Irala* 630 F 2d 876 (2d Cir 1980); *Kardic v Karadzic* 70 F 3rd 232 (2nd Cir 1995); *Sosa v Alvarez-Machain* 124 S Ct 2739 (2004).

[75] See, eg, Revak (2012) 1665f, who discusses the potential use of the ILO conventions in the context of the Alien Tort Statute.

[76] See for this argument Klösel (2012) 33f. For sceptical positions on the transformation of particularly ILO core labour conventions into hard law in German case law, see especially BGH NJW 1980, 2018 (in relation to unfair commercial practices law, further discussed in section 5.3.2.2. (p 202) in text and accompanying footnotes), and recently BVerwG NVwZ 2014, 527 (in relation to municipal law). An instructive and prominent case, however, where a court referred to the OECD Guidelines is the Dutch *Batco* case (NJ 1978, 220). Yet it should also be mentioned that, in this case, it was also not the OECD Guidelines per se that were treated as binding, but 'the fact that Batco Industries had accepted the OECD Guidelines as guidelines for its policy' by including a commitment on compliance with the OECD Guidelines in its annual report (see Genugten and Bijsterveld (1998) 173f, quote at 174). Thus, the decision could arguably equally be read as rendering the OECD Guidelines binding on the ground of commitment and reliance rather than on direct reference to the OECD Guidelines as hard law obligations.

[77] *cf* for these two aspects Baade (1980) 7ff, 12.

liability under the Alien Tort Statute quite significantly.[78] The rather reluctant position as to a court-initiated transformation of public codes of conduct into hard law certainly does not mean that this possibility is generally rejected. Yet, it is nevertheless predicted that this potential transformation of the above-mentioned public codes into binding hard law needs to be understood as a cumbersome and long process, which is probably also one of the reasons why the approach to developing international guidelines instead of hard law still receives criticism.[79]

The direct transformation of the public codes into domestic hard law with the help of national courts is accordingly deemed to be a highly uncertain option, the success of which can only be assessed in the future. Equally, the transformation of these public codes of conduct into or their replacement by international hard law obligations for corporations must at this stage be viewed as a long-term process with an open end.[80] However, these guidelines and recommendations still remain in their current form a valuable instance to trigger other processes through which the legal system might eventually come into play. Next to the possible integration of these codes within national legislation and policies,[81] their current potential lies particularly in their effect on private actors.[82] In fact, these public codes prove to

[78] 133 S Ct 1659 (2013). See also *Balintulo v Daimler AG*, No 09-2778-cv(L), 2013 WL 4437057 (2nd Cir, 21 August 2013). It has to be emphasised of course that the claim was not dismissed on the ground that corporations do not have obligations under international law, but mainly by declaring that the general presumption against extraterritorial application of US law also applies to the Alien Tort Statute. Thus, the recent development mainly imposes a hindrance on bringing to court violations of customary international law that occurred outside the US and involved non-US companies. However, even to the extent that the restrictions as to the extraterritorial Alien Tort Statute could be surmounted, several legal obstacles remain. It still remains questionable whether the Alien Tort Statute applies to companies. And even if this is answered in the affirmative, its use remains restricted to violations of a small set of human rights obligations and probably does not apply to all provisions in public codes of conduct concerning workplace standards and environmental protection. On this latter aspect, see also Revak (2012) 1666f.

[79] See, amongst the critical positions towards the regulatory approach taken by the UN Guiding Principles, especially Massoud (2013); Deva and Bilchitz (2013).

[80] See for the current discussions on an international treaty on business and human rights the very recent developments in the UN Human Rights Council. At its 26th session on 26 June 2014, the Council adopted with a highly divided vote (20 countries voting in favour, 14 countries voting against and 13 countries abstaining) a resolution by Ecuador and South Africa (A/HRC/26/L.22/Rev.1) that requests to 'establish an open-ended intergovernmental working group on a legally binding instrument on transnational corporations and other business enterprises with respect to Human Rights whose mandate shall be to elaborate an international legally binding instrument to regulate, in international human rights law, the activities of Transnational Corporations and Other Business Enterprises'. At this session, the Council also approved by consensus a resolution by Norway (A/HRC/26/L.1) that is directed, among other things, 'to launch an inclusive and transparent consultative process with States ... to explore and facilitate the sharing of legal and practical measures to improve access to remedy ... including the benefits and limitations of a legally binding instrument, and to prepare a report thereon'.

[81] For examples, see Ruggie (2014) 11f. Probably the most prominent integration of the UN Guiding Principles' due diligence concept into national legislation so far is the conflict mineral reporting under the US Dodd Frank Act, s 1502. Yet, it is currently a matter of controversy whether the provision is unconstitutional as a breach of First Amendment Protection; see especially the recent decision of the US Court of Appeals for the District of Columbia Circuit arguing in favour of First Amendment Protection, *National Association of Manufacturers et al v Securities and Exchange Commission et al*, No 13-5252, decided 14 April 2014.

[82] See, eg, Marrella (2007) 293: 'The real question then becomes the following: are codes elaborated by IGOs completely useless? My answer is no. I believe that such IGO-generated Codes of Conduct have a unique and very important value as external *benchmarks* for business-generated codes' (empha-

play an important role in shaping, influencing and further specifying the general debate on social responsibilities and, in so doing, they have had a considerable effect on another trend: the self-regulation in the private sphere and, more specifically, the development of private codes of conduct.

1.2.3.2. Private Codes of Conduct

The focus of the analysis so far has been set on codes of conduct that have been created by or at least with the significant participation of states as members of international organisations. Yet, the development towards codes of conduct on the level of international organisations is only one side of the coin; on the other side are the codes of conduct that are developed by the private sector. In specifying different forms of these codes, one can refer to model codes of business associations and NGOs that have as their aim to serve as a benchmark standard upon which companies can model their own policies. On the NGO side, one can refer in this context to, for instance, the Amnesty International Human Rights Principles for Companies or the Worker' Rights Consortium Model Code of Conduct. On the business side, famous examples of such model codes represent the sector-specific initiatives, such as the Chemical Industry's initiative Responsible Care, the Electronic Industry's Code of Conduct or initiatives addressing business in general, such as the International Chamber of Commerce Charter for Sustainable Development.[83] In addition, a plethora of different monitoring and certification programmes evolved that certify compliance with codes of conduct on workplace standards and environmental protection. However, at the core of the private codes of conduct development lie the codes that companies develop with the objective of setting benchmarks for their own global conduct and the conduct of subsidiaries and suppliers, and the following section will specifically focus on these corporate codes of conduct.

1.2.3.2.1. Global Guidelines on Socially Responsible Corporate Conduct

Corporate codes of conduct have been developed as a reaction to changing demands in society concerning their social role as well as a strategic response of companies to the emerging public codes of conduct in international organisations and the claims therein to take over social and environmental responsibility. The 1990s are frequently mentioned as a starting point when the first corporate scandals received media attention, such as Shell's planned sinking of the Brent Spar

sis in original); Ruggie (2007) 839: 'any successful regime needs to motivate, activate, and benefit from all the moral, social, and economic rationales that can affect the behaviour of corporations'; Teubner (2011) 34f: 'The Codes of the United Nations, the ILO, the OECD, and the European Union are mere constitutional impulses, which—*certainly with great influence*—international organizations send toward TNC' (emphasis added).

[83] A general collection of these and other influential codes of conduct from the private sphere is provided in the compendium of McKague and Cragg (2007).

platform in the North Sea or the sweatshop conditions in several garment factories. In reaction to these scandals, but also as a reaction to the increasing recommendations on corporate social responsibility as expressed in the public codes, companies began to develop their own responsibility codes.[84] Although initially subject to strong criticism as merely public relations campaigns, the corporate codes have evolved into an important part of the codification of aspects of corporate social responsibilities.

Since these corporate codes of conduct are expressions of the vision, culture and functioning of a particular company, it comes as no surprise that these corporate codes can differ quite significantly with regard to their content.[85] Differences can be identified between companies in different sectors. Labour issues tended to play a more important role in the codes of labour-intensive industries, such as the apparel, footwear and light manufacturing sectors,[86] whereas the extractive industries seemed in the first place to focus more on environmental standards.[87] Yet, this focus becomes understandable when taking into consideration that there are production-specific differences in companies. Companies in the garment industry, as a labour-intensive industry, were in the first place more vulnerable to the violations of labour standards of their huge network of suppliers. The extractive industries, in contrast, focused on the specifics of their operations to address issues of technical safety, such as healthy workplace conditions for employees, the risk of environmental pollution and the negative effect on communities.[88] An important additional reason for the difference in the codes is the different social pressures that companies encounter.[89] It is therefore no coincidence that the content of the code is also subject to change, particularly in situations where a company or even an entire sector is exposed to the public for not behaving in a socially responsible fashion. There are other elements that result in differences in the codes, such as

[84] *cf* the instructive diagram provided by Kolk and Tulder (2005) 6 on the explosion of corporate codes in the 1990s.

[85] For this observation, see initially Organisation for Economic Co-operation and Development (2001) 2: 'The codes examined differ considerably in terms of their content and degree of detail'; and Hepple (2000) 6.

[86] For this observation, see initially Organisation for Economic Co-operation and Development (2001) 2f: 'The content of the apparel codes, all of which cover labour issues, is quite different from the "average" content of the labour codes in the inventory. All of the apparel codes deal with child labour and the majority deal with bond labour, working environment and compensation. Codes from the extractive industry typically deal with a diverse array of issues and are much more likely to deal with the environment and the labour than the "average" code in the inventory'. See also subsequently with further references to empirical studies Kolk and Tulder (2005) 7; and World Bank Group (2003) Part I (Apparel, Footwear and Light Manufacturing, Agribusiness, Tourism) 6ff.

[87] World Bank Group (2003) Part II (Oil, Gas, Mining) 5ff (emphasising the less concise focus in these industries on issues such as child or forced labour) and 14ff (analysing the commitments concerning environmental aspects).

[88] On these sector-specific human rights impacts with an emphasis on the distinction between extractive industries on the one hand and the footwear and apparel industries on the other hand, see also Ruggie (2013) 23ff, in particular at 24.

[89] For this observation, see, eg, Organisation for Economic Co-operation and Development (2001) 2: 'The codes address a variety of issues, many appearing to arise from concerns of the general public'; Jenkins (2001) 28; Kolk and Tulder (2005) 7; McBarnet and Kurkchiyan (2007) 83.

the influence of the country of origin and thus the influence of the national political economy.[90] It is here that it is particularly noteworthy to mention the origin of codes of conduct as a development which is common in the US and that spilled over into Europe; a probable reason for this is the already broad reliance on voluntary social responsibility in this political-economic context and the structure of the system of corporate law as facilitating voluntary corporate philanthropy.[91]

Notwithstanding these differences between sectors, countries and individual companies, there seems to be at least a gradual development towards uniformity in terms of the substantive content. In general, the corporate codes of conduct can be broadly described as policy statements of companies that cover the three core substantive topics associated with corporate social responsibility, eg, decent profit making, responsibility for people in terms of human rights and labour, and responsibility for the environment.[92] From this broad focus on these diverse topics, there are two main elements that have crystallised as the core substantive aspects that are mainly focused in on the debate on corporate codes: the first relates to environmental protection and impacts on communities, while the second relates to particularly fundamental workplace standards.[93] It can at least be anticipated that, in the evolving discourse on the international level concerning business and human rights, general human rights aspects will also become a more important topic within codes of conduct. In addition to these general similarities in terms of substantive content, empirical studies suggest that there is also a tendency towards standardisation in the codes in terms of the specific aspects that they cover. This is not so much the case in the field of environmental protection, but it becomes increasingly observable in the field of workplace standards. In a recent study, the European Commission has analysed the codes of large European companies and has identified the UN Global Compact, the Universal Declaration of Human Rights and the ILO core labour rights as those that are most often referred to in the corporate codes or used as guidance.[94] This observation is partly shared by other empirical studies that emphasise the ILO core labour rights as the international framework that is frequently referred to,[95] in particular, the issues of child

[90] Kolk and Tulder (2005) 20f. *cf* on the need of a comparative perspective on CSR practices Williams and Aguilera (2008).

[91] See also on this aspect Hoffmann (2004) 1001, note 54: 'It is no accident that where a similar degree of security is *not* provided through institutional involvement, namely in LME forms of capitalism, multinational enterprises are taking the initiative themselves and adopting codes of conduct or corporate social responsibility' (emphasis in original).

[92] Marrella (2007) 295: 'Topics commonly treated are employment and labour relations; human rights, the environment; consumer protection and fighting corruption'; McBarnet and Kurkchiyan (2007) 65: 'a sweep of issues including business ethics, environment and human rights'.

[93] For this classification into workplace standards on the one hand and environmental topics on the other hand, see, eg, World Bank Group (2003) Part I (Apparel, Footwear and Light Manufacturing, Agribusiness, Tourism) and Part II (Oil, Gas, Mining) where the codes are categorised into those dealing with 'human rights and labour rights' on the one hand and 'environmental standards' on the other hand.

[94] European Commission, 'An Analysis of Policy References Made by Large EU Companies to Internationally Recognised CSR Guidelines and Principles', March 2013, available at: http://ec.europa.eu/enterprise/policies/sustainable-business/files/csr/csr-guide-princ-2013_en.pdf, at 7.

[95] eg, McBarnet and Kurkchiyan (2007) 66; Kocher (2008) 70; Kocher (2009) 419; Lin (2009) 720; Vytopil (2012) 166.

labour and forced labour.[96] Conversely, the OECD Guidelines and the UN Guiding Principles are less frequently referred to, although, in particular, with respect to the latter framework, the only recent adoption could be an important factor that might explain the reluctance of companies towards integrating it into their codes. Finally, an additional common aspect in corporate codes is the reference to compliance with national laws.[97]

As a result, one could indeed define corporate codes in their current form as voluntary declarations of companies that contain substantive standards on specific corporate social responsibility aspects. These codes represent policies that companies develop autonomously as their own applicable global standards on socially responsible conduct. While it is recognised that the corporate codes remain quite a diverse phenomenon with differences between sectors, countries and individual companies, there are nevertheless several common denominators. Corporate codes typically contain commitments to respect fundamental workplace standards, partly also broader human rights of communities and specific aspects related to environmental protection. In particular, in relation to workplace standards, a further standardisation can be observed where the ILO core labour rights play an important role as well as commitments to respect national law.

1.2.3.2.2. Guidelines for Corporate Groups and Supply Chains

However, the suggested importance of corporate codes does not simply rest on their status as corporate policies that specify substantive aspects concerning labour, human rights and environmental protection for the global operations. These codes are also important in specifying responsibilities in relation to corporate groups and contractual networks. It is emphasised as a common thread that these corporate codes are developed as group policies that are not only applicable to the head company; instead, companies generally present these codes as the underlying fundamental policy of the entire corporate group that also includes foreign subsidiaries.[98] In addition to the broad scope of worldwide operations of corporate groups, the corporate codes also became tools that addressed the responsibility of the contractual networks. By means of developing so-called supplier codes of conduct as an integral part of the overall corporate policy towards social responsibility, companies effectively presented to the public their intention to take over proactive responsibility for the adherence of their trading partners to social and

[96] World Bank Group (2003) Part I (Apparel, Footwear and Light Manufacturing, Agribusiness, Tourism) 6: 'Perhaps the greatest point of uniformity on every code of conduct examined was the prohibition against the use of forced labour.' At 7: 'Among the "leadership" firms examined, there appears to be an emerging trend that the minimum age for child labour must be at least 15, or the age for completing compulsory education, whichever is greater.'

[97] Picciotto (2003) 142; McBarnet and Kurkchiyan (2007) 67; Kocher (2008) 73. *cf* also Lin (2009) 721f, who observes that not only is adherence to local law included, but, in parts, also the multinational company's home country law.

[98] See extensively on the relevance of environmental codes of companies in relation to foreign direct investment Herberg (2007); Herberg (2008); and the reference to empirical studies by Kocher (2008) 69.

environmental standards, which is supported by means of including these codes into their supplier contracts.[99]

The corporate group standards as well as the supplier codes of conduct do not remain, in this regard, simply policy statements. On the contrary, the global policies are increasingly supported by dense internal control mechanisms and are thus integrated into the core operations of the company. In relation to the corporate group policies, specific auditing procedures exist that assign the parent company the role of a 'global executive organ' that implements global policies and attempts to identify and remedy breaches of the policies.[100] In the course of implementing these policies, concrete standards and norms are created, in particular standards concerning technical aspects of risk prevention.[101] In relation to supplier codes of conduct, it is equally the auditing and monitoring procedure that has evolved as the core mechanism to identify and track non-compliance. As a matter of fact, companies frequently include in their supplier contracts a right to inspect the factories and specific actions to deter non-compliance.[102] Monitoring the provision of the code is not only conducted by the company itself, it is also given into the hands of specialised auditors or NGOs.[103] Like the internal corporate policies, the supplier codes of conduct are equipped with specific procedures that aim to restore compliance and impose penalties on suppliers and, although seldom used, impose severe sanctions of termination or monetary penalties.[104] When it comes to the integration of the corporate policies into contractual networks, it is identified as a key component for the success of the codes that companies organise the code compliance in the spirit of collaborative partnership whereby both parties assist one another to safeguard and restore compliance with the code,[105] which is also how companies increasingly organise their supplier relations.[106] The relations between companies and their contractually affiliated suppliers have been described in this respect as a new form of corporate organisation whereby large companies begin to take over active responsibility for the behaviour of suppliers with respect to social and environmental standards.[107]

Based on these observations, one can define these corporate codes as global private standards on specifically environmental protection and labour standards that are used as benchmarks for the companies' global operations. In addition, the

[99] See particularly on the practice of supplier codes of conduct as contractual mechanisms the empirical studies of McBarnet and Kurkchiyan (2007) and Vytopil (2012).

[100] Herberg (2008) 27ff (quote at 28).

[101] ibid, 30ff.

[102] McBarnet and Kurkchiyan (2007) 74f.

[103] ibid, 74ff; Cafaggi (2013) 1602f.

[104] McBarnet and Kurkchiyan (2007) 78ff.

[105] See, eg, the studies of Frenkel and Seongsu (2004); Locke, Qin and Brause (2006).

[106] McBarnet and Kurkchiyan (2007) 68ff and Phillips and Lim (2009) 342ff both observe in their empirical studies that companies frequently describe their relations with suppliers concerning CSR requirements as a collaborative partnership, although it is also emphasised that this partnership approach is not followed in all respects. In particular, financial arrangements for renovations and improvements of the safety standards or higher wages for employees remain controversial topics; see for these specific aspects in detail McBarnet and Kurkchiyan (2007) 86ff.

[107] Phillips and Lim (2009) 350, with further references to the debate.

codes are also developed as standards for globally operating corporate groups as well as an evolving mechanism to develop responsibility within supplier networks. Thus, the corporate codes and the internal monitoring and sanctioning systems establish standards on socially responsible conduct for novel and more fragmented forms of corporate organisation.

1.2.3.2.3. A Transformation into Legally Binding Obligations?

In quite a similar manner to the public codes of conduct, these new forms of corporate self-regulation in the area of social and environmental standards increasingly influence the work of legal scholars and practitioners. Initially, legal contributions on these private initiatives mainly addressed the question of whether these codes ought to play a vital role at all in the regulatory architecture for companies. Proponents discussed in this context the inherent potential of these codes to serve as rules that, by means of monitoring and standardisation, could effectively change corporate behaviour in the absence of internationally binding rules. Moreover, reliance on corporate self-regulation in this field was, from this perspective, seen as beneficial since it allowed companies to develop individual rules that were tailor-made to the specific company culture and organisation, the sector and the particular countries of operation.[108] This rather positive assessment was contrasted with critical positions that emphasised the inherent problems with these voluntary efforts. Corporate codes were partly accused of being ineffective and of being mere public relations campaigns that were directed at improving the reputation of the adopting company rather than leading to real and long-term changes for those affected by corporate behaviour. Keywords such as 'smokescreens', 'paying lip-service' or 'public relations exercise' became influential characterisations by the critics. In addition, it was also emphasised that, being mere unilateral commitments by private actors on matters of public interest, corporate codes would face serious problems with regard to their legitimacy.[109]

However, more recently, this initial contrast between arguments for and against the value of these voluntary codes seemed to have moderated. Instead, in the more recent debate, a shift can be observed towards an amplified interest as to what the exact legal role is that these corporate codes could play. Discussions began to focus on questions of what possible legal effects such private codes could have and how these codes relate to hard law obligations of companies, and, like the public codes, there are two research perspectives that seem particularly promising. One can find, on the one hand, scholars who investigate corporate codes and the supporting auditing and sanctioning mechanisms from the perspective of whether these could qualify as emerging systems of non-state law and, quite differently from the public codes, tend to answer this question rather affirmatively.[110] Taking

[108] From the vast literature on the codes, see, eg, Baker (1993); Baram (1994); Toftoy (1998).

[109] For a critical perspective, see, eg, Anderson (1999) 484ff; Hong (2000); Blackett (2000) 411f; Jenkins (2001) 26ff; Arthurs (2005); Doane (2005).

[110] See especially Herberg (2005); Herberg (2007); Herberg (2008); Backer (2007); Backer (2008); Teubner (2009); Teubner (2011) and recently Podszun (2014). See also on the identified evolution of an

the concept of law in the tradition of legal pluralism or inter-legality respectively as a starting point, the codes and their internal control mechanism are described as an evolving autonomous non-state legal system that consists not only of primary norms that specify fundamental rules on socially responsible corporate behaviour, but also of secondary norms that consist of autonomous standards and specified requirements for particular constellations of corporate conduct. In this context, the auditing procedures and the internal operational standards in particular seem to play a crucial role.[111] On the other hand, the potential of these private codes to serve as the basis for legal obligations is also discussed with a view on whether they can become intertwined with the legal system, in particular the system of private law.[112] With respect to this research strand, this potential integration of corporate codes into formal law appears in the first place slightly less difficult in comparison to public codes. This is mainly due to the fact that private law recognises agreements and commitments of private actors as a valid source of legal obligations and, moreover, takes account of private self-regulatory standards that, even though treated as non-state social norms without direct legally binding effect, prove to be important for the interpretation of legal standards.[113]

The fundamentally different description of the codes as genuine non-state law and private self-regulation notwithstanding, one can still observe that both of these research perspectives share a common underlying assumption. The codes, so it is predicted amongst those who describe them as genuine systems of non-state law, can in the long term only be successful if they manage to interact with the formal legal system on a stable basis and make the legal system stabilise, and thus, to a certain extent, legitimise this autonomous legal order.[114] This is the

autonomous transnational law on corporate governance (excluding, however, corporate codes of conduct) Calliess and Zumbansen (2010) 181ff.

111 Herberg (2007), (2008) distinguishes three layers: the corporate guidelines that set the primary obligatory norms, the auditing procedure as an internal mechanism that enforces these norms and the operational internal standards that are concretely developed in the course of this internal auditing.

112 From the many contributions that discuss the potential of corporate codes to transform into legal obligations, see, eg, Picciotto (2003) 144ff; Webb and Morrison (2004); Murphy (2005); Sobczak (2006); Glinski (2007); Glinski (2011); Glinski (2014); Marrella (2007); the contributions in Dilling, Herberg and Winter (2008b); Kerr, Janda and Pitts (2009) 330ff; Phillips and Lim (2009); Heijden (2011a); Heijden (2011b), chs 5 and 6; Henning-Bodewig and Liebenau (2013); Torrance (2011); the contributions in Cafaggi (2012); Enneking (2012) 443ff, in particular 519ff; Revak (2012); Vytopil (2012); Cafaggi (2013); the contributions in Hilty and Henning-Bodewig (2014); Peterkova (2014a); Peterkova (2014b); Scheltema (2014) 396f, 399ff. See also on the interaction between private regulation and legal enforcement with a view to codes of conduct in the area of advertising and food safety Verbruggen (2014a) 101ff, 214ff.

113 See generally on the different strategies of the law to deal with non-state law Michaels (2005) 1227ff, who distinguishes here between four different categories: Non-state private standards could serve as the applicable law (which is, however, currently rejected), they can be incorporated into state law as norms (incorporation), they can be treated as facts that are relevant for the legal decision-making (deference) and they can be recognised as subordinated law (delegation).

114 See Herberg (2007) 36ff, 236ff, who, based on the theoretical perspective of inter-legality (see fundamentally on this concept Sousa Santos (1995) 473), envisages the interaction as a form of re-embedding an autonomous legal order into state law; and Teubner (2009) 271, who, based on the theoretical perspective of legal pluralism, envisages the interaction of the codes with state law as a collision of two autonomous legal orders that is 'one important condition for the success of corporate codes'. See also recently in the same direction Podszun (2014) 73ff.

point where the position is in line with the underlying assumption of scholars that focus on the links between corporate codes and formal law. Within this research strand, it is equally emphasised that the interaction of private self-regulation with formal law and thus the specification of criteria under which the law could recognise them as valid private ordering is a crucial prerequisite to make them more effective and to achieve greater legitimacy.[115] As Dilling, Herberg and Winter pointedly observe: 'By including the informal structures within its area of responsibility, formal law can enhance their degree of publicity, reliability, and substantial consistency and, therefore, their legitimacy.'[116] As a result, it seems to be a common thread in the literature that the success of the corporate codes and their potential to become relevant components in the future legal architecture on corporate social responsibility remains in the first place a matter of their ability to interact with the formal legal system and become recognised as valid self-regulatory standards. If so, the corporate codes could indeed serve as the next successful example for the reliance of the legal system on the productive potential of self-regulation in the private sphere. The codes could embrace the long tradition of the legal system to make use of self-regulation, as is evident from technical standards and standards for particular professions that inform the open-ended standards of due care or the delegation of law-making competences to private actors that are particularly apparent in the law of associations (articles of association), collective bargaining agreements or the recognition of standard contract terms in contract law.[117]

However, in spite of the frequently mentioned similarities between corporate codes and other types of self-regulation that the legal system has made use of so far, there are still important differences that render the incorporation of corporate codes more difficult. Several studies that have already focused on the possible interaction between formal law and corporate codes bring to the fore a noteworthy problem. Although manifold concepts exist in formal law through which social norms become relevant, the law as it stands still partly hinders the successful transformation of the codes into legally accepted standards.[118] Difficulties relate first

[115] Glinski (2007) 120; Glinski (2011) 89ff; Glinski (2014) 45f; and the contributions in Dilling, Herberg and Winter (2008b). See also Bachmann (2006b) 204ff; Joerges and Rödl (2008) 776f; Joerges (2011) 498ff; Mares (2010), pointedly at 285: 'Once the polarised voluntary-mandatory view of dealing with MNEs [Multinational Enterprises] and the limiting concept of CSR as "beyond compliance" are overcome, a start can be made … on the systematic examination of the mutual interaction between CSR and law through which responsible business practices strengthen the operation of regulatory regimes and law reinforces the CSR goal of respect for human rights.'

[116] Dilling, Herberg and Winter (2008a) 7.

[117] See, for these different forms of private self-regulation and their successful integration ('re-constitutionalisation') into the area of private law, especially Schepel (2005); Köndgen (2006) 481ff; Herberg (2007) 32f.

[118] In the existing studies, see only Arthurs (2005) 58f ('codes may theoretically be used to pour meaning and content into state … law even though they are not designed for that purpose. … so far, … the possibilities of creative interaction between state law and voluntary codes remain largely a matter of speculation'); Kenny (2007) 467 ('Ultimately … Wal-Mart's Code of Conduct … does not create a contractual obligation'); Estlund (2012) 262 ('Enforcement of lead firms' labour CSR commitments … is hardly on the horizon in private transnational labour regulation'); Revak (2012) 1667 ('Corporate codes of conduct are self-imposed, self-regulated, and voluntary, and therefore lack a definitive enforcement mechanism').

to the strategic way in which companies use their codes, which seems different from other types of self-regulation. In contrast to, for instance, technical standards or standard contract terms, companies seem to develop self-regulatory standards with the objective to avoid having them recognised in the law. Companies keep their codes as informal as possible and deliberately opt for forms other than those recognised as legally binding. For instance, the public declaration rather than a bilateral contract is chosen as the appropriate form and, in some codes, disclaimers are included to signal that no legal obligation is intended. This strategy of leaving the corporate codes deliberately informal obviously already renders it quite difficult to integrate the codes into formal law. It requires not only identifying possible links in private law that are already used to integrate private self-regulation into the law but also the development of novel responses within the legal system to deal with the specific character of these corporate codes. Yet it is not only the attitude of companies towards their codes that makes legal integration difficult. Moreover, it is also the underlying assumptions in the legal debate and the apparent lack of a uniform approach on how to address this new phenomenon of corporate codes that comes into play here. To be more precise, existing studies on corporate codes in private law so far seem not to have a shared understanding on the actual role that the legal system should play when approaching these codes. Should the legal system remain restricted to facilitating this new phenomenon by means of constituting incentives for companies to adopt corporate codes and, for the rest, leave the enforcement to social sanctions? Or do these voluntary corporate codes also need to be regulated? And, in the case of the latter situation, what is the right direction of regulation? Should the focus be on enforcing the code obligations and thereby effectively equipping the breach of the corporate code with legal sanctions? Or is it more appropriate to maintain a certain degree of scepticism and treat the codes as having an inherent potential to mislead the public that would have to be prohibited if no effort to comply with the code is present? It is these two particular problems that inspired this research and for which it consequently seeks to develop solutions. The objective is to do so by means of providing theoretically informed recommendations for the legal system on how to deal with these private corporate codes. Hence, this research is envisaged as contributing to the legal debate on corporate codes in the form of adding suggestions for further discussion on how to react appropriately to the new social phenomenon of corporate codes from the legal perspective.

Yet the complexity of the topic and the wide range of legal areas involved require, of course, that the exact focus for which such suggestions are developed be narrowed down. To that end, in this study the focus will be placed on proposals relevant for the area of substantive private law. The main reason for this choice relates to the fact that private law remains the core area that deals with self-regulation in the private sphere and is therefore expected to play a pivotal role for the future development of the codes as such. This choice for the area of substantive private law will, however, also have the result that some emerging and certainly also important discussions on corporate codes are excluded insofar as they are related to other areas of law. This concerns, among other things, the relevance of the codes and their potential conflicts with public law, such as constitutional and administrative law,[119] international economic law,[120] competition and anti-trust laws,[121] and the current proposals on the transformation of private international law in order to recognise the decisions of dispute-solving institutions that derive from the private sphere and their rules as the applicable law.[122]

As such, with a focus on the general private law debate on these private codes of conduct, the study seeks to discuss and systematise the studies that have already conducted research on the possible private law effects of corporate codes. Building upon their findings, the debate is taken one step further by not only discussing the status quo but also evaluating these proposals from the perspective of legal theory. In so doing, this book seeks to conclude with proposals on legal reform for the area of private law that should be initiated with respect to the emerging phenomenon of voluntary corporate codes.

1.3. TAKING CORPORATE CODES SERIOUSLY: UNFOLDING THE ARGUMENT

How should substantive private law react to the increasing adoption of corporate codes by companies? This question will serve as the general question that frames this research and it will—as already anticipated by the heading of this section—be developed as the core argument throughout the various chapters, that private law needs to recognise these corporate codes as evolving serious unilateral forms of regulation that derive from the private sphere. To that end, it is proposed that private law needs to develop appropriate concepts that render private law enforcement of these codes possible. In this context, one further restriction is made as to the scope and validity of this argument. The private law enforcement of corporate codes as envisaged in this study is specifically developed in relation to the enforceable obligations on the side of the corporate entity that adopts and publishes a corporate code, insofar as these obligations arise towards the respective company's external social environment. More precisely, the commitments laid down in the corporate codes are analysed in order to discover whether they could become enforceable private law obligations of the corporate entity concerned towards consumers, business partners and code beneficiaries, which would include primarily employees of subsidiaries and suppliers, and third parties that are directly affected by corporate irresponsible conduct.

This, as a main consequence, implies that the commitments laid down in the corporate codes are not discussed with respect to the internal relations within a corporate organisation, in particular the impact of the codes on rights and obligations of managers, shareholders and employees. To exclude this legal dimension of the corporate codes, that is, the commitments laid down in the corporate codes

[119] See especially Glinski (2011) 122ff.

[120] See Glinski (2014).

[121] On this topic, see, eg, Dubbink and van der Putten (2008); Ackermann (2014).

[122] See fundamentally on this question Fischer-Lescano and Teubner (2004); Michaels (2005); and with respect to particularly the corporate codes Teubner (2009) 271ff.

with respect to the internal relations within a corporate organisation, is of course not self-explanatory and therefore requires further justification. The main considerations behind ignoring the effects of the corporate codes on the internal organisation of the company are as follows. First, practical reasons led to this choice. If the effects of the corporate codes on the internal organisation of the company were included, the legal analysis would have had to be considerably broader in its scope, as it would, in addition to the already far-reaching area of general private law, also require an inquiry into the more specific rules on corporate law and labour law. Since, however, this study seeks not only to scrutinise the relevant legal issues thoroughly but also to engage in an interdisciplinary theoretical analysis, such a broad focus on very specific areas would remain inevitably highly superficial. Second, and more importantly, the decision to exclude the legal debates of the codes in labour law and corporate law has also been taken for a conceptual reason. It is based on the understanding that the legal questions and theoretical issues involved are different between internal and external relations. In the relations between companies and their external environment, the pressing issues are particularly whether and how the codes could become relevant in the absence of global mandatory rules on socially responsible business conduct. In other words, the question is mainly a matter of whether and to what extent the corporate codes are capable of becoming legal obligations and thus of assisting in closing the regulatory gap on a global level. When it comes to the internal relations that are influenced by a variety of mandatory rules that aim to protect specific social groups and interests, the discussions on private law enforcement would need to pay due respect to the potential conflicts between these mandatory rules and the autonomous code obligations. In this regard, research in the field of labour law would need to address the current conflicts of the corporate codes with mandatory labour standards if the rights conferred upon the employees by the codes are lower than those laid down in labour law or if the codes not only benefit the employees but also impose obligations on them that could violate labour law.[123] In the field of corporate law, in particular the legal effects of corporate codes on the duties of managers, the relevance of corporate codes would need to be specifically discussed in light of the legally codified managerial duties and the way in which such new social and environmental requirements have to be reconciled with the duties to act in the interests of the company.[124] While it is recognised that similar conflicts between corporate codes and mandatory rules are also likely to occur in the relations of companies with their external environment, once the codes become enforceable as new regulatory duties and mandatory rules are also

[123] This has become a prominent issue in the *Wal-Mart* dispute in Germany (ArbG Wuppertal, NZA-RR 2005, 476 LAG Düsseldorf, NZA-RR 2006, 81), where questions arose as to whether the private code of conduct would violate collective or individual labour law. See generally on the case and the subsequently following debate, amongst others, Backer (2007) 1768ff; Klösel (2012) 1ff.

[124] This is pointedly observed by McBarnet (2007) 22ff as the 'corporate social responsibility against the law', although the issue will become probably a more controversial issue in shareholder-oriented than in stakeholder-oriented corporate law. See also on the interplay between company law and voluntary CSR Sjåfjell (2011a); Sjåfjell (2011b).

increasingly adopted in countries with low labour or environmental standards,[125] it is nevertheless assumed that such conflicts prove to remain, for the time being, a less pressing issue compared with the question of whether and, if so, what actual effects the corporate codes may have.

As a result of this chosen focus, this study is particularly interested in the following questions:

(i) Should the corporate codes, from the perspective of private law, be interpreted as valid enforceable obligations and, if so, towards whom, ie, business partners, consumers, governments, code beneficiaries or even the global public, should such an obligation arise? And to the extent that an enforceable obligation represents an appropriate legal interpretation of these corporate codes, what would be the content of the legal obligation and what types of remedies are suitable to remedy breaches of the codes?
(ii) Moreover, should the corporate codes have an impact on the legal liability of companies towards detrimentally affected parties? Should they influence the scope of liability as a duty of care of the adopting company towards the addressees and beneficiaries? And should operational standards in corporate codes play a role in specifying the standard of due care?
(iii) Finally, in light of the current intense debate in the particular area of unfair commercial practices law, should the corporate codes also play a role in this field and, if so, what role should this be? Should the publication of a corporate code be regulated as a commercial practice that could be considered unfair if a company does not comply and what standard should apply to determine the unfairness? Or, conversely, should the corporate code be considered a reliable self-regulatory standard that could be used to specify the open-ended concept of fairness in unfair commercial practices law with the result that non-complying behaviour could also be interpreted as unfair trading behaviour?

With these specific questions in mind, the analysis will be structured as follows. The four chapters of *Part One* will be devoted to exploring the different possibilities for dealing with the codes in private law, focusing on the enforcement of the codes, their influence on civil liability and their regulation by unfair commercial practices law based on the current academic debate on these issues and, to the extent available, existing case law. To that end, the analysis will follow a functional and comparative approach as developed in chapter two, which relates the existing proposals in the corporate codes debate to the national private law rules of England and Germany. The comparative element in this legal analysis is, however, not envisaged as a genuine comparison that aims at identifying similarities or differences in the legal systems in relation to this particular problem. Although the differences and similarities in treating the corporate codes are mentioned on occasion and are explicitly encouraged to be worked out in further research, the main consideration behind including a comparative element in this study is different.

[125] See generally for first observations of such tendencies, in particular in relation to workplace standards in China, Lin (2007) 356ff.

The choice for a legal analysis with a comparative element ultimately serves the purpose of seeing whether and how uniform solutions to a common global phenomenon are possible. The comparative analysis thus seeks to signpost a way to use comparative law for the sake of developing harmonised approaches based on functional equivalence that pay due respect to national differences and the remaining territorial fragmentation of private law. In the course of the comparative analysis, additional inspiration is sought from other national debates on corporate codes, in particular the debate in US law. These occasional references to the situation in other legal systems and their potentially applicable legal concepts and doctrines are not part of the comparative analysis; rather, they occur as part of the conceptual debate and thus function as inspirations on what legal concepts could be applicable when linking corporate codes to private law. From the more detailed comparative analysis of corporate codes under German and English private law, the conclusion will be drawn that, in particular, two core topics are currently subject to uncertainty and thus give rise to controversy. First, it is debated how private law should approach corporate codes if these are only informal public declarations and are not incorporated into a binding contract. Next to the incorporation of corporate codes into contracts, can the unilateral commitment also be enforced in contract law and can such a declaration serve as a basis for establishing liability of the publicly declaring corporate entity? And how does the law on unfair commercial practices become relevant in relation to these public declarations? In addition, a second aspect in the private law debate on the codes that currently lead to contradicting proposals among private law scholars is identified in the specific character of these codes as intentional corporate efforts to regulate public interest matters. How does private law approach this specific function and content of the codes? Do the corporate codes represent agreements to which the general default rules and existing contractual remedies apply, ie, the rules on sales agreements or third party rights? Or are the codes new forms of public interest regulation that would need to be treated as new substantive private law obligations for which a novel remedial scheme is also required? And is it possible, and if so in what way, that these forms of regulation inform the open-ended standards in tort law and unfair commercial practices law?

Based on this preparatory work and the two core controversies identified, the three chapters in *Part Two* seek to lay the theoretical foundations on the normative proposals for private law reform based on, first, a closer analysis of the form of the corporate codes as public declarations and, second, their function in regulating public interest matters. In so doing, the study will employ the general theoretical framework of sociological jurisprudence that urges an appropriate response of private law to a new social phenomenon by combining an external interdisciplinary sociological analysis and the internal perspective of legal theory. This methodological framework is developed in chapter six. The sociological analysis, in this context, aims to provide a deeper understanding of the character of the corporate codes, thereby providing the system of private law with interdisciplinary insights into the functioning of the corporate codes in the broader context of society. With the help of legal theory, these interdisciplinary insights are subsequently assessed from the internal legal perspective with the objective of identifying the legal concepts that are most suitable to accommodate the corporate codes, based on this in-depth understanding. Concerning the debate on publicly declared corporate policies, the theoretical inquiry will address the following points. The interdisciplinary theoretical analysis will reveal, based on a socio-linguistic analysis of the actual code declarations, that these publicly declared corporate codes represent deliberate promises that result in an expectation of a binding effect in the specific social interaction between the market actors to whom it is addressed with the objective of inducing a contract. They also represent deliberate promises to establish an intensified trust relationship with the global public that, under the current conditions of distrust, requires specific legal protection. On the basis of this insight, the legal theory analysis seeks to discuss how the respective expectation of a binding effect in market relations and the intensified public trust could appropriately be reflected within the existing categories of private law. By relying on the theoretical debate on the legal enforcement of unilateral promises and on the protection of reliance on the expectations created by promises, the chapter will conclude with suggestions to enforce the corporate codes as unilateral promises when the corporate codes are introduced with the objective of furthering economic activity. In relation to the anonymous global public, it is suggested that the trust created by the corporate codes plays a role in the form of a tort law duty of care, the breach of which could result in an obligation to compensate a detrimentally affected party for incurred damages. When it comes to the second controversial issue, namely the regulatory character of the corporate codes, the interdisciplinary theoretical analysis, grounded in economic sociology, and recent political theory seeks to shed light on the character of the corporate codes as a new form of political regulation that is different from orthodox political regulation by the state. More concretely, on the basis of the distinction between politics and the political in recent political theory, in the tradition of functional differentiation and post-foundational thought, the codes will be described as new instances of political regulation by contract or public commitment, on the one hand, and by the deliberate choice to adhere to and pursue the policy recommendations developed in international politics, on the other hand. On the basis of this understanding, the legal theory debate will address the question of how this new form of political regulation could become relevant as a new dimension of public interests in private law. In relation to the enforcement of the codes within contracts and enforceable commitments, it is argued that this requires interpreting the corporate code obligation in light of its regulatory character and developing specific and novel forms of remedies.

Based on this theoretical analysis, the concluding chapter nine is devoted to translating the theoretical claims into concrete proposals for policy reform. These proposals are in the first place addressed to courts confronted with disputes involving corporate codes that are encouraged to use such occasions to develop the law further. However, to the extent that the proposals would inevitably result in a decision *contra legem*, they should also be read as being addressed to legislators as a proposal to consider statutory reform. In this context, first an attempt is made to develop theoretical claims for the enforcement of the publicly declared corporate codes, on the one hand, as terms in subsequently concluded contracts with the help of the existing rules on contract interpretation (Germany) and supplementation (England) and, on the other hand, as autonomous promises that were relied upon by further refining and broadening the scope of the common law doctrine of equitable estoppel (England) and the narrowly confined categories that make it possible to enforce promises that were made to consumers and that were relied upon (Germany). In relation to the beneficiaries of the codes, it is argued that the corporate codes should be interpreted as a form of an assumption of responsibility (England) and a *Verkehrspflicht* (Germany). When it comes to the regulatory character of the corporate codes, the proposals will more precisely address their interpretation as regulatory process obligations in contracts to which the remedy of specific performance applies and for which a novel form of collective enforcement should at least be considered. In addition, it is proposed to make use of the corporate codes as self-regulatory standards that could assist in specifying the standard of due care as an individually specified standard. Finally, with regard to the regulation of the corporate codes by unfair commercial practices law, the core proposal is to view the corporate codes mainly as self-regulatory, individually committed standards that could assist in specifying the fairness standard rather than addressing the matter as an unfair commercial practice. In a concluding section, the study seeks to contextualise these suggestions and to deliberate more in detail on the conditions of their success. To that end, specific social and legal parameters are pointed out that are crucial for the success of the suggested private law enforcement and indications are provided as to the feasibility of private law enforcement in the fragmentation of national legal systems and the remaining stable socio-economic and political patterns of evolution that the theory on the Varieties of Capitalism has revealed.

This proposed development 'towards private law enforcement of corporate social responsibility codes' is considered to contribute to the future regulation on corporate social responsibility aspects by enhancing the legitimacy of such private initiatives, but also by regaining the influence of the formal legal system that the process of globalisation and the recent changes in the corporate organisation have considerably diminished.

Part I

Linking Corporate Codes and National Private Law

2

Comparative Sociological Jurisprudence

A Method for Linking Global Self-regulation and National Private Law

> Once we acknowledge that the core institutional infrastructure of the global economy must be built at the national level, it frees up countries to develop institutions that suit them best.[1]

THE GENERAL OBJECTIVE of this book is to propose changes to private law in order to better deal with the global phenomenon of corporate codes. Yet, to be able to make such suggestions requires engaging in the first place in an analysis of the options in private law that are in principle available to deal with this phenomenon. The three chapters that follow this one in this part will therefore be devoted to this undertaking; they all seek to link in a different way global self-regulation through code of conduct with national private law. Before doing so, this introductory chapter seeks to focus on a theoretical and methodological framework that makes it possible to investigate the links between global self-regulation in the form of corporate codes and the legal system.

2.1. GLOBAL SELF-REGULATION AND FUNCTIONALLY DIFFERENTIATED PRIVATE LAW

In examining the corporate codes under private law, the study will adopt a functional understanding of the specific legal concepts involved.[2] It approaches legal concepts and doctrine with a view to how they deal with the specific social phenomenon of corporate codes of conduct. As a result, the legal analysis in the different chapters is thus not oriented on conceptual proximity between legal concepts and doctrines; instead, it is methodologically guided by the question of what function a particular legal concept can fulfil in relation to corporate codes and, in light of the comparative element, with a view to the functional equivalents in the different legal systems.

In approaching the corporate codes from this perspective, three functions are focused on in detail: the legal enforcement of corporate codes, their influence on the scope and content of civil liability and their influence on what is legally

[1] Rodrik (2011) 239.
[2] On this functional approach, see extensively with further references Michaels (2006).

understood as fair trading behaviour. This has some consequences for the structure of the following chapters. With regard to the function of enforcing corporate codes as positive obligations (chapter three), it is mainly the area of contract law that will be considered. This is due to the fact that contract law has evolved as the core area of private law that fulfils the function of enforcing the autonomous agreements and commitments of private parties as legal obligations.[3] In the course of discussing possible influence of corporate codes on the scope of civil liability (chapter four), the corporate codes will be related to the various rules in private law that establish liability for a private actor towards a detrimentally affected third party. Determining the scope of legal liability towards third parties is functionally primarily taken over by general tort law and it appears in particular in the rules for establishing a duty of care.[4] Therefore, these rules on establishing a common law duty of care, or *Verkehrspflicht* in German, will be relevant. In addition to tort law, this chapter will also discuss the potential of several other rules in private law that have the function of establishing liability towards third parties based on public declarations or bilateral agreements. This applies particularly to the rules on liability between parties in relations akin to contract (*culpa in contrahendo*) and liability towards third parties that are based on a contractual obligation to protect third parties (*protective effect of contracts*).[5] It is recognised that their functional interpretation, ie, as part of non-contractual legal liability of the corporate entity, could be criticised from the conceptual perspective as these concepts in some legal systems are seen as akin to contract rather than tort. However, the study is based on the assumption that a conceptual proximity to contract or tort depends on the characteristics of a particular national legal system, particularly on the evolved boundaries of contract law. Hence, these legal concepts can take the form of an 'escape into tort prompted by a rigidly conceived law of contract' as well as vice versa.[6] The final chapter in this part (chapter five) will focus on private law insofar as it fulfils the function to regulate the companies' use of corporate codes on the market as part of their trading behaviour. For this specific aspect, it is the narrowly confined area of unfair commercial practices law that plays an important

[3] See, eg, Collins (1986) 137, who declares the enforcement of contracts the 'core of contract doctrine'.

[4] See, eg, for the function of the duty of care in tort law to establish liability in relation to the common law Deakin, Johnston and Markesinis (2007) 102: 'The issue of the duty [of care] is … essentially concerned with whether the law recognises in principle the possibility of liability in a given type of situation. To put it differently, it helps demarcate the range of people, relationships and interests that receive the protection of the law from the effects of negligently inflicted harm.' For German law, see Markesinis and Unberath (2002) 86: 'The purpose of these duties of care [*Verkehrspflicht*] must be made clear. They are there to delineate the range of relationship which will be protected by careless interference; they are also there to limit … the range of persons who could be held liable for a particular harmful result.'

[5] The decision to relate these concepts of 'quasi-contractual liability' to tort rather than contract and also not to treat them as a third category is based on the consideration that both *culpa in contrahendo* liability as well as the protective effects of contracts primarily have the consequence that the scope of liability for a wrongful act is broadened. Conversely, in the law as it stands, these concepts cannot be used to *enforce* the voluntary agreement or commitment of a private actor. This renders them, in relation to the corporate codes phenomenon, from the functional perspective a part of determining legal liability rather than related to the proposed enforcement of the corporate codes as contractual obligations.

[6] Deakin, Johnston and Markesinis (2007) 20ff.

role, which is also the area of law where the particular issue of corporate codes is currently discussed prominently.

Each of these chapters will follow the same structure. The analysis starts with revealing the different angles through which the corporate codes could become relevant. This is followed by an analysis on how, pursuant to these options, private law would interpret the legal obligation deriving from a corporate code, the applicable remedies and what actors would be recognised as obtaining rights and remedies.

2.2. GLOBAL SELF-REGULATION AND TERRITORIALLY FRAGMENTED PRIVATE LAW

In pursuing the objective of developing recommendations on how private law should deal with the corporate codes phenomenon, a further choice has been made to develop these recommendations with a comparative focus on two national legal systems. The choice for a comparative methodological element in the analysis is based on the assumption that the corporate codes represent a novel global phenomenon to which the legal system as such needs to react uniformly. However, it is equally true that there is no such thing as a uniform global system of private law; conversely, private law still remains, to a great extent, fragmented into national legal systems. Given this territorial fragmentation of the system of private law, a legal analysis of the corporate codes is inevitably confronted with the difficulty of relating a global phenomenon (corporate codes) to a national context (private law) without either ignoring the national specifics or losing the global dimension in the focus on nationally shaped practices. How can this gap between a global social phenomenon and nationally shaped legal systems be bridged?

The studies that have researched the potential interaction between the global corporate codes and national private law have sought to overcome this gap by either pursuing what could be broadly framed as an overall global approach that discusses the corporate codes from the perspective of what is viewed as generally accepted principles of private law[7] or, conversely, by opting for the national perspective approach that discusses the interaction of the codes and private law in light of the specifics of one particular national legal system. The legal systems on the basis of which research on corporate codes has been conducted so far address particularly the national private laws of the US,[8] Canada and England,[9] the Netherlands[10] and Germany.[11] Yet both of these approaches are considered to have their limits. Exploring the legal status of corporate codes on the basis of existing European or international general principles of private law, such as the

[7] Picciotto (2003); Sobczak (2006); Marrella (2007); Koster and Eynde (2009); Peterkova (2014a) 11f.

[8] Kenny (2007); Coleman (2009); Phillips and Lim (2009); Estlund (2012); Revak (2012).

[9] Webb and Morrison (2004); Torrance (2011).

[10] Heijden (2011b); Heijden (2011a); Eijsbouts (2011); Vytopil (2012).

[11] Kocher (2002); Kocher (2008); Bachmann (2006b); Glinski (2007); Glinski (2008); Glinski (2011); Hilty and Henning-Bodewig (2014).

Principles of European Contract Law, the Draft Common Frame of Reference or the international UNIDROIT principles, can be criticised for ignoring that there is still inherent controversy over these principles and their legal character. Without taking a position on this matter, it is at least clear that there are immense difficulties involved in seeking to rely on these frameworks in national court proceedings. Against this background, this approach cannot be a viable option for a study that seeks to develop a model on serious private law enforcement of these codes.

Consequently, it is considered more feasible to connect to the latter approaches by using national private law as the legal basis to interpret the corporate codes. Yet this study seeks to take this national perspective a step further by not aiming to contribute to the further development of one particular legal system, but instead to engage in a comparative analysis of the corporate codes phenomenon. To approach the corporate codes phenomenon from a comparative legal perspective follows the idea of contributing to the debate on corporate codes in private law beyond the specifics of one particular legal system and thereby allowing inspiration from other legal systems and their solutions,[12] while at the same time respecting the necessity of developing autonomous solutions that take into consideration national idiosyncrasies.[13] The ultimate aim of this comparative analysis can thus be framed as developing recommendations for reform, particularly for the corporate codes in relation to two legal systems that aim to point to how a uniform solution to a global problem could be achieved in an era of remaining national diversity. This implies that the comparative analysis will be conducted differently than methodologically envisaged in orthodox comparative law. It has to be emphasised that this study will not directly compare the two legal systems and their approaches to corporate codes, but rather it will pursue a solution-oriented analysis on a comparative basis with a view to the specific problem of the corporate codes. More specifically, the study will explicitly not pursue a comparison in the strict sense and will not put the emphasis on their similarities and differences or discuss whether one legal system is better equipped to deal with the corporate codes phenomenon than another. Although such similarities and differences are occasionally mentioned and are indicated as an important topic for future research, the value of a comparative analysis is envisaged here as being able to develop a uniform response to a common global problem from the perspective of national private law that is based on functional equivalence.[14] This methodological approach follows primarily what Collins has framed as the methodology

[12] On this idea of using comparative law, see Smits (2009) 52ff; Smits (2014) 86.

[13] A first comprehensive attempt towards combining a comparative legal analysis to analyse the corporate codes phenomenon with a theoretical (economic) perspective is made by Cafaggi (2013), although such comparative elements are in fact already an inherent component of other contributions on this topic. Yet, so far, they do not appear in the form of a structured comparative analysis, but rather as occasional references to the (perceived) similar or comparable situation in other legal systems. Kenny (2007) and Revak (2012), for instance, refer to German labour law in their analysis of codes of conduct under US law; Bachmann (2006b) occasionally takes inspiration from US law in his analysis of German law. Glinski (2011) in her analysis on German law frequently mentions parallels to several other legal systems.

[14] Muir Watt (2007) 586ff.

of comparative (sociological) jurisprudence.[15] Although recognising the difficulty of developing a uniform solution for national legal systems that differ in their functioning, the approach of comparative sociological jurisprudence is based on the assumption that the pressure to harmonise private law in Europe, even in light of national diversity, requires exactly this undertaking.[16] Comparative jurisprudence serves accordingly as an analytical framework for developing solutions to a particular problem based on interdisciplinary insights from business studies, sociology and economics, with due respect for the different traditions, doctrinal evolution and cultures within the particular national legal systems.[17]

The two legal systems that are chosen as examples are the German and English systems of private law. This follows not only from the aim to develop proposals that should work in two of the most important legal traditions, eg, a codified system and a common law system, but the choice is also based on the consideration that there are substantive differences between these two legal systems in dealing with the corporate codes phenomenon that make them a particularly interesting comparison. First, when focusing on the corporate codes as a new phenomenon in private law, it is often mentioned in the current debate that a likely relevance of corporate codes in private law could be their use in the interpretation of open-ended concepts and blank clauses.[18] The frequent reference to this particular angle suggests investigating a system that is known for its various open-ended concepts through which social norms are integrated (Germany) and contrasting it with a legal system that retains a certain degree of scepticism towards such open-ended concepts and, instead, favours a pragmatic case-oriented approach that makes use of societal self-regulation as part of the facts of a particular case that assist in developing new and refining existing general rules for particular constellations (England).

In addition to their different ways of referring to social norms in legal reasoning, these two legal systems also show conceptual differences with regard to the legal concepts that are specifically relevant for the corporate codes. Such a conceptual difference is considered highly insightful in showing how uniform proposals for a particular new phenomenon based on functional equivalence can be envisaged when they need to be approached from conceptually different angles. With respect to the corporate codes phenomenon, it is here in particular where the stark contrast between a system that is known for its rigid and narrowly confined contract law with the doctrines of privity and consideration (England) and a system that has a considerably broader approach to contract law (Germany) can be seen. This particularly plays a role with regard to the enforcement of unilateral promises and the recognition of third party rights in contracts. Furthermore, such conceptual differences are also relevant in relation to the codes with regard to the rather strict distinction in English law between a contractual relationship and tort liability and,

[15] Collins (2008); Teubner and Collins (2011) 25ff.

[16] Teubner and Collins (2011) 28.

[17] Collins (2008) 253.

[18] See, eg, Herberg (2007) 33; Dilling, Herberg and Winter (2008a) 7; Eijsbouts (2011) 27, 40; Torrance (2011) 1605; Glinski (2014) 45.

conversely, the relaxation of this distinction in German law that treats relationships akin to a contract as a third category of quasi-contractual liability.

A third argument for choosing these two legal systems in particular is the fundamentally different, broader socio-economic context in which they are embedded. In the literature on the varieties of capitalism, these two countries are, in the European context, considered the representative examples of the two main variants of capitalism.[19] The UK serves in this theoretical framework as the paradigmatic example of the form of liberal market economies in which ownership and shareholder value are the core characteristics of economic activity, with a strong reliance on the competitive and deregulated market and formal contracting.[20] Germany, by contrast, is in this theoretical framework mentioned as a typical coordinated market economy that is less organised around the liberal market; it relies instead on coordination as its core organisational paradigm. Relational contracting, interfirm cooperation and long-term collaboration between companies, creditors, governments and trade unions are the central pillars of this capitalist structure.[21] These specific national, social, political and economic institutions of capitalism are generally used for the sake of explaining path-dependent evolutionary patterns on a national level and the evolution of national idiosyncrasies.[22] For the present study, the analysis of two legal systems that represent two opposing poles within the varieties of capitalism should serve as a useful starting point for the endeavour to find a common global response for the corporate codes phenomenon. The comparison between English and German law can also be considered as a test for the undertaking to realise uniform responses to a global problem in light of the remaining fundamentally diverging approaches to the regulation of corporations and market.[23] If it is possible to identify equivalent solutions for such differently organised forms of market activity and the related legal frameworks, such an undertaking could be successful on a greater scale overall. Yet the choice can also be read as drawing attention to the limits of the undertaking of finding equivalent solutions and thus provides a useful angle for further studies on the comparative dimension of CSR in relation to law.

Fourth, an important consideration behind the choice for these two legal systems is also their practical relevance. Having in mind that the objective is to suggest reform for private law and its enforcement structure for the corporate codes of transnational corporations, it is therefore also important to discuss examples of legal systems that prove to be relevant for companies in their global operations.

[19] Hall and Soskice (2001). See for the distinction between Rhenish and Anglo-Saxon capitalism Albert (1992).

[20] Hall and Soskice (2001) 8.

[21] ibid 8f. *cf* also Hoffmann (2004) 989ff.

[22] In this study, this already became relevant when explaining how a different understanding on CSR could evolve and the ideal typical distinction appeared between shareholder and stakeholder corporate law, see text in section 1.2.1. (p 4) and accompanying footnotes. See on the value of the varieties of capitalism approach as an explanatory framework for the evolution of the law with further references Calliess and Zumbansen (2010) 190ff.

[23] For a strong argument for maintaining these remaining national specifics when regulating world economy, see Rodrik (2011) xix, 233ff.

It is here that English and German law are also both important legal systems from the global perspective. When it comes to the area of contract law in the EU, English and German law are among the most preferred legal systems that are chosen in business contracts.[24] This of course does not apply to the rules on non-contractual liability where the law applicable concerning non-contractual liability for companies incorporated in Europe is generally the law where the damage occurred and not the country of incorporation.[25] However, in particular in relation to English law, it should be noted that, due to the characteristics of the common law system, developments in English law are highly important in influencing other Commonwealth countries. This also includes developing countries, in which alleged violations concerning labour standards and environmental protection often take place. As concrete examples, one can refer to the disputes involving environmental pollution and violation of social standards by companies in Nigeria, where English precedent influenced the legal decision even though it was ultimately based on Nigerian law.[26] Thus, proposing developments in the English common law—in particular, the tort of negligence—can also have a direct effect on the law of other countries. While this is certainly not an argument in favour of German law, one can refer here to the fact that this system remains important as the largest economy in Europe, rendering German law applicable to a number of globally operating multinational corporations. This is true to the extent that the narrowly confined exceptions in the European rules on choice of law apply that provide for an extraterritorial application of national law[27] and if such exceptions and the idea on a

[24] For empirical observations concerning choice of law in business contracts, see especially the study of the Oxford Institute of European and Comparative Law and the Oxford Centre for Socio-Legal Studies, 'Civil Justice Systems in Europe: Implications for Choice of Forum and Choice of Contract Law' (2008), available at: http://denning.law.ox.ac.uk/themes/iecl/pdfs/Oxford Civil Justice Survey—Summary of Results, Final.pdf, at 14f. The study indicates that in Europe, a preference exists among businesses to choose English, Swiss and German law.

[25] Article 4, para 1, Rome II Reg 864/2007/EC on the law applicable to non-contractual obligations [2007] OJ L199/40.

[26] Instructively on the influence of English common law doctrines on cases against companies on the oil pollution in Nigeria: Frynas (1999), in particular at 150, where it is concluded that 'English legal traditions, including strict standards of scientific evidence or statutes of limitation, decrease the chances of success for potential litigants in oil-related cases [in Nigeria]'; and recently Meeran (2011) 15. As a concrete example, one can refer here to the Dutch case against Shell on oil pollution in Nigeria, where the District Court of The Hague based the decision on Nigerian law, but in reaching its decision, it made use of recent developments in English law concerning the common law tort of negligence: *Akpan and others v Royal Dutch Shell and others*, District Court of The Hague, 30 January 2013, case number: C/09/337050/HA ZA 09-1580, para 4.10: 'In its conclusion of Nigerian law, the District Court *consulted English common law literature*, including handbooks regarding the specific torts alleged by Milieudefensie *et al*. After all, Nigerian law is a *common law system that is based on English law*' (official translation of judgment, emphasis added).

[27] Pursuant to the Rome II-Regulation, it is already possible for claimants to choose between the law where the damage occurs and where the event giving rise to the damage in case the dispute on non-contractual liability concerns environmental damages (art 7) or where 'the tort/delict is manifestly more closely connected' with another country (art 4, para 3). Besides, extraterritorial application of national law is the rule for overriding mandatory provisions (art 16). See generally on these and other relevant provisions that would allow applying the law of the home state extraterritorially Augenstein (2010) 70ff, paras 215ff.

necessary extraterritorial application of the law of the Member States of the EU in general are further pursued.[28]

Since the legal analysis will also include scholarly contributions and case law from other national legal systems (US law in particular), a few words are finally necessary on the rationale for this choice. These occasional references to the debate in other legal systems are not envisaged as part of the comparative analysis; the actual comparison remains emphatically restricted to the codes' place in the English and German system of private law. Yet, the overall objective of the following analysis is first and foremost to present and assess a variety of conceptual options on how to integrate corporate codes in private law. This in fact requires embracing the wider debate on corporate codes in private law and also taking account of suggestions and court decisions that are based on other national legal systems than those under scrutiny. In this context, the analysis seeks to remain careful when using material that is related to another legal system and its national specifics, and thus integrates them merely as conceptual inspirations and not as an integral part of the comparative analysis.

[28] For an argument to expand extraterritorial application of national law to human rights violations on the ground of the existing international duty of states to protect human rights, see Augenstein and Kinley (2013). See also generally on this issue Enneking (2012) 463ff.

3

Enforcing Corporate Codes by Private Law

The Role of National Contract Law

> Few of the commitments which companies normally sign up to in their voluntary CSR policies … are entirely free of legal obligation anyway … New legal tools are being evolved, and old ones used creatively to make what business have perceived as voluntary, or beyond the law, in fact legally enforceable.[1]

THAT COMPANIES CAN create a legally enforceable obligation by means of adopting a corporate code seems quite counterintuitive considering the common perception of corporate codes as entirely voluntary. However, the interpretation of corporate codes as the basis for a legal obligation effectively embraces nothing other than one of the most fundamental principles in private law: *pacta sunt servanda*. This core principle of contract law stresses the importance of keeping agreements and promises, and not deviating from them even if they were voluntarily created in the first place. Yet, in relation to corporate codes, their legal enforcement as contracts or promises is certainly not a given and uncontroversial fact. On the contrary, the corporate codes require further scrutiny as to whether they, pursuant to the rules on contract law, would qualify at all as a valid agreement or promise that the law recognises as legally binding. If so, it must be examined further what exact substantive legal obligation the code creates and who could rely on what types of remedies in case this obligation from the code is breached. This chapter will be devoted to these two broader issues.

3.1. CORPORATE CODES AS ENFORCEABLE OBLIGATIONS

To what extent is it possible to enforce legally the voluntary corporate commitments on socially responsible corporate conduct? In answering this question, three constellations need to be distinguished that existing empirical studies have identified as occurring frequently. The legal enforcement of corporate codes needs to be specified in relation to easy cases where corporate codes are incorporated into a bilateral contract (section 3.1.1), for comparably easy cases where the codes are

[1] McBarnet (2007) 31.

not an integral part of the contract, but appear in the ancillary documents of the contract (section 3.1.2) and, finally, the difficult and most controversial cases where corporate codes are detached from a bilateral contract and represent merely unilateral declarations to the public (section 3.1.3).

3.1.1. The *Easy* Case: Incorporation into Contracts

In empirical studies on the use of corporate codes by companies, a tendency can be observed within large enterprises to incorporate their own corporate codes explicitly into contracts with business partners. The prime examples in this context are the contracts of companies with their suppliers in which a reference is included to the company's corporate code. Increasingly, this strategy is also pursued for other types of contractual relations, eg, contracts that companies conclude with their respective customers or explicit contractual agreements with civil society groups.[2] If the corporate code appears explicitly in the contract terms, there are arguably no complex legal problems involved. Once a contract is concluded between a company and its contractual partner, any term that refers to the requirement to comply with the corporate code also becomes a valid and legally binding express term of the contract. The deliberate incorporation of corporate codes into contracts thus already represents one important constellation in which voluntary codes can be said to transform into legally binding obligations.[3] The following section will therefore merely analyse the most typical situations in which corporate codes are made part of a contract in order to identify the parties that become legally obliged to comply with the code and the parties that can remedy the code.

3.1.1.1. Supplier Contracts

The most frequently discussed contracts in which corporate codes currently play a role are the agreements of companies with their suppliers. As a matter of fact, large companies frequently incorporate their own corporate policies into supplier contracts, often in the form of a separate policy term that requires the business partner to follow the corporate policy of the company. Although these supplier contracts are not publicly available and companies keep them confidential, some

[2] Detailed empirical studies on the use of supplier codes of conduct have been conducted, particularly by McBarnet and Kurkchiyan (2007); Vytopil (2012); Cafaggi (2013). The latter constellations are dealt with by McBarnet (2007) 42f (mentioning business and governments as consumers that include social and environmental standards in contracts); McCrudden (2007) (focusing on social and environmental standards in public procurement contracts); Glinski (2011) 170 (mentioning contracts of companies with civil society groups and NGOs or local communities); Cafaggi (2013) passim (focusing on certification contracts between NGOs and companies); Coleman (2009); and Koster and Eynde (2009) (both focusing on contractual enforcement of agreements on social standards between companies and international trade unions).

[3] eg, pointedly, Kerr, Janda and Pitts (2009) 333: 'In this regard, codes of conduct adopted by companies … make the transition from a voluntary, self-regulatory instrument to contractual obligations that are legally binding on the contracting third party … and once again this represents a blurring of the putative legal/voluntary divide'; Torrance (2011) 1602.

evidence on the specifics of this incorporation can be derived primarily from empirical studies that have succeeded in accessing these codes.[4] Following their observations, a typical case represents a reference to a corporate code in a term in the contract that is separate from the 'ordinary' terms such as product quality, delivery date or payment.[5] A common phrasing of such a term is to make adherence to this corporate code an explicit obligation of the supplier.[6] This obligation is normally linked to several other provisions in the contract, which specify the right of the company to monitor compliance in the form of conducting audits.[7] In addition, the contract can also contain agreements concerning remedies that apply in an event of non-compliance, such as the obligation to set up an improvement plan or to participate in an employee and manager training and, in severe cases, the right to terminate the contract.[8] Consequently, when included in a supplier contract, the corporate code becomes a binding contractual obligation for the supplier, which can be enforced by the company as the contractual partner by invoking the contractually agreed remedies or the general remedies available under contract law. It has to be emphasised, however, that in this constellation, the provisions incorporating the corporate code most often solely create an obligation on the side of the supplier and merely entitle the company to enforce code compliance. Conversely, the terms that refer to the corporate code do not contain a contractual obligation for the buying company.[9] Hence, the incorporation of corporate codes into supplier contracts mainly has the result of creating an enforceable contractual obligation on the side of the supplying contracting party.[10]

3.1.1.2. Customer Contracts

Next to the prominent case of contractually included supplier codes of conduct, the incorporation of corporate codes is increasingly also observable in relations

[4] For examples of contractually included codes, see, eg, McBarnet and Kurkchiyan (2007) 69: 'By supplying the goods ... the Supplier expressly warrants that they will conform to all Policies, which are notified by the Company to the Supplier in connection with the supply of goods'; Vytopil (2012) 167: 'manufacturer is obliged to demonstrate that it is actively promoting good labour conditions for its workers'; Kerr, Janda and Pitts (2009) 333f: 'suppliers, partners and other third parties must know and agree to comply with the Code'. See also the different examples provided by Cafaggi (2013) in accompanying footnotes.

[5] For such observations in the supplier code of conduct of Gap Inc, see Backer (2008) 509ff.

[6] McBarnet and Kurkchiyan (2007) 65: 'Best practice is increasingly being treated as setting up a contractual obligation on suppliers to meet specified CSR standards'; Cafaggi (2013) 1562, 1576f and *passim*.

[7] See, eg, McBarnet and Kurkchiyan (2007) 74f: 'Best practice therefore involves sophisticated monitoring processes, and, as we have seen, the right to monitor compliance is likely to be expressly written into the terms and conditions of the contract: "[The Company] reserves the right to carry out a Social Accountability Assessment at the Supplier's premises".'

[8] McBarnet and Kurkchiyan (2007) 77ff; Backer (2008) 512; Cafaggi (2013) 1573ff.

[9] Cafaggi (2013) 1592: 'Rarely does the contract wording define and impose obligations on the main contractor or the retailer to monitor compliance in the interests of the final beneficiaries; rather, these are defined as rights, which the contractual party is free to exercise.'

[10] The follow-up question of whether a broader contextual interpretation or supplementation of the contract would arrive at a different conclusion and would also recognise duties on the side of the buying company will be focused on more in detail later in this part, see below section 3.1.3.2 (p 63), text and accompanying footnotes.

between companies and their customers. This tendency towards incorporating codes of conduct into contracts with large companies occurs primarily when the customers of the companies are public bodies, non-profit institutions or businesses that themselves attempt to source in a socially and environmentally responsible way. In fact, such contracts can be referred to as a first constellation in which corporate codes also result in a legal obligation not only for the supplier, but also the large buyer. As pointedly put by an observer, 'the consumers are both business itself and government, and consumer power is expressed in legal form through contractual obligation'.[11]

With respect to public bodies, one can mention the current strategy among governments and local administration to use their public procurement contracts to make adherence to social and environmental standards binding. In fact, the use of procurement contracts has become a widely used tool of governments, either as an alternative or a complementary policy measure to top-down regulation that aims at furthering social and environmental engagement by companies.[12] The increasing use of contracts by governments as a regulatory tool has also been caused by developments in public procurement law. It was in the first place the European Court of Justice and recently also the European legislator that have constantly broadened the catalogue of admissible criteria in public procurement procedures and, in so doing, have allowed and encouraged public bodies to give social and environmental criteria a decisive role in awarding contracts.[13] A clause on compliance with social and environmental standards integrated in a procurement contract then equally transforms an initially voluntary commitment to adhere to social and environmental standards into an obligation of the company that equips the government, as the contractual partner, with enforcement rights. A similar strategy to oblige businesses to comply with voluntary codes of conduct on social and environmental standards can be observed in relation to contracts that companies conclude with other businesses or institutions that themselves have the objective of being responsible customers. This strategy has recently received attention with respect to sponsoring contracts and contracts on the supply of sportswear and sports equipment between large apparel brands and

[11] McBarnet (2007) 43.

[12] See generally on this strategy McCrudden (2007). See also McCrudden (2004), in which he shows with rich empirical evidence that public procurement has throughout history frequently been used as a policy tool to achieve a social outcome.

[13] See the rulings of the European Court of Justice on social and environmental criteria in public procurement procedures: Case C-31/87 *Gebroeders Beentjes BV v The Netherlands* [1988] ECR-4635 (criterion directed towards combating unemployment); Case C-513/99 *Concordia Bus Finland* [2002] ECR I-07213 (environmental criteria); and Case C-448/01 *EVN Wienstrom GmbH* [2003] ECR I-14527 (requiring electricity to be supplied from renewable energy sources). For restrictions concerning such social and environmental criteria, see especially Case C-368/10 *European Commission v The Netherlands* (not yet reported). In its recent communication on CSR, the Commission also announced that it aims to 'facilitate a better integration of social and environmental considerations into public procurement'; see European Commission, A Renewed EU Strategy 2011–14 for Corporate Social Responsibility, COM(2011) 681 final 10f. Recent developments towards allowing social and environmental criteria to be better integrated into public procurement are Directive 2014/24/EU on public procurement [2014] OJ L94/65, art 18(2) and Directive 2014/25/EU on procurement by entities operating in the water, energy, transport and postal service sectors [2014] OJ L94/243, art 36(2).

US universities. By means of requesting that a code of conduct be included in such agreements, these universities seek to use their power as wholesale customers for the sake of making social and environmental standards contractually binding. A prominent example for such a term is the contract of Adidas with the University of Wisconsin, the interpretation of which became subject to a lawsuit. As this specific contract and the dispute on its classification will be more intensively analysed when focusing on the interpretation of the code obligation and its actual contractual enforcement, it should suffice to mention it, for the time being, as an illustrative example in which a contract of a large company with its customer contained a material term on compliance with a code of labour practice.[14] As a result, if included in a contract with a socially responsible customer, the corporate code can become a binding contractual obligation of the company that the customer, as the contractual partner, can enforce.

3.1.1.3. Contracts on Social and Environmental Compliance

In order to complete the overview of constellations in which voluntary codes on social and environmental standards become binding by means of being incorporated into a contract, one must also finally mention constellations in which companies and civil society groups or local communities directly contract on these standards. Such contracts can appear in the form of specific certification programmes in which the agreement is about the membership of companies in a particular certification programme. In these agreements, the membership contract specifies compliance with a code of conduct as a binding obligation of the company that becomes a member and is often also combined with extensive rights of the certifying organisation to inspect factories and remedy non-compliance.[15] The agreement usually refers to the social and environmental code of conduct of the particular certifier as an obligation for members, but also requires the company to reconcile its own corporate policy with this code. Prominent examples from the apparel industry are the *Fair Labor Association* and the *Fair Wear Foundation*. In their codes, it is specified that participating companies are obliged to adhere to the organisation's workplace code of conduct and the procedural rules specified therein, but it is also required that companies include this workplace code of conduct in their own corporate policies.[16] In exchange for this contractual obligation to comply with the code of conduct and accepting the procedures on monitoring and remediation applicable in the event of non-compliance, participating companies are entitled to advertise their membership with the logo of the association.

[14] In the contracting agreement, codes of labour practice are included as a material term, which obliges Adidas to 'ensure the socially responsible manufacture of goods' and 'to comply with the requirements of the codes'. *cf* on this point the claimant's complaint for declaratory judgment, available at: www.business-humanrights.org/Categories/Lawlawsuits/Lawsuitsregulatoryaction/LawsuitsSelectedcases/adidaslawsuitreuniversityofwisconsin, at 2.

[15] Different constellations of such certification contracts are discussed in Cafaggi (2013) 1603ff.

[16] Charter Fair Labour Association, pt IX (30 July 2013), available at: www.fairlabor.org/sites/default/files/fla_charter.pdf, at 12–13; Charter Fair Wear Foundation (October 2009), available at: www.fairwear.org/506/resources/ 9.

In spite of the differences between the various organisations and the requirements as to code compliance that is specified in these certification contracts,[17] the initiatives have as a common denominator the requirement that companies need to undertake strong efforts to achieve compliance with the code of conduct of the respective organisation on a constant basis in order to receive and maintain the certificate of the organisation.[18]

Apart from these specific certification contracts, codes on social and environmental standards can also become a mandatory obligation when companies contract with civil society groups explicitly on social or environmental aspects. Examples of this constellation are so-called International Framework Agreements (IFA), which are agreements between large companies and international trade unions on adherence to fundamental workplace standards.[19] In addition, there are also specific contracts between companies and civil society groups on specific code-relevant aspects.[20] This latter form of contracting recently became quite prominent. In the aftermath of the building collapse in Bangladesh that was described in chapter one, one of the core instruments to prevent similar tragedies in the future represented the Accord on Fire and Building Safety in Bangladesh. The Accord was negotiated by companies sourcing from Bangladesh, trade unions, NGOs and the ILO, and contained legally binding obligations for the participating companies to assist in improving the building and fire safety in the factories from which they source.[21] Hence, in addition to the general development towards incorporating a clause on compliance with social and environmental standards into commercial contracts, it is also through such very specific agreements that voluntary standards in corporate codes are initially transformed into legal obligations that are enforceable by contract law.

3.1.2. The *Comparably Easy* Case: The Ancillary Documents

The legal enforcement of the codes becomes slightly more complex when a corporate code does not appear in the form of an express term in the written contract, but is incorporated in its ancillary documents only. Empirical studies on the codes of conduct of large companies suggest that this is also frequently occurring, in

[17] An instructive comparison between the mandatory requirements of different certification programmes can be found in O'Rourke (2003) 12f.

[18] This focus on process obligations in certification contracts is emphasised by Cafaggi (2013) 1597.

[19] On these agreements, see especially the studies of Voss et al (2008); Kocher (2008) 68f. For the treatment of these Framework Agreements as enforceable contracts, see, eg, Coleman (2009) 621ff.

[20] Glinski (2011) 170.

[21] Accord on Fire and Building Safety in Bangladesh, available at: www.bangladeshaccord.org. First paragraph: 'The undersigned parties are committed to the goal of a safe and sustainable Bangladeshi Ready-Made Garment ("RMG") industry in which no worker needs to fear fires, building collapses, or other accidents that could be prevented with reasonable health and safety measures. The signatories to this Agreement *agree* to establish a fire and building safety programme in Bangladesh for a period of five years' (emphasis added). In s 5, the Accord also contains an arbitration clause and the consequence that 'any arbitration award shall be enforceable in a court of law of the domicile of the signatory against whom enforcement is sought and shall be subject to The Convention on the Recognition and Enforcement of Foreign Arbitral Awards'.

particular with respect to supplier codes of conduct. The parties to such contracts often choose to include their corporate codes not in the contractual document directly, but rather in the general terms and conditions[22] or, particularly in long-term relations, in the umbrella agreement that sets out the general conditions for an individually placed order for the supply of goods.[23] The enforcement of codes that appear in these documents is then merely a question of whether and to what extent these ancillary documents become contractually binding.

3.1.2.1. General Terms and Conditions

When made part of the general terms and conditions, contractual enforcement is first possible if the binding contract declares these general terms to be applicable and the particular term is not considered unfair.[24] By means of referring to them in the contract, the standard terms become express terms of the contract.[25] Moreover, contract law also recognises the general terms and conditions as part of the contract when they were present and handed over to the other party at the time of the formation of the contract[26] or, even if the particular terms were not referred to in the contract under dispute, they were still commonly included in previous transactions between the same parties.[27]

Yet, the interpretation of corporate codes as contract terms can become disputed in one particular situation. Once part of the general terms and conditions, the enforcement of corporate codes can be hindered by what is commonly referred

[22] Vytopil (2012) 166f.

[23] McBarnet and Kurkchiyan (2007) 69.

[24] One could in this regard also discuss more intensively whether the requirement to comply with certain social and environmental standards in general terms and conditions would have to be treated as an unfair term. One can mention here the financial investments that compliance with the code partly requires, which is often also phrased as a unilateral obligation of the supplier. However, given the high threshold for unfairness in commercial contracts, although it is possible, it seems that it is not too likely that a court would treat such terms as unfair. This applies in particular if, as will be discussed later (below section 3.1.3.2, p 63, text and accompanying footnotes), a contextual interpretation of this term is preferred that would interpret the obligation to comply with a code in light of the public declaration of the lead firm and thus would rather juridify the commitments to help achieving and maintaining compliance in the spirit of a partnership.

[25] On the details of incorporating supplier codes of conduct into the contract by means of reference, see Peterkova (2014a) 13f.

[26] Under German law, these requirements are set out in §§ 305ff BGB, which make as a condition for general terms of engagement that the party intending to incorporate them in the contract, explicitly or under exceptional circumstances by means of public notice, refers to them in the moment of the formation of contract, and the other party has the possibility to take notice of its content and accepts them. For the comparable situation in English law, see, eg, Collins (2003b) 223.

[27] If the parties are both commercial parties, the general terms and conditions could also be incorporated if these particular terms were not explicitly included in the contract under dispute, but were incorporated in previous contracts between the same parties; for German law, see, eg, BGH NJW 1964, 1788, 1789; NJW 1965, 1324, 1325; and for English law, see *British Crane Hire Corp Ltd v Ipswich Plant Hire* [1975] QB 303, in which a contract was concluded orally, but one party sent a written form to the other party shortly after delivery, which included reference to terms and conditions. The court concluded that both parties knew that the conditions were 'habitually imposed' by one party (evidence was taken from two previous transactions), so it was the 'common understanding' of the parties that the contract was to be concluded on the terms of one parties' general terms and conditions (per Lord Denning at 309).

to as the battle of forms. The battle of forms refers to a situation in which each party has in place its own set of general terms and conditions and the obligations laid down therein differ. With respect to corporate codes, this constellation occurs when both parties have included a code of conduct in their general terms and conditions and both attempt to incorporate their own set of general terms and conditions into the contract.[28] In this case, contract law has to decide whether and, if so, which of the differing sets of general terms and conditions eventually becomes binding and, consequently, also the corporate code of conduct therein. In general, there are different possible solutions on how to solve this problem of the battle of forms. In some systems, contradicting terms and conditions are treated as a dissent on the terms of the contract, with the result that none of them would become binding. Other legal systems deem binding the terms and conditions that were introduced first (those mentioned in the first offer) or those that were last introduced before the formation of the contract (those mentioned in the purported acceptance).

English and German law here have two different approaches and thus provide two different possible directions concerning the contractual enforcement of corporate codes that appear in general terms and conditions. In English law, it is the general approach to give priority to the last set of terms and conditions. Any introduction of own terms and conditions in response to the introduction of the other party is not considered an acceptance, but rather a counter-offer. This is due to the fact that the acceptance together with reference to one's own set of terms and conditions does not mirror the offer and thus cannot be interpreted as an unequivocal acceptance.[29] Pursuant to this understanding, a particular set of general terms and conditions can only become contractually binding if it is subsequently accepted without reference to one's own set of terms and conditions or if the other party accepted by means of beginning to perform the contract.[30] However, this approach did not remain uncontested. In giving a dissenting opinion in the Court of Appeal in *Butler Machine Tool Co Ltd v Ex-Cell-O Corp*, Lord Denning, for instance, suggested approaching the issue of the battle of forms differently by stating that: 'The terms and conditions of both parties are to be construed together. If they can be reconciled so as to give a harmonious result, all well and good. If the differences are irreconcilable—so that they are mutually contradictory—then the conflicting terms may have to be scrapped and replaced by a reasonable implication'.[31] His approach thus aimed at a solution that would attempt to reconcile the two opposing sets of general terms and conditions wherever possible and allow any differing clauses to be constructed by the court. However, since the other Lord Justices disagreed with this approach, it remains the rule that the terms included at the latest

[28] See especially on the relevance of the battle of forms problem for the corporate codes Vytopil (2012) 162f.

[29] This is also called the 'mirror image rule', which requires for a contract an offer that matches acceptance. The leading case establishing this rule is *Hyde v Wrench* (1840) 3 Beav 334.

[30] *BRS v Arthur v Crutchley Ltd* [1968] 1 Lloyd's Rep 271.

[31] *Butler Machine Tool Co Ltd v Ex-Cell-O Corp* [1979] 1 WLR 401 405. A similar approach is proposed by Beatson, Burrows and Cartwright (2010) 42.

before the conclusion of the contract will prevail.[32] With respect to the corporate codes, this approach to the battle of forms thus has the result that if made part of the general terms and conditions, the corporate codes would only become binding under the condition that they are part of the last terms and conditions that were introduced before the formation of the contract and if accepted by the other party explicitly or by means of performing the contract.

When it comes to the problem of the battle of forms in German law, it has previously equally been the rule that the terms and conditions that would prevail were the last ones introduced before the conclusion of the contract, provided that the other party accepted by performing the contract.[33] However, already by 1957, the Federal High Court of Justice issued a ruling that eventually turned out to become the prevailing approach to the battle of forms problem in German law.[34] In this case, the Court held that a constant reference by each party to its own set of terms and conditions would not result in the incorporation of any of the competing terms unless one party explicitly accepted the other party's set of terms and conditions. The parties' constant reference in their correspondence to their own terms and conditions results in incorporation only to the extent that the terms do not differ materially and can be reconciled with each other. For terms that are impossible to reconcile, none of the competing terms forms part of the contract; instead, they are legally treated as a partial dissent, with the result that conflicting terms are knocked out and default rules fill the gap.[35] With respect to the corporate codes, this has a different result regarding legal enforcement. In a battle of forms constellation, the corporate codes still become legally binding to the extent that they contain similar substantive obligations. Only to the extent that the codes differ in substance would corporate codes not become part of the contract and, since there are no default rules on social and environmental standards in contract law that could fill the gap, they would not be subject to contractual enforcement.

3.1.2.2. Umbrella Agreements

A different constellation of linking corporate codes to the contracting process without making it part of the contract is to include the codes in an umbrella agreement. In order to be able to answer whether corporate codes would become binding in this constellation, it is first necessary to provide some information on the character of these types of agreements. In long-term relationships between commercial parties on the continuous supply of goods or the provision of services, agreements between the parties are exhibited through a two-tiered structure. If two business

[32] However, in *Butler Machine Tool Co Ltd v Ex-Cell-O Corp* (ibid), the court also held that a party who signed a slip which contained reference to the other party's general terms and conditions accepted those terms and conditions even if the letter accompanying the slip stated that the party's own general terms and conditions would apply.

[33] For the development of the battle of forms problem under German law with further references to the debate, see generally Schlechtriem (1999) 36f.

[34] BGH BB 1957, 728, and in the same direction, BGH NJW 1973, 2106, 2107f; BGH WM 1974, 842, 842.

[35] Schlechtriem (1999) 37.

partners attempt to enter into a long-term relationship on the supply of goods or particular components, the terms specifying the general aspects of the business relationship are often set out in a general letter of agreement. This agreement is negotiated when parties start a relationship, and sometimes they are only informally agreed upon. The specific characteristic of these types of agreements is that they still lack specific arrangements as to the main performance obligation, such as the particular order of a number of specific goods and the price. The ordering process is instead subject to separate negotiations whereby the parties agree at regular intervals on the conditions that apply to a particular production and delivery of the goods for a specific period of time.[36] The reason for choosing this form of contracting is, among others, the ability for the buying party to maintain a certain degree of flexibility in order to be able to react to potential changes in consumer demand for such goods or price variations on the market and to simplify and facilitate the contracting process in complex transactions.[37] From the supplier perspective, this form of contracting has the advantage that the umbrella agreement already provides certainty in a long-term relationship and allows it to adapt its production accordingly. When determining whether such agreements, and thus the corporate codes included therein, are legally binding, first, an analytical distinction needs to be made between the interpretation of particularly the umbrella agreement as a binding contract and the possibility of the umbrella agreement becoming binding by means of being integrated into the specific agreement on the order of goods. If referred to in a contract that deals with any particular order of goods, if mentioned when the order is placed or if incorporated into previous orders on a sufficiently frequent basis, the umbrella agreement, and thus also the code of conduct therein, can become contractually binding as terms of the contract comparable to an express incorporation of general terms and conditions. The difficult question is whether the umbrella agreement can also, as such, be considered the legal basis for enforceable rights and obligations. Are the framework agreement and the corporate code therein the legal basis for a binding contract?

In English law, the leading case on this question is *Bair Textile Holdings Ltd v Marks and Spencer*,[38] in which the Court of Appeal decided that a long-term relationship between a retailer and a manufacturer, which lasted over 30 years and that was based on an informal agreement on further cooperation, could not be interpreted as a binding contract. The Court ultimately rejected the binding character of the agreement because it did not find sufficient evidence for an intention of the parties to create legal obligations when agreeing on this informal umbrella agreement. It was held that only the agreement on the specific order would be sufficiently specific to assume that the parties intended to be bound

[36] See generally for an instructive description of the interaction between these agreements Mouzas and Furmston (2008) and, with a view to specifically the arrangements in retailer–supplier relations, Mouzas (2009) 214ff; Collins (2009) 192ff.

[37] Mouzas and Furmston (2008) 40, 49.

[38] *Bair Textile Holdings Ltd v Marks & Spencer* [2001] CLC 999.

by it.[39] From this decision, it can be concluded that English law sets high threshold requirements for assuming that direct obligations are already created on the grounds of such a preliminary agreement. However, it should be noted that this case dealt with the constellation of an informal and oral agreement in which one party constantly made it clear towards the other that it would not want to treat the general agreement on long-term cooperation as a legally binding agreement and, on top of that, the evidence brought forward by the defendant on the content of this informal agreement showed that these obligations are quite vague in terms of content. In the event that the umbrella agreement remains less informal, is made in writing and contains more specific terms, it is thus more likely that the courts would interpret the terms of the umbrella agreement as a contract.[40] Provided that the umbrella agreement and the corporate code therein would sufficiently resemble a process of formal contracting, a different treatment is at least conceivable.

German law, in contrast, has a different approach to umbrella agreements. The courts have already treated these agreements as binding between the parties and, in this context, the Federal High Court of Justice also coined the term 'umbrella agreement' (*Rahmenvertrag*), which it defined as a general agreement between the parties that tied together the various individual contracts on the supply of goods.[41] Although the umbrella agreement does not specify main performance obligations, it already lays down sufficiently specific ancillary duties for the contracting parties. As such, the umbrella agreement is classified as a contract *sui generis*[42] that has as its content the commitment of both parties to enter into a long-term relationship from which particular obligations transpire.[43] However, in spite of this general possibility of treating the umbrella agreement as a binding contract, the Federal High Court of Justice also held that the sheer fact that parties maintain a long-term cooperative relationship does not per se indicate the existence of an umbrella agreement.[44] Against this background, it can be concluded that, pursuant to German law, it is at least possible in principle to interpret the umbrella agreement as a binding contract if the umbrella agreement is sufficiently specific. As a consequence, any corporate code that is included in an umbrella agreement can become a legally binding term of this separate framework contract.

[39] In fact, the court used two main arguments. First, the broad and rather informal 'supplier partnership agreement' was too vague to create legal relations. In addition, the purported lack of intention was explained by the fact that, in this particular case, the defendant had made clear towards the claimants on several occasions that it did not intend to create a binding contract that would govern the relationship. Both of these aspects are also emphasised by Mouzas and Furmston (2008) 46 as core obstacles that hinder the interpretation of umbrella agreements as binding contracts. They also focus on the doctrine of consideration that could provide an obstacle for treating umbrella agreements as contracts.

[40] See for a similar conclusion Mouzas and Furmston (2008) 48.

[41] BGH BB 1968, 61, 62.

[42] BGH NJW 1979, 1782, 1783.

[43] In BGH NJW-RR 1992, 977, 978, it was held that the umbrella agreement does not give rise to a duty to conclude and perform the individual contracts because the umbrella agreement does not deal in a sufficiently concrete manner with the main performance obligations. Yet, what can be derived from the contract is a duty to negotiate with the other party on individual orders, and a failure to do so can result in the payment of damages.

[44] BGH NJW 2002, 3695, 3696 (with respect to a banking contract).

3.1.2.3. Conclusion

As a result, next to the unequivocal enforcement of codes that are incorporated into bilateral agreements, a binding contractual obligation to comply with a code can also occur in constellations in which corporate codes are included in the documents that are ancillary to the main contractual document. Yet, with respect to this constellation, one can already identify different approaches between the legal systems involved. Under English contract law, in order for such ancillary documents to become contractually enforceable, they would need to be more formalised. They need to be part of the deliberate process of offer and mirroring acceptance. German law, by contrast, is also prepared to interpret as legally binding the more informal and underlying consensus, such as the implicit agreement on terms and conditions that do not differ in substance and the informal umbrella agreements.[45] To that effect, the enforcement of corporate codes would have a broader scope under German law. This legal system is thus more prone to also enforce the agreements on social and environmental standards that 'are normally set out in agreements designed at the "softest" end of the spectrum'.[46]

3.1.3. The *Difficult* Case: Public Declarations as Contract Terms

So far, the analysis has focused on constellations in which the binding character of the corporate code could be established with relative ease because the contracting parties explicitly included the corporate code in the contracting process by incorporating it either in the contractual document as such or in the documents that the law recognises as an integral part of the contracting practice. However, this affirmative conclusion on the contractually binding character of these types of codes of conduct conceals the underlying more difficult problem of whether a corporate code would even be enforceable if it remains a unilateral declaration. The question whether the publicly declared corporate code could become enforceable has already been subject to a court ruling. In the US case of *Doe v Wal-Mart Stores*,[47] it became an intensely debated question whether the publicly declared corporate code could become relevant in the interpretation of the supplier contract. Yet, apart from the discussed relevance of a publicly declared code for the interpretation of supplier contracts, this shift in focus from the bilateral agreement to the public declaration also leads to additional options concerning the actors that

[45] This conclusion could be explained with a view to the different forms of capitalism to which the respective legal systems relate. Being part of liberal market economies (LMEs) that are characterised by arm's-length exchange and discrete contracting, English law adheres to the idea of the formalised and explicit contract as an ideal. In the coordinated market economy (CME) of Germany, it is relational and incomplete contracting that appears as a main organising paradigm in the economy, which is also reflected in a more context-oriented contract law. See fundamentally on this difference in contracting between LMEs and CMEs Casper (2001); and Hall and Soskice (2001) 8f.

[46] McBarnet and Kurkchiyan (2007) 69.

[47] *Jane Doe and others v Wal-Mart Stores*, United States Court of Appeal for the 9th Circuit, 572 F 3d 677, opinion delivered by Judge Gould.

could eventually enforce such corporate codes, such as consumers that rely on the code when purchasing products or even the code beneficiaries.

3.1.3.1. A Controversial Case: Doe v Wal-Mart Stores

In 1992, a time when it began to become popular among large corporations to adopt codes of conduct related to minimum workplace standards, the large US retailer Wal-Mart also developed such a code and communicated it to the public. The main purpose of making the code publicly available was to emphasise the willingness of the company to improve working conditions worldwide. The code contained certain minimum standards regarding working conditions, such as adherence to local laws and local industry standards as to remuneration, working hours, the prohibition of forced and child labour, and non-discrimination, and it was incorporated into the contracts that Wal-Mart concluded with its foreign suppliers. Next to the substantive obligation of the supplier to adhere to minimum working conditions, the contract also contained a provision that reserved a right for Wal-Mart to inspect supplier factories and a right to terminate the contract if inspections were to reveal that the supplier failed to comply with the code.[48] Hence, this corporate code represented a contractual obligation on the side of the supplier and resembles the above-discussed constellation of contractually included supplier codes of conduct.[49]

It is this corporate code that eventually provided the basis for a class action lawsuit by employees of foreign suppliers that, interestingly, targeted Wal-Mart and not the contractually obliged suppliers. More precisely, the claimants argued that the corporate code not only created a contractual obligation for suppliers to adhere to the code but also an obligation on the side of Wal-Mart to improve workplace standards worldwide as it had promised in its publicly available corporate code. Essentially, Wal-Mart was accused for breaching this binding obligation to improve workplace standards by not monitoring supplier factories with sufficient frequency and accuracy. Pursuant to the facts of the case, the company allegedly ignored false records provided by suppliers during audits and the fact that suppliers obviously cheated them by showing them different workplaces and by preparing workers to answer the questions of auditors in a particular way. Moreover, the purported obligations to improve workplace standards worldwide were allegedly also breached by the active measures of the company that, rather than improving workplace standards, contributed to their aggravation. Setting short delivery periods and too tight price margins eventually made the supplier violate labour rights in order not to breach the contract on the production and sale of goods. As legal support for this claim, the claimants brought forward four different theories on which this duty to improve the working conditions could be based: a promise of Wal-Mart, implied in the contract with its supplier, to inspect suppliers factories properly to which claimants were third party beneficiaries; a duty of care based on

[48] The facts of the case are taken from *Jane Doe and others v Wal-Mart Stores* (ibid) 680f.

[49] See above, text and accompanying footnotes in section 3.1.1.1. (p 48).

either a voluntary assumption of responsibility or retention of control of Wal-Mart over working conditions due to the fact that it obliged the supplier to adhere to workplace standards; the idea that Wal-Mart was the joint employer of claimants because it effectively specified the conditions of employment; and a theory that referred to unjust enrichment because Wal-Mart directly profited financially from exploiting workers.

The District Court that was called upon to decide the case dismissed the claim.[50] In reviewing the appeal, the Court of Appeal discussed the different theories that the claimants had invoked and ruled that none of these theories could establish a positive obligation on the side of Wal-Mart towards the employees of suppliers. Insofar as the contractual aspects of the case were concerned, the court based the dismissal on the following arguments. First, it rejected the argument that a factual contract between the claimants and Wal-Mart existed that had made the company the joint employer solely because it regulated certain aspects of workplace standards. There was no day-to-day control of Wal-Mart over suppliers' working conditions to the extent that one could define Wal-Mart as the joint and factual employer.[51] Second, the court also ruled that the existing rules on contract interpretation did not support the argument that Wal-Mart intended to make the right to inspect an obligation to which claimants were third party beneficiaries.[52] Finally, the theories on negligence were also rejected due to the perceived absence of control of Wal-Mart over its supplier and the fact that a voluntary assumption of responsibility on the side of the company could not be identified.[53] It goes without saying that this case and the decision of the court received wide attention in scholarly literature. However, the astonishing aspect of the debate was that the critical positions did not predominantly argue that the court incorrectly or unconvincingly applied existing law. With only a few exceptions,[54] it was argued that the court could do nothing but dismiss the claim. It was stated that it 'properly decided the case under existing law',[55] that the outcome was 'due to the confines and interpretations of present law'[56] and that it is merely the law as it stands and not the interpretation of the court that turns out to be not 'very suitable to hold a transnational corporation liable for human rights abuses by its foreign suppliers'.[57] It is appropriate to pause here for a moment. What is actually the aspect in this case that, according to the critics, the law is not capable of dealing with? Or, to put it differently, why is it assumed in the comments to the decision that there should still be a binding obligation on the side of

[50] *Jane Doe v Wal-Mart Stores Inc*, No 05-CV-7307 AG (MANx), 2007 US Dist LEXIS 98102 (CD Cal, 30 March 2007).

[51] *Jane Doe and others v Wal-Mart Stores* (n 47) 682, B, paras 5f.

[52] ibid 681f, A, paras 2ff.

[53] ibid 683f, C, para 7.

[54] See Phillips and Lim (2009) 354, 362, 365, who argue that the court did not deal with the legal problems in a sufficiently in-depth way.

[55] Walle (2009) 597f.

[56] Revak (2012) 1667.

[57] Heijden (2011b) 177, who focuses on corporate codes under Dutch contract law, but in the course of the analysis also discusses intensively the *Doe v Wal-Mart* case. See also for a similar interpretation Peukert (2014) 250f.

the lead company even if the negotiated and legally binding contract with the suppliers explicitly states otherwise? Based on the theories presented by the claimants and the comments in the literature, there seem to be two main lines of arguments that are invoked.

The first frequently mentioned aspect justifying an obligation of a company that drafts and publishes a corporate code is the strong leverage of this company over its suppliers. In particular, critics argue that the contractual relations between large companies and their foreign suppliers are in reality not discrete contracts that are negotiated at arm's length, but are rather relations in which the lead firm has significant power over the suppliers—as was purported to be the situation in the *Wal-Mart* case. Hence, there is a need to complement this increasing power with the responsibility of the lead firm for the behaviour of the entities that it controls.[58] The publicly declared corporate policy of the large company that is incorporated in the contract is then also evidence of such a factual leverage of the company over its suppliers and its capability and factual intention to control workplace standards in foreign countries. The strong leverage of one entity over another can indeed serve as a valid argument to create obligations on the side of the controlling entity, which becomes apparent from the evolving general discussion in contract law on the obligations of lead firms in contractual networks towards detrimentally affected third parties.[59] Nevertheless, there also remains some difficulty with using this argument on an overall scale in relation to the corporate code that a company includes in its contract. Is it really the sheer presence of a corporate code and its integration in the contract as a unilateral obligation for the supplier that justifies a legal obligation of the buyer to use his contractual control? This is at least contested to the extent that this argument is considered generally valid for contractually imposed corporate codes. One can refer in this context to existing research on the organisation of global value chains that has identified remarkable differences between sectors concerning the actual control on the side of the lead firm. Global value chains do, depending on the particular sector and even the specific company, range from discrete market transactions and interdependent relational contracts to quasi-integration.[60] Against this background, it seems rather likely that the incorporation of the corporate codes into these value chains also follows different patterns and is organised in line with the general contractual relation. To refer to a corporate code in order to prove the strong leverage of the drafting company over its supplier can then be persuasive only when corporate codes are imposed on the contracting partner in a relationship that is generally characterised by strong economic leverage of the lead firm over its suppliers,

[58] For this argument, see Walle (2009) passim; Heijden (2011b) 182.

[59] See especially Collins (1990) 739f, 742f; Cafaggi (2008) 40ff; Teubner and Collins (2011) 235ff.

[60] See fundamentally Gereffi, Humphrey and Sturgeon (2005) 82ff, who propose a typology of global value chains based on evidence from different sectors along five different governance forms. Global value chains can be organised as: (1) market transactions; (2) modular value chains where certain specifications are imposed by customers, but suppliers take full responsibility for production and technology; (3) relational value chains where contracting parties are mutually dependent; (4) captive value chains where lead firms have a high degree of control over suppliers; and (5) a hierarchy that is characterised by vertical integration.

such as the apparel industry of which Wal-Mart is specifically part.[61] Conversely, for company–supplier relations that exhibit a mode of organisation that tends towards an arm's-length negotiation, the contractual incorporation of one party's published policy could hardly serve as evidence for recognising an accompanying obligation of the lead firm. In addition, the request on the side of one party to incorporate a corporate code into a supplier contract seems to become even less of a convincing argument for strong control in those constellations in which the buying firm takes a lead role. In particular, with respect to CSR standards, one must have in mind not only the imposition of standards by Western buyers but also the gradually evolving resistance of this imposition of workplace standards on the side of suppliers and their attempts to develop and insist on autonomous standards concerning workplace and environmental protection.[62] Moreover, one should also not forget that by means of supplying on a large scale to Western buyers, the presumed weak suppliers could become more powerful actors themselves.[63] Thus, it is not always the supplier that remains the structurally weaker party, even if the corporate code remains unilaterally imposed on it by contractual agreement. This is not to say that the argument of strong leverage is per se not convincing; yet it is crucial to emphasise that it remains an argument that would need to be carefully discussed with a view to the particularities of the relationship under scrutiny.

While the argument that refers to corporate codes as core evidence for strong leverage thus remains limited insofar as it only applies in specific constellations of strong control, there is, however, a second argument in the debate that is arguably more persuasive on a general level. The reason that seemed to disturb scholars with regard to the outcome of the *Wal-Mart* case was not solely a perceived dominance of Western buyers over suppliers in developing countries and the fact that the corporate code was imposed on the suppliers. A second, important line of argument targeted the courts' refusal to determine the obligations of the contracting parties in light of the impression that the company conveyed to the public and to its supplier.[64] It is noteworthy in this case that the company presented a strong commitment to the public to contribute to improving workplace standards worldwide, but that the Court, in deciding the case, did not pay attention to this public declaration at all—and, indeed, it is this aspect that reveals a core ambivalence in the codes in their current form. Companies present themselves to the public as actors that seek to improve social and environmental standards worldwide and to assist their contractual partners with achieving compliance with the code.

[61] But see on this point Gereffi, Humphrey and Sturgeon (2005) 91f, who describe the apparel industry even as only an initially captive value chain that has transformed into a relational value chain due to the increasing competence of East Asian suppliers.

[62] A good example in this regard is China, where suppliers, notwithstanding their dependence on large buyers from Western countries and the imposed obligations related to workplace standards, gradually begin to develop tactics of resistance towards the Western dominance of imposing labour standards and focus on the development of their own standards instead. For a detailed analysis of this development, *cf* Lin (2007).

[63] See pointedly Backer (2008) 523: 'Under the new regime it is possible for multinational enterprises to grow almost anywhere in the world. East Asia has evidenced the way in which shifts of economic power might affect the markets for beliefs and harmonising regulation in the future.' See also for a similar prediction Gereffi, Humphrey and Sturgeon (2005) 92.

[64] Phillips and Lim (2009) 371f; Revak (2012) 1667.

Yet, they nevertheless seek to avoid putting their own commitment in the legally binding form of a bilateral contract. Instead, the actual corporate code that contains the commitments of the company to act in a socially responsible manner is only part of an informal policy that is made available to the public. Hence, a major and reasonable ground for the discomfort of scholars that assessed the ruling in *Doe v Wal-Mart* is the concern that, by rejecting any responsibility of the company for its publicly declared code, the law appeared to have approved this Janus-faced strategy. Consequently, it marginalised 'the commitment of one of the world's largest private employers to afford minimum labour standards to their contractual suppliers' employees'.[65] Or, to put it differently, contract law as used here by the Court seems to be insufficiently prepared to look beyond the actual contractual agreement and to take into consideration other forms of unilateral commitments by private actors.

As a consequence, when analysing the potential of the corporate codes to become legally binding, next to the intentional incorporation of the code into the contract or in its ancillary documents, it is equally important to shift the focus to the question of how contract law actually deals with this ambiguous public statement and its potential enforcement as a binding contract or promise. In the *Wal-Mart* case in particular, the enforcement of the public declaration was primarily discussed in the course of interpreting a supplier contract in which a corporate code was included. Yet, the question about the enforcement of such publicly declared corporate codes also needs to be discussed with a view to other constellations. Considering a publicly declared corporate code also becomes relevant when focusing not only on such carefully negotiated contracts between companies and their suppliers, but also on other contracts that are concluded with the company. This applies, in particular, to the relevance of publicly declared corporate codes for mass transactions with end-consumers. In relation to consumers as contractual partners, a written contract does not exist normally and, consequently, no explicit reference to a corporate code can be made in a contract or the ancillary documents. Yet, this particular form of contracting is also characterised by a strong reliance of consumers on the public declarations of traders. The following sections will therefore focus more specifically on the potential enforcement of such public declarations within existing supplier and consumer contracts. In this context, currently the most prominent proposal is to make use of these publicly declared codes of companies when interpreting and supplementing subsequently concluded contracts (section 3.1.3.2). Furthermore, the focus on the publicly declared corporate code as such even suggests taking the debate further and investigating the potential direct enforcement of these public declarations by the addressees of the code, ie, the addressed consumers or even code beneficiaries (section 3.1.4).

3.1.3.2. Public Declarations in Contract Interpretation and Supplementation

The Court's ruling in the *Wal-Mart* case is indeed very straightforward. It does not contain any doubts among the judges or hints that a different interpretation would

65 Walle (2009) 589.

be conceivable. Yet in the scholarly literature on corporate codes, one can find contributions that offer perspectives on how such public declarations could become enforceable obligations. In this context, it has become a prominent suggestion to interpret these declarations as pre-contractual public statements that courts could read into the contract. Currently, this suggestion is, in particular, discussed with reference to a specific statutory provision that allows public statements of traders to be read into contracts when interpreting the characteristics and quality of the good that is subject to a sales contract.[66] The provision has its origin in the 1999 Consumer Sales Directive and reads that goods are presumed to be in conformity with the contract if they 'show the quality and performance which are normal in goods of the same type and which the consumer can reasonably expect, given the nature of the goods and *taking into account any public statements on the specific characteristics of the goods made about them by the seller, the producer or his representative, particularly in advertising or on labelling*'.[67] This provision is in fact a novelty to most European legal systems, which used to be quite restrictive with prescribing courts to take into account pre-contractual statements when determining the contractual obligations in a sales contract.[68] Based on the broad phrasing of the Consumer Sales Directive that specifies as product characteristics in the first place what the consumers can reasonably expect, it is argued that an incorporation of the specifically publicly declared corporate codes is necessary in order to react to the changing expectations of consumers that pay increasing attention to the social and environmental performance of a company and the way in which such commitments shape the expectations concerning the products that they buy.[69] In the following section, the potential and also current limits of this provision will be discussed in relation to reading the publicly declared corporate policies into the contract (section 3.1.3.2.1). Subsequently, it is proposed to shift the focus from this specific provision that remains rather narrowly confined in its scope to the general rules on contract interpretation and supplementation, and inquire as to their potential use with respect to publicly declared corporate codes (section 3.1.3.2.2).

3.1.3.2.1. Article 2 of the Consumer Sales Directive

When it comes to the possibility of relying on existing statutory provisions that prescribe reading public statements into subsequently concluded contracts, it has already been emphasised that the specific provision in the Consumer Sales Directive occupies a prominent position.

[66] Wilhelmsson (2002/2003) 91ff; Wilhelmsson (2004a) 233f; Kocher (2002) 269f; Dilling (2005); Glinski (2007) 124ff; Glinski (2008) 45ff.

[67] Article 2(2)(d) of the Consumer Sales Directive 1999/44/EC [1999] OJ L171/12 (emphasis added).

[68] See, eg, for German law Staudenmeyer (2000) 552: 'Such a clause is a new departure in most existing civil laws'; and for English law Watterson (2001) 208: 'The novelty for English law lies in the provision that the quality and performance which the purchaser can reasonably expect must be determined in light of public statements about the goods by the seller, producer or his representative.'

[69] Wilhelmsson (2002/2003) 96; Wilhelmsson (2004a) 233f; Dilling (2005) 288; Glinski (2007) 125; Kocher (2008) 78: 'If the market recognises this aspect of the product, then the mode of production would have to be considered a feature of the good itself'; Collins (2014) 634ff.

In English law, this provision has been implemented in section 14 of the Sale of Goods Act 1979 (SGA), which deals with terms that are generally implied in sale of goods contracts. According to section 14(2), it is an implied term in a contract on the sale of goods that the goods are of a satisfactory quality. Satisfactory quality is defined in subsection (2A) as meeting 'the standard that a reasonable person would regard as satisfactory, taking account of any description of the goods, the price (if relevant) and all the other relevant circumstances'. Referring to this section, section 14(2D) states that the 'relevant circumstances' also comprise 'public statements made by the seller, the producer or his representative, particularly in advertising or on labelling'. Hence, this statutory provision sets out three central conditions in order for a public statement to be relevant for a contract. First, due to the implementation in the SGA, the incorporation is only possible for these particular types of contracts. Second, the provision contains the condition that the buyer has to deal as a consumer. This means that under English law, the option to use public statements for specifying the product quality is restricted to consumer contracts, but does not represent a viable option in contracts between companies and their suppliers. Finally, in order to be admissible, the public statement needs to be a 'public statement on the specific characteristics of the goods', which implies that the consideration of public statements is limited to particular type of statements, namely those that concern the characteristics of the goods supplied.

For German law, the applicable provision implementing the requirements of the Consumer Sales Directive is § 434 I 3 BGB, which contains general rules concerning the agreed-upon properties of the goods supplied. § 434 I 3 BGB states that, in determining the properties of a product, the relevant characteristics are those that 'the buyer can expect from the public statements by the seller, the producer or his assistant, in particular in advertising or labelling about the specific characteristics of the object'.[70] Thus, this provision explicitly requires courts to take into account public statements on the characteristics of the product when interpreting the open-ended term of the 'agreed-upon properties' (*Beschaffenheit*) that the seller is obliged to deliver under a sale of goods contract. It should be noted in this context that the German legislator made the provision a general requirement for sales contracts and thus went beyond the requirements set out in the Consumer Sales Directive. The provision is not only applicable to consumer contracts as prescribed in the Consumer Sales Directive, but also to commercial contracts. Nonetheless, with respect to commercial contracts, it will remain limited in its application due to the fact that the provision becomes relevant only in cases in which no individual agreement on the properties of the product or the fitness for a particular purpose has been reached.[71] At least in relation to carefully negotiated sales contracts in which an agreement on the character of the goods has been reached, the provision remains of minor relevance. Apart from its broader scope, the requirements of this

[70] Translation taken from Kornet and Hardt (2013) 309.

[71] See, eg, Wunderlich (2002) 985: 'Allerdings kann eine Haftung für Werbeaussagen in der Vertragspraxis dadurch vermieden werden, dass die Beschaffenheit der Kaufsache … vereinbart oder die nach dem Vertrag erforderliche Eignung … bestimmt wird.'

provision resemble English law. The provision in German law is equally only a default rule for sales contracts and only applies to public declarations that specify the goods.

As a result, contract law in fact, since the implementation of the Consumer Sales Directive into national law, has at its disposal an explicit statutory provision that prescribes taking into consideration pre-contractual public statements. Its specific focus on public declarations renders it particularly attractive in dealing with the enforcement of publicly declared corporate codes within subsequently concluded contracts. Relying on this provision, these publicly declared codes could become relevant with respect to the contract term that obliges the seller to deliver a product with certain specifications and of a particular quality.

That being said, this statutory provision still has, at least in its current form, limited value, which is mainly due to its narrow scope of application. First, as this statutory provision has only been implemented in the default rules on sales contracts, it can only be used to read publicly declared corporate codes into contracts that qualify as such. Any suggestion to read publicly declared corporate codes into other types of contracts—for instance, contracts on the provision of services—would require interpreting the provision not as a specific default rule, but rather as revealing a general principle that, by means of an analogy or even statutory reform, should also apply to other types of contracts.[72]

Second, it should be noted that the provision has practical relevance merely for sales contracts of companies with individual consumers. In English law, this restriction is explicitly laid down in the Act. While this is not the case in German law, the provision is nevertheless in practice primarily relevant in consumer contracts given that it only applies to constellations in which no agreement on the properties has been reached between the parties. Consequently, in order to make use of the provision on a broader scale, it would be required to broaden the scope of the provision and treat it as a provision that not only has the objective to protect the expectations of consumers, but that also indicates the importance of public statements for the contracting process in general.[73] Third, the explicit restriction of this provision to public statements on the characteristics of goods in particular also hinders its general application to publicly declared corporate codes. Effectively, the provision can only be used for corporate codes that link the commitments to the particular product that the company sells in a sufficiently explicit manner. Corporate codes that contain general policy commitments of companies without reference to the products or even their own production method would most likely not be covered. Thus, the provision could only be of value for publicly declared corporate codes on a broader scale if the notion on the 'characteristics of

[72] For this suggestion, see Wilhelmsson (2004a) 235. An example of such a general provision on the relevance of pre-contractual public statements can be found in art 6:101, para 2 of the Principles of European Contract Law: 'If one of the contracting parties is a professional supplier who gives information about the quality or use of services or goods or other property when marketing or advertising them or otherwise before the contract for them is concluded, the statement is to be treated as giving rise to a contractual obligation unless it is shown that the other party knew or could not have been aware that the statement was incorrect.'

[73] For this suggestion, see Köndgen (2001) 239f; Wilhelmsson (2004a) 237.

the goods' is given a very broad interpretation.[74] Finally, even if all these proposals for a broad interpretation are followed, its potential still remains restricted. This is due to the fact that the provision in its current form prescribes that courts consider public statements only for the sake of determining the main performance obligation in a sales contract, namely the delivery of a particular product. This means that it would only be relevant in the case of a publicly declared corporate code if the code actually relates to this substantive obligation. Although, in the further analysis, this interpretation is treated as one important proposal in the debate,[75] it should be emphasised that it remains only one of the conceivable interpretations of corporate codes in contracts. Once a different interpretation is preferred, such as an obligation to confer a benefit upon a third party or a novel regulatory duty,[76] the provision cannot be applied directly. It could only be applicable to the corporate codes if it were further developed into a general rule on the interpretation of contracts that is not restricted to the process of determining the main performance obligation in a contract. An example of such a broad provision can be found in the Principles of European Contract Law.[77]

3.1.3.2.2. The General Rules on Contract Interpretation and Supplementation

Given the narrow scope of the statutory provision on public statements of traders in consumer sales contracts, it can also be an alternative to broaden the focus and analyse the corporate codes from the perspective of contract interpretation and supplementation in general. Arguably, in relation to publicly declared corporate codes, it is also possible to read corporate codes into subsequently concluded contracts by relying on the existing rules on contract interpretation and supplementation. The potential of the rules on contract interpretation and supplementation has not yet been explored in detail in the debate on corporate codes on social and environmental standards.[78] This lack of attention in the debate notwithstanding,

[74] For this suggestion, see Glinski (2011) 190f, who suggests interpreting even general image campaigns and information on the general policies as statements that influence the characteristics of goods.

[75] See below section 3.2.2. (p 110), text and accompanying footnotes.

[76] See below section 3.2.3 (p 126) on third party rights and section 3.2.4 (p 144) on regulatory contracts.

[77] Article 6:101, para 1: 'A Statement made by one party *before* or when the contract is concluded is to be treated as giving rise to a contractual obligation, if that is how the other party reasonably understood it in the circumstances taking into account (a) the apparent importance of the statement to the other party; (b) whether the party was making the statement in the course of business; and (c) the relative expertise of the parties' (emphasis added).

[78] The most comprehensive attempt to rely on the rules on contract interpretation and supplementation in order to read publicly declared corporate codes into contracts has been made by Barron (2007), who focuses on the publicly available general policies of banks and insurance companies that aim at consumer protection. The possibility of reading publicly declared corporate codes on social and environmental standards into supplier or consumer contracts is so far only indicated by Arthurs (2005) 59 in relation to contracts of companies with consumers and employees. The relevance of contract interpretation and supplementation is presumably also an inherent element in the analysis of Phillips and Lim (2009) 368ff, who argue that pre-contractual promises of companies to assist suppliers in achieving code compliance are effectively part of the subsequently concluded supplier contract, and Revak (2012) 1658, who discusses the interpretation of supplier contracts with a view to 'the circumstances surrounding the creation of the Standards'.

the following section seeks to reveal that reliance on these rules is in fact a promising undertaking when attempting to read the publicly declared corporate codes into contracts with business partners and consumers, and thus understand them as enforceable contract terms. In contrast to the above-mentioned specific provision in sales law, the general rules on contract interpretation and supplementation are badly equipped with regard to prescribing courts to take into consideration such public declarations. Nonetheless, due to their flexibility, they provide courts with the discretion to do so and thus can be of value once reasons are brought forward as to why this discretion should be used in relation to the corporate codes.

3.1.3.2.2.1. *English Law*

In English law, it is the general rule that the content of the contract and thus the mutual rights and obligations of the contracting parties are determined by the terms of the contract. In specifying these terms, English law distinguishes strictly between express and implied terms. Express terms are those explicitly agreed upon by the parties, whereas implied terms are those that courts read into the contract. Hence, in order to read the publicly declared corporate codes into the contract, one would need to suggest either treating them as express terms that were agreed upon by the parties or characterise them as pre-contractual statements that amount to a separate collateral contract next to the main agreement. Alternatively, one could also provide arguments for why a court should imply them in the contract.

3.1.3.2.2.1.1. Express Contract Terms

The starting point for the undertaking to determine the enforceable express terms of an agreement in English law is always the contractual document. English contract law departs from the general rule that the written document represents the contractual agreement and that this document is the sole repository of the terms of the contract. None of the parties should have the flexibility to claim at a later stage that other agreements and statements have been made, even though they did not find their way into the contractual document.[79] Following this understanding, contract interpretation is to be conducted within what is colloquially called the 'four corners' of the document. In this regard, English law traditionally adhered to a strict literal and objective approach meaning that the courts determined the contractual obligations from an objective perspective solely by giving the words that are used in the agreement an ordinary meaning.[80] With this literal approach to contract interpretation, it is of course very difficult to take into consideration public statements that were made prior to the conclusion of a contract and it is exactly this literal approach that seemed to have informed the court in the *Wal-Mart* case

[79] McKendrick (2013) 150.

[80] Cozens-Hardy MR in *Lovel and Christmas Ltd v Wall* (1911) 104 LT 85 88: 'it is the duty of the court, which is presumed to understand the English language, to construe the document according to the ordinary grammatical meaning of the words used therein, and without reference to anything which has previously passed between the parties to it'.

when it stated that 'based on the language and structure of the agreement', no obligation on the side of Wal-Mart could be identified.[81]

However, in English law, this orthodox literal approach has recently been subject to some modifications in favour of a more contextual approach. In particular, the speeches of Lord Wilberforce in *Prenn v Simmonds*[82] and *Reardon Smith Line Ltd v Yngvar Hansen-Tange*,[83] and later on Lord Hoffmann in *Investors Compensation Scheme Ltd v West Bromwich Building Society*[84] and *Mannai Investment Co Ltd v Eagle Star Life Assurance Co. Ltd*[85] proved to be particularly influential in this respect. In *Prenn v Simmonds*, Lord Wilberforce already acknowledged that there is a factual context in which the contract is concluded, which he famously framed as the 'matrix of fact'.[86] Subsequently, it was particularly Lord Hoffmann's re-statement in *Investors* that established the basis for a new contextual approach for interpreting contracts. In giving his speech to the court, Lord Hoffmann established several principles for contract interpretation. First, he emphasised that contract interpretation is not a matter of solely interpreting the words as to their literal meaning, but of ascertaining 'the meaning, which the document would convey to a reasonable person having all the knowledge which would reasonably have been available to the parties in the situation in which they were at the time of the contract'.[87] His second point was to make clear that the background is to be considered in the 'matrix of fact', which includes 'absolutely anything which would have affected the way in which the language of the document would have been understood by a reasonable man'.[88] Against this background, one could assume that the broad approach of 'absolutely anything' would provide a basis for an interpretation of contracts in light of public statements made by the parties in the negotiation and preparation phase. Yet, Lord Hoffmann immediately clarified in the third principle of contract interpretation that 'the law excludes from the admissible background the previous negotiations of the parties and their declarations of subjective intent'.[89] English law is in this aspect based on the assumption that the positions and intentions expressed by the parties in the pre-contractual stage remain preliminary and it is only the final document that fixes the consensus.[90] The exclusion of declarations made in the phase prior to contract formation would then most likely also include

[81] *Jane Doe v Wal-Mart Stores* (n 47) 681f: 'The language and structure of the agreement show that Wal-Mart reserved the right to inspect the suppliers, but did not adopt a duty to inspect them.'

[82] *Prenn v Simmonds* [1971] 1 WLR 1381.

[83] *Reardon Smith Line Ltd v Yngvar Hansen-Tange* [1976] 1 WLR 989.

[84] *Investors Compensation Scheme Ltd v West Bromwich Building Society* [1998] 1 WLR 896.

[85] *Mannai Investment Co Ltd v Eagle Star Life Assurance Co Ltd* [1997] 2 WLR 945.

[86] Lord Wilberforce in *Prenn v Simmonds* (n 82) 1384.

[87] Lord Hoffmann in *Investors Compensation Scheme* (n 84) 912.

[88] ibid 912f. In *Bank of Credit and Commerce International SA v Ali* [2002] 1 AC 251, Lord Hoffmann clarified that 'absolutely anything' means 'anything which a reasonable man would have regarded as relevant' and 'that there is no conceptual limit to what can be regarded as background' (at 269).

[89] Lord Hoffmann in *Investors Compensation Scheme* (n 84) 913.

[90] See already Lord Wilberforce in *Prenn v Simmonds* (n 82) 1984: 'By the nature of things, where negotiations are difficult, the parties' position, with each passing letter, are changing and until the final agreement, though converging, still divergent. It is only the final document which records the consensus.'

public declarations made by one party. This means that even the recent rules on contract interpretation, as re-stated by Lord Hoffmann, cannot be used to create additional terms that are not expressed in the document and that were only part of the pre-contractual negotiations. That being said, in giving his speech in *Chartbrook Ltd v Persimmon Homes Ltd*, Lord Hoffmann refined the scope of the general rule on the inadmissibility of extrinsic evidence by clarifying that such evidence could not be used 'for the purpose of drawing inferences about what the contract meant'. Yet he recognised that such evidence could still be admissible for other purposes, particularly in order to establish a fact, to support a claim for rectification or for estoppel.[91] It is from these purposes in particular that the possibility to use extrinsic evidence to establish a fact could be used in relation to corporate codes. More precisely, a pre-contractual public statement could be referred to as factual evidence for an actual implicit agreement between the parties that would have to be treated as an express term. Given that English law classifies the determination of terms in oral contracts as a question of fact,[92] one could interpret the corporate code as a term that has been agreed upon orally. This, however, requires a particular presentation of the facts. Express orally agreed terms of contracts are certainly not unilateral public declarations as such, but are only declarations on which the parties intended to make an agreement. Consequently, it is not the declaration that is open to a treatment as an express term. The public declaration can serve only as a basis for a term if the parties, based on factual evidence, negotiated and subsequently agreed that this public declaration should apply. The suggestion to treat the published corporate code as an oral express term is even more difficult in a constellation in which the subsequently concluded contract has been made in writing. In this regard, it is important to pay attention to the so-called parol evidence rule that generally prevents parties from bringing forward evidence to add to, vary or contradict the written document.[93] Although this rule has been relaxed and thus does not apply in absolute terms, it still remains a rebuttable presumption for written contracts that a document that appears to be a contract is considered the entire agreement.[94] Consequently, in order for a party to present evidence that a specific declaration in the pre-contractual phase represents an express term of an otherwise written contract, it is necessary to rebut this presumption by also presenting evidence that the agreement does not in fact represent the entire agreement between the parties.[95]

[91] Lord Hoffmann in *Chartbrook Ltd v Persimmon Homes Ltd* [2009] 1 AC 1101 1121: 'These are not exceptions to it. They operate outside it.'

[92] *Torbett v Faulkner* [1952] 2 TLR 659, 661 (per Romer LJ); *Maggs v Marsh* [2006] EWCA Civ 1058 [26] (per Smith LJ).

[93] *Bank of Australia v Palmer* [1897] AC 540, 545: 'parol testimony cannot be received to contradict, vary, add, or subtract from the terms of a written contract, or the terms in which the parties have deliberately agreed to record any part of their contract'. Cited in Beale (2012) 960, para 12-096; *Jacobs v Batavia and General Plantations Trust Ltd* [1924] 1 Ch 287.

[94] McKendrick (2013) 151.

[95] *Mercantile Bank of Sydney v Taylor* [1893] AC 317 321. See also GeoffreyLane LJ *in J Evans and Son (Portsmouth) Ltd v Andrea Merzario Ltd* [1976] 1 WLR 1078 1084, in which an oral statement prior to the formation of the contract was deemed a 'new express term which was to be included thereafter in the contracts between the plaintiffs and defendants'.

Following on from this understanding, it would only be possible under very exceptional circumstances to consider publicly declared corporate codes when constructing the contract and determining the express terms of the contract. The attempt to treat the corporate code as a fact that provides evidence for an additional express term of the contract remains limited to those constellations in which it can be proven that the commitments specified in a publicly available corporate code were actually explicitly agreed upon and, to the extent that a written contract exists, that supporting evidence exists for the fact that the parties did not intend their contract to represent the entire agreement. It is conversely not sufficient that one party simply took notice of the public declaration when concluding the contract. The potential of treating the corporate code as an express term is thus limited to the few situations in which it can be proven that the parties have reached consensus on compliance with social and environmental standards as specified in the publicly declared code with an explicit common understanding that this would be part of the actual agreement.[96]

3.1.3.2.2.1.2. Collateral Contracts

An alternative to the very difficult attempt to interpret public declarations as express terms of an orally concluded part of a contract could be the treatment of the codes as a collateral contract. Although treating a statement as a collateral contract should be reserved for rare constellations,[97] this concept actually turned out to be an important way to enforce pre-contractual assurances made either by one of the contracting parties[98] or by a third party[99] if these assurances induced another person to conclude a contract and where it was difficult to treat such an assurance as an express term of the principal agreement. In relation to the corporate codes, the rules on collateral contracts are particularly attractive. They make it possible to render pre-contractual statements of a trader contractually binding if these have been explicitly agreed upon as well as if the addressed party is merely induced by the statement to conclude a contract. In accordance with the rules on the formation of a collateral contract, the corporate code could be treated as a collateral contract if it was of crucial importance for the addressed party to decide to enter into the main agreement. In order to treat a pre-contractual assurance as a collateral contract, it is, however, necessary to qualify the statement in question as a contract term and not solely as a representation. The decision between a term and

[96] The argument of treating the corporate codes as commitments that have been factually agreed upon by the parties as part of the contract is employed by Phillips and Lim (2009) 371ff.

[97] See Viscount Haldane LC in *Heilbut, Symons and Co v Buckleton* [1913] AC 30, 37: 'It is contrary to the general policy of the law of England to presume the making of such a collateral contract in the absence of language expressing or implying it' and Lord Moulton (at 47): 'viewed with suspicion by the law. They must be proved strictly' and 'must from their very nature be rare'.

[98] See, eg, *Esso Petroleum Co Ltd v Mardon* [1976] QB 801, in which the pre-contractual statement on the annual throughput of a petrol station would amount to a collateral warranty because it was 'a vital factor in the calculations of both parties' (per Ormrod LJ). Since in this case, liability was established as a matter of a breach of contract as well as a negligent misstatement, the decision will also be consulted in the course of discussing tort liability.

[99] *Shanklin Pier Ltd v Detel Products Ltd* [1951] 2 KB 854.

representation primarily depends on the intention with which the statement was made.[100] In this context, the courts have used several criteria in order to infer the intention, one core aspect being the importance of the statement for the addressed party in relation to the decision whether or not to contract. Statements that are of importance for the other contracting party are more likely to be treated as a term compared to statements that only mention aspects of ancillary relevance.[101] As Lord Denning framed it in *Dick Bentley Productions Ltd. v Harold Smith*, 'it seems to me that if a representation is made in the course of dealings for a contract for the very purpose of inducing the other party to act upon it, and actually inducing him to act upon it, by entering into the contract, that is prima facie ground for inferring that it was intended as a warranty'.[102] Furthermore, the courts have also looked at the respective knowledge, skills and expertise of the parties to judge the statement[103] and the stage of the negotiations at which the statement was made, and have also taken into consideration whether a statement was made in a commercial or consumer contract.[104] With respect to corporate codes, this has the consequence that the possibility of treating corporate codes as collateral contracts could be an option if an argument can be brought forward that these publicly declared corporate policies were crucial for the addressed party when deciding whether or not to conclude a contract. Once the publicly declared compliance with a corporate codes becomes a decisive criterion when deciding whether or not to contract, it could also become an option to treat them as a contract that is collateral to the main agreement with a business partner or consumer on, for instance, a sale of goods or provision of services.

3.1.3.2.2.1.3. Terms Implied in Fact

From what has been stated above, it is consequently an option to treat the corporate codes as express terms either of the principal agreement if parties have agreed upon them or if they have directly induced the other party to conclude a contract. Yet, what about the frequently occurring case in which the corporate code remains a public declaration that the addressees notice, but that they neither explicitly discuss in the actual negotiations nor see as the core criterion for the conclusion of a contract? In such cases, the treatment of the corporate codes as express terms or collateral contracts is less likely. Reading the corporate codes into the contract only remains possible once the courts are prepared to treat the commitments in such public declarations as implied terms.

Implied terms are terms that are not explicitly stated in the agreement, but which the courts read into the contract for particular reasons.[105] English law has three different forms of implied terms: terms implied in fact, implied in law and

[100] McKendrick (2013) 145.

[101] See *Couchman v Hill* [1947] KB 554, in which the purchaser made explicit that the represented fact would be important for his decision to purchase.

[102] *Dick Bentley Productions Ltd v Harold Smith* [1965] 1 WLR 623 627.

[103] McKendrick (2013) 146.

[104] Howells and Weatherill (2005) 157.

[105] Peel (2011) 205, para 6-001; Beale (2012) 985, para 13-001; McKendrick (2013) 150.

implied by custom. The core rationale behind terms implied in fact is to supplement the contract with terms that give effect to the factual intention of the contracting parties, which are determined on the basis of several tests and criteria. Terms implied in law are standardised terms that are read into specific types of contracts on the basis of precedent or terms for which statute prescribes implication. Although the implication of terms in law was originally also seen as a matter of giving effect to the intentions of the parties to a particular transaction, it gradually became a matter of prima facie implication into specific types of contracts while allowing parties to deviate from them.[106] Finally, terms implied by custom represent a category of contract supplementation that allows the courts to read into the contract a relevant custom of the market, trade or locality.[107] As the idea of reading the publicly declared corporate codes into contracts focuses particularly on their relevance as part of the factual background that influences the conclusion of the contract, it is accordingly primarily the first form of implied terms that are of importance. Implying the code as a term in fact could become a viable option if it were possible to understand these codes as shaping the intentions and expectations of the contracting parties.[108] In the following, the potential will be explored to treat corporate codes as terms implied in fact in light of the general requirements for implying a term in fact.

When it comes to the category of terms implied in fact, one preliminary remark needs to be made as to its relation to contract interpretation. Since the rationale behind the implication is for this category to give effect to the presumed intentions of the contracting parties, it is seemingly in close proximity to the instrument of interpreting express contract terms.[109] Yet there is one crucial difference between these two approaches. English courts tend to have an inherent scepticism against the implication of terms as they deem it to be the responsibility of the contracting parties to make the contract and, conversely, not the task of the courts to write the contract for the parties. This is why it has been constantly urged that implication should be only 'sparingly and cautiously used'[110] and that the 'most usual interference' in cases in which the contract remains silent on a particular term is 'that nothing is to happen' and 'the loss lies where it falls'.[111] As a result, rather than adopting a broad contextual approach towards implied terms that uses manifold evidence from the contextual background to infer on the actual intention of the parties, English courts developed several narrowly defined tests that should guide courts in deciding whether a contract needs to be supplemented with a particular term. In this regard, the business efficacy test and the officious bystander test are

[106] On this development, see generally Kornet (2006) 211ff.

[107] Peel (2011) 234, para 6-046.

[108] The suggestion to apply this threshold in order to read publicly declared codes of banks and insurance companies into contracts with customers can be found especially in Barron (2007) 16ff. The general option of using the device of implying terms in fact in order to read self-regulatory consumer codes in contracts is also at least indicated in Howells and Weatherill (2005) 590f.

[109] Peel (2011) 222, para 6-032: 'a certain affinity between this form of implication and the interpretation of the express terms to which parties have agreed'.

[110] Lord Steyn in *Equitable Life Assurance Society v Hyman* [2000] 1 AC 408, 459.

[111] Lord Hoffmann in *Belize v Belize* [2009] 1 WLR 1988, 1993.

important to consider and the suggested implied term must be reasonable and necessary, must be capable of clear expression and must not contradict any express terms of the contract.[112] The business efficacy test goes back to the landmark decision in *The Moorcock*[113] and the central presumption behind this test is that there is an intention of the contracting parties to make a contract effective from a commercial perspective. Against this background, the courts are generally prepared to complete a contract with an implied term whenever the term is necessary to make the contract work. In this context, it has been emphasised that the criterion of implying a term is one of necessity and not reasonableness,[114] which means that a term can only implied when the contract is not workable without the term that should be implied.[115] The officious bystander test, for which the landmark case is *Shirlaw v Southern Foundries*,[116] refers to the strategy of looking at the contractual negotiations from the perspective of an officious bystander and, on this basis, assessing whether there is apparent evidence that the parties actually intended to include the missing term in the contract, but for some reason failed to do so.[117] Thus, in order for a term to be implied with reference to the officious bystander test, it is necessary that both parties would have had the joint intention to have this term included, although the often-differing commercial motives of the contracting parties will in most cases preclude this type of implication.[118] Moreover, a generally reluctant attitude is taken towards assuming that a particular term was obviously intended if the contracting parties have carefully drafted a written document. In addition to these tests, other criteria are relevant when determining whether a term can be implied. The term that is suggested for implication needs to be reasonable and equitable,[119] may not contradict the express terms[120] and must be capable of clear expression.[121]

With regard to the question of whether publicly declared corporate codes are capable of being implied in the contract on the basis of these different tests and criteria, one can seek guidance from a case in which the incorporation of the policy

[112] That all these different tests and criteria are relevant for the decision on whether a term is implied has been spelled out in *BP Refinery (Westernport) Pty Ltd Shire of Hastings* (1978) 52 ALJR 20, 26 (per Lord Simon) and (referring to the decision of the Privy Council in *BP Refinery*) *Philips Electronique Grand Public SA v British Sky Broadcasting* [1995] EMLR 472, 481.

[113] Lord Bowen in *The Moorchock* (1889) LR 14 PD 64, 68: 'In business transactions such as this, what the law desires to effect by the implication is to give such business efficacy to the transaction as must have been intended at all events by both parties who are businessmen.'

[114] *Liverpool City Council v Irwin* [1977] AC 239, 266: 'The touchstone is always necessity and not merely reasonableness' (per Lord Edmund-Davies).

[115] Beatson, Burrows and Cartwright (2010) 152.

[116] *Shirlaw v Southern Foundries* [1939] 2 KB 206.

[117] Lord MacKinnon in *Shirlaw v Southern Foundries* (ibid) 227: 'Prima facie that which in any contract is left to be implied and need not be expressed is something so obvious that it goes without saying; so that, if while the parties were making their bargain, an officious bystander were to suggest some express provision for it in the agreement, they would testily suppress him with a common "Oh, of course".'

[118] Beatson, Burrows and Cartwright (2010) 153.

[119] *BP Refinery (Westernport) Pty Ltd Shire of Hastings* (1978) 52 ALJR 20.

[120] *Duke of Westminster v Guild* [1985] QB 688.

[121] *Shell (UK) Ltd v Lostock Garages* [1977] 1 All ER 481, where it was held that a term that obliges one party not to 'abnormally discriminate' is too vague and ambiguous to be read into the contract.

of a bank was at stake. In *Suryia and Douglas v Midland Bank plc*,[122] the Court of Appeal had to deal with the question of whether the policy of a bank to advise clients as to new banking facilities could be implied in the banking contract with a firm of solicitors as a duty to inform the customers of such new banking facilities. In this case, the question was particularly relevant for the customers because if they were informed about the new banking facilities, they could have moved their account and received higher interest rates. Due to the fact that the bank did not inform them, they only realised after four years and claimed the missing interest on the basis that the bank breached an implied duty to inform them about new and beneficial facilities. The Court of Appeal, referring to *Philips Electronique Grand Public SA v British Sky Broadcasting*, applied the above-mentioned tests and criteria on implication and, in so doing, held that no implication would be possible. It would be 'onerous' for a bank to inform every single client with which it had contracts and that it would not be necessary to imply such a duty. From this decision, one can at least see that it remains a difficult undertaking to treat a publicly declared corporate code as a term implied in fact. The implication appears to fail primarily due to the requirement of strict necessity and the generally formalistic approach.[123] As a result, in order to bring forward the argument that a court should read the corporate codes into the contract, it would be, under the existing rules for the implication of terms in fact, crucial to provide the courts with an argument as to why incorporating this particular corporate policy is strictly necessary in order to effectuate the contract.

In order to argue for an implication of the codes, one could, as an alternative strategy, also rely on current developments in the rules for implying terms in fact as such.[124] It is, more precisely, an option to focus on the more recent decision in *Equitable Life Assurance Society v Hyman*, in which Lord Steyn focused on the reasonable expectations of the contracting parties as an important component in the undertaking of implying terms in fact. In this case, Lord Steyn (with endorsement of the other Lords) re-formulated the threshold for implication by stating that implying terms follow a 'standard of strict necessity', but necessity is to be viewed in light of whether a term is necessary to 'give effect to the reasonable expectations of the parties'.[125] Lord Hoffmann has recently taken this gradual shift from the established and very specific tests to the broader standard of reasonable expectations as a general threshold slightly further. In giving his speech to the Judicial Committee of the Privy Council in *Attorney General of Belize v Belize Telecom Ltd*,[126] he made 'some general observations about the process of implication'[127]

[122] *Suryia and Douglas v Midland Bank plc* [1999] 1 All ER (COMM) 612.
[123] Barron (2007) 16ff.
[124] This is the approach of Barron (ibid) 16ff, who, referring to *Timeload Limited v British Telecommunications plc* [1995] EMLR 459, argues that this perspective could also be reconciled with the parol evidence rule. In this case, it was held that a government licence, although not expressly part of the contract, represents 'an inescapable part of the background which falls to be considered' (at 466 per Sir Thomas Bingham MR).
[125] *Equitable Life Assurance Society v Hyman* (n 110) 459.
[126] *Attorney General of Belize v Belize Telecom Ltd* [2009] 1 WLR 1988.
[127] ibid 1993, para 16.

and, in so doing, offered a new perspective on this instrument and the relationship between the traditional tests that are applied so far. He held that the instrument of implying a term is essentially a question for the court as to 'whether such provision would spell out in express words what the instrument read against the relevant background would reasonably be understood to mean'.[128] In this regard, he emphasised that the tests and criteria for implying terms as set out in previous cases should explicitly not be understood as a 'series of independent tests', but 'rather as a collection of different ways in which judges have tried to express the central idea that the proposed implied term must spell out what the contract actually meant or in which they have explained why they did not think that it did so'.[129] One can thus read Lord Hoffmann's reappraisal on implying terms as an attempt to align the rules on contract interpretation and implication and to make the idea of the reasonable expectations fruitful in the context of implying terms.[130] These decisions have certainly been decided too recently for them to be understood as a comprehensive new approach or a substantial novelty in the rules on the implication of terms. The approach taken in these decisions has already been applied and referred to in a number of first instance cases.[131] That said, in a recent case decided by the Court of Appeal, the new approach was endorsed, but Lord Clarke also made clear that he did not interpret Lord Hoffmann's reappraisal as a new approach that deviates from the test of strict necessity and instead applies reasonableness as the relevant criterion for implication.[132] To him, the implication of a term remains an undertaking that is oriented on the threshold of whether the particular term is necessary to make the contract work.[133] In addition to this careful attitude of courts, there is also reluctance among contract law scholars to see the approach of constructing 'the meaning of the contract' as a new test for implying terms in fact. Partly, it is argued that the traditional tests should be used because these have 'stood for many years'.[134] It is also held that the 'unassisted direct resort' to the 'meaning of the contract' from the perspective of the reasonable expectations of the contracting parties remains so far an uncertain and open-ended criterion.[135] Yet, while these first reactions could indicate that this development towards using

[128] ibid 1993, para 21.

[129] ibid 1995, para 27.

[130] McKendrick (2013) 170. For a similar interpretation, see McCaughran (2011) 613.

[131] See Beale (2012) 987, para 13-005, note 17, who provides extensive evidence from recent case law.

[132] Lord Clarke in *Mediterranean Salvage and Towage Ltd v Seamar Trading and Commerce Inc (The Reborn)* [2009] 1 CLC 909, 916: 'Moreover, as I read Lord Hoffmann's analysis, although he is emphasising that the process of implication is part of the process of construction of the contract, he is not in any way resiling from the often stated proposition that it must be necessary to imply the proposed term. It is never sufficient that it should be reasonable.'

[133] ibid 919: 'Is the proposed implied term necessary to make the contract work? That seems to me to be an entirely appropriate question to ask in considering whether a term should be implied on the assumed facts in this case.'

[134] Beatson, Burrows and Cartwright (2010) 154: 'Although Lord Hoffmann's statement was characteristically bold, the test for implied terms developed by the Courts have stood for many years and it may therefore be premature to regard them as less helpful than a direct search for the meaning of the contract.'

[135] Beale (2012) 988, para 13-005: 'Nevertheless … it is submitted that the principles developed by the courts, which have stood for many years, must still be regarded as of importance in assisting the court to arrive at a conclusion'; Peel (2011) 223, para 6-033: 'It is too early to tell if that view is entirely correct.'

the 'meaning of the contract' and the 'reasonable expectations of the contracting parties' does not substantially reform the threshold for terms implied in fact in general, nevertheless, it offers a refreshing perspective that has the potential to lead to a different outcome on the implication in some constellations.[136] The potential supplementation of a contract with a publicly declared code might be one of these. Framing as a threshold the necessity to protect the reasonable expectations of the contracting parties arguably makes it slightly easier to imply publicly declared corporate codes into any subsequently concluded contract. In this context, one would not need to focus on the question whether the corporate codes are strictly necessary in order to make a contractual agreement between a company and its contractual partner work or whether the publicly declared code spelled out clearly the joint and obvious intentions of the parties. Instead, implication would already be possible if it could be shown that incorporating the publicly declared corporate codes is necessary in order to spell out what the contracting parties reasonably expect from the contract.

To conclude, the rules on terms implied in fact offer the general option for courts to supplement the contract with terms that parties have not explicitly agreed upon. There are, however, quite high threshold requirements in order to be able to use them in relation to publicly declared corporate codes. It is necessary to justify why such a publicly declared code would be necessary in order to effectuate the contract and to allow the parties to perform their contractual obligations or spell out a joint intention, which is certainly difficult. Alternatively, one could also suggest taking the recent developments in the rules on implying terms in fact further and interpret them as statements that merely spell out what the parties reasonably expect from their contract.

3.1.3.2.2.2. German Law: Contextual Contract Interpretation

When attempting to read public statements into subsequently concluded contracts, the rules under German law differ quite significantly from English law. In German law, the relevance of pre-contractual statements for determining the obligations of the contracting parties is, in general, a matter of contract interpretation. Contract interpretation is possible in this legal system with respect to the express terms of a written agreement as well as terms that are considered to spell out the implicit agreement. In the absence of an express term in the contract dealing with a particular matter, German law specifies the rights and obligations from the perspective of what the contracting parties' presumed intention was in this respect. In this context, contract interpretation under German law is of a highly contextual nature and thus makes it possible to read into the contract statements that the contracting parties have spelled out in the final contract incompletely, or have even

136 See for this interpretation McCaughran (2011) 622, who predicts that the decision between adopting the traditional approach in *Philips Electronique* and the new approach in *Belize* will in most cases not matter. Yet he also submits that the preference for one test or the other could matter for some 'hard cases', such as *Equitable Life Insurance*, in which Lord Hoffmann's reappraisal could lead to a slightly easier implication.

failed to incorporate at all, provided that arguments can be brought forward that these statements are part of the actual agreement of the parties. It is this broad approach towards contract interpretation that can be relied upon to make the publicly declared public corporate codes part of the enforceable contract between the company and its contractual partner. The broad contextual perspective on the entire contractual relationship upon which the rules on contract interpretation are based also renders it in this context considerably easier to treat public declarations as terms in contracts as opposed to the more formal approach in English law on the final agreement.

In German law, the undertaking of contract interpretation has to depart from the provision of § 133 BGB, which deals with the interpretation of declarations of intent, and § 157 BGB, which specifies rules on the interpretation of contracts. It has, however, become the prevailing opinion that these provisions are to be read together as the basis for the interpretation of both declarations of intent and contracts.[137] Pursuant to §§ 133 and 157 BGB, contract interpretation is not primarily a matter of interpreting the express terms and their particular meaning; rather, it is the role of the court to identify the actual intentions of the contracting parties beyond the express words of the agreement. The courts are consequently prepared to use the rules on contract interpretation to read into the contract terms that were not part of the agreement but that the courts considered as being an expression of the 'tacit' intentions of the parties.[138] Pursuant to § 133 BGB, the most important component is to determine the actual will of the party making the declaration of intent. It is, however, recognised that the process of interpretation has to approach the meaning of the declaration as it is understood from the perspective of the addressee.[139] Thus, contracts are interpreted by looking at the interests and intentions of the speaker, but also by considering the perspective of the addressee. From these two perspectives, the 'normative will',[140] eg, what the parties could reasonably have intended, is derived. When determining the content of this 'normative will' inherent in the declaration of intent, German courts generally use a variety of documents. Although § 133 BGB declares the actual will to be decisive and not how the will has been literally expressed, it has nevertheless become the prevailing opinion that it is not the internal will of the speaker that represents the starting point of contract interpretation, but rather the available declaration of intent and the words used in a contractual document.[141] In addition, the courts

[137] eg, Palandt-Ellenberger § 133, para 2; Medicus (2010) 129, para 319ff; AK-BGB-Hart §§ 133, 157, para 2: '§ 133 und § 157 müssen heute als Ausdruck eines (weitgehend) einheitlichen Auslegungsprogrammes für Rechtsgeschäfte interpretiert werden.'

[138] Markesinis, Unberath and Johnston (2006) 139 explain this approach on the basis of decision RGZ 117, 176, in which a vendor sold his business to a merchant. The latter promised him a share in profits for the following ten years. The court ruled that it was a duty under the contract that the vendor would not set up a competing business, which the parties 'tacitly' agreed upon.

[139] The so-called 'Auslegung nach Empfängerhorizont', which is established case law, eg, RGZ 119, 21, 25; BGH NJW 1961, 2251, 2253; NJW 1988, 1378, 1379; NJW 1990, 3206, 3206; Palandt-Ellenberger, § 133, para 9; Erman- Arnold § 133, para 19.

[140] Medicus (2010) 131, para 323.

[141] BGH NJW 1993, 721, 722; NJW 2001, 144, 144; NJW-RR 2007, 976, 977.

also pay attention to the surrounding circumstances and the presumed interests of the parties.[142] A particularly important component in the course of this interpretative undertaking is, in this regard, the so-called history of the declaration (*Entstehungsgeschichte*).[143] The courts are generally prepared to consider the process of how the contract has been formed and to take into account statements made by the parties in the course of their negotiations. On this basis, the courts have used pre-contractual correspondence between the contracting parties and their communication during the negotiations when interpreting contracts and declarations of intent.[144] They also have referred to prospectuses, flyers or other statements that have been made available by one party to the other as important documents that give an indication as to the intentions of the contracting parties.[145] Draft versions of contracts have been taken into consideration as well.[146] Interestingly, the literature also explicitly mentions public advertisement by a commercial seller as admissible evidence in contract interpretation.[147]

Against this background, a corporate code in the form of a public declaration could certainly be seen as admissible evidence when specifying the terms of the contract. That being said, there is nonetheless an important aspect that is capable of preventing the incorporation of publicly declared corporate codes into the contract. In spite of the general admissibility of pre-contractual public declarations in the process of interpreting contracts, German law restricts the use of extrinsic evidence when weighing this contextual material. To be sure, there are no general rules as to when the contextual background has to be considered and the courts have quite wide discretion in determining whether they consider the background material important in order to infer on the tacit intention. Yet one can still observe some caution among the courts to use extrinsic evidence very widely. The contextual background of a declaration, in particular the declarations that parties made in the course of their dealings, is mostly taken into consideration when there is ambiguity in the declaration and the contractual agreement does not fully reflect the presumed interests and expectations of the contracting parties. This is not to say that contracts do not require an interpretation if the parties have used clear wording; even clear and unambiguous wording in a contract might, at least in principle, require interpretation.[148] Yet the more explicit the parties have been in their declarations, the less there is a need to take into consideration the contextual

[142] See, eg, BGHZ 156, 335, 346: 'der erklärte Wille, wie er auch aus den Begleitumständen und nicht zuletzt der Interessenlage hervorgehen kann. Im Zweifel gilt, was nach den Maßstäben der Rechtsordnung vernünftig ist und der recht verstandenen Interessenlage entspricht'.

[143] Palandt-Ellenberger § 133, para 16; MüKo-Busche § 133, para 17; Erman-Arnold § 133, para 25.

[144] BGH NJW 1983, 672, 673; BGH NJW 1990, 441, 441; BGH NJW 1999, 3191 3191; BGH NJW 2002, 1260, 1261.

[145] BGH NJW 1981, 2295; ZIP 2004, 843, 844.

[146] See, eg, BGH NJW 1987, 2437, 2438.

[147] Schiemann (2010) 117, para 47; Medicus (2010) 147, para 359; Soergel-Wolf § 145, para 6.

[148] That clear wording in the contract would make the rules of contract interpretation inapplicable was in fact the previous approach of the courts; see, eg, BGH NJW 1981, 1736. This has been criticised in the literature, eg, MüKo-Busche § 133, para 53 (2012); Erman-Arnold § 133, para 13; Soergel-Hefermehl § 133 para 27, and is not followed in more recent decisions: BGH NJW 1983, 672; BGH NJW 2002, 1260, 1261.

background of the contractual agreement.[149] In relation to written contracts that are subject to mandatory form requirements, the Federal High Courts even established a presumption in favour of the completeness of such a written contract, with the result that evidence from the contextual background can only be taken into consideration in exceptional circumstances.[150] As pointedly observed by a contract law scholar: 'In practice, the previous negotiations and the subsequent conduct, let alone a party's statements of subjective intent, will extremely rarely be used to add to, vary or contradict the text of the instrument.'[151] Focusing on publicly declared corporate codes, this implies that the incorporation cannot be justified with a view to the sheer possibility of treating them as admissible material. Instead, it is necessary to provide an additional argument as to why these codes should be given strong weight in the course of contextual contract interpretation. Possibly, the courts could be inclined to assume that there is no need to take these publicly declared corporate codes into consideration when, as in the *Wal-Mart* case, the corporate code was already included in the contract with the clear phrasing that compliance with the corporate code remains the sole obligation of the supplier.[152] Similarly, it is possible that the courts would reject the relevance of the commitments laid down in the corporate code even when no such clear term is included in the contract. Once other relevant and important factors in contract interpretation, such as the presumed interests of the parties and the purpose of the transaction, already provide sufficient clarity as to the actual agreement of the parties, it seems less likely that additional material will be consulted. If, for instance, the main agreement of the parties is an agreement on the sale of goods, it is not entirely certain whether a court would also consult the public statement on compliance with social and environmental standards on the side of the company as being a part of the agreement.

As a result, pursuant to the rules on contract interpretation in German law, it is already possible to use public declarations as evidence when determining the terms of the contract. There is thus no need to develop the existing rules further in order to read publicly declared codes into the contract. Yet, due to the margin of discretion of courts and the reluctance to use extrinsic evidence for contracts that do not at first sight require such a broad interpretation, additional arguments are equally necessary in order to convince the courts that these publicly declared corporate codes need to be given weight in the process of interpreting contracts.

3.1.3.2.2.3. Interim Conclusion

The previous analysis focused on the existing options in contract law to use the rules on contract interpretation and supplementation in order to interpret the

[149] Soergel-Hefermehl § 133, para 25: 'Ist z.B. der Wortlaut einer Erklärung besonders klar und vollständig, so werden auch unter Berücksichtigung des Vertrauensschutzes nur gewichtige Umstände eine dem Wortlaut nicht entsprechende Auslegung rechtfertigen können.' See also Kornet (2006) 106: 'the clearer and more self-contained the wording used, the less need there is to search for alternative interpretations'.

[150] BGH NJW 2002, 3164, 3165, with further references.

[151] Vogenauer (2007) 138.

[152] See the reasoning in the *Wal-Mart* case, above n 81.

corporate codes as a term in subsequently concluded contracts. In so doing, it could be revealed that there are indeed options in both legal systems that could be used to transform the published corporate codes into enforceable terms of a contract. First of all, it is already possible to read into the contract public statements of a trader that characterise the goods for sale due to the specific provisions in the default rules on sales contracts. For publicly declared codes that do not qualify as such, it was suggested that the incorporation of publicly declared corporate codes could become an option only if this specific provision would be broadened and understood as codifying a general principle of contract interpretation or if the rules on contract interpretation and supplementation are applied.

In relation to the general rules on contract interpretation and supplementation, it was revealed that English law remains reluctant to allow declarations to be read into the contract that do not form part of the actual contractual agreement, but that, under certain circumstances, it is nonetheless possible to treat publicly declared codes as contract terms. Depending on the facts of the case, public declaration could represent additional oral agreements between the parties or a collateral contract. The courts could also imply them in the contract if normative reasons so require. However, in the English rules on contract interpretation and supplementation, a generally reluctant attitude could be identified to recognising as contract terms declarations of the parties that are not expressly mirrored in the contractual document. In German law, the suggestion to enforce the corporate codes as terms in contracts between companies and suppliers could be related to the contextual approach to the rules on contract interpretation. For this legal system, it was observed that the existing rules already provide for a broad admission of extrinsic evidence and thus equip a court with the discretion to derive a contract term from material that was present in the pre-contractual stage, including public statements of one of the contracting parties. Yet, although the rules in their current state already allow public statements to be read into contracts, there is nevertheless a need to develop further arguments in order to convince the courts that in the specific constellation of publicly declared codes, the courts would need to use this discretion and also give these codes strong weight when interpreting contracts.

3.1.4. Taking the Debate to the Next Level: Enforcing Publicly Declared Codes

Looking at the potential enforcement of corporate codes discussed so far, it is apparent that the ultimate legal basis for the enforcement of corporate codes is not the corporate code as such, but a bilateral contract between the company and its business partners. Yet, what about the enforcement of corporate codes as such? Is contract law even prepared to enforce the public declaration separately if it is not linked directly to any bilateral contract? More precisely, can the publicly declared corporate code as such be treated as a valid binding contract (section 3.1.4.1)? Or can the corporate codes qualify as unilateral promises of a kind that contract law is prepared to enforce (section 3.1.4.2)? These questions are addressed in the following sections with a view to the general debate in contract law about enforcing public unilateral declarations.

3.1.4.1. *Public Declarations as Contracts*

Is there a possibility in contract law to interpret a publicly declared corporate code as an offer to contract that becomes binding once a member of the public accepts? For the corporate codes under scrutiny, this option so far seems not to have become a prominent topic for debate.[153] Yet when broadening the focus to other types of corporate self-commitments, in particular unilateral self-commitments of companies or industries that are made in the course of national policy processes, one can indeed find such proposals in the scholarly debate as well as in the decisions of lower courts. In order to understand this suggestion and be able to translate the presented arguments in order for them to apply to the informal and transnational corporate codes that are scrutinised in this study, some background information is required on the character of the self-commitments on the basis of which the interpretation as contracts is proposed. The suggestion appears specifically in the debate on unilateral self-commitments of companies or industry associations in the national context that are developed and published in cooperation with national policy makers. Areas in which such self-commitments appear frequently are environmental policy[154] and policies on financial regulation.[155] Recently, the value of unilateral self-commitments also received attention in the debate on gender quota in management and supervisory boards. Self-commitments of individual companies or industry associations are in these contexts envisaged as an alternative to regulation by statute. They represent firm commitments of a whole industry or individual firms to pursue a specific policy objective, for instance, to reduce carbon emissions in a particular period or to make available certain financial services to everyone regardless of their financial solvency. In exchange for this self-commitment, the idea is that the government, in reliance on the self-regulation by the sector or by individual companies, informally agrees to refrain from regulating this particular field.[156]

In the legal debate, such specific self-commitments of companies are from the orthodox perspective treated as voluntary in nature that cannot be enforced as a

[153] So far, it is mainly Kenny (2007) who discusses the possibility of whether the code can be interpreted as an implied contract between companies and suppliers' employees pursuant to US law. Some arguments in favour of a contractually binding character with, however, a cautious conclusion as to the possibility under current contract law can also be found in Glinski (2011) 217f (towards consumers for public commitments in advertisement) and 328ff (towards third parties detrimentally affected by the operations of a subsidiary by means of drawing an analogy to public declarations of companies to pay debts of a subsidiary that benefit creditors). The option of interpreting a corporate commitment on workplace standards as a unilateral contract is also at least briefly indicated by Webb and Morrison (2004) 122f; Sobczak (2006) 171; Koster and Eynde (2009) 139f; and Peterkova (2014a) 17f.

[154] For an overview of these different types of environmental self-commitments, see generally Paton (2002) 38ff, who distinguishes four different types: unilateral initiatives by firms, private codes by industry associations or NGOs, government-sponsored programmes and negotiated agreements between governments and companies.

[155] One can mention here in particular the Guidelines of the Central Credit Agency (*Zentraler Kreditausschuss*) on the provision of bank accounts that banks that are members also post on their websites and the Banking and Insurance Codes that Barron (2007) 3, note 1 deals with.

[156] There is also the constellation in which the government formally agrees not to regulate. Yet these cases are rather classified as genuine norm-substituting contracts between governments and companies, which are not too relevant in the discussion on unilaterally and publicly declared codes.

legally binding contract.[157] However, in spite of this common understanding, there are, at least in the German debate, equally scholarly contributions,[158] as well as some lower court decisions,[159] that suggest interpreting such corporate self-commitments to the public as genuine contracts. The debate has so far addressed in particular the question of whether a public declaration to comply with the Guidelines of the Central Credit Agency and specifically the commitment therein to provide a bank account to every customer could be legally enforceable by the beneficiaries of this commitment. Among those that treat these self-commitments as enforceable, one core suggestion is to view these public self-commitments as contracts that the self-committing companies have concluded with the government. The two lower German courts mentioned above, for instance, had to deal with the public commitment of a company on its website to follow the recommendations of the Central Credit Agency. The courts were called upon to decide whether such a public statement would result in an obligation to follow the guidelines and provide a bank account to everyone.[160] Effectively, the commitment was treated as an offer addressed to the government to conclude a contract that the latter accepted by refraining from regulating the field in question.[161] Since the core purpose of this contract between the company and the government was interpreted as conferring a benefit upon the individuals that sought to open a bank account, this agreement between companies and the government resulted in a separate enforcement right of the individuals as third party beneficiaries.[162] In the scholarly debate, one can

[157] For self-commitments in the environmental sector, see, eg, Di Fabio (1997) 970; for self-commitments in the financial sector, see, eg, Berresheim (2005); Segna (2006). *cf* also the comments in a Scottish case, *Mumford and Smith v Bank of Scotland* 1996 SLT 392, to which Barron (2007) 3, note 2 refers: 'the orthodox view has been that any argument based on non-observance would be doomed to failure'.

[158] Affirmative with respect to environmental self-commitments: Frenz (2001). 228ff, and with respect to self-commitments as to the provision of financial services Derleder (2003); Kohte (2005b); Knops and Bamberger (2009) 1129f.

[159] The prominent decisions in favour of the contractually binding character of unilateral self-commitments are LG Berlin WM 2003, 1895 (binding decision, appeal from AG Charlottenburg BKR 2004, 41, further appeal denied); LG Bremen, file number 2-O-408/05, judgment 16 June 2005 (overruled by OLG Bremen, ZIP 2005, 798) and against the interpretation of self-commitments as contracts OLG Bremen, ZIP 2005, 798; AG Stuttgart, judgment 22 June 2005—14 C 2988/05; AG Nürnberg, judgment 24 March 2005—34 C 9121/04.

[160] It has to be emphasised that in the particular debate on self-commitments concerning the provision of financial services, further complexity is involved due to the fact that the discussion on the binding character of such self-commitments was carried out with respect to the statements on the homepage of the individual banks and the guidelines of the central credit agency as such. With respect to the latter, the debate surrounded the question whether the published guidelines could bind the companies as members of the credit agency. The following analysis will, however, relate the arguments that were raised in this debate more generally to the publicly declared self-commitments of companies.

[161] In LG Bremen, file number 2-O-408/05, judgment 16 June 2005, the court argued that the government accepted by not undertaking regulatory measures in this field. Evidence for this acceptance was taken from the BT-Drucks. 14/3611 and 15/2500, in which it was explicitly laid down why Parliament refrained from regulation by referring to self-commitment. In LG Berlin WM 2003, 1895, the court used as supporting evidence a press conference of the local administration from which it became clear that the administration relied on this statement and, as a result, refrained from initiating binding legislation. On this aspect, see generally Kohte (2005b) 416f.

[162] LG Bremen, file number 2-O-408/05, judgment 16 June 2005 ('Durch Auslegung nach den §§ 133, 157 BGB ergibt sich das Vorliegen eines Vertrages zugunsten Dritter. Begünstigter dieses abstrakten Schuldversprechens zugunsten Dritter ist gemäß der Selbstverpflichtung Jedermann'). The possibility of interpreting corporate codes as constituting contractual third party rights is discussed in this part; see below section 3.2.3. (p 126), text and accompanying footnotes.

also find support for this decision.[163] Thus, one conceivable way to treat public self-commitments as enforceable contracts is to interpret them as bilateral contracts between companies and the regulator where the self-commitment is made in exchange for the government's promise to refrain from regulation. In addition, the scholarly literature provides for another interpretation. In the course of the debate, it is in fact also suggested that these public self-commitments be interpreted as offers of a company that are directly addressed to the consumers that benefit from the particular commitment. According to this suggestion, a public self-commitment would represent an offer to the public that can be accepted by the beneficiaries simply by making use of the promised services and entering into a contract.[164]

The arguments above have been developed with respect to public self-commitments that deal with specific policy issues and these commitments are a reaction to political debates on whether or not to regulate the particular field. Although the corporate codes that are discussed here are less formalised and definitely not in a comparably firm way linked to legislative processes, the respective suggestions can nevertheless also be made fruitful for the type of corporate codes that are discussed in this study. Based on the existing suggestion, the possible interpretation of publicly declared corporate codes as contracts is conceivable for three different constellations. Following the suggested interpretation of public self-commitments as contracts with the government, one can equally argue that the public declaration to comply with certain social and environmental policies could be qualified as an offer addressed to the government to self-regulate this field, which can be accepted by the latter by refraining from regulating this particular area in reliance on the effectiveness of self-regulation. In addition, one could also discuss whether corporate codes should be treated as offers to the public that become enforceable by a customer either by notifying the company or by relying on the promised behaviour when deciding whether or not to purchase a product.[165] Finally, it is also conceivable that the corporate codes amount to direct contractual offers towards the beneficiaries of the code, ie, the employees of subsidiaries and suppliers or other third parties that benefit from the code, that becomes an enforceable contract once the beneficiaries accept.[166]

In order to determine whether these are viable interpretations under the current contract law, the following section will assess these arguments from the perspective of the English and German rules on contract formation.

[163] Derleder (2003) 964; Kohte (2005a) 353f.

[164] For this suggestion with a particular view to environmental self-commitments, see Frenz (2001) 229f; and for self-commitments as to the provision of financial services, see Kohte (2005a) 352f; Knops and Bamberger (2009) 1129.

[165] Both these arguments have also been used by Glinski (2011) 129, 217f.

[166] On the basis of US law, this possibility is discussed but eventually rejected by Kenny (2007) 463ff. Kenny sees the potential offer in the fact that the publishing company requires the code of conduct to be distributed globally to all supplier factories and made available to beneficiaries in the form of posters. Acceptance is identified here in the fact that employees continue to work, but Kenny concludes that an interpretation of this published code of conduct reveals that it is too vague to be counted as an offer. For a similar perspective on the basis of US law, see also Revak (2012) 1664ff. A comparable suggestion of treating a corporate self-commitment as directly binding towards the beneficiaries, such as local communities, is at least briefly indicated by Glinski (2011) 170, 330.

3.1.4.1.1. English Law

In English law, the general requirements to conclude an enforceable contract are that there is an offer, which is accepted. Moreover, a well-known characteristic of the English rules on contract formation is the requirement that the offeree gives or promises something in exchange for the offer (so-called consideration). Ever since the famous case *Carlill v Carbolic Smoke Ball Corp*[167] case, it is recognised that an offer to contract can also be made to the public. Thus, offer and acceptance do not necessarily require personal interaction between the contracting parties, but can also be concluded between remote parties. As is well known, in this case the court held that a company made a contractual offer in the form of a public advertisement in newspapers that advocated a newly developed smoke ball as a way to prevent influenza and promised to pay £100 to anyone who got sick with influenza after using the smoke ball in the described way. The particular offer to the public could in this case be accepted without notifying the offeror by merely performing the conditions set out in the contract.[168] Since the case still represents the landmark case on contract formation between remote parties and, moreover, specifically deals with statements in advertisements,[169] it provides particularly useful guidance for the question of whether corporate codes could also be viewed as a contract that is concluded by means of an offer to the public. In addition to the presence of offer and acceptance by performance, in English law it is crucial for every contract to identify consideration, eg, the person making the offer has to receive something in return for promising an action. In English law, contracts are only given 'the badge of enforceability'[170] if they are based on a bargain and create obligations for both parties. Conversely, agreements not supported by consideration are not enforceable unless they are made in a deed.[171] As the presence of a deed is a highly unrealistic constellation in relation to publicly declared corporate codes, an interpretation of the corporate codes as contracts is thus dependent on whether one can identify valid consideration in relation to the publicly declared code. Based on these requirements for contract formation, there are essentially two questions that require specific attention. First, are the publicly declared corporate codes capable of being qualified as an offer to contract? And, if so, can one identify valid consideration in this constellation?

[167] *Carlill v Carbolic Smoke Ball Corp* [1892] EWCA Civ 1.

[168] ibid 262 (per Lord Lindley).

[169] The advertisement in this particular case was particularly published in newspapers. Arguably, however, it is possible to apply the requirements spelled out in this case to the conventional types of unilateral declarations that appear in modern forms of marketing communication, in particular declarations on websites or public posters. As far as the latter form is concerned, *Bowerman v Association of British Travel Agents* [1996] CLC 451 already provides an illustrative example in which the requirements set out on *Carlill v Carbolic Smoke Ball* were applied to a public poster.

[170] McKendrick (2013) 68.

[171] Beatson, Burrows and Cartwright (2010) 93; Peel (2011) 71, para 3-001 166ff, para 3-170ff; Beale (2012) 293, para 3-001.

3.1.4.1.1.1. Binding Offers to the Public

English law defines an offer as a statement of a party that reveals an intention to be legally bound on the stated terms. In general, there is no formal requirement as to how the offer is made; it can be made orally, in writing or by conduct. In *Carbolic Smoke Ball*, Lord Bowen, referring to *Spencer v Harding*,[172] held that it is also possible to make an offer to the public with the result that such a statement becomes enforced by anyone who accepts it before it is retracted.[173]

Following the objective approach in English law towards contract interpretation, in order for a public statement to qualify as an offer, it would need to express in a sufficiently specific manner the intention to be legally bound. In particular, in relation to statements in public advertisements, the requirement of an intention to be bound is generally analysed very thoroughly. The court, when confronted with a public declaration, needs to draw a distinction between an offer and mere 'puff'[174] by reading the 'advertisement in its plain meaning, as the public would understand it' and asking: 'How would an ordinary person reading this document construe it?'[175] This requirement to identify an intention to be legally bound in publicly declared corporate codes and not see them as a mere puff already represents a first hurdle. In this regard, a sceptical perspective seems to prevail that infers from the generally vague phrasing of the codes that the companies do not actually intend to create a binding obligation.[176] The language used in the codes often seems 'to be merely a general statement of company policy and guidelines for employer-employee conduct' rather than 'precise and absolute phrasing'.[177] As support for this scepticism, one can also refer to a case in English law that dealt with a party's reference to its general corporate policy in the course of contractual negotiations. In *Kleinwort Benson v Malaysia Shipping*, the Court of Appeal ruled that a statement of a party that merely contains a reference to the policy of a company is not an offer supported by an intention to be legally bound by the terms of this policy. The party's reference to its general policy did not give rise to a legal obligation, but was considered 'a moral responsibility only'.[178] As a result, a first hindrance that is likely to prevent the contractual enforcement of corporate codes can be found in the reluctance in English contract law to treat statements that refer to a particular corporate policy as having been made with an intention

[172] *Spencer v Harding* (1870) LR 5 CP 561.

[173] Lord Bowen in *Carlill v Carbolic Smoke Ball Corp* (n 167) 268: 'It is an offer made to all the world; and why should not an offer be made to all the world which is to ripen into a contract with anybody who comes forward and performs the condition?' See also Lord Lindley (ibid) 261: 'they are offers to anybody who performs the conditions named in the advertisement, and anybody who does perform the condition accepts the offer'.

[174] Lord Lindley (ibid) 261.

[175] Lord Bowen (ibid) 266.

[176] See especially Kenny (2007) 463ff, who deems the vague phrasing a core hindrance for a potential contractual enforcement; see also Revak (2012) 1655f.

[177] Kenny (2007) 464f.

[178] *Kleinwort Benson v Malaysia Shipping Corp* [1989] WLR 379, 391 (per Lord Justice Gibson). In this particular case, the policy in question was an assertion by one party that it was its policy 'to ensure that the subsidiary was able to meet its debts'.

to be legally bound. Conversely, the phrasing, as guidelines and policies, instead suggests a treatment as non-binding informal and aspirational statements.

In addition, the requirement of an intention to be legally bound on the stated terms is not only relevant when distinguishing sufficiently specific offers from mere puffs. The intention to be legally bound is also used as a criterion to categorise public declarations as either offers or so-called invitations to treat. In contrast to an offer, the invitation to treat is defined as a statement that expresses the willingness of someone to enter into further contractual negotiations, but that is not yet made with an intention to be directly legally bound on the terms.[179] Following the general objective approach in English contract law, the decision between an offer and an invitation to treat effectively depends in each specific case on whether an intention to be legally bound can be derived from the objectively available statement.[180] Yet, English courts have provided guidance for 'certain stereotype situations' in which the distinction is determined, at least on a prima facie basis.[181] English law thus also contains a general presumption for particular types of statements as to whether they would qualify as offers or invitations to treat. In this context, it is the general rule that statements to the public are generally treated as invitations to treat and only exceptionally as offers. This applies to statements made in public advertising as well as those presented to the public in the form of distributed catalogues, leaflets or posters[182] and displaying goods for sale in a shop window.[183] Against this background, one can also define the general presumption in contract law of treating statements made to the public as invitations to treat rather than binding offers, an additional obstacle that needs to be overcome when seeking to enforce the corporate codes as contracts.

In fact, the presumption can only rebutted if a particular advertisement is qualified as an offer to conclude a *unilateral* contract, as was the case in *Carbolic Smoke Ball*. A unilateral contract is concluded by an offer to pay a sum of money or perform an action in which the conditions are already set out that the addressee of the promise will have to do in order to complete the contract.[184] Unilateral contracts are constellations in which a party already includes in its offer all the terms that are necessary to conclude a binding contract, with the result that the potential addressee only needs to accept or perform the action. In such cases, the intention to be legally bound on the terms is inferred from the fact that the speaker does not realistically expect any further negotiations with the addressee before entering

[179] McKendrick (2013) 26f: 'did the maker of the statement intend to be bound by an acceptance of his terms without further negotiation, or did he only intend his statement to be part of the continuing negotiation process?'.

[180] Peel (2011) 11, paras 2-006 and 2-002.

[181] ibid 12, para 2-007; Beale (2012) 172, para 2-003.

[182] *Partridge v Crittenden* [1968] 1 WLR 1204 (an advertisement to sell wild birds is not yet an offer).

[183] *Pharmaceutical Society of Great Britain v Boots Cash Chemists (Southern) Ltd* [1953] 1 QB 401; *Fisher v Bell* [1961] 1 QB 394 (displaying a flick knife in a shop window is not an offer to contract).

[184] For examples, see generally the case law cited in Beale (2012) 216, para 2-078: *Rogers v Snow* (1573) Dalison 94, *Great Northern Railway v Witham* (1873) LR 9 CP 16 (promise to pay a sum if the other walks from London to New York); *Hamer v Sideway* (1881) 124 NY 538 (promise to pay money for giving up smoking for a year).

into a contractual agreement and thus presumably already seeks to contract rather than only negotiate.[185] Thus, in order for a corporate code not to be treated as an invitation to treat but as an offer, it would need to set out all conditions that are necessary to conclude a contract.

3.1.4.1.1.2. The Doctrine of Consideration

This leads to the second requirement of contract formation, namely the requirement of consideration. In order for public declarations to become binding, they need to already contain the request for valid consideration. Consideration in English law is generally defined as a 'right, interest, profit, or benefit that is given to the offeror or some forbearance, detriment, loss or responsibility that is given, suffered or undertaken'[186] by the offeree. For valid consideration, the following rules are fundamental. First, consideration has to be sufficient, but need not be adequate. This means that the focus is solely on whether something of value has been exchanged, not whether whatever is given is an adequate value for the promise made by the offeror.[187] Second, past consideration is not sufficient, which implies that promises to reward someone for having performed an act prior to making the promise are generally not enforceable.[188] Third, consideration must move from the promisee. A third party cannot make a contract enforceable by providing consideration.[189] As consideration must be given in return for the promise, it is finally necessary that consideration is requested by the promisor. Mere reliance of the addressed party on the promise is not sufficient.[190] This criterion is particularly important in relation to unilateral contracts that are concluded by an offer to the public. With regard to declarations to the public, the consideration requirement has to appear in a particular form. As addressed already, the public declaration needs to specify the exact conditions that need to be performed by the addressees in order to receive the benefit. In *Carbolic Smoke Ball*, the court held that consideration was specified in the public offer in the form of two components that were set out in the advertisement: the effort of the addressed consumers to buy[191] and the inconvenience to use[192] the smoke ball. A similar argument was made in a more recent case applying the principles set out in *Carbolic Smoke Ball*. The decision *Bowerman v Association of British Travel Agents*[193] dealt with the question of whether a poster placed prominently in the offices of associated travel agents by

[185] Peel (2011) 14, para 2-010.

[186] Justice Lush in *Currie v Misa* (1875) LR 10 Ex 153, 162.

[187] *Bolton v Madden* (1873) LR 9 QB 55, 56 (per Justice Blackburn): 'the adequacy of the consideration is for the parties to consider at the time of making the agreement, not for the court when it is sought to be enforced'.

[188] Beatson, Burrows and Cartwright (2010) 95 provide the example that 'if A saves B from drowning, and B later promises A a reward, A's action cannot be relied on as consideration for B's promise'.

[189] ibid 98.

[190] ibid 92.

[191] Lord Lindley in *Carlill v Carbolic Smoke Ball Corp* (n 167) 264.

[192] Lord Bowen (ibid) 271: 'Inconvenience sustained by one party at the request of the other is enough to create a consideration.'

[193] *Bowerman v Association of British Travel Agents* (n 169).

the defendants could be interpreted as an offer to contract. The posters contained the promise that the Association of British Travel Agents would protect travellers in case of insolvency of the agent if they booked a trip with an associated travel agent. The Court of Appeal held that booking a trip with a travel agent was set out as a condition to receive insolvency protection and that this would amount to sufficient consideration.[194]

However, the requirement of specifying and requesting an action or forbearance in the public declaration is where the crux lies with respect to the corporate codes. Where is it laid down in corporate codes that the performance of an action or forbearance is conditional to make the corporate code effective? Based on what has been presented above, there are in general several potential candidates for consideration. The public self-commitment could be interpreted as being addressed to the government with the request to abstain from regulating this field. It would thus be forbearance on the side of the addressed regulators that would represent consideration. In addition, the fact that the self-commitment is used for marketing purposes and is addressed to the public could be used to argue that consideration is present on the side of the addressed members of the public if they reward the company with an increase in sales. With respect to the potential beneficiaries, in particular employees in subsidiary or supplier factories, a request for consideration could be seen in the fact that these employees continue working after having noted the code.[195] In the corporate code debate, one can finally also find the proposal to view as valid consideration the fact that the global public, including addressed and benefiting local communities or NGOs, abstain from protesting and thus damaging a company's reputation.[196] In general, one could deem that all of these conditions in substance amount to valid consideration in the eyes of law. In relation to the addressed governments as well as the local communities, the valid consideration would represent forbearance from regulating respective protesting that benefits the company. With respect to the public and the purchase of products, the sufficiency of consideration can be explicitly derived from the rules on consideration spelled out in *Carbolic Smoke Ball*. Finally, with regard to the employees in supplier and subsidiary companies, valid consideration can be identified in the performance of a contractual duty owed to a third party, which, in contrast to the performance of an existing contractual duty towards the promisor, English law accepts as sufficient and real consideration.[197]

[194] Lord Hobbhouse (ibid) 463: 'ABTA's members prominently market themselves as members of ABTA and anybody who chooses to do business with them is certainly giving consideration to ABTA for any contract or "collateral" contract which may ensue.'

[195] See especially for this argument Kenny (2007) 464.

[196] See on this point Glinski (2011) 170. The suggestion to consider forbearance of protests as valid consideration in the law is also made in relation to Global Framework Agreements between companies and trade unions; see, eg, Coleman (2009) 628: 'Under an IFA, the MNC promises to respect and not interfere with core labour rights. In return, the GU [Global Union] promises not to engage in a negative publicity campaign that damages the company's reputation and affects sales.'

[197] See fundamentally *Shadwell v Shadwell* (1860) 9 CB (NS) 159. See also *Pao On v Lau Yiu Long* [1980] AC 614, 632 (per Lord Scarman): 'Their Lordships do not doubt that a promise to perform, or the performance of a pre-existing contractual obligation to a third party can be valid consideration.'

Taking a closer look at these different candidates, however, there is one particular problem that prevents viewing all these elements as valid consideration. The corporate codes under scrutiny are highly ambiguous due to their informality concerning the action or forbearance that the company expects in exchange for making the code. Concerning the potential consideration by governments, it should be noted that these types of codes are not directly embedded within a legislative process, with the result that a direct link between the self-commitment and a purported requested forbearance in the form of abstaining from regulation is immensely difficult to construct. Although companies may adopt and publicly commit themselves to complying with a corporate code, also with the objective of pre-empting public regulation, this motive remains but an informal expectation and emphatically not a directly expressed request. With regard to the potential consideration on the side of other market actors that reward such a declaration with an increase in sales, it is equally true that this increase in sales is only in rare constellations included in the code as an explicit request from the company.[198] The same holds true for the forbearance of local communities from protesting and the reliance of employees on the self-commitments when continuing to work. By means of adopting corporate codes, companies may also have the objective of convincing the public that they are reliable actors against which no protests would need to be initiated and that they adopt standards that beneficiaries can rely upon. However, it would certainly go too far to define this as being explicitly requested as a condition for the corporate code to become effective.[199] In short, it is one core problem that none of the proposed forms of consideration appears in the codes in a sufficiently specific and explicit manner as a requirement that is necessary for the code to become effective. Yet, on the other side, it seems equally unsatisfactory to reject enforcement for lack of consideration and view the codes as unenforceable, merely gratuitous promises. In fact, the corporate codes would be best placed as public declarations that are somewhere in between a promise made with the clear request for consideration and a purely gratuitous promise for which nothing is received in return; they are declarations that are based on the expectation that such a commitment would be rewarded by the market, the regulator and the global public. Yet the expectation remains implicit, highly diffuse and thus quite difficult to grasp. Hence, when seeking to enforce publicly declared corporate codes as contracts, one would need to focus more specifically on whether and to what extent the English doctrine of consideration is capable of also recognising diffuse

[198] Examples of such conditional promises are provided by Glinski (2011) 217. Glinski specifically focuses on public promises of companies to cooperate with an NGO in order to protect the environment if consumers buy the product. However, she also emphasises that such statements will mostly be present in ad hoc advertising campaigns and explicitly not in the publicly available corporate code itself.

[199] Here, one can also identify a difference between publicly declared corporate codes that in general do not contain any indication that the company expects something in return for its public commitment and international framework agreements that are negotiated between companies and trade unions. In the latter case, one can indeed occasionally find explicit clauses on forbearance to protest; see Coleman (2009) 628, note 128, who refers here to the Chiquita Framework Agreement that contains a clause that the parties: 'Avoid actions that could undermine the process … such as public international campaigns.'

and implicit hopes or expectations for a reward as valid consideration. Recognition can be based on two arguments, which rely on a very broad understanding of the doctrine of consideration and which certainly would be read not merely as an application, but rather as a further development of the doctrine as such.

First, one can refer to the case law on the rule that consideration needs to be sufficient but not adequate. This rule has already led in some cases to the courts recognising trivial acts specified in public advertisements as sufficient consideration and it is the reasoning of the codes that is particularly noteworthy. Interestingly, when justifying why even a minimal action can amount to sufficient consideration, the courts have referred to the fact that the request for the performance of this particular action is effectively linked to an implicit and underlying broader purpose that ultimately benefits the speaker. In *Chappell & Co v Nestle*,[200] for instance, the House of Lords interpreted a poster containing the offer to give gramophone records to anyone who sent a minimal amount of money to cover the costs of posting the promised records together with three wrappers from Nestlé's chocolate bars as an offer supported by sufficient consideration. In this decision, the Law Lords made clear that good consideration must effectively be what the contracting parties agree even if this is, from the perspective of the court, only a trivial and inadequate benefit.[201] Yet the trivial act was also justified as sufficient consideration because it was effectively based on the broader implicit objective to increase sales. In this particular case, Lord Somervell said that because 'the whole object of selling the record … was to increase the sales of chocolate, it seems to me wrong not to treat the stipulated evidence of such sales as part of the consideration'.[202] A similar reasoning can be found in *Carbolic Smoke Ball*, in which Lord Lindley said: 'It is quite obvious that in the view of the advertisers a use by the public of their remedy, if they can only get the public to have confidence enough to use it, will react and produce a sale which is directly beneficial to them.'[203] In a similar vein, the Court of Appeal in *Bowerman v Association of British Travel Agents* held that a benefit was present on the side of the Association of British Travel Agents because a contract concluded with one of its agents would effectively also be a promotion for it. What is noteworthy is that the court emphatically found that '[a] picture was presented (...), *wholly unrealistically*, of ABTA as some benevolent body which gained no benefit from and had no interest in travellers choosing to deal with ABTA members'.[204] From these decisions, one can see that the courts at least exhibit a particular scepticism towards a purported gratuitous character of promises that a commercial actor makes to the public in the course of a public advertisement campaign. Yet, despite such observable tendencies towards paying due respect to the underlying and implicit purpose of public advertisement when

[200] *Chappell and Co v Nestle Co Ltd* [1959] AC 87.

[201] See especially the statement by Lord Somervell (ibid) 114: 'A contracting party can stipulate for what consideration he chooses. A peppercorn does not cease to be good consideration if it is established that the promisee does not like pepper and will throw away the corn.'

[202] Lord Somervell (ibid) 114f.

[203] Lord Lindley in *Carlill v Carbolic Smoke Ball Corp* (n 167) 264.

[204] *Bowerman v Association of British Travel Agents* (n 169) 465 (per Lord Hobhouse) (emphasis added).

determining consideration, it is also true that the respective public advertisement in all these cases still contained an explicit request of the respective company to perform an act even if it was trivial or indirect. The consideration was the explicit request to buy and use the advertised smoke ball (*Carbolic Smoke Ball*), the purchase of chocolate and the sending of the wrappers (*Chappell v Nestle*) or the booking of a holiday with an associated travel agent (*Bowerman v Association of British Travel Agents*). The reasoning of the courts in these cases thus remains difficult to apply to public declarations when only implicit and diffuse expectations are apparent, but no formal request whatsoever has been made on the side of the company. In order to also treat such cases as containing valid consideration, it would be necessary to shift the focus from an implicit broader purpose that formally appears in a trivial act to only accepting an implicit broader purpose as valid consideration.

In light of the difficulty to also consider as valid consideration an implicit and diffuse expectation, a second argument could be made that makes use of the recent slight tendency in English law towards relaxing the strict requirement of consideration. The decision that is most prominently referred to in relation to this development is *Williams v Roffey Bros*.[205] This case dealt with a promise of defendants for which the claimants promised to perform their duties under the existing contract. In deciding the case, the Court of Appeal held that a promise to perform a duty would amount to sufficient consideration because fulfilling the contractual duty on time would amount to a 'practical benefit' for the defendants.[206] In the context of the corporate codes, one could consider making use of this notion of a 'practical benefit' in order to capture indirect and implicit benefits that companies may have when publishing a corporate code in the form of less regulation by the government, an increase in sales or a more positive attitude towards the company from civil society. Yet, this argument is also certainly highly controversial and can easily be criticised. *Williams v Roffey Bros* is a narrowly confined exception that refined the consideration requirement in relation to the modification of existing contracts. Conversely, it did not attempt to develop rules concerning the necessity of consideration for the formation of contracts as such. The decision had the concrete purpose to 'refine and limit the application'[207] of a very specific principle set out in *Stilk v Myrick*,[208] in which the enforcement of a promise in an existing contract was rejected when the promisee promised in return to merely perform his legal obligations under the contract. It is this narrow scope on the specific factual constellation of promises in existing contracts that render it difficult to use as a first step for a general relaxation of the consideration requirement. Moreover, even if a broad application were nevertheless suggested, it also remains questionable whether, in

[205] *Williams v Roffey Bros* [1991] 1 QB 1.

[206] ibid 16 (per Glidewell LJ). McKendrick (2013) 78f summarises this practical benefit as having the following factual advantages for the claimant: (1) the claimant continued to work, (2) defendants spared trouble and expenses for finding someone else to complete the work, (3) the defendants avoided a penalty clause for delay in their contract with their customers, (4) a co-ordinated method of payment was promised, (5) the defendants could use their trades to do work in the completed flat, which otherwise would have been held up.

[207] *Williams v Roffey Bros* (n 205) 16 (per Glidewell LJ).

[208] *Stilk v Myrick* (1809) 2 Camp 317.

relation to the corporate codes, a practical benefit as envisaged in *Williams v Roffey Bros* could be identified. The promise in *Williams v Roffey Bros* was one that was made in a personal meeting between the contracting parties, whereas the corporate codes appear in highly informal relations of the company and the external public. An immediate 'practical benefit' provided to the companies by politics, the market or the global public is more difficult to identify.

Against this background, the strict requirements of consideration as a benefit that needs to be requested by the promisor and that must move from the promisee represents a third obstacle that currently hinders the enforcement of publicly declared codes as contracts.

3.1.4.1.2. German Law

Like English law, the German rules on contract formation require the presence of offer and acceptance for the conclusion of a legally binding contract, but, as is frequently emphasised by scholars of comparative law, the German legal system, in contrast to English law, does not have a requirement of consideration.[209] On the contrary, German law is prepared to enforce contracts on bilateral exchange, such as the sales contract (§ 433 BGB), as well as contracts without consideration, such as lending free of charge (§ 598 BGB) or the promise to give a gift (§ 516 BGB). The criterion to distinguish between contractually enforceable and social agreements remains the intention of the party when making a declaration. Provided that an intention to be legally bound can be inferred from the statement and its surrounding context, German law is in principle prepared to interpret such a declaration as a binding offer that, once accepted, becomes a valid contract. However, with regard to agreements that do not have as their objective a reciprocal exchange, German law still has in place certain additional requirements that need to be met in order to enforce such unilateral declarations as contracts. Of particular relevance in this context are the mandatory form requirements for promises for which nothing is received in return. Consequently, when seeking to enforce publicly declared corporate codes as contracts, particular attention is required as to the presence of an intention to be legally bound and any applicable mandatory form requirements.

3.1.4.1.2.1. Binding Offers ad incertas personas

Comparable to English law, German law also accepts the possibility of making a contractual offer to the public, a so-called offer *ad incertas personas*.[210] As a general rule, an offer *ad incertas personas* is present if a declaration to the public is sufficiently concrete and specifies all the essential components that are necessary for the conclusion of the contract (*essentialia negotii*).[211] This requirement is met when

[209] From the many authors dealing with this matter, see eg, Zweigert and Kötz (1998) 397f; Markesinis, Unberath and Johnston (2006) 87: 'In German law the seriousness of the parties is not determined by any doctrine even remotely akin to that of consideration.'
[210] Palandt-Heinrichs § 145, para 7; MüKo-Busche § 145, paras 13, 17.
[211] Palandt-Ellenberger § 145, para 1; Prütting/Wegen/Weinrich-Brinkmann § 145, para 4.

the declaration leaves no need for further negotiation and it can be accepted by a simple 'yes'.

The specification of the *essentialia negotii* is crucial in this context as it serves as the criterion to distinguish between an offer and a non-binding invitation to treat, and it represents, comparable to English law,[212] the general rule that posters, leaflets or the display of goods in a shop window are treated as invitations to treat rather than as offers.[213] The same applies to presentations on websites.[214] This general presumption suggests that the courts would, in a similar vein as in English law, due to their form as public declarations, be more inclined to treat published corporate codes as an invitation to treat than as offers. However, it should be noted that there are also cases in which German courts have interpreted statements to the public as binding offers provided that they were sufficiently concrete and showed a certain degree of seriousness. Interesting examples for such offers to the public can in this regard be found particularly in the case law of the lower courts. A famous example comes from the Higher Regional Court of Frankfurt. The court interpreted as an offer a statement made by the spokesman of a bank at a press conference that contained the commitment to compensate craftsmen suffering from insolvency of another company financed by this bank.[215] Notwithstanding the fact that a press conference is an unusual setting for making an offer, it was held that the statement was not spontaneous, but rather was sufficiently well considered and prepared, which is why one could assume that there was an intention to create a legal obligation. Other examples are the warranty statement of a producer on a website that was interpreted as an offer to conclude a warranty contract with the end-consumer[216] or the presentation of goods on the website of an online auction if the general terms of the online auction stated that the goods would be sold to the person that bids the highest price.[217] Even a declaration on a product that is offered for sale can count as an offer to everyone who buys the product.[218] It is this line of cases on which the suggested interpretation of corporate codes as public offers to contract could accordingly be based.

Yet, even if the attempt is made to define publicly declared corporate codes as comparable to these exceptional constellations in which courts interpreted a declaration to the public as an offer and not an invitation to treat, the ultimate decision as to whether a binding offer is present still depends on whether one could interpret the particular corporate code under scrutiny as a sufficiently serious declaration that is made with an intention to be legally bound. Pursuant to the German rules on contract formation, this depends on the content of the actual declaration,

[212] For the similarities between English and German law with respect to the specific distinction between invitations to treat and offers, see generally Lando and Beale (2000) 162.

[213] Palandt-Ellenberger § 145, para 2; MüKo-Busche § 145, para 12; Soergel-Wolf § 145, para 7.

[214] See, eg, AG Butzbach, NJW-RR 2003, 54.

[215] OLG Frankfurt, NJW 1997, 136.

[216] OLG Frankfurt, EuZW 2010, 77, 78.

[217] BGHZ 149, 129—Riccardo.de. In this case, the Federal High Court decided that activating the website in which the goods are presented is a declaration of intent. However, the court left open the question of whether this act represents an offer or the 'anticipated acceptance' with the highest bidder.

[218] BGH NJW 2007, 2912.

eg, the specificity of the declaration and the language used.[219] Moreover, pursuant to the general contextual approach towards the interpretation of declarations of intent and contracts, one would need to also consider the context in which the declaration was made, the interests of the parties and the purpose of the particular declaration.[220] Yet in the current debate on public commitments to comply with a corporate policy, there seems to be instead a tendency against understanding such declarations as being made by companies with an intention to be legally bound. Already in the debate on national self-commitments to provide financial services that are posted on websites, it is predominantly argued, despite the few lower court decisions, that the content of the declaration and the context in which it is made does not indicate the presence of an intention to be legally bound.[221] In fact, the authors who favour an interpretation of unilateral self-commitments of companies concerning the provision of financial services as binding offers base their qualification on the argument that it is not merely the intention of the speaker, but the impression of the declaration from the perspective of the addressees and their interests that should be decisive when determining whether or not a declaration is binding.[222] Yet, even from this perspective, the interpretation as a declaration of intent can be questioned. Self-commitments, for the most part, do not, as would be required for an offer *ad incertas personas*, specify the *essentialia negotii*, at least not as far as the actual characteristics of the contractual partner are concerned. An important argument here is the fact that companies foreseeably and with reasonable interest reserve a right to further decide about their contractual partner, which is obviously not yet specified in the public declaration.[223] A similarly sceptical attitude can be identified in the related debate on public declarations of companies to comply with the corporate governance codes. Even for these more formal and even legally required declarations,[224] it is the prevailing opinion that such public commitments are not made with an intention to be legally bound, but merely represent non-binding aspirational policy statements.[225]

Against this background, it comes as no surprise that the few scholars who also focus on the specific and more informal corporate codes that are discussed in this

[219] ibid.

[220] See especially BGHZ 21, 102 107: 'Art der Gefälligkeit, ihr Grund und Zweck, ihre wirtschaftliche und rechtliche Bedeutung, insbesondere für den Empfänger, die Umstände unter denen sie erwiesen wird, und die dabei bestehende Interessenlage der Partien … sind daher für die Beurteilung der Frage eines Rechtsbindungswillens … heranzuziehen.'

[221] In this direction, see, eg, OLG Bremen, ZIP 2006, 798, 799f; Segna (2006) 12. A similar position against the intention to be bound, but based on the argument that the declaration is not properly received by the addressees as required by contract law, is taken by Berresheim (2005) 425f.

[222] See especially Kohte (2005b) 406ff. See also Koch (2006) 2248 and for environmental self-commitments Frenz (2001) 229.

[223] Segna (2006) 13f. This argument is also accepted by Koch (2006) 2248f, who, however, continues by suggesting an interpretation of such unilateral commitments as offers to contract that are made under the condition that the publicly declaring company remains free to inquire about the financial solvency of the person who, by accepting, would eventually become a party to the contract.

[224] *cf* § 161 AktG (German Stock Companies Act).

[225] Lutter (2002) 468; Schmidt/Lutter-AktG-Spindler § 161, para 78 with further references; MüKo-AktG-Goette § 161, para 43, and with a view to the German code on mergers (*Deutscher Übernahmekodex*), Hopt (1997) 402.

study also take a rather sceptical position as to the presence of an intention to be legally bound on the side of the publishing company. Partly, the scepticism is justified by the presumption that, realistically, companies could not have had the intention to make such informal policy statements legally binding to the global public; moreover, it is also the aspects of a vague phrasing of the codes, the risk of liability associated with such a declaration to the global public and, finally, their substantive content as voluntary and flexible policies that are used as arguments.[226] This generally sceptical attitude towards statements in public advertisements in general and public self-commitments in particular can thus be seen as important obstacles that make the enforcement of public self-commitments as contracts quite unlikely.

3.1.4.1.2.2. Mandatory Form Requirements

Considering the difficulty of qualifying the codes as promises to pursue a genuine bilateral exchange as already discussed intensively in the analysis in English law,[227] it seems more likely that the codes would under German law be interpreted as contracts that create only a unilateral obligation on the side of publishing company. Although German law is generally prepared to enforce agreements with unilateral obligations as contracts once the benefiting addressees accept, they are nonetheless often subjected to a mandatory form requirement.[228] In order to identify any form requirements that could be applicable to the corporate codes, it is necessary to identify the applicable type of contract in this constellation. Based on the content of the corporate codes, ie, to comply with certain social and environmental standards, one may suggest a classification either as a promise to make a financial contribution to beneficiaries or civil society groups, or a promise to perform an action or refrain from doing something. On the basis of this understanding, two standard types of contracts are suitable. As regards the payment of a monetary sum, a probable qualification would be the promise to make a gift or donation.[229] As far as the promise to undertake particular measures is concerned, such as

[226] Bachmann (2006b) 297f distinguishes between corporate policies that are addressed to political institutions that he considers to be based on an intention to be politically, but not legally, bound, declarations on websites that increase the risk of liability too significantly for assuming an intention to be bound and policies addressed to a 'specific group' that could possibly be interpreted as being made with an intention of being legally bound. Glinski (2011) distinguishes between self-commitments that are made in informal cooperation with governments or an administration in which an intention to be legally bound could in principle be assumed (at 130) and informal self-commitments in advertising or on the Internet in which this is most likely not the case (at 217). She takes a similar sceptical position concerning an intention to be legally bound with respect to public commitments by which a parent declares that it is responsible for the behaviour of its subsidiaries (at 330ff). See also Krebber (2008) 174ff, who interprets codes of conduct generally as 'typically non-binding' and declares even mutual agreements of companies with trade unions concerning fundamental labour standards as 'non-binding, below a legal agreement, comparable to a gentlemen's agreement' (at 181).

[227] See above section 3.1.4.1.1.2. (p 88), text and accompanying footnotes.

[228] See pointedly Markesinis, Unberath and Johnston (2006) 88: 'most of these transactions are regarded as potentially "dangerous" by German law and therefore subjected to strict requirements of form'.

[229] *cf* § 516 BGB: 'A donation by means of which someone enriches another person from his own patrimony is a gift if both parties are in agreement that the donation occurs gratuitously' (translation taken from Kornet and Hardt (2013) 311).

environmentally friendly production methods or the improvement of workplace standards, the corporate codes could be interpreted as an abstract promise to perform an action, which resembles the contract type of a bare acknowledgement of debt (§ 780 BGB).[230] To the extent that corporate codes qualify as gifts or donations, pursuant to § 518 BGB, it would be a mandatory requirement to have the contract made in writing and authenticated by a notary.[231] It goes without saying that it is highly unlikely that the corporate codes will fulfil this requirement. As far as promises to perform an action are concerned, § 780 BGB requires such promises to be generally in writing and not in electronic form. If the acknowledgement is made as part of a gift or donation, it may even fall under the strict requirements of § 518 BGB.[232] The form requirement for bare acknowledgements of a debt can equally be a hindrance in relation to publicly declared corporate codes whenever they are made publicly available on websites or are even referred to in oral commitments of company representatives in press conferences, interviews or shareholder meetings. Yet, in relation to this qualification, a specific provision in the commercial code could be applicable that waives the mandatory form requirements laid down in § 780 BGB for constellations in which the debtor is a commercial party.[233] This, as a consequence, would mean that there would be no mandatory form requirements that could hinder the enforcement. Accordingly, it also comes as no surprise that the question whether a public self-commitment of a company would be subject to mandatory form requirements remains disputed so far.[234]

Hence, in relation to German law, it is very possible that a court would deem a publicly declared code unenforceable for failing to fulfil the mandatory form requirements that are laid down in §§ 518 I and 780 BGB.

3.1.4.1.3. Interim Conclusion

To sum up, when relating the publicly declared corporate codes to the current rules on contract formation under English and German law, several obstacles can be identified that are capable of hindering their interpretation as enforceable contracts. Three core obstacles could in this context be identified as particularly relevant.

[230] In the debate on the self-commitments concerning the provision of financial services, § 780 BGB seems uncontroversial as the main applicable type; see, eg, the suggestion of Derleder (2003) 964 and affirmatively: Kohte (2005b) 406; Segna (2006) 7.

[231] *cf* § 518 I 1 BGB: 'For the validity of a contract by which a performance is promised as a gift, the notarial authentication of the promise is required' (translation taken from Kornet and Hardt (2013) 312).

[232] *cf* § 518 I 2 BGB: 'The same applies to a promise or declaration of acknowledgement when a promise to fulfil an obligation or the acknowledgement of an obligation in the manner referred to in §§ 780 and 781 is made as a gift' (translation taken from Kornet and Hardt (2013) 312).

[233] *cf* § 350 HGB (German Commercial Code).

[234] *cf* only Segna (2006) 8, note 45, who criticises the Regional Court of Bremen for classifying the public self-commitment as a bare acknowledgement of a debt pursuant to § 780, but fails to address the applicable mandatory form requirement; and Koch (2006) 2244, who insists on the application of § 350 HGB for the banks that post the commitment on their websites and thus concludes that such public commitments would not be subject to mandatory form requirements.

The first and most problematic aspect of an interpretation of publicly declared codes as contracts was seen in the necessity to identify an intention to be legally bound that underlies the particular code declaration. There seems to be a generally sceptical attitude towards interpreting reference to voluntary and often vaguely phrased corporate policies as statements that companies make with an intention to be legally bound.

An additional obstacle was identified in the general tendency to qualify statements to the public as non-binding invitations to treat rather than contractual offers. It is only by rebutting this general prima facie assumption that the interpretation of corporate codes as contractual offers is conceivable.

Finally, the contractual enforcement of corporate codes can also fail on the ground that the corporate codes are difficult to classify as clear reciprocal agreements. In relation to English law, their character as informal commitments, unsupported by clearly requested sufficient consideration, has the inevitable result that they would qualify as unenforceable gratuitous promises. Although German law is more prone to also enforcing promises that do not exhibit reciprocity, the contractual enforcement may still become difficult due to the fact that mandatory form requirements could apply.

3.1.4.2. Public Declarations as Relied-upon Unilateral Promises

Given the several difficulties involved when seeking to interpret publicly declared corporate codes as ordinary contracts that are concluded between remote parties, it is considered a promising alternative to search for categories in private law that provide for the enforcement of public declarations. The corporate codes could in particular be interpreted as unilateral promises that become binding once they are declared by the company and taken seriously and relied on by the addressed public. In the corporate codes debate, this idea is indeed occasionally presented. Corporate codes, pursuant to this understanding, are interpreted as unilateral promises that ought to be treated as binding on the ground that another party has relied on them to his or her detriment[235] or reasonably trusts and expects that the promise will be fulfilled.[236] As far as the specific legal basis of this proposal is concerned, there are currently two main reasons offered for allowing this category of enforcing declarations. The enforcement is considered to derive from general principles in contract law, in particular estoppel and *venire contra factum proprium*.[237]

235 Herberg (2007) 115; Phillips and Lim (2009) 375ff.

236 Marrella (2007) 302 explicitly does not take detrimental reliance of another party as a criterion, but the mere expectation of another party that the promise will be fulfilled. See presumably in a similar direction also Bachmann (2006b) 254 ('Orientierungsmaßstäbe liefern die unter dem Rubrum der positiven "Vertrauenshaftung" entwickelten Fallgruppen'); Glinski (2011) 130 ('Vertrauensbasierte Rechtswirkungen').

237 Bachmann (2006b) 254f; Herberg (2007) 115 refers broadly to 'tort law' and 'reliance liability'; Marrella (2007) 302 refers to the fact that the protection of expectations in serious promises is an important doctrine 'in international business law' and the 'applicable law'. See also Glinski (2011) 130, who argues both on the basis of the rules on contract formation as well as the possibility to rely on general principles in the law that are used to establish reliance-based liability, such as *culpa in contrahendo*, good faith or estoppel.

In this context, some authors refer to Article 2:107 of the Principles of European Contract Law as this provision indicates the enforceability of a unilateral promise.[238]

However, a suggestion that is more specifically oriented to a currently existing legal doctrine is made in the analysis of the corporate codes under US law in the form of relating the codes to the doctrine of promissory estoppel, as laid down in the Restatement (Second) Contracts.[239] This doctrine declares unilateral promises binding if someone relies on the promise. The doctrine is applicable if there is no valid bilateral reciprocal contract between the parties and no intention to be legally bound characterises the declaration, provided that, first, the promisor can foresee that the other party relies on the promise and, second, justice requires the promise to be enforced.[240] Thus, the doctrine of promissory estoppel embraces the principle that a promise is binding if it successfully induces reliance on others and there are valid reasons that justify the legal enforcement. From the conceptual perspective, this doctrine of promissory estoppel is difficult to grasp as it sidesteps the existing dichotomy between contract and tort. In general, promissory estoppel remains outside contract because it is only applicable when a contract has not been concluded either because of the lack of an intention to be legally bound on the side of the party that makes the promise or because there is no clear consideration. Moreover, the constitutive component of reliance of another party also brings it into close proximity with tort rather than contract and there are indeed cases in which the courts have used the doctrine to hold the promising party merely liable to compensate the promisee for its reliance losses only.[241] That being said, empirical studies on the use of promissory estoppel by courts also demonstrate that the concept is frequently given a contractual gloss. Courts also award claimants in estoppel cases contract remedies, eg, claims as to specific performance or damages aimed at expectation interest.[242] When drafting the section on promissory estoppel in the Restatement (Second) Contracts, it was even discussed whether the primary remedy for promissory estoppel should be enforcement of the promise.[243] Focusing on the proposal to invoke the doctrine of promissory estoppel in relation to corporate codes, there are two different constellations in which an application of the doctrine could provide for an enforcement of the codes. First, the corporate codes could qualify as promises that become enforceable by beneficiaries that reasonably rely on the codes in the expectation that the company would comply with

[238] See especially for this suggestion Bachmann (2006b) 296f; and Glinski (2011) 129.

[239] Phillips and Lim (2009) 376. See also in this direction Bachmann (2006b) 252ff.

[240] Section 90(1) of the Restatement (Second) Contracts: 'A promise which the promisor should reasonably expect to induce action or forbearance on the part of the promisee or a third person and which does induce such action or forbearance is binding if injustice can be avoided only by enforcement of the promise. The remedy granted for breach may be limited as justice requires.'

[241] A famous case for an award of reliance losses is *Hoffmann v Red Owl Stores* 133 NW 2d 267 (1965). The understanding of promissory estoppel as a quasi-tort law remedy allowing the recovery of reliance losses is also brought forward in the common law debate on equitable estoppel in Australia; see, eg, Robertson (1998).

[242] Farber and Matheson (1985); Yorio and Thel (1991). For similar observations in the Australian doctrine of equitable estoppel, see, eg, Cooke (1997).

[243] *cf* Fuller and Perdue (1936) 63f and accompanying note 14.

the promised standards to their benefit.[244] Second, based on the fact that the company addresses primarily the market public, one could also argue for a promissory enforcement towards those who rely upon these codes when taking decisions on the market.[245]

In the following sections, these proposed forms of enforcement will be analysed from the perspective of English and German contract law with the objective of identifying whether such an exceptional reliance-based enforcement of publicly declared commitments to comply with corporate codes is possible. With respect to English law, the potential enforcement will be discussed on the basis of the doctrine on promissory or equitable estoppel. For the analysis of German law, several statutory categories to enforce unilateral promises and developments in case law on reliance liability are analysed that are in scholarly debate interpreted as evidence for a gradually evolving reliance-based enforcement of declarations.

3.1.4.2.1. English Law: Equitable Estoppel

As stated above, one core legal basis for the proposal to enforce relied-upon promises was identified in the doctrine of promissory estoppel in US law. This doctrine is, however, not specific to US law, but it has evolved as a general common law doctrine. Consequently, it is also known in English law, but, in contrast to the US, its scope of application is narrower. Promissory estoppel under English law can only be used as a defence against claims of the promisor. Conversely, it is not possible to rely on this doctrine as a cause of action, ie, when seeking to enforce a promise. The doctrine is thus solely applied in constellations in which the parties are already contractually bound, but one party makes a promise to waive, modify or suspend its contractual rights.[246] In such constellations, promissory estoppel declares the promisor to be estopped from going back to the initial agreement and thus equips the promisee with a defence when the promisor seeks to enforce the initial rights that he has waived, modified or suspended. Ever since the landmark decision of *Combe v Combe*, this is colloquially described as the established rule that promissory estoppel can only be used as a shield, not as a sword.[247] This narrow scope of application, in contrast to the situation in the US or other common law systems,[248] renders the enforcement of promises based on reliance or trust of an

[244] Phillips and Lim (2009) 376: 'The promise would be that the buyer will assist, monitor, and sanction the supplier in order to avoid this mistreatment. The buyer also arguably promises not to impose production pressures leading to code violations. If the buyer fails to keep those promises, and the worker establishes a causal link to her damages, a colourable claim may arise.' See also Herberg (2007) 115: 'Eine entsprechende Fallkonstellation läge etwa dann vor, wenn die Belegschaft einer der Produktionsstätten sich darauf verlassen hat, dass das Unternehmen das sicherheitstechnische und betriebsmedizinische Wissen, das an anderen Standorten über die Jahre gesammelt wurde, auch in dem betreffenden Betrieb berücksichtigen werde.'

[245] This seems more the idea of Bachmann (2006b) 297f.

[246] Beatson, Burrows and Cartwright (2010) 123.

[247] *Combe v Combe* [1951] 2 KB, 215 224 (per Lord Birkett) with reference to Lord Denning's speech in *Central London Property Trust v High Tree House* [1947] KB 130, 136.

[248] In addition to the US, one can mention in this context the Australian legal system, where promissory estoppel since *Waltons Stores (Interstate) v Maher (1988)* 164 CLR 387 has been recognised as a doctrine that can be relied upon as a cause of action.

addressed person considerably difficult. Yet, it is equally true that the doctrine of promissory estoppel is quite a complex concept. It is part of the broader doctrine of equitable estoppel, which encompasses different categories of reliance-based estoppel.[249] Within this broader category of equitable estoppel, there are some categories where estoppel can serve as a cause of action. The core field in which this is the case is property law.[250] The exception covers two categories of equitable estoppel that are defined as proprietary estoppel. First, promises can be enforced on the ground of reliance when someone improves land in the mistaken belief that he is the owner and the actual owner 'stands by' or, second, when a promisee relies on a promise of the landowner that he will be given an interest in the land in the future.[251] In *Thorner v Major*, three conditions are set out that have to be fulfilled in order to use proprietary estoppel as a cause of action. A promise or representation needs to be made on the acquisition of an interest in property, the promisee needs to have reasonably relied upon the promise and there needs to be detriment of the side of the claimant as a consequence of the reliance.[252] This narrow relaxation suggests that there is also in principle an existing possibility in English law to enforce promises that an addressee relied on and for which it would be unconscionable to allow the promisor to insist that no obligation was created.

In spite of the existence of this category that allows promises to be enforced with reference to estoppel, it should be noted that proprietary estoppel in its current form only applies to very specific promises regarding land and has not yet been extended to other types of promises. An instructive, relatively recent case that shows this reluctant attitude is the decision of the Court of Appeal in *Baird Textile Holdings v Marks & Spencer*, which was already important for analysing the binding character of an umbrella agreement.[253] In this case, the court not only refused to understand the long-term cooperation between the commercial partners as an implied binding framework contract, it also denied the claimant the possibility of basing the claim to enforce the promise on estoppel. The court used two arguments against the use of estoppel in this constellation, which are relevant for the discussion on enforcing corporate codes. First, it was held that the purported promise made by the defendant that the relationship between the parties would be a long-term cooperation was not sufficiently specific. On top of that, the promising company expressed that it did not understand this informally promised cooperation as creating a legal obligation. In other words, the promise in this particular case did not provide sufficient grounds for the promisee to reasonably rely on it. This argument could also be relevant in relation to corporate codes in case the company includes disclaimers in its codes to express its unwillingness to

[249] Halsbury's Laws, vol 47, estoppel, paras 302, 306.

[250] See, eg, *Tanner v Tanner* [1975] 1 WLR 1346; *Crabb v Arun District Council* [1976] Ch 179; *Pascoe v Turner* [1979] 1 WLR 431; *Western Fish Products Ltd v Penwith DC* [1981] 2 All ER 204; *Greasley v Cooke* [1980] 1 WLR 1306; *Jennings v Rice* [2002] EWCA Civ 159; *Thorner v Major* [2009] 1 WLR 776.

[251] Beatson, Burrows and Cartwright (2010) 127; McKendrick (2013) 97.

[252] *Thorner v Major* [2009] 1 WLR 776, 786 (per Lord Walker). In explaining the model of promissory estoppel, Collins (2003b) 83ff adds as a fourth (normative) criterion that it would also need to be 'unfair, or unconscionable, to permit someone to go back on his or her original promise or undertaking'.

[253] See above section 3.1.2.2. (p 55), text and accompanying footnotes.

create a legal obligation.[254] Yet, even if this hurdle is overcome, either because the company has not (yet) included a disclaimer or because reasons can be brought forward as to why the disclaimer would in such cases be invalid, the claim for enforcement of corporate codes would not be successful, namely, because a second element of the reasoning in the decision of the court comes into play. In *Baird Textile Holding v Marks & Spencer*, the court emphatically underlined that even if the promise had been clear and the facts would justify reasonable reliance, the law as it stands would not allow the promise to be treated as binding, because such an enforcement would contradict existing law by sidestepping established doctrine.[255] In general, the courts remain immensely reluctant to extend the scope of estoppel as a cause of action from promises related to land to other types of promises that concern the performance of an action because accepting this possibility would effectively circumvent the requirement of a bargain, which is considered a fundamental prerequisite under English law for creating an enforceable obligation.[256] In short, recognition of promissory estoppel as a broad cause of action, as is the case for proprietary estoppel, is prevented by the doctrine of consideration. Against this background, the suggestion to enforce the corporate codes as relied-upon promises is difficult to construct with the existing categories due to the general concern in English law that recognising such a category would effectively abolish the doctrine of consideration as such. Consequently, any proposal to enforce the corporate codes as relied-upon promises is only possible if an argument is made why the doctrine of promissory estoppel needs to be further developed into a cause of action comparable to the category of proprietary estoppel. Moreover, such a claim would also have to address carefully how such a proposal could be reconciled with the valid and strong perception in English law that the doctrine of consideration must not be abolished.

3.1.4.2.2. German Law: Enforceable Unilateral Promises

Under German law, the starting point for the analysis of the enforcement of unilateral relied-upon promises is to be found in § 311 I BGB. In this provision, it is laid down that enforceable obligations can only be created by contract if the law does not say otherwise. This provision embraces the general rule under German law that private actors are generally allowed to create enforceable obligations only when they rely on the form that the law provides for, namely the bilateral contract and the specific legally recognised exceptions of unilateral actions.[257] As a result,

[254] On this use of disclaimers in corporate codes as an important hurdle precisely for promissory estoppel claims, see Phillips and Lim (2009) 376.

[255] *Baird Textile Holdings Ltd v Marks & Spencer* [2001] CLC 999, 1009 [38] (per Sir Andrew Morritt V-C.)

[256] Lord Denning in *Combe v Combe* (n 247) 221 and Roskill LJ in *Brikom Investments Ltd v Carr* [1979] QB 467, 486: 'it would be wrong to extend the doctrine of promissory estoppel, whatever its precise limits at the present day, to the extent of abolishing in a backhanded way the doctrine of consideration'.

[257] The question of whether § 311 I BGB has to be understood as specifying the contract and the legally codified exceptions as exclusive forms to create legal obligations is, however, controversial. On this debate with further references, see generally Bachmann (2006b) 266ff, 296.

the enforcement of a unilateral promise is only possible to the extent that it can either be interpreted as an offer to conclude a bilateral contract or be related to such an exception.

Focusing on the statutory exceptions, the most important categories of unilateral binding acts are the foundation (§§ 80 and 81 BGB), the public offer to pay a reward (§ 657 BGB), prize notifications (§ 661a BGB) and the legacy (§§ 1939 and 2147 BGB).[258] In addition to these statutory exceptions, there are, however, also cases in which the courts were prepared to enforce promises even without reference to these statutory exceptions. In these cases, the enforcement of promises was not interpreted as an exception to the contract principle; instead, these promises were qualified as contracts and the existence of a contract was justified by referring to the apparent seriousness of the promise (instead of a detailed analysis of the intention to be legally bound) and the expectations and reliance on the side of the addressees (instead of a detailed analysis of the acceptance). Examples are informal promises or assurances in the construction industry to pay outstanding debts if the other party would continue the work. In such constellations, an intention to be legally bound is generally difficult to identify, but often the promisee nonetheless takes seriously such promises to his detriment.[259] In this context, one can also refer to the existing option in labour law to treat unilateral promises of an employer to pay a benefit to its employees as creating an enforceable obligation on the side of the employer if the beneficiaries rely on them (so-called *Gesamtzusage*).[260] These different examples, although not qualifying as a statutory exception, also provide an indication that German law has tools available to it to treat promises as binding that an addressed party relies on. In addition, one could at least consider classifying a publicly declared corporate code as a declaration that would fall under one of the statutory exceptions. In this regard, first § 657 BGB, ie, the legally binding public offer to pay a reward, could be relevant. This is due to the fact that this provision deals specifically with unilateral declarations to the public. Moreover, one might also consider the specific provision that deals with prize notifications by a trader. This latter provision seems interesting to consider because it introduces for the first time an option to enforce a unilateral declaration prior to contract if such a declaration is sent to other market actors with the objective of inducing them to conclude a contract on the sale of goods.

Focusing on the first possibility, § 657 BGB renders binding a unilateral promise to the public to pay a reward for an action that is specified in the promise. Consequently, in order to qualify as a unilateral binding promise, it is thus necessary that the corporate code would be interpreted as a declaration of intent, which requires the presence of an intention to be legally bound on the terms specified in the promise.[261] This effectively means that § 657 BGB does not per se allow binding promises that others rely upon to be enforced, but it only narrowly applies

[258] Enumeration taken from Palandt-Grüneberg, § 311, para 4; Erman-Kindl § 311, para 2.

[259] See generally for examples Stoll (1978) 760f, fns 91–93.

[260] See generally on this category with further references Bachmann (2006b) 285ff.

[261] Palandt-Sprau § 657, para 1; Soergel-von Reden § 657, para 5; Staudinger-Bergmann § 657, para 48.

to promises that the promisor issues with an intention to be legally bound. As a result, an interpretation of the corporate codes in light of the statutory exception of § 657 BGB eventually faces the same difficulties that have already been discussed in relation to their interpretation as public offers to contract. In addition, it is also fairly uncontroversial that the public offer to pay a reward applies solely to promises that are made to the public to pursue a reciprocal exchange. If at all, an analogous application to non-reciprocal promises is only accepted under the condition that the mandatory form requirements for gift-making promises are fulfilled.[262] § 657 BGB is thus a provision that attempts to fill a legal enforcement gap in constellations in which a promisor aims to receive something in return for paying a benefit, but where the formation of a contract would fail because the offer is not strictly speaking accepted by a potential addressee who performs the required action. It should essentially provide the possibility for someone to receive the promised benefit if he fulfils the requirement specified in the public offer, even if he did not notice that the offer was made, and failed to deliberately accept it.[263] It is no coincidence, against the background of these two conditions, that this possibility to enforce unilateral promises, although treated in German law as a statutory exception that allows a party to create obligations in a form other than the contract, is in comparative scholarship referred to as an equivalent to the common law concept of the unilateral contract rather than to the doctrine of promissory estoppel.[264] In the context of this study, this merely has the result that the option to enforce the corporate codes as public offers to pay a reward is only possible if, as was already suggested for the English concept of the unilateral contract, the corporate codes were either interpreted as serious promises that are akin to reciprocal agreements or if an analogy of § 657 BGB is suggested that would allow unilateral promises to perform an action, without further form requirements, to be considered binding where the promise is made with the implicit objective to receive a reward.

An alternative in German law would be to consider relying on §661a BGB in order to enforce the corporate code promises.[265] This provision allows specific types of promises to be enforced even if the promisor did not intend the statement to create a legal obligation.[266] The main component necessary in order to enforce a promise on the basis of § 661a BGB is that the average (but not the specifically addressed) consumer perceives the statement as serious.[267] In fact, this narrowly confined provision specifically on prize notifications that address consumers already provided

[262] Staudinger-Bergmann § 657, para 44, with further references to the debate.

[263] Bachmann (2006b) 280f.

[264] See pointedly Weller (2009) 137: 'Im berühmten Carbolic Smoke Ball-Fall wird das Vertragsprinzip selbst auf eine Auslobung angewendet. Demgegenüber findet das Vertragsprinzip nach deutschem Recht auf eine Auslobung gerade keine Anwendung, weil diese nach §657 BGB als einseitig-bindendes Leistungsversprechen konzipiert wird.' See also Kleinschmidt (2009) 1122.

[265] This idea is in relation to public self-commitments of companies indicated by Bachmann (2006b) 298 ('nach dem Gedanken der §§116, 661a BGB'); Bachmann (2006a) 261.

[266] BGH NJW 2004, 1652, 1652; NJW 2006, 230, 232; Palandt-Sprau § 661a, para 1; Prütting/Wegen/Weinrich-Mörsdorf-Schulte § 661a, para 10; MüKo-Seiler § 661a, para 4.

[267] Palandt-Sprau § 661a, para 1; Erman-Ehmann § 661a, para 2. But for a different interpretation, see Staudinger-Bergmann § 661a, para 26.

the ground for a more fundamental debate concerning the appropriate classification of this particular obligation in the existing private law system. The Federal High Court of Justice, being called upon to decide whether the provision was in accordance with the constitution because of its purported punitive nature, ruled that the obligation deriving from §661a BGB would neither qualify as a criminal sanction nor provide the liability in tort.[268] In a similar vein, the European Court of Justice held that the provision was akin to contract rather than non-contractual liability due to the fact that these notifications are intended to induce a contract.[269] The legal character of the provision also became a topic in the scholarly debate. Current suggestions are as diverse as to classify §661a BGB as liability in tort with a punitive character,[270] as a new form of non-contractual relation created by statute that is different from tort[271] or as an ordinary declaration of intent that represents a sub-category of § 657 BGB.[272] Moreover, new categories were developed, such as the 'statutory simulation of a contract',[273] as a private law norm in its own right that has a punitive character comparable to penalty clauses in contracts[274] or a novel form of liability that is justified on the ground of reasonable reliance.[275]

This brief overview on the general conceptual debate of the provision has in this context mainly the purpose of underlining that this specific statutory exception is, like the common law doctrine of promissory estoppel, difficult to grasp with the established categories of contract and tort. The provision uses as its starting point the behaviour and declarations of a trader who, although not having the objective to conclude a contract, seeks to induce an addressed party to rely on the statement in its further behaviour. In fact, the provision is closely related to other provisions introduced relatively recently, in particular to §§ 241a[276] and 434 I 3 BGB,[277] that seek to protect reliance of addressees of public marketing by attaching legal consequences to the public declarations and the sending of material to consumers. Taken together, these provisions could thus be read as evidence for the fact that German private law is already in its current form prone to attach legal consequences to promises if these are directed towards inducing particular behaviour on the side of consumers, and, as explicitly laid down in § 661a, such consequences could also include enforcing a promise. Based on such an interpretation of this statutory

[268] BGH NJW 2003, 3620.

[269] Case C-96/00 *Gabriel* [2002] ECR-I-06367; Case C-27/02 *Engler* [2005] ECR-I-481 (both decisions are, however, based on the Austrian equivalent provision, eg, § 5j of the Austrian Consumer Protection Law).

[270] See, eg, Lindner (2006) 96ff.

[271] This seems the classification of the Federal High Court of Justice in BGH NJW 2003, 3620, 3621 ('einseitiges Rechtsgeschäft oder geschäftsähnliche Handlung'). See also Lorenz (2000) 3308, who draws parallels to the quasi-contractual *Rechtsscheinhaftung*; MüKo-Seiler § 661a BGB, para 4, suggesting an 'application of selected rules on the declaration of intent', but also emphasising the quasi-tortious character of the provision.

[272] Prütting/Wegen/Weinreich-Mörsdorf-Schulte § 661a BGB, para 3.

[273] MüKo-Micklitz § 13, para 47.

[274] Schäfer (2005) 984f.

[275] Alexander (2002) 172f.

[276] For the parallels between §241a BGB and § 661a BGB, *cf* Prütting/Wegen/Weinreich-Mörsdorf-Schulte § 661a BGB, para 2.

[277] For the parallels between § 661a BGB and § 434 I 3 BGB, *cf* Bachmann (2006a) 261.

exception, one could conceive understanding it as an expression of a more general rule that promises that are relied upon by addressees could not only give rise to pre-contractual liability but could also be enforced as a legally binding obligation.

Such an interpretation could then make it particularly valuable when attempting to enforce corporate codes as publicly declared relied-upon promises. That being said, it is also emphatically emphasised that such a suggestion cannot be achieved with a mere application of the provision as it stands. It is clear that in its current form, § 661a BGB deals only with the enforcement of declarations that have as their content the notification that a prize is won and will be paid and, moreover, only applies to declarations by a trader who addresses a consumer. Thus, comparable to the situation in English law concerning promissory estoppel, the provision can only be invoked if it is treated as spelling out an evolving general principle that a public declaration that is relied on needs to be kept and can be enforced.

3.1.4.2.3. Interim Conclusion

Pursuant to the analysis above, it is indeed possible for both legal systems to identify categories that provide for the enforcement of unilateral promises that an addressee relies on. Yet in both legal systems, the scope of application of these existing categories remains too narrow currently to make use of them in relation to the publicly declared corporate codes. The doctrine of promissory estoppel in English law can, on an overall scale, only be invoked as a defence. In English law, so far, only proprietary estoppel can be used as a cause of action to enforce promises that have as their content land rights. In the context of German law, there are provisions in the Civil Code and concepts developed in case law that at least suggest that this legal system is prepared to enforce unilateral promises on the ground of reasonable reliance of an addressee. Yet, the explicit restrictions to public declarations of intent that are made with the request to perform an action in § 657 BGB and to specific declarations that approach consumers with the information that they have won a prize in § 661a BGB render both categories, at least in their current forms, not feasible as a basis upon which the enforcement of publicly declared corporate codes could be built.

This implies that the enforcement of publicly declared codes as relied-upon promises is only conceivable in conjunction with proposals to broaden the scope of these existing categories. However, in this context, it should be noted that such a development necessarily needs to address how it would relate to the established principle that the creation of enforceable obligations requires the existence of a contract based on an intention to be legally bound (Germany) respectively is dependent on the existence of a bargain (England).

3.1.5. Conclusion

The core topic of these first four sections (3.1.1.–3.1.4.) has been to investigate whether existing private law could potentially enforce the corporate code as legally binding obligations. There is one core result of this inquiry and that is that there is no generally valid answer as to whether or not corporate codes are legally enforceable. Instead, one needs to distinguish clearly between different forms in which the codes appear. First, there are constellations in which one can interpret the corporate codes as enforceable obligations from the perspective of contract law. This is primarily the case when companies deliberately incorporate their corporate codes in a legally binding contract or at least incorporate them in documents that are generally accepted in contract law as ancillary documents that also specify the rights and obligations of the contracting parties, such as general terms and conditions or umbrella agreements.

That being said, next to these rather uncontroversial constellations in which the code becomes enforceable, the codes also appear in a form for which current contract law does not seem to already have a clear-cut answer. Whenever a company avoids relating the corporate code to a bilateral contractual agreement with its business partner or a civil society group and, instead, prefers to keep the code informal by making it publicly available, the legal rules do not provide for a clear decision on how these statements should be dealt with. One could, as observed in the decision of the trial court and the Court of Appeal in the *Wal-Mart* case, simply ignore such public declarations as a potential source of legal obligations. Yet, as has been stated in the current legal debate on the corporate codes, an enforcement of such public declarations is not inconceivable. First, pursuant to the current rules on contract interpretation and supplementation, it is possible to treat the corporate codes as pre-contractual public statements that could be enforced as a term in subsequently concluded contracts. Yet one can even consider a separate enforcement of publicly declared corporate codes, although from a doctrinal perspective, this would be difficult to construct. In this context, two potential directions were presented. Publicly declared corporate codes could be related to the rules on contract formation as an offer to the public that becomes contractually enforceable once accepted by the public. Alternatively, such public declarations could be viewed as unilateral promises that induce reliance on the side of the public or the beneficiaries, which could be enforced by relying on specific exceptions where private law makes it possible to enforce promises that are not made in a contract. This is thus one topic that the further course of this study will discuss more intensively with regard to which of these proposals for the enforcement of unilaterally publicly declared codes private law should follow.

3.2. THE ENFORCEABLE OBLIGATION AND APPLICABLE REMEDIES

Having analysed the general potential to enforce the codes in private law, the focus is shifted to the question of how the identified enforceable code obligation would be qualified and what remedies could be applicable in case of a breach. As a matter of fact, a closer look at the existing contributions in the corporate code debate reveals that there are currently different proposals for this issue. A lawsuit initiated recently by the University of Wisconsin against Adidas for alleged breach of its contractually incorporated code should serve as an introduction to reveal the controversy in this context.

3.2.1. Setting the Scene: *University of Wisconsin Madison v Adidas*

In July 2012, the University of Wisconsin Madison filed a claim in the US Federal Court against its general sponsor and supplier of university apparel and sportswear, Adidas, alleging a breach of contract for a violation of labour standards at the factory sites of one of the company's suppliers. According to the claimant and undisputed by the defendant, the contract between the two parties contained a labour code of conduct that obliged Adidas to comply with the standards laid down therein and it remained equally undisputed that this contractual incorporation would be a valid express contract term. One of the core requirements of this binding code was that the sportswear company 'complies with all applicable legal requirements of the countries of manufacture' and 'shall provide legally mandated benefits' to workers where apparel is produced. In performing the contract on the delivery of sportswear, the company was allowed to subcontract with local suppliers, but the contract also stated that the company would have to in this case still remain 'fully responsible' and that the manufacturing process would fulfil the requirements as specified in the Licensing Agreement, hence the labour code.[278] In short, the parties to the contract concluded a code of conduct with a contractual term that required the defendant to comply with labour standards and make sure that these standards were also followed by any subcontractors that the company would make use of.

A dispute between the parties arose on the interpretation of this clause after the organisation Workers' Rights Consortium (WRC), an NGO specialised in monitoring labour standards in supply chains, identified problems at one of Adidas' suppliers named PT Kizone in Indonesia.[279] The particular allegations were that PT Kizone failed to pay workers severance wages from September 2010 and, shortly thereafter, stopped remunerating the employees completely. In addition, the supplier was accused of not compensating the families of workers who died in the course of their employment. Adidas did not dispute that all these wages and benefits were regarded as legally mandated benefits under Indonesian law. After PT Kizone became insolvent and was consequently not able to pay the required wages and compensation, NGOs and activists launched several campaigns in order to raise public awareness of this problem. They publicly appealed to the responsibility of the retailers that contracted with PT Kizone for the workers and urged them to pay the employees of its suppliers these benefits; several US universities that maintained sponsor or sportswear supply contracts threatened to terminate their

[278] Evidence taken from Claimant's Complaint for Declaratory Judgment, available at: www.business-humanrights.org/en/adidas-lawsuit-re-university-of-wisconsin#c18941.

[279] The contract even stated that the findings of the WRC as to non-compliance with the code are an immediate event of default; see Claimant's Complaint for Declaratory Judgment, para 17.

contracts. After Adidas refused to pay compensation or to contribute to a fund, the University of Wisconsin eventually decided to sue the company for breach of contract for not complying with the code.

In the course of the proceedings, the main legal issue turned out to be the interpretation of the labour code of conduct and, more particularly, what obligation it would create for Adidas. It comes as no surprise that the parties had quite different views on this aspect. While the University of Wisconsin asserted that the obligation to comply with the labour code of conduct would have to be read as a duty to pay the legally mandated benefits directly to the workers,[280] Adidas argued that the corporate code would have to be read as a bilateral duty obliging Adidas to ensure adherence to the specified social standards in the manufacturing process and merely to cease sourcing from suppliers that turned out to violate fundamental labour standards as specified in the code.[281] In other words, the defendant favoured an interpretation of the corporate code that put the company under an obligation to comply with a specified manufacturing process and deemed the obligation to be enforceable primarily by the other contracting party in the form of seeking an injunction order against subcontracting or by a right to reject the manufactured goods of the particular supplier. Conversely, the claimant interpreted the code as making the company directly responsible for the payment of the legally specified wage as indicated in the code and thus interpreted the contract term as an obligation to confer a direct benefit upon suppliers' employees. Since Adidas, bowing to the pressure from NGOs, eventually agreed to contribute to a fund that was set up by several retailers that ought to compensate the workers, the University of Wisconsin subsequently withdrew its claim for a declaratory judgment. Yet the missing precedent from the court notwithstanding, the contradictory opinions in this case suggest that in the course of a legal dispute, the appropriate qualification is likely to become a pressing issue. In fact, in the current scholarly debate, proposals for the contractual interpretation of corporate codes can already be found that resemble the positions taken by the parties to the lawsuit. There is, on the one hand, one important strand in the debate that, in quite a similar manner to the position of Adidas, sees the codes as related to the part of the contract that specifies the manufacturing process and, thus, in a broad sense the goods that the seller is obliged to deliver. Pursuant to this understanding, the corporate codes are related to the default rules that specify the typical performance obligations and applicable remedies in sales contracts. The suggestion is developed for consumer contracts on the basis of the existing possibility to read the publicly declared corporate codes into contracts in which no agreement on the product specification has been made,[282] as well as for constellations in which the corporate code is incorporated in a (mostly commercial) contract.[283] There are,

280 ibid, para 24.

281 See the response by Adidas, available at: www.business-humanrights.org/en/adidas-lawsuit-re-university-of-wisconsin#c18941.

282 See above section 3.1.3.2.1. (p 64), text and accompanying footnotes.

283 See above section 3.1.1. (p 48), text and accompanying footnotes.

on the other hand, also proposals, like the University of Wisconsin claim, that contractually incorporated codes have to be effectively read as provisions that directly benefit the beneficiaries and, as such, would need to be related to the rules on contractual third party rights. Although this latter suggestion is currently primarily suggested for constellations in which the codes are explicitly included in commercial contracts or contracts with civil society groups, it will be discussed whether it can also be viable for constellations, in particular for consumer contracts, if the code remains a public declaration.

In addition, one can also find noteworthy contributions that seek to qualify the codes as novel duties in contracts that do not fit within the generally accepted scheme of contractual obligations and remedies for breach of contract and that, on this basis, explore what new paths would need to be taken when determining the actual obligation.

3.2.2. The Default Rules on Sales Contracts

When investigating the option to interpret the corporate codes in light of the default rules on sales contracts, it is important to distinguish between two different approaches. First, the suggestion to view corporate codes as part of the performance obligations for sales contracts appears with respect to consumer sales contracts. The focus here is set specifically on whether the corporate codes or even public codes of conduct would be used in the course of determining the characteristics and quality of the good pursuant to the expectations of the consumer.[284] Second, the idea of viewing corporate codes as a specification of the good can also be found in the discussion on ethic clauses in commercial contracting. One may in this context refer particularly to scholars who focus on the interpretation and enforcement of commercial contracts under the Vienna Convention on Contracts for the International Sale of Goods (CISG).[285]

In one way or another, there is one core problem with such an interpretation: how can the corporate codes become relevant in determining the agreed-upon or reasonably expected product characteristics or quality if the adherence to social and environmental standards does not have a direct influence on the physical characteristics of the goods? A key element in the argumentative strategy of proponents here is to suggest a broad interpretation of the term of 'characteristics' of the product which the parties determine in their contract or expect from a public declaration as part of the conformity requirement.[286] On the basis of a broad

[284] See Kocher (2002) 271f; Wilhelmsson (2002/2003) 95ff; Glinski and Rott (2003) 652f; Dilling (2005); Glinski (2007) 124ff; Glinski (2008) 45f; Kocher (2008); Castermans (2009) 46ff, 55ff; Glinski (2011) 187ff; and recently Collins (2014).

[285] Schlechtriem (2007) 97ff; Schwenzer and Leisinger (2007) 262ff; Schwenzer (2010) art 35, para 9; Schwenzer, Hachem and Kee (2012) 371, para 31.48, 381, para 31.86ff.

[286] This broad interpretation of product characteristics according to what the parties have subjectively intended is suggested by Schwenzer and Leisinger on the basis of the broad approach towards non-conformity in the CISG; see Schwenzer and Leisinger (2007) 265f. See also Schwenzer, Hachem and Kee (2012) 381, para 31.87. Glinski and Rott (2003); Dilling (2005); and Kocher (2008) argue for the

interpretation, three possible links between the corporate codes and the product characteristics are presented. First, it is argued that any social and environmental standard needs to be read as an explicit specification of the production process and, accordingly, be treated as characterising the products as such.[287] Second, the contractually agreed compliance with the ethical clause is interpreted as significantly influencing the market value and the price of the goods sold and thus raising the quality of the product. Goods delivered by a seller who does not comply with the code would then consequently exhibit a quality standard that falls below what had been agreed upon or what the buyer should reasonably expect.[288] Finally, a third link is made related to the purpose for which the products are bought. In this context, the corporate code could serve as indicating the purpose for which the goods are bought. In relation to supplier contracts, compliance with a corporate code on the side of the seller could be interpreted as an agreement that is included in a contract to indicate that the buyer intends to resell the products either in a particular market segment[289] or as products for which the brand is sensitive in relation to social and environmental standards. As a result, non-compliance with social and environmental standards could thus make the goods unfit for resale due to the suspicion among consumers that the goods could have been produced under environmentally unsustainable or socially irresponsible conditions.[290] As far as a contract with an end-consumer is concerned, the fitness for the purpose is affected if not only the use of the product as such but also the end-users' objective to pursue an altruistic objective is accepted as a valid purpose.[291]

In the following, the feasibility of these arguments is explored from the perspective of the current default rules on sales contracts, ie, the English SGA and the German default rules on sales contracts that determine the characteristics of the goods (§ 434 BGB). The second part of the analysis will focus on the remedies that, pursuant to this suggestion, would be applicable in case the code is breached and the actors that are entitled to invoke these remedies.

subjective and broad understanding of non-conformity under German law on the basis of the understanding of non-conformity introduced by the Consumer Sales Directive that is modelled after the CISG. See also Castermans (2009) 47, who states that Dutch law already seems to favour such a broad interpretation, and Wilhelmsson (2002/2003) 89, who reveals similar tendencies for Nordic sales law.

[287] With respect to consumer contracts, see Glinski and Rott (2003) 652; Glinski (2011) 188; Collins (2014) 634ff. With respect to ethical clauses in commercial contracts, see Schwenzer, Hachem and Kee (2012) 371, para 31.48.

[288] With respect to consumer contracts, see Glinski (2007) 125. *cf* also Collins (2014) 637f, who suggests that even the sheer reputation of the good can be a relevant quality aspect (at 638: 'If goods can possess a reputation, then reputation might also include a reference to how it was produced down the supply chain … if the Apple iPhone name stands for … an ethical and legal production process, in substantial compliance with their Code of Conduct, the products could be said to possess the quality of being produced according to good labour standards'). With respect to ethical clauses in commercial contracts, see Schwenzer and Leisinger (2007) 266, 379f; Schwenzer, Hachem and Kee (2012), para 31.79-81.

[289] Schwenzer and Leisinger (2007) 266.

[290] *cf* Maley (2009) 116f.

[291] See resumably in this direction Glinski and Rott (2003) 653; Glinski (2007) 124.

3.2.2.1. Corporate Codes and Product Characteristics

3.2.2.1.1. English Law

In the context of the English rules on the sale of goods, there are three main rules that are applicable when relating corporate codes to the characteristics of the good. The argument of treating the corporate codes as an explicit specification of the manufacturing process could be realised when treating the codes as a description. This would have the result that the code would be an element of the condition in the sales contract that the goods have to correspond with the description (section 13 SGA). When it comes to the suggested influence of corporate codes on the quality standard, the main option is to interpret the codes either as an agreed term on quality or as specifying the satisfactory quality (section 14 SGA). Finally, the codes, as indicators for the particular purpose of reselling the products in a particular market segment or pursuing ethical consumerism, would have to be analysed on the basis of section 14 (3) SGA, which specifies as an implied term in sales contracts that goods have to be reasonably fit for a particular purpose.

3.2.2.1.1.1. Sale by Description

It is an established rule that parties can describe the goods. Such descriptions made by the seller determine what good the seller is obliged to deliver. If the goods are described in the contract, the sale is interpreted as a sale by description.[292] It is, however, also recognised that not all descriptive words are automatically a description pursuant to section 13 SGA. Descriptive words may also have no legal force at all; they may be representations or they may be express terms in the contract other than a description.[293] In general, the description is a statement that defines a particular class or kind of goods or a substantial ingredient of the 'identity' of the thing sold.[294] However, the question whether or not a particular statement is a description proves in this regard to be very difficult since the courts have not yet devised a clear test to identify descriptions in a contract.[295] This difficulty notwithstanding, one could answer the potential of interpreting the codes as a description by focusing on particular cases where the courts determined a term to be a description.

In *Joseph Travers & Son Ltd v Longel Ltd*, it was stated that a sale by description can be divided into two categories, namely sales of unascertained or future goods as being of a certain kind or class or specific goods that the buyer agrees to buy in reliance on the description given.[296] In addition, section 13(3) makes clear that a sale of description is also possible when the goods are exposed for sale and rent and are selected by the buyer. As a result, the option of interpreting a contract with

[292] Halsbury's Laws, vol 91, *Sale of Goods*, para 73.
[293] Burrows (2007) 876–77, para 10.30.
[294] Halsbury's Laws, vol 91, *Sale of Goods*, para 75.
[295] Burrows (2007) 876. *cf* also Guest (2006) 536, para 11-02, who describes s 13 of the SGA 'one of the most troublesome in the whole Act'.
[296] *Joseph Travers and Son Ltd v Longel Ltd* (1948) 64 TLR 150, 153 (per Sellers J).

a code of conduct as a sale by description would then primarily become relevant in relation to commercial contracts in which the parties agree upon the delivery of goods with certain specifications that still need to be manufactured by the supplier or when the goods are chosen by the buyer on the basis of being exposed by the seller. In these contracts, the corporate code could in principle be a description of how these future goods should be produced. This, however, depends on whether specifications as to the manufacturing process that do not describe the good as such could be qualified as a description. In this context, one can refer to cases in which the courts made stipulations as to the surrounding circumstances of the product as an integral part of the description if the parties made them so. These were particularly statements as to the packaging of the goods if the parties made them into a description[297] and statements as to time and the method of shipment of the goods.[298]

On the basis of these decisions, one can indeed argue that, comparable to the specification of the delivery time or the way in which they should be packed, it is also the particular production method that parties can make into a description. This implies that corporate codes could indeed be interpreted as terms that describe the products as 'fair and ethically traded' or produced under environmentally friendly conditions, which would make goods manufactured in breach of the code different from the goods that were contracted for.[299] However, in this regard, it must also be taken into account that there is a strict standard once it is concluded that a statement qualifies as a description. Since section 13(1A) SGA determines correspondence with the description a condition, non-compliance with the corporate code would put the buyer in a position to be able to reject the goods and to avoid the contract even if only minor deviations from the description are concerned. In accordance with the existing rules, the buyer does not need to be satisfied with comparable goods even if these are merchantable.[300] With respect to corporate codes in contracts, this would mean that even a minor event of non-compliance, such as a short-term extension of the agreed working time or paying less remuneration than agreed, would amount to a breach of contract resulting in these strong entitlements for the buyer. It is then also against the background of these far-reaching consequences that the contract has to be interpreted with a view

[297] *Re Moore and Co and Landauer and Co* [1921] 2 KB 519.

[298] See, eg, *Bowes v Shand* (1877) 2 App Cas 455 (a term in the contract that the goods must 'be shipped during the months March and/or April' can be a description); *Macpherson Train and Co Ltd v Howard Ross and Co Ltd* [1955] 1 WLR 640 (the words in the contract 'due London approximately 8th June' can be interpreted as part of the description); *J Aron and Co Inc v Comptoir Wegimont* [1921] 3 KB 435.

[299] This argument is made by Schwenzer, Hachem and Kee (2012) 381f, para 31.90: 'whether an ethical manufacturing process amounts to a distinguishing feature of a narrower genus. It would appear that this question must be answered in the affirmative'.

[300] See, eg, *Arcos Ltd v EA Ronaasen and Son* [1933] AC 470, where it was held that delivered goods that do not correspond with the description entitle the buyer to reject the goods 'if he finds convenient so to do' (at 480, per Lord Atkin) even if it only concerns a minor deviation from the description (in this case the thickness of staves).

to what the parties would have reasonably agreed upon. In this context, one can follow the dictum of Lord Diplock in *Ashington Piggeries Ltd. v Christopher Hill Ltd* that

> [T]he 'description' by which unascertained goods are sold is … confined to those words in the contract which were intended by the parties to identify the kind of goods, which were supplied. It is open to the parties to use a description as broad or narrow as they choose. But ultimately the test is whether the buyer could fairly and reasonably refuse to accept the physical goods proffered to him on the ground that their failure to correspond with that part of what was said about them in the contract makes them goods of a different kind from those he had agreed to buy.[301]

Against this background, the suggested broad understanding of a description in relation to corporate codes would have to be carefully evaluated. Given the far-reaching consequences, it is more likely that a differentiation would be made between different types of codes of conduct depending on the weight that the parties give them. If the corporate code is included as a very specific agreement as to how the production should be organised and contains indications that the ethical standards are included in making the goods specifically labelled 'fair trade products', one could indeed justify seeing the code as a description that is in place to distinguish the goods from those that cannot be sold as such explicit 'fair trade products'. Yet, in cases in which the corporate code generally requires adherence to ethical standards without a direct reference to an expected fair trade character of the product, it is submitted that they would be less likely to qualify as a description. This applies in particular if the parties did not even include a corporate code in the section of the contract that contains the description of the goods, but instead incorporated it as a general term that merely requires the seller to comply with the social and environmental policies in its course of doing business.

3.2.2.1.1.2. The Requirement of Satisfactory Quality

An alternative to treating corporate codes as descriptions is to interpret the codes as statements that influence the quality standard of the goods either as an explicit agreement on the quality or as an indication that the courts can use when specifying the objective standard of 'satisfactory quality'.[302] In this context, one must, however, have in mind the strong influence of the *caveat emptor* principle in English sale of goods law. This principle stated that the risk of receiving a product of lower quality than expected is generally on the side of the buyer, who accordingly cannot remedy the fact that he receives lower quality than expected. Yet, although this principle has proven to be highly influential on the English rules on the sale of goods, it is equally accepted that it has been considerably moderated over time. First, it is accepted that parties can make express stipulations in their contracts as to the quality, with the result that the delivery of less-than-agreed quality amounts to a breach of contract.[303] This implies that an express term in a contract on

[301] *Ashington Piggeries Ltd v Christopher Hill* [1972] AC 441, 503f.

[302] For this latter option in relation to CSR commitments made towards consumers, see Collins (2014) 633.

[303] Guest (2006) para 11-024; Adams and MacQueen (2010) 142.

compliance with a corporate code can result in an obligation of the seller to deliver products of a higher 'ethical' quality, provided that ethical standards are actually considered to have an influence on the quality of the product.[304] In addition to this possibility of a particular agreement on quality, in cases in which goods are sold in the course of business, it is an implied term in sale of goods contracts that goods are of satisfactory quality (section 14 SGA).[305] As a result, the corporate codes could, even if not part of an explicit agreement on quality, still become relevant in the interpretation of satisfactory quality. As regards the understanding of 'satisfactory quality', this term is specified in the law as 'the standard that a reasonable person would regard as satisfactory, taking account of any description of the goods, the price (if relevant) and all other relevant circumstances' and includes 'their state and condition', the 'fitness for all purposes for which goods of the same kind in question are commonly supplied', 'appearance and finish', 'freedom from minor defects', 'safety' and 'durability'.[306] The answer to whether the codes could be read as part of the quality would need to be identified when focusing on the specific aspects mentioned in section 14(2B) SGA.

The physical aspects, such as the state and condition, appearance and finish and freedom from minor defects, as well as the safety and durability of the product, are obviously difficult to apply with respect to the codes. Yet, one could relate the codes to the criterion of price and 'other relevant circumstances'. However, as to the relevance of the criterion of price, this criterion seems not to fit entirely in relation to the codes because the price argument would be used differently than intended by the Act. Pursuant to section 14(2A) SGA, it is the price that serves as a relevant criterion in determining the quality of the product, with the result that someone paying a higher price can expect a better quality;[307] yet the argument in relation to the corporate codes is that compliance with environmental and social standards could result in a higher quality expectation because the products can achieve higher prices on the market. The criterion of the price could then only be used if parties had agreed on a higher price as a result of including the obligation to comply with the corporate code in the contract. This constellation could be interpreted as akin that in *Clegg v Anderson*, in which it was held that in cases of a 'high-priced quality good, the customer may be entitled to expect that it is free from even minor defects, in other words perfect or nearly so'.[308] Yet, the codes could come into play as 'other relevant circumstances', which is also the criterion for which advertisement or statements on the Internet play a role.[309] In addition to statements in advertisements, which could most likely encompass publicly declared corporate codes, one could also consider treating an agreed general term on compliance with a code as 'other relevant circumstances'. The contractually

[304] Schwenzer, Hachem and Kee (2012) 377, para 31.70.
[305] It should be noted that the requirement of selling in the course of business is given a broad interpretation; *cf* Halsbury's Laws, vol 91, *Sale of Goods*, para 79.
[306] SGA, s 14(2A), (2B).
[307] *Clegg v Andersson* [2003] EWCA Civ 320.
[308] ibid [72] (per Lady Justice Hale).
[309] Adams and MacQueen (2010) 177.

included or publicly advertised corporate code could then be used as an indication of satisfactory quality if the argument is followed that the ethical behaviour of a trader has a direct influence on the quality because the market rewards ethical conduct and sanctions non-ethical conduct in the form of an increase and decrease of sales, respectively.[310] Assuming this were the case, the corporate codes could be treated as an aspect that specifies the generally expected standard of satisfactory quality of the good for sale. This would have the result that the corporate codes would be related to the implied condition[311] in a contract on the sale of goods that the seller has to deliver a good of satisfactory quality. As a result, non-compliance with the code could be interpreted as a breach of that condition.

3.2.2.1.1.3. The Fitness for a Particular Purpose

Finally, this section will turn to the suggested interpretation of the corporate code as a statement by which the buyer makes explicitly or implicitly known the fitness for a particular purpose pursuant to section 14(3).[312] In the context of supplier contracts, this purpose could be the purpose of reselling, either in a particular market segment where ethical standards are important or under a particular brand that is sensitive to ethical aspects. The corporate code would then be interpreted as a (contractual or pre-contractual) statement that makes this purpose either explicitly or implicitly known to the seller. With respect to consumer contracts, the particular purpose would be socially responsible consumption, which would either be explicitly made known by including a corporate code in a contract or be treated as being implicitly known because the consumer would, foreseeably for the company, rely on an advertisement on compliance with a code.[313] In general, in section 14(2B), it is laid down that it is an implied term in sale of goods contracts that the goods in question are fit for any particular purpose and that, following section 14(3), being fit for any particular purpose requires that this purpose has been made known to the seller. In relation to the purpose of reselling in a particular market segment, one can draw the analogy to the resale of a product on a particular foreign market, which has been treated as a particular purpose that the buyer needs to make known to the seller.[314] As regards the objective to buy a good with the altruistic objective to have positive effects on the environment or to support companies that improve the social situation, one could refer to a case in which the environmental quality of a product with the objective of obtaining a better energy rating was also a particular purpose.[315]

[310] See Schwenzer, Hachem and Kee (2012) 379f, para 31.79–81, who argue that this assumption would have the advantage of being able to 'relieve the parties from the necessity of drafting extensive definitions of quality in their contract'.

[311] SGA, s 14(6): 'As regards England and Wales and Northern Ireland, the terms implied by subsections (2) and (3) above are conditions.'

[312] Pursuant to Schwenzer and Leisinger (2007) 266f, it would go too far to assume that adherence to ethical standards would qualify as part of the general use.

[313] On this constellation, see Collins (2014) 632f.

[314] *Teheran Europe Co Ltd v ST Belton* [1968] 2 QB 545.

[315] See *Jewson v Boyan* [2004] 1 CLC 87, where this purpose was deemed to be a particular purpose that would need to be made known to the seller.

Thus, non-compliance could be treated as a breach of this term, if the party requiring compliance with a corporate code can provide factual evidence that he made known to the seller the necessity of adherence to the code in order to be able to use the goods for this purpose. Relevant evidence could be any express incorporation of such a purpose in the contractual document, other communication that took place between the parties, or the reference to the purpose of the contract.[316]. This particular purpose could also be surmised from the fact that the buyer reasonably relied on the skill or judgement of the seller to understand this purpose.[317] As regards the latter aspect, one can bring forward the argument that this is at least the case in relation to suppliers that produce the goods for a large brand-sensitive corporation. Such suppliers could, based on their skills, be reasonably aware of the fact that compliance with the corporate code would be necessary for the company in order to be able to sell the products on a particular market or with a brand name on it.[318] The argument of a particular purpose is more difficult in relation to end-consumer contracts when the consumer did not make his intention explicit to the company, but, as is probably more common, the consumer only relied on the publicly declared code when making a purchase decision. Here, the only way to rely on the code is to argue that by making its corporate policy publicly available by explicitly including it in an advertisement, the company could have foreseen that consumers would rely on it when making ethical purchase decisions. This specific purpose could at least be foreseeable by the company if it offers the product in a particular market segment that targets particularly socially responsible consumers or if it explicitly advertises its goods with an emphasis on its ethical aspects, with the expectation that consumers would buy it for exactly this reason. Yet, admittedly, there are quite some 'ifs' involved, which indicate that such an interpretation is not very likely.

3.2.2.1.1.4. Interim Conclusion

To sum up, this analysis of the English default rules on implying terms in sale of goods contracts has revealed several possible interpretations of the corporate code as part of the product characterisation. Yet, these interpretations depend very much on the factual constellation under scrutiny. Once the corporate code appears to be a specific term that is included in the contract section that describes the goods for sale, one could consider interpreting the code as a description and thus qualify the code as part of the obligation that the seller has to deliver goods that correspond to the description. For the vast majority of corporate codes that are less specific or where the parties have not included them in the section dealing with the description of the goods, one could nevertheless consider interpreting the codes either as an express term on a particular quality or as relevant circumstances

[316] For the relevance of these aspects with further reference to case law, see Guest (2006) 572, para 11-055.

[317] ibid 573, para 11-055.

[318] This argument can be found in Schwenzer and Leisinger (2007) 266: 'where the buyer's firm, i.e. the company's name, contains information in this regard or where its reputation in context with ethical values is widely known in the trade sector concerned'.

that the courts could take into consideration when determining the standard of satisfactory quality. This would have the result that the codes would be seen as an obligation of the seller to deliver a product of satisfactory or agreed quality. Goods of sellers that do not comply with the codes would fall below the quality standards. Finally, in relation to supplier contracts, it is at least also conceivable that the corporate codes could be interpreted as an indication in the contract that the goods are sold for the particular purpose of marketing and reselling them in a particular market. If so, the corporate code would become related to the implied term that establishes an obligation of the seller to deliver goods that reasonably fit this purpose.

In one way or another, pursuant to this interpretation, the corporate codes would not be interpreted as creating a separate obligation for the seller, but, instead, as an indication that the law uses when specifying the main performance obligation of the seller, eg, to deliver a product with certain specifications and of a particular quality.

3.2.2.1.2. German Law

With respect to German law, the arguments presented in English law are essentially very similar, yet they would need to be related to the interpretation of § 434 BGB. This provision specifies the main duty of the seller in a sales contract, which is to deliver a good free from material and legal defects. In this regard, § 434 BGB determines that the goods are considered free from physical defects if they have the agreed-upon properties (*Beschaffenheitsvereinbarung*). If no agreement as to the properties has been made, the product needs to be suitable for the intended use or have the properties that are usual in objects of the same kind. Thus, in German law, the corporate code could either be interpreted as a relevant element for determining the 'agreed upon properties' or an indication of the 'intended use' or, finally, as an indication of the 'usual properties' in sales contracts, which are determined by statements made in an advertisement.

3.2.2.1.2.1. The Agreed-upon or Expected Properties

The main source from which the duty of the seller to deliver a product free from defects can be determined is the agreement between the parties on the properties and German law departs from a subjective understanding of the properties, eg, it determines the properties primarily on the basis of what the parties agreed upon.[319] It remains, however, a point of controversy whether the agreed-upon properties remain restricted to the physical aspects of the product. Prior to the reform of the BGB in 2002, the Federal Court of Justice adhered to a narrow understanding of what would qualify as part of the properties and thus remained reluctant to extend it to aspects that are not part of the physical characteristics of the product.[320] However, following the reform, it became a matter

[319] MüKo-Westermann § 434, para 9; Staudinger-Matusche-Beckmann § 434, para 38.

[320] In BGH NJW 1990, 1659, 1660, the court held, for instance, that agreed release from custom taxes cannot form part of the agreed-upon properties.

of controversy whether this understanding could still be upheld in light of the broader understanding of properties of the Consumer Sales Directive. In the course of the debate, different understandings about the properties followed. Some authors argued for a narrow interpretation that would only recognise physical aspects as properties, while others claimed that the properties have to be interpreted broadly on the basis of what the parties intended and could also extend to non-physical elements.[321] Having in mind that compliance with a particular manufacturing process cannot be directly related to the physical aspects of the product, the option to interpret the corporate codes as part of the product specification requires favouring a broad interpretation. This broad understanding can be justified by referring to the requirement that the provision must be interpreted in accordance with the Consumer Sales Directive that equally favours a broad understanding,[322] by drawing analogies to the broad interpretation in the CISG that served as a model for the Directive[323] and by referring to the decisions of lower courts that considered non-physical aspects, such as the country of origin or an agreement on the organic quality of a product, as part of the properties.[324]

If, on the basis of these arguments, a broad interpretation is favoured, it will have the effect that the parties are allowed to make binding agreements as to the 'fair trade' or 'environmental' character of the goods. In cases in which the corporate code is phrased in a broader way and contains more general requirements as to the sellers' adherence to social and environmental standards in the manufacturing process, one may discuss whether a contractually included code provides an indication of the expected quality of the goods. To my understanding, the decision of whether the corporate code could be interpreted as a quality indication depends, comparable to the discussion in English law, on whether the agreed adherence of the trader to social and environmental standards can be linked to the market value of the goods that he delivers.[325]

Consequently, based on a broad understanding of the term 'properties' in § 434 I BGB, one can indeed argue that a corporate code either in the form of an agreement on the production method or the general compliance of the trader in adhering to certain social and environmental standards could be interpreted as part of the properties of the good and, as such, become relevant for the duty of the seller

[321] A narrow interpretation is favoured by, eg, Grigoleit and Herresthal (2003) 124 and more recently Ostendorf (2011). The position of favouring a broad interpretation is taken by Berger (2004); MüKo-Westermann § 434, para 9; Staudinger-Matusche-Beckmann § 434, para 54.

[322] Glinski and Rott (2003) 652f; Dilling (2005) 300ff; Glinski (2011) 185f.

[323] See Glinski (2011) 188ff, who refers to the OLG München, NJW-RR 2003, 849, in which the nonconformity requirement was given a broad interpretation on the basis of art 35 CISG.

[324] The case primarily referred to is LG Ellwangen, NJW 2003, 517 518, although it should be noted that the decision determining the country of origin as part of the agreed-upon properties was eventually overruled. The Court of Appeal decided for this case that the 'properties' have to be interpreted narrowly; see OLG Hamm, NJW-RR 2003, 1360. Additional indications from case law for a broad interpretation from prior to the 2002 reform is provided by Dilling (2005) 300ff. For recent developments in case law towards a broad interpretation of properties beyond physical aspects, *cf* Staudinger-Matusche-Beckmann § 434, paras 54, 55.

[325] See above n 310.

to deliver a good free from physical and legal defects. The same would apply if the corporate code would remain a public declaration. Insofar as no agreement on the properties of the product has been made, the public declaration would become relevant in determining the properties that the buyer can reasonably expect (§ 434 I 2 No 2, 3 BGB).

3.2.2.1.2.2. The Intended Use

In addition to the possible interpretation either as an agreement on the properties or as an indication of the agreed-upon or objectively expected properties, this section will finally turn to the perspective on the codes as evidence for the particular purposes of reselling the product on a particular market or the objective of ethical consumerism. This interpretation becomes particularly relevant if the broad interpretation suggested above is not followed, since the intended use is understood to be broader in comparison to the agreed or ordinary properties.[326] Concerning the purposes behind buying a product that are accepted as part of the 'intended use', the Federal High Court of Justice has so far at least left open the issue of whether reselling the product could generally qualify as an 'intended use under the contract',[327] but given the generally broad interpretation of the intended use, there are at least good reasons to do so. The same applies to consumer contracts. On the basis of existing case law on particular preferences and altruistic purposes as part of an intended use, one could argue that the altruistic purpose of ethical consumption could also be interpreted as part of the legally relevant intended use.[328] Provided that both purposes are generally capable of qualifying as part of the intended use in accordance with § 434 I No 1 BGB, the crucial question is whether this specific use has been made known to the seller. This can be the case if the intended use is made explicit in the contract in the form of linking code compliance to the particular purpose of reselling or, alternatively, it is equally possible that this link is established on the ground that the buyer, in the course of the negotiations or at the time that the contract is concluded, expressed this intention by emphasising that code compliance would be necessary in order to fulfil the purpose. If, however, an explicit link between the corporate code and the intended purpose is not established by the buyer, the possibility of relating the corporate code to the duty to deliver goods that are suitable for the intended use depends very much on whether one can assume that the parties implicitly assumed this purpose.[329] It is on this aspect that, comparable to English law, one would accordingly need

[326] Palandt-Weidenkaff § 434, para 20; MüKo-Westermann § 434, para 19.

[327] BGH NJW 2009, 2808. See especially from the case law prior to the 2002 reform BGH JZ 1970, 28, where the delivery of meat that was under suspicion of having been contaminated with salmonella due to a particular country of origin would be interpreted as not having the agreed properties due to the fact that the meat could not be resold on the market. But see Fabricius (1970) 30f, who suggests that such cases could be more appropriately solved by applying not the specific rules on sales of goods contracts, but the general rules on breach of contract (*positive Vertragsverletzung*) or *culpa in contrahendo*.

[328] See Dilling (2005) 302ff.

[329] Palandt-Weidenkaff § 434, para 22; MüKo-Westermann § 434, para 18; Erman-Grunewald § 434, para 17.

to invoke the argument that the supplier reasonably knew the brand sensibility of a particular buyer. In relation to a company's sales agreement with an end-consumer, one would need to refer to the knowledge of companies of the increasing importance towards ethical consumerism when they sell in a market segment that targets ethically responsible consumers.[330]

3.2.2.1.2.3. *Interim Conclusion*

With respect to German law, it could be observed that the corporate codes are generally capable of becoming part of the product specification, although it should be noted that this interpretation needs to depart from a broad understanding of the agreed-upon properties and the understanding of the intended use. Yet, if a broad interpretation is argued for, it indeed becomes a viable option to relate the corporate codes specifically to the duty of the seller to deliver goods free from material defects.

3.2.2.2. *Applicable Sales Law Remedies*

After having discussed the general possibility to qualify the code obligation in light of the default rules on sales contracts, this section will now discuss the enforcement structure that would derive from this particular interpretation. Who can, pursuant to this proposed interpretation, enforce the corporate codes and what remedies could be invoked when the code obligation has been breached?

Based on an interpretation of the codes as part of the duty of the seller to perform his main obligation under the sales contract, non-complying behaviour has to be interpreted as a breach of contract in the form of either poor or non-performance in the delivery of the goods. Since this duty remains a relative duty towards the buyer, this interpretation merely has the result that enforcing the corporate code is placed in the hands of the respective buyers. Thus, breaches of corporate codes can be remedied by large companies towards their suppliers and by consumers towards companies that they bought products from and that publicly declared to have complied with a code. Moreover, the proposed interpretation of non-compliance with the corporate code as an event of poor or non-delivery automatically results in general sales law remedies as the applicable remedial scheme. In relation to German law, § 437 BGB determines as main sales law remedies the claim for specific performance, avoidance of the contract, price reduction and damages, and in this regard does not explicitly distinguish between consumer and commercial contracts. Specific performance is the main remedy; avoidance

[330] With respect to end-consumers, however, it should be noted, that German law does not allow the interpreting of internal motives of the buyers as part of the 'intended use'; *cf* Staudinger-Matusche-Beckmann § 434, para 76. This implies that in relation to end-consumers, the altruistic purpose can only be interpreted as part of the intended use if it is not only an important aspect for the consumer, but is also known to the seller. This knowledge could possibly be assumed by referring to his choice to serve a particular market for socially responsible goods or to an advertisement of the goods that contain an emphasis on the socially or environmentally responsible manufacturing process.

is dependent on additional requirements[331] and damage compensation is available in accordance with the general rules on damage compensation for breach of contract (§§ 280ff BGB). In English law, the situation is slightly more complex. In relation to consumer contracts, the remedy of specific performance has equally been made available to consumers in case the goods do not conform to the contract,[332] but this remedy is generally not available in commercial contracts. For both commercial and consumer contracts, English law has as the main remedy for breaches of contract, including breach of the terms related to the conformity of the delivered goods, actions for damages. These would consequently be available for breach of corporate codes if these were considered part of the obligations under sales law.[333] In case the breach concerns a condition, it is also possible for the buyer to reject the goods and avoid the contract. Next to the remedies available pursuant to the default rules on sales contracts, there is also the possibility of using remedies that are specified in the contract or in the code, such as any penalty or liquidated damages clauses or explicit rights to terminate the contract in case of non-performance or poor performance.[334] It is thus primarily these remedies that the buyers can make use of when attempting to remedy non-compliance with the code. Yet, in spite of their general availability for breaches of corporate codes, there are a few specific aspects that would need to be taken into consideration in that respect.

Focusing on the claim for specific performance, it has already been emphasised that this remedy does not seem to fit with the situation of the codes. Specific performance in the form of a claim for repair is difficult to conceive and its replacement by a 'non-contaminated' product does not seem to be a viable option.[335] The use of this remedy raises important questions as to how specific performance could work in practice, given that this 'non-contaminated' character of the product cannot be identified on the basis of inspection. Moreover, an important reason why specific performance does not seem to fit in this context is that it is solely the product delivery and not the actual non-complying behaviour that can be remedied by a claim for specific performance.

The difficulty concerning the action for damages is related to the undertaking of determining the measurable damage that the buyer can claim. In relation to end-consumer contracts, the delivery of the product results primarily in disappointed expectations, but not in direct financial damage. In relation to commercial contracts in which goods are resold, the possibility to claim damages remains an option. Here, one could either claim damages for a loss of profits if the buyer could

[331] § 323 I BGB declares termination possible only after a period for specific performance is set: 'If the debtor, in the case of a synallagmatic contract, does not render the performance which is due, or does not render it in conformity with the contract, the creditor may withdraw from the contract, if he has determined for the debtor without result, an appropriate period of time for performance or subsequent fulfilment' (translation taken from Kornet and Hardt (2013) 307).

[332] Sections 48A, 48B and 48F SGA lay down that non-conformity means a breach of 'an express term of the contract or a term implied as to the correspondence with the description or satisfactory quality'.

[333] Collins (2014) 638.

[334] Schwenzer, Hachem and Kee (2012) 633, para 44.266.

[335] Glinski (2011) 191f; Peterkova (2014a) 23.

only resell the goods at a lower price[336] or claim a non-pecuniary reputation loss on the side of the buyer.[337] This general possibility notwithstanding, these damages are still difficult to calculate. As regards loss of profits, there are several practical hurdles involved concerning how these damages can be measured.[338] Insofar as the possibility of claiming non-pecuniary losses in the form of reputation damage is concerned, it has to be emphasised that current sales law only very exceptionally recognises reputation loss as part of the damages for which monetary compensation can be claimed.[339] These difficulties could potentially be met if the breach of a corporate code could give rise to a claim for exemplary or even punitive damages.[340] However, with respect to this suggestion, it must be emphasised that both English and German contract law do not make it possible to claim exemplary or punitive damages for breach of contract.[341]

Given these difficulties in relation to specific performance and the problems in identifying a measurable financial damage that contract law recognises as a valid basis for an action for damages, it seems that, in the debate on corporate codes in sales, primarily avoidance or withdrawal of the contract are considered viable remedies.[342] However, if the parties have not explicitly agreed on this right, it has to be borne in mind that the right to avoid the contract is generally dependent on an additional condition. In German law, in order to be able to avoid the contract, the buyer would need to provide arguments as to why the breach was not trivial.[343] A similar, even higher threshold for the entitlement to reject the goods and avoid the contract is required under English law. In order to avoid the contract, it is generally accepted that the breach has to concern either condition or,

[336] Dilling (2005) 290, 305; and Schwenzer and Leisinger (2007) 268f. Schwenzer, Hachem and Kee (2012) 630, para 44.250 also focus on this possibility, but they argue that the claim for damages for non-compliance with ethical standards would need to be directed primarily at skimming-off the profits that the seller made by not complying with the code. However, since this approach does not focus on the principle of compensating the buyer for his loss, but rather allows him to claim the amount that the seller has obtained, it seems more in proximity with a possible claim based on unjust enrichment or the category of punitive damages, as the breach of the code is primarily sanctioned based on the consideration that the seller should not benefit from a breach of contract.

[337] Schwenzer and Leisinger (2007) 268ff; Schwenzer, Hachem and Kee (2012) 611, para 44.160, 618, para 44.188.

[338] Schwenzer, Hachem and Kee (2012) 630, para 44.251.

[339] On this option in general, see also critically Schlechtriem (2007) 97ff; Peterkova (2014a) 23. Schwenzer, Hachem and Kee (2012) 618, para 44.190 equally emphasise that several legal systems (including Germany and England) deny recovery for loss of goodwill and reputation.

[340] *cf* for this idea of allowing punitive damages for breach of agreements on ethical or environmentally friendly manufacturing practices Wilhelmsson (1998) 65 (with respect to consumer contracts); and Schlechtriem (2007) 99 (with respect to commercial contracts).

[341] See for England the narrowly framed possibility for exemplary damages in relation to tort as set out in *Ross v Barnard* [1964] AC 1129. However, concerning contracts, it remains the general rule that these types of damages cannot be awarded; *cf* with extensive references to case law on this aspect Peel (2011) 1000f, para 20-020; and with reference to the position of the Law Commission on exemplary damages, see Burrows (1998) ch 7 140. For the generally sceptical perspective on non-compensatory, ie, exemplary and punitive damages in Germany, see especially BGHZ 118, 312.

[342] Dilling (2005) 307; Glinski (2011) 192.

[343] § 323 V 2 BGB: 'If the debtor has not effected performance in conformity with the contract, the creditor cannot withdraw from the contract if the violation of duty is trivial' (translation taken from Kornet and Hardt (2013) 307).

if not, it must be so fundamental to the buyer that avoidance is justified. Insofar as the corporate code qualifies as a description or is interpreted as part of the satisfactory quality, the SGA already qualifies correspondence with the description and delivery of goods of a satisfactory quality as a condition and thus entitles the buyer to this remedy. Concerning the interpretation of the corporate code as an agreement on the quality, the question about the nature of this term is, however, more complicated. In the absence of an express remedy specified in the contract, the term will often be treated as an innominate term and thus requires a decision as to whether the breach is so fundamental that avoidance of the contract is justified.[344] As a result, avoidance of the contract is a remedy that requires not merely a breach, but a severe breach of the contract. Concerning this additional requirement, proponents bring forward several arguments. With respect to commercial contracting, it is argued that ethical production is 'of such an essential nature' for the buyer because realistically he cannot market 'ethically contaminated' products.[345] In relation to consumer contracts, the main argument is the reference to the increasing relevance of compliance with social and environmental standards for the purchase decision of consumers, which suggests that non-compliance should not be treated as minor.[346]

Provided that these arguments are followed, the most viable enforcement option would indeed remain the buyers' entitlement to avoid the contract with a non-complying contractual partner. That being said, even if considered viable pursuant to the rules on sales contracts, the use of this remedy remains limited for practical reasons. As the breach of a corporate code does not affect the general usability of the product, it seems quite likely that the remedy will not be used very often. Consumers, assuming they could prove the 'defect' of non-complying behaviour, will most likely not be inclined very often to give back 'contaminated' products.[347] In relation to commercial contracting, an important counter-argument against the practical relevance of this remedy is that companies, if not attempting to resell the products with a specific fair trade certification, still have an interest in receiving the goods in order to avoid shortages and the risk of breaching the follow-up contracts with their distributors and retailers. Against this background, in many cases, it would thus not make commercial sense to reject the goods, avoid the contract and undertake the effort to find a different source on the market if the corporate code has been breached. In addition, a commercial buyer may not want to risk terminating a long-term relationship with its otherwise reliable supplier. In particular, the latter aspect is also supported by empirical evidence on the use of codes in commercial contracts, which reveal that the instrument of termination is seldom used because buyers have a strong interest in continuing the relationship

[344] Adams and MacQueen (2010) 142.

[345] Schwenzer and Leisinger (2007) 268 argue here that incorporation of ethical standards already 'sufficiently made clear that compliance is of special interest to the buyer'. See also on this point Schwenzer, Hachem and Kee (2012) 382, para 31.91.

[346] Wilhelmsson (2002/2003) 91; Glinski (2010) 192.

[347] Wilhelmsson (2002/2003) 99; Glinski (2010) 192.

and, if disputes arise, to solve them informally.[348] Therefore, proponents of the sales law interpretation merely argue that the future of private law enforcement of contractually binding corporate codes relies on a particular use of this remedy.

On the one hand, the potential of this remedy lies in its value for singular 'grass-roots action' of consumers[349] or as a remedy that becomes effective when collectively organised in the form of protests by NGOs that urge consumers to boycott certain brands and return their products.[350] In addition, it could become effective if reliance is placed on the conviction that a 'buyer convinced of his ethical values' would feel obliged to abstain from contracting and forgo the eventual individual profits that he could gain from such a contract.[351] On the other hand, private law enforcement of the corporate codes is also envisaged in conjunction with a suggested reform of the enforcement system of sales law in the form of the introduction of an additional collective enforcement mechanism. The main suggestion in this regard is to give collective institutions that act in the interest of consumers a stronger role in enforcing product-related obligations of companies in sales contracts by, for instance, seeking an injunction order against traders that bring products onto the market that do not comply with advertised social and environmental minimum standards.[352] Yet, even if these practical problems are met by extending the enforcement structure of sales law, one must finally also mention the criticism that this remedy faces as an ineffective and possibly unethical private law enforcement mechanism. It should be noted in this context that in the broader debate on the corporate codes, it is also discussed whether a legal remedy of avoidance or termination, even if available, should be used. In fact, the use of this particular remedy can have the potential to worsen rather than improve the situation for those that should benefit from the code. In fact, if companies terminate or avoid their contracts with suppliers, it is very possible that suppliers run out of business, with far-reaching adverse effects for those that ought ultimately to benefit from the code.[353] Based on these considerations, the potential of the suggested private law enforcement in sales law does not lie in the actual use of this remedy; it is instead the mere threat of using this sanction that could have a disciplining effect and, as such, could play an important role in the private law enforcement of the codes.

[348] McBarnet and Kurkchiyan (2007) 78ff.

[349] Wilhelmsson (2002/2003) 101 ('green micropolitics').

[350] Glinski (2011) 193.

[351] This option is presented, but it is based on an understanding of the cultural relativity of ethical values rejected by Schlechtriem (2007) 100–01.

[352] Wilhelmsson (2002/2003) 101; Glinski (2011) 193.

[353] This is why, for instance, the UN Guiding Principles urge that companies would also need to pay due respect to the adverse consequences of contract termination when attempting to remedy adverse human rights impacts that are directly linked to their business operations; see especially Commentary on Principle 19 UN Guiding Principles. See also on this point Collins (2014), pointedly at 626: 'The well-intentioned consumer who avoids products made using child labour, such as cotton clothing from Asia, may discover that the main group who suffer from a consumer boycott are the children themselves, who may be forced to survive by accepting even worse kinds of jobs such as prostitution.' For the awareness of this problem among companies, *cf* also McBarnet and Kurkchiyan (2007) 82: 'Contract termination would in many instances lead to factory closure and job loss, and setting that sequence of events in play could be seen as extreme corporate irresponsibility.'

3.2.2.3. Conclusion: Corporate Codes and Sales Law

The previous section focused on the potential of interpreting the corporate code in light of the default rules on sales contracts based on the assumption that these codes represent either agreements on the particular manufacturing process or at least have an influence on the agreed or expected quality of the product and their potential use. On the basis of the English SGA and the German provisions concerning sales contracts, it could be shown that this interpretation is indeed viable, but only if a sufficiently broad interpretation would be favoured concerning the definition of product specification and quality. If so, an interpretation of the codes in light of the default rules on sales contracts would have the result that the corporate codes would become an integral part of the performance obligation of the seller to deliver a product with certain specifications. Focusing on the actual enforcement of the code obligation interpreted in this way, the possibility of avoiding the contract in an event of non-compliance was identified as currently the most viable legal remedy. Although this particular remedy currently faces limitations as to whether it is a practically relevant and, moreover, a desired private law enforcement mechanism, there are two directions that could enhance its practicability and effectiveness. It could become a practically relevant remedy if developed into a collective enforcement mechanism and it could at least be viewed as an effective remedy to the extent that the threat of its potential use could already have a disciplining effect on companies.

3.2.3. Third Party Rights in Contracts

The above-mentioned interpretation of contractually incorporated codes remains by no means uncontested in the corporate codes debate. On the contrary, in the course of the debate, it is also mentioned that the strong focus on the entitlement of consumers and large buyers does not pay due respect to the beneficiaries that the codes seek to protect.[354] Important concerns regarding the interpretation of corporate codes through the lenses of (consumer) sales law were that the interests of consumers and those of the beneficiaries can also conflict, and that consumer sales law enforcement of codes would result in a selectivity of the code obligations that would be practically enforced according to the preferences of consumers.[355]

In searching for alternative interpretations, it evolved as the most prominent proposal to interpret the contractually binding codes as obligations that would

[354] A very critical position on the interpretation of the codes in light of the sales law rules is expressed by Heijden (2011b) 11: 'Private enforcement through contractual liability in a consumer context is not dealt with, because such enforcement is not considered to be viable in holdings TNCs liable.' A more cautious position is taken by Estlund (2012) 253: 'the remedies would run not to workers but to consumers and might reflect only the price premium paid for sweat-free goods (assuming such a premium could be proven)'.

[355] Sobczak (2006) 175ff.

have to be interpreted in light of the rules on third party rights in contracts.[356] The proposed interpretation of codes as third party rights already received some prominence in *Doe v Wal-Mart* as far as supplier contracts are concerned. In the debate that took place in the aftermath of this lawsuit, it could be revealed that the court, although eventually refusing to recognise a contractual promise on the side of Wal-Mart to benefit the workers, in its reasoning nevertheless implicitly interpreted the contractually incorporated code of conduct as an obligation to benefit third parties, yet on the side of the supplier.[357] In addition, the argumentative strategy of the claimants in this case and contributions to the scholarly debate suggest that a contractual obligation to benefit third parties on the side of the large buyers in supplier contracts could be extracted from the publicly declared policies to the extent that they can be read into the supplier contracts.[358] In addition to supplier contracts, the dispute between the University of Wisconsin Madison and Adidas reveals that the interpretation of codes as contractual third party rights could equally apply in relation to contracts of companies with their customers, at least if these contracts contain a clause that require compliance with the code of conduct. This was in fact the suggested interpretation of the claimants, who argued in their statement of claim that the corporate code creates an obligation on the side of Adidas to benefit the employers directly by paying the legally mandated benefits. Finally, the interpretation of the code creating a third party right is also at least conceivable with respect to the public declaration as such if parallels are drawn with the public self-commitments in the national context. In interpreting the self-commitments of companies in the national context, it was not only the courts, but also parts of the scholarly literature that interpreted such self-commitments as unilateral contracts (with the governments or consumers) that would benefit third parties.[359] Hence, once an understanding of the corporate codes as unilateral contracts with governments or other market actors would be followed, even the publicly declared corporate code could in principle be open to a qualification as an obligation to benefit third parties.

Regardless of whether the supplier or the customer contract or even the public declaration, in its interpretation as a unilateral contract, is taken as the basis for

[356] For this understanding, see Phillips and Lim (2009) 368ff; Heijden (2011b), ch 5; Heijden (2011a) 6f; Vytopil (2012) 161f; Geis (2012) 1176ff; Peterkova (2014a) 18f. A comparable interpretation with respect not to corporate codes in particular, but to clauses in private contracts that oblige one contracting party to refrain from discriminating its employees can be found in Ayres and Brown (2006). An interpretation as third party clauses is equally discussed in relation to bilateral International Framework Agreements on adherence to fundamental workplace standards between companies and international trade unions: Koster and Eynde (2009) 138f.

[357] Coleman (2009) 630: 'Had the plaintiffs asserted standing as direct, rather than third- party, beneficiaries, or sued the suppliers rather than Wal-Mart, it is not clear that the court would have dismissed their claim.' See also Phillips and Lim (2009) 368ff, who argue that the corporate codes would qualify based on the surrounding circumstances as terms that treat the code beneficiaries as intended and not merely incidental beneficiaries.

[358] See especially Phillips and Lim (2009) 371ff.

[359] See above section 3.1.4.1. (p 82), text and accompanying footnotes. This suggestion appears particularly in German debates as an interpretation of public self-commitments as bare acknowledgements of a debt that benefits a third party (§§ 780, 328 BGB); see generally on this possibility: Kohte (2005a) 353; Segna (2006) 7; and the court decisions referred to above (n 162).

this obligation of the contracting parties to confer a benefit on a third party, the feasibility of interpreting the corporate codes depends effectively on whether and to what extent contract law allows such an exception in light of the general principle of the privity of contracts. Can the term that specifies an obligation for one of the contracting parties be interpreted as a binding obligation to confer a benefit upon a party that is a stranger to the contract? And, as a result of such an obligation, could the benefiting third party acquire an autonomous enforcement right in addition to[360] or instead of[361] the other contracting party, or, if not, is it at least possible to interpret the corporate codes as a bilateral obligation to confer a benefit upon third parties? Among proponents of this suggested interpretation of the codes, there are two core perspectives on the corporate codes that are offered as to how the creation of third party rights could be envisaged in relation to the corporate codes. First, an interpretation of the codes as enforceable third party rights is considered a feasible option with respect to those provisions in the corporate codes that contain either an explicit enforcement right for a third party[362] or an obligation that can only be conceived as being for the benefit of a third party. The most apparent examples of such uncontroversial benefits are code obligations that are phrased as direct benefits for employees, such as the payment of minimum wages, the obligation not to exceed specified working hours or explicit agreements not to discriminate where this anti-discrimination clause is explicitly included in a contract in order to benefit employees.[363] Partly, reference to such explicit agreements can also be found in the discussion on environmental codes if such agreements contain, for instance, an explicit right for the local communities.[364] Second, a more difficult constellation is to be found in codes that are not very specific in conferring benefits upon third parties but, instead, more broadly give rise to an obligation to 'improve fundamental workplace standards' or 'protect the environment'. In relation to such agreements in which the contracting parties have not made explicit their intention whether or not to create rights directly for third parties that benefit from the improvement of such standards, the argument is presented that the third party right can be established by way of interpretation. It is here the main argument that, even if not making it explicit, it still represents the most likely

[360] This seems to underlie the suggestions of Phillips and Lim (2009) 368ff; Heijden (2011b) 172; Heijden (2011a) 6f; Vytopil (2012) 161.

[361] Ayres and Brown (2006) 1698 suggest that the contracting party should agree to waive its rights to sue the promisor for a violation of the standards and give the exclusive right to enforce the Fair Employment Standards to the third party beneficiaries; Geis (2012) 1777f suggests that in agreements on CSR aspects, the promisee should, in giving up his rights, solely retain a right to monitor compliance with the standards.

[362] One can mention in this context as an illustrative example the Accord on Fire and Building Safety in Bangladesh, as discussed above, section 3.1.1.3. (p 51), text and accompanying footnotes. The Accord as signed by the participating companies could, due to its clear phrasing, be interpreted as creating third party rights for beneficiaries to initiate complaints (para 18), possibly even remedying breaches of the agreement in an arbitration procedure (para 5).

[363] It is these explicitly designed third party agreements that Ayres and Brown (2006) have in mind. It also resembles the situation analysed by Heijden (2011b) 171f that a corporate code is negotiated as an explicit third party clause.

[364] See especially Geis (2012) 1178; see also, presumably in a similar direction, Glinski (2011) 170.

interpretation that the contracting parties made such codes a contractual obligation for the purpose of benefiting not themselves, but instead the beneficiaries as third parties.[365]

In the following sections, these two possible interpretations will be analysed with regard to how they could be realised in light of the existing possibilities to create third party rights by contracts. In the context of English law, the corporate codes will consequently be related to the existing common law exceptions from the strong doctrine of privity and the recent statutory reform in the form of the Contracts (Rights of Third Parties) Act 1999. In German law, the analysis will discuss this interpretation on the basis of the rules on third party rights (§§ 328ff BGB), which are recognised as the core exception from the otherwise applicable principle of the relativity of contractual obligations. After having identified the option under current contract law to interpret the corporate codes as conferring a benefit upon a third party, the second part of the analysis will focus on the enforcement structure that would follow from this interpretation of the code.

3.2.3.1. Corporate Codes and Third Party Benefits

3.2.3.1.1. English Law

3.2.3.1.1.1. The Doctrine of Privity

When analysing the general possibility under English law of creating an enforcement right for a party that is a stranger to the contract, it is important to bear in mind that third party rights in contracts have to be viewed in light of the strict doctrine of the privity of contracts and it is this doctrine that for a long time in fact prevented *any* possibility of creating third party rights in a contract. In fact, in the past, it represented a general principle of English law that parties who were strangers to a contract could not enforce a term of a contract and refer these strangers to tort law, which would, however, limit their rights to the compensation of narrowly confined types of damages. This principle has its origin in the landmark case *Tweedle v Atkinson*[366] and was subsequently reaffirmed on several occasions.[367] Although it was prominently criticised by different Law Lords in their speeches[368] as well as in the academic literature,[369] it prevailed as a general rule and relaxations

[365] Phillips and Lim (2009) 368ff. See also Cafaggi (2013) 1592f: 'A third-party beneficiary contract can be said to exist, even if the beneficiary is not expressly named, nor identifiable, nor in existence even at the time of execution.' A critical perspective on this approach is, however, taken by Estlund (2012) 254f.

[366] *Tweedle v Atkinson* (1861) 121 ER 762.

[367] *Dunlop Pneumatic Tyre Co Ltd v Selfridge and Co* [1915] AC 847; *Scruttons Ltd v Midland Silicones Ltd* [1962] AC 446; *Beswick v Beswick* [1968] AC 58.

[368] See only the speeches of Lord Denning in *Smith and Snipes Hall Farm Ltd v River Douglas Catchman Board* [1949] 2 KB 500 514 and in *Beswick v Beswick* [1966] Ch 538, 552–54, 557; Lord Steyn in *Darlington BC v Wiltshier Northern Ltd* [1995] 1 WLR 68 76; Lord Goff in *The Pioneer Container* [1994] 2 AC 324 335; *White and Jones* [1995] 2 AC 207; and Lord Diplock in *Swain v Law Society* [1983] 1 AC 598, 611 ('an anachronistic shortcoming that has for many years been regarded as a reproach to English private law').

[369] See, eg, Markesinis (1987) 396f.

of the strict approach only evolved in the form of very narrowly confined common law exceptions for particular types of contract. Among these exceptions, the most prominent became the field of carriage of goods by sea and the third party effect of exemption clauses in these contracts. In this area, the question about third party rights was primarily approached in relation to the right of third parties to rely on exemption clauses that restricted the scope of liability of the contracting parties in the event of a breach and the courts gradually recognised the right of the third parties to benefit from the exemption clauses in contracts by means of using them as a defence against the claims of one of the contracting parties.[370] However, as corporate codes do not represent terms that exempt or limit liability, but, on the contrary, are terms that create a basis for additional liability on the side of the promisor, this exception seems not to fit entirely.

Yet, in addition to the area of exemption clauses, the rigid privity rule also became affected by developments in the area of tort law when the courts interpreted a breach of contract as a breach of the tort law duty of care. The constellations dealt with by the courts concerned liability of the promisor towards a third party when the negligent performance or non-performance of the contractual obligations detrimentally affected a third party, but the party did not have a right to enforce the contract. While it was clear that the third party could not enforce the contract, the tort of negligence served as the legal angle to develop the right of a third party to obtain compensation for breach of the contract in the form of a breach of the duty of care.[371] One of the most prominent decisions in this regard is *White and Jones*, which concerned the role of parties benefiting from a will that a solicitor had agreed to set up in relation to a client. In giving his speech to the court in this case, Lord Goff justified the right in constellations in which a contract benefits third parties, but considered that a contractual solution 'in this country could be open to criticism as an illegitimate circumvention of … long established doctrines'.[372] In relation to the corporate codes, this exception in the form of tort law liability does indeed become relevant as a way of allowing a third party to hold the contracting parties liable for breach of contract. That being said, this exception seems not to fit with the arguments presented above, given that applying this doctrine would neither be capable of establishing a right of a third party to enforce the code in a contract nor create a direct obligation to confer a benefit upon a third party; it remains restricted as a cause of action for liability in tort in case the contract is negligently performed and affects a third party. It is due to

[370] See fundamentally *NZ Shipping Co Ltd v AM Satterthwaite and Co Ltd (The Eurymedon)* [1975] AC 154. It should be noted, however, that reliance on the exemption clause was not justified on the ground of recognising the exemption clause as a third party right. It was rather constructed as a unilateral binding contract between the contracting party and the third party based on the exemption clause in the bill of lading. See also for this construction Lord Hobhouse in *Homburg Houtimport BV v Agrosin Private Ltd (The Starsin)* [2004] 1 AC 715, 785: 'It is the bill of lading that the mutual contract between the relevant persons must be found … Through the agency of the contracting carrier, the third party becomes a party to a contract contained in the bill of lading.'

[371] *Ross v Caunters* [1980] Ch 297; *Henderson v Merrett Syndicates Ltd* [1995] 2 AC 145; *White v Jones* [1995] 2 AC 207.

[372] Lord Goff in *White and Jones* (n 371) 266.

this focus on mere liability for breach of the contract and not enforcement of the contract that the potential of this doctrine will be dealt with in the context of tort liability.[373] Consequently, it can be concluded that these very specific common law exceptions from the doctrine of the privity do not fit with the constellation of the corporate codes. This accordingly makes it necessary, in relation to the possibility of third party rights in corporate codes particularly, to focus on the recent statutory reform in the form of the Contracts (Rights of Third Parties) Act that passed the Parliament in 1999 after an extensive report was published by the Law Commission where reform was recommended.[374]

3.2.3.1.1.2. The Contracts (Rights of Third Parties) Act 1999

In order to analyse the relevance of this Act for the interpretation of the codes, it is necessary to focus briefly on the actual changes that this Act brought about and the conditions that render it possible for a third party to acquire rights under the contract. First, it has to be noted that the Act does not change the law fundamentally; it remains the rule that parties that are strangers to the contract generally cannot enforce one of its terms. The Act only provides for a very specific exception for particular types of terms in which the parties have intended to make a term enforceable by a third party. In addition, it should be noted that the Act does not replace the existing common law that has been briefly described above; thus, the possibility of creating rights of third parties pursuant to the existing common law exceptions remains.[375]

As regards the conditions under which a third party right is created, the Act states that a third party right is created either if the contractual term expressly provides for the right to claim a contractual benefit (first test) or, in the absence of a sufficiently clear expression, if a term 'purports to confer a benefit on' a third party (second test).[376] In case a term only fulfils the latter test, it is the rule that a presumption is established in favour of a third party right that can be rebutted by the promisor. In order to rebut the presumption, the promisor needs to prove that, on the basis of a proper construction of the contract, the parties did not intend to give the third party an enforcement right.[377] At the time that the new Act came into force, there were three aspects that remained subject to uncertainty. First, in particular, the test pursuant to section 1(1)(b) became an important aspect in the debate and the question arose with regard to when a term should be considered to

[373] See section 4.1.1.1. (p 151), text and accompanying footnotes.

[374] Law Commission, No 242/1996, 39ff, para 3.1.ff. As main reasons for reform of the strict rule, the Commission brought forward the importance of protecting the intentions of the parties in contract law and of respecting their freely negotiated agreements, the necessity to protect the expectations of the third party that ought to have faith in receiving a benefit that parties agree upon as part of their contract, the recognition of commercial realities, and the fact that other Member States of the European Union, as well as several common law countries, already recognise the possibility. For a detailed analysis of the history of and the reasons for reform, see generally Kornet (2009) 153ff.

[375] Deakin, Johnston and Markesinis (2007) 23; McKendrick (2013) 117f.

[376] Section 1(1) of the Contracts (Rights of Third Parties) Act 1999.

[377] ibid, s 1(2).

'confer a benefit upon a third party'. Moreover, the quality of the presumption was discussed and, more precisely, the threshold for a party to rebut the presumption. Finally, it was discussed whether the third party would gain the right to enforce the contract or whether its rights would have to be determined separately for every term in the contract.[378] This last question seemed not to lead to intense controversy due to the clear language of the Act and it appeared to have become the prevailing opinion that the third party right would need to be discussed for every term separately.[379] In relation to the other two aspects, there is still no full clarity on the issue. In light of this remaining uncertainty, the following section will discuss the interpretation of the corporate codes, primarily on the basis of the tendencies that can be inferred from the cases that have been decided by the courts in the aftermath of the adoption of the Act. Assuming that constellations in which the third party right for the affected beneficiaries is laid down either in the code or in the contract directly would easily pass the first test, the following section will focus primarily on those constellations in which it is not explicit in the code whether or not a third party right should be created and where the parties have even included a disclaimer in their code. In so doing, the first question to be addressed is whether such codes would in the first place pass the second test, with the result that a presumption is set up in favour of a third party right. Subsequently, the conditions are analysed under which the contracting parties could rebut the presumption by including a disclaimer.

3.2.3.1.1.2.1. Terms that 'Purport to Confer a Benefit'

As regards the first point, in order to set up the presumption in section 1(1)(b), it is necessary to focus on the intention of the parties and examine whether the parties intended the term to create a benefit for a specific third party. Since the undertaking to determine the intentions of the contracting parties is primarily a matter of objective contract interpretation, the second test is primarily a matter of interpreting the term in light of the contract. In this regard, it has already been decided that a term that represents the legal basis for an obligation of one of the contracting parties to pay a direct benefit to a third party would pass this second test.[380] This also seems to be in line with how Burrows, a member of the Law Commission drafting the Act, envisaged the provision. He argued that the provision is based on:

> [T]he idea that, if you ask yourself, 'When is it that parties are likely to have intended to confer rights on a third party to enforce a term, albeit that they have not expressly conferred that right', the answer will be: 'Where the term purports to confer a benefit on an *expressly identified* third party.'[381]

[378] For an extensive analysis of these problems, see MacMillan (2000) 724ff.

[379] Beale (2010) 224. In fact, the uncertainty seemed rather to stem from the fact that the Commission's Bill referred to the third party as being competent to enforce the contract.

[380] In *Nisshin Shipping Co Ltd v Cleaves and Co Ltd* [2003] 2 CLC 1097, the court held, for instance, that a term requiring the payment of a commission fee to two named third parties is to be interpreted as conferring a direct benefit upon each of these parties, with the result that a presumption is set up that each of the named parties has its own enforcement right.

[381] Burrows (2000) 544 (emphasis added).

Based on this view, it is also possible to interpret those codes as capable of creating a third party right when the third party beneficiaries are expressly named as those that should receive a specified benefit. This particularly applies to codes that provide for an obligation to pay the minimum wage or other financial benefits for workers or codes in which neighbours of factories are expressly mentioned as those that ought to benefit from the strict environmental standards of factories.

Yet, what about cases in which a particular term does not specify a direct benefit, but only contains obligations that have the indirect consequence that the situation for a third party is improved? Is it possible to interpret a term that makes it an obligation of one of the contracting parties to 'adhere to fundamental workplace standards' or to 'assist in improving the human rights situation' equally as a term that confers a benefit upon a third party? In this regard, it should first be noted that the decision whether a term purports to confer a benefit remains an objective test that departs from the language used in that term and the relation of that term to other contract terms. In *Dolphin Maritime and Aviation Services Ltd v Sveriges Angfartygs Forening*, Justice Christopher Clarke emphasised that, in order to pass the second test, it is necessary to find evidence that the term has been set up by the parties with the purpose of benefiting a third party. Conversely, the fact that a term does simply improve the situation for a third party does not suffice.[382] Whether parties have this purpose and intention is a matter of construction, but it was also already decided that it is not necessary that this purpose to benefit a third party is the sole or even predominant purpose behind the term.[383] Thus, in order for a term to be enforceable by a third party, one needs to determine whether the parties agreed on the term with the underlying purpose to benefit the third party or whether the improved situation only represents the positive side-effect of the contractual performance. From the existing decisions, one can identify a tendency not to put too high a threshold requirement on this purpose.[384]

Following this interpretation of the second test, it is in fact also possible for corporate codes to pass this second test if they do not directly specify a financial benefit for specific beneficiaries, but merely contain obligations that the contracting parties agree upon with the aim of improving the situation for the beneficiaries. In fact, one can argue that the parties must have had this inherent purpose if they wanted their codes to be taken seriously at all. It seems in this context difficult to conceive that the contracting parties would not have intended the corporate codes to become obligations that should benefit third parties. Even if it probably remains the more important consideration behind including the term that negative reputational effects for the contracting parties are mitigated, the requirement of identifying the third party benefit as one, but not necessarily the main, purpose behind

[382] *Dolphin Maritime and Aviation Services Ltd v Sveriges Angfartygs Forening* [2009] 1 CLC 460, 486. See also Burrows (2000) 544: 'not designed to cover consequential or incidental benefits stemming from the promisor's performance'.

[383] *Prudential Assurance Co Ltd v Ayres* [2007] EWHC 775 (Ch) [28]: 'no requirement that the benefit on the third party shall be the predominant purpose or intent behind the term or that it denies the applicability of s 1(1)(b) if a benefit is conferred on someone other than the third party'. See also *Laemthong International Lines Company Ltd v Abdullah Mohammed Fahem and Co* [2005] 1 CLC 739 749 (per Clarke LJ).

[384] See in this direction McKendrick (2013) 120.

the term would probably allow such an interpretation. That being said, although it is following the broad interpretation of the criterion of the 'purpose' principally possible to interpret even codes as terms that 'confer a benefit upon a third party' where the benefit may also only have been a side-issue, there is nevertheless an additional criterion in the Act that is capable of preventing setting up the presumption of a third party right. Pursuant to section 1(3) of the Act, it is necessary that the third party, although not required to be named in person, needs to be identifiable as a member of a group specified in the contract. This essentially means that one needs to derive from the contractual term an identifiable group to which the individual beneficiary belongs;[385] conversely, it is not sufficient that the identification is possible by mere implication.[386] With respect to the corporate codes, this requirement becomes problematic in constellations in which, on the basis of the code, it is not possible to identify a particular group that is to be considered a beneficiary. This applies in particular to general obligations in the codes that deal with respect for human rights or environmental protection and that, in addition, do not simultaneously specify a concretely identifiable group as the beneficiaries, such as members of a (specified) local community or the individuals living in the immediate vicinity of factories. It can also be relevant in relation to workplace standards for those standards in relation to which an explicit group of beneficiaries cannot be determined on the basis of the contractually included term. Against the background of the clear wording in the Act, it seems difficult to qualify the latter constellations as falling under the Act.[387] This then accordingly narrows down the possible interpretation of corporate codes as conferring a benefit upon third parties to constellations in which the codes are sufficiently specific with regard to the group for the benefit of which the code has been set up. This requirement is then primarily met in relation to codes that deal with specific labour rights, as these codes specify adherence to workplace standards as benefits of employees, but it will remain difficult to establish in relation to those obligations in a code that deal with issues that could potentially affect a variety of different groups and individuals, such as environmental protection or general human rights protection.

To conclude, pursuant to the Contracts (Rights of Third Parties) Act 1999, it is possible to interpret corporate codes as creating a presumption in favour of a third party right if it is possible to derive unambiguously from the codes the group that should receive the benefit. With respect to those codes in which a group cannot be identified because the benefit of the codes affects a large and indefinable number

[385] eg, *Prudential Assurance Co Ltd v Ayres* (n 383), in which 'any previous tenant' was seen as sufficient; and *Kharegat v Deloitte* [2004] EWHC 1767, in which 'entire group' was interpreted as conferring a benefit upon several individuals appearing on a separate list. See also on this issue Kornet (2009) 156, who states that 'stevedores, independent contractors' is sufficient to identify the third parties as a group.

[386] Bridge (2001) 87f.

[387] The situation seems comparable to the example provided by Bridge (ibid) 90, who argues that s 1(3) would be applicable if someone purchases a wedding present in a store with the order to the seller to deliver it to a particular person, but that this would not be the case if the wedding present is simply bought 'as a gift'. In the latter case, the impossible identification of the beneficiary on the side of the seller would most likely not result in a right for the party to receive the gift to enforce the contract, if, for instance the gift turns out not to be of satisfactory quality.

of groups, a respective interpretation would only be possible if the requirement in section 1(3) were relaxed to also accept third party rights when the contract does not explicitly specify a group of beneficiaries but when this group can be determined only by way of implication.

3.2.3.1.1.2.2. Rebutting the Presumption

Assuming that there are accordingly constellations in which the codes can be interpreted as a term in the contract that purports to confer a benefit, it still needs to be discussed whether and under which conditions the promisor can rebut the presumption of a third party right. With respect to the corporate codes, this is primarily a question of how to treat disclaimers in the codes.

In general, in the academic literature on the Act, it was held that the presumption is a strong one that puts the party wishing to rebut the presumption in the position of having the 'onus of proof' and having to bring forward evidence that no intention is present.[388] Although the Act refers to the rebuttal in terms of the parties not having the intention to create a third party right, it is clear that this again is a test in which the intention is determined on the basis of what the contract states. Accordingly, as much as setting up the presumption, the rebuttal is an objective test where the words of the contract and, since Lord Hoffmann's re-statement on contract interpretation, also the surrounding circumstances are taken into consideration.[389] The courts so far seem to have developed an approach that renders it difficult for the parties to rebut the presumption. In *Nisshin Shipping*, for instance, it was, explicitly held that it is not sufficient to rebut the presumption by bringing forward that the contract otherwise remains neutral on this issue.[390] This suggests that the presumption for an enforceable third party right can realistically only be rebutted if there is an express term negating the enforcement right or if the solution recognising the third party right would lead to an inconsistency in the contract. In *Mentmore International v Abbey Healthcare*, it was also indicated, although eventually not decisive and therefore eventually not decided upon, that it would not be sufficient that the contract contained a standard clause that the agreement would not have intended to benefit third parties.[391] In addition, it should be noted that the party rebutting the presumption not only needs to prove its lack of intention but also the intention of both parties, because it is stated in the Act that it has to be the intention of both parties not to benefit the third party.[392]

[388] This was the position by Law Commissioner Burrows and it is so far followed in the literature; see, eg, McKendrick (2013) 119; Beale (2012) 1439, para 18-091. But see critically Roe (2000) 889.

[389] Roe (2000) 889f.

[390] *Nisshin Shipping Co Ltd v Cleaves and Co Ltd* [2003] 2 CLC 1097, 1104 (per Colman J).

[391] *Mentmore International v Abbey Healthcare* [2010] EWCA Civ 761 [33], [34]. In this case, it was held, although not finally decided, that a clause at the end of the contract stating that the agreement is not 'intended to benefit or be enforceable by' anyone other than the parties could probably not be sufficient if this latter clause 'appears to be a standard form clause'. For a different position that would allow a standard disclaimer to be sufficient, see Burrows (2000) 545: 'simple standard term … can be included'.

[392] Peel (2011) 685, para 14-093; Beale (2012) 1440, para 18-091.

With respect to the corporate codes, one can accordingly assume that an otherwise neutral contract is not sufficient for the company as a rebuttal of presumption. Moreover, following the considerations in *Mentmore International*, it is also possible that the standard disclaimer in the contract would not suffice in order to rebut the presumption. The situation would then only be different if the contract would contain a disclaimer that the specific term is not enforceable by third parties. Although in relation to the corporate codes the validity of a disclaimer would very much depend on the actual phrasing, it seems likely that the standard disclaimers in contracts would not be sufficient, but that certainly explicit disclaimers in the codes themselves, declaring that no right is intended to be created for a third party, would be capable of rebutting the presumption.[393] This implies that primarily the observed constellations in which the corporate code contains an explicit disclaimer would resist an interpretation as terms that create an enforcement right on the side of the third party, with the result that the obligation to confer a benefit upon a third party would remain a bilateral duty between the contracting parties.

3.2.3.1.2. German Law

In German law, the relativity of contractual obligations also represents a fundamental principle of contract law with the result that, generally, rights and obligations created by contracts are valid between the contracting parties only.[394] However, in spite of this general principle, there are several exceptions, the most notable being the rules laid down in §§ 328ff BGB. It is thus these rules that will be discussed in the following section with the objective of determining whether they could become applicable to the contractually enforceable codes.

3.2.3.1.2.1. Third Party Rights in the BGB

Pursuant to § 328 BGB, it is recognised that parties are capable of creating an agreement in favour of a third party with the result that the third party acquires a right to claim performance of the contract against the contracting party that is under the obligation to confer the benefit upon him. In addition, on the basis of case law, an analogy of the § 328 BGB category was developed in the form of an agreement that has a protective effect vis-a-vis a third party. The difference between these two forms is, first, that the former agreement, colloquially also referred to as the 'genuine' third party contract (*echter Vertrag zugunsten Dritter*), sees the reason for allowing third parties to enforce a right as a matter of giving effect to the intention of the parties; conversely, in the latter constellation, also known as the 'not genuine' third party contract (*unechter Vertrag zugunsten Dritter*), the courts have developed the possibility that a third party could be protected by the contract.

[393] On this issue, see McKendrick (2013) 120: 'parties who wish to exclude the third-party right would be well advised to say so expressly and clearly in their contract'; and Beale (2012) 1440, para 18-091.

[394] See, eg, Palandt-Grüneberg Introduction to § 241, para 3; MüKo-Gottwald § 328, para 1; Erman-Westermann § 328, para 1.

An important difference is that § 328 BGB allows the third party to claim performance of the contract, whereas the latter constellation only allows a third party to claim compensation for losses that have been incurred due to the reliance on the proper performance of the contract. Due to the focus on the potential contractual enforcement of the codes and in line with the analysis of English law, the decision is to focus solely on the qualification of the corporate code as a 'genuine' contract in the following section and leave the possible interpretation of the code as a contract with protective effect to the following chapter, in which the relevance of the codes for extending the scope of liability will be discussed.[395]

3.2.3.1.2.2. Contracts for the Benefit of a Third Party (§ 328 BGB)

In order for parties to create an enforceable right for a third party to claim performance of the contract, it is necessary that the agreement of the contracting parties can be qualified as a contract in favour of third parties. The contract in favour of third parties is not a particular type of contract, but rather represents a specific qualification that can in principle apply to all types of agreements—even binding agreements prior to the conclusion of a contract or contracts with unilateral obligations can represent an agreement in favour of a third party.[396] A qualification of a contract in favour of a third party is first possible when, on the basis of the contractual documents, the parties have expressly agreed to give the third party a right to enforce the benefit. Thus, comparable to the solution presented for English law, pursuant to German law, it is the case that a third party right arises once the contracting parties have explicitly stated such a right in their contract, with the result that contractually binding codes that are explicitly phrased as a financial benefit could generally be capable of being qualified as third party contracts.

In the absence of a term that expressly mentions the benefit for a specified third party, the existence of a third party contract depends on the interpretation of the contract in light of the surrounding circumstances. Hence, the question whether a third party should acquire an enforceable right is in German law determined on the basis of general contextual interpretation of the contract with a view to what the parties have reasonably intended by reaching a specific agreement.[397] In addition to the application of the general rules on contract interpretation, there are also specific interpretative rules for the interpretation of third party agreements in particular. A crucial criterion in order to determine whether a contract represents a contract in favour of a third party is in this regard the 'purpose of the contract' (§ 328 II BGB). Focusing more specifically on this specific criterion of the 'purpose', German courts have developed on a case-by-case basis typical constellations in

[395] See section 4.1.1.2. (p 153), text and accompanying footnotes.

[396] It is, for instance, possible to conclude a pre-contract (*Vorvertrag*) in favour of a third party (Palandt-Grünberg § 328, para 1) or, as is particularly relevant insofar as the publicly declared corporate codes are interpreted as a binding contract, ie, an acknowledgement of a debt, that ought to benefit third parties (§§ 780, 328 BGB).

[397] BGH NJW 1975, 344, 345; NJW 1985, 1457, 1457; Bayer (1995) 131ff; Rösch (2006) 103ff. For the relevance of contextual contract interpretation with respect to corporate codes, see above, section 3.1.3.2.2.2. (p 77) text and accompanying footnotes.

which contracts are deemed to have the purpose to benefit third parties, such as widows' pensions in employee contracts, contracts of parents contracting for medical treatment of their child, savings accounts stipulating the performance to a third party, certain carriage contracts and as 'the paradigm of contracts for the benefit of third parties' insurance contracts.[398] With respect to the corporate codes, one would accordingly need to determine whether the codes were included in the contract with the purpose of benefiting a third party and it is in this context that similar arguments can be brought forward, as have already been discussed with respect to English law. In addition, one can bring forward the argument that, since German law does not have a comparably strong tradition of the relativity of contractual obligations as English law, it seems here considerably easier to justify the existence of a third party right. However, in spite of this broad scope of interpretation, the difficulty in German law lies hidden in the detail. While it is certainly true that there is a wide degree of discretion when attempting to qualify a contract as being in favour of a third party,[399] it is equally true that the courts make use of additional criteria when determining whether the contract has the purpose to give the third party an enforceable right. It is first not sufficient that the contract simply lays down an obligation of one party to confer a benefit on a third party, as such an agreement could also mean that the parties simply wanted to create a benefit without going so far as to give the beneficiary the right to claim performance.[400] Hence, already in the course of interpreting the agreement, it is necessary to distinguish between different types of third party contracts and identify what the parties reasonably intended. Did the parties intend to conclude a genuine contract in favour of a third party with an autonomous right on the side of the third party to claim performance? Or does the agreement suggest that the contract only confers a benefit on a third party with the result that the third party is put in the position of accepting performance but not claiming it? Or is the third party benefit only an incidental purpose, with the result that there is not even an obligation for one of the contracting parties to benefit a third party? As indications of an enforceable right, several criteria play a role, in particular whether performance of the contract should benefit the third party solely or also one of the contracting parties.[401]

Concerning the corporate codes, this would in fact provide an argument in favour of a third party contract, given that the actual improvements specified in the codes are of little use to the contracting parties. Moreover, it also has an influence on whether the contracting party that is the promisee is personally responsible for the third party.[402] Thus, the more remote the promisee and the third party,

[398] For this categorisation with extensive explanations, see Markesinis, Unberath and Johnston (2006) 187ff (quote taken from 194).

[399] Bayer (1995) 134f.

[400] For the category of third party contracts that constitute a contractual obligation to confer a benefit upon a third party, but restrict the enforcement of this obligation to the contracting parties, see, eg, Palandt-Grüneberg, Introduction to § 328, para 1; Prütting/Wegen/Weinrich-Medicus § 328, para 12.

[401] Bayer (1995) 135–36; Rösch (2006) 104ff; Palandt-Grüneberg § 328, para 3; Prütting/Wegen/Weinrich-Medicus § 328, para 13.

[402] Erman-Westermann § 328, para 12. But see critically on this aspect as the sole criterion Bayer (1995) 135.

the less the courts seem to be inclined to interpret a contract as one concluded for the benefit of a third party. This may provide an argument against an interpretation of the code as a term that benefits a third party, given that the affected third parties often represent a large group for which the contracting parties do not owe personal responsibility. In addition, the question whether the party should obtain an enforcement right also depends on whether conferring a benefit was the general purpose of the contractual agreement or was only a secondary purpose or a side-effect of an obligation that ought ultimately to benefit the contracting parties. To provide an illustrative example, a case in which the purpose to benefit the third party was not deemed to be the case was an assurance of a party to pay the study expenses of a student if this declaration was made towards the administration for immigration purposes. In this decision, it was held that the *primary* purpose of the declaration was not to benefit the student, but merely to serve the interests of the public administration of having an assurance. The party benefiting from this declaration could thus not claim the benefit, although the declaration explicitly mentioned that party as a beneficiary of the promised benefits.[403] On the basis of the additional criterion of the third party benefit as having to be the primary purpose, one would need to distinguish more in detail between different aspects that are relevant for the codes. Based on this criterion, the courts could in principle deny a third party right based on the argument that the contracting parties had in the first place the objective of furthering their reputation and not of giving a third party the right to claim performance. The interpretation seems here to depend primarily on the context in which the contract is concluded. In relation to corporate codes that have been included in contracts with the primary objective of improving the situation of employees or local communities, an interpretation as a contract in favour of a third party seems more likely. In particular, with respect to contracts between companies and NGOs, or when socially responsible customers insist on incorporating a corporate code with the objective of improving the situation for particular groups, one could more easily assume that the parties had the intention to benefit the third party.[404] This could thus be a viable option for constellations such as the labour code of conduct that was under dispute in the *University of Wisconsin v Adidas* lawsuit. While in cases of supplier contracts, this interpretation seems equally possible, it could also be the case that, based on the context, the courts would deem the primary purpose behind the code to be the specification of certain ethical standards for the purpose of gaining reputational benefits rather than benefiting third parties. Second, with regard to the latter codes, in which the purpose of benefiting third parties does not suggest itself, the existence of a third party contract in light of the reasonable interest of the contracting parties would depend on whether the code contains improvements that primarily benefit third parties. This criterion seems most likely to be fulfilled specifically in relation to codes on

403 BGH NJW 1991, 2209.

404 See in a similar direction Glinski (2011) 170: contracts with local communities or NGOS, if they are 'designed' as contracts for the benefit of third parties or as contracts with protective effect vis-a-vis third parties.

workplace standards. In case the corporate code contains a specific financial benefit, such as 'payment of legally mandated benefits', an interpretation of the codes as a contract in favour of a third party represents a viable option, considering that the employees as beneficiaries can easily be inferred from the context and such benefits are only conceivable as third party benefits. Finally, insofar as the code obligation benefits the contracting parties as well as a large number of third parties, it could also become relevant how the code is phrased and how large the group of potential beneficiaries could be. Certainly, German law does not contain explicit limitations as to the number of third parties that the contracting parties can make a beneficiary; parties can also make an agreement in favour of not yet existing persons and it is generally sufficient that the third party is identifiable as a person or as a member of a group.[405] Yet, in spite of this generally wide discretion of the parties to create enforcement rights of a large and not yet specified number of third parties, the courts will probably be less prepared to interpret a corporate code as a contract in favour of third parties the less specific the parties have been and the more the risk of third party liability increases for the obliged contracting party.[406] Against this background, it is again useful to distinguish between different constellations. More generally phrased codes, such as 'adhere to fundamental workplace standards', are difficult to interpret as being in favour of third parties. In relation to these generally phrased codes, it might still be possible on the basis of supplementary contract interpretation to determine employees of the company and specified affiliated entities (subsidiaries and suppliers) as a confined group of beneficiaries and consequently interpret such terms as nevertheless conferring a benefit. However, with respect to the obligation in the code to comply with general social and environmental standards where it is already difficult to identify a benefiting group or where the scope of potential beneficiaries seems difficult to oversee for the obliged contracting parties, it seems rather unlikely that courts would be prepared to interpret these codes as third party rights.[407] A possible third party enforcement right could in these cases only be established by means of a statutory reform whereby, for instance, environmental organisations, trade unions or human rights groups are considered to obtain a private right to enforce contractually agreed benefits for public goods.[408]

As a result, in the context of German law, the interpretation of the corporate codes as contracts in favour of third parties remains a viable option even for codes that contain vague phrasing, provided that the general rules on contract interpretation and supplementation render it possible to identify a group of beneficiaries. In this context, it is particularly the main purpose of the contract and several additional criteria, such as the relationship between the contracting parties and the

[405] This is established case law, eg, BGH NJW 1979, 2036 2036; BGH NJW 1995, 2028, 2030; BGH NJW-RR 2008, 683, 684.

[406] Prütting/Wegen/Weinrich-Medicus, para 14; Erman-Westermann § 328, para 6.

[407] See for a similar prediction, but with a view to international principles on contract law, Peterkova (2014a) 18.

[408] See for this suggestion especially Glinski (2011) 173.

third parties and the risk of additional liability, that are important to consider. On the basis of these criteria, it seems accordingly possible to qualify as a contract in favour of third parties corporate codes that do not mention or specify a particular group of beneficiaries, provided that the purpose of the contract clearly signals that this benefit was intended.

Finally, a few words must also be said about the option of the contracting parties to exclude the right for a third party by means of a disclaimer. It seems to be quite clear that, in a similar vein to English law, a clause indicating a lack of intention needs to be taken into consideration in the process of interpreting the contract. A likely result of using such disclaiming language would be an interpretation of the corporate code as a contract that creates an obligation of one party to benefit a third party that, however, remains enforceable by the contracting parties only.

3.2.3.1.3. Interim Conclusion

The previous analysis dealt with the proposal to qualify the corporate code as terms that benefit third parties and, as a result, to give the third party and the contracting party the right to enforce the code by means of claiming performance. The suggestion has been discussed on the basis of the available tools in English and German contract law and the extent to which they recognise relaxations of the general principle of the privity of contractual rights and obligations. In this regard, it has been argued that both jurisdictions generally allow parties to make an agreement that creates an enforcement right of a third party and that these rules are generally prepared to interpret the existence of a third party enforcement right for those codes that either expressly contain a third party right or are very precise as to the benefit that a third party receives. In addition, based on the criterion of the 'purpose', it is generally also possible to interpret corporate codes as creating third party rights when they are more vague in their phrasing. In relation to English law, the limit for an interpretation as a third party benefit was identified in the requirement to mention expressly in the term at least the group that should receive the benefit. Due to the possibility of contextual contract interpretation and supplementation, this aspect is not problematic in the context of German law.[409] With respect to German law, the limit for an interpretation as a third party contract is the requirement to deem the third party benefit as one of the core purposes of the contract. However, since both legal systems generally recognise the right of the contracting parties to exclude the right of a third party to enforce the contract, it is not possible to interpret the codes as creating a third party right once the contracting parties have included a specific disclaimer in the code.

[409] This is also emphasised as a general difference between the English and German conception of contractual third party rights; see generally on this aspect Müller (2003) 153, who emphasises that this requirement makes the scope of third party rights in English law considerably narrower compared to other jurisdictions and the Principles of European Contract Law. See also Rösch (2006) 125.

3.2.3.2. *Applicable Remedies for Contracts with Third Party Benefits*

In analysing the possible enforcement of the corporate code that derives from this interpretation, based on the results above, it is necessary to distinguish between two constellations.

First, to the extent that the corporate codes fulfil all requirements of the Contracts (Rights of Third Parties) Act or § 328 BGB and do not contain a disclaimer, the rules on third party rights declare that the contractual term can be enforced not only by the contracting parties, but also directly by the beneficiaries. With respect to English law, section 1(5) of the Contracts (Rights of Third Parties) Act 1999 in this regard explicitly states that 'there shall be available to the third party any remedy that would have been available to him in an action for breach of contract if he had been a party to the contract'. Thus, as Andrews pointedly puts it, 'the Act creates a direct obligation, tie or vinculum iuris, between the promisor and the third party'.[410] This means that the third party can claim the damages as to his expectation interests or, at the discretion of the court and if not precluded on equitable grounds, also specific performance.[411] The third party is precluded from self-help remedies, such as termination of the contract[412] and, in the course of enforcement, any exemptions or restrictions apply to him in the same way as they would apply to the promisee.[413] In addition, section 1(4) also states that the promisee, eg, the other contracting party, retains the right to enforce the contract. Hence, both the promisee and the third party obtain the right to enforce the contract. With respect to German law, § 328 BGB states explicitly that the contract in favour of a third party has the result that the third party gains an autonomous right to claim performance, although the courts have made clear that he does not become party to the contract.[414] Due to the fact that German law determines specific performance as the first remedy in case of a breach of contract, it is also this remedy that is available to the third party. With respect to other remedies, such as termination or damages, the situation is more complex and depends inter alia upon whether the remedy has consequences for the bilateral contract or whether it only affects the third party.[415] It is accepted, however, that rights that only affect the third party, such as damages for late delivery or damages related to the integrity interest, can be claimed.[416] In the context of the corporate codes, this has the result that the benefits specifically mentioned in the codes could be claimed directly by the third party and, moreover, that this very third party could seek redress for non-compliance by means of invoking the remedies that the respective legal system has available for breach

[410] Andrews (2001) 359.
[411] ibid 361.
[412] Beatson, Burrows and Cartwright (2010) 631.
[413] Contracts (Rights of Third Parties) Act 1999, s 3. See generally and extensively on the different constellations involving defences Beale (2012) 1444, para 18-095.
[414] BGH NJW 1970, 2157, 2157; BGH NJW-RR 1993, 770, 771; Palandt-Grüneberg § 328, para 5.
[415] Rösch (2006) 181f.
[416] Bayer (1995) 342; Rösch (2006) 182; Palandt-Grüneberg § 328, para 5. The situation is more complex with damages instead of performance, termination or rescission. For an extensive overview of the academic debate on this issue, see generally Bayer (1995) 339ff.

of contract. Employees of suppliers could, for instance, not only claim damages for losses incurred in relying on the fact that the obliged contracting party would adhere to the code; it would equally be possible to claim payment of the required wages or even seek an injunction against an employer discriminating or requiring specific performance with regard to health and safety standards.

Second, in constellations in which the interpretation of the codes suggests that they create a benefit for a third party, but where the parties have excluded the default consequence of an enforcement right for the beneficiary by means of a disclaimer, the corporate code could still qualify as a contractual obligation to confer a benefit upon a third party. However, in this constellation, the enforcement remains a sole entitlement on the side of the innocent contracting party that could remedy a breach of the code by means of invoking the general remedies available for breach of contract. When it comes to third party benefits, the main remedy is the claim for performance in the form of requiring the obligated party to confer the promised benefit. This is generally the main remedy under German law for breach of contract. Yet, it is also in these types of contracts that English courts have in the past exceptionally deemed specific performance as the appropriate remedy based on the consideration that the damages for the breach of contract were nominal and that only this remedy would do justice in these cases.[417]

3.2.3.3. Conclusion: Corporate Codes and Contractual Third Party Rights

Analysing the corporate codes in light of the rules on third party rights in contract has revealed that a respective interpretation of the corporate codes is in principle a viable option. The analysis above suggests that the interpretation is particularly suitable if the corporate codes explicitly name the beneficiaries and specify the benefit. In relation to those codes that are broader in their phrasing, the interpretation as a third party right depends particularly on whether the group of beneficiaries is expressly named (the English approach) or if, on the basis of a contextual contract interpretation and supplementation, the intention to benefit a third party can be identified as the main purpose underlying the contract (the German approach). On this basis, an interpretation of the codes was considered suitable for codes that specify particular benefits for employees. Possibly, the interpretation of codes as establishing third party rights could also be realised for generally phrased codes that make adherence to fundamental workplace standards a contractual obligation. The same applies to codes on environmental or human rights standards insofar as they specify a particular group as beneficiaries, such as neighbours of factories in a particular distance or members of a defined local community. However, insofar as the codes remain more abstract obligations in this area, an interpretation of the codes on the basis of third party rights seems to be more difficult. To the extent that the purpose of creating a benefit for a third party can be derived from the phrasing or the surrounding circumstances, the corporate codes would, pursuant to the rules on third party rights in contracts, qualify as a contractual obligation to confer the benefit upon these third parties, as agreed upon by the contract that is

[417] See especially *Beswick v Beswick* (n 367) 89 (per Lord Pearce).

enforceable not only by the innocent contracting party but also by the beneficiaries themselves. That being said, as parties are capable of opting out of these rules in the form of excluding the third party right, it is also possible that, with respect to contracts that include disclaimers as to third party rights, the corporate codes only remain a bilateral obligation to confer a benefit upon a third party that can consequently only be enforced by the contracting parties.

3.2.4. Corporate Codes as Regulatory Contracts

Although it is fair to say that the two qualifications of corporate codes in contracts presented so far represent the core suggestions in the debate, it should be noted that there are also authors who deviate from both of these approaches and indicate a preference for an entirely different qualification and enforcement. These proposals all seem to have in mind slightly diverging conceptualisations, but what they have in common is, first, that they understand the corporate codes as *novel* terms in contracts that cannot be fully captured with the help of the general default rules on contract interpretation and the existing remedies. Second, the contributions also have in common that they describe these codes as provisions that have in the first place a regulatory function.[418] This regulatory character cannot be fully grasped with the orthodox rules of contract law due to the fact that these regulatory provisions follow a logic that differs quite significantly from the logic of contractual exchange.[419] Yet, although the regulatory character of the codes represents a common point of departure, the contributions point in different directions as far as the appropriate rules are concerned that should be applicable to specify the code obligation and remedies.

One core proposal in this context is to understand the corporate codes as terms that render the self-regulatory corporate policy as such part of the contract. More precisely, corporate codes constitute a novel contractual duty, the exact content of which is specified in the first place by the self-regulatory rules without the use of default rules.[420] A main consequence of this understanding is to understand the breach of a contractually incorporated code as having multiple legal effects. Breaching, for instance, a contractually included labour code of conduct can be simultaneously qualified as a breach of the commercial contract, the employment contract, the self-regulatory code of conduct of the company, and possibly also an existing certification contract with a multi-stakeholder initiative.[421] Hence,

[418] Coleman (2009) 631 ('agreement not to violate labor rights'); Sobczak (2006) 169 ('codes of conduct, i.e. norms that belong to consumer law, regulate labour relations within supply chain that are formally excluded from the scope of labour and employment law') and passim; Backer (2008) 508ff (at 509: 'self-referencing regulatory communities'); Cafaggi (2013) 1558ff (at 1558f: 'a growing regulatory section'); Verbruggen (2014b) 82f ('such standards go beyond regulating simple safety and quality attributes of the exchanged commodity only; they also concern matters that have traditionally been associated with public policy').

[419] Backer (2008) 509ff; Cafaggi (2013) 1559 and passim.

[420] See generally on this possibility Backer (2008); Cafaggi (2013).

[421] Cafaggi (2013) 1557.

the contractually enforceable corporate code results in several duties for which several remedial regimes are available which are not necessarily interlinked. The innocent party can invoke the remedy specified in the self-regulatory code, the remedy generally available pursuant to contract law for breach of contract or, possibly, remedies specified in the certification contract.[422] To that end, the remedies specified in the corporate policy, the private law remedies for breach of contract and the remedies specified in a certification contract are viewed as complementary ways of enforcing the regulatory provision in the contract.[423] Another contribution discusses the potential of qualifying the corporate codes as provisions that attempt to regulate labour relations.[424] Based on this understanding, it is conceivable that the corporate codes could be interpreted by means of applying the rules on employment and labour law when determining the content and enforcement of the codes.[425] A slightly different suggestion is to interpret contractual agreements on the improvement of labour standards with the help of public codes of conduct, in particular the ILO conventions, as the applicable rules that determine content and remedies.[426]

It is clear that these proposals remain in their current form rather general ideas that offer a different perspective on the corporate codes in contracts; conversely, they should not be read as concrete proposals for private law on how to interpret and enforce the corporate codes in contracts in light of this regulatory dimension. For the time being, therefore, it has to suffice to interpret these suggestions as introducing a different, namely regulatory, understanding of the codes that could have the result that not only are the rules that regulate contracts in general applicable but so too are the rules that are capable of specifying more concretely this regulatory objective, eg, the international or national rules on labour or environmental law or the content and remedies in the self-regulatory policies. It is this novel approach to viewing the corporate codes as a regulatory duty akin to state regulation that will be relied upon in the theoretical analysis and taken further.

3.2.5. Conclusion

To sum up, in the previous section, an attempt was made to qualify the corporate codes in terms of contractual obligations and identify how they can be enforced accordingly. In so doing, three different perspectives were offered that each focus on a different element of the codes. First, the focus was placed on the potential

[422] ibid 1611ff.

[423] ibid 1589, 1613, 1615.

[424] Sobczak (2006).

[425] Indicated in ibid 175: 'by broadening the sphere of application of labour law norms as well as the circle of people authorised to take collective actions, the use of consumer law tools to regulate labour relations within supply chains constitutes an opportunity for labour lawyers'.

[426] Coleman (2009) 632: 'courts can turn to the ILO's Conventions and Recommendations and the Committee on Freedom of Association to clarify the intent of the parties and the material terms of the contract'.

influence of the corporate code on the specification and quality of the goods that are agreed upon in a sales contract, with the result that the enforcement would be specified by the sales law remedies. Second, based on an emphasis of the corporate codes as obligations that are included not merely for the benefit of the contracting parties, but rather with the objective of improving the situation for parties external to the contract, it was discussed whether it was equally possible to qualify the codes as obligations of the contracting parties to directly benefit these third parties that could be enforced by the contracting parties and the beneficiaries. Provided that the corporate codes are sufficiently specific in terms of the actual benefit and the group that ought to receive the benefit, it was argued that such an interpretation is in principle possible, although any disclaimer inserted into the code as to the exclusion of a third party right would, pursuant to the current rules on third party rights, have the result that the duty to confer a benefit would remain bilateral. Finally, it was briefly presented that there are also contributions in the debate that propose an interpretation of the corporate codes as terms that introduce a regulatory dimension in contracts that instead requires an interpretation in light of the rules that specify this regulatory objective, eg, the self-regulatory corporate policies, the rules on labour law or the international public codes of conduct.

Against the background of these different available options, the following analysis will have to focus particularly on what option is to be preferred when suggesting a strategy for private law enforcement of the corporate code. Bearing in mind that the presented options each depart from a different understanding of the codes, the appropriate strategy depends in the first place on the understanding of the character of the codes and it is this element that the following analysis will focus on more in detail.

3.3. OVERALL CONCLUSION: CORPORATE CODES UNDER CONTRACT LAW

In this chapter, the corporate codes were analysed from the perspective of contract law with the objective of identifying whether contract law is generally prepared to enforce the corporate codes and, in the course of the analysis, two main aspects were identified that require further scrutiny.

3.3.1. The Status of Publicly Declared Codes

While contract law is generally prepared to enforce the corporate codes in constellations in which companies explicitly include them in contracts or in the ancillary documents, the situation is less clear if the corporate codes remain solely declarations to the public. From the perspective of contract law, there are several options available on how to treat the publicly declared corporate codes. Contract law could, as was the case in the *Wal-Mart* case, simply ignore these published declarations based on the understanding that it is not the unilateral self-commitment, but solely the binding and written contract that is enforceable.[427] However, it was equally considered an option to interpret the corporate codes as pre-contractual statements that, due to their influence on the contracting process and the eventual agreement, could be read into the contract either by a broad interpretation of the statutory provision on pre-contractual statements in (consumer) sales contracts[428] or with the help of the general rules on contract interpretation and supplementation.[429] In addition, one could also conceive of an interpretation of these publicly declared corporate codes as commitments of companies that have an autonomous binding effect. An interpretation of public declarations as unilateral contracts was discussed, although the analysis has shown that, pursuant to the current rules on contract formation, this option remains difficult to realise due to a general scepticism against the binding character of commitments of companies to comply with a corporate policy, the general presumption in contract law against an intention to be bound in public statements and the focus of contract law on the enforcement of reciprocal and not merely unilateral agreements.[430] As an alternative, it was discussed whether the codes could be enforceable as unilateral promises towards those that reasonably rely on them. While it has been argued that such a reliance-based enforcement of promises is not unknown in contract law, it was shown that the current scope of these exceptions, eg, equitable estoppel in English law and the statutory provisions on binding promises in German law, remains too narrow for capturing the codes, with the result that this option could only be invoked if the scope of these exceptions were broadened.[431]

In the course of discussing how the corporate codes ought to be treated from the perspective of private law, the focus will consequently be put precisely on the character of these publicly declared corporate codes and the underlying question whether or not they ought to be enforceable by contract law.

3.3.2. The Code Obligation and Applicable Remedies

In addition to this specific focus on the enforcement of corporate codes that are publicly declared, there are also several options concerning the rules that should apply when qualifying the exact code obligation and determining the applicable remedies. First, the courts could rely on the default rules on sales contracts and apply sales law remedies provided they consider the main contribution of the codes in contracts as describing the product, influencing the quality standard of the products or indicating a particular purpose for which the goods are used.[432] Second, one could consider linking the corporate codes to the rules in contract law

[427] See the arguments by the court discussed above, section 3.1.3.1. (p 59), text and accompanying footnotes.
[428] See the arguments discussed above, section 3.1.3.2.1. (p 64), text and accompanying footnotes.
[429] See the arguments discussed above, section 3.1.3.2.2. (p 67), text and accompanying footnotes.
[430] See the conclusion above, section 3.1.4.1.3. (p 97).
[431] See the conclusion above, section 3.1.4.2.3. (p 106).
[432] See the arguments discussed above, section 3.2.2.1. (p 112), text and accompanying footnotes.

that deal with contractual third party benefits and third party rights.[433] Finally, one could also interpret corporate codes as separate sections in contracts that introduce a novel regulatory dimension in contracts, which would require developing specific rules that apply when qualifying the code obligation and the applicable remedial scheme for breaches.[434]

In light of these available options and the different perspectives that were offered as to the contractual interpretation of the codes, the second topic for further analysis is a closer investigation into the actual function of the codes in contracts and the rules that ought to be applicable for determining the code obligation and the remedial scheme that is applicable for breaches of the code.

[433] See the arguments discussed above, section 3.2.3.1. (p 129), text and accompanying footnotes.

[434] See the arguments discussed above, section 3.2.4. (p 144), text and accompanying footnotes.

4

Liability for Breaching Corporate Codes

The Role of National Civil Liability Rules

> Characteristics that make the field of private law very suitable ... as an instrument for global business regulation include ... its flexibility, its open norms and the fact that its reflexive nature leaves a good deal of room to its regulatory addressees to develop their own standards and best practice.[1]

PRIVATE LAW IS prepared not only to enforce the agreements and promises of private actors, but also to consider private standards and established practices in the course of specifying what conduct would qualify as legally wrong and thus could give rise to liability. This means that the legal effects of corporate codes are not exhausted by their potential enforcement as legal obligations. Corporate codes could also become relevant as standards that influence what is legally expected from a company that holds itself out to comply with a code. From this perspective, corporate codes could determine what a committing company can be held liable for in case it does not live up to this standard and causes harm to others. In order to specify the actual legal effects of corporate codes on the scope of liability, a more detailed analysis is required of how contractual agreements and public declarations are actually capable of influencing the scope of legal liability. To that end, the analysis will, comparable to the discussion on the contractual enforcement of corporate code, assess the possible links between contractually incorporated and publicly declared corporate codes and the rules on non-contractual liability (section 4.1) and, on this basis, define what specific legal obligation the code could give rise to and how a breach can be remedied (section 4.2).

4.1. THE INFLUENCE OF CORPORATE CODES ON LEGAL LIABILITY

With regard to the relevance of the corporate codes for determining the scope of liability, it has to be clear right from the start that tort law already specifies as a legally wrongful act the active infringement of specific rights of another person if this causes damage. This merely implies that the breach of specific aspects that are laid down in a corporate code can in part already amount to a wrongful act even

[1] Enneking (2012) 522.

if the wrongfully acting company does not have a corporate code in place. This applies to, for instance, the prohibition of forced labour or adherence to health and safety standards. A company that forces people to work, that provides an unsafe workplace for its employees or that pollutes the land of another person by factory emissions can, in accordance with the general rules on tort liability or any specific statutory liability, already be liable to compensate the victims regardless of whether a code has been adopted and made publicly available. However, in addition, there are also rules in private law that broaden the scope of liability for parties that conclude a particular contractual agreement and for constellations in which a party makes a (public) declaration.

4.1.1. Contractually Enforceable Corporate Codes

It has already been observed in the previous chapter that corporate codes can be enforced if they are included in contractual agreements. This section will now focus on the question of whether this contractually included code of conduct is also capable of resulting in the liability of the party that is contractually obliged to comply with the corporate code when the contractual obligation is not performed at all or not properly and a third party is detrimentally affected. The potential influence of a contractually included code on the scope of liability towards third parties seems, so far, to be still underexplored in the debate. It is merely mentioned occasionally as a side aspect in a few contributions.[2] Yet, in the lawsuit between the University of Wisconsin and Adidas, this proposal could actually become practically relevant. So far, the parties in this particular lawsuit focused on the question of whether the code of conduct as incorporated into the contract could be interpreted as a clear contractual obligation of the company to pay legally mandated benefits to their suppliers' employees. Due to the phrasing and the admissible contextual background, it is very possible that a third party right would be difficult to extract from the code and the perspective would need to be taken that the code obligation had been intended to create bilateral obligations only. This, however, does not mean that the ultimate beneficiaries would be left without any remedy. On the contrary, one could argue that the incorporation of a labour code of conduct into a contract has the result that the benefiting workers become

[2] Glinski (2011) 172f; Cafaggi (2013) 1594. A suggestion that is presumably functionally equivalent appears in the analysis of Heijden (2011b) 174ff. In her analysis of the legal effects of corporate codes under Dutch private law, she analyses not only whether contractually incorporated codes could result in a contractual third party right in the form of an explicit clause, but also whether a contract with a corporate code could have an effect on third parties, which could be relevant for the Dutch contract law concept of *derdenwerking* and the tort law rules on negligence. The idea of third party protection by contract also appears in the arguments of the claimants in the *Doe v Wal-Mart* case in relation to the theory of third party beneficiary negligence. The court, however, rejected this argument because, in this contract, it was the supplier and not Wal-Mart that was under an obligation to comply with the code: *Jane Doe and others v Wal-Mart Stores* 572 F 3d 677, 684. Finally, one can also refer to the analysis of Osieka (2014) 165ff, who discusses the German contract with protective effect towards third parties as a potentially viable interpretation for transnational supplier contracts (even regardless of whether a corporate code has been incorporated) at least insofar as the protection of employees of suppliers is concerned.

at least incidental beneficiaries of the codes that are affected by the performance of this contractual obligation. Incidental beneficiaries do not obtain rights to enforce the contract, but it is possible that a duty of care exists on the side of the contracting party not to harm them when performing the obligations under the contract. According to this understanding, a breach of the contractually incorporated corporate code then represents a breach of contract that can be remedied by the direct contractual partner. Yet, in addition, it also amounts to a breach of this specific duty of care owed to beneficiaries that, in relying on the proper performance of the contractual obligations, suffered losses.[3] In other words, this suggestion aims at broadening the scope of liability of a party towards detrimentally affected third parties for losses that are caused by an incorrect performance of the contractual obligations.

In German law, such constellations are generally discussed as contracts with protective effect towards third parties (*Vertrag mit Schutzwirkung zugunsten Dritter*). In English law, the equivalent[4] doctrine that needs to be consulted is the specific refinement of the tort of negligence that the House of Lords established for constellations in which a negligently performed contract detrimentally affects a third party and where, due to the privity of contract, the third party would otherwise be left unjustly without remedy.[5]

4.1.1.1. English Law: Negligent Performance of a Service

Pursuant to English law, it is the general rule that a party can be held liable outside the boundaries of a valid contract primarily for committing a tort that is specified either by statute or by common law. In this regard, the broadest common law tort is the tort of negligence, as established in the famous case of *Donoghue v Stevenson*.[6] The tort of negligence is a common law cause of action to remedy breaches of a duty of care that the defendant owes to a claimant when he has caused the kind of damage that is recognised by English law. In the context of further refining the tort of negligence and spelling out its conditions for various constellations, the most important requirement in order to establish liability *in principle* in a given type of situation has proven to be the existence of a duty of care.[7] The conditions of the

[3] In the lawsuit *University of Wisconsin v Adidas*, such an interpretation could have the result that Adidas, even if not contractually obliged to pay directly the benefits to employees of its suppliers, could still be obliged to compensate them. This would become possible if the company had performed its bilateral contractual obligations (that had protective effect) negligently by failing to ensure that its supplier would adhere to fundamental labour standards and thereby caused harm to employees who continued working and suffered loss due to the insolvency of their employer.

[4] With respect to this particular concept, the respective development in the tort of negligence can quite uncontroversially be defined as the equivalent, given that the House of Lords explicitly relied on the German concept of contracts with protective effect when establishing this particular category of a duty of care; see *White v Jones* [1995] 2 AC 207, 262 (per Lord Goff). Moreover, it seems to be quite uncontroversial that, even after the statutory reform in 1999, such a constellation would not fall within the ambit of the Contract (Rights of Third Parties) Act 1999; see only Deakin, Johnston and Markesinis (2007) 23.

[5] *Ross v Caunters* [1980] Ch 297; *Henderson v Merrett Syndicates Ltd* [1995] 2 AC 145; *White v Jones* (n 4).

[6] *Donoghue v Stevenson* [1932] AC 562.

[7] Deakin, Johnston and Markesinis (2007) 102.

duty of care are, in a premature form, already spelled out in *Donoghue v Stevenson* as the so-called neighbour principle[8] and were further developed over time. In *Caparo plc v Dickman*, it was established that the existence of a duty of care in English law is generally determined on the basis of the three-stage test. A duty of care exists when: first, it is foreseeable for the defendant that claimant would suffer harm; second, a relationship of 'proximity' between claimant and defendant exists; and, third, it is 'fair, just and reasonable' to impose a duty.[9] Whether such a situation of 'proximity', also described as a 'pre-tort relationship' between the claimant and the defendant,[10] is recognised by the courts depends particularly on the facts in a given case. In this regard, in recent decisions it was established as a rule that a duty of care exists between a party to a contract and a third party if the third party is typically affected by the performance of the contract and it is foreseeable for the contracting party that the third party could suffer loss. Two of the landmark cases that have established this rule deal specifically with the contract to set up a will.[11] On the basis of this constellation, it was decided that the contractual obligation to set up a will remains bilateral with only the contracting parties as the direct beneficiaries. However, the party obliged to set up the will and those eventually benefiting from this will are in proximity because the third parties are closely affected by the contractual performance, which was also foreseeable for the defendant.[12] In discussing whether it would be fair, just and reasonable to establish a duty, several reasons were brought forward, the most important being the famous statement of Lord Goff, who argued that establishing a duty of care follows the 'impulse to do practical justice',[13] not to leave the party that suffers ultimately and in major parts from the defective contract performance without compensation. As a result, when determining whether a contractually incorporated code could establish liability for negligence in principle, it is relevant to focus on whether the performance of this contractual obligation typically affects third parties and is foreseeable for the company, and whether it is fair, just and reasonable to establish this duty.

When discussing the first condition of whether the contractual obligation established by a contractually included code typically affects third parties, the various suggested qualifications of the corporate code obligation in contracts would need to be taken into consideration. To start with the easy constellation, it seems quite obvious to declare a corporate code as typically affecting the beneficiaries if an interpretation is preferred that views the code as a term that confers a direct benefit on a third party. In relation to this interpretation, the application of the tort of negligence would merely have the result that the third party would obtain

[8] Lord Atkin in *Donoghue v Stevenson* [1932] AC 562, 580: 'You must take reasonable care to avoid acts or omissions which you can reasonably foresee would be likely to injure your neighbour. Who, then, in law is my neighbour? The answer seems to be—persons who are so closely and directly affected by my act that I ought reasonably to have them in contemplation as being so affected when I am directing my mind to the acts or omissions which are called in question.'

[9] *Caparo Industries v Dickman* [1990] 2 AC 605, 617f.

[10] Deakin, Johnston and Markesinis (2007) 113.

[11] *Ross v Caunters* (n 5); *White v Jones* (n 4).

[12] *White v Jones* (n 4) 247.

[13] ibid 259ff.

an additional remedy to claim compensation next to its contractual remedies to enforce the contract. The situation is slightly more complex if the code is deemed to be part of the sales law obligation. With respect to this interpretation, the obligation to manufacture and deliver a product with certain specifications and a particular quality incidentally affects at least the third parties that are involved in the manufacturing process. As support for this, one can refer to the fact that, pursuant to this interpretation, the codes represent an agreement on the specific good manufacturing practice. It is by means of extending the obligation to deliver a product to the specific way of manufacturing that this obligation becomes an incidental benefit for those affected by the manufacturing of the goods. Finally, to the extent that the corporate codes are interpreted as a contractual obligation to regulate, the ultimate beneficiaries of the codes could become incidental beneficiaries as the explicit and immediately affected objects of this regulatory undertaking.[14] Thus, with respect to all potential qualifications of the codes in contracts, one can identify an immediate link between the respective code obligation and the code beneficiaries, and thus argue that there is proximity between the party that is obliged to comply with the code and the third party, and that the defective performance of the code obligation also typically affects the code beneficiaries.

With regard to the requirement of the foreseeability of this extended scope of liability, a strong argument in favour of foreseeability is the fact that the parties have also included the code obligation with the intention of improving the situation for parties outside the contract. Against this background, they must also foresee that external parties would rely on it. This leaves the question of whether a duty of care exists with regard to the criterion of whether it would be fair, just and reasonable to impose a duty of care in this particular constellation. It is here that additional normative criteria would need to be brought forward that support why, in the particular constellation of the contractually included codes, it is justified to impose a duty of care on the contracting parties that are obliged to comply with the corporate code towards detrimentally affected third parties.

4.1.1.2. German Law: Contracts with Protective Effect Towards Third Parties

With regard to German law, the arguments that can be brought forward in favour of an interpretation of contractually incorporated corporate codes as contracts with protective effect towards third parties are quite similar, although they have to be related to other criteria. In general, the contract with protective effect is a concept developed on the basis of case law. It effectively broadens the scope of liability to oblige a contracting party not only towards its immediate contractual partner, but also towards a third party to the extent that the defective performance of the contract amounts to a breach of a duty of care (§ 241 II BGB). Effectively, the contract with protective effect towards third parties represents a private law doctrine at the intersection of contract and tort liability. Although initially developed by

[14] For this observation, see pointedly Backer (2008) 518: 'the people actually affected … are passive participants, the objects rather than subjects of this system'.

the courts as an analogy to § 328 BGB for contracts in which the parties implicitly agreed to protect third parties,[15] it has become a common understanding in the scholarly literature to treat it as an exception of tort liability where a duty of care is imposed on one of the contracting parties towards the third party.[16] The following considerations will be based on the latter understanding and thus will not merely discuss whether the phrasing of corporate codes or the intention of the parties suggest an interpretation as an agreement to protect third parties. Instead, the focus will be placed on whether the corporate codes could qualify as contractual agreements for which the criteria developed by the courts would apply and thus result in legal liability towards third parties.[17]

As regards the conditions for a contract to have protective effect, first, comparable to English law, it is required that the third party is in proximity to the contractual performance (*Vertragsnähe*) and that the liability is foreseeable for the debtor. The criterion of proximity is fulfilled if the main contractual performance is either intended to benefit or mainly affects the third party.[18] In this context, one can refer to the arguments already presented in the context of English law. In short, in relation to contractually incorporated codes, the ultimate beneficiaries are those primarily affected by the performance either as direct third party beneficiaries, as the object of the agreement on ethical manufacturing practices or as the object of the agreed regulatory undertaking. In addition, German law requires that for a contract with protective effect, the extended risk of liability is foreseeable for the debtor.[19] With respect to this criterion, one can, as in English law, argue that the corporate code has been intentionally included in the contract in order to improve the situation for particular beneficiaries, which renders it foreseeable to the obliged contracting party that the third party is affected by improper performance of the code obligation and would rely on this. In this context, it can also be mentioned that German courts have accepted foreseeability even if the exact number and identity of protected third parties is unknown to the obliged contracting party.[20]

The most difficult requirement to establish a contract with protective effect is represented by the reasonable interest of the contracting parties to include the third party in the protective scope of the contract. This requirement is, as such, already controversially discussed and it is so far merely specified in relation to two

[15] See, eg, BGHZ 9, 316, 318; 24, 325, 327; BGHZ 69, 82, 86; BGH NJW 1971, 1931, 1931f. This position is affirmed in the literature, eg, Palandt-Grüneberg § 328, para 14; Soergel-Hadding, Annex § 328, para 6.

[16] See fundamentally Larenz (1956) 1194; and Bar (1980) 314. From the recent literature with further references to the different positions, see Zenner (2009) 1030, 1033f.

[17] Following the understanding of Zenner (2009) 1033f, one can use the concept of the contract with protective effects in two different ways. It could be applied when an agreement contains a clause on third party protection and it is also applicable when seeking to impose liability on the contracting parties towards third parties if normative reasons, such as good faith, so require. It is then the latter view on this concept that will be employed.

[18] eg, BGHZ 70, 329, 393; BGH NJW 1968, 885, 887; BGH NJW 2004, 3035, 3037; Palandt-Grüneberg § 328, para 17; MüKo-Gottwald § 328, para 178 ('drittbestimmte Hauptleistungspflichten … bei dem der Schaden aus der Pflichtverletzung erkennbar gerade dem Dritten droh[t]').

[19] MüKo-Gottwald § 328, para 184; Soergel-Hadding Annex § 328, para 17. Erman-Westermann § 328, para 15.

[20] BGH NJW 1995, 392, 392; NJW 2004, 3035, 3038.

different typical constellations in which it is considered reasonable that the contracting parties would have wanted the third party to be protected. From its origin, the contract with protective effect towards third parties was primarily developed for constellations in which a third party is likely to suffer damages to its bodily integrity or property in the same way as the contracting parties and in which one of the contracting parties, due to a statutory duty, has an interest that the third party's integrity is protected ('Wohl und Wehe').[21] The second—in this context more relevant—constellation covers contracts in which, despite the presence of contradicting interests of the third party and the contracting parties, the interest to include the third party in the protective scope follows from the content of the contractual performance.[22] Yet, although this required 'interest' has been established for these two typical constellations, it is recognised that the decision whether it has been in the interests of the contracting parties has to be discussed for every constellation separately.[23] In discussing this latter constellation, the scholarly literature has frequently emphasised that it is not only the presumed interests of the contracting parties that are relevant when determining whether a protective effect was reasonable, but also normative criteria, for instance, the interest of the public in the proper functioning of standardised processes that consumers typically rely on[24] market-relevant criteria[25] or the protection of independent expertise.[26] Thus, comparable to the discussion in English law on whether it would be fair, just and reasonable to establish a duty of care, the core question when interpreting a contractually incorporated corporate code as having protective effect towards the beneficiaries remains whether comparable normative reasons can be brought forward as to why a duty of care of the party would need to be established.

4.1.1.3. Interim Conclusion

When it comes to the options of broadening the scope of liability in relation to codes that are included in contracts, it could be a possibility to interpret these codes as contracts that establish a duty of care towards the beneficiaries. This conclusion has relied primarily on the argument that, first, the corporate code obliga-

[21] Established in BGHZ 51, 91, 96. See also on this category Palandt-Grüneberg § 328, para 17a; MüKo-Gottwald § 328, para 179; Soergel-Hadding Annex § 328, para 15.

[22] The core constellations decided by the courts are contracts that constitute an obligation to provide expertise that is subsequently used in the context of other contractual negotiations, eg, BGHZ 127, 378; 159, 1, 5; 167, 155.

[23] MüKo-Gottwald § 328, para 181 ('Interessenbewertung im Einzelfall'); Soergel-Hadding, Annex § 328, para 15; Grundmann and Renner (2013) 382 ('Das Kriterium der Gläubigernähe ist ... konturlos geworden und durch einzelfallbezogene Interessenbewertung ersetzt worden').

[24] See the previous case law of the Federal Court of Justice on inter-banking agreements. The reason for an interpretation of these agreements as contracts with protective effects towards consumers was justified by the reasonable reliance of the public on the proper functioning of such standardised mass transfer systems, eg, BGH NJW 1977, 1916, 1916; NJW 1986, 249, 250; NJW-RR 1988, 559, 560; OLG Düsseldorf NJW 1977, 1403, 1404. Recently, however, the Federal High Court of Justice changed its position; see BGH NJW 2008, 2245, 2247f: 'Der Charakter des bargeldlosen Zahlungsverkehrs als einheitlich praktiziertes Massengeschäft ist entgegen der bisherigen höchstrichterlichen Rechtsprechung nicht geeignet, den personenrechtlichen Einschlag als Abgrenzungskriterium zu ersetzen.'

[25] Grundmann and Renner (2013) 383.

[26] Teubner (2003).

tion, regardless of how it is eventually qualified as a contractual obligation, mainly affects the code beneficiaries and that, second, the extended risk of liability is foreseeable for the party. What has been left open is whether the required normative reasons for extending the scope of liability would also be fulfilled. The normative question of whether it is eventually justified and desirable to extend the scope of liability for contractually incorporated codes will be focused upon in more detail in the theoretical analysis.

4.1.2. Publicly Declared Corporate Codes

In addition to this possible influence of a contractually incorporated corporate code on the scope of liability, there are also categories in the rules concerning legal liability where statements play a role and, consequently, publicly declared corporate codes possibly also play a role. In fact, in the *Wal-Mart* case, the claimants did not only rely on a contractual interpretation of the codes; they also put forward arguments as to why the publishing company would be liable in tort. Effectively, it was brought forward that Wal-Mart was liable for the violations of workplace standards, even if the supplier directly committed the said violations, because the company was under a duty of care to prevent harm to the parties that benefited from the code. In seeking to justify this duty of care on the side of the company, there were two different elements that played a role. First, an attempt was made to establish a duty of care based on the fact that the company effectively retained control over suppliers' working conditions, which, however, was dismissed by the court on the grounds that the company only exercised 'minimal or no control over the day-to-day work'.[27] Considering the difficulty of using publicly declared corporate codes as evidence for such an extensive control of one company over another,[28] this argument will not be dealt with in depth. Second, claimants presented an alternative theory that seems to be worth considering for the purposes of this study. In arguing for negligence on the side of Wal-Mart, the claimants presented to the court the fact that Wal-Mart voluntarily attempted to protect the claimants by means of committing itself to improving working conditions, actually conducted audits and, furthermore, that the beneficiaries suffered harm having relied on the commitment and the voluntary behaviour.[29] Hence, the argument in favour of liability targeted the voluntary commitment of the company to improve the working conditions and the apparent behaviour to fulfil this commitment, and sought to interpret both as behaviour that could in principle

[27] *Jane Doe and others v Wal-Mart Stores* (n 2) 684. Similar attempts to establish liability of a company on the grounds of the criterion of retention of control can be found in the general literature on parent company liability and the liability of companies in supplier relations; see, eg Glinski (2011) 343ff; Saage-Maaß (2011) 13ff.

[28] See section 3.1.3.1 (p 59), text and accompanying footnotes. A similar position is taken by Phillips and Lim (2009) 367, who consider (based on empirical evidence) that the current efforts undertaken by Western buyers to improve social and environmental standards for suppliers are insufficient for assuming a retention of control that could result in negligence.

[29] *Jane Doe and others v Wal-Mart Stores* (n 2) 684.

give rise to liability. This of course raises the question of how, pursuant to the rules on non-contractual liability, such voluntary public commitments and gratuitous behaviour could result in legal liability. In approaching the relationship between the corporate code and the scope of liability, there seem to be essentially two forms of liability that could play a role in this context.

First, the act of publicly declaring a corporate code could be a wrongful act that gives rise to liability towards those that rely on it to their detriment if the public declaration contained false or misleading information and promises. When interpreted in this way, the corporate codes would influence the scope of liability as a specific liability for making a negligent misstatement (section 4.1.2.1). Alternatively, one can also take the corporate codes as evidence of an assumption of responsibility of the company towards the beneficiaries specified in the corporate code by words, conduct and, on this ground, refer to it as establishing a duty of care of the company to protect the beneficiaries and prevent harm to them (section 4.1.2.2). From this perspective, the corporate code could assist in broadening the scope of liability to also cover pure omissions.[30]

4.1.2.1. *The Public Declaration as the Basis of Liability*

The interpretation of publicly declared corporate codes as misleading statements that are negligently published is not prominently debated. One can refer in this context only to Dam, who mentions the potential of published corporate codes resulting in prospectus liability to the extent that the corporate code contains false information.[31] However, in spite of the little attention given to the category of prospectus liability in the corporate code debate, this option is, in fact, intensively debated with respect to a different type of publicly available corporate commitment, namely corporate governance codes. In relation to the public declaration of companies to comply with the corporate governance code, it is suggested in the current debate that this declaration can be interpreted as a reason for the liability of the company or the members of management and the supervisory board towards the public that relies on the honest publication of the code declaration.[32]

4.1.2.1.1. English Law: Negligent Misstatement

In English law, liability for the act of making a negligent misstatement follows the *Hedley Byrne* principle. In the landmark decision after which the principle is named, the Law Lords overturned the previous established authority that limited liability

[30] *cf* for these two ways of conceptualising liability in relation to public statements under English law: Lord Hoffmann in *Sutradhar v Natural Environment Research Council* [2006] UKHL 33 [25]; and, in analysing this decision in relation to a civil law system (the Netherlands), Enneking (2008) 503.

[31] Dam (2008) 50. A comparable suggestion to adapt the rules on prospectus liability cautiously to the realities of publicly declared corporate codes can also be found in Bachmann (2006b) 240ff.

[32] See for this suggestion Lutter (2002) 469ff; Ulmer (2002a) 171f; Ulmer (2002b) 168f. For similar attempts concerning the German code on mergers (*Deutscher Übernahmekodex*), see Hopt (1997) 402f. But see critically on this attempt MüKo-AktG-Goette/Schall § 161, para 102; Bertrams (2004) 233ff.

for false, fraudulent statements of fact.[33] In this case, a rule was established according to which a claimant can bring an action for losses, including economic losses,[34] incurred by reliance on a statement provided that a 'special relationship' existed between the claimant and the defendant.[35] The court held that liability principally exists between two parties where 'a person takes it upon himself to give information or advice to, or allows his information or advice to be passed on to, another person, who, as he knows or should know, will place reliance on it'.[36] The main requirements for liability for negligent misstatement in accordance with *Hedley Byrne* are, first, that information is provided or advice is given. This means that liability is restricted to making a false statement of fact. Moreover, the tort of negligent misstatement is only applicable in constellations in which the defendant 'voluntarily assumes responsibility' for his statement and could foresee that the other party reasonably relies on it.[37] Finally, in order not to undermine the rules on contract law, the Law Lords famously declared that the duty of care is reserved for 'special relationships' between the defendant and the claimant that are akin to contract.

Pursuant to the first requirement, liability for negligent statements would, in relation to corporate codes, only be possible if they contain facts and not merely represent statements of opinion or statements of intent. However, with respect to this requirement, it should also be noted that the distinction between a statement of fact and one of opinion or intent is not always clear and is open to interpretation. In one prominent decision, the courts interpreted a statement that could prima facie be considered one of a future intention in fact as a statement of fact about the present state of mind of the speaker.[38] In other decisions, statements that seemed to express merely an opinion could be treated as statement of facts because of the superior knowledge of the speaker.[39] Regarding the corporate codes, one would probably need to distinguish here between the different aspects in the codes. There is a likely situation that the corporate commitment not only contains a statement about what it will do in the future but also contains information as to the present efforts of companies to protect the environment or improve labour standards. For these statements, liability for negligent misstatement would in principle be

[33] *Chandler v Crane, Cristmas and Co* [1951] KB 164.

[34] In general, under English law, recovery for pure economic losses outside a contract is not accepted; see *Murphy v Brentwood District Council* [1991] 1 AC 398, 475 (per Lord Reid): 'economic losses are only recoverable if they flow from breach of a relevant contractual duty, but here again, in the absence of a special relationship of proximity they are not recoverable in tort'.

[35] *Hedley Byrne and Co Ltd v Heller and Partners Ltd* [1964] AC 465.

[36] ibid 503 (per Lord Morris).

[37] Deakin, Johnston and Markesinis (2007) 144.

[38] *Edgington v Fitzmarice* (1885) 29 Ch D 459, 483 (per Lord Bowen): 'The state of a man's mind is as much a fact as the state of his digestion.'

[39] One can here refer in particular to the different treatment of statements made by a party as to an estimate of potential costs or benefits of an object that the parties negotiate to contract on. In *Economides v Commercial Union Assurance Co plc* [1998] QB 587, the Judicial Committee of the Privy Council held that a statement by a 21-year-old student on the costs of replacing the contents of a flat was a mere statement of opinion. In *Esso Petroleum Co Ltd v Mardon* [1976] QB 801, the statement of one party on the estimated annual throughput of petrol of a petrol station was held to be a statement of fact due to the superior knowledge and experience of the seller. A similar conclusion was reached in *Smith v Land and House Property Corporation* (1884) 28 Ch D 7, in which the statement that a hotel was let to a 'most desirable tenant' was held to be a statement of fact due to superior knowledge.

possible if it could be proven that the factual situation is different and that the company negligently made this representation. The situation with respect to the future-oriented commitments in the codes is slightly less clear, but such commitments could still qualify as a statement of fact. More concretely, the liability of the codes in terms of a negligent misstatement would be possible if it could be proven that the company made the statement dishonestly in the first place and thus never intended to undertake the promised efforts. In this constellation, the corporate commitment to comply with its code could, in accordance with *Edgington v Fitzmaurice*, be viewed as a false statement of fact about the present state of mind of the speaker. To the extent that this state of mind cannot be proven, liability in relation to the corporate code will only be possible if the law would be developed further and a category of liability would be recognised for constellations in which a party detrimentally relies on a promise.[40]

As far as the second requirement of assuming responsibility for the statement is concerned, it is explicitly possible that liability is prevented if a disclaimer is placed in the code that reveals that the company did not want to assume legal responsibility for the given words.[41]

Yet, even insofar as the corporate codes would qualify as statements of fact and it can be stated that the company assumed responsibility for them, the third requirement set out in *Hedley Byrne* remains problematic in relation to the codes. It is generally accepted that liability for a false statement of fact only arises if such a statement is made in the course of a 'special relationship' between the claimant and the defendant. As Lord Reich made clear: 'It would be one thing to say that the speaker owes a duty to a limited class, but it would be going very far to say that he owes a duty to every ultimate "consumer" who acts on those words to his detriment.'[42] This condition was further clarified in the famous case of *Caparo Industries v Dickman*,[43] which dealt with the liability of auditors, in the context of a takeover bid, for preparing accounts of a company. The prepared accounts gave the false impression that the company was making profits, although it was effectively worthless. By setting up the three-stage test of requiring foreseeability, proximity and a justification of why it is fair, just and reasonable to impose a duty of care, the House of Lords ruled that, in this particular case, it could not be foreseen that the account would be used for this purpose.[44] From this argument, one can already identify the tendency to narrowly interpret potential liability for negligent

[40] See McKendrick (2013) 101f, who presents the option that promissory estoppel could equally develop into a cause of action to allow recovery for reliance losses in relation to a promise. The wrong on the side of the promisor would in this case be identified in that he acted unconscionably by means of making a promise that the other party relied upon and thereafter breached the promise.

[41] In *Hedley Byrne and Co Ltd v Heller and Partners Ltd* (n 35) 532 (per Lord Devlin), the requirement of assuming responsibility for the statement was rejected because the statement contained a disclaimer that made it clear to the claimants that the statement was made 'without responsibility'.

[42] ibid 483, per Lord Reich.

[43] *Caparo Industries v Dickman* (n 6).

[44] In determining foreseeability, Lord Oliver set out the following conditions for foreseeability in *Caparo Industries v Dickman* (n 6) 638: (1) advice is required for a purpose, which is made known to the adviser; (2) the adviser knows that the advice will be communicated to advisee for that purpose; (3) it is known that the advice is likely to be acted upon by the advisee without independent inquiry; and (4) it is so acted on by the advisee.

misstatement and reduce it to constellations in which the purpose of the statement is known to both the speaker and the addressee, and the speaker can foresee that the addressee relies on this statement for this particular purpose. Can such a situation of a 'special relationship' be conceived for corporate codes?

First of all, it is clear that the character of the corporate codes as statements made to the public will most likely not be interpreted as resulting in liability towards a detrimentally affected member of the public, even if these codes have the purpose of informing the general public of their corporate efforts. One can only establish liability towards particular members of the public insofar as a special relationship can be identified to which the corporate codes relate. Such a relationship could be discussed specifically as arising between a company and its commercial partners or maybe even towards the beneficiaries of the code. With respect to commercial relations, it could be noted that there is a general reluctance towards recognising liability for statements between commercial parties negotiating at arm's length. As a result, even the negotiation phase is not per se a sufficiently close relationship giving rise to a general duty of care in the form of making factual statements with care.[45] With respect to the corporate codes, this has the result that liability for publishing a corporate code is already difficult to establish in relation to a party if this party is close to concluding a contract with the company.[46] In fact, so far, there is primarily one main situation in which a duty of care was established in relation to a negligent misstatement. In *Smith v Eric S Bush* and *Harris v Wyre Forest District Council*,[47] individual consumers were attempting to buy a house and a professional surveyor was providing the information as to the value of the property. More concretely, these cases, heard jointly, dealt with valuation reports for housing that aimed to establish the value of a house that a purchaser would buy on loan. The purchasers relying on the report made the purchase decision and later it turned out that the house contained defects that required considerable additional investment. In this particular case, the House of Lords held that the surveyors were liable for making a false valuation report not only towards their contractual partners but also towards the purchasers who relied upon the report. In so deciding, the courts put forth as the main argument in favour of the duty of care that it is unlikely that the purchasers would order an independent report and that the surveyors could have known this with respect to this particular housing market.[48]

[45] See, eg, Deakin, Johnston and Markesinis (2007) 146: 'each side will have to rely on its own judgement or obtain the opinion of a third party. Thus, with reason, the courts take the view that parties to pre-contractual negotiations will primarily look to their own interests and not to those of each other' and further in note 274: 'There are alternatives to *Hedley Byrne* for framing liability for disappointed expectations, but these are rarely, if ever, available in English law.'

[46] Only when a contract has been concluded after a false statement of fact has been made to the speaker is liability possible under s 2(1) of the Misrepresentation Act 1967: 'Where a person has entered into a contract after a misrepresentation has been made to him by another party thereto and as a result thereof he has suffered loss, then, if the person making the misrepresentation would be liable to damages in respect thereof had the misrepresentation been made fraudulently, that person shall be so liable notwithstanding that the misrepresentation was not made fraudulently, unless he proves that he had reasonable ground to believe and did believe up to the time the contract was made the facts represented were true.'

[47] *Smith v Eric S Bush and Harris v Wyre Forest District Council* [1990] 1 AC 831.

[48] ibid 964f (per Lord Griffiths).

In *Morgan Crucible v Hill Samuel*, Lord Hoffmann provided an additional potential explanation as to why a duty of care was established in the *Smith* and *Harris* case, despite the restrictions set out in *Caparo*. He held that the respective cases dealt with 'different economic relationships between the parties and the nature of the markets in which they were operating' and that the former case dealt with 'a person of modest means and making the most expensive investment of his or her life', whereas the latter concerned 'an entrepreneur taking high risks for high rewards'.[49] Thus, it appears that the existence of a duty of care to make statements of facts with care is also influenced by factors such as the necessity to protect one of the parties, the presence of unequal bargaining power and the severity of the losses caused for the affected party.[50] Following Lord Hoffmann's interpretation, one could at least argue that a duty of care exists not to make a false statement in relations in which the potential addressees require protection because they cannot obtain and rely on other independent information. One could argue that with respect to corporate codes, such a constellation is present. The code of a company is made publicly available to the beneficiaries with the objective of making them explicitly aware of the efforts that are undertaken to improve their situation and it is here the company that presents itself as a professional reliable organisation to beneficiaries that require such protection.

However, in spite of this general possibility to establish a 'special relationship' based on the reasoning that a company could be considered a professional party and that there is a necessity to protect the beneficiaries, this possible interpretation is considerably restricted by a recent decision with similar facts. In *Sutradhar v Natural Environment Research Council*,[51] the House of Lords decided on liability for negligent misstatement of the Natural Environment Research Council for publishing a report that contained statements as to the water quality and the possible contamination of drinking water with arsenic in Bangladesh. According to the court, such a publicly available report does not result in a duty of care towards the population of Bangladesh and thus would make the Research Council in no way liable for issuing a false report about the good quality of the drinking water. In relying on Lord Denning's dissenting judgement in *Hedley Byrne*, Lord Hoffmann held that liability for a publicly available statement is subject to several restrictions and would require at least a 'measure of control over and responsibility for the potential situation'.[52] In the commentary, it was again underlined that 'the test of proximity in negligent misstatement is narrower than that for conduct causing direct physical injury'.[53] As a result, the decision indicates that the relationship of proximity between the company and the beneficiaries of a public statement cannot solely be justified by the necessity of protecting the beneficiaries and the particular

49 *Morgan Crucible v Hill Samuel* [1991] Ch 295, 302.

50 See explicitly on this interpretation Deakin, Johnston and Markesinis (2007) 152. See also Giliker (2002) 114, who holds that the court in *Smith v Eric Bush* and *Harris v Wyre Forest* seemed strongly guided by 'concerns of social justice'.

51 *Sutradhar v Natural Environment Research Council* (n 30).

52 ibid [38].

53 ibid, commentary to case, para [C3], provided for in [2007] Env LR 10, 187.

expertise of the speaker if the two parties are located in remote countries. It is an additional requirement that the party making the statement also has control over or takes over responsibility for the source of danger. However, in relation to the codes, one could bring forward as an argument in favour of an existing 'responsibility for the potential situation' the fact that the company not only presents its code of conduct to the public as a commitment to improve the situation of particular groups, but that it is also capable of controlling the situation by conducting audits and guiding their contractual partners into achieving code compliance. It is this additional factor that could play a role as an indication that the company is capable of influencing the situation of the beneficiaries. Yet, it has to be clear that it is only the combination of these various factors read together that could possibly be used as arguments to establish proximity between the company and the beneficiaries and, as a result, establish a duty of care that obliges the company not to make a false or dishonest statement towards them.

4.1.2.1.2. German Law

In German law, the rules on liability for negligent misstatements are not to be found in the law of tort. Instead, they are part of the rules on quasi-contractual liability and rules that deal with liability for situations in which, typically, particular trust in a statement is present. In this regard, it is important to consider two main sources of such quasi-contractual reliance liability when discussing the potential liability for publicly declaring compliance with a code. First, it is recognised that a person can be held liable for making a statement if the statement was made within the pre-contractual phase of negotiation and initiating a contract (§ 311 II BGB). This so-called *culpa in contrahendo* is a form of quasi-contractual liability between two parties. This category of liability derives from the assumption that the phase prior to the conclusion of a contract is based on intensified mutual trust, which the law needs to protect by allowing the recovery of reliance losses. Second, in addition to the general reliance liability, a specific form of liability for making a statement is the so-called prospectus liability.[54]

4.1.2.1.2.1. Culpa in Contrahendo Liability

In general, it is recognised that the detrimental reliance of a party on the behaviour of the other in the phase prior to the conclusion of the contract can amount to a breach of the quasi-contractual duty to deal fairly and can consequently result in liability for the speaker (*cf* §§ 311 II, 280 I BGB). The conditions for liability in the pre-contractual stage are, in this regard, the existence of a relation of *culpa in contrahendo* pursuant to § 311 II BGB or a comparable *Sonderverbindung*. Moreover, the act of making the statement needs to be interpreted as a breach of the duty to deal

[54] Specific statutory provisions on prospectus liability are laid down in §§ 44ff BörsG; § 20 VermAnlG. In addition, a general prospectus liability was developed by case law with §§ 311 II, III BGB as legal basis; for an overview, see Palandt-Grüneberg § 311, para 71; Erman-Kindl § 311, paras 52ff.

fairly. These two requirements need to be fulfilled in order to hold a person liable for making a statement if reliance on the statement has caused damage and there is at least negligent behaviour on the side of the speaker.

Liability requires, first, comparable to the English criterion of a relation 'akin to contract', that the statement is made when parties either negotiate a deal (§ 311 II No 1 BGB) or are in the prior phase of initiating a contract (§ 311 No 2 BGB). The negotiation phase begins when the parties begin to get in contact with the ultimate aim of concluding a contract.[55] In the constellations under scrutiny, such a relationship is definitely present when the company negotiates a contract with a potential supplier or a customer on, for instance, the supply of goods. In addition, a relationship of *culpa in contrahendo* is also present in the phase where a contract is initiated, which is interpreted in a broad fashion. A contract can even be initiated by the unilateral behaviour of one party if the ultimate aim of this behaviour is to induce the other party to conclude a contract. Classical constellations are customers entering a shop for the sake of buying a product or even if a company sends advertising material to a potential consumer.[56] Based on these rules, one can argue that a relationship of *culpa in contrahendo* can equally arise between a company and potential consumers, provided that the corporate code is sent to the party or made publicly available for the sake of inducing the other party to conclude a contract. However, given that the objective of this chapter is to investigate primarily the liability for the statement towards the beneficiaries of the codes that rely on the codes to their detriment, the ultimate question is whether German law would even recognise such a relationship of *culpa in contrahendo* between the company and the beneficiaries of the code. Focusing on the criteria of either starting negotiations or initiating a contract, there is reason for skepticism as to whether they are met in such constellations. One could, however, consider qualifying the relationship between the company and the beneficiaries as a constellation falling within the ambit of § 311 II No 3 BGB, which only requires loose commercial contact between the parties. Courts have accepted, for instance, the fact that a commercial contract pursuant to this provision also arises if different parties enter into negotiations with a party.[57] Based on this provision, one could at least conceive that a relationship of *culpa in contrahendo* could be present towards those parties that the company directly addresses with a code with the objective of inducing them to start or continue working in a particular factory that is run by a supplier. Yet, it should be noted that this represents quite a far-reaching understanding of the scope of the pre-contractual relationship that is protected by § 311 II.

To the extent that a relationship of *culpa in contrahendo* can be assumed, German courts are generally prepared to interpret as a breach of the duty to negotiate fairly the fact that one party makes a statement that influences the other party to his detriment. More concretely, it was, for instance, held that a party providing false information on the existence of insurance for the car or information in a

[55] Erman-Kindl § 311, para 20.

[56] Beaucamp (2003); Palandt-Grüneberg § 311, para 22; Erman-Kindl § 311, para 21; MüKo-Emmerich § 311, para 48.

[57] MüKo-Emmerich § 311, para 50; Erman-Kindl § 311, para 22.

prospectus handed over to the other party in the course of the negotiations would qualify as a breach of the duty to negotiate fairly.[58] However, a breach of the duty to trade fairly has also been recognised with respect to statements of intent. This applied in particular to letters of intent that represented a breach of the duty to deal fairly if the party issuing this letter did not seriously consider concluding the contract.[59] From these decisions, one can draw parallels with corporate codes that contain false factual information on the current company performance as well as constellations in which it can be proven that the publication of the code was made dishonestly, eg, that an intention to comply with the commitment was not present.

Consequently, it can be concluded that liability for false statements is a viable option for the publication of the codes towards those parties that are in a relationship of *culpa in contrahendo* with the company that publishes the code. However, insofar as this relationship only arises between the company and its potential customers or suppliers and would not be so easily accepted in relation to the potential beneficiaries, the potential of this *culpa in contrahendo* liability remains limited. This is due to the fact that, on the side of the parties towards whom the company is potentially liable, the losses incurred amount primarily to a disappointed expectation in the general confidence of the corporate code as a commitment made for the benefit of other parties. While a potential customer or supplier could theoretically pursue an action against a company for publishing a corporate code claiming that he has relied on the code, it may be difficult to prove that reliance upon this statement has resulted in a measurable damage to the extent that compensation can be sought. The measurable damage that is caused by non-compliance with a corporate code occurs merely on the side of the beneficiaries. The only option to overcome this separation of claim and loss is then to allow the entitled consumer or supplier to compensate the damages of the third party that were caused by non-compliance with the corporate code. Pursuant to German law, this is in fact possible within the narrowly confined boundaries of the doctrine of transferred losses (*Drittschadensliquidation*), which requires that the separation of claim and loss is only a matter of coincidence. The general idea behind allowing a party to claim damages on behalf of the affected party is that the party breaching a duty and causing damage should not benefit from the fact that its (potential) contractual partner was damaged, but that, as a matter of coincidence, the damage occurred only to a third party.[60] When applying the doctrine of transferred losses, it is the general rule that the party entitled to compensation can claim the damage. Thus, the doctrine of transferred losses does not entitle the negatively affected party to claim his own losses; instead, the entitled party can claim the damages on behalf of the affected party. If this doctrine is applied to the liability for negligently declared

[58] For examples, *cf* BGH NJW 1977, 1583 (information on annual turnover of the company); BGH NJW 1979, 1449 (information on a property in an advertisement prospectus); BGH NJW 1980, 2408 (information on the debts of a company); BGH NJW 2004, 1732, 1734 (false information in a prospectus on a commission fee), BGH NJW-RR 1997, 144 (information on the current use of a property).

[59] MüKo-Busche, Introduction to § 145, para 58 with further references.

[60] See, eg, RGZ 62, 331, 334; 90, 240, 246; 93, 39, 40; 170, 246, 250f; BGHZ 15, 224, 227f; 25, 250, 258; 40, 91; 49, 356.

corporate codes, it can have the result that consumers and suppliers would have to claim compensation for any damage occurred on the side of a third party that has relied on the corporate code. Considering that the constellation of the corporate codes does not fit with the established categories for which the doctrine has been developed,[61] an application would need to be proposed in conjunction with the claim to broaden its scope to cover third party losses for other types of constellations.[62] However, one core problem of applying the doctrine in relation to the corporate codes remains the condition of coincidence. In situations in which a statement is made publicly available, there is always a chance that different parties rely on it; this mere fact does not make it a coincidence that loss and claim are separated. The coincidence of the separation of claim and loss could in relation to the corporate codes only be justified by referring to the fact that the separation of claim and loss is in this constellation based on the specific character of the corporate code that seeks to protect beneficiaries, but are merely used by companies to induce other parties to enter into a contract. It is, in short, the deliberate use of the code in a different context (marketing) than prima facie suggested on the ground of its content (protection of specified third parties) that could render the separation of a *culpa in contrahendo* claim and reliance loss coincidental.

4.1.2.1.2.2. Prospectus Liability

As an alternative to the certainly complex undertaking of relating the corporate codes to liability in a relationship of *culpa in contrahendo* combined with the doctrine of transferred losses, it could also be an option to link liability for declaring compliance with a corporate code with the rules on prospectus liability, at least insofar as a corporate code contains false information. Naturally, liability for issuing a prospectus does not fit in its current form due to the obvious fact that published codes do not fall within the definition of a prospectus. Although there is no statutory definition of a prospectus and the Federal High Court of Justice has ruled that, so far, the definition is not entirely clear,[63] it is still accepted that normal advertising material as well as public information such as newspaper advertisements, flyers and normal exposés are not covered.[64] The rationale behind prospectus liability is that, in constellations of capital investment, the prospectus is often

[61] The factual constellations to which the doctrine of transferred losses applies are: (1) indirect agency; (2) mandatory transfer of risk in contracts involving a carrier; (3) contracts on the storage of goods where the goods belong to a third party; (4) fiduciary relationships; and (5) explicit contractual agreements on compensation of third party losses. See, eg, on these categories MüKo-Oetker § 249, paras 296ff; Prütting/Wegen/Weinrich-Medicus § 249, paras 94ff.

[62] For this possibility, see, eg, Kollhosser (1966) 305: 'Die Lehre von der Liquidation des Drittinteresses ist noch kein abgeschlossenes, dogmatisch festes Gebilde, sondern der Erweiterung fähig.' From the more recent literature, see MüKo-Oetker § 249, para 290. A recent suggestion for a broad scope of application of the doctrine of transferred losses in order to handle the specific liability risks produced by the financial crisis has been made by Grundmann and Renner (2013) 380f.

[63] BGHZ 177, 25, 28 ('noch nicht abschließend geklärten Kriterien des Prospektbegriffs').

[64] BGH NJW 1981, 2810, 2811; OLG Karlsruhe ZIP 2010, 1036, 1038; MüKo-Emmerich § 311, para 161; Erman-Kindl § 311, para 52.

the only information material available for the party taking an investment decision and therefore reliance on this statement needs to be protected.[65] Thus, liability for issuing a prospectus mainly arises if the information provided in the statement proves to be important for an investment decision. The narrow scope on statements that contain information necessary for an investment also makes this form of liability difficult to apply to corporate codes that contain general information on social and environmental standards. As a result, this specific form of liability could only become applicable if, following some contributions in the scholarly debate, a broader scope of application would be suggested that not only focuses on the specific types of prospectus on investments but also applies to other information that is provided in advertisement material.[66] However, even if this suggestion were followed, it would primarily have the result that liability would arise in relation to those parties that rely on the codes when making investment decisions and not necessarily those that are affected by the non-compliance.[67] Effectively, the possibility of holding the company liable for the information provided or promises made in its public declaration would then be similar to the situation of *culpa in contrahendo* and would depend ultimately on whether it would be possible for the addressed parties to claim the losses of the beneficiaries.

4.1.2.1.3. Interim Conclusion

The previous section dealt with the suggestion of holding a company liable for not complying with its publicly declared corporate code based on the rules on liability for false and misleading statements. In analysing the codes under the English and German rules on this form of liability, it was revealed that the publication of a corporate code could generally result in liability if it occurred in a relationship 'akin to contract' or a relationship of *culpa in contrahendo*. With respect to this requirement, however, it was emphasised that such a relationship is not so easily recognised and is thus difficult to establish in particular between a company and the beneficiaries of the codes. As a result, making use of the rules on liability for negligent misstatement is only possible on the basis of a very broad understanding of such a 'special relationship' or *Sonderverbindung* that pays due respect to the characteristics of the codes as public declarations and recognises the need to protect public reliance on such statements. Alternatively, it is at least considered to be possible in

[65] BGHZ 111, 314, 317; BGH NJW 1992, 228, 229; BGH WM 2001, 25, 26.

[66] See especially Köndgen (1983) and specifically in relation to declarations of companies to comply with corporate governance codes Lutter (2002) 473ff; Ulmer (2002b) 168f; Ulmer (2002a) 171f. For similar attempts concerning the German code on mergers (*Deutscher Übernahmekodex*), see Hopt (1997) 402f. A cautious suggestion to broaden the scope of prospectus liability to public declarations of companies in general is provided by Bachmann (2006b) 240ff, 254.

[67] This problem is also emphasised by Bachmann (2006b) 256: 'Schon das Beispiel der kapitalmarktrechtlichen Prospekthaftung macht … deutlich, dass Konzepte einer „Vertrauenshaftung", sei sie negativ, sei sie positiv dort an praktische Grenzen stoßen, wo es nicht um die Exekution konkreter vermögensbezogener Pflichten (Geldzahlung), sondern um die allgemeine Erwartung des Verkehrs geht, bestimmte selbst gesetzte Standards würden auch wirklich eingehalten. Hier ist mit geldmäßiger Kompensation nicht gedient.'

German law to apply to the codes the doctrines that allow parties in a relationship akin to a contract to compensate the losses of third parties, ie, beneficiaries.

4.1.2.2. Non-compliance as the Basis of Liability

Apart from interpreting non-compliance with the corporate codes as a form of liability for false or misleading statements, one could also link the corporate codes to the rules on liability in a different way. In fact, the corporate codes could also be interpreted as evidence for the fact that a company voluntarily assumed responsibility for the parties specified in the codes as beneficiaries. This would have the result that the company would not only be liable in case it directly harms the beneficiaries, but also if it, contrary to its promise in the code, does not contribute to improvement by, for instance, tolerating harm that is done by others. In the case against Wal-Mart, this argument was presented in the form of the allegation that the company condoned the violations of suppliers, although it presented to the public that it would not do so and, moreover, made the beneficiaries rely on its commitment by conducting audits to discover and remedy violations of the code that conveyed the impression that the corporate commitment was reliable and would be followed.[68] Although not accepted by the courts, this suggested interpretation received quite some attention in the scholarly debate on the codes. In the US debate, scholars related the codes to the existing Good Samaritan tort law duties that oblige someone who provides a voluntarily, gratuitous service to do so with reasonable care in order to prevent harm to those that benefit from the service.[69] It is held that, in particular, companies that 'put forth codes of conduct and publicise their measures to improve foreign working conditions'[70] could be considered as voluntarily assuming responsibility towards the beneficiaries and thus as being under an obligation to prevent harm to them. Although this suggestion is currently most prominently proposed in relation to the US Good Samaritan duties, one can also occasionally find equivalent proposals on codes as a voluntary assumption of responsibility in other scholarly contributions.[71]

This suggested interpretation of the codes will be, in the following, related to the English and German contexts. To that end, the analysis will discuss corporate codes as a potential assumption of responsibility in English law that could justify the existence of a duty of care that also covers omissions. In German law, the corporate codes are discussed from the perspective of whether they are capable of

[68] *Jane Doe and others v Wal-Mart Stores* (n 2) 684: 'one who "undertakes to provide protective services to another" must exercise a duty of care'.

[69] Phillips and Lim (2009) 351ff; Revak (2012) 1662ff. On the discussion of deducting Good Samaritan Duties under US tort law from voluntary environmental and social compliance programmes of companies, see also Natale (1988); Crawley (1993).

[70] Revak (2012) 1664.

[71] For the attempt to interpret a corporate code as establishing a duty of care on the basis of Dutch law of 'proper social conduct', see Heijden (2011b) 194ff. With respect to German law, one can also find this approach in the form of a proposed interpretation of corporate codes as a category of *Verkehrssicherungspflichten* that will be discussed more intensively below, section 4.1.2.2.2. (p 171), text and accompanying footnotes. For this suggestion, see Saage-Maaß (2011) 13ff.

resulting in a *Verkehrspflicht* that requires the company with a publicly available code to prevent harm to the parties that it has undertaken to protect.

4.1.2.2.1. English Law: Voluntary Assumption of Responsibility

The common law tort of negligence can be read as a general cause of action for cases in which the defendant, by a positive act, causes physical losses or damages to property. Outside the boundaries of this clear constellation, however, liability is restricted and subject to additional requirements. Specific additional requirements were already discussed in relation to the potential liability for statements that cause harm, but they also exist for other forms of liability, especially liability for omissions. Following Lord Goff in *Smith v Littlewoods Organisations*, it is a general rule that 'the common law does not impose liability for what are called pure omissions'.[72] This implies that someone can in general not be held liable for not preventing harm even if he was practically in a position to act.[73] Such a duty to act can only be established when one party assumes responsibility towards the other.[74] In determining whether a party assumes responsibility, there are several criteria that play a role. Responsibility can be assumed by means of a contract[75] or it could be derived from the fact that a protective statutory duty exists between the defendant and the party that causes harm to the claimant.[76] In addition, it is frequently the criterion of whether the defendant was able to control the dangerous situation or the party that plays a role.[77] In a recent case, Lord Hope framed it as a general rule that in order to establish a duty of care to prevent others from harm based on an assumption of responsibility, it is necessary that 'the person who is said to be under that duty has by his *words* or *conduct* assumed responsibility for the safety of the person who is at risk'.[78] Against this background, it is indeed possible that a court called upon to determine whether a party assumed responsibility takes into consideration his words in the form of a commitment to protect this party. With respect to the assumption of responsibility in terms of words, however, it is necessary to refer again to *Sutradhar v Natural Environment Research Council*, which has already been consulted when discussing liability for negligent misstatement. In this case, the House of Lords explicitly rejected the argument of the claimants

[72] *Smith v Littlewoods Organisations* [1987] 2 AC 241, 271.

[73] See, eg, Lord Diplock in *Home Office v Dorset Yacht Co Ltd* [1970] AC 1004, 1060: 'The very parable of the good *Samaritan (Luke 10, v 30)* which was evoked by Lord Atkin in *Donoghue v Stevenson* illustrates, in the conduct of the priest and of the Levite who passed by on the other side, an omission which was likely to have as its reasonable and probable consequence damage to the health of the victim of the thieves, but for which the priest and Levite would have incurred no civil liability in English law.'

[74] *Smith v Littlewoods* (n 72) 272 (per Lord Goff).

[75] *Stansbie v Troman* [1948] 2 KB 48.

[76] This was the case in *Home Office v Dorset Yacht Co Ltd* (n 73). In this case, several boys escaped custody and damaged the property of third parties; it was ruled that this would result in liability for negligence on the side of the institution that had generally control over them in custody.

[77] On this relationship between control and assumption of responsibility with further references to case law, see Petrin (2013) 612ff.

[78] *Mitchell v Glasgow City Council* [2009] 1 AC 874, 890 (emphasis added).

that the mere act of drafting and publishing a report on the quality of drinking water would qualify as an assumption of responsibility towards the population in Bangladesh. In dismissing this claim, several arguments were brought forward. First, it was held that the organisation that published the report was not put under an obligation to test the water;[79] moreover, it was held that evidence for a voluntary assumption of responsibility could not be found in the report[80] and, finally, the argument was made that the Research Council did not have any control over or responsibility for the dangerous situation.[81] Although one could argue that the decision could be potentially decided differently in relation to public statements that contain more specific evidence for a voluntary commitment to protect particular parties than the scientific report that was subject to this case, this decision still suggests that the mere fact of voluntarily publishing a statement seems not to suffice for an assumption of responsibility. Therefore, one would need to argue that the situation concerning publicly declared corporate codes differs from the facts in this case.

In this context, one can argue here, first, that in relation to the corporate codes, the publishing companies do not make this commitment entirely voluntarily. On the contrary, the companies take responsibility for the beneficiaries on the ground of an implicit request by the public and it is often reliance of the public and governments on these voluntary efforts that provide an incentive to abstain from other regulatory measures.[82] In addition, one can also argue that by means of conducting audits, the publicly declaring companies were, contrary to the situation in *Sutradhar v Natural Environment Research Council*, actually in a position to influence their supplier. Moreover, one can also rely in this context on a recent noteworthy development of the 'assumption of responsibility' that dealt particularly with workplace standards in companies and the way in which companies can assume responsibility for the employees of its subsidiaries on the grounds of a corporate group health and safety policy. In *Chandler v Cape*, the Court of Appeal applied the notion of assuming responsibility in parent–subsidiary constellations, with the result that a duty of care was established for a parent towards employees of a legally separate subsidiary with respect to health and safety measures.[83] It was particularly noteworthy in this case that the duty of care was not understood as a matter of piercing the corporate veil or of effective day-to-day control of the parent over the subsidiary.[84] Instead, one main reason for establishing a duty of care was the fact that the parent had developed a group policy on health and safety standards that it organised on the level on the parent company, which was considered sufficient for assuming responsibility for the benefiting employees. It was the group policy together with the technical and medical assistance of the parent concerning health

[79] *Sutradhar v Natural Environment Research Council* (n 30) 27.
[80] ibid [29] et seq.
[81] ibid [38].
[82] Revak (2012) 1663.
[83] *Chandler v Cape plc* [2012] 1 WLR 3111.
[84] See ibid 3128, per Arden LJ: 'I would emphatically reject any suggestion that this court is in any way concerned with what is usually referred to as piercing the corporate veil ... There is no imposition or assumption of responsibility by reason only that a company is the parent company of another company.'

and safety measures that was interpreted as putting the parent in the position of having superior knowledge. This superior knowledge effectively represented the reason for assuming responsibility towards those who benefited from and in a foreseeable way relied on this superior knowledge. It was also held that liability is not dependent on the active intervention of the parent in the particular situation that resulted in the wrongful act. Already a general practice of intervening in the operations of the subsidiary was sufficient as a criterion for treating reliance of the employees as reasonable and on the side of the parent that this reliance was foreseeable.[85] One can interpret this case as a first indication to broaden the scope of liability. It is accordingly not only a high level of control of one entity over the other that could lead to an assumption of responsibility and thus justify the existence of a duty of care, but also superior knowledge based on a cooperative organisation of workplace standards at the parent company level.[86] This cooperative organisation is evidenced by, among other things, the general corporate policy. On the basis of this recent decision, one can argue that a duty of care could potentially also be established in constellations in which a company has in place a supplier policy or a general policy as to the global improvement of workplace standards towards the protected beneficiaries, in particular employees. One can in this regard argue that such a policy puts the company in a position of superior knowledge and that, due to the frequent audits on the factory sites of subsidiaries and suppliers, a similar practice of intervening in the operations also exists. The publication of the corporate code combined with the common practice of auditing and training could then, read together, serve as the justification to view reliance on the side of the employees as being reasonable and the extended liability risk on the side of the company as being foreseeable. Together, this could then result in an assumption of responsibility and thus a duty of care to prevent harm to the beneficiaries.

One must, however, still be sceptical as to whether the assumption of responsibility would be extended on the basis of a corporate policy insofar as it concerns other groups than specifically employees, such as third parties living in the vicinity of factories that suffer losses from violations of environmental standards. This is first due to the fact that the court in *Chandler v Cape* could base the assumption of responsibility towards employees on previous cases that already provided indications for such a possibility in principle.[87] This is different with respect to other beneficiaries, such as third parties affected by factory operations or environmen-

[85] More specifically, the court developed four criteria in *Chandler v Cape plc* (n 83) 3131 (per Arden LJ): '(1) the businesses of the parent and subsidiary are in a relevant respect the same; (2) the parent has, or ought to have, superior knowledge on some relevant aspect of health and safety in the particular industry; (3) the subsidiary's system of work is unsafe as the parent company knew, or ought to have known; and (4) the parent knew or ought to have foreseen that the subsidiary or its employees would rely on its using that superior knowledge for the employees' protection.'

[86] A similar interpretation of this decision as broadening the scope of liability beyond the accepted criterion of control, but with a critical tone that it would open the 'floodgates' for unforeseeable liability, is taken by Petrin (2013) 611ff.

[87] *Adams v Cape Industries* [1991] 1 All ER 929; *Connelly v Rio Tino Zinc Corp* [1999] CLC 533, in which, despite eventually dismissing claims of an employee of a subsidiary against the parent for violations of health and safety standards, Wright J indicated that 'in appropriate circumstances' a duty of care could be owed by a parent towards employees of subsidiaries concerning health and safety standards

tal pollution, where a more reluctant attitude will probably be taken towards an assumption of responsibility.[88] This is particularly true when broadening the scope to another recent case on the assumption of responsibility under the common law of negligence in relation to corporate group liability. Although surely not representing an authority for English law, one can in this context refer to the case concerning Shell's operations in Nigeria that was recently decided by a District Court in the Netherlands. In *Akpan v Shell*, the District Court of The Hague decided on the basis of the common law tort of negligence as the applicable law that, although an assumption of responsibility based on proximity of the parties was established in *Chandler v Cape* between parent companies and the employees of their subsidiaries, the criteria established in this case does not lead to a similar result for people living in the vicinity of a factory.[89] One of the main reasons brought forward by the court was the concern that broadening the scope of liability towards third parties other than employees would render the risk of liability for the company unforeseeable.[90]

Consequently, if one has in mind the careful approach towards establishing a duty of care to prevent harm to third parties in English law, one needs to remain sceptical as to whether a general duty of care towards all different groups of incidental beneficiaries would be established on the ground of a publicly declared corporate policy that is put into practice by means of intense monitoring and auditing. So far, it seems more likely to limit this option to employees of subsidiaries and possibly suppliers. However, based on a careful further refinement of the criteria established in *Chandler v Cape*, it might be possible over time to broaden carefully, but constantly, the scope of beneficiaries towards which responsibility is assumed.

4.1.2.2.2. German Law: *Verkehrspflichten*

In the context of German law, the proposal to interpret the corporate codes as evidence for the existence of a duty of care towards the beneficiaries needs to be related to the main and broadest category of liability in tort, eg, § 823 I BGB. Pursuant to this provision, a person is liable in tort for infringing upon what is colloquially called the enumerated 'absolute rights' of life, body and health, freedom, property and narrowly allowed other rights of others if the behaviour represents an unlawful act (*Pflichtverletzung*). Whether an act is unlawful depends on whether

(at 538); and *Lubbe v Cape plc* [2000] 1 WLR 1545, in which Lord Bingham specified aspects to be taken into consideration when discussing the assumption of responsibility of companies towards employees of subsidiaries for violations of health and safety standards (at 1555f). *cf* further on this issue *Busisiwe Ngcobo v Thord Chemical Holdings* [1995] WL 1082070 and *Sithole v Thor Chemicals Holdings Ltd* [1999] WL 477489, which concerned similar constellations, but mainly dealt with conflict of laws questions.

[88] But for a broader interpretation of the scope of *Chandler*, see Petrin (2013) 614f: 'Chandler can even be read to suggest that parent companies might also be liable to non-employee third parties, considerably broadening their liability exposure.'

[89] *Akpan and others v Royal Dutch Shell and others*, District Court of The Hague, 30 January 2013, file number: C/09/337050 / HA ZA 09-1580.

[90] ibid, para 4.29 ('a duty of care in respect of a virtually unlimited group of people in many countries').

the person alleged to have caused the damage owed the party affected in its absolute rights a *Verkehrspflicht*, which resembles the common law duty of care.[91] Thus, in German law, it is the context of establishing a *Verkehrspflicht* in which the corporate codes could play a role. In general, there is no overall rule on the existence of a duty of care; instead, there are different categories. One may, in the first place, refer to duties of care that relate to a person's own conduct or one's own property if the conduct or the property is capable of infringing upon the rights of others. For these constellations, it is accepted that this party has a duty of care not to affect detrimentally another person's absolute rights.[92] The situation is, however, more difficult as far as someone else's behaviour is concerned. In the event that it is a third party or the party suffering loss alone that causes the actual harm, an omission not to prevent harm only represents an unlawful act if there is a duty to act on the side of the claimant.[93] Thus, in order for a company to be held liable for not preventing harm to beneficiaries of the code, it is necessary to justify why the company has a duty to act in relation to the parties benefiting from the code. There are two prominent types of duties that require a party to act in order to prevent harm: *Verkehrssicherungspflichten* and *Fürsorgepflichten*. Both will be discussed as to whether they can be justified with the existence of a corporate code.

The former duties of care have been developed by case law for constellations in which a party creates a source of potential danger in relation to his property or his behaviour and obliges him to ensure that the interests and rights of others are not violated if they are affected by this potential danger.[94] Hence, a *Verkehrssicherungspflicht* creates legal responsibility towards everyone to prevent harm, but its existence remains dependent on the factual capability to control the potential source of danger.[95] *Verkehrssicherungspflichten* have been recognised, for instance, for organisers of sports,[96] for owners of restaurants or shops[97] and for organisers of mass spectacles,[98] and it remains a characteristic that these duties are owed to everyone who can be potentially affected. In relation to the corporate codes, such a *Verkehrssicherungspflicht* is obviously difficult to establish by referring solely to the publicly declared code of the company. However, comparable to English law, if the corporate code is put into practice by active monitoring, advice-giving and training, it is in principle possible to argue that the company, based on its code, effectively influences the decisions of independent third parties, eg, subsidiaries or suppliers, to an extent that it is responsible for the third parties' dangerous

[91] For the perception of equivalence of the common law duty of care and the German *Verkehrspflicht*, see especially Markesinis and Unberath (2002) 82: 'If one looks at the substance rather than the form, the duty of care is as much a central concept to German tort law as it is to the common law.'

[92] MüKo-Wagner § 823, para 317.

[93] RGZ 106, 283, 285; BGHZ 71, 86, 93. See also on this issue Markesinis and Unberath (2002) 86; MüKo-Wagner § 823, para 318; Erman-Schiemann § 823, para 77.

[94] See extensively on the different categories Palandt-Sprau § 823, paras 45ff; MüKo-Wagner § 823, paras 320ff; Erman-Schiemann § 823, paras 89ff.

[95] *cf* Bar (1980) 122ff.

[96] BGH NJW 1983, 801.

[97] BGH NJW 1991, 921

[98] BGH NJW 1990, 905.

behaviour.[99] It is clear that in order to establish a *Verkehrssicherungspflicht* on the side of a publishing company not only to monitor the hazards of its own factory operations but also those of other independent organisations, it is necessary not only to refer to codes as such, but also to bring forward evidence that the corporate code is put into practice in the form of a direct influence of the subsidiary or supplier. Consequently, it is merely the active intervening behaviour on the side of the publishing company, not the public commitment per se that could serve as an argument in favour of a *Verkehrssicherungspflicht*.

Alternatively, it could also be an option to relate the corporate codes to the other category of duties of care that establish liability for omissions in principle. The *Fürsorgepflichten* (duties to protect others) represent duties of care that a defendant owes a particular individual or group and that obliges him to take active measures to prevent harm to the person. In contrast to the *Verkehrssicherungspflicht*, the *Fürsorgepflicht* does not result in a duty of care towards everyone, but only towards a specific party. However, while the *Fürsorgepflicht* is confined as to the scope of protected parties, it is wider than the *Verkehrssicherungspflicht* as it does not require a strong influence over the source of danger that may affect this party in its absolute rights.[100] Thus, deriving a *Fürsorgepflicht* from the publicly declared code would have the result that the company would have a duty to protect the specified beneficiaries from harm even if it does not have a strong influence over the potential source of danger. However, due to the fact that a *Fürsorgepflicht* requires a party to intervene actively in another party's autonomous sphere in order to prevent harm, it is the general rule in German law that there is no general responsibility of someone to protect others actively from harm. German law does not know a general Good Samaritan duty outside the scope of narrowly confined criminal liability.[101] A protective duty of care primarily exists when the defendant has a guarantor position (*Garantenposition*) and there are several possibilities as to how this position can be created. First, it is recognised that the *Fürsorgepflicht* exists when a party is under a statutory duty to protect, such as a parent towards children or partners in a marriage.[102] Moreover, it is also possible to be in the position of a guarantor in the form of a contractual assumption of responsibility, even if this contract is not qualified as a contract with protective effect towards third parties. A prominent example from case law is the contract between a hospital and a patient that obliges the hospital to protect the patients from harm that is caused by visitors or other patients.[103] Next to a contract, a *Fürsorgepflicht* has also been justified by a factual assumption of responsibility, for instance, of a doctor

[99] An even wider interpretation of codes of conduct is presented by Saage-Maaß (2011) 15f, who argues that a *Verkehrssicherungspflicht* to monitor suppliers could be extracted from the due diligence requirement of the UN Guiding Principles.

[100] MüKo-Wagner § 823, para 319.

[101] BGH NJW 1999, 573, 574. See also MüKo-Wagner § 823, para 319, 333; Markesinis and Unberath (2002) 90. In principle, breach of Good Samaritan duties under German law could be sanctioned by criminal law (§ 323c StGB), but generally it does not result in liability in tort.

[102] eg, BGH NJW 1979, 973; NJW 1988, 2667, 2668f.

[103] eg, BGH NJW 1976, 1145, 1146; BGH NJW 2005, 1937, 1937.

who undertakes treatment even if no contract exists.[104] In this particular case, the *Fürsorgepflicht* was justified by the fact that this factual behaviour establishes trust on the side of the patient with the result that the latter refrains from undertaking precautionary measures himself.[105] Finally, there are also decisions in which the *Fürsorgepflicht* was justified on the grounds of a particular profession.[106] With regard to the corporate codes, these criteria could play a role in different ways. First, in the absence of a valid contract between the company and the beneficiaries, it is possible to justify the existence of a *Fürsorgepflicht* from the fact that the company factually promises and performs a voluntary service that creates reliance on the side of the other party. In fact, it is very possible that, on the grounds that a company has in place a corporate commitment and undertakes to fulfil this commitment by frequent audits, beneficiaries rely on this statement and thereby, as a result, fail to undertake precautionary measures themselves.[107] An additional argument could be to refer to the accepted category of a *Fürsorgepflicht* created by a contract and argue that the creation of such a duty by unilateral self-commitment is effectively comparable. Finally, it is also possible to derive the *Fürsorgepflicht* from the role of the company as a professional, although the difficulty here is in identifying the particular profession that the publishing company holds itself out to have by means of publicly declaring compliance with a corporate code. As a specific professional role, one could only refer to its purported role as a particularly socially responsible company that adheres to higher standards in its global operation. Yet, given the very narrow recognition of duties to protect that derive from professions, it seems highly questionable whether this argument would be successful.

To sum up, it could be shown that there are two possible ways through which the corporate codes could become relevant in the course of establishing a duty of care. In relation to the *Verkehrssicherungspflichten*, the corporate codes could give rise to a duty of care towards the public for behaviour of a third party, such as a supplier or subsidiary, provided that the corporate code is put into practice in the form of active monitoring, advice and training and, in so doing, leads to a stronger influence of the company over the dangerous behaviour of the third party. It is, however, also possible to relate the corporate codes to the category of *Fürsorgepflicht* by treating them either as akin to a contractual assumption of responsibility for particular groups or as a factual assumption that triggers reliance on the side of the beneficiaries and has the result that one's own precautionary measures are not undertaken. It has to be clear, however, that in both cases,

[104] BGH NJW 1979, 1248.

[105] ibid 1249: 'Mit der Fallübernahme erweckt der Arzt bei dem Patienten in der Regel *das Vertrauen*, dieser werde ihm unter Einsatz seine ärztlichen Kenntnisse und Fähigkeiten beistehen, ihn weiter zu behandeln … Der Kranke *verläßt* sich auf diese Obhut und wird nicht mehr versuchen, anderweitig Hilfe zu erlangen' (emphasis added).

[106] eg, BGH NJW 1962, 959; NJW 1988, 1380, 1381; NJW-RR 1990, 1245, 1246: 'oblag *aufgrund ihrer beruflichen Stellung* auch die deliktische (Garanten-)pflicht, dafür zu sorgen, daß keiner der Besucher … zu Schaden kam' (emphasis added); NJW-RR 1991, 1240, 1241.

[107] See for this argument Revak (2012) 1663. See also Herberg (2007) 115.

it is never the corporate code alone but rather the public self-commitment in conjunction with active efforts to fulfil the commitment that justifies the existence of a duty of care.

4.1.2.2.3. Interim Conclusion

In analysing the options to use the code as evidence for the existence of a duty of care on the side of the company, it could be revealed that the publicly declared code could in principle assist in establishing a duty of care. However, in spite of this potential, it also became clear that there are additional factors that play a role. In English law, a reluctant attitude has been identified towards establishing a duty of care solely on the basis of a unilateral public declaration. The potential of the corporate code to be counted as an assumption of responsibility was, in accordance with English law, identified in the active behaviour of the company to put the corporate code into practice by actively advising subsidiaries or suppliers. In this context, the currently most promising constellation would, due to the recent decision *Chandler v Cape*, particularly represent an assumption of responsibility of the company towards employees. With regard to German law, this behaviour of putting into practice a publicly declared corporate policy was also identified as a possibility to broaden the scope of liability in principle when interpreting the corporate code as resulting in a *Verkehrssicherungspflicht*. In addition, on the basis of the case law on the *Fürsorgepflicht*, an alternative perspective was offered where the corporate codes could play a role. More specifically, it was discussed whether the code could be interpreted as akin to a factual assumption of responsibility towards beneficiaries based on public self-commitment that is to be interpreted as akin to a contract.

4.1.2.3. Conclusion: Liability for Publicly Declared Codes

To conclude, the analysis on the current options in private law to make use of the publicly declared corporate codes when determining the scope of liability has discussed two potential links. First, the corporate code could become relevant as resulting in liability for making a false or dishonest statement towards those that rely on the statement, including detrimentally affected beneficiaries. However, this option depends on the additional requirement that the company that publicly declares that it complies with its code and the detrimentally affected beneficiary are in a relationship 'akin to contract' or *Sonderverbindung*. This possibility notwithstanding, the argument remains difficult to construct in relation to parties that are spatially only very remotely connected. Second, it is also possible that the corporate codes could be used as an argument to broaden the scope of liability for the company with a publicly available code to also cover omissions if the code is interpreted as an assumption of responsibility towards the beneficiaries specified in the code. In the course of investigating this option, it became clear that this is only possible if the published policy is combined with active behaviour to fulfil the commitment that triggers reliance on the side of the beneficiaries, provided that reliance is justified.

4.1.3. Conclusion

The analysis has so far generally focused on whether the corporate codes could assist when specifying the legally expected conduct for the company that holds itself out to comply with the corporate code by contract or self-commitment. Based on the previous analysis, there are arguably two topics that would require attention from the normative perspective.

First, while it could be shown that there are several options to interpret the corporate code as a relevant component when determining what conduct a company can be held liable for, it was equally emphasised that these options require a normative justification as to why the additional liability for non-compliance with a code should be imposed. This already became clear when interpreting the codes as a contractual assumption of responsibility under English law and a contract with protective effect under German law, respectively, on the condition that the existence of a duty of care towards incidental beneficiaries must be justified as fair, just and reasonable (England) or in the reasonable interest of the contracting parties (Germany). It has also played a role when discussing whether reliance on the publicly declared code was present in a relationship akin to a contract or whether reliance on the code could be interpreted as a voluntary assumption of responsibility towards particular third parties. As a result, in the further course of the analysis, a core focus will have to be placed on this additional justification and the underlying question whether there are normative reasons why the corporate codes ought to be a considered a factor that should influence the scope of liability for the party that undertakes to be bound by the code.

Second, in the course of analysing the publicly declared codes in particular, two different options were presented on how the corporate codes could become relevant when specifying liability. The act of publicly declaring a corporate code could be understood as an event of creating liability in the form of making a false or misleading statement.[108] Alternatively, the code could be used as an argument that the company voluntarily assumed responsibility and thus is also liable for omissions.[109] Due to the fact that these two options in general are both conceivable, it is also necessary to decide in the further course of analysis what form of liability is to be preferred in relation to the corporate codes.

4.2. THE CODE OBLIGATION AND THE APPLICABLE REMEDIES

Having discussed the potential influence of corporate codes on the scope of liability on the side of company, the following section will now focus on how the corporate codes would be qualified in terms of a legal duty and what remedies are available for breaches of this duty.

[108] See above, section 4.1.2.1. (p 157), text and accompanying footnotes.
[109] See above, section 4.1.2.2. (p 167), text and accompanying footnotes.

4.2.1. Corporate Codes as a Duty of Care

To start with, it is quite uncontroversial that the corporate code, in the interpretation above, would result in a tort law duty of care. It would be a duty of care that the company that is contractually bound to comply with the code or had publicly declared to comply with it owes to the beneficiaries of the codes. It is in this context primarily the exact characteristics of this duty of care that differ. With regard to the proposal to establish a duty of care on the basis of a contract, the duty of care would be interpreted as a duty to take reasonable care in the course of performing the contractual code obligation and to preserve the integrity and economic interests of those benefiting incidentally from the contract.[110] Insofar as the corporate code is related to the category of liability for negligent misstatements, the code would be an integral part of the legal duty on the side of the publishing company to make statements with reasonable care in a relationship akin to a contract.[111] If interpreted as *evidence* for a voluntary assumption of responsibility towards the specified beneficiaries, the code would become part of the legal duty to take reasonable care in order to prevent harm to beneficiaries and would oblige the company to also prevent harm from occurring.

In one way or another, these different forms of the duty of care all require the publicly declaring companies to take reasonable care in their operations. This, however, raises the additional question of how the standard of reasonable care is specified and, in particular, whether operational standards specified in corporate codes could also play a role in this respect. In fact, in the corporate codes debate, in several contributions one can already find the proposal to view the corporate codes as self-regulatory standards that influence the standard of due care and thus assist in determining whether the company breached the duty of care and thus acted negligently.[112] One core idea in this context is to draw analogies to technical standards and standards of particular professions that also play a role in determining what the law understands as reasonable care. To that end, one may argue that non-compliance with operational standards specified in corporate codes could provide the law with the indication of negligent behaviour or, conversely, compliance could signal that the company has not acted negligently.

[110] For English law, see Lord Browne-Wilkinson in *White v Jones* (n 4) 276: 'the law imposes a duty to the intended beneficiary to act with due expedition and care in relation to the task on which he has entered'. For German law, see Palandt-Grüneberg § 328, para 13; MüKo-Gottwald § 328, para 161 ('vertragliche Schutz- und Sorgfaltspflichten zugunsten Dritter').

[111] For English Law, see, eg, Collins (2003b) 182: 'The Law imposes a duty of care on parties to negotiations for a contract when they make statements to each other'; In German law, this would qualify as part of the general duty to negotiate in good faith; see, eg Palandt-Grüneberg § 311, para 11.

[112] Webb and Morrison (2004) 125ff; Glinski (2007) 133ff; Glinski (2008) 47f, 50ff, 57ff; Glinski (2011) 265ff; Herberg (2007) 219ff; Torrance (2011) 1603. See presumably in a similar direction Heijden (2011b) 196. Comparable suggestions to use commitments of companies as self-regulatory standards can be found in the legal debate on corporate governance codes: Hopt (1997) 402; Ulmer (2002b) 166f.

4.2.1.1. *The Standard of Taking Reasonable Care*

Focusing on the interpretation of the applicable standard of due care tort law, it should be noted that it represents a general principle in tort law that this standard is determined on an objective basis. In English law, this is reflected in the standard of the 'reasonable man'[113] or, in relation to professionals, the 'standard of the ordinary skilled man exercising and professing to have that special skill'.[114] In German law, the standard for negligence is, pursuant to § 276 BGB, one of 'reasonable care' that is determined on an objective basis.[115] The fact that the standard of reasonable care represents an objective one primarily has the result that the courts refer to objective factors and not to the individual character, capabilities or expertise of the person who is under a duty of care. In determining the objective standard, the courts take into consideration a variety of factors. It has to be clear that there are some factors used by the courts that do not play a role in the analysis of corporate codes. This applies, for instance, to the factors that are taken from the specific situation in which the harm occurs[116] or general economic factors, such as the risk involved in a particular undertaking[117] or the relationship between the cost of preventing harm and the harm that has been caused.[118] In addition to these more general factors, it is, however, accepted that the standard of reasonable care is also influenced by self-regulatory rules and it is here that the corporate codes could also play a role. In this context, one can distinguish between two possible ways in which the corporate codes could come into play. First, the corporate codes could be classified as an autonomously committed individual self-regulatory standard and could thus become relevant in specifying the individual standard for a particular company.[119] Second, the corporate codes could be interpreted as a broad self-regulatory standard that, comparable to the standards of particular professions or technical standards, is capable of specifying the standard of due care on an objective basis.[120]

[113] See especially the famous speech of Greer LJ in *Hall v Brooklands Racing Club* [1933] 1 KB 205, 224, who describes the reasonable man 'as "the man in the street", or "the man in the Clapham omnibus", or, as I recently read in an American author, "the man who takes the magazines at home, and in the evening pushes the lawn mower in his shirt sleeves"'.

[114] *Bolam v Friern Hospital* [1957] 1 WLR 582, 586.

[115] Established case law since RG RGZ 68, 422; BGH NJW 1953, 257.

[116] For situation-specific standards of due care in English law, one may refer to the event of an emergency, sports events or traffic situations: Deakin, Johnston and Markesinis (2007) 201ff. In German law, a prominent example for a lower standard of reasonable care based on situation-specific circumstances are sport injuries (BGH NJW 1976, 957, 958) and a prominent example for situations in which the standard is higher due to the specifics of the situation is road traffic (BGH NJW 1988, 909, 909).

[117] *Glasgow Corp v Muir* [1943] AC 448, 456 (per Lord MacMillan): 'There is no absolute standard, but it may be said that the degree of care required varies directly with the risk involved'; and *Paris v Stepney Borough Council* [1951] AC 367, 375 (per Lord Simonds).

[118] For English law, see *Tomlinson v Congleton BC* [2004] 1 AC 46, 82 (per Lord Hoffmann) and *Shine v Tower Hamlets LBC* [2006] EWCA Civ 852 [25] (per Buxton LJ), quoting *Bolton v Stone* [1951] AC 850 as authority. For German law, see Palandt-Grüneberg § 276, para 19 with further references to relevant case law.

[119] Glinski (2007) 135; Glinski (2008) 47ff; Herberg (2007) 218ff.

[120] Webb and Morrison (2004) 125ff; Glinski (2007) 136ff; Glinski (2008) 50ff; Podszun (2014) 64.

4.2.1.2. *Individual Components*

Interpreting the corporate codes as an expression of an individually committed or agreed higher standard of due care on the side of the publishing company is in this context the more difficult category to rely on. Having in mind that the standard of due care is generally an objective one, individual components in the person of the tortfeasor can only play a minor role at best. The success of this proposal thus depends mainly on whether a particular legal system accepts individual aspects as relevant factors for specifying the standard of due care. It is in fact in relation to this aspect that the English and the German legal systems differ to a certain extent.

Focusing on English law, it is the general rule that the standard of reasonable care remains entirely impersonal. In general, it is thus impossible to raise the standard with reference to individual factors,[121] as is equally the case with respect to the undertaking of lowering the standard due to individual factors.[122] Following this reluctance to take into consideration individual factors in the person alleged to be in breach of a duty of care, it seems quite difficult to argue that the influence of the corporate codes creates an individually higher standard of care. However, an important exception is the decision in *Stokes v Guest*,[123] in which the individual knowledge of an employer actually informed the objective standard of what can be expected from a prudent employer. In this decision, it was decided that the overall test for the standard of due care for employers as to the health and safety of employees remains an objective one that is determined by the general and recognised practice in this field. It is noteworthy, however, that the court held that the objective standard of a prudent employer is also influenced by a specific above-average knowledge in relation to the accepted practice: 'where he has in fact greater than average knowledge of the risks, he may be thereby obliged to take more than the average standard precautions'.[124] Hence, notwithstanding the generally objective standard in English law, it is still possible that a specific individual knowledge or expertise raises the standard of reasonable care. Following this interpretation, it is accordingly possible to treat the corporate codes equally as indications of a higher level of individual knowledge and expertise[125] that is capable of informing the objective standard of due care and thus requires that the respective company takes more precautions as they are specified in the commitment.

[121] Deakin, Johnston and Markesinis (2007) 201; Rogers (2006) 243.

[122] A famous example for this objective standard is *Nettleship v Weston* [1971] 2 QB 691, in which the Court of Appeal held that the standard of an ordinary, reasonably competent driver would even apply to a learner driver that has individual lower skills. The narrowly confined exceptions where a lower standard is accepted relate primarily to children or people with disabilities; see *Mullin v Richards* [1998] 1 WLR 1304.

[123] *Stokes v Guest* [1968] 1 WLR 1776.

[124] ibid 1783 (per Swanwick, J). See also at 1785: 'Such knowledge, however … brings its own responsibilities.'

[125] Affirmatively Glinski (2008) 47: 'The reason for this legal effect of private regulatory instruments on their authors is not party autonomy but the expertise that the instruments give evidence of.' A more detailed account on the relation between individual corporate codes and expertise can be found at Herberg (2007) 174ff; Herberg (2008) 31.

Slightly different from the rather strict objective approach in English law, it is in the context of German law a little easier to use individual standards when determining the standard of reasonable care. This is due to the fact that individual aspects of the person who is accused of acting negligently are recognised as exceptions to the generally objective standard insofar as they result in a higher diligence standard.[126] In this context, the courts have used particular individual competences of a person as reasons for raising the standard of due care compared to what would generally be required in a particular situation. Aspects that the courts have considered important were in this regard, for instance, the knowledge of a person[127] or a skill that the person had.[128] Based on this recognition, it is an option to interpret the corporate codes as an individual standard of due care if the operation standards in the corporate codes could be read as an individual expertise or skill that the company holds itself out to have.

Hence, it is generally possible in both legal systems to interpret the corporate codes as factors that could specify the standard of due care for the company that holds itself out to comply with the code.

4.2.1.3. *Industry Self-regulation and Practice*

Next to treating the codes as factors that specify an individual standard of due care for the particular company, it is also debated whether the codes could influence the objective standard of due care more generally. When determining the standard of due care, it is accepted that the rules of private professional bodies and accepted industry practices are taken into consideration.

In the context of English law, reference to professional and industry standards are quite common for determining the standard of due care for a particular profession.[129] In particular, the rules concerning medical practice represent professional standards that specify the standard of due care,[130] but such private standards are also important with respect to, for instance, engineers. Concerning the latter, the most prominent self-regulatory standards that are taken into consideration are the technical standards of the British Standards Institute.[131] In English law, these self-regulatory standards are interpreted as expressing professional standards that are generally used to specify what amounts objectively to negligent behaviour.[132]

[126] MüKo-Grundmann § 276, para 56; Erman-Westermann § 276, para 10. But see critically on this prevailing opinion that an individually higher standard is accepted Staudinger-Löwisch/Caspers § 276, para 30 ('in dieser Allgemeinheit nicht richtig').

[127] BGH VersR 1958, 94 (individual knowledge related to the traffic situation), OLG Koblenz, NJW-RR 2004, 1025 (an eight-year-old child had better knowledge of gas tanks than could be expected).

[128] See prominently BGH NJW 1987, 1479, where a specifically skilled medical doctor, more precisely the Chief Medical Doctor, was held to a higher standard than the ordinarily skilled doctor.

[129] Rogers (2006) 247ff; Deakin, Johnston and Markesinis (2007) 205ff.

[130] See fundamentally *Bolam v Friern Hospital* [1957] 1 WLR 582 concerning the professional standards of medical art.

[131] *Ward v Ritz Hotel* [1992] PIQR P315.

[132] ibid 327 (per McCowan LJ): 'the judge gave too little weight to the British Standard … they represent the consensus of professional opinion and practical experience as to the sensible safety precautions'.

In addition, these standards have also at least partly been used to establish a safe harbour. In some cases, compliance with these standards was used as an argument that the alleged tortfeasor had actually taken reasonable care and thus was not negligent.[133] Examples of relevant self-regulatory standards in the German context are, for instance, the standards of medical doctors or lawyers that are developed by the associations of these particular professions.[134] Other examples are the informal guidelines of the banking sector on the provision of financial services.[135] The most prominent example are the standards developed by the German Standards Institute (*Deutsches Institut für Normung* (DIN)) that the courts frequently consider in the course of specifying the standard of reasonable care.[136] In applying these standards, the courts have emphasised that these standards do not have statutory force as a legally binding standard; they merely represent indications as to what is an accepted practice and thus can objectively be expected as reasonable care.[137] Therefore, these standards do not represent a generally applicable standard and the failure to comply therewith automatically results in negligence. Non-compliance can only be treated as providing a strong indication that the standard of reasonable care has not been met. Conversely, however, it is accepted that the mere compliance with DIN norms does not have the result of an automatic finding that a person has not acted negligently.[138] Thus, within German law, self-regulatory standards do not establish a safe harbour.

Focusing on the corporate codes and their potential to be treated as self-regulatory standards, one could first at least consider interpreting the individual corporate codes as an admissible self-regulatory standard that specifies the industry practice. However, there are two main problems involved with such an interpretation. One problem is the lack of a generally sufficient degree of uniformity that would justify an interpretation of the corporate codes as a generally accepted practice. Thus, the interpretation of individual company codes as a general self-regulatory industry practice is only possible to the extent that common operational

[133] This was particularly discussed in relation to medical art, especially *Bolam v Friern Hospital* (n 130) 587 (per McNair, J): 'he is not guilty of negligence if he has acted in accordance with a practice accepted as proper by a responsible body of medical men skilled in that particular art'. However, the courts also established criteria that prevented the treatment of professional standards as a safe harbour; *cf Sidaway v Bethlem Royal Hospital* [1985] AC 871, 900 (per Lord Bridge) and *Bolitho v City and Hackney Authority* [1998] AC 232, 241ff (per Lord Browne-Wilkinson). For the incapability to exclude liability by referring to compliance with an accepted banking practice, see also *Lloyd's Bank v Savory* [1933] AC 201, 235 (per Lord Wright): 'they claim that this regrettable consequence resulted from their following the ordinary practice of bankers, sanctified by long and successful usage. I do not think this is a sound argument. The practice, on its very face, is inconsistent with provident precautions against a known risk, and the mere fact that it is usual and long established is not a sufficient justification'.

[134] For Germany, see, eg, Staudinger-Löwisch/Caspers § 276, para 42; Erman-Westermann § 276, para 12.

[135] OLG Köln NJW 1990, 2261, 2262.

[136] BGH NJW 1984, 801, 802; 1988, 2667; NJW-RR 2005, 386, 387.

[137] BGH NJW 1998, 2814 2815 ('Die DIN-Normen sind keine Rechtsnormen, sondern private technische Regeln mit Empfehlungscharakter').

[138] A prominent example in which negligence was present despite compliance with DIN norms is BGH NJW 1984, 801, 802. See generally on this question Prütting/Wegen/Weinrich-Schmidt-Kessel § 276, para 11a.

standards exist among a sufficient number of companies in the same sector.[139] In addition, in contrast to the self-regulatory standards that are accepted in the law as relevant to specify the standard of due care, such as technical standards, corporate codes are developed and adopted differently. They are not developed by private associations that are recognised as having a particular expertise or even the official assignment to develop common standards, such as the Standard Institutes in Germany or Britain.[140] It is instead individual companies that develop their own standards for their individual operations and these standards are developed internally or at best in informal cooperation with other companies in the field. Other suitable candidates for an interpretation as standards that express a generally followed practice could then be seen in the public codes of conduct, eg, the recommendations and guidelines by international political organisations on socially responsible business conduct. Their recognition as standards that inform the standard of due care could be based here on the increasing and uniform reference to these standards in private codes. As such, one could propose treating these public codes as an evolving industry practice that specifies the standard of due care for socially responsible globally operating companies.

4.2.1.4. Interim Conclusion

The discussion on corporate codes as standards that are capable of specifying the standard of due care has revealed two different angles through which operational standards specified in corporate codes could become relevant. First, one could interpret the corporate codes as an individual standard of due care that specifies the standard of reasonable care for a particular company. This option primarily depends on whether the corporate codes could be interpreted as instances that reveal a particular skill or knowledge of the company. Second, while a sceptical position was taken as to whether individual company codes would qualify as self-regulatory standards that are capable of specifying an industry practice, it was presented at least as an option that this role could be assigned to the more standardised public codes of conduct that companies increasingly refer to in their own codes.

4.2.2. Applicable Remedies

With regard to the suggested interpretation of corporate codes as part of the legally expected conduct of a company, the enforcement structure for breaches is not very

[139] See pointedly Herberg (2007) 216f with respect to the chemical industry: 'In der Chemiebranche besteht die Grundeinheit industrieller Selbstregulierung, zumindest was transnationale Problemlagen betrifft, zwar nach wie vor in den einzelnen Konzernen, die sich aus eigenem Antrieb um die Installation geeigneter Steuerungssysteme bemühen und hierbei jeweils ihr eigenes, organisationsinternes „Binnenrecht" schaffen; gleichsam als Nebeneffekt dieser Bemühungen kristallisiert sich aber nach und nach ein einheitliches Mindestniveau an Sorgfaltsmaßstäben heraus.' See also for the conditions of this requirement of uniformity among corporate standards Glinski (2011) 266ff.

[140] On this public recognition of the standard-setting bodies in England and Germany, see generally Schepel (2005) 117ff, 126ff.

difficult to classify. It follows the general rules on non-contractual liability and thus gives those detrimentally affected a cause of action to claim compensation for the incurred losses. However, in this context, a particular restriction needs to be mentioned as to the types of losses that can be compensated by affected third parties. In general, liability in tort in both legal systems only allows compensation to be claimed for damages to property and bodily integrity; thus, not all losses incurred in reliance on the corporate code can be compensated. In English law, this becomes apparent in the restrictions of the types of damages that can be compensated on the basis of the tort of negligence, which in principle covers only physical losses and losses to property and, only in the exceptional situation that there is a 'special relationship', also economic losses.[141] In the context of German law, the limitation to the recovery of losses related to bodily integrity, health and property already becomes apparent from the fact that they are enumerated rights, the violation of which can lead to liability in tort. Conversely, it is the general rule that economic losses are not considered an absolute right the infringement of which could be remedied with the rules on tort liability.[142]

For the liability for non-compliance with corporate codes, this has the result that only parts of the non-complying behaviour can be remedied. While a tort law perspective on the corporate code may be used to accommodate claims for what can be broadly phrased as fundamental breaches of particular rights, such as the breach of health and safety standards, it is less feasible with regard to the many other commitments in the corporate codes. In particular, rights as to adequate remuneration, excessive overtime or trade union representation are difficult to remedy on the basis of tort law.[143] Having said that, the recovery of economic losses in particular is in principle possible, but depends on how the corporate codes become relevant for specifying liability. For constellations in which the affected beneficiaries base their claim on a contractual assumption of responsibility based on the incorporation of the corporate code into a contract, recovery of financial losses incurred due to reliance on the proper performance of the contract can be recovered. This is due to the fact that English law recognises this form as a specific constellation in which it is exceptionally possible to also recover economic losses[144] and German law treats the applicable contract with protective effect as part of the rules on contractual liability that allow recovery of the reliance interest, including pure economic losses.[145] The same holds true for the option to interpret non-compliance with corporate codes as a form of liability for negligent misstatement. This form of liability represents the second main constellation in

[141] *Murphy v Brentwood District Council* [1991] 1 AC 398, overruling the previous authority of *Anns v Merton London Borough Council* [1978] AC 728.

[142] This is established case law, eg, BGHZ 27, 137; NJW 1978, 2031, 3032; Soergel-Spickhoff § 823, para 87.

[143] Saage-Maaß (2011) 8f.

[144] See especially *Henderson v Merrett Syndicated Ltd* [1995] 2 AC 145, 181 (per Lord Goff): 'for if a person assumes responsibility to another in respect of certain services, there is no reason why he should not be liable in damages for that other in repsect of economic loss which flows from the negligent performance of those services'. See also *White v Jones* (n 4) 268 (per Lord Goff).

[145] See, eg, BGH NJW 1965, 1955, 1957; BGHZ 133, 168, 171f.

which recovery of economic losses is accepted insofar as the losses are a result of the reliance on the correctness of the statement.[146] In these cases, it is possible for beneficiaries of the code to recover not only the physical harm and losses to their property but also financial losses.

4.3. OVERALL CONCLUSION: CORPORATE CODES UNDER CIVIL LIABILITY RULES

After having described the different options of relating the corporate codes to the legal liability of the company that undertakes to be bound by the code, the concluding remarks here seek to identify the core aspects that deserve further attention from the normative perspective. The analysis focused on two particular angles through which corporate codes could become relevant: first, corporate codes could be relevant for determining the scope of liability of the company that is contractually obliged to comply with the code or publicly commits itself to comply with the code; and, second, the codes could be a private standard that is capable of specifying the standard of due care. With respect to both of these angles, several possible patterns were identified that require further attention.

In the course of analysing the potential of the corporate codes to influence the liability of the corporate entity, it became clear that this option is generally possible. However, in this context, it has also become clear that private law requires additional normative criteria in order to justify the existence of such a duty of care. In the context of English law, this became apparent in the criterion of whether it would be 'fair, just and reasonable' to establish a duty[147] and also in the context of determining whether the company and the detrimentally affected beneficiaries were in a 'special relationship'.[148] With respect to German law, these criteria became relevant when seeking to determine whether the protective scope of the contract was in the 'reasonable interest' of the contracting parties[149] and, when discussing the justification for treating the relationship between the company and the beneficiaries as a *Sonderverbindung*, whether that gives rise to liability for misleading statement[150] and, in the course of discussing the options of interpreting the behaviour of the company, as a *Verkehrspflicht*.[151] As all these possible interpretations were, so far, only presented without focusing on whether one of these options ought to be realised, the following theoretical analysis will focus more specifically on whether and for what reason it would be justified to let the scope of liability be influenced by the presence of a corporate code. Yet, an additional

[146] For English law, see generally Deakin, Johnston and Markesinis (2007) 143ff. With respect to German law, the general rule for the recovery of economic losses stems—comparable to the contract with protective effect—from the fact that liability in a *Sonderverbindung* is viewed as being related to the rules on quasi-contract and not tort liability.

[147] See above, section 4.1.1.1. (p 151), text and accompanying footnotes.

[148] See above, section 4.1.2.1.1. (p 158), text and accompanying footnotes.

[149] See above, section 4.1.1.2. (p 153), text and accompanying footnotes.

[150] See above, section 4.1.2.1.2. (p 162), text and accompanying footnotes.

[151] See above, section 4.1.2.2.2. (p 171), text and accompanying footnotes.

topic for further debate was identified. In the course of determining the potential influence of the codes on the scope of liability, two options were presented as to how private law could approach legal liability in particular for publicly declared corporate codes. The corporate codes could become important for liability as a false or misleading declaration to the public that the beneficiaries rely on to their detriment. It was, however, also an option to view the publicly declared codes as evidence of a voluntary assumption of responsibility on the side of the company. This suggests that one should also take a closer look at which option is to be preferred for dealing with corporate codes. This means that one of the core aspects of the theoretical analysis will be to develop a normative perspective on whether the corporate codes ought to give rise to liability and, if so, discuss further what form of liability is most appropriate. A second way is to make use of corporate codes as self-regulatory private standards that could assist in specifying the standard of due care. With respect to this suggestion, the question was not only whether the corporate codes or the more standardised public codes become relevant, it is also the appropriate classification, eg, their treatment as an individual standard[152] or even as a general standard of accepted industry practice,[153] that seems to require further scrutiny. As a result, the specific self-regulatory character of the corporate codes and the public codes will be focused on more specifically in the course of the theoretical analysis.

[152] See above, section 4.2.1.2. (p 179), text and accompanying footnotes.
[153] See above, section 4.2.1.3. (p 180), text and accompanying footnotes.

5

Corporate Codes and Unfair Trading Behaviour

The Role of Unfair Commercial Practices Law

> [S]uits by misled consumers constitute one indirect but potentially effective and underutilized way of enforcing CSR commitments on behalf of workers.[1]

THE FIELD OF unfair commercial practices law has probably received the most attention in the corporate codes debate so far. Nearly all research on corporate codes at least mentions this field as a handy category for regulating corporate codes.[2] This is astonishingly the case despite the fact that this rather specific area is narrowly confined to the regulation of business-to-consumer practices and does thus not even fulfil the function of regulating social and environmental corporate behaviour. The particular prominence of this area in the corporate codes debate is most likely related to the fact that two important lawsuits on codes of conduct have been initiated in which unfair commercial practices law served as the legal basis. In the first place, the US case *Kasky v Nike*[3] case triggered a discussion about whether unfair commercial practices law is called for to regulate public statements of companies by which they declare compliance with their corporate codes if these codes deal specifically with workplace standards in production, general respect for human rights or environmental protection. Despite being initially closely related to the US legal system and the debate on the scope of the constitutional protection of free speech, the decision also crossed the Atlantic and resulted in a debate on the scope of European unfair trading laws in relation to corporate codes. A couple of years later, a consumer organisation and NGOs filed a claim relating to a misleading advertisement against the retailer Lidl for

[1] Estlund (2012) 253.

[2] See, eg, Kocher (2002) 275ff; Kocher (2005); Webb and Morrison (2004) 133ff; Joseph (2004) ch 5; Murphy (2005) 431; Sobczak (2006) 171ff; McBarnet (2007) 40ff; Glinski (2007) 126ff, 130ff; Glinski (2008) 46f, 48ff, 53ff; Glinski (2011) 193ff, 279ff; Dam (2008) 49f; Wouters and Chanet (2008) 285ff; Heijden (2011b) 217ff; Henning-Bodewig (2010); Henning-Bodewig (2011); Henning-Bodewig and Liebenau (2013); Revak (2012) 1667ff; Estlund (2012) 252f; and very recently Hilty and Henning-Bodewig (2014).

[3] *Kasky v Nike* 93 Cal Rptr 2d 854 (California Court of Appeal); 45 P 3d 243 (California Supreme Court); 123 S Ct 1776 (US Supreme Court).

non-compliance with its publicly declared code.[4] This case can be read as initiating a follow-up discussion that focused on whether and how the use of corporate codes would be regulated by unfair commercial practices law. In the following, these two related legal debates on corporate codes are introduced, using the two cases as a starting point.

To start with, some general remarks will be given on how the general comparative analysis pursued in this study is envisaged in light of the maximum harmonisation of this field (section 5.1). The analysis will continue by focus on *Nike v Kasky* and the controversy on the scope of the Unfair Commercial Practices Directive and the extent to which this instrument as implemented in the national legal systems regulates corporate codes (section 5.2) and the different ways in which corporate codes could be regulated (section 5.3). The final section will then analyse the legal consequences that the regulation of corporate codes by unfair commercial practices law can have (section 5.4).

5.1. THE COMPARATIVE APPROACH TO UNFAIR COMMERCIAL PRACTICES LAW

Before addressing the specific questions that arise when seeking to relate the use of corporate codes to unfair commercial practices law, some preliminary remarks on the comparative approach in this chapter need to be made. It remains the general approach of this study to analyse the interaction between corporate codes and private law on the basis of two different national legal systems. However, in the particular context of unfair commercial practices law, a strict application of this methodological focus seems to be quite difficult due to the complexity of this area in terms of the legal area that it is related to in different national legal systems, the national differences in the enforcement structure, and the interaction between the national rules and the European legislation in this field.

It should be noted that the field has been subject to several maximum harmonisation attempts on the European level in the form of Directives and Regulations, [5] the most relevant for this study being the Unfair Commercial Practices Directive.[6] Therefore, to the extent that these harmonised rules are already relevant for the corporate codes or, more precisely, the provisions as they have been implemented in the national legal systems on the regulation of advertisements and unfair

[4] *Verbraucherzentrale Hamburg v Lidl*, Statement of Complaint filed 6 April 2010, case settled on 14 April 2010. Detailed information is available at: http://business-humanrights.org/en/lidl-lawsuit-re-working-conditions-in-bangladesh.

[5] Council Directive 84/450/EEC concerning misleading advertisement [1984] OJ L250/17; Directive 97/7/EC on the protection of consumers in respect of distance contracts [1997] OJ L144/19; Directive 98/27/EC on injunctions for the protection of consumers' interests [1998] OJ L166/51; Directive 2002/65/EC concerning the distance marketing of consumer financial services [2002] OJ L271/16; Regulation (EC) 2006/2004 on cooperation between national authorities responsible for the enforcement of consumer protection laws [2004] OJ L364/1; Directive 2006/114/EC concerning misleading and comparative advertising, [2006] OJ L376/21.

[6] Directive 2005/29/EC of 11 May 2005 concerning unfair business-to-consumer commercial practices in the internal market [2005] OJ L149/22.

competition, these harmonised rules will be used as the legal basis for the following analysis. However, it is still recognised that, in spite of the strong harmonisation in this particular field, the implementation of the Directive and its interpretation by the national authorities is still likely to produce different outcomes. This is first due to the fact that the implementation of the Directive can be found in the national rules on advertising and market behaviour that have different regulatory characters. In fact, it is particularly the German and the English systems that differ here quite significantly. The German regulation of unfair commercial practices is comprehensively regulated by the Unfair Competition Act (*Gesetz gegen den unlauteren Wettbewerb* (UWG)), which is enforced in the civil courts. The regulation of unfair trading behaviour is therefore characterised by a long-lasting evolution of detailed and complex case law and an intense scholarly debate on the interpretation of the various provisions.[7] In England, by contrast, the area of unfair commercial practices is, to a large extent, a matter of self-regulatory codes on advertising practices developed and enforced by non-judicial advertisement bodies. This emphasis on self-regulation in this particular area has a long-standing tradition in the UK and is appreciated for being cost-efficient, speedy and cooperative.[8] Concerning the self-regulatory system, the most important sources are the Advertising Codes developed by the Committee of Advertising Practice (CAP)[9] that are subject to a self-regulatory enforcement procedure that is located at the Advertising Standards Authority (ASA).[10] This system of self-regulatory advertisement control is complemented by subsidiary statutory regulation in the form of administrative and criminal law enforcement. The most important statutory sources are the criminally oriented Trade Descriptions Act 1968 and the administrative regulations that aimed at consumer protection.[11] Noteworthy in this context particularly is the Consumer Protection from Unfair Trading Regulation 2008,[12] which implements and echoes verbatim[13] the Unfair Commercial Practices Directive and replaced some parts of other existing Acts. In addition, it also needs to be emphasised that the regulation of advertisement and the interpretation of 'fairness' is influenced by

[7] It should be noted that there are also self-regulatory systems that deal with commercial practices in particular fields. Yet, in the legal debate, these self-regulatory mechanisms are not viewed as being equally positive. It is instead emphasised that the self-regulatory systems are incomplete because they operate on a voluntary basis and do not always lead to appropriate results. A concise overview of the self-regulatory systems and the main points of criticism in the German debate is provided by Baeter (2011) 26ff.

[8] Howells and Weatherill (2005) 422f.

[9] These are primarily the UK Code of Non-broadcast Advertising, Sales Promotion and Direct Marketing and the UK Code of Broadcast Advertising, available at: www.cap.org.uk/Advertising-Codes.aspx.

[10] For an overview on the structure, organisation and operation of the ASA with a discussion on the advantages and criticism of this self-regulatory approach, see generally Parry (2000).

[11] The most important are the Consumer Protection Act 1987 and the Control of Misleading Advertisement Regulations 1988, which implemented Directive 84/450/EEC on misleading advertisement [1984] OJ L250/17.

[12] The Consumer Protection from Unfair Trading Regulations 2008, SI 2008/1277. The other important recent effort in relation to unfair trading is the Business Protection from Unfair Trading Regulations 2008, SI 2008/1276.

[13] See the Report of the European Commission on the application of the Unfair Commercial Practices Directive, COM (2013) 139 final 3.

different national cultures that lead to different perceptions and interpretations of what decent trading behaviour entails.[14] Against this background of diversity, it is indeed quite likely that the different regulatory structures will also influence the interpretation of unfair commercial practices in relation to corporate codes in the national legal systems, even if they are based on a common regulatory framework.

Therefore, when analysing the corporate codes in this area, a difficulty arises in terms of taking into consideration the discussions at a European level and the maximum harmonisation of this field, and of paying due respect to the national specifics and the fact that the harmonised system is imposed on systems that differ quite significantly. Yet the purpose of this study is neither a comprehensive analysis of the success of harmonisation in the field of unfair commercial practices law, nor the interaction between national law and European rules, but the specific topic of examining the relevance of corporate codes in this particular field. Therefore, the methodological choice is to modify the comparative approach in this particular field slightly. The following considerations will be taken from the assumption that the field is characterised by maximum harmonisation.[15] This means that the discussion on the corporate codes will depart from the harmonised rules on unfair commercial practices that are laid down in the Directive and refers to these provisions as the basic rules for both countries. However, in order to be able to analyse the corporate codes under the harmonised rules, the national debates and related case law will also be consulted, in particular with regard to the interpretation. In this regard, the analysis in German law will take into consideration the academic debate and the existing case law on corporate codes that are discussed in the UWG. The legal status in English law will focus on any guiding documents given by the Office of Fair Trading, requirements on fair advertisement as laid down in the Advertising Codes of the CAP and the ASA and, to the extent available, related decisions of criminal or administrative proceedings against traders. By using this combined approach, it will be possible to adhere consistently to the general approach taken in this study to conduct a solution-oriented analysis of the problem of the corporate codes while also paying due respect to the regulatory complexity of this particular field.[16]

5.2. THE SCOPE OF UNFAIR COMMERCIAL PRACTICES LAW

5.2.1. Setting the Scene: From *Kasky v Nike* to Europe

The debate on whether the corporate codes would fall within the ambit of unfair commercial practices law is closely related to the case *Kasky v Nike*. In this case, a

[14] See extensively on the problem of the European Fairness concept and different national perceptions Micklitz (2006a) 86ff.

[15] *cf* Collins (2010) 118, who calls the Directive a 'more aggressive approach towards harmonisation of national laws than we have witnessed in previous consumer measures'.

[16] For similar methodological approaches in the corporate debate, *cf* in particular Glinski (2011) 196ff, who refers to the provisions of the Directive and relates them to German case law on the Unfair Competition Act; and Heijden (2011a) 217, who bases her analysis primarily on the provisions of the Consumer Sales Directive and only refers to the Dutch rules in footnotes.

Californian public interest lawyer sought to explore the possibilities of enforcing the publicly available corporate code of the sportswear company Nike with the help of unfair commercial practices law. The background of the lawsuit was the public statement made by Nike in the aftermath of a public outcry regarding its working conditions in supplier factories at the end of the 1990s. After civil society groups and the media accused the company of exploiting workers in foreign countries where it produced sportswear, Nike reacted by launching a campaign that was directed towards underlining its ongoing commitment to improve working conditions; editorial advertisements in magazines were placed, press releases were published and letters were sent to universities. The company on several occasions emphasised the fact that it had developed and published a code of conduct that should further compliance with fundamental workplace standards in supplier factories, but it was careful enough to avoid relating the campaign directly to its products. After NGOs revealed that working conditions had in the meantime still not improved, Marc Kasky filed a claim on the basis of the Californian Unfair Competition and False Advertising Law,[17] alleging that Nike had misled the consumer public by its campaign that purportedly contained false statements about the working conditions in the company's supply chain.

The core issue in this lawsuit was whether such general statements concerning labour standards are actually subject to the regulation of fair trading laws. This issue was framed as the question whether the statements would qualify as political speech, which due to the high protection of free speech would prevent advertising laws from being applicable. Actually, the first two instances in the proceedings interpreted the company's reference to its corporate code as political speech.[18] The California Supreme Court, however, disagreed and overruled the decision. It declared that the statements were commercial speech because the company was a commercial speaker addressing a commercial audience with a commercial purpose.[19] The situation as to whether public declarations of companies on labour standards would effectively qualify as political or commercial speech remained to a certain extent uncertain because the US Supreme Court refused to decide on this question in substance and the case was eventually settled. Yet the decision of the California Supreme Court as the last court that ruled on this matter points at least slightly in the direction of denying companies free speech protection when they make public statements concerning their policy on social and environmental issues. The scholarly debate seemed to be undecided on this

[17] California Business and Professions Code, ss 17200ff, 17500ff.

[18] *Kasky v Nike*, California Court of Appeal (n 3) 861: 'Information about the labor practices at Nike's overseas plants thus constitutes data relevant to a controversy of great public interest in our times.'

[19] *Kasy v Nike*, California Supreme Court (n 3) 259: 'Because in the statements at issue here Nike was acting as a commercial speaker, because its intended audience was primarily the buyers of its products, and because the statements consisted of factual representations about its own business operations, we conclude that the statements were commercial speech for purposes of applying state laws designed to prevent false advertising and other forms of commercial deception' and at 262: 'An advertisement primarily intended to reach consumers and to influence them to buy the speaker's products is not exempt from the category of commercial speech because the speaker also has a secondary purpose to influence lenders, investors, or lawmakers.'

matter.[20] The particular controversy about whether statements related to working conditions would qualify as commercial or political speech certainly needs to be viewed against the US background, in which the protection of free speech is an issue of particular importance. Although the fundamental right to free speech is also by no means irrelevant for the debates on advertisement in the European context,[21] fundamental rights in general seem on the European side of the Atlantic at least not to form a core obstacle for the application of unfair commercial practices law to CSR communication.[22] These differences notwithstanding, the *Kasky v Nike* case did effectively trigger a debate amongst European scholars as to whether the rules on unfair commercial practices law would in fact be equally applicable for the public commitments of companies to comply with their corporate codes. The debate currently addresses two particular topics that relate to recital (7) and Article 1 of the Unfair Commercial Practices Directive (UCPD). First, in a similar vein to *Kasky v Nike*, yet not in the guise of the protection of free speech, it became an issue whether the substantive content of corporate codes, ie, social and environmental standards, could represent an obstacle for their regulation by unfair commercial practices law. This was debated, on the one hand, by discussing whether such statements would qualify as matters of taste and decency, which are excluded from the scope of the Directive. On the other hand, at least in the beginning, it was not entirely certain whether such statements would be outside the scope of the Directive because they do not affect the 'economic interests' of consumers as explicitly required in Article 1 UCPD. Finally, a more intense discussion emerged with respect to the definition of *commercial* practice and whether corporate codes could qualify as such.

5.2.2. The Environmental and Social Content of Corporate Codes

The first two issues seemed to have been solved quite quickly. It became the prevailing opinion that statements related to social and environmental aspects would hardly qualify as a matter of taste and decency.[23] What was slightly more controversially debated was whether statements on social and environmental aspects would be excluded due to the reference in Article 1 to behaviour affecting the consumers'

[20] For those in favour of commercial speech and regulation of publicly declared corporate codes by advertising laws, see, eg, Lu (2000) 627; Joseph (2004), ch 5, 101ff. For those arguing for free speech protection, see, eg, McIntyre (2004); Sutton (2004).

[21] For similarities between the US debate and the debates in Germany triggered by the landmark decision on the Benetton advertisement (BVerfGE 102, 347—Benetton I; BVerfG WM 2003, 1033—Benetton II), see Kübler and Kübler (2003) 922f.

[22] See more in detail on this aspect Streinz (2014).

[23] See, eg, Henning-Bodewig (2011) 1018. A probable reason why the restriction of 'taste and decency' became an issue in the first place is that the Commission's Proposal for the Directive stated that 'matters of taste, decency and *social responsibility* will be outside the scope'; see European Commission, Proposal for a Directive concerning unfair business-to-consumer commercial practices, COM (2003) 356 final, para 39 (emphasis added). But see the partly sceptical perspective of Glinski (2008) 46f, who predicts that 'statements made regarding the use of environmentally sound or ethical production methods may not even come under the Directive'.

'economic interests'. The practical relevance of the discussion was the following. If the law on unfair commercial practices were applicable to all sorts of corporate statements, the rules could potentially conflict with national or European rules in the field of environmental or social policy.[24] Yet, based on the understanding that environmental and social aspects prove to play an increasingly important role for the purchase decisions of consumers, a tendency could be observed in favour of treating such interests as being relevant.[25] Following this argument, the corporate codes can fall within the ambit of the regulation of unfair commercial practices to the extent that and as long as companies deliberately link them to their marketing communications and consumers use these communications as criteria in their purchase decisions. It is thus the assumption of the deliberate use of corporate codes on the consumer market and their influence on the decision of other market actors that eventually allows unfair commercial practices law to be as applicable to the codes.

5.2.3. Corporate Codes as Commercial Practices

5.2.3.1. Public Communication on Corporate Codes

When focusing on the companies' use of corporate codes on the consumer market, one topic for debate still remains. To what extent do the corporate codes qualify as commercial practices? The facts of *Kasky v Nike* indicate that it is primarily the reference to the corporate code in various forms of marketing communication that represents a commercial practice. In this context, however, it is debatable whether all types of communication on the code would be covered given that, pursuant to the Directive, a commercial practice refers only to commercial communication that is '*directly* related to influencing consumers' transactional decisions *in relation to products*'.[26] Moreover, recital (7) reads that the Directive excludes 'commercial practices carried out primarily for other purposes … such as annual reports and corporate promotional literature'. Consequently, while it is obvious that corporate code communication in product advertisements represents a commercial practice, it is less clear whether corporate communication on the code in other forms of communication would also qualify as such. This applies in particular to sustainability reporting, public relations communications or online communications, for which generally a classification as commercial practice remains contested.[27] In relation to the corporate codes, there seems arguably to be a slight tendency in

[24] Wilhelmsson (2006) 62.

[25] ibid 63: 'If consumers' economic interests are understood sufficiently broadly, it should be possible to condemn such statements with the help of the Directive, as they most certainly may affect the transactional decisions of some consumers'; Glinski (2011) 198f.

[26] Article 2(d) UCPD (emphasis added).

[27] A broad interpretation of commercial practice also covering these forms of communication is favoured by, among others, Wilhelmsson (2006) 54; and Keirsbilck (2011) 229. A narrow interpretation is favoured by, among others, Köhler and Lettl (2003) 1034–35; Ernst (2010) 1311 ('kaum Fälle denkbar'); and Birk (2014) 171ff (who argues against interpreting sustainability reports as commercial practices).

favour of treating such broad public relations statements as covered if they are used for marketing purposes towards the consumer and not only as information on the corporate policy.[28] This position also resembles the US position, as illustrated by the California Supreme Court, which argued that regulation is necessary to capture 'statements made in the context of a modern, *sophisticated public relations campaign*' that has eventually directed towards increasing sales.[29] However, it is equally true that applying this understanding to all types of communication would effectively render it practically impossible to draw a distinction between communications covered by the Directive and those that are not, as it is difficult to imagine that there is any corporate communication that is not capable of influencing the consumer.[30] Thus, the criterion to determine whether communication on the corporate codes is covered will have to focus not only on the potential influence that the corporate code may have, but also on the purpose that the company pursues with its code communication. On this basis, it could be possible to qualify merely those forms of communication as a commercial practice in which companies refer to their corporate code with the objective of seeking an advantage on the market and improving their reputation.[31]

5.2.3.2. *Non-compliance with Corporate Codes*

An additional evolving issue in the current debate on corporate codes is whether unfair commercial practices law is also capable of regulating non-complying behaviour of companies with their code. More precisely, from the perspective of unfair commercial practices law, one could focus not only on the use of the corporate codes for marketing purposes as a behaviour that could be unfair but also on the actual violation of social or environmental standards to the extent that they result in an unfair competitive advantage on the market.[32] In general, it should be noted that the restriction of the UCPD to business-to-consumer commercial practices renders it difficult to cover practices that do not directly influence the consumer.[33] However, taking into consideration the national perspectives, it remains at least conceivable to regulate corporate conduct that violates social or environmental standards insofar as this conduct has an influence on the marketing and the distribution of a product. With respect to English law, one can refer to the Guidance of the Office of Fair Trading on the Consumer Regulations on Unfair

[28] See, eg, Glinski (2011) 198f with further references; Henning-Bodewig and Liebenau (2013) 755f. See also Köhler (2014) 163ff, who differentiates between CSR statements in posters that address consumers and on websites, which would qualify as a commercial practice, and CSR statements in magazines that are directed towards informing other businesses, which would not.

[29] *Kasky v Nike*, California Supreme Court (n 3) 313 (emphasis added).

[30] On this point, see Köhler and Lettl (2003) 1035: 'dass eine klare Abgrenzung zwischen unmittelbarer und (nur) mittelbar absatzfördernden Maßnahmen in der Praxis kaum möglich ist'.

[31] See in this direction Henning-Bodewig (2010) 1103ff; Henning-Bodewig (2011) 1020 ('Als *Faustregel* wird man jedoch sagen können, dass … nicht die good governance Regeln als solche … dem Lauterkeitsrecht unterliegen, sehr wohl jedoch ihr *Einsatz zu Marketingzwecken*' (emphasis in original).

[32] This aspect is dealt with by Kocher (2005) 648f; Kocher (2008) 79ff; Glinski (2011) 292ff; Henning-Bodewig (2010) 1103ff; Henning-Bodewig (2011) 1020ff.

[33] See generally on this restriction Wilhelmsson (2006) 69f.

Trading that deems the definition of commercial practices to be broad and also covering 'acts and omissions, which occur further up the supply chain' if the product is eventually sold to a consumer.[34] In the context of German law, one can refer to the fact that the Federal High Court of Justice at least indicated that breaches of social standards in the manufacturing process could also become relevant in unfair commercial practices law provided that this internal behaviour leads to a direct competitive advantage on the market.[35] Consequently, in the context of unfair commercial practices law, it becomes at least a conceivable option to include in the regulation not only the act of communicating corporate codes but also actual non-complying behaviour with the voluntary standard provided that such internal and pre-trading behaviour has an influence on the market.

5.3. CORPORATE CODES AS UNFAIR COMMERCIAL PRACTICES: FROM *KASKY v NIKE* TO *VERBRAUCHERZENTRALE HAMBURG v LIDL*

After having focused on whether the scope of unfair commercial practices law on the regulation of trade practices allows for the regulation of corporate codes, the following section will shift the focus and will discuss how corporate codes would be regulated by this area. In fact, while scholars were still debating the scope of unfair commercial practices law, NGOs[36] were already busy preparing another lawsuit against a company that had allegedly failed to comply with its corporate code of conduct. Their efforts eventually resulted in filing a claim against the German retailer Lidl in 2010.

In this particular case, the consumer association that officially filed the lawsuit focused on two communicative contexts in which reference to the corporate code was included. First, the allegations of unfairness related to the internet presentation of the company in which the retailer stated that it was a member of the Business Social Compliance Initiative (BSCI) and presented itself as a responsible member that campaigns for worldwide minimum workplace standards and has in place a corporate code to improve working conditions worldwide. Second, the company advertised its membership of the BSCI and its commitment to improving workplace standards in its regular product flyers that were distributed to households across Germany. After an investigation of one of the NGOs at the companies' supplier factories in Bangladesh revealed that the working conditions in Lidl's supplier factories were not in compliance with what it publicly described in its communication as 'fair', the claim was filed with the allegation that these public declarations represented an unfair commercial practice. Since the retailer

[34] Office of Fair Trading (2008) 14 (para 4.3).

[35] BGHZ 120, 320—Tariflohnunterschreitung (not paying the minimum wage is not per se a commercial practice, but it would be qualified as such if used for the purpose of gaining a competitive advantage on the market). Yet, interpreting the violation of environmental standards in the production process as unfair trading behavior was seen sceptically in BGHZ 144, 255—Abgasemissionen (violation of environmental law in the production is not per se a commercial practice).

[36] In this case, the NGOs involved were the European Center for Constitutional and Human Rights and the Clean Clothes Campaign in cooperation with the Consumer Advice Center Hamburg.

immediately signed a declaration of omission, the case was not decided, which naturally gave rise to speculation on how the court would or should have decided.

Due to the fact that Lidl published its commitments in conjunction with product advertisements, at least as far as the product flyers were concerned, the debate on the scope of the Unfair Commercial Practices Directive in terms of the covered communication did not become directly relevant. What became the crucial issue of this case instead was whether reference to the corporate policy and the commitment to comply with the code of conduct of the BSCI was misleading for consumers because the product flyer contained false or misleading information on the actual violations or even misled consumers by omitting information on the actual efforts and the membership requirements of the BSCI. Thus, from the perspective of unfair commercial practices law, the publication of the code was discussed as a potentially unfair commercial practice in the form of providing misleading information on the 'nature of the trader',[37] the 'extent of the trader's commitments'[38] or the 'nature of the product',[39] respectively. In the subsequent debate, one can also find the suggestion to categorise CSR communications even as constellations in which the misleading omission could play a role.[40] Based on the fact that the brief statements of the company on their CSR policies are not always very specific, it could be argued that effectively material information on the actual engagement of the company was omitted that would have been necessary for the consumer to make an informed decision.[41] This latter suggestion would of course even go one step further. It would effectively oblige companies not only to refrain from providing misleading information in the CSR communication that they decide to publish, but would also require them to provide information on their CSR policies in the first place. Given the far-reaching impact of this proposal, however, this suggestion remains highly contested.[42] Apart from these different options to interpret the corporate code communication or even the lack thereof as an unfair commercial practice, the potential link to the corporate code could also be the non-complying behaviour. In this context, the most prominent suggestion currently is to relate corporate codes to Article 6(2b) UCPD, which declares 'non-compliance with a code of conduct' to be an unfair commercial practice.[43] Occasionally, it is suggested in this context to interpret the non-complying behaviour as a breach of

[37] Article 6, para 1(f) UCPD, implemented in Germany in § 5 I No 3 UWG and in England in s 5 (4)(j) Consumer Protection from Unfair Trading Regulations 2008.

[38] Article 6, para 1(c) UCPD, implemented in Germany in § 5 I No 3 UWG and in England in s 5 (4)(c) Consumer Protection from Unfair Trading Regulations 2008.

[39] Article 6, para 1(a) UCPD, implemented in Germany in § 5 I No 1 UWG and in England in s 5 (4)(a) Consumer Protection from Unfair Trading Regulations 2008.

[40] Article 7 UCPD, implemented in Germany in § 5a UWG and in England in s 6 Consumer Protection from Unfair Trading Regulations 2008.

[41] Fezer-UWG, Introduction E, para 239f. See also MüKo-UWG-Micklitz, EG F, para 204, who, however, distinguishes between environmental information that would qualify as material information in the sense of art 7 UCPD and social criteria that would not (yet).

[42] Birk (2011) 203; Birk (2014) 177ff; Henning-Bodewig and Liebenau (2013) 756.

[43] McBarnet (2007) 41, note 130; Wouters and Chanet (2008) 288; Heijden (2011b) 221; Grabosch (2011) 171f; Cottier and Wermelinger (2014) 90f. See also Podszun (2014) 55: 'Zahlreiche CSR-Aktivitäten, die eine gewisse Regelungsintensität erhalten, werden dem Begriff des Verhaltenskodex entsprechen.'

the law or an internationally accepted consensus that specifies the general clause on unfair trading.[44]

5.3.1. Regulating Communication on Corporate Codes

To start with, the rules on unfair commercial practices already specify that the publication of false information can qualify as an unfair commercial practice insofar as it is related to the products, the corporate performance or the extent of the traders' commitments. One can therefore assume that clear statements in advertisements, such as 'we do not contract with factories that employ children' or 'we are bound by the code of an industry association', are uncontroversial examples in which a statement could be prohibited if children are found in factories or the code did not have the quality of a binding commitment, but was merely an aspiration.[45] The crux with regard to the corporate codes lies, however, again in the vague phrasing of the code that describes the commitment in a less specific fashion and thus renders it difficult to determine whether a particular code is true or false. Yet, while the vague character is a core obstacle when seeking to interpret the codes as contractual obligations,[46] this is not equally true in the context of unfair commercial practices law. This is due to the fact that the threshold in this area is not only the truthfulness of a statement, but also whether a particular statement is objectively misleading. Based on this threshold, it is considerably easier to treat statements that have a vague content also as an unfair commercial practice. In fact, in particular with respect to environmental aspects of the products or the company performance, vague claims are viewed as having a high potential of being misleading if not sufficiently substantiated. A different approach can only be identified if the corporate code is used in relation to a communication on the environmental or social engagement.

5.3.1.1. Communication on Products and Corporate Performance

Within the context of unfair commercial practices law, it remains a general presumption that information on environmental aspects has a high potential of being misleading. In its guidance on the Unfair Commercial Practices Directive and more precisely in its Staff Guiding Document, the European Commission already emphasised that environmental claims need to be 'clear, truthful, accurate and not misleading'.[47] Moreover, in its recent report on the implementation of the Unfair Commercial Practices Directive, it has suggested applying two principles when determining whether environmental marketing is misleading: first, the environmental information needs to be presented in a 'specific, accurate, and unambiguous

[44] See Meessen (1981) and, more recently, Kocher (2005); Kocher (2008) 81f; Glinski (2008) 53ff; Glinski (2011) 285ff; Podszun (2014) 73ff.

[45] Henning-Bodewig (2010) 1103.

[46] See sections 3.1.4.1.3. (p 97), text and accompanying footnotes.

[47] Commission Staff Working Document, Guidance on the implementation/application of Directive 2005/29/EC on unfair commercial practices, SEC (2009) 1666 38.

manner'; and, second, the trader must have scientific evidence as support for the claims and must have this evidence available when its claim is challenged.[48]

A similar approach can be identified in the interpretation of misleading advertisements in the English as well as in the German debate on environmental claims. The self-regulatory UK advertisement codes, for instance, contain rules that require companies to be able to substantiate those claims that a consumer would regard as objectively relevant.[49] This general requirement has been particularly specified with respect to environmental claims. The specific provisions dealing with environmental marketing state that 'all terms in marketing communications must be clear to consumers' and that 'absolute terms must be supported by a high level of substantiation'.[50] Equally, the ASA declared on several occasions that vague claims are not allowed without further substantiation. For instance, it held that an advertisement was in breach of the advertisement code in which words such as 'sustainable' were used to characterise an oil company and its current efforts to mitigate environmental pollution. It was held that the word 'sustainable' is too ambiguous and thus, in order not to be a misleading advertisement, would need to be substantiated by data.[51] In a similar vein, the advertisement of a palm oil firm was held to be misleading because claims that the palm oil industry is 'sustainable' and that 'the industry practices are held to high environmental standards' are not sufficiently substantiated and true when it is still subject to controversy as to whether this form of production is in fact sustainable.[52] With regard to product advertisements, there are also requirements as to statements that deal with comparisons and advertise a product as 'greener' or 'friendlier'.[53]

German courts have equally adopted quite a strict approach towards environmental claims in advertising and it seems accepted that environmental advertisement has a high potential of being misleading. Courts have interpreted company-related claims as misleading when a company declared that it actively protects the environment. Such a statement gives the impression that the company is in general environmentally friendly, which is misleading if the majority of the products it offers have a negative impact on the environment.[54] The threshold requirements are even higher when the statement is related particularly to the product, which in unfair commercial practise law also includes information on the production process. Companies are only allowed to advertise the environmental

[48] Report of the European Commission on the application of the Unfair Commercial Practices Directive, COM(2013) 139 final 20. See also on this issue European Commission, A renewed EU Strategy 2011–14 for Corporate Social Responsibility, COM (2011) 681 final 9.

[49] UK Code of Non-Broadcast Advertising, Sales Promotion and Direct Marketing, 3.7 and 3.8; UK Code of Broadcast Advertising, 3.9.

[50] UK Code of Non-Broadcast Advertising, Sales Promotion and Direct Marketing, 11.1 and 11.2; UK Code of Broadcast Advertising, 9.2 and 9.3.

[51] ASA Ruling, *Shell International Ltd*, 13 August 2008, Complaint Ref: 506657.

[52] ASA Ruling, *Malaysia Palm Oil Council*, 9 September 2009, Complaint Ref: 94637.

[53] UK Broadcasting Code, 9.4: 'Comparative claims such as "greener" or "friendlier" can be justified, for example, if the advertised product or service provides a total environmental benefit over that of the advertiser's previous product or service or competitor products or services and the basis of the comparison is clear.'

[54] KG Berlin, NJW-RR 1991, 622—Schützt unsere Umwelt!

quality of a product if it is environmentally friendly in comparison to comparable products and if the referred environmental standards are actually met.[55] With regard to labels, the statement has to contain the reasons for awarding the label[56] and, obviously, the trader has to be entitled by the labelling organisation to carry the label.[57] Certainly, the strict rules on substantiation have primarily been developed so far specifically for environmental claims and thus cannot immediately be translated to the field of corporate codes that contain social standards. However, one can at least argue that advertisements related to social issues, such as child labour or benefits for employees, arguably have a similar potential to mislead the consumer and thus would require a similarly high threshold as to specificity.[58] Here, it is not so much the issue that scientific uncertainty on the actual environmental impact makes this form prone to being considered misleading, but rather the complexity of the worldwide production patterns and the lack of access to external reliable information could be a reason why companies should equally be required to be specific on their social claims.

As a result, the act of publishing a vague code that contains information or a commitment related to products or the company performance is in principle capable of being qualified as an unfair commercial practice, although the actual unfairness will of course depend on the particular case.

5.3.1.2. *Communication on Social and Environmental Engagement*

However, individual corporate codes as well as the codes of other associations or even public codes that companies refer to in their communication do not always contain a direct link between the companies' products or their general performance and the code. The codes are often framed as commitments to initiate a change that should in the long run lead to an improvement of working conditions or reduced environmental pollution. In part, they also contain commitments concerning a continuous engagement in a particular project or association. The message that these codes convey is thus that the company, beyond making profits, remains committed to taking an active role in society. A closer look at the statements of Lidl seems to confirm this. The company stated that it 'campaigns for minimum workplace standards', that it 'contributes to the improvement of workplace standards' and that it 'does not tolerate human rights violations'. The sheer fact that NGOs provided evidence of violations of workplace standards in the supplier factories neither makes such statements incorrect, nor can it simply be assumed that this

[55] Eg BGH WRP 1996, 299—Umwelfreundliches Bauen. For a detailed overview of the different categories: Köhler/Bornkamm-UWG § 5, para 4.163ff.

[56] In particular, for the use of labels BGHZ 105, 277—Umweltengel (private labels in advertisement certifying the environmental quality of a product need to indicate the reasons why the label has been awarded).

[57] Birk (2014) 175.

[58] This understanding also seems to be followed by the European Commission, A renewed EU Strategy (n 47), in which 'environmental and social credentials' are equalised. An understanding on treating social and environmental claims alike also seems to underlie the contributions of Glinski (2008) 46f; and Henning-Bodewig (2010) 1104 .

would make a statement misleading because it provides the impression that the company is sourcing from suppliers that do not violate social standards. Instead, one could equally define them as statements that do not even seek to describe the production process of the products or characterise the company as such, but, instead, put the emphasis on the general aspirations of the company. With respect to such general statements on social or environmental engagement, however, the rules on unfair commercial practices law are generally less clear as to whether such a statement would be misleading.[59] Looking at the existing case law and decisions of self-regulatory advertisement bodies on these types of statements, a considerably less strict attitude can be identified.

Such general statements were so far primarily interpreted as misleading if they were not separated clearly enough from the product advertisement. If the statement appeared in too close spatial proximity to the product, it was held that the average consumer would understand it as a statement characterising the product. In Germany, for instance, a lower court held that it would be misleading to use the slogan 'we do not support child labour' if it appears in a flyer directly next to the advertised product.[60] In a ruling dealing with the ISO 14001 environmental management standard, the ASA stated that statements as to compliance with this standard must not be used in conjunction with information on the general environmental performance, since the ISO standards are explicitly not outcome standards but management standards.[61] And in the above-mentioned palm oil case, it was also ruled that reference to the participation in the Roundtable on Sustainable Palm Oil was misleading if it was mentioned in conjunction with the purported sustainable production of the company.[62] Having said that, apart from this requirement to separate the product advertisement from general statements as to social or environmental engagement, a less strict threshold applies to these types of statements. German courts, for instance, only allowed an injunction against statements that convey the impression that the company actually contributes to a social or environmental project if it turns out that no such contribution is made on the side of the company.[63] In general, however, the social and environmental engagement of companies and their use of this in advertisement campaigns are not regulated very heavily. This is particularly obvious in German case law in which, for instance, the advertisement of companies on their engagement in a social or environmental project was not treated as misleading even if no specific information was given.[64] The most prominent decision in this regard is the

[59] See for similar observations on the basis of US law Peukert (2014) 237.

[60] LG Stuttgart, WRP 2006, 1156. For a similar treatment of advertisement of ISO management standards, see OLG München WRP 1999, 965.

[61] ASA Ruling, *Shell International Ltd*, 13 August 2008, Complaint Ref: 506657.

[62] ASA Ruling, *Malaysia Palm Oil Council*, 9 September 2009, Complaint Ref: 94637, Claim 3.

[63] OLG Stuttgart, WRP 1999, 45—Schokolade für die Umwelt. The unfair commercial practice was in this case the fact that the logo of an environmental organisation was put on the products together with a description of an endangered species and an invitation to consumers to make a donation.

[64] Eg, BGH NJW 2006, 149—Artenschutz, in which the BGH decided that a company statement to 'generally support the foundation for endangered species' would not be misleading; and OLG Hamburg, NJW-RR 2003, 407—Bringt die Kinder durch den Winter, in which the court held that the promise to support a foundation that supports children for every sold product would not be misleading provided that the company actually makes a contribution.

Krombacher decision, in which the Federal High Court of Justice had to deal with the cooperation of a company with an environmental NGO, which it advertised with the claim that it would financially support the organisation for every product that was sold. The court not only decided that making an environmental engagement dependent on the purchase of a product is not an unfair commercial practice as such it also stated that even a vague phrasing as to the actual financial contribution would most likely not mislead the average consumer.[65] The ASA rulings seem in this regard to be slightly stricter and thus more inclined to treat a broad statement on the social engagement, without further substantiation, to be misleading. The ASA in its ruling on a statement by Food Brands Corp held that a company's commitment in the form of a sticker on a product that 'every pack raises money for Children in Africa' is misleading if no indication is made as to how the contribution to this organisation is actually calculated.[66] In this case, the ASA held that it is also not sufficient to refer to the website as providing further information on the social engagement—the main aspects of the engagement would need to be specifically mentioned on the product.

With respect to communication on corporate codes in particular, this less strict approach would probably have the result that reference to a corporate code that contains a commitment as to social or environmental engagement would in general be less likely to be treated as misleading than a code that specifically linked the commitment to the production of its product or its current company performance. Yet, it has to be emphasised that this conclusion is based on the insight from only a few cases that dealt with the misleading character of general declarations on corporate policy.

5.3.1.3. Interim Conclusion

It must be emphasised that the unfairness of a particular code can only be determined on an individual basis with a view to the particular code. Yet the previous analysis could also reveal some general trends as to whether a corporate code is likely to be qualified as misleading. It seems quite clear that the event of publishing a corporate code would generally qualify as an unfair commercial practice if it contains objectively false information on the actual performance of the company or its product. Insofar as a corporate code or a reference thereto in an advertisement only contains factually correct but quite unspecific information, the situation is more complex. Due to the strict approach towards product-related statements on environmental matters, one can predict that the use of a corporate code for the purpose of characterising the companies' product or informing about the corporate performance is likely to be misleading even if vague and promotional language is used. A different standard seems to apply for codes that are published with the apparent purpose of emphasising the social or environmental engagement of the company. In this context, the approach seems to encourage rather than restrict

[65] BGH NJW 2007, 919—Krombacher I; BGH NJW 2007, 922—Krombacher II.
[66] ASA Ruling, *Food Brands Group*, 7 January 2009, Complaint Ref: 65142, Claim 1.

this form of communication, although there are restrictions as to the use of such general statements in the course of a product- or company-related advertisement.

5.3.2. Taking *Lidl* Further: Regulating Non-compliance with a Corporate Code

In the *Lidl* case, the claimants sought to apply unfair commercial practices law with the objective of targeting the company's use of the corporate code as a marketing tool and thus of sanctioning the company for providing inaccurate, incomplete or misleading information on its code commitment. However, given that unfair commercial practices law not only regulates the publication of misleading information but also allows the sanctioning of other forms of trading behaviour, it could also be an option to focus on whether and how in the context of the *Lidl* case the non-complying behaviour could be targeted by unfair commercial practices law. In the corporate codes debate, particular attention is in this context drawn to a provision in the UCPD that determines as an unfair commercial practice 'non-compliance with commitments in a code of conduct that the trader has undertaken to be bound by'.[67] At first sight, this provision seems particularly suitable to deal with corporate codes. Not only does it explicitly refer to commitments in a code of conduct that a company declares to comply with, a careful reading of the provision also reveals that it determines explicitly not the provision of information on the commitment, but instead the actual non-compliance with the code of conduct as the unfair commercial practice.[68] However, against the background of the general intense debate on self-regulatory codes of conduct as specifying the fairness of a commercial practice and the general EU policy on self-regulation,[69] this is not so clear. Moreover, national legal systems differ quite significantly in their approach towards self-regulation in this field.[70] The following section seeks to provide some general remarks on the European approach and subsequently assess the debate in German and English law on this provision with the objective of identifying whether the rules in these legal systems would enable it to be applied to the corporate codes.

5.3.2.1. *Codes of Conduct in European Unfair Commercial Practices Law*

Pursuant to Article 2(f) UCPD, a code of conduct is defined as 'an agreement or set of rules not imposed by law or regulation or administrative provision of a Member

[67] Article 6(2)(b) UCPD, implemented in Germany in § 5 I No 6 UWG and in England in s 5 para 3b Consumer Protection from Unfair Trading Regulations.

[68] See generally on this clarification and the problems of interpretation due to the ambiguous phrasing in the German provision implementing this requirement: Dreyer (2007) 1300; Götting/Nordemann § 5, para 6.6: 'Der Unternehmer *hält* einen Verhaltenskodex *nicht ein*, auf den er sich verbindlich verpflichtet hat, obwohl er dies in der Werbung oder durch andere Angaben auf die Einhaltung des Verhaltenskodexes hinweist' (emphasis in original).

[69] Howells (2006) 199ff.

[70] ibid 197.

State, which defines the behaviour of traders who undertake to be bound by the code in relation to one or more particular commercial practices'. In order for an event of non-compliance with a code of conduct to be considered a misleading commercial practice,[71] it is also required pursuant to Article 6 UCPD that: first, the code is 'not aspirational, but firm' and 'capable of being verified'; second, the company has to indicate in a commercial practice that it is bound by the code; and, third, that the commercial practice is likely to mislead the average consumer. The provision follows the generally affirmative position of the European Commission towards using self-regulation as a complementary measure in the field of consumer protection. As already stated in the Green Paper on Consumer Protection: 'The introduction of a legal consequence for commitments made through codes of conduct and other voluntary commitments could possibly help business and consumers … More rigorously enforced commitments through self-regulation would provide a stronger case for less substantive regulation.'[72] The respective provision in the UCPD represents an element of this broader objective to use self-regulatory standards by traders by deeming them to be a tool to determine the fairness of a commercial practice.[73] In this context, it should also be noted that the Commission favours a broad understanding of what would be considered a code of conduct by emphasising that the provision would apply not only to codes that contain rules on a particular trade practice, but also to codes of conduct that contain commitments in relation to environmental protection.[74] Hence, pursuant to this understanding, it can indeed be an option to rely on this provision in order to sanction conduct that amounts to a breach of the commitments made in social and environmental codes. As will be shown below, however, the two legal systems of Germany and England have quite different approaches towards the use of codes of conduct in unfair commercial practices law[75] and, as a consequence, would probably also provide different answers as to whether non-compliance with CSR codes could generally be capable of qualifying as an unfair commercial practice.

5.3.2.2. *German Law: Controversy Over Codes of Conduct*

In the German debate, the particular provision on non-compliance with the corporate code has in fact triggered an intense debate about its actual scope of application. Already prior to the implementation of the Directive, German courts remained reluctant to use self-regulatory codes for specifying the fairness standard and only

[71] The following analysis will not focus on other provisions in the UCPD that deal with codes of conduct. Annex I ('Black list') deems as an unfair commercial practice the reference to a code of conduct in which the trader incorrectly declares to be a signatory to the code while not being (No 1) or purports that the code has been endorsed from a public or other body, although this is not the case (No 3). Both constellations seem not to play too strong a role in relation to the corporate codes under scrutiny.

[72] European Commission, Green Paper on European Union Consumer Protection, COM (2001) 531 final 14.

[73] Howells (2006) 206; Cafaggi (2011) 119ff.

[74] European Commission Staff Working Document, Guidance on the Implementation/Application of the Directive 2005/29/EC on Unfair Commercial Practices, SEC (2009) 1666 44f.

[75] Howells (2006) 197ff.

occasionally deemed non-compliance with a self-regulatory code to be an indication of the unfairness of a commercial practice.[76] In line with this scepticism, the German legislator, in its explanations on the Act that implemented the Unfair Commercial Practice, also explicitly stated that the provision in the European Directive on non-compliance represents a novelty in German unfair commercial practices law that cannot be integrated into the established categories.[77] Against this background, it seems no coincidence that the debate is currently characterised by a variety of suggestions as to how the provision is to be interpreted in relation to the CSR codes of companies.

The controversy begins already with the general definition of a code of conduct in the Directive as implemented in § 2 I No 6 UWG. Some commentators argue that neither individual codes of companies nor the social responsibility codes of business associations or the international publicly initiated codes, such as the UN Global Compact, could be qualified as a code of conduct in the sense of § 2 UWG. The main argument invoked is that a code of conduct in the sense of unfair commercial practice law can *per definition* only mean a code that set rules with respect to fair commercial practices and not to fair production.[78] Others argue that only individual codes of companies would strictly speaking be excluded from the definition of a 'code of conduct' because the definition requires the code to be a set of rules developed by several traders and not a self-created policy of an individual company.[79] According to this understanding, the individual corporate policy of a trader would not fall within the definition, while commitments in an individual code that refer to the code of an external association, such as the BSCI or the UN Global Compact, could potentially be covered. In addition to these more sceptical positions, there are also scholars who suggest defining the code of conduct in a broad fashion and covering both the codes of trade associations as well as individual codes of companies that deal with social, environmental and ethical standards.[80] The complexity increases when focusing on the second element of a code of conduct that needs to be present in order for non-compliance with the code to be qualified as an unfair commercial practice. Since non-compliance can only be an unfair commercial practice if the code is firm and capable of being verified, the argument is made that the corporate codes or the commitments of industries would not be sufficiently firm, but would rather qualify as aspirational statements.[81] Others, however, suggest treating internal compliance guidelines

[76] See, eg, BGH GRUR 1991, 462, in which the court held that non-compliance with the self-regulatory rules of private actors that constituted rules on fair and honest commercial practices does not release the court from investigating autonomously a breach of unfair commercial practices law.

[77] BT-Drucksachen 16/10145 17: 'Dem UWG ist diese Fallgruppe bisher unbekannt.'

[78] Köhler/Bornkamm-UWG § 2, para 113; Glinski (2011) 209. See also Birk (2011) 201 for, in particular, the code of conduct of the BSCI that Lidl referred to on its website and Birk (2014) 174 for public codes as the OECD Guidelines or the ILO core labour conventions.

[79] Harte-Bavendamm/Henning-Bodewig-UWG-Keller § 2, para 163; Birk (2011) 199f.

[80] Dreyer (2007) 1295; Kopp and Klostermann (2009) 157; Götting/Nordemann-UWG § 5, para 6.8.; Fezer-UWG § 5, para 419 and accompanying note 2702.

[81] Birk (2011) 201 with respect to the UN Global Compact.

and ethics codes as sufficiently firm and capable of being verified, in particular if they have internal control and sanctioning mechanisms.[82]

The uncertainty in the literature is also supported by the attitude of the courts in dealing with this provision. There is little case law available that deals with self-regulatory codes or international soft law, but the few decisions available also seem to indicate scepticism on the side of the courts. In the famous asbestos decision that in the absence of newer case law on specifically international social standards needs to be considered as guidance, the Federal High Court of Justice dealt with the question whether the event of supplying and distributing products that were produced in violation of an ILO convention would represent an unfair commercial practice. The court made clear that the ILO conventions are not capable of determining the fairness of a commercial practice because they are not yet based on an internationally accepted universal consensus.[83] In a more recent decision focusing on the relevance of a code of conduct in determining the fairness of a commercial practice, the court also decided that non-compliance with a code of conduct on trade practices could not be used as the sole criterion to justify the unfairness of a commercial practice.[84] On the contrary, the court held that even after the adoption of the European Directive, non-compliance with a corporate code does result in a prima facie assumption or even a rebuttable presumption of the unfairness of a commercial practice.[85]

Given how difficult it is to define a corporate code as a code of conduct in accordance with the Unfair Competition Act, an alternative proposal is currently made. In the course of the proposal to treat non-complying behaviour as an unfair commercial practice, it is also brought forward that such behaviour could even be interpreted as violating a legal norm (§ 4 No 11 UWG) or as the breach of an international consensus on fair trading practice that becomes relevant for specifying the general clause on 'unfairness' (§ 3 I UWG).[86] In developing this interpretation, proponents consider the ILO core labour rights,[87] specifically the prohibition of child labour,[88] or other codes enacted by international organisations[89] as the most viable candidates for such an international consensus. However, the suggestion

[82] Götting/Nordemann-UWG § 5, paras 6.8 and 6..; Fezer-UWG § 5, para 420.

[83] BGH NJW 1980, 2018—Asbestimporte.

[84] BGH GRUR 2011, 431—FSA Kodex although it should be noted that it was in this case more difficult to interpret non-compliance with the self-regulatory code as a misleading practice due to the fact that the defendant did not—as required under art 6 UCPD—undertake to be bound by the code. See also on this issue BGH WRP 2006, 1113—Probeabonnement, paras 19, 20.

[85] BGH GRUR 2011, 431 432: 'Auch nach Umsetzung der Richtlinie 2005/29/EG über unlautere Geschäftspraktiken sind Verstöße gegen einen Verhaltenskodex, zu dem sich Verkehrsbeteiligte verpflichtet haben nicht bereits als solche unlauter.'

[86] On the potential of international codes of conduct to inform the general clause in unfair commercial practices law, see especially Meessen (1981) and more recently Kocher (2005). Glinski ((2008) 52ff; (2011) 285ff) discusses the potential of self-regulatory corporate codes to inform the fairness standard. See very recently on this suggestion Podszun (2014) 73ff.

[87] Kocher (2005) 649f.

[88] Glinski (2008) 49.

[89] Meessen (1981) 1131 refers particularly to the UN Code of Conduct for Multinational Enterprises and the OECD Guidelines for Multinational Enterprises.

also extends to self-regulatory codes that could equally contribute to setting such general standards on fair trading practices.[90] In this context, however, it also has to be emphasised that this suggestion also remains contested in the literature[91] and that it also still contradicts the interpretation of the Federal High Court of Justice in the Asbestos case that explicitly held that the ILO Occupational Cancer Convention[92] does not represent an existing or emerging international consensus that specifies the fairness of trading behaviour.[93]

As a result, on the basis of the German debate on codes of conduct in unfair commercial practices law, it seems difficult to identify a clear direction on whether this option would be viable. On the contrary, the controversy on the relevance of codes of conduct and international policy frameworks on social standards suggests that there are several possible directions that could be taken. An interpretation of corporate codes could be suggested as a code of conduct that specifies the unfairness standard for a company that undertakes to be bound by it, with the result that non-complying behaviour could be treated as an unfair commercial practice pursuant to § 5 I No 6 UWG. Moreover, one could also conceive interpreting the codes either as a quasi-legal norm the violation of which could qualify as an unfair commercial practice pursuant to § 4 No 11 UWG. Finally, the code could also become relevant for specifying the general fairness standard set out in § 3 I UWG and thus non-compliance could become an indication of the unfairness of the commercial practice.

5.3.2.3. *English Law: Self-regulation as Specifying the Fairness Standard*

In stark contrast to the intense and detailed debate among German academics and the generally reluctant attitude of German courts, the English debate on this issue seems not to be comparably controversial. In fact, the general perception towards using codes of conduct as a specification of the fairness standard seems affirmative. In assessing the UCPD, Collins, for instance, argues that the provision does even not go far enough. While behaviour representing non-compliance with a code of conduct would result 'in an automatic finding of unfairness', he argues that the opposite is not the case, with the result that traders would probably be discouraged from, rather than being encouraged to, subscribe to code of conduct.[94] The reason for this positive perspective on the codes and the suggestion to use self-regulatory codes as a general standard that specifies fairness seems here closely related to the scepticism in the common law towards open-ended standards such as 'unfairness'. Having this in mind, the recognition of self-regulatory codes could be a valuable tool to concretise this open-ended standard and

[90] Kocher (2005) 650 refers particularly to the private initiatives of the Fair Labor Association and Social Accountability International in which companies can participate; Glinski (2008) 53ff focuses on corporate codes to the extent they contain similar topics.

[91] See, eg, Henning-Bodewig (2011) 1021; Birk (2011) 197f.

[92] ILO Convention No 139 concerning Prevention and Control of Occupational Hazards caused by Carcinogenic Substances and Agents, adopted in Geneva, 59th ILC session on 24 June 1974.

[93] BGH NJW 1980, 2018, 2018.

[94] Collins (2005) 424.

provide more concrete guidance for traders.[95] This general affirmative position on self-regulatory standards of companies or industries as tools specifying what is considered fair business practice also becomes apparent from case law in the context of unfair commercial practices law. Two decisions illustrate this. In *Director General of Fair Trading v Tobyward*, Hoffmann J explicitly stated in the course of an injunction against a misleading advertisement that 'courts should support the principle of self-regulation'.[96] In a similar vein, in *VG Vehicles (Telford) Ltd*, self-regulatory codes also played a role when determining whether a trader was guilty of an offence laid down in the Trade Descriptions Act. The court held that the trader was criminally liable for falsely claiming to comply with the voluntary Motor Industry Code of Practice.[97]

While this underlines the general affirmative position on self-regulatory codes as standards specifying the fairness standard and thus makes it possible to interpret non-compliance with a code of conduct in principle as an unfair commercial practice, it does not yet provide any indication as to whether the specific corporate codes under scrutiny would be covered. In specifying the types of codes of conduct that could generally be relevant for substantiating the fairness standard, Howells states that the code of conduct definition would merely cover codes that consist of rules related to commercial practices, for example, those dealing with advertising, direct marketing, data protection or the sale of alcoholic beverages.[98] A broader interpretation is, however, provided by the Office of Fair Trading in its guidance on the Consumer Protection from Unfair Trading Regulation 2008. In this guidance, the Office of Fair Trading provides as a clear example a breach of a code on environmental sourcing that it would interpret as an unfair commercial practice in the form of non-compliance with a code of conduct. The example provided concerns a constellation in which a trader indicated that it was bound by a code that promotes the sustainable sourcing of wood. With respect to this code, the Office of Fair Trading emphasises that selling products that have been produced in violation of this code would contradict the expectations of an average consumer and therefore would amount to a breach of the consumer protection regulations.[99] Thus, the fact that such an example is used by the Office of Fair Trading can provide an indication that codes of conduct that contain rules on the environmentally responsible sourcing of products are considered as 'code of conduct' in the sense of unfair commercial practices law.

Based on this guidance, one can conclude by viewing it at least as an option to treat non-compliance with corporate codes on social and environmental standards as an unfair commercial practice provided that the trader has indicated that it is bound by the code. However, one problem in relation to the codes of conduct could be the requirement of the code to be firm and capable of being verified. While one may give this requirement a broad interpretation, it is emphasised that statements

[95] ibid 423f; Howells (2006) 213.
[96] *Director General of Fair Trading v Tobyward* [1989] 1 WLR 522.
[97] *VG Vehicles (Telford) Ltd* (1981) 89 ITSA Monthly Review 91.
[98] Howells (2006) 205.
[99] Office of Fair Trading (2008) 33.

using primarily promotional and aspirational language are less likely to be qualified as firm and verifiable commitments.[100] Due to the fact that the vagueness and the use of aspirational language is, as mentioned throughout the analysis, a core criticism against the corporate codes, one may on this ground maintain a certain scepticism as to whether the provision would eventually apply to the particular types of codes under scrutiny. The vague phrasing could thus be a core obstacle when seeking to treat non-complying behaviour as an unfair commercial practice.

5.3.3. Conclusion

The previous section dealt with the regulation of the corporate codes in the context of unfair commercial practices law and, in so doing, discussed two possible options for approaching the codes in this context. First, the regulation of corporate code communication was discussed, as this also seems to be the current regulatory focus in unfair commercial practices law. Moreover, it was presented as an additional yet more disputed option to focus on the non-complying behaviour as an unfair commercial practice. From the current debates on the use of self-regulatory codes for specifying the fairness standard, it could be revealed that it is particularly problematic whether the codes would qualify at all as a relevant code of conduct or alternatively as a general standard that specifies fair trading behaviour and whether, if so, it would qualify as sufficiently firm and capable of being verified. On the basis of this analysis, two topics for the further debate are emphasised and addressed below.

First, quite comparable to the discussions in tort law, a decision in unfair commercial practices law would need to be made as to the regulatory focus in relation to the codes. Is it primarily the communication on the code and the use of codes in the marketing that ought to be regulated as a potentially misleading provision of information? And, if so, how far should the scope of unfair commercial practices law in terms of regulated communication reach? Or is it rather the non-complying behaviour that ought to be the focus of regulation and, if so, how far could unfair commercial practices law be potentially applied with regard to acts and omissions in the production phase that precede the actual trading behaviour on the consumer market? In addition, it has also been discussed how corporate codes could assist in specifying the open-ended standard of fairness. More concretely, can a corporate code qualify as a self-regulatory code as envisaged by the Directive or can it be considered an unwritten consensus or even a quasi-legal (§ 4 No 11 UWG) standard that specifies the open-ended concept of fairness? It is thus these two aspects that need to be specifically dealt with when developing suggestions on how unfair commercial practices law should assist in the private law enforcement of the codes.

[100] See Howells (2006) 208f, who distinguishes between statements in advertisements (such as 'hope to be able to' or 'will strive to') that will probably qualify as aspirational and clear statements (such as 'we will deliver within seven days') that will qualify as firm. In addition, he also discusses the problem of 'capable of being verified' that could exclude commitments with vague content, such as 'carry out work reliably'.

5.4. APPLICABLE REMEDIES

As a final element in the discussion on this area of law, this section will focus on the applicable enforcement mechanisms in case non-compliance with a corporate code would result in liability for the committal of an unfair commercial practice. The objective here is to identify the remedies and parties that are entitled to invoke these remedies. In so doing, however, a distinction needs to be made between the different options that have been presented in the previous sections. To the extent that unfair commercial practices law regulates the publication of the corporate code and the communication about it, the consequence is that the act of declaring the corporate code to the public without adhering to it would qualify as an unfair commercial practice that is sanctioned. If, conversely, the regulatory focus is put on the provisions dealing with non-compliance with a code of conduct or the breach of a legal norm, the remedial scheme will be directed towards sanctioning the non-complying behaviour instead. This distinction is of crucial importance when determining the content of the injunction order ('stop now' order) that represents the most important collective enforcement mechanism in this area.[101] In one way or another, however, unfair commercial practices law is already in its current form quite well equipped to provide for private law enforcement of corporate codes. For this specific area, a specific collective enforcement mechanism is in place (section 5.4.1) in addition to the general private enforcement by individual traders and consumers (section 5.4.2).

5.4.1. Collective Enforcement

Focusing in the first place on the collective enforcement of unfair commercial practices law, one can refer particularly to Article 11 UCPD, which prescribes that Member States have to ensure the effective enforcement in the interests of consumers. More concretely, the Member States have to have in place mechanisms by which organisations having a legitimate interest in combating unfair commercial practices may take legal action or bring a complaint before an administrative authority against an unfair commercial practice by a trader. In this regard, the most relevant enforcement procedure in case of a breach of the duty to deal fairly is the injunction order.

Under English law, this procedure is conceptualised as an administrative procedure by which particular institutions that are deemed to represent the collective interests of consumers have the right to seek an injunction order against a trader committing an unfair commercial practice. The institutions competent to enforce the Consumer Protection from Unfair Trading Regulation 2008 are laid down in

[101] Thus, in relation to the first option (the publication of corporate codes as an unfair commercial practice), the injunction order would be sought against the further publication of the code, as did the claimants in the *Lidl* case. In relation to the second option (non-compliance as an unfair commercial practice), the injunction would have to be sought against the non-complying behaviour insofar as is covered by unfair commercial practices law; see extensively on this latter aspect Glinski (2011) 272ff.

Part 8 of the Enterprise Act 2002,[102] with the Office of Fair Trading being the most important institution.[103] These different collective bodies can seek an order for injunction against an unfair commercial practice, although it should also be noted that the strong influence of self-regulation is also apparent with respect to the enforcement of unfair commercial practices law. Most unfair commercial practices, in particular regarding misleading advertisements, are still primarily subject to the self-regulatory advertisement bodies.[104] In addition to the collective enforcement that is directed towards seeking an order for injunction against an unfair commercial practice, the UK regulation on unfair commercial practices is complemented by a particular emphasis on a system of criminal sanctions for particularly reckless forms of breach.[105]

In Germany, the collective enforcement procedure against unfair commercial practices is a legal action in the civil courts that can be initiated by qualified private associations that are deemed to act in the interests of consumers. In order to be qualified as such, the institution needs to be included in a list that is set up and frequently updated by the Federal Office of Justice.[106] In addition, the right to seek an injunction order is also given to incorporated trader associations insofar as they further the interests of traders on a stable basis.[107] It is these collective organisations that could, if applicable, remedy non-compliance with a corporate code by seeking an injunction order against the publication of the corporate code.

Next to the possibility of seeking an injunction order, the German collective enforcement system in the field of unfair commercial practice law also contains other very specific remedies. In this context, it is particularly the possibility to skim off the profits obtained through an unfair commercial practice that has to be mentioned.[108] This remedy is unique and provides for sanctioning the trader by claiming the restitution of obtained profits. However, it should also be noted that, in practice, the skimming-off profits procedure is only seldom used for several practical reasons.[109]

[102] Consumer Protection from Unfair Trading Regulation 2008 s 26; Enterprise Act 2002, s 213.

[103] Enterprise Act 2002, s 213(1).

[104] See Howells and Weatherill (2005) 426f, who also emphasise that the attitude to give enforcement in the first place in the hand of self-regulatory bodies is also actively furthered by the courts.

[105] The criminal sanctions are primarily laid down in the Trade Descriptions Act 1968 and the Consumer Protection Act 1987. For an extensive analysis of these provisions and the enforcement, see generally Howells and Weatherill (2005) 397ff.

[106] § 8 III No 3 UWG. The most recent list of institutions can be found at: www.bundesjustizamt.de/DE/SharedDocs/Publikationen/Verbraucherschutz/Liste_qualifizierter_Einrichtungen.pdf?__blob=publicationFile&v=29.

[107] § 8 III No 2 UWG. The necessity to require a stable organisational structure and a long-term activity in the field of both trader and consumer associations is emphasised by Micklitz (2006b) 228.

[108] This provision is based on the preparatory study of Micklitz and Stadler (2003b) and is controversially debated; for an overview of the legislative reform and the relevant debates, see generally Alexander (2010) 501ff.

[109] Micklitz and Stadler (2003a) 562 refer to the problem that the consumer associations are not given sufficient incentives to make use of this costly procedure, given that the obtained profits cannot be kept, but need to be claimed for the public treasury; Alexander (2010) 514f refers to the requirement of an intentional wrongdoing on the side of the trader that the courts often use to reject the claim for skimming-off profits; Kocher (2012) 1409f also mentions the difficulty of identifying causality between the obtained profits and the unfair commercial practice.

5.4.2. Individual Enforcement

In addition to this specific collective enforcement mechanism, individuals and companies are also entitled to remedy a violation of fair trading laws provided they are negatively affected by a breach. This applies, on the one hand, to other traders who may have a competitive disadvantage from the unfair commercial practice of a competitor and, on the other hand, to consumers who may be caused by the unfair commercial practice to enter into a contract that they otherwise would not have concluded.

The right of competitors to seek redress for an unfair commercial practice is already directly referred to in unfair commercial practices law. Article 10 UCPD in this regard already states that persons who could be able to enforce breaches of the Directive include competitors, but that the rights of competitors to enforce a breach are still regulated differently in the Member States. The UK government has interpreted this aspect of the Directive as being optional and eventually decided not to extend the possibility of seeking an injunction order to competitors.[110] Germany, in contrast, also gives individual competitors the right to seek an injunction order.[111] The possibility for consumers to sanction a breach of the duty to trade fairly is not part of unfair commercial practices law, but it remains primarily a matter of general private law. In this regard, the unfair commercial practices law makes explicit that any finding as to unfairness 'is without prejudice to contract law' (Article 3(2) UCPD). This implies that a breach of the duty to act fairly does not immediately allow the finding that the party having relied on the unfair practice in the form of concluding a contract can also remedy the breach. Whether this is the case is instead determined by the rules on rescission, misrepresentation and pre-contractual liability. The rules on private law, however, already show different interactions with the rules on unfair commercial practices that can also be relied on to remedy the unfair trading practice of a trader and, consequently, the code-relevant behaviour. It should be noted, however, that the remedies presented below focus primarily on the interpretation of the codes as an unfair commercial practice in the form of providing misleading information and not primarily on remedies for non-complying behaviour.

5.4.2.1. English Law: Misrepresentation and Recent Reform

It has already been emphasised when discussing the possible incorporation of a code into a contract as well as the possibility of holding the company liable for negligent misstatement that English law exhibits an inherent reluctance to impose obligations on the parties prior to the conclusion of a contract. Exceptions to this are the rules on misrepresentation that allow a party to the contractual negotiations to be held liable for making a false statement of fact in the pre-contractual stage. Insofar as the misrepresentation results in a contract, the Misrepresentation

[110] On this implementation problem, see particularly Collins (2010) 112.

[111] In Germany, the right to obtain damages is laid down in § 9 UWG.

Act 1967 applies, with the result that the party having relied on such a statement to its detriment may hold the party making the statement liable by rescinding the contract and by seeking compensation for losses incurred due to the misrepresentation.[112] Thus, insofar as it is the code communication that is to be remedied, it is possible for the consumer to rescind a subsequently concluded contract provided that the communication contains a false statement of fact. Insofar as a commercial practice is not unfair on the ground of providing false but only misleading information, the remedy specified in the Misrepresentation Act is, however, not applicable.[113]

That being said, this limitation to statements of fact is likely to change in the near future as the rules on misrepresentation are currently subject to reform. Despite an initial reluctance towards a private right of action for consumers in relation to misleading commercial practices, the Law Commission and the Scottish Law Commission were asked to assess the implication of introducing a private right of redress for consumers with respect to unfair commercial practices. In 2012, the Law Commissions published an extensive report with recommendations for reform.[114] One of the main findings of the Law Commissions was that the current system is too complex and may have the likely result that 'consumers become lost in a bewildering array of remedies, all with their own complexities and uncertainties'.[115] Therefore, the Law Commissions proposed reforming the law on misleading commercial practices and recommended specifically introducing a new act that would give consumers a redress against traders that commit an unfair commercial practice as specified in the Consumer Protection from Unfair Trading Regulation 2008.[116]

The suggested private right of action should in the first place consist of a right to unwind the contract or to claim a discount. In addition, consumers should be able to claim damages to compensate them for indirect losses, which should include economic damage, distress and inconvenience provided that the consumer can prove that the practice has actually caused damage.[117] Other authorities, such as the Office of Fair Trading, endorsed the report and recommendations of the Law Commissions[118] and, in August 2013, the UK government reacted by announcing that it would attempt to amend the Consumer Protection from Unfair Trading Regulations by including a private right of redress for consumers that have

[112] For the use of the rules of misrepresentation in relation to corporate CSR statements in advertising and its limits, see Collins (2014) 629f.

[113] On this problem, see generally Collins (2010) 115.

[114] The Law Commission and the Scottish Law Commission, Consumer Redress for misleading and aggressive practices, No 226, March 2012.

[115] ibid 41, para 4.2.

[116] ibid 53, para 5.6.

[117] ibid 54ff, paras 5.18ff.

[118] Office of Fair Trading, Response to the Law Commission and Scottish Law Commission on Consumer Redress for Misleading and Aggressive Practices, July 2012, available at: http://lawcommission.justice.gov.uk/docs/lc332_consumer_redress.pdf. The Office of Fair Trading suggested an even wider reform that should give consumers redress in relation to all breaches as laid down in the Consumer Protection from Unfair Trading Regulations 2008, particularly 4, para 1.4: 'The OFT believes that an effective redress system in relation to unfair commercial practices would cover the whole scope of the Consumer Protection from Unfair Trading Regulations 2008.'

been victims of misleading and aggressive practices, as proposed by the Law Commissions.[119] This eventually resulted in the adoption of the Consumer Protection (Amendment) Regulations 2014,[120] which now provide for individual rights of consumers that can be used to sanction misleading and aggressive commercial practices. Consumers can unwind the contract, receive a discount and seek damages beyond the existing rules on misrepresentation. Comparable to the possible enforcement of the codes on the basis of sales law remedies,[121] the threat of using this sanction can potentially be effective in preventing future code violations.

5.4.2.2. *German Law: Private Law Remedies*

Although in the course of reforming the UWG, the German government went as far as to explicitly envisage the remedies laid down in the UWG as an exhaustive regulation of the possible remedies for committing an unfair commercial practice,[122] private law scholars have emphasised several private law remedies that are still available for consumers that are affected by an unfair commercial practice.[123] First, the rules on rescission are considered applicable for consumers that concluded a contract after the trader provided false or misleading information.[124] Second, the misleading statement could also become relevant for liability for *culpa in contrahendo*. Since, within a relationship of *culpa contrahendo*, a false or misleading statement is considered to be a breach of the duty to negotiate fairly, it would give the innocent party the right to claim liability, which includes unwinding the contract.[125] Finally, insofar as the code is read as a relevant product characteristic, it would be possible to invoke the sales remedies.[126]

5.5. OVERALL CONCLUSION: CORPORATE CODES UNDER UNFAIR COMMERCIAL PRACTICES LAW

To sum up, on the basis of the European rules on unfair commercial practices and their interpretation in national law, it could be revealed that this area of law offers several possibilities to regulate public declarations to comply with corporate codes and render them subject to legal sanctions. In the context of discussing the scope of unfair commercial practices law, it could be shown that the corporate codes relate to commercial practices insofar as either when the company uses the code as part of its marketing communication on the consumer market or when the

[119] UK Government, Department for Business Innovation and Skills, Reform of Consumer Law: Draft Regulations. Government Response to Consultations on Misleading and Aggressive Commercial Practices and the European Consumer Rights Directive, August 2013.

[120] Consumer Protection (Amendment) Regulations 2014, SI 2014/870.

[121] On this option, see section 3.2.2.2. (p 121), text and accompanying footnotes.

[122] BT-Drucksachen 15/1487 22.

[123] See, eg, Alexander (2002); Sack (2004).

[124] See, eg, Alexander (2002) 100ff; Sack (2004) 626.

[125] §§ 311 II, 241 II, 280 I, 249ff BGB. See for this option: Micklitz and Stadler (2003b) 37f; Sack (2004) 628. A more reluctant position towards this possibility is taken by Alexander (2002) 134ff.

[126] Alexander (2002) 182ff; Sack (2004) 627f.

non-complying behaviour in the sourcing process has effects on the market. In the course of discussing the potential perspective of unfair commercial practices law on the codes, it was, comparable to the analysis on tort law, emphasised that there are in principle two options for how the code could influence the liability. Unfair commercial practices law could regulate the publication of the code as a potentially misleading action or focus on the non-complying behaviour as a potentially unfair commercial practice. As a result, comparable to what has been concluded with respect to the area of tort law,[127] the further theoretical analysis will have to address the question of which of these regulatory approaches in unfair commercial practices law is ultimately preferable.

When analysing the latter option, another element of controversy could be identified. In the course of the analysis on non-compliance with a code of conduct as an unfair commercial practice, it was revealed as a matter of dispute whether corporate codes could be of help when specifying the fairness standard. On that point, the role of self-regulatory corporate codes and public codes of conduct seems as much disputed as the use of self-regulatory standards in unfair commercial practices law as such. As a result, a core topic for further analysis must also be an inquiry into the potential of the corporate codes as self-regulatory standards and the justification for only restrictively recognising self-regulatory standards in this particular area.

[127] See the conclusions drawn in section 4.3. (p 184).

Part II

Theorising Corporate Codes and National Private Law

6

Comparative Sociological Jurisprudence

A Normative Method for Theorising Global Self-regulation and National Private Law

> [S]ociological jurisprudence is a pipe dream. After a heated debate for almost a century, lawyers know that, logically speaking, it is an oxymoron—like a white raven. Practically-speaking, it necessarily falters in the normative closure of the legal system.[1]

> The project of comparative sociological jurisprudence is doubly impossible, because it adds to the existing problem of finding adequate modes of communication between law and socio-economics the further problem of establishing communications (or transplants) between autonomous national legal systems.[2]

IN THE PREVIOUS part, the analysis sought to explore the currently existing options in private law to deal with corporate codes and systematise the related legal debate. Yet, so far, an attitude was taken that aimed to remain as neutral as possible with respect to assessing the presented options and expressing preferences for one proposal or another. From the normative perspective, the different options were treated as equally valid. However, in order to take the functioning of the legal system seriously and the necessity of deciding on new phenomena, it is considered crucial for legal scholarship not to be satisfied with such mere possibilities and end the analysis by 'simply suggest[ing] anarchy, free choice, or nothing'.[3] Instead, it is my firm belief that legal scholars need to go further and develop solutions for the law in terms of how it should deal with a new social phenomenon and that they need to do so in a way whereby the solutions can be perceived by the law as 'rational, reasonable and just'.[4] This normative objective of legal scholarship of course raises the question about the foundation, the normative basis, on which proposals can be based. How can proposals be developed that the legal system could accept as 'rational, reasonable and just'?

[1] Teubner (2006a) 3.
[2] Collins (2008) 254.
[3] Luhmann (2004) 428.
[4] ibid.

An answer can be found in legal theory, which is the area that fulfils the function of informing the legal system by employing the expertise of the system of science.[5] To that end, legal theory and its interdisciplinary links to other scientific fields can 'irritate' the legal system and provide it with external insights on how the law ought to be.[6] Against this background, it is the core objective of this second part of the book to engage in a theoretical analysis on what the relation between global self-regulation through corporate codes and national private law should look like.

In the light of this general objective, this introductory chapter is devoted to establishing the link between the past legal and the coming normative theoretical perspective on global corporate codes under national private law. It seeks to do so by focusing, in the first place, on identifying the relevant topics in the previous legal analysis that actually require closer scrutiny from a theoretical perspective and, on that basis, on suggesting a methodology for conducting a theoretical inquiry of these topics.

6.1. A NEED FOR THEORY ON CORPORATE CODES IN NATIONAL PRIVATE LAW

As observed in the various previous chapters, from the perspective of national private laws, different approaches can be taken when attempting to regulate corporate codes and there are indeed several constellations for which the private law consequences of corporate codes seem to be quite clear and thus are not a matter of controversy. The most apparent examples of such uncontroversial constellations are corporate codes that are directly incorporated into contracts or at least in the ancillary documents. Corporate codes appearing in such a form are enforceable as contractual obligations.[7] In a similar vein, to the extent that companies make their codes publicly available in marketing and advertising, it is possible that these codes are subject to unfair commercial practices law and could be interpreted as a potentially misleading provision of information to consumers, especially if reference to products is included.[8] As a result, no specific theoretical inquiry is deemed necessary for these constellations.

There are, however, also aspects where the situation from the private law perspective seems less clear and several directions in the law are conceivable. Analysing the conclusions of the three different chapters,[9] one can arguably identify two core characteristics of the corporate codes that run as a thread through the entire analysis and can be identified as a cause of this legal uncertainty. These

[5] For this understanding of legal theory, see Buckel, Christensen and Fischer-Lescano (2006), Introduction VII–IX; Vesting (2007) 8ff.

[6] Smits (2014) 82f.

[7] See, section 3.1.1. (p 48) and 3.1.2 (p 52), text and accompanying footnotes.

[8] See section 5.3.1.1. (p 196), text and accompanying footnotes.

[9] See sections 3.3. (p 146), 4.3. (p 184), 5.5. (p 212) respectively.

are, first, the question of how corporate codes should be treated in private law if these remain solely a public declaration and, second, whether these corporate codes could be characterised as self-regulatory rules that assist by specifying the obligations under private law of the respective corporate entity and that have an influence on the remedies applicable to a breach of a corporate code.

6.1.1. The Status of Public Declarations in Private Law

While it was fairly uncontroversial that contractually incorporated codes can be enforced on the basis of contract law, a less clear position characterises the debate on publicly declared corporate codes. In relation to contract law, the *Doe v Wal-Mart* case served as an example to introduce the different approaches that could possibly be taken by contract law in terms of whether or not to enforce such public declarations. Should contract law, as the trial court and the Court of Appeal did in this specific case, interpret these publicly declared corporate policies as voluntary aspirations that are not legally relevant? Or should these public declarations be used when interpreting and supplementing subsequently concluded contracts with a business partner or consumer and thus become enforceable contract terms? Could these public declarations even be enforced autonomously and, if so, on what legal basis is this conceivable? Are such public declarations a contract that is concluded between remote parties or could they qualify as unilateral promises that are enforceable once someone relies on them?

Difficulties on the treatment of these public declarations equally arose when determining the influence of corporate codes on the legal liability of the corporate entity. In this context, private law does not seem to have a clear position on whether the publicly declared codes are at all capable of influencing legal liability for the publishing company in the form of representing a voluntary assumption of responsibility. Moreover, the analysis also revealed that there are different ways of relating such public declarations to the categories of legal liability. On the one hand, publicly declaring an intention to comply with a corporate code could be viewed as assuming responsibility for the reliability of such statements towards the addressees and could result in liability for negligent misstatements. Alternatively, the corporate code could also be used as a basis to expand the scope of liability in principle. Pursuant to this understanding, the publicly declared code would be treated as evidence for the fact that the company voluntarily assumes responsibility for the beneficiaries of the code. As a result, it is thus not only a question of whether these publicly declared codes ought to influence the scope of liability but also of how such liability should be envisaged and what category of liability would be most suitable. Concerning the latter aspect, similar problems were also identified in the regulation of the codes by unfair commercial practices law. For this area of law, it is not merely the question of whether publicly declared codes would be regulated that is relevant, but the question of the suitable category. Currently, corporate codes are primarily approached with a view to whether the public declaration to comply with a corporate code could represent an unfair commercial practice. Yet it was also presented as an alternative to focus on the regulation of the actual non-complying behaviour insofar as it has an effect on the consumer market by understanding the corporate codes as guidance on what would qualify as fair trading behaviour.

This uncertainty in the law suggests defining as one core topic for the theoretical inquiry the character of these public declarations with a view to identifying the concepts and doctrines in private law that are appropriate to accommodate them.

6.1.2. The Status of Corporate Regulation in Private Law

In addition to this controversy on publicly declared corporate codes, a second core reason for uncertainty in the law seems to be the actual character of the corporate codes. From a doctrinal perspective, this appeared in the question of whether and how the codes could become relevant as rules and standards that specify the private law obligations of the companies and, specifically in relation to contractual enforcement, determine the applicable remedies and entitled parties.

The question of how the corporate codes could help in specifying the obligation was intensively discussed in the course of analysing the contractual enforcement of corporate codes. In this area, several proposals exist on how to characterise the corporate codes as terms in a contract. There are two main proposals that both treat the corporate codes as an ordinary contractual agreement to which either the default rules on sales contracts or the rules on third party rights apply. In addition, however, a new perspective was introduced that describes these corporate codes as novel duties in contracts that integrate self-regulatory corporate policies or even public codes of conduct into the contract. Pursuant to this latter understanding, it would be consequently these global self-regulatory frameworks on CSR that represent the default rules and thus determine the actual content of these regulatory contractual obligations and remedies.

The self-regulatory character of the corporate codes also became an issue in tort law in the course of discussing whether the codes represent self-regulatory standards that are capable of specifying the standard of reasonable care. In this context, two options were presented. The corporate codes could represent an individual standard of due care that applies to companies that have such corporate code commitments in place. In addition, the corporate codes or the public codes referred to in individual codes could play a role as recognised self-regulatory standards that specify a particular industry practice. Indirectly, the question on the self-regulatory character of corporate codes also became an issue in the context of unfair commercial practices law when discussing whether the corporate codes would qualify as self-regulatory codes of conduct or even the expression of a generally accepted global consensus or quasi-legal standard that is capable of specifying fair trading practice.

Based on these observations, a second core topic for further analysis is identified, namely to focus more in detail on the character and functioning of the corporate codes in terms of their regulatory character and an appropriate response of the law.

6.2. COMPARATIVE SOCIOLOGICAL JURISPRUDENCE AND CORPORATE CODES

But how then can a theoretical analysis be conducted that aims to find an appropriate response in private law in relation to these specific topics? What theoretical framework is suitable to investigate thoroughly two such different phenomena, ie, unilateral public declarations and private regulation, and their appropriate treatment in private law? To start with, the following inquiry is based on the assumption that a suitable theoretical framework is to be found in the approach of sociological jurisprudence.[10] This follows two main considerations.

First, it is the understanding that corporate codes and the two constituting characteristics represent a broader social phenomenon that has effects beyond the individual company that adopts and publishes such a code. These new unilateral publicly declared forms of private regulation have to be perceived as a widely employed response of private actors to changing social expectations that fundamentally affects the organisation of society at large. This indeed suggests an analysis of the corporate codes with an approach that is capable of providing insights into these broader social effects and that is explicitly not, as approaches in business studies and economics on voluntary corporate social responsibility claim, restricted to the criterion of profitability for the corporate entity or economic efficiency.

Second, the choice for sociological jurisprudence is based on the firm conviction that this theoretical framework provides a persuasive understanding of the character of the legal system and thus its realistic capability to implement changes triggered from outside by describing it as a social practice that is directed towards coherent decision making on the basis of positivised law as well as a prescriptive set of rules, which fulfil the function of providing guidance for society on what behaviour is normatively acceptable.[11] A theoretical analysis that is based on this understanding of the law is particularly valuable when seeking to develop proposals on what an appropriate response to a specific phenomenon would be. It emphasises, on the one hand, the normative dimension of the law and thus the question of what behaviour the law should define as acceptable. On the other hand, it also urges sensitivity with regard to the organisation of the legal system as a specific practice and, accordingly, the question of how such normative considerations on what ought to be acceptable can be realised in light of the law's very own functioning and its existing constraints.

These considerations suggest that the approach of sociological jurisprudence is indeed immensely valuable when seeking to find normative answers to a new social reality for the law. Sociological jurisprudence convincingly describes changes in the law as following a necessity to be sensitive to the normativity of a new social phenomenon as well as the Eigen-normativity and internal coherence of the (national) legal system. It is, however, exactly this attempt that also renders

[10] See fundamentally Friedman (1975); Teubner (1983); Teubner (2006a); Collins (1999); Collins (2008); Wielsch (2009); Teubner and Collins (2011).

[11] *cf* for these two elements of the law and the consequences for legal science Tuori (2002) 285f.

comparative sociological jurisprudence impossible. In the end, it requires an immensely difficult translation of the normativity of a social practice, here unilateral declarations by companies and private regulation, into the normativity of the law. The following two sections therefore seek to develop a methodological way of how this 'impossible necessity'[12] of bridging two types of normativity can be approached in relation to the corporate code phenomenon and its two constituting characteristics.

6.2.1. The Social Responsiveness of the Law

Despite important differences in their approaches, scholars in the tradition of sociological jurisprudence share as a common ground the understanding that the legal system needs to be responsive towards social change and thus be prepared to integrate such new social phenomena. In fact, this common understanding can be found in studies that depart from an understanding of the law as a system that is generally open to its social environment as well as in theories that insist on the fact that the legal system is autopoietically closed. Concerning the former understanding, one can most prominently refer to the theoretical account developed by *Lawrence Friedman* which emphasises the importance of the legal system to interact with its social environment and strongly advocates that the legal system and the arguments employed by law makers and courts effectively represent responses to how they envisage changes in society.[13] Hence, the legal arguments that are perceived as persuasive—or 'rational, reasonable and just'[14]—and thus the normative direction of the legal system are essentially determined by changes in the social context.[15] As far as proponents of the autopoietic theory of law are concerned, it is in particular Teubner who emphasises the necessity of the legal system to be responsive to its social environment even in light of its operational closure.[16] The criterion of social responsiveness appears in this theory in the description of new social phenomena as 'reflexive social practices' that become apparent in 'social institutions, the normative expectations, social demands, political rights and utopian hopes of individual participants within them, as well as principles gained in political conflicts on the ground, principles that concern their overall social purposes and their contributions to different constituencies'.[17] Such societal demands effectively signpost the normative direction in which the legal system ought to develop.[18] Whenever new social phenomena represent a productive innovation that could be beneficial for society, it will be the legal system in particular that

[12] Teubner (2006a) 3.
[13] Friedman (1975) 269ff; Friedman (1999) 534ff.
[14] Above n 4.
[15] Friedman (1999) 534, 538.
[16] See fundamentally Teubner (1983) 257ff; and, more recently, Teubner (2006a) 10, 12f; Teubner and Collins (2011) 85: 'socially appropriate concepts'.
[17] Teubner (2006a) 10.
[18] Francot-Timmermans and Christodoulidis (2011) 187f; Fischer-Lescano (2012).

is called upon to develop categories that foster this new development. However, the same holds true when such social developments produce risks for society at large or result in fundamental social conflicts and inequalities. Here, 'pressure is brought to bear to the law to innovate'[19] and the legal system needs emphatically to take over the role as 'gentle civilizer of social systems' and 'offer one amongst several fora for peaceful settlement'.[20] Translated into the relevant question for this study on how private law ought to react to the increasing adoption of corporate codes, this proposes that an appropriate response requires identifying the social potential of these codes that private law needs to further and the inherent risks that these corporate codes are likely to produce. This requires first of all gaining a more in-depth understanding of this particular social phenomenon and it is in this aspect that an interdisciplinary social theory analysis of the corporate codes proves to be particularly insightful. The analysis of the corporate codes from the perspective of social theory can provide the legal system with a deeper understanding of its characteristics and, on this basis, its broader social implications can already indicate what reactions are appropriate for the legal system, such as reluctance or regulation, stabilisation or prohibition.

Yet what particular theoretical description within social theory should be employed for this undertaking? Once accepted that an overall generally valid theoretical framework that the law can rely on does not exist,[21] the appropriate theoretical framework to describe and evaluate a particular social phenomenon can only be determined in close proximity to the problem at stake.[22] With respect to the corporate codes, this means that the appropriate theoretical framework to shed light onto its characteristics will have to be determined with a view to the problems and issues that are relevant in the legal debate. An appropriate theoretical framework for dealing with the first topic of enforcement and liability for the publicly declared corporate codes needs to be particularly well equipped to shed light on the binding effect of the corporate codes, given that this represents the underlying core of current legal controversy. Considering further that this legal debate primarily uses the declared intention on the side of the corporation and the reasonable reliance on the side of those addressed by the codes as decisive criteria, a theoretical approach is called for that combines a linguistic approach on the binding effect of declarations and the use of language from the perspective of a reasonable speaker[23] with

[19] Ellis (2010) 61.

[20] Fischer-Lescano and Teubner (2004) 1045.

[21] Wiethölter (2005) 68ff. A recent attempt to frame theoretically the necessity of the law to distance itself from the ideal of a comprehensive and generally valid theory has been made by Teubner (2014) 188ff. See also Smits (2009) 50: 'the question about proper methodology of normative legal scholarship can only be answered by reference to the core of the normative approach. This core is that, in finding what normatively belongs, there is not one objective truth … Law is about conflicting normative positions'.

[22] Teubner (2014) 196: 'if the law insists on the partiality of the various social theories and only opens itself up to their influence to the extent that they make statements which are valid for their social sphere … This would not be any arbitrary "pick and choose", but a self-imposed obligation to carefully examine the claims of all theories in order to do justice to the plurality of social rationalities'.

[23] Searle (1971); Austin (1976 [1962]).

a theory that focuses on the social effects of language and the expectations that it creates in light of the fragmentation of social communication.[24] With regard to the character of the corporate codes as self-regulatory frameworks and the appropriate response of private law when determining the respective companies' obligation, this study proposes that a combination of the insights of economic sociology[25] and political theory in the tradition of social differentiation[26] will prove to provide valuable insights. The main reason for this particular theoretical focus relates to the fact that the core question among private law scholars currently addresses the appropriate interpretation of agreements and commitments of private actors within economic relations that attempt to pursue a political objective and their relationship to national and international political regulation in the field of social and environmental standards.

To that end, the linguistic-sociological analysis on the binding effect of publicly declared codes and the sociological-political analysis on the regulatory character of corporate codes in general ultimately seek to inform the legal system on how it ought to deal with this new social phenomenon.

6.2.2. The Eigen-normativity of the Law

In addition to the need to develop responses for private law with a careful view to the characteristics of the new social phenomena, the idea of sociological jurisprudence also rests on the need to maintain the autonomy of the legal system and the importance of respecting the internal normative constraints within the legal system, ie, its Eigen-normativity. All claims for the need for a socially responsive legal system notwithstanding, the closure and autonomy of the legal system and its orientation on its own rules, doctrines and principles remain an equally important prerequisite for its existence and its proper functioning. The law needs to take predictable decisions that are based on a coherent application of its own founding principles and is thus certainly influenced by the social context, but it is ultimately determined by its autonomous structure.[27] This renders it difficult to translate interdisciplinary insights on how the law ought to deal with a social phenomenon directly into proposals for legal reform. It instead requires subjecting the insights obtained by means of an interdisciplinary analysis to an analysis that takes into

[24] As a general framework, see Luhmann (1979); Luhmann (1995). For specific studies on the character of communication in commercial contracting and corporate advertising, see in particular Köndgen (1981); Lüsing (2010); Lüsing (2012).

[25] Polanyi (2001 [1944]).

[26] Luhmann (2000); Marchart (2007).

[27] Luhmann (2004) 102: 'Persons, interactions, and organisations are venues for the introduction of a communication to the legal system and for its removal from the system. The legal system … does not pursue imperialist interests to attract as much communication as possible and to retain it in the system. It is not an attracting system. It only predicates: *if* law is to be used, that is, if there is a question as to law and injustice, it can be used only *on the terms set by the legal system*' (emphasis in original).

consideration the underlying principles of the law that may be affected.[28] As pointedly framed by Tuori: 'Legal scholarship is not and does not pretend to be sociology, nor should it be judged as a defective version of that discipline ... Sociology's talk about law has first to be transformed into legal science's talk in law.'[29]

For the present study, this has the consequence that the inquiry into corporate codes in private law also needs, in addition to obtaining interdisciplinary insights, to reverse the perspective and assess the observed social practice as to how it relates to the normative criteria that underlie private law. In the course of this undertaking, attention will have to be given to the available concepts in private law with a view to identifying an appropriate one to deal with the corporate codes phenomenon and to discuss whether there are justified constraints in private law to treat the corporate codes in a different way from that proposed by the interdisciplinary analysis. Concerning the binding effect of the publicly declared corporate codes, this autonomous legal perspective will focus on the question of whether and on the basis of what concepts private law is capable of translating the socially binding effect into a legal obligation or whether there are valid constraints against rendering unilateral declarations legally binding. In the course of analysing the regulatory character of the codes, this internal legal perspective will play a role when assessing how the regulatory role relates to the established legal perceptions on the public/private divide and the recognition of public interests in private law. Bearing in mind the comparative element in this study, the criterion of the autonomy of legal systems and its Eigen-normativity requires in fact twofold sensitivity. It not only refers to the respect for the autonomy of the legal system in general, but also takes into consideration the territorial fragmentation of the legal system and thus the autonomy of nationally shaped concepts and doctrines.[30] For the objective of developing policies for private law for the corporate codes phenomenon, this has the result that the theoretical analysis will need to distinguish between the sociological and the legal analysis of the codes as well as between the treatment in English and German law within the legal analysis to the extent that the applicable concepts and doctrines differ.

[28] Nonet and Selznick (1978) 73ff, 77: 'A responsive institution retains a grasp on what is essential to its integrity while taking account of new forces in its environment'; Teubner (2006a) 4: 'Private law doctrine can only be persuaded to develop conceptual innovations by its own path-dependent evolutionary logic'; Teubner and Collins (2011) 19: 'In order to preserve the authority of the legal system and for it to remain faithful to its organising principles, such as treating like cases alike, legal rules must fit within an intelligible and justifiable normative scheme of principles.'

[29] Tuori (2006) 39.

[30] Collins (2008) 254; Teubner and Collins (2011) 25ff.

7

Firm Commitments

Theorising Public Declarations in National Private Law

The corporate codes are an almost paradigmatic example of how private actors, by their own means, manage to establish norm systems of considerable binding effect.[1]

WHENEVER A COMPANY decides not to integrate its code into its contracts, but addresses the public directly with a unilateral declaration, private law is confronted with uncertainty: it can either enforce or refuse to enforce the corporate codes. It can furthermore opt for applying the rules on legal liability or unfair commercial practices law to the event of publicly declaring compliance with a code or leave them in the realm of 'voluntariness'. Ultimately, the decision whether such declarations ought to be treated as relevant for creating legal obligations depends on whether and in what way companies effectively create a binding effect with such declarations (section 7.2) and to what extent the law is prepared and willing to transform this binding effect into a legal obligation (section 7.3), which requires in the first place that the criteria that determine whether a binding effect is created are identified (section 7.1).

7.1. ELEMENTS TO CREATE A BINDING EFFECT

7.1.1. Revisiting the Debate on Intention, Declaration and Reliance

Earlier, it was emphasised that the legal debate on publicly declared corporate codes is currently characterised by a wide range of diverse proposals with a proposed enforcement of these declarations on the one side of the spectrum and an interpretation as purely voluntary aspirational policy statements on the other side. Yet, a closer look at the substantive arguments in the debate reveals that it is not only the characterisation of these corporate codes as such that differs but also the underlying criteria to justify this decision.

Proponents of an enforcement of these public declarations refer here predominantly to the need to protect the expectations created by such statements. Corporate codes would need to be enforced in subsequently concluded contracts because the

[1] Herberg (2008) 25.

expectations of the contracting parties would need to be protected.[2] The publicly declared codes should purportedly also be enforced as unilateral promises due to the need to protect the expectations of the addressed public in the publicly declared codes, which might even include the often remotely located beneficiaries that rely on the codes to their detriment.[3] Similar arguments on the need to protect reliance of the public appear in the discussion on corporate codes in tort law and unfair commercial practices law. In these fields, the public declarations to comply with a corporate code are considered relevant for specifying liability because they shape the expectations of consumers on the market (unfair commercial practices law)[4] and of those third parties that are detrimentally affected by relying on the commitment (tort law).[5] It is thus the need to protect the expectations created by the code or detrimental reliance of the public on the declaration that essentially serves as a criterion to justify the legally binding effect. In contrast, the sceptical positions employ a different criterion in order to argue against the private law effects of corporate codes. In the course of analysing the potential interpretation of publicly declared corporate codes as contracts, a core argument against the legal enforcement remains the intention to be bound. Partly, it is assumed that a company realistically did not publish its corporate code with an intention to be bound[6] or it is referred to the possible risk of liability as an indication that the company could not have reasonably meant to make this statement legally binding.[7] The purported lack of an intention to be bound is also explained by referring to the vague phrasing of the publicly available declaration.[8] Hence, it is the intention of the company as expressed in the objectively declared intention that is taken as the decisive criterion, which according to the sceptical position is not present.

[2] See most explicitly Glinski (2007) 122f: 'Relevant legal effects can be based on the legal protection of the addressees' *legitimate expectations*' and the 'confidence in promises'; Glinski (2011) 174ff; Barron (2007) 16: 'I will attempt to demonstrate that in a suitable case, the court could use … *reasonable expectations* in order to hold that a failure to follow the terms of a self-regulatory code amounts to a breach of contract' (emphases added).

[3] See Phillips and Lim (2009) 376, who argue that a binding character of the corporate codes towards workers is primarily a matter of whether reliance of the addressed workers was reasonable. In this context, they deem 'conceivable, that workers who relied on buyer promises about wages, hours, or working conditions, could show an injustice if the promises were not kept' and support this by the normative argument that 'compensation is particularly central to any worker's decision to take and remain in a job.' See also Marrella (2007) 302: 'a unilateral statement becomes binding if and insofar as it has determined a *legitimate expectation* (or expectation interest) … In other words, individual codes of conduct, as any other unilateral statement, become legally binding if *the other party proves* that without fault he or she *has considered such declaration as serious*' (emphasis added).

[4] See especially Glinski (2008) 44: 'The related legal effects are based on the legal protection of *legitimate expectations* in the compliance with these promises … in the law on misleading advertising' (emphasis added).

[5] This became particularly apparent in the debate on corporate codes as an assumption of responsibility where the foreseeability of *reasonable reliance* was a crucial criterion.

[6] Glinski (2011) 217: 'ein entsprechender (Selbst-)Bindungswille gegenüber beliebigen Mitgliedern der Öffentlichkeit höchst unwahrscheinlich'.

[7] Bachmann (2006b) 297: 'Ansonsten ist darauf abzustellen, ob sich der Versprechende einem für ihn kalkulierbaren Risiko ausgesetzt sieht.'

[8] See especially Kenny (2007) 463ff, who argues against the contractual enforcement of the public code declaration that the code 'merely *contains general statements* of company policy and guidelines' (at 464) and 'Wal-Mart's *language* leaves too much room for interpretation' (at 465) (emphasis added).

Whether the corporate codes can be described as declarations with legally binding effect thus depends in the first place on the criterion that is deemed decisive. Is the legal obligation dependent on the (presumed) intention of the company to create such an obligation or is it the objectively declared intention as apparent in the code that decides on the binding nature of the code? Or does the discussion on the binding effect require focus to be placed on the expectations that are created by the corporate codes and explain the binding nature with the need to protect these expectations? Essentially, the legal debate on the publicly declared corporate codes touches upon one of the classical and most fundamental debates in private law here, which is concerned with the question of what weight the elements of will, declaration and reliance are to be given in the creation of obligations under private law. Is it thus in the first place the internal will of the speaker that serves as the reason that private actors are bound, as Will Theory[9] and Promissory Theories[10] claim? Or is a reliance-based perspective on private law obligations more appropriate[11] that justifies the existence of private law obligations with the necessity to protect expectations and reliance regardless of whether the respective actor intended to be bound? The following section will assess the debate on these fundamental theories with the objective of choosing the perspective that will subsequently be employed to analyse the binding nature of the publicly declared corporate codes.[12]

[9] Will Theory represents one of the most important historical theories to explain the binding character of contractual obligations; see prominently Savigny (1840) vol III, 258: 'Denn eigentlich muß der Wille an sich als das einzig Wichtige und Wirksame gedacht werden.' For an historical overview of Will Theory, see Gordley (1991) 161ff. See, as proponents for taking the internal will as the decisive criterion of legal obligations in the German debate, eg Mayer-Maly (1965) 518ff; Flume (1979) 4f, 116f; Lobinger (1999) 89ff.

[10] Promissory Theories represent a theoretical approach, mainly in common law theory, that seeks to explain the binding character of contracts with the autonomy of parties to make promises. Promissory theories of contracting have been strongly influenced by the seminal work of Fried (1981). See especially at 4: 'so long as we see contractual obligation as based on promise, on obligations that the parties have themselves assumed, the focus of the inquiry is on the will of the parties'. For a recent account of Promissory Theory, see, eg, Smith (2004) 103.

[11] In German legal theory, an account of a reliance-based model of contractual obligations is provided by Bydlinski (1967) 131ff. Yet, so far the most comprehensive and influential theory on reliance as the justificatory basis for private law obligations in the German context has been provided by Canaris (1971). In the common law theory on contracts, reliance-based contract theory is significantly influenced by the work of Fuller and Perdue (1936) 58f: 'while the will theory undoubtedly has some bearing on the problem of contract damages, it cannot be regarded as dictating in all cases a recovery of the expectancy … certainly as to most types of contract, it is vain to expect from the will theory a ready-made solution for the problem of damages'. The reliance-based approach has also been strongly influenced by the seminal work of Atiyah (1979), who describes the recent developments in contract law from being oriented on the will (at 405ff) towards a benefit- and reliance-based form of liability (at 764ff).

[12] In this context, it must of course be noted that these theories aim predominantly to explain the binding nature of *contractual* obligations and thus do not focus intensively on obligations that derive from the rules on legal liability (tort, quasi-contract). Arguably, however, the theories can also be of value in relation to the binding effect of non-contractual legal obligations in private law *to the extent* that these obligations are not merely imposed by law for a particular reason, but are justified with reference to the intentional act of the speaker (eg, voluntary assumption, objective words and conduct) and reasonable reliance of the addressees.

7.1.2. Towards a Combined Approach

In the theoretical debate on the weight of will and reliance in explaining the existence of private law obligations, the arguments exchanged indicate that critical points can be raised against both a purely reliance-oriented theory and a pure will and promissory theory. In its strictest form, a reliance-based perspective seems problematic because it effectively abandons the principle of autonomy that underlies private law by considering enforceable obligations not as created by a party, but instead as imposed by law due to reliance.[13] However, the will-centred perspective seems equally incomplete because it tends to reduce the role of private law to this very idea of safeguarding autonomy and thereby inevitably ignores the fact that private law also needs to fulfil the objective of providing certainty in social interaction and order social relations.[14] Hence, once respect for the autonomy of private actors as well as the need to protect integrity and order of social interaction are both accepted as important objectives of private law, the justification of private law obligations would need to start by deeming both the autonomous contribution of the speaker and the expectations as crucial to creating enforceable private law obligations.

7.1.2.1. The Intention Component

It is the core idea of Will Theory and Promissory Theories to explain the binding nature of a statement by referring to the internal will of the speaker to be bound by the expressed terms.[15] If this valid objective is taken seriously, private law needs to treat as an obligation that the private actor chooses to make a binding commitment. Yet, courts using the criterion of the intention still face the general problem of how to determine the internal motives of the speaker.[16] This is in the first place a problem of judicial fact-finding and it is therefore no coincidence that in Will Theory, it is emphasised that the intention, in order to become binding, needs to be expressly declared.[17] This, however, already leads to a slight shift away from the intention to the *declared intention* as the legal criterion to explain why a legally binding obligation has been created. However, the shift from intention to declared intention leads to problems when the intention and declaration differ. For constellations in which an objectively available declaration suggests an intention to be bound, although the speaker has mental reservations, the so-called Declaration theory evolved. Declaration Theory suggests giving the objectively declared

[13] *cf* prominently for this provocative understanding of contractual obligations Gilmore (1974).

[14] See pointedly Bydlinski (1967) 136: 'Von der "Verkehrssicherheit", die insoweit mit der Ordnungsaufgabe des Rechtes überhaupt identisch ist, bezieht also das Verpflichtungsgeschäft mit seine Verbindlichkeit. Gerade diese läßt sich … nicht einfach aus der Selbstbestimmung erklären, sondern bedeutet vielmehr deren Einschränkung für die Zukunft.'

[15] Fried (1981) 57: 'The moral force behind contract as promise is autonomy; the parties are bound to their contract because they have chosen to be.'

[16] For this aspect, see Kornet (2006) 235f, 275. An additional closely related problem is emphasised by Bydlinski (1967) 69. He highlights that the focus on the internal intentions essentially implies making dependent the binding nature from a fact that is by nature fluid and therefore difficult to fix.

[17] Gordley (1991) 162f.

will preference over the internal motives of the speaker.[18] This preference is also expressed in current contract law in which it is not the internal will, but rather the objectively available declaration that determines the existence and content of a legal obligation.[19]

In the more recent debate, two noteworthy and persuasive attempts are referred to that scrutinise the relationship between declaration and intention in more detail and, to that end, seek to reconcile them In the Continental German debate, the so-called Validity Theory (*Geltungstheorie*)[20] has persuasively argued that a party is eventually bound because he expresses a commitment to do something and, in so doing, assigns this declaration the role of creating the obligation.[21] It is accordingly in the first place the *act of declaring* as apparent in the declarations, ie the use of a particular committing language, that creates the binding effect.[22] However, in order to bind a speaker on the grounds of such an expressed commitment, this very commitment needs to be made deliberately and consciously by the speaker; a binding effect can thus only be produced if the speaker remains responsible for its existence and the content, and if the declaration is attributable to him.[23] In the common law theory, the Consent Theory of contracts can be employed as a theoretical account that seeks to combine the focus on the objective declaration with the intention as the reason why private actors are bound.[24] Pursuant to this understanding, private law obligations are not created by the will, but rather by the objectively manifested and visible assent to alienate rights.[25] It is the conventional use of 'language itself' that binds the speaker,[26] provided that it reveals 'a manifestation of an intention to alienate rights'.[27] This emphasis on the objective declaration notwithstanding, Consent Theory equally recognises that the consent originates ultimately from the individual will and autonomy, as these bring about

[18] See generally Schapp (1986) 27ff with further references to Declaration Theory.

[19] See generally Kornet (2006) 238ff, 275f.

[20] Larenz (1966) 45; Larenz, Wolf and Neuner (2012) § 30, 337ff, paras 1ff.

[21] See Larenz, Wolf and Neuner (2012) § 30, 338f, para 6, who compare the declaration of intent with a statute that once adopted is also binding as such, and not only to the extent and as long as the legislators have a respective intention.

[22] See pointedly ibid § 30, 338f, para 6: 'Teile ich einem anderen lediglich mit, ich wolle jetzt dies oder jenes, bin ich dadurch nicht gehindert, alsbald anderes zu wollen. Sage ich dagegen, ich *verpflichte* mich dazu, dies oder jenes zu tun, hat diese Erklärung den Sinn der Endgültigkeit. Sie besagt nicht, dass etwas so sei oder sein werde, sondern dass die zum Ausdruck gebrachte Rechtsfolge fortan *gelten solle*.'

[23] Larenz (1966) 88 ('eigenes, bewusstes Tun'); Larenz, Wolf and Neuner (2012) § 30, 338, paras 8, 10: 'dass die Freiheit *a priori* die Verantwortung für missglückte Formen der Selbstbestimmung miterfasst'. For similar positions, see Canaris (1971) 419f and MüKo-Säcker, Einleitung, para 162 ('im Begriff der ausgelegten Willenserklärung werden vielmehr Momente der individuellen Selbstgestaltung wie der auferlegten Verantwortung für den zurechenbar gesetzten äußeren Erklärungstatbestand zusammengedacht').

[24] Barnett (1986) 301: 'In contrast to will theory, a consent theory's recognition of the dependence of contractual obligation on a rights analysis is able to account for the normal objective-subjective relationship in contract law.'

[25] ibid 302.

[26] ibid 303 and further: 'Language itself—the way that assent to a transfer is manifested—is as much a convention as those conventions governing rights acquisitions. If the word "yes" ordinarily means *yes*, then the subjective and unrevealed belief that "yes" means *no* is generally immaterial to a regime of entitlement allocation' (emphasis in original).

[27] ibid 304.

and determine the ultimate consent.[28] Pursuant to these theoretical explanations, the first decisive criterion of binding oneself is represented by the actual declaration to the extent that it contains language that is commonly or conventionally used to signal that a binding effect is created, provided that the existence and content of this declaration is attributable to the speaker and its deliberate choice to issue this declaration. The following analysis will embrace this particular understanding of the creation of private law obligations and will consequently analyse the publicly declared corporate codes by focusing on the actual declaration and its interaction with the intention. Since this undertaking requires revealing the meaning of language and its conventional use to create a binding effect, guidance on this issue will be sought primarily in the field of linguistics. A theoretical framework that is generally capable of explaining the effects of the intentional use of particular language and that is therefore considered particularly suitable is, in this regard, the linguistically inspired Speech Act Theory developed by Austin and Searle, which will consequently be consulted when seeking to identify the intended socially binding effect of publicly declared corporate codes.

7.1.2.2. The Reliance Component

Nonetheless, as stated above, the perspective of the speaker as to whether he reasonably intended to create an obligation remains an insufficient basis to justify the existence of legally binding obligations. The perspective effectively ignores the fact that the declaration and thus the language used by the speaker takes place in a particular social interaction in which the declared intention is perceived in a particular way and expectations deserving protection are created. It is for this element that reliance-based theories of private law obligations are relevant, as they emphasise the need to also consider the perspective of the addressee and the social context in which a particular declaration or behaviour takes place. However, when using the criterion of reliance to justify the existence of private law obligations, some specifications need to be made. First, reliance as the basis to justify the existence of private law obligations faces essentially similar practical problems as the criterion of intention insofar as reliance is highly dependent on the internal motives and characteristics of the addressees. Whether or not someone relies on a declaration and expects it to be binding depends equally on personal and emotional components in the person of the individual addressee and a court can hardly use this criterion as a basis.[29] It is therefore not individual reliance but the social and institutional dimension of reliance that can serve as the criterion. As a result, the analysis on the binding effect of a statement from the perspective of the addressees is determined on the basis of sociological analysis that focuses on whether and what type of reliance is created in a particular form of social interaction in light of the particular communicative rules of the context. Second, a main

[28] ibid 319.
[29] See AK-BGB-Teubner § 242, para 56: 'viel zu sehr mit privaten, persönlichen, gefühlsmäßigen Konnotationen belasted, so daß es eher der individuellen … Ebene … zuzuordnen wäre'.

and valid critical point in relation to the criterion of reliance is the difficulty for the law to use reliance as the decisive criterion due to its ubiquitous presence in social life.[30] As a matter of fact, private actors rely on the declarations and behaviour of others in such manifestly different situations that the criterion to protect reliance as such is likely to overburden the law. Against this background, the reliance-based criterion can only be convincing if it justifies legal obligations not with the sheer presence of reliance in social interaction, but instead provides persuasive arguments for why the reliance in the specific behaviour or declaration under scrutiny ought to be protected.[31]

For the analysis of the corporate codes, this has the following consequences. When determining whether the corporate codes can bind the publishing companies, next to the intentional use of particular language of the code declaration, it is equally important to take account of the perspective of the addressees. In order to obtain a better understanding of the perspective of the addressees and the way in which language is perceived in different social contexts, the second part of the analysis will subject the insights of Speech Act Theory to a social theory analysis that explains how language becomes visible in social interaction as social communication that determines the expectations of the addressees. This sociologically inspired analysis of the publicly declared corporate codes will depart here from an understanding of social communication as fragmented, which has the result that a particular language, as reasonably used by the speaker, may be perceived differently depending on the particular social communication to which it is connected. The understanding of fragmented social communication here follows, among others, Wittgenstein's understanding of the fragmentation of language into different language games,[32] as well as the distinction in Systems Theory between consciousness (*Bewusstsein*) and autonomous forms of socially differentiated fragmented communication.[33] Pursuant to this sociological perspective, the binding effect then becomes not only a matter of whether a speaker uses language in a reasonable way in order to create a binding effect, but also depends on whether in a particular social context, this binding effect is confirmed and thus relied upon by an observer in the further interaction.[34] To that end, the sociological analysis should also shed light on whether, from the sociological perspective, there are valid arguments for why the created reliance is reasonable and thus ought to be considered worth being protected.

[30] See on this problem with further references Lüsing (2010) 105. See also pointedly Teubner (2003) 344: 'whether a social trust relation should be supported by legal sanctions or not, cannot be answered by the inner structure or by the intensity of the trust relation itself'.

[31] Teubner (2003) 344: 'Unlike contract, which contains in itself the conditions under which a legal obligation is created, trust is in itself legally empty. For its promotion to legal status it needs external criteria'; Lüsing (2010) 105.

[32] Wittgenstein (1968) § 23, 11

[33] Luhmann (1995) 137ff, 255ff.

[34] ibid 143f: 'In every instance every individual communication is recursively secured in possibilities of understanding and the control of understanding as the connective context for further communication; otherwise, it would never take place. It is an element only as an element of a process, however minimal or ephemeral that process may be.'

7.2. THE SOCIALLY BINDING EFFECT OF PUBLICLY DECLARED CODES

The central question addressed in this section is whether the publicly declared corporate codes are capable of binding the respective company and, if so, identify towards whom such a binding effect is created. To that end, the interaction between the three components of the content of the code declaration, the intention of the company and reliance of the addressees will be discussed, whereby each component will use, as a starting point, the available evidence that empirical studies have provided, which is subsequently assessed from the theoretical perspective. The ultimate aim of this analysis is to advocate an understanding of publicly declared corporate codes as instances that create a binding effect in relation to two social contexts. With regard to potential contractual partners of the company, the corporate codes represent preparatory declarations that significantly determine further cooperation and thus influence any potential explicit consensus that this cooperation may bring about. In relation to the addressed global public, the corporate codes are binding in the form of serious attempts to regain trust that, due to the high level of distrust towards companies in this interaction, requires external stabilisation. From an interdisciplinary perspective, the corporate codes are accordingly described, as indicated by the chapter heading, as 'firm commitments' that seek to restore trust in corporations.[35]

This conclusion on the intentionally created and reasonably relied-upon binding effect will then provide the starting point for the last section, which addresses whether and how this observed *socially* binding effect can be recognised as a *legally* binding obligation.

7.2.1. The Declaration: Corporate Codes as Binding Promises

7.2.1.1. Observing the Content of Corporate Codes

When focusing on the actual content of the declaration and the question of whether the published documents could produce a binding effect, empirical studies suggest that there is evidence for committing language in the corporate codes. In the following, an overview on the form and phrasing of the corporate codes as discussed in empirical studies will be presented, followed by a brief presentation of two concrete examples of publicly declared corporate codes. The analysis of these two codes serve in this context merely as an illustration of the general overview; conversely, it is not the objective to conduct an empirical study, which is also why these examples were selected on a random basis.

To start with, some general characteristics discussed in the literature will be presented. Published CSR statements of companies are often quite brief; they are usually one to three pages long.[36] There are some differences between the

[35] Inspired by the title of Mayer (2013).
[36] Herberg (2008) 25.

codes concerning the degree of specificity. An empirical survey of corporate codes in the sporting goods industry, with a particular focus on the topic of child labour, for instance, demonstrated that the substantive content of the section on child labour seems quite specific in comparison to the model codes of business associations, but is vague if it is compared to the codes of NGOs and public codes of conduct.[37] Another study using a similar analytical framework suggests that there are also differences in the corporate codes and that there are examples of codes with very specific phrasing as well as codes that are comparably vague.[38] In addition, the evidence suggests that corporate codes tend to develop and become more specific after a company or an entire sector has been subject to scandals.[39] Notwithstanding these differences in the actual codes as to their specificity, there are still some general patterns that can be mentioned. It is a main characteristic that the published corporate codes remain programmatic statements; they are guidelines for decent corporate conduct that are formulated in a very general manner and express the overall company values.[40] These guidelines often use headlines such as 'our constitution' or 'our commitment'.[41] As a justification for adopting and publishing corporate codes, companies invoke the authority of 'generally accepted standards' and standards that reflect the values of the companies' 'investors and consumers'.[42] The texts are introduced by reference to the values that guide the companies, but an emphasis is also placed on the general relevance of environmental protection, economic success[43] and compliance with the expectations of stakeholders and society.[44] The published statements may have a specific addressee in terms of setting obligations for suppliers or the company; yet, in general, they address the general

[37] Kolk and Tulder (2005) 11f; Bondy, Matten and Moon (2004) 454 distinguish between principle and commitment codes. While commitment codes refer to CSR policies that are formalised with specific statements on intended actions and allowed behaviour, principle codes are statements that remain quite vague and give little indication about how the company intends to engage in CSR.

[38] See Kolk and Tulder (2005) 14f with respect to the specific issue of child labour; see also Vytopil (2012) 165f, who identifies that corporate codes could range from 'weak codes' where 'The wording was general and left much room for interpretation' to 'strong codes' that had very specific phrasing and referred for specification to international and national policy frameworks.

[39] An early striking example is provided by Baram (1994) 47, who analysed the code of Dow Chemical in the aftermath of the Bhopal tragedy. Such tendencies have also been observed in relation to codes in the sporting goods industry and coffee sector by Kolk and Tulder (2005) 12f, with further references to the studies. Backer (2013) 847ff describes this progress concretely on the basis of the CSR policy of Apple Inc, in which the company in the first place used its CSR statements and reports as an alternative to third party monitoring, but in the aftermath of public scandals increasingly incorporated external standards in order to render its statements more concrete. Estlund (2012) 242f puts the emphasis on the improvements in the code of conduct of Wal-Mart in the aftermath of the lawsuit for violations of labour standards.

[40] Herberg (2007) 69f.

[41] ibid 94; Herberg (2008) 25. A concrete example here is the CSR policy of Apple with respect to the environment, which is phrased as 'our commitment' (www.apple.com/uk/supplier-responsibility/environment) and with respect to labour standards, which is entitled the 'Accountability' section and is introduced by the headline 'We Believe in Accountability—For Our Suppliers and for Us' (www.apple.com/uk/supplierresponsibility/accountability.html).

[42] For this interpretation with respect to Apple, see Backer (2013) 832.

[43] Herberg (2008) 25.

[44] Backer (2013) 832f.

public. With respect to the presentation to the public, it should be noted that the codes are not always very well organised; information on the CSR profile is, in some cases, spread over a company's website. Statements can be found in different sections, which makes the identification of the actual content relating to the different aspects of environment, labour and human rights, as well as ethical compliance, sometimes quite difficult to find within the manifold of other promotional statements.[45]

As examples of code commitments, I will briefly describe the 'sustainability statement' that Adidas published and framed as its 'commitment to manage our business in a responsible way' that 'is rooted in the Group's values and principles'.[46] In this commitment, Adidas refers to the core company values and the 'rules that society expects from a responsible company'.[47] In order to fulfil these rules, Adidas states that it seeks to design products that are 'environmentally sound' and to reduce the adverse environmental impact of its own operations and its supply chain. Another effort that Adidas presents to the public is 'about setting workplace standards for … suppliers and helping them to ensure fair, safe and healthy conditions in their factories'.[48] Adidas declares further to adhere to all applicable laws, directives and guidelines. In the sustainability section of the website, Adidas concretises this commitment by stating that it fosters contact with stakeholders from civil society[49] and states in a quite concrete way that 'our suppliers *must* safeguard their workers' health and safety and ensure environmentally sound factory operations'.[50] One can thus see that the language used in the corporate codes appears in a strong manner, tending towards a clear language of a commitment and not merely an aspiration. This is demonstrated by, among other things, the heading of 'sustainability statement', 'our commitment' and the frequent use of words such as 'must' or 'will'.[51] However, in spite of this strong language, it should be noted that the substantial obligation remains quite programmatic. An obligation to 'design environmentally friendly products' and to 'facilitate workplace improvements' still remains quite abstract as it does not define what exactly an environmentally friendly product entails or in which direction workplace standards should be improved. This observation appears to be in

[45] ibid 851: 'Apple presents a patchwork of interconnected, disjointed, and occasionally out-of-date HTML and PDF documents, making the task of locating specific information about the company's current policies in CSR practices a difficult task.'

[46] www.adidas-group.com/en/sustainability/managing-sustainability/general-approach/#/our-sustainability-statement.

[47] www.adidas-group.com/en/sustainability/managing-sustainability/general-approach/#/our-sustainability-statement. In the following, the different aspects of the commitment will be described, which are all taken from this publicly available commitment.

[48] www.adidas-group.com/en/sustainability/managing-sustainability/general-approach/#/our-sustainability-statement.

[49] www.adidas-group.com/en/sustainability/managing-sustainability/general-approach/#/our-sustainability-statement.

[50] www.adidas-group.com/en/sustainability/partnerships/civil-society (emphasis added).

[51] For similar observations in relation to environmental codes in the chemical industry on the basis of Henkel, see Herberg (2007) 102f. For the use of similar language in publicly available International Framework Agreements, see Coleman (2009) 623.

line with what empirical studies have discovered about the degree of specificity in relation to the content of the corporate codes.[52]

Another example of a corporate code is the commitment of the Swedish fashion company Hennes & Mauritz (H&M). H&M uses the headline 'H&M conscious' in order to describe its intentions with respect to a sustainable company culture.[53] It refers quite broadly to its 'vision',[54] which is 'based on a drive for continuous improvement' and its 'responsibility towards everyone who contributes to our success, including those who are not employees of H&M'.[55] Despite the fact that these statements are indeed quite vague and (possibly deliberately) use words such as 'responsibility' and 'vision' instead of 'commitment' and 'obligation', there are also sentences that are stronger in their phrasing, such as 'We *have* to ensure that our employees' human rights are not violated, and the same applies to employees of our suppliers and cooperation partners'.[56] In some parts, the 'vision' of H&M does not merely describe what it intends to do in the future, but rather describes what it is actually doing.[57] The company seems to put in its commitment as to future and current efforts a rather brutal honesty on past failures, against which the current commitments are measured. Moreover, the company describes the efforts mentioned in its sustainability vision and informs on current efforts in terms of classifying them as 'started', 'more to do' and 'on track'.[58] Thus, the company already concedes in the statement where it finds the current situation to be improvable and what aspects it will give its attention to in the future.

On the basis of these examples, together with the observations of the other authors that were consulted above, some general characteristics about the corporations' public declarations can be summarised. The phrasing already seems to reveal quite a contradiction in itself. On the one hand, the corporate codes are predominantly phrased in terms of strong words that indicate a commitment for their present and future behaviour. This becomes visible with terms such as 'commitments', 'will' and 'have to' that are used quite frequently; one might be tempted to say that these words are overused in order to make sure that the public puts faith in the strong intention of the company to take the code as the core and binding guideline for its behaviour. In some cases, such as Adidas, these strong words are even used in the heading. Yet, in other cases, such as H&M, softer words of 'responsibility' or 'vision' are used to describe the CSR policy, although it is astonishing that this vision is accompanied by the use of strong words in the content and the blunt description of failures in the past, which seems to underline the

52 See, eg, Kolk and Tulder (2005) 11f; Herberg (2007) 102 ('Unschärfe der Texte') 104 ('holzschnittartige Verlautbarungen').

53 http://about.hm.com/en/About/sustainability/hm-conscious/conscious.html#cm-menu.

54 http://about.hm.com/en/About/sustainability/hm-conscious/sustainability-vision.html#cm-menu.

55 http://sustainability.hm.com/en/sustainability/about/governance/vision-and-policy.html.

56 http://sustainability.hm.com/en/sustainability/about/governance/vision-and-policy.html (emphasis added).

57 H&M states that 'we apply the precautionary principle in our work', 'We take a clear stand against all forms of corruption' or 'We engage in dialogue'.

58 http://sustainability.hm.com/en/sustainability/commitments/choose-and-reward-responsible-partners/about.html.

company's claim for credibility of the statement.[59] Yet, this interpretation seems to be, on the other hand, compromised by the fact that the content of this commitment is often described in a very vague manner, such as 'improve workplace standards', 'design environmentally sound products' or 'engage with stakeholders'.[60] Partly, these commitments become understandable if additional information and additionally provided guidelines (such as the employee code of ethics or a specific supplier code of conduct or reference to mentioned international guidelines) are consulted, but in other cases 'internal guidelines that are in place' or a 'code of conduct that suppliers must sign' are referred to without making these additional references publicly available. Another factor that compromises the interpretation of the code as a strong commitment is the, at least, occasional use of disclaimers that are included in corporate codes[61] or an explicit emphasis that the adoption of the corporate code follows a moral responsibility of the respective company.[62] In terms of the content, it could moreover be identified that companies do not always distinguish between current actions and future efforts. Instead, they often combine sentences about a commitment ('we commit to respect safety standards') with reports on current company projects. One possible interpretation of such links is that the company not only makes a commitment with respect to the future, but also seeks to convey the message that it already adheres to it in the form of undertaking concrete measures. The statements and reports can then be considered as a means to underline the seriousness of the commitment by emphasising how the company already lives up to what it declares. Viewed this way, the statements on current efforts could be interpreted as being an attempt to add additional credibility to the declaration on future behaviour.

7.2.1.2. Theorising the Content as Promissory Language

In order to gain a deeper understanding of the character of these publicly declared codes and the consequences of the particular language used therein, these obser-

[59] For this interpretation, see Sutton (2004) 1166: 'Transparency requires that companies acknowledge failures and problems in operations … stakeholder groups … are more likely to engage and acknowledge progress when a corporation is candid about its mistakes.' See also Herberg (2008) 25: 'By presenting their codes of conduct to the public, the corporations put behind them the failures of the pasts; the texts claim credibility.'

[60] The fact that corporate codes are phrased in a flexible way has also been observed by McBarnet and Kukchiyan even for supplier codes of conduct that are directly incorporated in the contract. See McBarnet and Kurkchiyan (2007) 70ff, pointedly at 70: 'The "soft" contract … gives ample flexibility to both sides in deciding the actual level of standards.'

[61] The presence of disclaimers ('This code should not bind the signatories' or 'This code is not intended as creating legal obligations') seems so far not to be too relevant an issue for currently available codes. However, the problem of disclaimers is still dealt with in the analysis as it is anticipated that recognition of the potential binding effects of corporate codes may have the result that companies focus on the potential liability for their declaration more intensively and seek to avoid the risk by including disclaimers more often. For the problem of disclaimers in relation to codes, see generally Herberg (2007) 115; Phillips and Lim (2009) 362, 374, 376.

[62] This explicit emphasis on the moral responsibility became, for instance, apparent in the public declarations of companies in the aftermath of the building collapse in Bangladesh; see, eg, the public declaration of Benetton: 'We will contribute to providing support to the families of the victims of this tragic event, as we feel that everyone in our industry *is morally obligated* to do so as this is an issue

vations will now be assessed from the theoretical perspective. As stated above, Speech Act Theory will serve here as the main theoretical framework in order to determine whether these publicly declared codes can be defined as promises that bring about a binding effect, as descriptive statements or as statements that would have to be categorised entirely differently. When analysing the corporate codes, for this undertaking the study can partly rely on the analysis based on Speech Act Theory as conducted by Herberg, who focused particularly on the codes of large companies in the chemical industry. His theoretical considerations will be taken into consideration but also complemented by additional aspects that have been discussed in the literature more recently and that need to be addressed based on the evidence above.

7.2.1.2.1. The Social Effects of Language

One of the striking aspects of publicly declared corporate codes is probably the fact that they are statements in which companies frequently use the words 'we commit' and 'we are responsible', although one is nevertheless tempted to assume that the companies effectively did not intend their codes to be interpreted in such a strong way. This seeming divergence between the presumed motives and declaration is, according to Speech Act Theory in the tradition of Austin[63] and Searle,[64] solved in favour of the express declaration. In fact, Speech Act Theory derives from the assumption that statements are more than a factual reflection of the internal motives of the speaker; they are utterances in which the used language has a meaning on its own. Speech Act Theory is, in this aspect, related to language philosophy in the tradition of Wittgenstein, which assumes that describing the world (and the expressing one's internal motivations) is only one among several functions of language. Language can have an autonomous meaning and fulfil the function to perform an act.[65] In Speech Act Theory, the orthodox idea of treating language only as a means of describing the factual reality is criticised as 'descriptive fallacy'.[66] Instead, it is assumed that language can also be used for so-called 'performative utterances'. Performative utterances are expressions that do not describe facts and can therefore never be true or false; rather, they are statements that create a fact simply by means of expressing it with words. To say something is not just to say something; to say something is already doing something.[67] Or, as Searle puts it: 'You make it the case that you promise by saying, "I promise".'[68] Following this theoretical framework, the speaker can be socially bound by a

that touches the entire sector.' Declaration available at: www.business-humanrights.org/Documents/Bangladeshbuildingcollapse#140287 (emphasis added).

[63] Austin (1976 [1962]).

[64] Searle (1971); Searle (2010).

[65] Wittgenstein (1968) § 7, 5: 'I shall also call the whole, consisting of language and the actions into which it is woven, the "language-game"'; § 23, 11: 'Here, the term "language-*game*" is meant to bring into prominence the fact that the *speaking* of language is part of an activity, or of a form of life' (emphasis in original).

[66] Austin (1976 [1962]) 3.

[67] ibid 4ff.

[68] Searle (2010) 12.

particular declaration if the declaration contains the relevant performative words and is issued in a way that a reasonable speaker would do. In light of the general understanding of Speech Act Theory, two conditions need to be fulfilled in order for publicly declared codes to be considered as speech acts. First, it is necessary to investigate whether language is used as is conventional for the particular type of speech act (the illocutionary force of the words) and whether the utterance in fact brings about the effects that such types of speech acts conventionally have (the perlocutionary force of the words).[69] Since the focus of Speech Act Theory remains primarily the illocutionary act,[70] the theory will be primarily consulted when classifying the corporate codes in terms of the expressed declaration. While the consequential effects of promises as envisaged by Speech Act Theory will also be briefly outlined, the inquiry into the actual social effects of this speech act will remain subject to the later sociological analysis that discusses more in detail how the intended act is perceived and confirmed by the addressee.

7.2.1.2.2. Corporate Codes as Promises to the Public

With respect to the qualification of the corporate codes as a particular type of speech act, the committing language in the corporate codes suggests an interpretation as a unilateral promise.[71] For some elements in the corporate codes, it seems fairly straightforward to use the category of promise considering the main words they contain. Some codes contain unequivocal phrases such as 'we commit' or 'we will do something', sometimes they even explicitly specify the code as 'our promise'.[72] Here, it is the use of 'performative verbs [that] serve the special purpose of making explicit … what precise action it is that is being performed by the issuing of the utterance',[73] which makes such statements in codes promises. Yet, even if the explicit performative is not used for every aspect of the code,[74] one can nevertheless argue that the overall purpose of the language used in the corporate codes is to signal the performance of a promise. Even a specific element in the code that signals only an 'intention' or 'vision' rather than a 'promise' or

[69] Austin (1976 [1962]) 95ff. See also at 109: 'we also perform illocutionary acts such as informing, ordering, warning, undertaking, &c, i.e. utterances which have a certain conventional force. Thirdly, we may also perform perlocutionary acts: what we bring about or achieve by saying something, such as convincing, persuading, deterring, and even, say, surprising or misleading'.

[70] For this interpretation of Speech Act Theory, *cf* Alexy (1978) 79.

[71] See Herberg (2001) 28; Herberg (2008) 25, who refers for this classification not only to Austin, but also to the concept of generally socially accepted communicative categories as developed by Luckmann. See instructively Luckmann (1986) 201: 'Demgegenüber gibt es wohl in allen Gesellschaften kommunikative Handlungen, in denen sich der Handelnde schon im Entwurf an einem Gesamtmuster orientiert, als dem Mittel, das seinen Zwecken dient. Dieses Gesamtmuster bestimmt weitgehend die Auswahl der verschiedenen Elemente aus dem kommunikativen "Code" und der Verlauf der Handlung ist hinsichtlich jener Elemente, die vom Gesamtmuster bestimmt sind, verhältnismäßig gut voraussagbar.'

[72] *cf* the introductory section of H&M Conscious: 'it's our *promise* to bring you more fashion choices that are good for people, the planet and your wallet'. Available at: http://about.hm.com/en/About/sustainability/hm-conscious/conscious.html (emphasis added).

[73] Austin (1976 [1962]) 61.

[74] *cf* for a concrete example again the statement of H&M as discussed above, where also partly less concrete language ('our responsibility', 'our vision') could be identified.

'commitment' could still be considered part of the promise once it is used in a particularly emphatic manner considering other strong words and utterances that are used in the context.[75] Such an emphatic manner is arguably present to the extent that the corporate code contains other closely related statements with stronger words, or the company underlines the seriousness and credibility with reference to its changing behaviour after past failures, or the code contains information on how its 'vision' is put into practice by current efforts. In general, when identifying the performative and classifying the act, it is necessary to take into consideration the broader communicative context of such publicly declared promises and their classification as public relations communication.[76] An interpretation of the corporate codes language needs to remain sensitive to the conventional use of promotional language for such types of declarations and therefore focus not only on the meaning of one particular word in the code, but also on the declaration in general and the overall message that the language used conveys to the public.

In relation to the corporate codes, however, it is not so much the necessity of using the relevant performative words that is problematic. A core and important criticism in relation to corporate codes is here rather that the corporate codes, even if they use the performative of a promise, do not perform a *convincing* or successful promise because the content of the code does not comply with the pragmatic rules on promising. From this perspective, the codes may only be interpreted as misleading promises in which a promise is indicated by the use of particular words, but where the language read together with the context does not amount to a promise. In this context, four lines of criticism deserve further scrutiny.

First, one main criticism of the corporate codes is that they are not successful promises because they only re-state aspects that the company is under an obligation to do anyway. In Speech Act Theory, this criticism could be phrased as a breach of the pragmatic rule that promises, in order to be successful, need to create new binding obligations and not merely refer to ones that already exist.[77] In other words, promising does not cover trivial promises.[78] If the seller of a product, for instance, expresses towards the buyer that he 'promises to deliver the product' after having reached a contractual agreement, which is also fixed by written consensus, it is difficult to assume that this is the performance of a self-standing promise. It is instead likely that the utterance is understood as a statement that emphasises the already existing obligations and assures the buyer that the obligation will be fulfilled. Hence, it would not qualify as an act of promising that brings about a binding effect, but rather as a descriptive statement of fact, eg, not a performative but a constative utterance.[79] In this context, Herberg holds that, as

[75] For this argument, see Atiyah (1981) 101: 'it would be generally agreed that a person may say he intends to do something in such an emphatic manner that, given other appropriate circumstances, his statement amounts to, or includes, a promise'.

[76] This aspect is more extensively dealt with below, section 7.2.3.2.2. (p 255), text and accompanying footnotes.

[77] See fundamentally Searle (1971) 49.

[78] Herberg (2001) 34.

[79] Herberg (2001) 34 uses the example of an employee who promises the employer to work well, which can equally not be understood as a promise because the employee is already under an obligation on the basis of the employment contract. In contrast to the perspective taken here, however, he defines

such, the corporate codes could possibly be considered trivial promises because the codes merely follow an economic necessity and thus promise something that the company would do anyway because it is economically worthwhile to develop environmentally friendly products and to respect the rights of employees. Yet, he also argues, with good reason, that this argument can only be valid if either the code contains such reservations, eg, if a company had made explicit that it produces 'environmentally friendly only if it is profitable' or 'adheres to high workplace standards because it is profitable', or if the statement gave the overall impression that the promised action is limited to cases in which it does not contradict economic motives.[80] However, his analysis of the codes of large companies in the German chemical industry shows that both elements cannot be found in the codes. On the contrary, some companies even explicitly assure in their codes that economic constraints do not have priority over matters of security, environmental protection and health and safety matters and thus make explicit that the promised actions are on an equal footing with economic objectives.[81] This is in line with what has been stated in the overview above, namely that stakeholder expectations and social values are referred to as a main impetus for adopting corporate codes and explicitly not merely economic motives. An additional criticism relating to the triviality of the promise could, however, be the fact that statements appear frequently in corporate codes that ensure 'adherence to local law and compliance with all applicable laws, regulation and directives'. Thus, one could argue that such statements, in fact, do not go beyond what companies are in any case obliged to do: to comply with the law. Again, this criticism can only be valid if it is supported by the texts of the corporate codes. Nevertheless, looking more closely at the corporate codes, it can also be observed that they contain the condition that local law is only the minimum standard and that, whenever the corporate code defines higher standards, these latter standards are applicable and supersede compliance with local law.[82] In addition, even from the statement to comply with local law wherever the company operates, a valid promise beyond an existing obligation can be extracted. This is due to the fact that such statements cannot only be interpreted as a promise to adhere to local law but also as a promise to undertake actions in order to enforce the law and thus to take over not only a rule-obeying but also an active regulatory role.[83] The statement in which a company refers to the fact that it requires that 'suppliers *must* safeguard their workers' health

these statements not as a mere description of an existing fact, but goes further by arguing that such statements would turn into their opposite. Someone who promises something that he is obliged to do will encounter distrust and scepticism on the other side.

[80] ibid 35.

[81] For an example of such a code, see the published code of BASF, which Herberg (2007) 85 refers to: 'Wirtschaftliche Belange haben keinen Vorrang gegenüber Sicherheit, Umwelt- und Gesundheitsschutz.'

[82] The prime example are commitments related to child labour, in which it is frequently mentioned that the minimum age is either the age that local law prescribes or the age laid down in international guidelines, whichever is higher. For this aspect in the codes, see McBarnet and Kurkchiyan (2007) 67f.

[83] The specifics of this regulatory role as constituted by the codes will be discussed more intensively in the second part of the theoretical analysis, namely ch 8.

and safety and ensure environmentally sound factory operations in compliance with local law' can be interpreted as a promise to enforce applicable health and safety regulations by means of using contracts.[84] It is thus a promise that contains not only the commitment to comply with local law, but also one directed towards proactive contractual regulation of the supply chain in the absence of a properly working governmental body in particular countries.

Second, corporate codes are also criticised as unsuccessful because, as it is argued, it can be observed that companies do not behave according to their commitment; actually, they never intended to fulfil their promises. This criticism appears most prominently in the categorisation of corporate codes as 'greenwashing', 'bluewashing' or 'socialwashing'.[85] However, since the internal motives of whether or not the speech act will be performed are irrelevant in relation to the question of whether an act is performed, this criticism against the promissory character of the corporate codes can only be valid insofar as it refers not to the unwillingness, but to the obvious incapacity to fulfil the promise at the time that it is made. Later factual deviations from a code do not destroy their character as promises, but rather amount to a breach of the promise, and mental reservations not to fulfil the promise are, as stated above, not valid. Yet, an initial and obvious incapacity of the speaker to perform the promise could indeed be a relevant criterion to compromise the success of a promise.[86] This aspect is not so much a problem when discussing promises by individuals, but it becomes relevant in the context of promises by large and complex organisations. In the context of corporate codes, this could be relevant if the department that develops and finally decides to declare public compliance with the code is not allowed to speak in the name of the entire organisation that is ultimately bound. If, for instance, the head firm declares worldwide compliance with health and safety standards, one may question whether the firm is at all capable of ensuring compliance in a decentralised corporate organisation. However, this criticism can be met when looking at the actual organisation of large worldwide operating companies. Despite the transformation from hierarchical into heterarchical organisations, there are still tendencies to organise certain aspects of an organisation in the headquarters,[87] to which the adoption of corporate codes for globally operating groups belong.[88] In fact, one may even find in corporate codes assurances that the code is developed for and applies to all parts of a globally operating company and, notably, also the statement that they are restricted to those that the head firm has control over as

[84] This argument is also brought forward by McBarnet and Kurkchiyan (2007) 66f.

[85] The term 'greenwashing' refers to the criticism that companies deliberately intend for economic motives to create the impression of being an environmentally friendly company without having the actual intention to protect the environment. It has been coined by the environmentalist Jay Westerveld and has become a catchphrase to describe and criticise 'false' environmental statements by companies; *cf* Cherry and Sneirson (2012) 141. Increasingly, not only is the term 'greenwashing' used, but so is 'bluewashing' for commitments related to the UN Global Compact (the blue flag of the United Nations) if the publishing company does not behave accordingly; *cf* Weschka (2006) 651. Sometimes, one might also find the term 'socialwashing' for commitments related to social aspects.

[86] Herberg (2001) 37f.

[87] Muchlinski (2007b) 50f.

[88] Herberg (2001) 38f.

the head of a corporate group.[89] The British–Dutch joint venture company Shell, for instance, explicitly states in its commitment that 'All Shell companies, contractors and joint ventures *under our operational control* must manage HSSE [Health, Safety, Security and the Environment] and SP [Social Performance] in line with the commitment and policy'[90] and also makes explicit with which managerial systems it intends to control the implementation of the promised behaviour within the complex joint-venture structure of the company.[91] The situation is slightly different insofar as promises are concerned that deal with the behaviour of suppliers that are not under the direct and intense control of the head company. Here, it is difficult to assume that a company has the authority to make a commitment for all the separate and autonomous entities. However, a closer look at the public declarations reveals that the promises that the companies issue are often not promises, based on the content, that all the mentioned contractual partners adhere to social and environmental standards; instead, the promise is precisely framed as a commitment to also *support* adherence on the side of contractually affiliated entities, to choose the contracting partners accordingly and to engage in a long-term partnership.[92] Consequently, since the code declaration already makes clear that the promise covers those entities that the company hierarchically controls and otherwise specifies promises on cooperation with entities that are not under its control, the authority to make the promise is present.

Third, the most important criticism that may compromise the promissory character of corporate codes remains their vague phrasing. Pursuant to this criticism, companies do not make any substantive commitment when publishing a code, but rather frame them as programmatic aspirations or policies. Although the codes contain strong words, particularly 'we are committed to', the substantive obligation remains quite abstract as the codes refer to actions such as 'protect the environment' or 'respect fundamental workplace standards'. With respect to the pragmatic rules on promising, this becomes relevant insofar as the action or forbearance that is promised needs to be sufficiently concrete in order to understand what the promise is about or at least indicate how the action is specified in the future.[93] In everyday life, it also makes a difference whether someone promises

[89] See pointedly ibid 38: 'Die Antwort, die in den Unternehmensleitlinien erteilt wird, ist eindeutig. Viele Texte enthalten den expliziten Hinweis, daß die definierten Standards konzern- und weltweit gelten.'

[90] www.shell.com/global/environment-society/s-development/our-commitments-and-standards/hse-com-policy.html (emphasis added).

[91] www.shell.com/global/environment-society/s-development/our-commitments-and-standards/hse-manuals.html.

[92] See again the commitment of H&M in its supplier code of conduct, available at: http://sustainability.hm.com/en/sustainability/commitments/choose-and-reward-responsible-partners/code-of-conduct.html#: 'We are therefore committed to working closely with our suppliers and business partners to achieve a long-term, sustainable social and environmental standard in the factories that manufacture H&M's products and in the operations of other business partners'. See also http://about.hm.com/en/About/sustainability/commitments/responsible-partners.html: 'We must also hold ourselves to an exceptional standard of partnership. We do this by offering long-term contracts, providing training in good business and sustainable practices, and rewarding partners who consistently meet or exceed our expectations.'

[93] Herberg (2001) 32f.

'to give back the borrowed money tomorrow' or whether he promises 'to possibly give back the money sometime'.[94] Some corporate codes[95] in fact partly contain commitments without an indication of the specific time period in which the actions will be fulfilled and, moreover, do not even define a specific action that will be undertaken. In this context, however, it should be noted that even high degrees of abstraction do not necessarily mean that the substantive promise is meaningless. On the contrary, in the case of the corporate codes, it can be argued that a high degree of abstraction is actually needed in order to qualify them as serious. Abstract and indeterminate phrasing is nothing particular to the codes. In fact, it equally appears in the law where blank clauses and indefinite terms, abstract and broad phrasing do not have the result that they lack promissory character. The discussion on the allowed degree of abstraction appears particularly in the area of environmental law.[96] Despite some strong criticism of this abstract form of law from legal scholars,[97] it has been underlined here that the abstract phrasing of provisions is not to be avoided, but, on the contrary, it is even necessary due to the specific characteristics of the subject matter. In the field of environmental protection, one of the central reasons for abstract and flexible phrasing is the high degree of scientific uncertainty, which requires that the regulatory authorities use flexible forms in order to be able to incorporate scientific developments.[98] Taking into consideration this general tendency of abstract formulation in the field of environmental protection, one can also bring forward the fact that the vague phrasing of the corporate codes is only a way to align the codes to the general regulatory character in the respective field and thereby connect appropriately to the general discourse in the area in which the self-commitment is effectively placed.[99] Hence, in a similar vein to environmental laws, it is also environmental corporate codes that need to exhibit open-ended and flexible phrasing in order to pay due respect to the scientific uncertainty and the need to adapt to new insights.[100] While this argument of aligning the codes to the regulatory specifics concerning environmental issues would allow less specific phrasing for commitments on environmental protection, there are other reasons why rather abstract phrasing is required in other areas

[94] For this example, see ibid 32.

[95] As the degree of specificity varies quite significantly between different codes (above references in n 38), this criticism is of course not applicable to all codes, but merely to those that empirical studies have qualified as 'vague' or 'weak codes'.

[96] Ladeur (1995); Hansjürgens and Lübbe-Wolff (2000).

[97] Hansjürgens and Lübbe-Wolff (2000) 11ff.

[98] Ladeur (1995) 11. Other reasons for such abstract and symbolic phrasing are listed by Matten (2003) 218f, who particularly mentions the productive potential of such abstract forms of regulation as an 'integration and social orientation by symbols' and a valuable 'communication of abstract scientific concepts' that increases the relevance of these issues in social communication.

[99] Herberg (2001) 41ff interprets this as a separate communicative rule, but he acknowledges that it is also an important component of the rule that the promise has to be specific enough. See in a similar direction Matten (2003) 221f: 'The crucial element seems to be that companies have to be aware of the fact that the public assesses their actions in environmental issues with a certain normative judgement and the corporation has to know which are the public's political preferences and effectively communicate that it actually lives up to these requirements.'

[100] For more on this relationship between the character of environmental law and private codes of conduct on environmental protection with a focus, however, not on corporate codes, but on privately organised environmental certification schemes, *cf* Ellis (2013) 1051ff.

such as workplace standards or human rights. For these issues, the vague phrasing becomes understandable when taking into consideration the political dimension of the subject. Workplace standards and human rights aspects are subject to controversial political debates and, as a result, differ significantly from one country to another. The fact that the commitments expressed in the corporate codes are adopted as guidelines for globally operating companies actually renders the use of abstract formulation necessary in order to prevent contradictions between a code and the local law in a specific country. An overly specific code on workplace standards may put the company or its suppliers in a situation in which they either breach the code or break the law. The necessity of solving this problem can be read as a solution for the contradicting expectations that the public has towards the company. Companies are, on the one hand, expected to apply the high standards of their home country on a global scale, but, on the other hand, they are confronted with the expectation that they should remain sensitive to the political, economic and cultural situation of the country in which they operate and should not impose their, eg, Western, perceptions and conviction on other countries.[101] Against this background, vague phrasing is not necessarily a tactic of companies to avoid making a meaningful promise; it can equally represent a reasonable solution in order to make a convincing promise in the contested field of global social rights. This, however, can certainly not mean that any statement in the field of environmental protection or social standards can be classified as a successful promise irrespective of its specificity. The fact that the codes are connected to areas that are in a state of flux and require a high degree of abstraction can certainly not have the result of an 'anything goes' approach. For statements in this field to be successful promises, notwithstanding a respected higher degree of abstraction, it is necessary to extract at least a minimum content. Otherwise it would obviously be impossible to determine whether the promisor has fulfilled the promise by means of undertaking a certain action. In this regard, however, it can be argued that even vague codes can be interpreted in a way that renders it possible to determine what behaviour is in conformity with the promise. Herberg discusses this on the basis of a corporate commitment 'to produce products that are non-hazardous for humans and animals' and states that such a commitment can only be fulfilled if the product does not cause damage or if it is properly labelled in order to warn its users. Although such statements can surely be classified as very vague, it is still possible to distinguish between behaviour in conformity with the promise and behaviour that is not in conformity: selling products that have caused death and serious health problems among children is not an action that is in compliance with the guideline. Hence, although there is still a 'grey area' of behaviour that is difficult to judge, it is nevertheless possible to extract a minimum content for hard cases and decide whether these amount to compliance with the promise.[102] Moreover, the high degree of abstraction in the code can also be reduced when

[101] For this problem in the context of commitments of companies to regulate suppliers by means of contract, see McBarnet and Kurkchiyan (2007) 70ff.

[102] Herberg (2001) 33.

taking into consideration that companies in the 'preamble' of the codes also refer to various other values and guidelines, such as international policy frameworks or the expectations of specific stakeholders. To the extent that such references are included in the code, the declaration provides interpretative guidance that allows the content to be further specified.[103] Thus, it can be stated that, although not in all cases, even from more abstract and vaguely phrased codes, a meaningful promise can be extracted which sets the basis to evaluate behaviour on whether specific corporate behaviour is in compliance with the code. One could even go as far as to argue that a higher degree of abstraction in fact does not render a promise unsuccessful; rather, it increases the risk for the speaker that ambiguities on the content are solved by other materials and information that is indicated in the code from the perspective of how a reasonable speaker would understand it.

Finally, the promissory character of the corporate codes, in particular its character as a speech act that binds the speaker, could be prevented by the use of disclaimers that indicate that the corporate code should not bring about the conventional effects of the promise, which is essentially a question as to how contradictions in promises are dealt with. How should declarations be interpreted when the general interpretation of the language suggests the performance of a promise, but one aspect in the declaration provides evidence that these effects should not be created? More concretely, how can corporate codes be dealt with that use clear promissory language and state at the end that 'the code is not intended to create new or additional rights for any third party'?[104] Two solutions are possible to deal with such a contradiction in the corporate code. First, taking into consideration the main assumptions of Speech Act Theory that it is the utterance that brings about the particular effect and not the intention, any statement mentioning a lack of intention could potentially be interpreted as not being capable of destroying the performative force of the language. Austin illustrates this using the concrete example of Hippolytus, which reads: 'my tongue swore to, but my heart (or mind or other backstage artiste) did not'.[105] Despite the fact that Hippolytus makes visible his internal motivation not to swear, Austin argues that by means of swearing, by means of saying 'I swear to', he nonetheless swears. He performs it simply by means of uttering the required words.[106] Austin confesses that a speech act can become misleading if at the same time a contradicting intention is expressed; however, the sheer expression of the lack of intention does not change the very

[103] A good example of such an interpretation could again be Apple's code. In its supplier code of conduct, in which it commits to 'ensuring that working conditions in Apple's supply-chain are safe, that workers are treated with respect and dignity, and that manufacturing processes are environmentally friendly', it is stated that the code 'is modelled on and contains language from the Electronic Industry Code of Conduct' and that 'Recognized standards, such as the Universal Declaration of Human Rights, and standards issued by organizations such as the ILO, Social Accountability International and the Ethical Trading Initiative were used as reference in preparing this code and *may be useful sources of additional information*' (emphasis added). Hence, it is specified in the code what additional sources can assist in determining the content.

[104] Apple Supplier Code 2014 8, available at: www.apple.com/supplierresponsibility/accountability.html.

[105] Quote taken from Austin (1976 [1962]) 9.

[106] ibid 10.

nature of the utterance as a speech act.[107] If this solution were preferred, the result would be that corporate codes with disclaimers could still qualify as promises, but rather as misleading and unsuccessful promises. Yet, with respect to the corporate codes, one can (and it is arguably preferable) to interpret corporate codes with disclaimers differently. In general, disclaimers can be read as a standardised way to express the intention not to bind oneself *legally*. Against this background, disclaimers emphatically do not have the purpose to prevent *any* binding effect of a promise. It is hardly conceivable that a disclaimer is included to refer to the lack of an intention to create a moral or social obligation. Provocatively speaking, for companies that rely on sophisticated marketing strategies, this would be communicative nonsense.[108] On the contrary, companies instead use the corporate codes in order to create at least a moral threshold for their future corporate behaviour. Against this background, a disclaimer does not amount to a real contradiction since it does not refer to the effects of the promise as a binding obligation, but only excludes, in a rather standardised way, the possible *legally* binding effects. However, as such, the disclaimer is not necessarily a breach of the pragmatic rules on promising and therefore not always capable of preventing a binding effect. It only aims to prevent specifically the legal consequences of this promise by framing it as a socially binding promise. Whether such an exclusion is valid is then not primarily a matter of linguistic rules, but it remains subject to the autonomous decision within the law where other criteria, such as reasonable reliance, also play a role.[109] This, as a result, implies that the use of disclaimers will be addressed when analysing the transformation of any identified socially binding effect created by a corporate code into a legal obligation.[110]

To sum up, this section has sought to analyse the corporate codes declaration by focusing on the language used therein, with a particular view to the most important critical points that are raised against a promissory character. In so doing, it was argued that the corporate codes can, due to adherence to the pragmatic rules of promising, be described as successful promises that are generally capable of bringing about the conventional effects of promising.

7.2.1.2.3. The Conventional Effect of Promises

When analysing the consequences of performing the speech act, it should be noted that, as far as Speech Act Theory is concerned, it is mainly the utterance as made by the speaker that brings about a certain effect. It is furthermore based on the assumption that there are conventional effects for each specific speech act. In this regard, an important distinction is made. A particular speech act can be embedded in a conventional procedure that brings about a certain conventional effect[111] and

[107] ibid 11.

[108] One need only imagine the presence of a disclaimer in a corporate code that reads: 'This code should not be interpreted as a moral or social commitment from our side.'

[109] Köndgen (1981) 183ff; Herberg (2007) 115.

[110] See below, section 7.3.1. (p 266), text and accompanying footnotes.

[111] Austin (1976 [1962]) 26ff, 117. Examples of such conventional speech acts are 'marrying', 'christening', 'betting' or those declarations that are legally or socially institutionalised as having a certain effect; see Lüsing (2012) 138.

thus can have this particular effect. Or, if such a conventional procedure is lacking, the main effect of the speech act remains that a reaction is provoked and required from the other party.[112] Following this understanding, the promise generally has the conventional effect 'to commit the speaker to a certain course of action'.[113] The fact of promising thus has the conventional effect that the speaker is bound to do the promised action; deviations will have to be considered a breach of the promise. With respect to the corporate codes, this would eventually mean that publicly declaring the corporate code has the consequence that the company is bound by its statement and is effectively prevented from declaring non-compliance as a change in the general company strategy or its intentions.[114] Yet it remains to be seen whether and in what form this binding effect is actually confirmed and relied upon in the course of specific social interaction. This will be discussed more specifically when focusing on the reliance component and the consequences of promises within different forms of social interaction. For the time being, it must suffice to conclude that, from the perspective of a reasonable speaker, the publicly declared corporate codes can qualify as promises that have the conventional effect of binding the speaker on the promised terms.

7.2.2. The Intention: Corporate Codes as Deliberate and Strategic Promises

This emphasis on the actual code declaration and its potential to create a binding effect by the use of language notwithstanding, the intention on the side of the companies cannot be entirely ignored. This is also recognised in Speech Act Theory, according to which the internal motives are by no means irrelevant. On the contrary, in order to bind the speaker, speech acts require explicit coherence between the declaration and the intention. Whether this is the case in relation to corporate codes will be discussed in this section with a view to the underlying motives of companies.

7.2.2.1. Observing Motives behind Adopting and Publishing Codes

The most difficult component in the analysis of corporate codes is presumably the identification of the actual motives that induce companies to adopt and publish corporate codes. The fact that the internal decision-making processes of a company are, to a large extent, confidential and that the publishing companies are complex organisations makes an investigation into the actual motives quite cumbersome. Despite this difficulty, one may nevertheless discuss in this context empirical studies that attempt to shed some light on the motives. Such studies can be found in microeconomics that focus on motives to adapt CSR policies from the perspective of what would be strategically beneficial for corporate managers

[112] Austin (1976 [1962]) 117f.
[113] ibid 157.
[114] Herberg (2008) 25.

and qualitative empirical analyses in social sciences that conducted interviews in companies. It comes as no surprise that these studies do not find clear evidence for an intention to create a legal obligation by publicly declaring a corporate code. In fact, the only constellation in which an intention to create an obligation is discussed so far is when corporations deliberately choose to make the corporate code part of a contractual agreement in order to steer and control the internal processes in the company and the production at supplier factories.[115] In these constellations, it is suggested that an intention to create an obligation is present.

Among the motives that are mentioned as decisive for adopting and publishing a code, the most prominent is the purported intention to react to public pressure and to fulfil claims for greater transparency about internal decisions and intentions.[116] Hence, companies appear to use the corporate codes as a means to inform their stakeholders about their philosophy.[117] The publication of a corporate code may also be caused by pressure from other companies in the same industry, since those may fear a reputational risk for the entire sector and may thus call for collective transparency on CSR.[118] Another important factor that is emphasised, particularly in the debate in microeconomics, is the motive of companies to gain a competitive advantage.[119] Companies publish their corporate codes in order to position themselves strategically so as to attract investors, consumers and highly skilled employees. Further support for this assumption comes from Gunningham, Kagan and Thornton. Based on extensive surveys on corporate environmental policies in companies from different sectors, these authors identify that, with respect to environmental performance, the majority of companies that have corporate codes and environmental programmes in place can be described as environmental strategists.[120] Strategists are characterised by the fact that they deem environmental performance to be a relevant means to improve economic performance and that they use the publication for strategic purposes. Published documents are reviewed carefully and only selective information is made available in order to ensure that the published documents cannot be turned against the company by its competitors or by environmental groups.[121] Finally, it is also mentioned that corporate policies are partly based on the strategy to pre-empt governmental regulation in the particular field[122] or to fill existing regulatory voids in the country of operation.[123]

[115] See explicitly Bondy, Matten and Moon (2004) 467: 'if corporations are using the codes to regulate the behaviour of their employees or suppliers, the codes may … operate as a type of quasi-legal documents'. For the presence of an intention to be bound behind CSR clauses in contracts, see also Cafaggi and Randa (2012) 19.

[116] See, eg, Diller (1999) 101; Bondy, Matten and Moon (2004) 450 (with further references to studies in economics); Sutton (2004) 1162.

[117] Bondy, Matten and Moon (2004) 461.

[118] Gunningham (2007) 489ff uses the term 'collective license to operate' to describe this pressure.

[119] This motivation discussed by, amongst others: Diller (1999) 101; Bondy, Matten and Moon (2004) 461.

[120] For this conclusion, see Gunningham (2007) 477ff, where the empirical studies they conducted are also referred to.

[121] ibid 478 with further references to the studies conducted.

[122] Diller (1999) 101; Cafaggi and Randa (2012) 20.

[123] See Jackson (2014) 26ff, pointedly at 28f: 'The statistical results show that the degree of CSR adoption is positively associated with the company exposure to country environments characterized by

To conclude, from what has been discussed in the literature so far, the motives for adopting the corporate codes could be classified into two categories.[124] One important motive is to provide information about the corporate philosophy and be transparent about the internal organisation in order to react to or even pre-empt public scandals and build and regain public trust towards society. And, second, the literature on corporate codes suggests that the CSR profile including the corporate code follows the strategic objective of obtaining a competitive advantage in the form of a better market position of the company or pre-empting governmental regulation. Thus, in short, adaption and publication of a corporate code follows the motive to inform and persuade.

7.2.2.2. Theorising the Motives as an Interaction Between Intention and Language

In what way are these motives relevant when discussing the binding effect of the corporate codes? In the course of discussing Speech Act Theory and the debate above, it has been stated that the binding effect is already created by the use of particular language (provided that it is confirmed within the social context, as will be discussed below). Within Speech Act Theory, it is emphasised that the speaker needs to deliberately and intentionally perform the particular speech act in order to make it successful.[125] After all that has been said, it is clear that this intention does not need to be an intention to be bound,[126] but it is necessary that the internal state of mind must be coherent with the declaration and the effects it is supposed to have.[127]

When applying this idea to the corporate codes, it implies that the motives, however heterogeneous they eventually may be, can still sufficiently support the created binding effect as autonomously and intentionally created. This is possible even if no direct intention to be bound is present, as long as an intention can be observed to issue the declaration in a particular context for which the speaker is aware and accepts that his intentional declaration may have the particular effect. Applying this threshold, one can argue that the strategic motives to persuade and the motive of being transparent on corporate policies, culture

weak formal labor law and absence of the rule of law, as well as high degrees of actual human rights abuses or documented cases of labor standards violations.'

[124] This is not to say that these are the only motives. Other motives that are discussed in the literature with further references to the relevant empirical studies can be found in, eg, Kerr, Janda and Pitts (2009) 330f.

[125] See Searle (1971), 48ff, who also specifies this intention to bring about the speech act by several rules, in particular that the speaker and hearer are 'conscious of what they are doing', that the speaker 'intends to do' the required action, that he 'intends that the utterance will place him under an obligation' and that he 'intends that the utterance will produce in the addressee a belief'.

[126] The difficulties in identifying this direction are also emphasised by Atiyah (1981) 101: 'What is that extra something which creates the obligation? The natural temptation is to say that it is the intention of the speaker to commit himself to an obligation; but once it is conceded that even the dishonest speaker who intends to make no such commitment is bound by a promise, it becomes exceedingly difficult to formulate any other set of conditions, which explain what is to count as a promise.'

[127] Lüsing (2010) 394 ('Kohärenz zwischen Gemeintem und Erklärten'), 396 ('gelungene Sprechakte, bei denen das Erklärte dem Gemeinten entspricht').

and future intention are sufficient to achieve coherence between intention and declaration. In fact, the corporate code is part of what the publishing company deliberately aims to contribute to the debate on social and environmental responsibilities. It is not an accidental way of interacting with the public, but rather is a carefully organised and strategic way of communicating. This is also supported by the fact that developing a corporate code is generally not a task that is taken over by the marketing department. Instead, the corporate codes are confirmed by several other departments, such as the senior management and possibly even the legal department.[128] Unlike short-term marketing campaigns or spontaneous statements by managers, the corporate codes are subject to many internal checks and balances, in which the content and the potential effects are carefully analysed. In addition, in particular, the strategic motive to use the code in order to prevent governmental regulation and gain competitive advantages on the market suggests an intentional participation in a context that brings about a binding effect. In fact, the strategic objective to pre-empt governmental regulation and gain competitive advantage can also, from the perspective of the company, only be realised if a declaration is made that deliberately conveys the impression that the company is bound to undertake the action. It seems to be difficult to assume how the company could otherwise have sought to convince and persuade. In short, the strategic motive to persuade and regain trust *requires* a deliberate and intentional 'play' with the binding effects of the promise. One could even go one step further and presume a deliberate purpose to take as much advantage of the potential binding effect considering the expertise in large companies in the different departments (communication experts, legal department and market analysts) that carefully prove the way in which communication with the public can be strategically used in light of its effects.

Against this background, one can argue that the necessary components as to the intention on the side of the speaker also seem adequate in order to assume a sufficient interaction between the declaration and the intention. The corporate codes neither represent the type of promises that are made accidentally or unconsciously, nor are they promises where the potential binding effects of the declaration are not sufficiently taken into consideration the very moment it is expressed.

7.2.3. Reliance: Social Effects of Code Promises Contextualised

After having discussed the requirements as to the declaration and its coherence with the interaction, the focus will finally be put on the effect that the declaration has in social life. Already in Speech Act Theory, this distinction is made by means of clarifying that the illocutionary act, eg, use of a particular language in order to bring about conventional effects, is only one factor. Attention also needs to be paid

[128] Herberg (2007) 77. In this context, it should also be noted that the public codes of conduct explicitly require companies to have their corporate codes developed in consultation with experts and approved by the senior management; see most explicitly Principle 16(a), (b) of the UN Guiding Principles.

to the actual effects from the perspective of the addressee and the way in which the effects are institutionalised in the course of social interaction. A speaker may have deliberately used the language in, from the perspective of linguistics, a reasonable and logical way; however, in the particular social interaction, the success of these reasonably intended effects depend on whether the addressees would perceive the statement as such. Consequently, the success of an utterance is a matter not only of using language in a way that makes sense linguistically, but also of adhering to the specific rules that govern a social context. Hence, in order to be able to reveal the actual social effects of corporate codes, eg, whether they become binding eventually, it is necessary to relate the insights of linguistics to a social theory analysis that explains how a declaration and the use of particular language is perceived by the addressees in the form of social communication. The analysis on the actual effects of promising will thereby be conducted with a view to the specific social expectations that are created by such promises pursuant to the rules of the contexts in which the codes become relevant.

7.2.3.1. Observing the Social Context of Corporate Codes

The most important context of the corporate codes is, in this regard, the website of the respective company and the general corporate communication. Companies post corporate codes and sustainability commitments on their website and use the Internet to provide quite extensive information about their performance. The information on the content of the corporate codes has also been taken primarily from the respective websites of the companies.[129] To be more precise, the corporate code can often be found in a specific 'sustainability' or 'social responsibility' section that is clearly separated from the product presentation. In some cases, there can even be a specific website that contains information about the structure of the corporate group, career prospects and the social and environmental engagement. This website can be clearly distinguished from the website that contains the product advertisement. It has a different URL and the link to the product advertisement cannot be found that easily.[130] This separation of the code and the product information is probably influenced by legal requirements. As was mentioned in the course of analysing the corporate codes in the context of unfair commercial practices law, the courts held statements and certifications on the company performance and policies to be misleading if they appear in too close proximity to concrete product information.[131] Next to the website, the corporate codes are also often referred to

[129] This applies to the statements of Adidas and H&M as well as the information taken from the studies of Backer and Bondy, Matten and Crane, since they also make extensive use of the companies' websites.

[130] As an example, one can refer again to the website of Adidas—www.adidas-group.com/en is the company page, whereas www.adidas.com (which is directly linked to the respective company websites .nl, .de, .co.uk) is a separate site that advertises the products that Adidas sells. On the latter website, reference to the company website is included only at the very bottom, where a sitemap of the entire page is given. Conversely, the corporate group website only refers to the different products at the very bottom where the logos of the brands are posted.

[131] On this aspect, see section 5.3.1.1. (p 196), text and accompanying footnotes.

in other general public relations communications such as prospectuses and are visualised in symbols that create the corporate identity.[132]

As was stated above, companies not only make commitments with respect to future behaviour, they also use their codes as a basis for reports. The corporate codes and a report on actual efforts in a particular period are, in this regard, either included in the general annual report in the form of so-called integrated reporting[133] or in the form of a specific social or environmental 'progress report'.[134] Here, it has to be distinguished between information on the actual progress and the expression of future commitments. The latter is particularly mentioned as a basis against which the reported actions are evaluated. The Adidas sustainability report, for instance, mentions the corporate code commitment, followed by facts and figures that highlight the progress in the past year, and sets new commitments for the following year.[135] These reports are primarily addressed to shareholders and potential investors, but they are also used as a means to inform stakeholders. In addition, an important social context in which companies include reference to the sustainability commitment is advertising. An example of this strategy is the 'we agree' campaign of Chevron, which was published in the aftermath of the Deepwater Horizon catastrophe in the Gulf of Mexico. The company used an advertisement campaign to present itself as a sustainable and green company by declaring that it agrees 'to develop affordable, viable alternatives to fossil fuels', to use its profits 'in future energy supplies, employing workers at good wages' and 'to support the communities they are part of'. The campaign reflects and attempts to make publicly visible Chevron's statement on sustainability, which is entitled the 'Chevron way'.[136] Next to such campaigns that can be broadly described as mere image campaigns, corporate codes can also be used (often shortened) in the context of product advertisement. The facts of the case against the German retailer Lidl, as discussed in chapter five, can be a good example in this respect. Lidl not only used the website to announce that it adheres to the highest labour standards, but also mentioned in a product leaflet that was distributed to mailboxes of

[132] A good example of this strategy is the former marketing campaign of BP, in which it not only made commitments with respect to renewable energy, but also developed a general marketing campaign that went even as far as changing the name from 'British Petroleum' into 'Beyond Petroleum'. For the BP marketing, the environmental commitments and the focus on the change of the entire brand in detail, see Cherry and Sneirson (2011) 1002ff.

[133] Integrated reporting means that the company includes a report on non-financial information in its annual financial statement. Integrated reporting is also strongly recommended by the Global Reporting Initiative, a leading non-profit initiative that focuses on the development of global reporting with respect to non-financial information. For the Global Reporting Initiative's statement with respect to integrated reporting, see: www.globalreporting.org/information/current-priorities/integrated-reporting/Pages/default.aspx.

[134] This is, for instance, the strategy employed by Apple, which posts on its website an annual 'progress report': www.apple.com/supplierresponsibility/reports.html.

[135] See the sustainability report at www.adidas-group.com/de/nachhaltigkeit/berichte-policies-und-daten/nachhaltigkeitsberichte/. In the reporting part, the actual commitment is partly used as an introduction against which the actual performance is measured. These commitments are entitled 'Milestones'.

[136] For an extensive analysis of the Chevron commitment and the advertising campaign, see generally Cherry and Sneirson (2012) 134ff.

consumers: 'we trade in a fair way! … Lidl campaigns for fair labour conditions worldwide'. In the context of this advertisement, the company also referred to its corporate values and its membership of the Business Social Compliance Initiative.[137] Less frequently, corporate codes also appear in product advertisements. This is particularly the case when a company uses a commitment to participate in a fair trade initiative to label its product as 'fair trade products'. Evidence for this strategy can be taken from the case law, as discussed in chapter five within the context of unfair commercial practices law.

To sum up, this overview suggests that the corporate codes primarily appear on the website within the communication with which the company attempts to inform the public (website and public relations communication), its shareholders and investors (sustainability reports) and other market actors (image campaigns and advertisement). Moreover, the corporate code is mostly published in the course of providing general information on the company history, values and culture (public relations, website), giving information on the general company performance (reports and advertisement) or in some cases also related to the products that the company attempts to sell on the market (mostly advertisement). Both insights will, in the following discussion, be related to the theoretical analysis. The former aspect provides evidence as to the question of what social context the corporate codes are embedded in and thus what observer perspective needs to be taken. The latter element is relevant insofar as it provides evidence for the particular object of the expectations.

7.2.3.2. *Theorising Corporate Codes as Differentiated Social Communication*

7.2.3.2.1. The Transformation of Language into Social Communication

The analysis on the social effects of promises from a social theory perspective is based on the general assumption that there is a fragmentation of language into various distinctly separate forms of social communication, which follows particularly Wittgenstein's notion of fragmented language games[138] and Luhmann's idea of social communication as differentiated into different self-referential processes.[139] The understanding that language always appears in society in the form of differentiated social communication implies, in the first place, that the language, as reasonably used by the speaker, does not necessary coincide with

[137] Evidence for this advertisement has been brought forward by the claimants in the statement of claim, which is available at: www.vzhh.de/recht/30332/Lidl_Klage.pdf.

[138] Wittgenstein (1968) § 23, 11: 'But how many kinds of sentences are there? … There are *countless* kinds: countless different kinds of use of what we call "symbols", "words", "sentences". And this multiplicity is not something fixed, given once for all; but new types of language, new language-games, as we may say, come into existence, and others become obsolete and get forgotten' (emphasis in original).

[139] Luhmann (1995) 137ff, 144: 'From the assumption that communication is a basally self-referential process that coordinates three different selections in each of its elements, it follows, according to Systems Theory, that there *can be no environmental correlate* for communication. The *unity* of communication corresponds to nothing in the environment. Therefore communication *necessarily* operates by *differentiating*' (emphasis in original).

how the addressee perceives it. Focusing concretely on the effects of promises, this implies that a promise made by a reasonable speaker, with the objective of creating a binding effect, could actually be prevented if this binding effect is not confirmed by the speaker and relied upon in the further course of social communication. The purported and deliberately created binding effect is only created if the particular rules applicable to the interaction between speaker and addressee were to confirm the promises as binding.[140] Since the universality of having a convention that promises are binding is disputed from the perspective of social differentiation, the binding effect is only created if it is constantly understood, confirmed, repeated and ultimately stabilised as a firm expectation in a particular type of social interaction.[141] This can be concretely illustrated when comparing the effects of a promise to host the next get-together the morning after a long wild party night and a promise made in the course of a commercial relationship to continue business relations. Although it is fair to say that a promise was made in both cases,[142] the effects are still different. An important component for the different effects is thus a way in which the addressed party perceives and confirms the promise pursuant to the rules of the particular context, which will, in the following, be analysed with respect to the corporate codes.

7.2.3.2.2. Social Expectations Created by Code Communication

This undertaking requires, in the first place, identifying the relevant social context to which the corporate codes relate. Pursuant to the overview above, the corporate codes appear primarily in the context of public relations communication of the company. Yet, to what social context is such public relations communication effectively linked? As the name already indicates, public relations communication represents a form of communication by which someone conveys information to the general public without already addressing a particular person or a particular group in order to start communication. The sociological literature on public relations has, in this regard, specified the characteristics of public relations by describing it as a communicative attempt by which closed organisational or social systems provide information to their social environment in order to allow further interaction.[143]

[140] The condition of an accepted rule or convention that promises are binding also underlies in fact Promissory Theories, in particular Fried (1981) 16: 'An individual is morally bound to keep his promises because he has intentionally invoked a *convention* whose function it is to give grounds … for another to expect the promised performance. To abuse this confidence now is like … lying: the abuse *of a shared social institution*' (emphasis added). See in detail on this aspect in Fried's promissory theory Kimel (2003) 14ff.

[141] Luhmann (1995) 142: 'The ability to differentiate between functionally specific acts or functional dominances of one or the other selection horizon is possible only if the unity of the communicative synthesis is guaranteed in advance as something normal.' See also Atiyah (1981) 129: 'So the end, I suggest, the assumption that promises do in general create binding obligations entails … a social group whose judgment *determines* the initial question of entitlement' (emphasis added). And later: 'He [the speaker] cannot just create … rules or … obligations by what he does, because he is not in charge of relations between himself and other members of the group.

[142] Assuming of course that similar words are used, such as 'I promise' or 'I will definitely' and that the general language rules are fulfilled.

[143] From the perspective of sociological public relations theory, see Ronneberger and Rühl (1992) 111ff.

Accordingly, this form of communication could be defined as comparable to the communication of individuals when they introduce and present themselves to others; it is akin to the self-presentation of individuals in everyday life.[144] Attempts in sociology to describe the character of self-presentation have, in this regard, focused on the social function of self-presentation to introduce the speaker to social interaction and, moreover, to underline the qualities of the speaker. As a result, communication on self-presentation is by no means neutral and only descriptive information; it is already a way that influences the perception in others about oneself.[145] Even more, public relations communication is an institutionalised way of building social trust by revealing the qualities of a person or an organisation and of convincing other social actors to foster a social contact.[146] Translated into the self-presentation of companies, this form of communication is consequently a way in which companies introduce themselves as social actors and reveal their hidden qualities in the form of internal policies, corporate culture and philosophy. The main function of this communication is to reduce the anonymity between the company and the public and to intensify social interaction. In this regard, public relations communication proves particularly important in a market context where it is directed towards attracting the attention of customers and investors, but also employees with the objective of being considered by them as a trustworthy actor. With respect to the CSR communication, this attempt to build trust is, however, in fact even broader as it is not only linked to the market public, but also represents a way to create general trust towards the global public in order to maintain the social licence.[147] However, in addition to this effect of public relations communication on the creation of social trust, there is a second function of such general public relations communication that exceeds plain self-presentation and trust-building: public relations communication can more appropriately be classified as what Köndgen has defined as intentional self-presentation.[148] Intentional self-presentation goes beyond introducing the speaker and presenting him as trustworthy; it is a way to deliberately create expectations in other actors in order to induce them to perform a certain action.[149] In relation to public relations communication and company statements on websites and in PR campaigns, this implies that this form of communication also follows the deliberate function to start communication on the anonymous market for the sake of inducing addressees to enter into further cooperation, negotiation and ultimately contractual consensus. Consequently, communication of companies

[144] See fundamentally on the sociological concept of self-presentation of individuals Goffman (1959). The understanding of public relations communications of companies as a form of organisational self-presentation has been (with reference to Goffman's idea of individual self-presentation) coined by Köndgen (1981) 175.

[145] For this persuasive character of individual self-presentation Goffman (1959) 3f.

[146] See Ronneberger and Rühl (1992) 237ff, particularly at 242: 'Das PR-System kann die unsichere Kommunikations- und Interaktionssituation dadurch stabilisieren, daß es mit Vertrauen besondere *Ordnungsleistungen* erbringt' (emphasis in original).

[147] Herberg (2007) 75: 'Die Verhaltenskodizes der Konzerne sind daher nicht einfach ein Mittel der Imagepflege wie jedes andere, sie sind ein spezielles Mittel der Werbung um *öffentliches* Vertrauen, und zwar, so sei hinzugefügt, unter den Bedingungen erheblicher Legitimations- und Vertrauensprobleme' (emphasis added).

[148] Köndgen (1981) 174ff.

[149] ibid 174.

to the public is not only linked to the communication with an anonymous global public by invoking the social institution of trust, it is already loosely connected to the more specific social context of the market with the aim of initiating cooperation and contracting. In this context, it is comparable to an initial assurance about the qualities of the speaker as a potential contractual partner upon which further interaction is built.[150]

Considering these two communicative contexts of public relations communications, this form can be sociologically framed as an interaction with the anonymous public to further trust and the more specific interaction of inducing cooperation. This, however, raises the question of the consequences that a specific promise made by corporate codes could have in these respective communicative contexts. What social expectations does it give rise to in these contexts and are there reasons why these expectations deserve protection?

7.2.3.2.2.1. Persuading Promises on the Market

What are the consequences of promises in the process in which a contract is induced, planned and ultimately agreed upon? Does a promise pursuant to the rules of this social interaction immediately result in a situation in which the promise is confirmed as socially binding? In general, it is fair to assume that the entire undertaking of creating an agreement between actors on the market is the typical context in which a binding effect is created. However, it is equally true that not all promises made within the course of this undertaking are immediately and irrevocably binding. On the contrary, in the course of inducing cooperation and negotiation with the objective of contracting, manifold communications take place that parties do not necessarily treat as irrevocably binding. So far, it is merely the final explicit consensus that fulfils this role. A first indication about whether the corporate codes create binding effect can thus be taken from the actual place of the corporate codes in this process. Public relations communication is included at an early stage of this particular form of communication. The declarations made therein are directed towards inducing the entire process. As a result, they seem not to be entirely comparable to the declaration that amounts to the final offer and that is perceived by the addressee as the basis for an ultimate consensus; initial statements and public relations communications are rather a way to convey information and make general and abstract commitments that structure the further contractual negotiations.[151] The integration of the corporate codes in such forms of initial information therefore renders it unlikely that they are perceived as declarations that bind the speaker as final offers; on the contrary, the corporate codes are instead a way to initiate a cooperative relationship and provoke a reaction of the other party to confirm or reject the proposed commitment.[152]

[150] ibid 178.
[151] ibid 187f.
[152] See Herberg (2007) 116: 'Die Selbstverpflichtungen der Konzerne sind selbst kein Vertrag, sie spezifizieren aber die Rahmenbedingungen rechtskräftiger Verträge.'

However, their character as initial declarations certainly does not mean that no binding effect is created whatsoever. Considering that the process of contractual negotiations and pre-contractual cooperation is not a loose social interaction without rules, but rather is an institutionalised form of social interaction in which previous communication is relied upon in further interaction, it could be argued that participants in this process nevertheless confirm such promises and the commitments made therein as binding, even though they might be treated as informal and thus only a merely informal confirmation of the binding effect.

Such an interpretation follows from the perspective on the process of contracting as a particular language game, ie, communication on planning.[153] The function of this specific form of communication is to reach a consensus and the starting point is always a proposal of the conditions under which the further interaction and cooperation should take place.[154] A promise included at the beginning of this planning dialogue would then have the character of a proposal, which could be either confirmed and relied upon by the addressee or rejected. Whenever the proposal is accepted and relied upon in the further course of planning, it has the result that the binding effect occurs, as this proposal structures the further course of the dialogue and limits the range of possibilities that the parties can opt for.[155] Initial and informal promises, such as corporate codes, then represent what dialogue analysis has framed as a 'commitment in dialogue',[156] which the parties can make already in the course of their social interaction and not only when explicitly recording the consensus. By means of already including a promise in this dialogue when seeking to induce cooperation, the proposed binding effect is then effectuated once it receives a confirming reaction of the addressed party, either in the form of acceptance or a proposition that reveals reliance on the initial proposal and thus determines the further process of cooperation.[157] As a result, someone who promises in the language game of planning and cooperation that he will perform an action in the form of a proposal incurs a performance obligation once it is relied upon by the other party. He who promised may not then simply refuse to do the action without running the risk of being socially sanctioned.[158] However, the rules of this particular dialogue can permit the loss of a commitment by retracting

[153] For the classification of the process of contracting as a language game, see Campbell and Collins (2003) 34f; Lüsing (2010) 363ff. The specific characterisation of contracting as a language game of 'planning' is suggested by Lüsing (2010) 382ff on the basis of dialogue analysis that is developed by, among others, Walton and Krabbe (1995). On the interpretation of contracting as a language game, see also Teubner (2000a) 403, 407ff, who, however, conceptualises the language game of contracting not only as interpersonal communication but also as a social discourse between the different socially institutionalised discourses of economy, law and the productive social system. This dimension of contracting will also become discussed, see section 8.3.2.1. (p 348), text and accompanying footnotes.

[154] Lüsing (2010) 382.

[155] ibid 365: 'Die grundlegende Einsicht des Paradigmas des Sprachspiels ist damit die Einsicht, dass man mit jeder sprachlichen Handlung bestimmte Festlegungen eingeht, die den weiteren Dialogverlauf in der Weise bestimmen, als dass sie bestimmte sprachliche Handlungen eröffnen oder versperren.' See also Hawickhorst (1987) 132.

[156] Walton and Krabbe (1995) 31: 'Perhaps the most obvious way is for a speaker to incur a commitment through his own direct or indirect speech act.'

[157] See on this aspect the detailed analysis of Lüsing (2010) 382.

[158] ibid 382f: 'Wer vorschlägt zu x-en legt sich damit insbesondere auf Folgendes fest: … dass er selbst bereit ist zu x-en … Wer vorschlägt zu x-en, dem ist es verboten … sich zu weigern, zu x-en.'

one's own commitments or by getting released from a promise.[159] In that sense, this implicit way of proposing and confirming is less formalised and definite than the final consensus. Until such a release or retraction happens, however, the particular commitment must be considered as binding.[160] From this perspective, one can understand the corporate codes as proposals by the speaker to create a binding effect. Once such proposals are accepted by other participants in the form of basing further cooperation on it, they can be interpreted as being confirmed and thus becoming an implicit consensus on the specific aspect of corporate social and environmental responsibility as declared in the code, even though other aspects of the contractual relationship might not have been fixed yet.

This understanding of the binding character can also be based on treating the specific social context of inducing a contract not as a dialogue-based language game of planning that follows particular dialogue rules, but as a social relationship that is institutionalised as dependent on mutual reliance on initially provided information and assurances. Köndgen advocates this understanding of contracting with a view to contracts between traders and consumers on the anonymous market. He emphasises that in the social interaction between remote parties, which are seeking to conclude a consensual relationship on the consumer market, reliance on the various types of pre-contractual information is a constituting feature. This is due to the fact that, in the absence of personal interaction, parties, when seeking to cooperate, need to rely on other forms in order to specify the particularities of the deal and the person with whom to contract.[161] It is here the wide range of information and habits of both parties that already structure, in parts, the particularities of the deal and thus create an expectation on the side of the addressee that the self-commitments will be fulfilled.[162] Thus, a promise included in a communication that is addressed to the anonymous market results in creating a binding effect because the addressee perceives such information in the absence of intense personal interaction as the sole and ultimate basis for any deal that is concluded. However, in contrast to the promises that form the explicit consensus between remote parties, Köndgen emphasises that, from the perspective of the addressees, the expectations created by this form of pre-contractual information always remains pending, implicit and diffuse, and comes to the fore only when the decision to conclude a contract is finally taken.[163] Pursuant to this understanding,

[159] Walton and Krabbe (1995) 36ff.

[160] ibid 41: 'In the language of negotiation dialogue, sometimes a distinction is made between binding and nonbinding agreements. It is tempting to infer that a parallel distinction can be made between binding and non-binding commitments, where the latter type is retractable and the former is not. However, this is an illusion. For there are no nonbinding commitments since the term *commitment* means that you are bound to something … even a retractable commitment is binding.'

[161] Köndgen (1981) 186.

[162] ibid 187f, pointedly at 187: 'Selbstbindungen strukturieren mithin den Erwartungshorizont künftiger Geschäftspartner vor, liefern eine Situationsdefinition für den ersten geschäftlichen Kontakt und bereiten so den Boden für das im engeren Sinne rechtsgeschäftliche Handeln. Sie versprechen noch keine konkrete vertragliche Leistung, aber sie spezifizieren zumindest teilweise schon deren Rahmenbedingungen.'

[163] ibid 188: 'Die Werbung des Warenherstellers prüft fraglos die Vorstellungen des Werbeadressaten hinsichtlich der Produktqualität. Aber diese Erwartungen werden aktuell erst, wenn der Verbraucher den angepriesenen Artikel erwirbt und in der Hand hält.'

corporate codes, as included in public relations communications or advertising campaigns, are equally confirmed as binding even in the particular situation of mass contracting. The corporate codes are part of the material that is, in the context of the market, institutionalised as the reliable basis for further cooperation, which, even though only implicitly, already shapes the expectations of the addressees in their decisions as to whether or not to intensify cooperation and ultimately to contract. The codes then represent relied-upon declarations that influence the decision making on the market.

As for the binding effect of corporate codes, the analysis of the social interaction of planning cooperation and inducing a contract suggests that the binding effect, as reasonably intended by the publishing companies, is actually confirmed by the addressees by accepting it or relying on it as a prerequisite for further cooperation. Yet, an important characteristic of this identified binding effect in the interaction is the fact that the binding effect occurs even before the overall consensus is reached on the cooperation as such and that it remains less formalised than the ultimate contract or transaction that records the entire consensus.

However, the fact that expectations are created in the binding effect in this form of social interaction does not yet say anything about the particular content of these expectations and codes, and their importance for the functioning of this social interaction. Yet, an answer to this question is crucial in order to determine whether these expectations would need to be protected and thus whether the law needs to be responsive by equipping the disappointment of these expectations with legal sanctions. Concerning the content of the created expectations, it should first be noted that the corporate codes are included in different corporate communication strategies. They appear as isolated promises concerning future responsible behaviour as well as elements in image campaigns or product advertising. Therefore, the concrete content of expectations may differ and thus different substantive expectations need to be distinguished. In general, one can say that the corporate codes as such create an expectation as to the future socially responsible conduct of the corporate entity and the company's active role in regulating worldwide compliance with social and environmental standards as a private actor. Having said that, the overview above has also emphasised that the corporate code is not always an isolated promise as to future regulatory behaviour; the code partly appears in other communicative contexts as well. In this regard, two important contexts have been identified. The corporate code is partly related to information on the current company performance, as is the case, for instance, with respect to sustainability reports or company-focused advertisements, and it is partly explicitly integrated into product advertisement. Focusing on the former constellation, the close proximity of the corporate code promise with the communication on the actual performance can have the result that the code is not perceived by the addressees as an isolated promise as to the future behaviour or the ongoing regulatory role, but, more generally, as an expectation about the social and environmental character of the future contractual partner. Accordingly, the object of expectations is then not the future behaviour, but the character of the publishing company in relation to which the corporate code assists in personalising the company. An even more drastic shift in the expectations takes place when the corporate code is directly related to product advertisement. A company advertising its products with an intention to produce under environmentally friendly conditions or by adhering to social standards does not equally create an isolated expectation that the company actively promotes future good corporate practice. The expectations about compliance with the corporate code instead seem to merge with product-related expectations as to the characteristics and quality of the product. The expectations as to the corporate codes then become merely an expectation in the substantive character of products.[164]

Thus, corporate codes can result in expectations that are related to the products that the company sells, the character of the company and its current performance or, if they remain an isolated commitment, an expectation as to the future behaviour of the company. However, despite their different objects, all of these expectations prove to be important for the functioning of the particular social interaction and thus would require protection. First, it seems fairly uncontroversial to assume that, in the market context, expectations and confidence in products are crucial and, accordingly, ought to be protected. The main reason here is the crucial importance of goods as a tool for the proper functioning of the market.[165] This distinct position of the goods could then justify extending the scope of protection to the expectations that relate to the environmental or social characteristics of the goods. In addition, sociological research also suggests that, notwithstanding the crucial importance of protecting confidence in goods for the functioning of the market, the anonymous market still has not led to a diminishing importance of expectations that are directed to the integrity of the contractual partner.[166] Against this background, it makes sense to also qualify the social and environmental character that the company declares to have, its current social and environmental integrity, as expectations that are crucial for the functioning of this relationship. Yet, what about the most general expectation concerning socially and environmentally responsible corporate conduct in the future, which represents the core of the corporate code promise? Is there a need to also protect the substantive expectation that the other person will behave responsibly in the future and undertake the promised measures even if no link to the actual current performance or to the sold products is made? There are, in fact, two arguments that support a specific form of protection. One general argument in favour is to refer to the increasing relevance of future ethical behaviour for market transactions—keyword ethical

[164] It is this relationship between corporate codes and the expectations in the products the company sells that is often emphasised in the literature; see, eg, Glinski (2007) 125f; Herberg (2007) 116f.

[165] This importance of product-related expectations has already been emphasised by Weber. In fact, it is one of his core observations that the development of a specific market rationality has eventually resulted in a situation where only the interest in products and not in persons is relevant. See Weber (1968) 636: 'The market community as such is the most impersonal relationship of practical life into which humans can enter with one another … The reason for the impersonality of the market is its matter-of-factness, its orientation on the commodity and only to that. Where the market is allowed to follow its own autonomous tendencies, its participants do not look toward the persons of each other but only toward the commodity.'

[166] For the importance of these expectations as to the person with whom to contract, see generally for long-term business relationships the empirical study of Macaulay (1963) 58f, and for the 'seemingly' anonymous discrete consumer transactions, see Köndgen (1981) 203ff (with references to empirical studies).

consumption and trading.[167] However, the more specific argument that can only be briefly indicated here with reference to the further theoretical analysis relates to the regulatory role that companies increasingly take over by means of their codes and the importance of preserving the expectations in this new regulatory role.[168]

*7.2.3.2.2.2. **Trust-Building Behaviour towards the Global Public***

Yet, as has been stated above, public relations communication is not only related to the social interaction of inducing and planning a contract as initial statements, it has also been described as communication that is directed towards building trust between an (economic) organisation and the public. What consequences does a promise have in this undertaking in relation to building public trust? Since the codes are in this regard promises that are made in a social interaction of complete anonymity, the situation seems to be comparable to a promise between strangers. In analysing promises that are made between persons in situations of anonymity, Kimel has argued that such promises do not fail beforehand for the very reason that there is no underlying social practice or convention in place between the parties that allows for an a priori expectation that the promise will be fulfilled. Promises between strangers fulfil another important function. They become part of the trust-building behaviour from the side of the speaker and, in this capacity, can help to 'restore her reputation *as a trustworthy person*'.[169] Following this understanding, a promise made within public relations can assist in strengthening general public trust if the promisor also attempts to fulfil the promise. Hence, by means of making a promise to the public in the form of a corporate code, the company can further the public perception of being a trustworthy entity, thus resulting in intensified social trust between the company and the global public as an addressee. The sociological literature on the institution of trust has shown that such forms of trust-building are crucial for society in order to function properly.[170] In fact, trust is essential to keep society running because it allows decisions to be defined as rational and justified under conditions of risk and uncertainty. As Luhmann pointedly states: 'The *lack of trust* ... simply withdraws activities. It reduces the range of possibilities for rational action ... It prevents, above all, capital investment under conditions of uncertainty and risk.'[171] The absence of trust may consequently cause a shrinking or entire disappearance of social systems because distrust prevents necessary

[167] This tendency towards ethical consumerism is discussed more in detail later, see section 8.2.1.2. (p 314), text and accompanying footnotes.

[168] See conclusion of section 8.2.3. (p 334). The argument to protect the trust in the regulatory role is also indicated in the analysis of Bachmann (2006b) 240ff, 254f, who refers to the importance of protecting the parties' reliance in private regulation (*Regelvertrauen*), in particular the declarations that give the impression of a regulatory norm (at 255: 'Wer dadurch einen herausragenden Vertrauenstatbestand schafft, dass er seinen Erklärungen äußerlich den Anschein einer (dauerhaften) Rechtsnorm gibt (etwa durch Gestaltung als "Kodex" oder "Ordnung") wird sich ... daran festhalten lassen müssen').

[169] Kimel (2003) 20f (quote at 20, emphasis in original).

[170] For an analysis of the role of trust in social theory, see, eg, Luhmann (1979); Gambetta (1990); Sztompka (1999); Teubner (2003).

[171] Luhmann (1988b) 104 (emphasis in original).

decisions from being taken and system-running operations from being pursued. The presence of trust conversely produces social order and stability.[172] Since trust is not an a priori-existent social fact, but needs to be constantly created, gained and maintained, it is necessary for societies that trustworthy conduct is undertaken and that it is consistently manifested and repeated. Consequently, the corporate codes fulfil an important function within society: they are instances that seek to build public trust and to establish the general expectation that companies remain reliable players in the global economy that contribute to the functioning of society.

However, this necessary attempt of public trust-building is, in this constellation, not simply one among of ordinary trust-building attempts with an anonymous global public. The corporate codes are in fact not merely included in a social relationship of anonymity as a mere way to increase trust. Instead, they are apparent in relationships that are characterised by a high level of distrust of companies after their failures in the past. How, then, can trust-building behaviour be successful when included in a relationship characterised by low trust or distrust? Or, to put it another way, what effects does a promise have if not included in an interaction between strangers not knowing each other, but in a context in which the promisor is explicitly distrusted? In fact, the corporate codes do not represent an ordinary promise; they are promises that convey the paradoxical message 'trust me, although I know you do not trust me'. Against this background, is it possible that the public eventually accepts the trust-building attempt? Or is it more likely that such promises are perceived as solely empty gestures? While one could of course argue that such promises are worthless because of the anticipated distrust, a sociological analysis suggests a slightly different interpretation. Following the sociological understanding on the mechanisms to create social trust under conditions of distrust, trust-building behaviour is in these situations not entirely in vain, yet the conditions of distrust make such trust-building behaviour particularly vulnerable and risky undertakings. This is due to the fact that, in situations of distrust, distrust constantly 'endorse[s] and reinforce[s] itself in social interaction'.[173] Under conditions of distrust, a 'self-enhancing vicious spiral of deepening cynicism and suspicion will start.'[174] If there is thus a negative bias towards expecting untrustworthy conduct, the likely consequence is that a person is still distrusted even if he attempts to behave in a trustworthy manner. This tendency in fact becomes particularly apparent when looking at the perception of corporate codes by the public. Here, the present and strong distrust towards companies seems to have infected the perception of their corporate codes rather than vice versa. The discussion on the corporate codes currently seems to be caught in the logic that 'the uglier the company, the more makeup it uses'.[175] It still remains one of the first public reactions to the efforts of companies to establish trust to blame such attempts as 'green washing', 'blue washing' or 'social washing'[176] rather than referring to the possible positive efforts that might have been or at least could be achieved. The sociological

172 Sztompka (1999) 106.
173 Luhmann (1979) 74.
174 Sztompka (1999) 111.
175 Sjåfjell (2011a) 126.
176 Above text in n 85.

perspective teaches us that such situations of immense distrust are difficult to solve and give a different direction. Definitely, an occasional attempt to re-establish trust is not sufficient.[177] Trust can only be re-established and the 'vicious spiral' of distrust can only be reversed once trustworthy conduct is repeated steadily and if it is adhered to over a long period, with the eventual result that distrust becomes unjustified.[178] With respect to the corporate codes, this effectively means that the corporate codes cannot be successful in establishing trust if one considers them from a short-term perspective. The trust-building function can only be achieved on a long-term basis if promising companies combine promising trustworthy conduct with underlying trustworthy behaviour, eg, if they promised and show efforts on compliance with the promise on a long-term basis.

Against this background, the trust-building function of the corporate codes currently remains in an ambivalent stage. The corporate codes generally have the potential to be successful in establishing public trust, yet they can only realise this potential if they are supported by constant trustworthy conduct. However, the fact that this process is easily undermined by a single event that gives rise to justified distrust implies that a limited number of promising, but non-complying, companies may already have more implications than just the fact that it might disappoint expectations in this particular company. One non-complying company can be a threat for the entire success of the complete attempt to build trust by publicly declaring compliance with corporate codes. It is this fragility of public trust created by the codes that provides a strong argument why the created trust ought to receive additional protection. Under conditions in which trust is difficult to institutionalise but easy to undermine, it seems difficult to conceive that the social mechanism of trust-building will be powerful enough to transform the ongoing breeding of distrust into trust. Social trust-building mechanisms may possibly suffice in constellations in which dense community rules are in place that are prepared to sanction directly an event of disappointed trust in the form of exclusion; yet, in the constellations of the corporate codes, this possibility seems not to be sufficient. In the global arena, the loose ties and different interests are most likely not strong enough to take over the role of sanctioning disappointments of trust alone. It is then also the legal system that needs to play a role. To be clear, an argument for a role of the legal system to protect trust would by no means put the legal system in the position to create trust in the corporate codes; the legal system obviously cannot make the corporate codes into trustworthy declarations. Nevertheless, the legal system can be important for stabilising the expectation that one may have trust in the corporate codes by treating reliance on them as reasonable and legitimate. In other words, although even a legal stabilisation may not increase the likelihood that a company effectively complies with its corporate code, the law nevertheless sends the signal that disappointing the expectation in a complying company will be legally sanctioned. Translating public trust into legally stabilised reasonable public trust then translates the created trust from purely a matter of

[177] Good (1988) 43: 'If an untrustworthy person behaves well on one occasion, it is not nearly so likely that the converse inference will be made.'
[178] Sztompka (1999) 111.

trusting the distrusted companies into trusting that the law will sanction cases of disappointed trust. The advantage of this transformation is that disappointments following the untrustworthy behaviour of companies can be more easily captured because at least the trust in the effectiveness of the legal sanctions will remain intact. Or, to put it in the words of Luhmann, disappointments can then be taken with a 'higher degree of composure; at least one knows that one will not be discredited for one's expectations. One can afford a higher degree of uncertain confidence or even of mistrust as long as one has confidence in law'.[179]

7.2.4. Conclusion

This previous analysis has sought to focus more in detail on the question of whether the corporate codes can be described as instances that bind the company in the course of social interaction. Seeking inspiration from a theoretical framework that identifies the binding character in a particular interaction between an intention of the publishing company, the code declaration and the language used therein and the expectations created on the side of the addressees in a particular context, it could be revealed that the corporate codes do in fact create a binding effect in a twofold way. First, the binding effect occurs in the social interaction of inducing cooperation and planning an agreement that becomes binding when relied upon by the contracting parties in the further course of their cooperation. Second, the corporate codes can bind the company towards the global public in the form of intensified public trust. With respect to both social relations where the codes bind the speaker, it was emphasised that the substantive content of this binding effect, eg, the obligation to act socially responsibly in the future, represents an important aspect of the novel regulatory role that is taken by companies. It is this aspect that the legal system needs to be responsive to by developing mechanisms to stabilise the created expectations in this regulatory role and uphold them in case of disappointment.

7.3. PRIVATE LAW ENFORCEMENT OF CODE PROMISES

Having analysed the way in which corporate codes become binding in social interaction and having revealed the need for the law to be responsive to this socially binding effect, the following section seeks to discuss more in detail how this social responsiveness could be institutionalised in the law. To that end, it will be scrutinised whether private law is, in light of its own rules and criteria, first of all generally capable of treating the observed socially binding effect as legally binding (section 7.3.1). Answering this in the affirmative, the analysis will proceed by focusing on the appropriate concepts and doctrines to accommodate this binding effect in relation to, on the one hand, the particular social relationship in which the code promise was introduced to initiate further cooperation and ultimately

[179] Luhmann (2004) 148.

conclude an agreement (section 7.3.2) and, on the other hand, in relation to the global public and the need to protect general public trust in the promised future good corporate behaviour (section 7.3.3).

7.3.1. From Socially to Legally Binding Effect

The theoretical analysis has so far inquired as to the binding effect of the code declaration from the interdisciplinary perspective of linguistic and sociology, which resulted in conclusions about the socially binding effect of the codes. The following considerations will discuss how this socially binding effect can be recognised as a legal obligation. The general sociological and linguistic arguments, with regard to this question, certainly have an influence in informing the law. Yet, their influence on the legal perception notwithstanding, it also has to be clear that their insights cannot be undertaken uncritically; for the interpretation of the corporate codes as legally binding obligations, it is eventually the normative criteria in the law that need to be consulted.[180] This certainly does not mean that the conclusions as to the socially binding effect are not valid. On the contrary, in many aspects that are relevant for the corporate codes, the law (specifically the system of private law) would arrive at similar conclusions.

First of all, promises made by private actors are not only from the linguistic and sociological perspective binding, it is also fairly uncontroversial to describe such promises in general as the conventional basis to create legal obligations. In particular, contract law is, from an orthodox understanding, primarily concerned with the enforcement of the promises that parties make. Yet, it is equally fairly uncontroversial that not all promises are treated as legally binding, but that private law has in place several additional criteria when determining whether the particular promise ought to be enforced. In relation to the corporate codes, these additional criteria partly resemble the linguistic and sociological criteria that have been discussed above. Comparable to the analysis on the socially binding effect, corporate codes would also from the legal perspective only under exceptional circumstances be considered invalid for their vague content. By the same token, the mental reservation of the party not to be bound would generally not be considered an obstacle for creating a legal obligation. Concerning the vague content, private law is prepared to treat even promises with vague content as legally binding if a minimum content can be extracted.[181] By the same token, it is accepted in private law that the speaker

[180] For the necessity of distinguishing between the sociological and legal perspective when seeking to transform social obligations into legal obligations, see fundamentally Teubner (1983) 279 ('In creating its own reality from the perspective imposed by the exigencies of conflict resolution, the legal system abstracts highly selective models of the world, thereby neglecting many politically, economically, and "socially relevant" elements') and particularly in relation to self-commitments with socially binding effect, see Bachmann (2006b) 77f; Ackermann (2007) 86f.

[181] In the context of English law, one can refer here to *Dicker v Scammell* [2005] EWCA Civ 405, H3, in which it was held that: 'For an agreement to be void for uncertainty, it must be legally or practically impossible to give it any sensible meaning. Courts should strain to be preservers, not the destroyers, of bargains. "That is certain *which can be rendered certain*".' See also *Hillas and Co v Arcos Ltd* (1932) 147 LT 503, 514 (per Lord Wright): 'It is … the duty of the Court to construe such documents fairly and broadly, without being too astute or subtle in finding defects.' With respect to German law, the general rule is

cannot avoid creating a legal obligation by a deliberately issued declaration simply by having mental reservations about the legal consequences.[182]

That being said, there is also one element in the corporate codes in which the legal perspective of the corporate code differs from the sociological perspective. As already indicated above, it is the integration of disclaimers in the codes or the explicit declaration of companies that their codes should not be considered a legally binding obligation. From the linguistic perspective, it was concluded that promises with express reservations not to be bound could still be defined as successful promises if the reservation is interpreted as an attempt to exclude the legally binding effect.[183] Yet, from the legal perspective, an explicit contradiction in the form of making a promise while excluding its legal consequences requires a slightly different assessment. In such constellations, private law respects, on the one hand, the expressed intention of the speaker, who has the freedom to determine whether or not to create a legal obligation.[184] With this rule in mind, companies can indeed avoid being legally bound by a publicly declared code if they use clear disclaiming language in their codes. However, the freedom of the speaker to make a promise and exclude its legal consequences is not respected absolutely. On the contrary, whenever a sufficiently specific promise is made, the possibility to exclude legal consequences for the declaration is assessed in light of another important principle: the rule that parties ought not to behave in a contradictory way or, to put it the other way around, that they have a duty to induce reliable assumptions. This principle appears in the principles of *venire contra factum proprium*[185] and estoppel,[186] and it fulfils the function of safeguarding the reliability of behaviour in social interaction. In fact, in relation to promises, private law pursues the objective not only to protect the freedom of a party to make a promise but also to ensure the reliability of promising as an institutionalised form to cre-

equally to render the content of a declaration certain with the help of contextual interpretation before deeming it void; see, eg, MüKo-Busche § 145, para 6: 'Da die *Bestimmbarkeit des Inhalts* genügt, reicht es aus, wenn die wesentlichen Vertragspunkte unter Anwendung der §§ 133, 157 … durch Auslegung ermittelt werden können' (emphasis added). The importance of interpreting corporate codes with vague content and seeking to identify a minimum content before deeming them void for vagueness is explicitly argued for by Glinski (2007) 123; Kocher (2009) 424. But for a critical perspective on the possibility of legally enforcing vaguely phrased codes of conduct, see Peterkova (2014a) 15f.

182 With respect to German law, the irrelevance of mental reservations is explicitly set out in § 116 1 BGB: 'A declaration of intention is not void because the declarant has made a mental reservation that he does not intend the declaration made' (translation taken from Kornet and Hardt (2013) 298). In English law, the irrelevance of mental reservations derives from the objective test applied to contract formation and interpretation, which looks at the declaration rather than the intention for determining the existence and content of private law rights and duties; see eg, *Percy Trentham Ltd v Archital Luxfer Ltd* [1993] 1 Lloyd's Rep 25, 27 (per Lord Steyn): 'English law generally adopts an objective theory of contract formation. That means that in practice our law generally ignores the subjective expectations and the unexpressed mental reservations of the parties.'

183 See above, section 7.2.1.2.2. (p 239), text and accompanying footnotes.

184 For English law, see, eg, Collins (2003b) 121 with reference to *Attorney-General of Hong Kong v Humphreys Estate (Queen's Gardens) Ltd* [1987] AC 114. For German law, see, eg, Palandt-Ellenberger § 145, para 4 with further references and recently in relation in particular to declarations to the public on the Internet: OLG Düsseldorf, MMR 2014, 165.

185 *cf* Singer (1993) 313ff, in particular at 347ff.

186 *cf* Spence (1999) 1ff.

ate legal obligations and to protect those who rely on this practice.[187] Therefore, in order to fulfil the latter function, it must be treated as unfair to let the speaker benefit from the assumptions of the binding effect that he deliberately creates in others by means of invoking the socially institutionalised practice of promising, but, at the same time, allow him to opt out of the general consequences that using this practice brings about.[188] In fact, in private law, this principle has been embraced by the courts when they ruled that priority is to be given to the overall behaviour over an express reservation to exclude legal consequences.[189] Against this background, the decision whether or not a legal obligation is created if a corporate code promise is made with the contradictory indication not to be legally bound on its terms depends, from the legal perspective, ultimately on the weight that each of the principles is given in this particular constellation. In the corporate code debate, the argument is already made that corporate codes with strong words indicating that a promise is made would need to be treated as binding, even if the reservations not to create a legal obligation are not present. If such disclaimers are not sufficiently clear and unambiguously phrased and placed in a way that the addressees can immediately note them, so that an assumption as to the binding character does not reasonably arise on the side of the addressees in the first place, the disclaimer could be ignored.[190] From this perspective, the legal decision of whether or not a publicly declared corporate policy

[187] On this function of contract law in relation to the enforcement of promises, see Raz (1981) 933ff.

[188] See pointedly, from the perspective of a common law scholar, Atiyah (1981) 168: 'No doubt there are circumstances in which such a disclaimer may be legitimate, but there are also many circumstances in which it is not. The putative promisor may well be attempting to have things both ways in speaking thus: on the one hand, he wants to raise expectations in the mind of his hearers—what, indeed, is the purpose of making statement of this kind if he does not want them to raise expectations? And on the other hand, he wants to reserve complete freedom of action. In some circumstances this sort of disclaimer is thus a disreputable attempt to obtain the benefit of raising expectations and inducing actions in reliance without accepting the corresponding obligations.' See also from the perspective of a scholar of German law Bachmann (2006b) 251: 'Das gegebene Wort ist eben mehr als die versehentliche Schaffung eines Rechtsscheins; es ist das Instrument dessen Einsatz die Rechtsordnung nur um den Preis der rechtsgeschäftlichen Bindung schafft.'

[189] So-called *protestario facto contrario non valet*. In this regard, however, it should also be noted that there might be different outcomes between national systems of private law. In German law, the Federal High Court of Justice (BGHZ 21, 319, 333ff) ruled in a prominent decision, for instance, that a contractual obligation could be created by invoking a socially typical practice that is institutionalised as signalling the intention to be legally bound (in this case using a paid-for parking spot), despite an express declaration that no such legal relationship was intended. English law, in contrast, seems to have a more reluctant attitude towards ignoring formal reservations and treating them as a matter of implied contracts or liability for statements; on this aspect in relation to contractual obligations, see, eg, Collins (2003b) 121 ('express reservations indicating an unwillingness to enter into a contract will normally prevent an inference of consent'); McKendrick (2013) 110; and in relation to tort, see Deakin, Johnston and Markesinis (2007) 144. Yet, English law also consists of several statutory rules and doctrines, such as the Unfair Contract Terms Act, the doctrine on implied contracts, contracts that are concluded by performance or estoppel cases, which are handy devices for constructing a contract or liability even in the light of an express reservation.

[190] Against the background of the identified differences between the legal systems (see above n 189), it comes as no surprise that this suggestion appears mostly in the German and not so often in the common law debate on corporate codes; see, eg, Bachmann (2006b) 254f; Koch (2006) 2244; Herberg (2007) 115; Glinski (2011) 178. In the common law debate on corporate codes, the possibility of using express disclaimers seems, conversely, more accepted as a potential hindrance to exclude the binding effect; see especially Phillips and Lim (2009) 376f.

eventually has legally binding effect is decided by focusing on the relationship between declared promise and the related disclaiming language. A company that declares with strong words that it will perform a particular act and expects to receive a benefit creates a strong impression that this promise is performed; thus, standard disclaiming language that is on a regular basis included in the code or is expressed at a later stage may not be sufficient to destroy the overall impression that the company deliberately invokes a socially institutionalised practice that is directed towards creating a binding effect. In such constellations, one would consequently arrive at the conclusion that the company is bound. From this, conversely, it follows that the situation could be different with respect to corporate codes that contain a clear emphasis on their aspirational and non-binding character. Such codes could be also interpreted as non-binding. However, for the majority of codes, where the emphasis is set on the objective to persuade and present to the public a serious commitment, the strong commitment inducing the assumption that an obligation is created supersedes the expressed intention to avoid the legal consequences.

As a result, it is also from the private law perspective generally possible to interpret unilaterally and publicly declared corporate codes as promises that not only have socially but also genuine legally binding effect. Nonetheless, further scrutiny is required as to the appropriate legal consequences that this legally binding effect may have.[191] In this context, the following sections will argue that the legal consequences of this particular type of promissory declarations need to be determined with respect to the particular relation in which they are included. Here the legal consequences for publicly declared corporate code promises in the social context of contracting, on the one hand, and their legal consequences in relation to the global public in general, on the other hand, require separate attention.

7.3.2. Corporate Codes in Market Relations

Insofar as the relevance of the corporate code promise for the relationship between corporations and their contractual partners is concerned, the legal consequences of promises are determined by the rules that regulate this specific relationship. In this context, chapter three revealed that the concepts that are in principle available in contract law are in particular a contractual enforcement of publicly declared corporate codes, their interpretation of the codes as terms in subsequently concluded contracts, and the option to enforce the codes as separate relied-upon promises. The following sections will be devoted to a closer analysis of the potential of these three concepts.

[191] This necessity to focus not only on the legally binding character of self-commitments but also on the appropriate legal concepts in light of the legal consequences is also emphasised by Ackermann (2007) 86.

7.3.2.1. *Corporate Codes as Enforceable Contracts?*

The main option available in contract law to give effect to a promise is the enforcement of such declarations as contracts. Given that the corporate codes have been described as a promise, a contractual enforcement thus seems at least plausible at first sight. However, it should be noted that the rules on contract formation are not prepared to enforce all types of promises; these rules also contain constraints that effectively confine the scope of the contractual enforcement to particular types of promises. From the various doctrines that fulfil this purpose, chapter three has identified three conditions that currently likely hinder the contractual enforcement of the corporate codes promises in particular. First, there is the internal restriction in contract law to enforce only promises that are made in a relationship of reciprocity or, conversely, its reluctance towards enforcing unilateral promises that are not made in a bargain. Second, on the basis of the criterion of an intention to be legally bound, a tendency could be particularly identified in the current case law against enforcing declarations of companies that contain a commitment to comply with their corporate policies. Third, equally in the course of discussing the intention to be legally bound, a presumption could be identified not to enforce as contracts specific declarations to the public if they are expressed in advertisements or marketing statements.[192] Thus, when attempting to enforce the corporate codes as contracts, it is necessary to analyse the underlying justification of this restriction and whether they are valid in relation to the corporate code promises. In addition, the analysis will also take account of another, so far widely ignored, criterion that could, and in fact should, prevent the contractual enforcement of corporate codes: the requirement of acceptance and the underlying assumption that the formation of a contract requires consensus.

7.3.2.1.1. Reciprocity

One of the core legal obstacles for a suggested contractual enforcement of the corporate codes has been identified in the focus in contract law on enforcement of agreements that have as their objective a reciprocal exchange and the reluctance to enforce in a similar vein promises that only create unilateral obligations. This restriction was identified in particular in the context of English common law, namely in the applicable doctrine of consideration. In the German debate, a comparable restriction was identified in the mandatory form requirements that need to be met when attempting to enforce non-reciprocal agreements. Thus, for the present theoretical inquiry, the confining role of consideration (England) and form (Germany) needs to be revisited with a view to whether it reasonably justifies not enforcing the corporate codes as contracts.

One of the policies of the common law behind the focus on restricting enforcement only to reciprocal agreements and those meeting a high formal threshold (deed) is to insist on consideration as a necessary formality in order to signal to the

[192] See conclusion drawn in section 3.1.4.1.3. (p 97).

law the presence of a serious agreement.[193] As a formal criterion, it should protect the parties from binding themselves too quickly without careful reflection. Consideration and form requirements are effectively a criterion that allows contract law to determine whether the parties have carefully reflected before binding themselves, are conscious about the fact that an agreement is reached and signal to the law that their agreement should be taken seriously.[194] However, this justification rests on a specific presumption concerning seriousness that seems questionable with respect to the codes. It is based on the understanding that an agreement in which each party gives something in exchange for a benefit is meant seriously and follows careful deliberation.[195] Conversely, contract law departs from an inherent concern towards gratuitous promises, namely that they are not based on an equally careful reflection and seriousness, and that the promisor did not intend for them to be legally binding. This inherent skepticism is overcome by requiring a particular form for unilateral promises that provides the necessary indication for the seriousness, the careful deliberation on the side of the promisor and the intention to be legally bound.[196] A similar rationale can be found for civil law systems with respect to mandatory form requirements for unilateral promises.[197] Yet, this inherent suspicion against the seriousness and the need to require on this ground an additional formal signal does not entirely fit with the character of corporate codes as promises that are explicitly, deliberately and strategically conveyed to the public with the objective of improving the companies' reputation. The apparent strategic objective to persuade the public can, in fact, only be successfully realised if companies also take their publicly declared commitments seriously and understand them as binding guidelines for future behaviour.[198] In addition, in relation to the codes, a formal indication of seriousness and sufficiently careful reflection on the side of the companies can already be identified in the fact that the publication of such declarations is in the organisation of globally operating groups subject to careful internal revisions and confirmation by different departments.[199] The strategic objective of such declarations and the internal checks and approvals could therefore be deemed, from the legal perspective, to be comparable formal criteria to signal to the law that the promise was meant to be serious and could therefore replace, for such specific types of promises, the requirement of reciprocity or mandatory form in relation to the codes.

However, the reciprocity requirement is by no means viewed in the legal debate as the only formal criterion to determine the seriousness of an agreement

[193] Zweigert and Kötz (1998) 390ff; Smith (2004) 216ff.

[194] These three aspects are discussed in Fuller (1941) 800ff in the form of the evidentiary, the cautionary and the channelling function.

[195] Eisenberg (1982) 643: 'And because bargain promises are typically rooted in self-interest rather than altruism, they are likely to be finely calculated and deliberately made.'

[196] Smith (2004) 217.

[197] Zweigert and Kötz (1998) 395ff; Smith (2004) 216f.

[198] Herberg (2007) 75: 'wäre die PR-Katastrophe im Grunde schon vorprogrammiert'.

[199] See pointedly Herberg (2007) 77: 'ist es wichtig zu sehen, dass die PR-Abteilung des Unternehmens die Grundsätze nicht eigenmächtig formulieren kann. Die Bestimmungen müssen detailliert mit dem Top-Management abgestimmt sein, da nur diesem die Befugnis zukommt, dem Gesamtkonzern die Marschroute vorzugeben und unternehmerische Strategien in für die Zukunft zu entwerfen'.

or declaration. In the common law debate, an additional substantive reason for requiring consideration or a particular form is identified in the need to preserve the intangible character of altruistic promises from legal enforcement.[200] In particular, Eisenberg argues in this direction by stating that the 'world' of unilateral promises is one 'driven by affective considerations like love, affection, friendship, gratitude, and comradeship'.[201] To allow the contractual enforcement of such gratuitous promises would, from this perspective, inevitably destroy the very character of promising, as it would inevitably alienate the altruistic gift from its original function and translate it into a commodity.[202] Hence, the justification for only enforcing reciprocal agreements relates here to the need to preserve the integrity of the process of promising and gift making and to prevent the law from destroying this process by means of legal enforcement.

However, the argument on the intangible value of the promise is in fact not an argument against the refusal to enforce promises in general; rather, it has particularly in mind the need to keep free from legal regulation the gift-making procedure between parties in a personal social relationship. In such contexts, it is indeed highly plausible not to enforce donative promises unless the parties have made explicit that they want to do so. However, the justification not to enforce unilateral promises expressed by a commercial actor on the market context seems not to be affected in a comparable manner by such concerns of 'commodifying' the relationship. In fact, such promises are implicitly highly commodified. It seems in relation to this justification, as already suggested in the literature on consideration, more appropriate to distinguish between gift promises in relation to which the law ought to carefully check whether or not to intervene and promises in a commercial context in which the 'gift' serves an implicit commercial purpose.[203] In the latter constellations, the necessity for an additional form requirement or the requirement of reciprocal exchange could be relaxed if the promise serves, even indirectly, the purpose of inducing a commercial exchange. With respect particularly to the corporate codes, the underlying justification not to enforce a unilateral promise because of the need to protect the intangible value of the promise seems here even less convincing if one has in mind the codes' ambivalent character. They are promises that, notwithstanding their deliberate phrasing as an altruistic undertaking, are effectively directed towards less regulation by politics or reputational advantages, which should result in an increase in sales. They appear, although at first sight as altruistic commitments, to be highly 'commodified'. Against this

[200] See for this argument especially Eisenberg (2001) 229f.

[201] ibid 230.

[202] ibid. According to this understanding, the focus on reciprocity is necessary in order to prevent what Eisenberg sees as 'commodifying the gift relationship' and '[degrading donative promises] into the bills of exchange'.

[203] This aspect is also relevant in Gordon (1990) 992f and 1004, who discusses whether adhering to a 'commercial-gift dichotomy' would be more appropriate as opposed to the bargain-gift dichotomy as inherent in the doctrine of consideration. *cf* also for the broader perspective Pound (1959), who argues that the enforcement of promises follows from the organisation of our society as an industrial and commercial society, pointedly at 456: 'in a commercial and industrial society a claim or want or demand that promises be kept and that undertakings be carried out in good faith, a social interest in the stability of promises as a *social and economic* institution, becomes of the first importance' (emphasis added).

background, a specific form of protection for the gift-making procedure or the parties involved does not seem necessary.

Yet, the justification for the focus on reciprocity in contract law is not exhausted by these two reasons. In addition, an important realistic[204] justification for having the requirement to enforce only reciprocal contracts is raised in particular in the common law debate. It sees the value of requiring consideration as serving an umbrella concept that the courts use in the legal decision in order to accommodate other aspects, such as fairness, reliance or duress. The most prominent defender of this justification of consideration is Atiyah. He puts forward the idea that, in the decisions of courts, the underlying question is ultimately not the character of the agreement in question, eg, whether it is reciprocal or not, but rather whether courts in the past were guided by other normative considerations that were only ultimately presented as a question of whether or not there was reciprocity in the agreement.[205] The reason these normative reasons were eventually related to the doctrine of consideration is the influence of formalist theories of law that made the courts frame their reasoning in technical language and, in so doing, use consideration.[206] The most obvious evidence for this approach represents, in this regard, the conception of the unilateral contract. Unilateral contracts are characterised by the reliance of one party on the promise of another rather than a clear exchange relationship and courts are still prepared to enforce such promises as contracts.[207]

Translated into the constellations of corporate codes, the reference to the lack of reciprocity and bargain would effectively only be the apparent and superficial reason to justify why, in particular, the corporate codes are not enforced, but it would effectively be based on other normative reasons, such as aspects of fairness, lack of detrimental reliance or good faith in general. Yet, other relevant criteria that are discussed in the guise of consideration, in particular reasonable reliance and the indirect benefits on the side of the promisor, do in fact rather support the enforcement of the codes. An argument in favour of enforcing the corporate codes from the perspective of the addressee is the reasonable reliance on the regulatory role of the company, the alignment of the further cooperation strategy of the addressees and the dependence on this code for the ultimate decision whether or not to contract with a publicly declaring company. An additional argument from the perspective of the speaker is the close proximity of such a promise made in

[204] See for this interpretation Smith (2004) 225ff.

[205] Atiyah (1986) 181: 'The truth is that the courts have never set out to create a doctrine of consideration. They have been concerned with the much more practical problem of deciding in the course of litigation whether a particular promise in a particular case should be enforced … It seems highly probable that when the courts first used the word "consideration" they meant not more than that there was a "reason" for the enforcement of a promise.' A similar argument is presented by Collins (2003b) 64, who holds that the doctrine of consideration is merely an 'instrument policing the boundaries of enforceable contract' whereby: 'The crucial device employed by the courts is to discover an implied request to perform an act whenever they wish to enforce a donative promise'.

[206] Smith (2004) 226. See also Collins (2003b) 80, who argues that the unilateral contract could also be interpreted as a reliance-based model of enforcement.

[207] Smith (2004) 229. An alternative view is provided by Collins (2003b) 4f, who argues in relation to *Carlill v Carbolic Smoke Ball Corp* (extensively discussed in section 3.1.4.1.1., p 85) that contractual enforcement was recognised in order to pursue the objective of discouraging misleading and extravagant claims in advertising.

a commercial context to the background expectation that a benefit is received.[208] Thus, effectively, the exchange is also present in a more nuanced way in relation to the corporate codes.

So far, the normative justification for the restriction in contract law on enforcing reciprocal agreements and those fulfilling a requirement of form have been discussed primarily on the basis of one core justification that is equally brought forward in the civil law and common law debate and those that mainly characterise the common law debate on consideration. One additional historically important justification in the civil law debate for being reluctant towards enforcing agreements outside a reciprocal exchange and requiring additional requirements, such as acceptance and form, has been identified in the need to protect the promisee from being obliged to accept a gift.[209] The original rationale behind also recognising a need to protect the addressee here has been the consideration that accepting a promise to make a gift can also be accompanied by quite a considerable burden on the side of the promisee or may cause him to feel obliged to give something in return. In the recent debate on promises, this justification has been partly criticised as not being practically relevant and for being an outdated understanding.[210] In response to this criticism, however, it has also been emphasised that the need to protect the addressee of an altruistic promise is still partly irrelevant today, when research reveals that humans want, and socially institutionalised rules suggest the inherent (socially or psychologically) obligation, to give something in return for any promise received.[211]

That being said, while the need to protect the addressee particularly makes sense with respect to the promises made in the context of interpersonal relations, this objective does not fit entirely with how the corporate codes function as promises. In situations in which a promise is addressed to the public, and thus the addressee remains anonymous, the need to protect the addressee from receiving the gift and prevent him from feeling obliged to reward the promisor seems to be less important.[212] In addition, there is an additional argument against the necessity to protect the addressees of the corporate codes. The corporate codes effectively represent a response to the ongoing claim of the public for a more concrete and sincere social responsibility after a phase of public scandals, which could be rather interpreted as a constellation whereby companies seek to make good failures from the

[208] Atiyah (1986) 241f: 'For instance, there are promises made in a commercial context which may appear gratuitous, but where the promisor expects some return in a rather more indirect way than the present doctrine of consideration recognises. There is a lot be said for the view that such promises are really bargain promises, and should be fully enforceable, even while executory, to the same extent as ordinary contracts.'

[209] This so-called principle of *beneficia non obtuduntur* was already debated before the codification of the BGB and represents one of the classical justifications against rendering unilateral promises binding. On this principle with further references, see Kegel (2002) 108; Bayer (1995) 220; Bachmann (2006b) 294ff.

[210] Wennberg (1966) 77; Hawickhorst (1987) 149.

[211] This argument is particularly developed by Bachmann (2006b) 295, who refers to the psychological studies of Lersch and the sociological insights of Köndgen of reciprocity as a background expectation in social interaction.

[212] ibid 296.

past. In such constellations, the promise must be interpreted as a way to provide compensation and react to the request of the public. The public perceives these corporate codes not as a gratuitous promise for which they have to give something in return, but rather as reciprocal compensation for previous harm.

Hence, the decision in contract law not to enforce the corporate codes for their lack of reciprocity and for not meeting the high threshold requirements of form are based on underlying reasons that do not fit in relation to the corporate codes. This, as a result, suggests that the lack of reciprocity in the corporate codes should not be considered an obstacle and, instead, that the specific requirement of reciprocity or mandatory form in this particular constellation should be relaxed.

7.3.2.1.2. The Social Context of Contracting

To the extent that the focus in contract law on the enforcement of reciprocal agreements is relaxed in relation to corporate codes, a second obstacle for the potential contractual enforcement of the corporate codes needs to be addressed. In the course of the legal debate, a general tendency in contract law could be observed to treat the declaration of companies that they will comply with their corporate codes as non-binding, because these are presumably not based on an intention to be legally bound. Certainly, the enforcement cannot be rejected on the grounds that an intention to be bound is not present, considering that the theoretical analysis has revealed that a sufficient interaction between the intention and the declaration is present in the code. Once it is accepted that the intentional and deliberate use of committing language sufficiently respects the autonomy of private actors to create socially[213] and legally[214] binding obligations, it would be contradictory to re-introduce the intention to be legally bound in this context as a decisive criterion 'through the back door'. However, the criterion of an intention to be bound is also used to accommodate other reasons and it is these underlying reasons that could justify not enforcing the corporate codes. The intention to be legally bound is, in contract law, also used as a broader criterion to reject the enforcement of particular types of agreements, in particular, agreements in the context of family relations.[215] The underlying argument against the enforcement of agreements within the context of family or social relations is here also not in every case the factual state of mind of the parties, e,g whether they had the serious intention to be legally bound.[216] Instead, this requirement is used to prevent the particular social sphere of the family from being regulated by the law.[217] Viewed through this lens, the presumed lack of an intention to be legally bound can be better interpreted as a self-limitation of the law to prevent the legal regulation of particular social

[213] See the arguments above, section 7.2.2.2. (p 250), text and accompanying footnotes.

[214] See the arguments above, section 7.3.1. (p 266), text and accompanying footnotes.

[215] Collins (2003b) 67; Smith (2004) 213.

[216] Smith (2004) 213: 'Domestic agreements are often extremely serious.'

[217] Teubner (2000b) 391: 'familiare Kommunikation ist … von ökonomischem Druck freizuhalten'; Collins (2003b) 97: 'using … these legal doctrines in order to establish a limit to the application of market justice to family relationships'; Smith (2004) 214: 'the mere threat of legal enforcement can change the character, and hence the value, of domestic agreements'.

spheres and thus to avoid a complete 'contractualisation of social life'.[218] The main argument for not enforcing, for instance, agreements within family relations with reference to the lack of an intention to create a legally binding promise seems to be primarily a concern in the law that contractual enforcement would effectively impose a structure that is antithetic to the functioning of social relations. Family relations are based on shared interests[219] and are, in their functioning, highly individualistic;[220] imposing the structure of the standardised and self-interested contract on such relations would then be capable of destroying or at least corrupting the integrity of such relations.

Although the particular concern in relation to families is clearly not an issue in relation to the codes, it is nevertheless the general concern of corrupting a particular social sphere that could also become relevant here. One can at least consider for a relevant reason not to enforce the corporate declaration to comply with a particular social or environmental code that such declarations ought to be left unenforceable because of the sensitive political issues involved and the need to free the political sphere from legal intervention. This argument already appears in relation to other agreements in which governments or state officials are involved,[221] and it is in particular controversial in the debate on contractual enforcement of a specific type of agreement on policy issues, namely coalition agreements. For these agreements, it is held that, notwithstanding the seriousness of the political parties and their apparent intention to conclude a binding agreement, the specifics of political processes represent a strong argument not to render them subject to a legal regime and allow judicial enforcement.[222] Parties to coalition agreements need to be able to react to policy changes or changes in the public opinion, which is detrimental to the binding and enforceable character of contracts.[223] If this is accepted, it actually represents a valid argument that the formal or informal participation of companies in political regulation in the form of public promises on sensitive and rapidly changing policy issues and their political role would also need to enjoy the same degree of informality and thus remain free from any intervention from contract law.[224]

Yet, there are in fact several arguments that can be brought forward against this perspective. The first argument already appears in the debate on the contractual enforcement of political agreements as such. A closer look reveals that it is by no means a uniform understanding that political agreements and declarations would need to be kept free from legal regulation. On the contrary, particularly in the

[218] Collins (2003b) 94ff.
[219] Smith (2004) 214.
[220] Teubner (2000b) 393.
[221] See generally Collins (2003b) 99ff.
[222] See with further references to the debate Schlieffen (2005) 692f, para 9: 'Essenz des Arguments ist: Koalitionsvereinbarungen dürften nicht verrechtlicht werden, damit die Politik nicht noch mehr verrechtlicht werde.'
[223] Kewenig (1965) 189f.
[224] The similarities between political coalition agreements and corporate self-commitments are explicitly discussed by Bachmann (2006b) 31, 279, 297, who also concludes that at least corporate self-commitments that are clearly addressed to politics should be viewed as 'politically, but not legally binding'.

debate on coalition agreements, it is equally argued that a possibility must also be given to parties to enforce such agreements as contracts, to the extent that there is a visible tendency towards formalising these agreements and an apparent request for certainty among the partners of the coalition on an agreed political objective.[225] In other words, once the political sphere becomes more formalised and governed by legal relations, the same would need to be assumed for corporate codes. A second argument follows from the analysis above where the inherent flexibility and informality has already been addressed. When discussing the phrasing of the corporate codes, the analysis has developed the argument that the corporate codes, in order to be convincing in sensitive policy areas, require informal and vague phrasing to a certain degree.[226] From the legal perspective, this strengthens the argument that the required informality and flexibility of sensitive policy issues has already been sufficiently respected in the course of determining the substantive content of the declaration. The need to react flexibly to changes in the policy processes to which the codes are connected could also be sufficiently preserved by means of allowing a strong contextual interpretation of the content of the commitment in light of the developments in the particular policy area. The third argument relates to the specific regulatory character of the corporate codes, which will be discussed more intensively in the following chapter. In this section, it will be developed as one of the core arguments that the corporate codes represent a form of politicisation that is different from the formal political system. Thus, the regulatory role that companies take over with their codes differs from the regulatory role of actors in the formal political system.[227] Based on this understanding, it can be assumed that the integrity of the official policy processes remains fully intact even if the corporate codes are enforced. In fact, one main observation of the political character of the corporate codes is that the enforcement seems to be rather a prerequisite for the success of this new political sphere.

Thus, the argument not to enforce the corporate codes because they are substantively related to the political sphere also does not seem to be an argument against the enforcement of the corporate codes.

7.3.2.1.3. The Invitation to Treat

Having argued that neither the focus in contract law on reciprocal agreements nor the politically sensitive context represents valid justifications against a contract enforcement of the corporate codes, this section will finally turn to the final obstacle in contract law that has been identified. Contract law treats public declarations made in advertisements as non-binding invitations to treat rather than as contractually binding offers based on the general presumption that such public advertisements are not made with an intention to be legally bound. Again, the theoretical analysis, in particular the description of corporate codes as initial promises that seek to persuade other market actors to further interaction, does in fact support

[225] See with further references Schlieffen (2005) 692f, para 9 and 696f, para 12.
[226] See above, section 7.2.1.2.2. (p 239), text and accompanying footnotes.
[227] On this aspect extensively section 8.2.2. (p 318), text and accompanying footnotes.

an interpretation as invitations to treat and not as final offers. However, given their observed socially and legally binding character, one could argue that such initial declarations could also be seen as contractually enforceable, as is already exceptionally the case.[228] Thus, the crucial task is again to analyse more closely the presumption of interpreting public declarations of traders as invitations to treat and, as a result, not enforceable and to identify whether it is valid in relation to the corporate code.

In contract law, this assumption against an enforcement of invitations to treat is partly justified by referring to the fact that companies, as a matter of fact, do not have an intention to be bound when publishing an advertisement.[229] As already stated above, this reference to a merely purported missing internal intention not to be bound is viewed as unconvincing in relation to the codes. Yet, effectively, this presumption also serves as a criterion to accommodate another valid reasoning. To that end, contract law scholars have emphasised that the category of the non-binding invitation to treat serves as an important tool in contract law to decide on the moment of contractual responsibility.[230] The invitation to treat can thus be interpreted as an internal decision in contract law to specify, with regard to the moment of full contractual responsibility, only declarations that are made after a phase of intense social interaction, negotiation and persuasion in which both parties are given the chance to deliberate on the deal. The main reason for not enforcing contracts such as pre-contractual declarations is the value of preserving a phase prior to the deal in which the parties are given room to manoeuvre, to solve ambiguities and to reflect carefully upon whether or not they are willing to create a full contractual relationship.[231] A late moment of contractual responsibility is particularly in the interests of the party that makes a public promise as it allows his to investigate whether the potential future contractual partner is reliable and financially solvent.[232] Moreover, a late moment of responsibility can also be in the interests of the addressed party as it gives his the opportunity to require, if necessary, additional material, clarify existing ambiguities for the sake of being able to take an informed decision or require changes.[233]

[228] One may refer here in the English context to the category of the unilateral or collateral contract and in the German context to § 657 BGB. One may, in the German context, even consider invoking the noteworthy developments concerning the specifics of contract formation of sales contracts concluded over the Internet where the invitation to treat is no longer treated in every respect as non-binding and irrelevant for the eventual formation of the contract, if it is technically fixed; see especially BGH NJW 2005, 976. On this constellation, see also Mankowski (2003) 854: 'Der wertungsmäßige Vergleich mit der Lage, wie sie sich ergeben würde, wenn die invitatio verbindlich wäre, drängt sich geradezu auf.'

[229] Smith (2004) 187f: 'there is a rebuttable presumption that advertisements are invitations to treat. Such presumptions are in part merely generalizations; in the common law world, most advertisements do not, as a matter of fact, indicate an intention to be bound and so courts will make a prima facie assumption that any particular advertisement reveals a similar intention.'

[230] ibid 188; Collins (2003b) 171f: 'a court must make a discretionary choice between them [eg the various moments of responsibility], concealing the real grounds for the decision by the formalist reasoning of offer and acceptance'.

[231] Collins (2003b) 173f.

[232] Staudinger-Bork § 145, para 4; Palandt-Ellenberger § 145, para 2.

[233] This is particularly emphasised by Collins (2003b) 173: 'These exploratory discussions perform a valuable service, for the parties to become better informed about the details of the transaction, and they resolve possible ambiguities.'

In addition, enforcing as contracts promises in this prior stage could then have a negative effect on this free flow of pre-contractual communication and negotiation; it would probably make the parties considerably more cautious when declaring something in this phase for fear of already creating a full contractual relationship with the party they so far may only want to inform or convince that they should conclude a contract.

This justification, however, did not remain uncontested.[234] In particular, Köndgen argues that the need to provide parties with room for negotiation does not fit with the modern reality of contracting, at least as far as mass consumer contracts are concerned. To him, giving the parties a phase for communication and interaction assumes quite unrealistically that the consumer addressed by a public advertisement would realistically have the option to negotiate a deal that is advertised to him, which is quite far-fetched in the reality of modern mass contracting.[235] This argument of the fixed and specific character of advertisements is in fact particularly valid with respect to the corporate codes. In relation to product advertisements that are characterised by their short-term objectives of drawing the attention of the public to a particular product or service, one may have good reason to provide the respective trader with the possibility of room for manoeuvre. For short-term campaigns, there is a indeed a reasonable interest on the side of the trader to retract an advertisement without further consequences if he runs out of stock or to refuse to enter into a contractual relationship on an advertised complex financial product before inquiring about the financial solvency of his future contractual partner. In these cases, it might suffice to recognise a binding effect of advertisement only to the extent that a contract is concluded[236] or to treat such public declarations as binding, yet understand them as revocable and subject to the condition that the product is available and the customer is financially solvent.[237] However, as far as corporate codes are concerned, this interest of retracting the code or leaving it non-binding because of the need to further negotiate the particularities of the deal seems less convincing. Although corporate codes are certainly an integral part of marketing strategies and are included in short-term campaigns, they go beyond this short-term objective. By means of publicly declaring that they will comply with a corporate code, the company presents a fixed and binding guideline to the public that should set a long-term benchmark for the company as to its conduct. This long-term objective behind this declaration renders the interest of retraction and further negotiation on its term less relevant and, consequently, its treatment as non-binding not entirely convincing.

Hence, the specific difference between advertisements in general and corporate codes in particular finally also renders the generally valid reasons behind treating public advertisements usually as non-binding invitations to treat unsuitable in relation to the corporate codes.

[234] Köndgen (1981) 291ff. See also AK-BGB-Hart § 145, para 16.
[235] Köndgen (1981) 292.
[236] This is also recognised by Köndgen (1981) 293.
[237] For this suggestion, see Koch (2006) 2248.

7.3.2.1.4. Acceptance and 'Meeting of the Minds'

After all that has been argued above, one can draw the conclusion that the initially presented restrictions are based on reasons that may be relevant in other contexts, but not in relation to the corporate codes. Consequently, it is indeed possible to propose the contractual enforcement of the corporate codes by applying the rules on contract formation to them. Yet, some intuitive discomfort with this conclusion remains. The purpose of corporate codes and the general circumstances in which they occur still differ in relation to the procedure through which contracts are commonly concluded. Provided that the rules on contract formation effectively apply to the corporate codes, how are contracts on publicly declared corporate codes concluded in practice? Are the codes offers to contract that become binding once 'accepted' by a member of the public? Or are they unilateral contracts that do not even require acceptance on the side of the addressed public and thus become binding without any corresponding behaviour on the side of the addressed public? The focus inherent in the rules on contract formation on consensus, on a meeting of the minds and thus on the paradigm of offer and corresponding acceptance between two parties in personal interaction seems here not to fit entirely with the reality of the relationship between the company and the market public.

So far, this aspect has not been specifically problematised in the corporate code debate. In particular, the discussion on whether acceptance on the side of the market public is required and, if so, how it has to take place given the remoteness of the contracting parties is not at all a matter of controversy.[238] The lack of attention to this requirement is most likely caused by the fact that, in relation to offers made in the form of public declarations and remotely concluded contracts, the courts have so far had a mere technical view concerning the requirement of acceptance by arguing that the acceptance is the performance of an act in reliance on the promise. The existing case law notwithstanding, this interpretation is still open to criticism as an apparent formalistic attempt to fit the enforcement of public declarations, which are made to persuade others and induce cooperation, into the rules on contract formation that is based on an artificial understanding of acceptance and consensus, and does not fit with the real facts of the case. Accordingly, it comes as no surprise that the interpretation of public offers as contracts is, in academic scholarship, defined as merely a legal 'fiction'[239] or as a constellation in which the courts pay 'lip-service to the rules of acceptance'[240] and do nothing more than 'twisting the facts to fit them into the rules'.[241] Indeed, once the rules on contract formation are taken seriously, public unilateral declarations cannot be

[238] In the debate on corporate codes, the requirement of acceptance is for the most part either only briefly mentioned and not discussed (see, eg, Webb and Morrison (2004) 122 and Glinski (2011) 130) or viewed as a criterion that is uncontroversially fulfilled (Kenny (2007) 464: 'little debate' that the offer is accepted; Revak (2012) 1655).

[239] Lüsing (2010) 342. See also Bachmann (2006b) 279: 'Diese Argumentation mag das Rechtsgfühl befriedigen, bleibt aber dogmatisch unbefriedigend.'

[240] Collins (2003b) 166.

[241] ibid 170.

considered contractually binding.[242] And this debate on whether acceptance needs to be taken seriously or can be fictionally constructed is, in relation to the corporate codes, arguably not only of academic interest; it has, in this particular constellation, important practical implications concerning to whom and when the corporate code becomes enforceable. In general, the requirement of acceptance becomes particularly important when turning to the question whether the public declaration becomes binding towards members of the addressed public or only those that are aware of the declaration and accept it by relying on it. If acceptance is required and the rules on contract formation are taken seriously, a logical distinction would have to be drawn between members of the public towards whom the public commitment is enforceable and those that are unaware of its existence.[243] This, however, seems immensely difficult to realise on a practical level. Once the practically and intuitively more viable perspective is taken and both constellations are treated alike, the requirement of acceptance is effectively abolished. As was indicated above, it seems that currently the latter option is preferred. In the course of interpreting such public declarations as unilateral contracts, the courts have so far held that an offer to the public can be accepted by the addressees merely by performing the contract and that companies have waived their right to require the communication of acceptance by means of addressing the public as a whole.[244] Thus, in the current case law, the requirement of acceptance is replaced by fictional acceptance. The Principles of European Contract Law go even further here by simply declaring promises comprehensively legally binding even without acceptance.[245]

In spite of this currently available possibility to waive factually the requirement of acceptance, there is an important difference between corporate codes and other unilateral public declarations for which a contractually binding obligation is created without acceptance. In relation to the so far accepted unilateral promises, it indeed seemed possible to relax the requirement of acceptance because of another specific and identifiable criterion that could be taken to determine the moment of contractual responsibility and the actors between which such an obligation would be created. Pursuant to the rules set out in *Carlill v Carbolic Smoke Ball Co* (England) and § 657 BGB (Germany), respectively, the performance of a particular action as specified in the public declaration could serve as a criterion to specify when

[242] Bachmann (2006b) 279: 'Nimmt man das Vertragsprinzip ernst, kann eine einseitige Selbstverpflichtung in all diesen Fällen nicht mit bindender Wirkung begründet werden.'

[243] For this argument already, see Anson and Gwyer (1923) ch 2, No. 3, at 24: 'It is … laid down that a reward cannot be claimed by one who did not know that it had been offered. The decision seems undoubtedly correct in principle. One who does an act for which a reward has been offered, in ignorance of the offer, cannot say either that there was a *consensus* of wills between him and the offeror, or that his conduct was affected by the promise offered. On no view of contract could he set up a right of action' (emphasis added).

[244] In English law, this has been established in the landmark case *Carlill v Carbolic Smoke Ball Corp*, see section 3.1.4.1.1.1 (p 86), Text and accompanying footnotes. In the context of German law, it is either § 151 BGB that is considered applicable, see section 3.1.4.1.2.1. (p 93), text and accompanying footnotes, or the public offer is treated as a binding offer to pay a reward (§ 657 BGB) that is binding if the specified action is performed, see section 3.1.4.2.2. (p 102), text and accompanying footnotes.

[245] Article 2:107 of the Principles of European Contract Law: 'A promise which is intended to be legally binding without acceptance is binding.'.

and towards whom contractual responsibility arises. In other words, the lack of acceptance is in these cases compensated by the visible reciprocity. The range of liability for the promisor is reduced to those that actually conferred a reciprocal benefit upon him. Due to the significantly more implicit reciprocity in the corporate codes, this explicit substitute criterion is not in a similar vein available in relation to the codes. Using the underlying implicit expectation on the side of the company that the publicly declared compliance with the corporate code would be rewarded would obviously be difficult, if not impossible, to use in practice. To relate the rules on contract formation to the publicly declared corporate codes would thus effectively require *a combination* of relaxing the formal requirements of both reciprocity and acceptance, which would effectively reduce contract formation to solely the requirement of an offer, as envisaged in the Principles of European Contract Law. It would mean that the unilateral promise to comply with the code is immediately binding without acceptance. Suggesting such a construction would, however, result in a second difficulty. The corporate codes also differ from clearly expressed unilateral promises as they are envisaged, for instance, in the Principles of European Contract Law. What these rules on the enforcement of unilateral promises have in mind, according to the commentary, are public declarations that either have as their content a sufficiently specific action that the promisor seeks to fulfil or that is addressed to an identifiable group of addressees for a particular purpose.[246] However, this is not the reality of the corporate codes, which are addressed to the public and contain promises to undertake a long-term and timely unspecified engagement. Interpreting such promises as contractually binding once they are publicly declared, without further requirements, would then have the effect that a legally binding and irrevocable promise is created towards the global public on a long-term basis. This would indeed raise concerns as to the foreseeable risk of liability. Yet, more importantly, it would also not fit with the identified character of the corporate codes, which can, as revealed by the interdisciplinary analysis, be described as public declarations that fulfil two distinctly different purposes in social interactions. They are directed towards obtaining a benefit from specific actors, such as consumers or regulatory bodies, but they are also a way to inform and develop the trust of the global public.[247] Treating them as contractually binding unilateral contracts that create a unilateral obligation once declared would then not pay due respect to these two different purposes and would thus fail to differentiate sufficiently between the specific characteristics of the binding effect in each of these contexts.

Against this background, there remain valid concerns about 'forcing' the corporate codes into the rules on contract formation by modifying the rules to an extent that only an offer, but neither acceptance nor reciprocity, is required. Instead, it is considered worth investigating conceptually alternative solutions in private

[246] See Lando and Beale (2000) 157, who use the two examples of, first, a public promise to set up a fund to compensate victims of the Gulf War to which the declaring company would be bound and, second, a promise of a company sent in a letter to the creditors of its subsidiary that it will ensure that the debts of the subsidiary are met.

[247] See above, section 7.2.3.2.2. (p 255), text and accompanying footnotes.

law that could more accurately reflect the binding effect of such pre-contractual persuading promises. As will be argued below, such alternatives can be found in the rules on contract interpretation that allow treating pre-contractual promises as enforceable contract terms once a contract is concluded and in the current debate on reliance liability that provides a suitable basis for the equitable enforcement of unilateral promises that are made in a relation to the objective to persuade others to intensify further cooperation and eventually conclude a contract.

7.3.2.2. Corporate Codes as Enforceable Terms in Contracts

Although the previous analysis concluded that the rules on contract formation do not fit entirely with the specific type of promises made by corporate codes, it would be too quick to conclude that the enforcement of the codes is doomed to fail in general. A different possibility to recognise the binding effect of declarations that are made in a phase before a contract is concluded represents, in this regard, their treatment as a contractual term in a subsequently concluded contract. With respect to a potential interpretation of the codes as contract terms, chapter three revealed two important aspects. First, a distinction could be observed between the statutory provision for sale of goods contracts that explicitly prescribe reading into the contract's pre-contractual public statements that characterise the goods for sale[248] and the general rules on contract interpretation and supplementation in which pre-contractual declarations are used as extrinsic evidence when determining the enforceable obligations of the parties.[249] Hence, contract law exhibits, in its current state, a different treatment within the rules on contract interpretation and supplementation between product-related declarations in sale of goods contracts as a prescribed part of the contract terms and other types of declarations for which the courts have the discretion to consider public declaration if they find them pivotal to infer the content of the contract. In light of the theoretical analysis above, this distinction would have the result that a treatment as part of the contract terms would be likely between corporate codes that are related to products and for codes in which the general performance or the future behaviour is emphasised. In this context, the first issue is to focus on the underlying justification for giving product-related declarations in sale of goods contracts such a distinct role in comparison to other declarations and whether it is convincing in relation to the corporate codes. Second, the legal analysis has revealed that there are differences as to the treatment of pre-contractual statements between the German and the English rules on contract interpretation and supplementation. In this regard, English law seems to be more reluctant to consider evidence that is extrinsic to the formalised contractual document than is the case in German law. This suggests making a distinction in the analysis between the legal systems and focusing particularly on the justification for this reluctant attitude in English law and its validity in relation to the codes.

[248] See section 3.1.3.2.1. (p 64), text and accompanying footnotes.
[249] See section 3.1.3.2.2. (p 67), text and accompanying footnotes.

7.3.2.2.1. A Focus on Products?

The different treatment of product-related and other statements in terms of contract interpretation becomes understandable against the historical background of the provision that deals with product-related statements, namely its origin in the Consumer Sales Directive. As set out in the recitals, the main objective underlying the Consumer Sales Directive is to ensure a high level of consumer protection and safeguard the functioning of the internal market.[250] In relation to the objective of consumer protection, the specific provision relies on the assumption that the expectations of consumers are, in modern forms of contracting, more influenced by public statements made in the pre-contractual phase than by the personal interaction with the immediate seller or the signing of the contractual document.[251] However, in the debate on this provision, it has also been emphasised that this influence of pre-contractual behaviour is a common feature in consumer contracting in general.[252] In fact, it is not even a specific characteristic of consumer contracting; the importance of pre-contractual material becomes equally important in relation to business contracts.[253] Against this background, it seems more appropriate to see the distinct position of product-related marketing in sales law not as intrinsically related to the characteristics of consumer sales contracts, but instead as a first step towards reconciling contract law with the realities of contracting where marketing and pre-contractual publicly available information generally tend to play an increasingly important role. The relevance of marketing in sales law could then be the starting point at which new rules are introduced that are subsequently expanded to other constellations.[254] This general provision on the relevance of pre-contractual public statements for sale of goods contracts could then be viewed as a general principle that can inform the general rules on contract interpretation and supplementation, and could thus apply to non-product-related statements as well.

7.3.2.2.2. The Flexible Rules on Contract Interpretation and Supplementation

However, this consideration for a stronger emphasis on pre-contractual statements for specifying the terms of the contract rests fundamentally on the normative criterion to protect the substantive expectations of the contracting parties to the extent that they are shaped by marketing material and other types of public information in the social and environmental production of products, company performance and

[250] Consumer Sales Directive 1999/44/EC [1999] OJ L171/12, recital (1)–(5).

[251] See, eg, Staudenmeyer (2000) 552: the consumer 'is probably more influenced by the advertising statements of the producer. Given the consumers' reliance on such statements, it is important to include them in the assessment of conformity with the contract'.

[252] Wilhelmsson (2004a) 235.

[253] See generally again the analysis on the influence of marketing for the process of contracting in Köndgen (1981) 174ff and Herberg (2007) 114: 'so sind die Wirtschaftsakteure unter heutigen Bedingungen in wachsendem Maße darauf angewiesen, sich auf … Werbeaussagen, Produktinformationen, Gütezeichen, vorvertragliche Zusagen und informelle Abreden erlassen zu können'.

[254] Wilhelmsson (2004a) 237: sales law as 'paradigmatic for contract law in general'.

future behaviour. Hence, it is based on the assumption that contract interpretation and supplementation are, in general, oriented to this normative objective. This normative assumption is not particularly problematic in relation to the German system of contract interpretation, where the rules on contextual contract interpretation adhere to the principle that the 'normative will' of the parties, eg, their respective intentions and expectations in light of the overall behaviour, is the decisive point and not the formal declaration of intent. It is in this context already explicitly accepted that initial promissory statements that influence the formation of the contract, such as the invitation to treat, can become a contractual term if the promisor does not revoke the statement and thus destroys the binding effect before the contract is concluded.[255] However, a similarly affirmative answer to the treatment of pre-contractual statements does not explicitly characterise the English system. It is in this legal system the formal contract rather than the informal and implicit factors in the contractual relationship that marks the starting point for contract interpretation and also supplementation. Hence, a closer analysis of this understanding is required with the objective of identifying whether its underlying justification is valid in relation to the corporate codes.

The difficulty in English law of interpreting promises by parties made in the phase prior to closing the deal as contract terms relates here to the historically evolved approach of enforcing as contracts only the final mutual and formalised consensus and the discrete transaction. The traditional justification for adopting such a strict approach in contract interpretation and implication is the reluctant attitude of courts in relation to interfering in the contractual relationships. In short, it is for the parties and not the courts to write the contracts and 'the court must not make the contract speak where it was intentionally silent'.[256] One can interpret this as an approach to give parties wide freedom on whether and how to use the contractual document and to take a cautious and reluctant attitude towards legal intervention. Yet, as has been rightly emphasised in the contract literature, this approach is part of the classical understanding of contract law that derives from the assumption that parties use the contract as a freely negotiated tool to conduct a discrete transaction.[257]

In spite of this strict focus on the express terms of the contract, English law has in fact also developed exceptions to this orthodox understanding that can be used in relation to the corporate codes. One can refer here in the first place to the collateral contract that is already applied to enforce declarations in the pre-contractual stage that significantly influence the contracting process. The collateral contract, which gives rise to binding enforceable terms next to the subsequently concluded main contract, fulfils the function of enforcing deliberate declarations that generally represent invitations to treat provided that the promisee acted directly upon this

[255] See explicitly Medicus (2010) 147, para 359: 'Dass der Verkäufer zunächst nur eine Aufforderung zu Anträgen erklärt, schließt jedoch nicht aus, dass hierbei miterklärte konkrete Werbeaussagen in den später geschlossenen Vertrag eingehen können, wenn der Verkäufer sie nicht rechtzeitig (also vor Vertragsschluss) richtig gestellt hat.'

[256] Kornet (2006) 181f (quote at 182).

[257] MacNeil (1978) 863; Campbell and Collins (2003) 26.

promise.[258] It represents a tool to circumvent the rigours or the parol evidence rule for factual constellations when it was apparent that a particular pre-contractual declaration strongly influenced the parties in their decision.[259] Thus, for the specific constellations in which the party negotiating a deal with the company can prove that the promises made in the code were decisive for the eventual contractual decision, it is also already possible under the current rules in English law to enforce corporate codes as contractual terms. This possibility notwithstanding, it is also true that this tool is not handy in terms to being able to consider as terms all types of pre-contractual statements and thus also not corporate codes in general. For declarations that are made with the purpose of informing and persuading another party to enter into a contract, including declarations in marketing or other types of public declarations that induce contractual negotiations and structure the expectations of the parties, such an explicit and direct reliance is difficult to construct. Thus, when the code, next to product advertisement, descriptions of the good or direct statements of the seller, only remains one of the relevant factors that influence what the addressed member of the public expects from a contract, the device of the collateral contract reaches its limits. It is only here that the rules on implied terms could be invoked. That being said, the existing rules on implied terms do not quite fit, since, based on their development in the common law, they have not used the reasonable expectations of the contracting parties as the general benchmark. In fact, the rules on implied terms do not fulfil the function of reading in the contract what the parties had actually intended and expected; implied terms in fact rather operate on the basis of specific tests with a particular presumption about what the parties had intended.[260] The officious bystander test in this context aims at giving effect to constellations in which, from the perspective of a bystander that was present at the formation of the contract,[261] the parties obviously intended to use the contract in a specific way and when a term that is logical to fulfil this commonly intended purpose did not find its way into the final document. It thus seems justified by the objective to give effect to the apparent and, from the perspective of an observer clearly visible, joint intentions of the parties on how to use the contract for which 'few could doubt that the term represents their original intention'.[262] The business efficacy test deviates slightly from this understanding because it forgoes the rationale to respect the apparent intentions of the parties by setting up a presumption on what the parties have intended. To that end, it is assumed that the parties can only have intended to use the contract as a *workable* tool that serves the commercial purpose that is laid down or derived from the contract. In this sense, it is based on the rationale that the courts are prepared to

[258] *cf* the instructive example in Collins (2003b) 214f on the implied collateral contract created by a public bid for tenders.

[259] Beatson, Burrows and Cartwright (2010) 136.

[260] Kornet (2006) 185: 'The foundation for the implication of a term in fact is the presumed intention of the parties.'

[261] Although there is no uniform approach of whether the officious bystander is a subjective bystander who proposes terms that the parties would from their perspective have agreed on or is an objective bystander that proposes terms according to the standard of a reasonable person in the position of the contracting parties; see generally on this controversy Kornet (2006) 191ff.

[262] Collins (2003b) 245.

supplement the contract if the identified commercial purpose of the transaction so requires.[263] In other words, the general justification for the reluctant attitude towards a broad interpretation does arguably follow the rationale to interfere as little as possible in an agreement combined with the explicit aim to pay due consideration to the parties' apparent and jointly expressed intentions and the commercial purpose of contracting. This, however, is too narrow to pay respect to the corporate codes. The codes, first, do not in an apparent but a subtle way, shape the expectations of the parties and, second, they are not directly linked to the explicit commercial purpose of the transaction. Thus, in order to enforce publicly declared codes as terms in subsequently concluded contracts, a broader approach towards implying terms would be required and there are two supporting arguments for this proposal.

The first argument refers to the already expressed external critique in English law that questions the narrow underlying rationale of implied terms and suggests that other underlying purposes, particularly the protection of the reasonable expectations of the parties, should be, and in fact are, already considered by the courts as a threshold for implied terms. One of the leading advocates for protecting reasonable expectations in contract law in this context is Lord Steyn. In several extra-judicial writings, he emphasised that there are already notions of good faith and fair dealing in English law, and held that, in the further development of the common law, these notions should be given more weight as principles particularly underlying the law of contract.[264] In one of his early writings on this topic, he argued that these principles are by no means a threat to the valid objective of providing certainty and predictability in commercial transactions, for these notions seem to work almost perfectly 'in the hard school of litigation and international commercial arbitration'.[265] Insisting on the English heritage of pragmatic reasoning and the orientation on concrete problems, however, the role of these notions should, to him, not become a basis for dealing with contracts in every possible respect. What he had in mind was particularly the area of consumer law where he considered the careful drafting and negotiation between the parties to be a myth.[266] Having in mind the character of the corporate codes as public declarations, where equally negotiation and changes are unlikely, his suggested threshold of the reasonable expectations could indeed make sense, particularly in relation to the corporate codes. In fact, as already indicated in the legal analysis, his position, which he also expressed in several speeches to the courts,[267] has recently influenced the development of the rules on implying facts[268] and it is thus also this development that can be relied upon when seeking to imply publicly declared corporate codes as terms in contracts. Lord Steyn's understanding of an increasing

[263] ibid 240.
[264] Steyn (1991); Steyn (1996); Steyn (1997).
[265] Steyn (1991) 140.
[266] ibid 140f.
[267] *Percy Trentham Ltd v Archital Luxfer Ltd* [1993] 1 Lloyd's Rep 25, 27; *First Energy (UK) Ltd v Hungarian International Bank* [1993] BCC 533, 533f; *Total Gas Marketing Ltd v Arco British Ltd* [1998] CLC 1275, 1286.
[268] See section 3.1.3.2.2.1.3. (p 72), text and accompanying footnotes.

relevance of the reasonable expectations of the contracting parties rather than the narrow commercial purpose of the transaction has been taken up in other scholarly contributions.[269] Interestingly, when discussing the reasonable expectations of the parties as a threshold for English contract law when implying terms, scholars also emphasise that this notion is not only a recent development in case law, but has also implicitly influenced the existing tests of implied terms in a number of decisions.[270] In other words, in the guise of the established tests for implied terms, the courts today already use fairness and reasonable expectations as the decisive benchmark.[271] On the basis of this rather realist position, it could become possible in relation to the publicly declared codes to justify the implication also by reference to the existing tests and, in so doing, to develop the argument of the reasonableness of the expectations as to the binding effect of the corporate codes within the 'the vagueness of the business efficacy test'.[272]

A second argument to broaden the scope of implying terms relates to an evolving change in the underlying threshold for implying terms and the increasing use of the normative criterion of the reasonable expectations. It departs from the original underlying objective of protecting the freedom of contract and the autonomy of the parties and the respect for the way that they intended their commercial transaction, but it argues that this objective can only be fulfilled with a stronger focus on the entire contractual relationship. This argument is developed in the socio-legal research on contracting.[273] This strand of research emphasises that the current rules on contract interpretation and supplementation fail to fulfil the objective of enforcing the contract as intended by the parties by focusing on the contractual document.[274] If the underlying objective remains to enforce the autonomously negotiated agreement of commercial parties, one would need to have in mind the characteristics of this commercial reality. In particular in commercial relations, the contracting process is effectively not organised as a process in which every potential detail of the transaction is fixed within the contractual document. Instead, the parties will, in the course of their negotiations, realistically exchange several documents and discuss manifold issues, but the contractual document will most likely not be able to codify all of these issues.[275] The formal agreement only adds the

[269] See especially Yee (2001); Barron (2007) 11ff with further references to the scholarly debate on reasonable expectations in other common law countries.

[270] See pointedly Yee (2001) 204, who states with respect to the business efficacy test and the officious bystander test that: 'The theme underlying these malleable tests may be that without the implied duty, a party would be prevented from fulfilling his or her contractual expectations. Hence, parties' reasonable expectations are essentially controlling.'

[271] See pointedly Kornet (2006) 189: 'There are cases in which the business efficacy test is used in order to mask a normative assessment of the way in which the risks of a particular contract are allocated. At times, the court will imply a term stating that it is necessary to give business efficacy to the agreement, when it is in fact basing its decision on the court's own view of what is fair and reasonable with respect to the bargain struck between the parties.'

[272] Kornet (2006) 189.

[273] MacNeil (1978); Campbell, Collins and Wightman (2003).

[274] Campbell and Collins (2003) 27 call this the 'disfunction of law'.

[275] ibid 41. Several points are raised in this respect. First, they argue that the focus on express terms puts pressure on the parties to put as much into the contractual document as possible, which, from an economic perspective, only increases transaction costs. Second, the parties may need to consult lawyers

specific allocation of risks and the remedies for breach.[276] Thus, in order to adhere to the objective of preserving freedom to contract and enforce the agreements made by the parties to govern their contracts, attention would need to be paid not only to 'the paper deal', but also to the underlying 'real deal'.[277] In addition to the research on the implicit dimensions of contracting, the claim to focus in contract law on the entire contractual relation, the mutual understandings and cooperation, and not only on the contractual document is also furthered by the relational theory of contracting.[278] The express contract terms are, pursuant to this empirically informed theory, also deemed to be only one aspect in very complex relationships, and it is the entire contractual relationship rather than the discrete transaction that needs to be focused on.[279] As MacNeil pointedly stated, 'contract always means relations among people who have exchanged, are exchanging, or expect to be exchanging in the future, i.e. exchange relations'.[280] Against this background, it is held that the 'express terms are, from both practical and intellectual perspectives, a singularly inappropriate starting place for the analysis when dealing with most contract cases and issues.' Even worse: 'Starting with the express terms and the classical contract approach almost invariably skews the analysis of the circumstances in which they are embedded.'[281] Thus, when seeking to enforce contracts as agreed upon by the parties, an understanding of the contract is necessary that goes beyond the discrete exchange fixed in a formal agreement and concluded by offer and acceptance, by taking into consideration the constant interaction between the parties in which the actual and implicit agreements are reached. This argument is also of particular relevance in relation to the codes. In fact, the relationship between publicly declared corporate codes and subsequently concluded contracts can instead be described as one in which the unilaterally declared policy serves as the ultimate basis for the implicit agreement and not the contractual document. In fact, even in cases in which the contracting parties undertake the effort to include the corporate code explicitly into the contractual document and thus render it binding, this is apparent. The contractual clause often merely repeats the commitments laid down in the publicly declared code; it sometimes even refers to a corporate policy that is attached to the contract.[282] Given these specifics, the focus on the contractual document and not the contextual background provides an incomplete understanding

in order to clarify whether the contract as drafted by lawyers accurately reflects what they have agreed upon, which is equally more costly for the parties. Third, it is doubtful whether the lawyers are even capable of bringing all the tacit agreements between the parties into one single document. Fourth, if having the aim to take seriously the enforcement of the parties' agreement, the law could actually not ignore other evidence simply for reasons of formality. Fifth, some obligations are even only mutually assumed by the parties and, in the absence of clear legal knowledge, parties will not be able to distinguish between assumed and agreed obligations.

[276] Campbell and Collins (2003) 38.

[277] Macaulay (2003).

[278] MacNeil (1978); MacNeil (2000); MacNeil (2003).

[279] MacNeil (1978) 890: 'In a truly relational approach the reference point is the entire relation'; MacNeil (2003) 207ff 207: 'the core of relational contract theory is little more than a belief that analysis of transactions must always start with their context'.

[280] MacNeil (2000) 432.

[281] MacNeil (2003), both quotes at 211.

[282] See section 3.1.1. (p 48), text and accompanying footnotes.

not only for the contracting process in general, but in particular in relation to the corporate codes and the obligations as parties have intended to agree on them.

Based on these arguments, it is concluded that also in English law, the existing tests for implying terms can, notwithstanding their first appearance as narrowly confined and thus not suitable tests, be applied to transform the corporate code promises into enforceable terms in subsequently concluded contracts.

7.3.2.3. Corporate Codes as Enforceable Promises

Having focused on the possibility of making use of the rules on contract interpretation and supplementation in order to enforce the corporate codes as contract terms, finally, it needs to be discussed whether private law could also accommodate the binding effect by an autonomous and separate enforcement of corporate codes. Given the conceptual difficulties of enforcing the corporate codes as contracts, the question will be confined to the discussion on whether private law has, in addition to the rules on contract formation, conceptual alternatives at its disposal to enforce promises that are made in a relationship that is akin to a contract and have the objective of persuading an addressed party to behave in a way that benefits the promisor. To clarify this point, contractual enforcement of such promises was considered a possibility, but still a conceptually artificial interpretation of the corporate codes that would result in further difficulties as to the actors and the moment when contractual responsibility arises. Given the observed difficulties in the rules on contract formation, is it possible for contract law to be responsive to the binding effect of the codes by allowing the enforcement of binding promises that are made in the course of pre-contractual negotiations and social interaction that is directed towards inducing a contract? Are there rules in private law to deal with promises that appear in the 'no-man's land' between a contract based on explicit consensus and non-contract? An answer to this question depends here very much on whether concepts are available in the rules that govern the pre-contractual phase where contracts are induced and prepared. The significantly different approaches towards regulating this pre-contractual phase in the legal systems that are chosen as examples here render it necessary to differentiate between the German and the English legal systems in the search for appropriate concepts.

7.3.2.3.1. The German Debate: Binding Promises in the Pre-contractual Phase

With regard to the rules governing the pre-contractual stage, ever since the foundational work of Jhering, it is a well-established rule under German law that this phase prior to the contract can give rise to obligations of the contracting parties due to their reliance on one another.[283] Since 2002, the pre-contractual liability also represents a codified third category[284] of quasi-contractual liability that is conceptually located between tort and contract liability. However, it is so far equally

[283] Jhering (1861).
[284] § 311 II BGB.

accepted that the obligations pursuant to § 311 II BGB are mainly restricted to ancillary duties (§ 241 II BGB) and that breach of these ancillary duties, also in the form of making a public promise, generally has the legal consequence that a claim can be made for reliance losses; conversely, reliance protection in the pre-contractual phase does not go as far as to protect the positive reliance that the promise will be fulfilled.[285] In more recent decisions, the courts also became increasingly prepared to grant, in exceptional cases, compensation as to the expectation interest,[286] but the enforcement of the promise is still not a viable option. However, in the current academic debate, this possibility of also recognising positive binding obligations in private law outside contractual agreement has received increasing attention. Interestingly, in the course of this debate, arguments are not only presented concerning whether such a secondary enforcement model could be justified; several contributions also revealed that such a quasi-contractual relationship with positive binding obligations in fact characterises private law and has already been employed by the courts. So far, this inherently accepted enforcement of pre-contractual unilateral promises has only been concealed in an artificial interpretation of this obligation as a bilateral binding contract. Thus, in order to allow the publicly declared corporate codes to be treated as binding enforceable obligations in the quasi-contractual relations and thus establish a category of autonomous enforcement outside of contract, the following section embraces the theoretical debate on reliance liability with a view to how it could justify the enforcement of the particular pre-contractual public promises apparent in the codes.

As an initial and influential attempt to establish the reliance-based creation of legal relationships as an additional category next to contracts, one can refer to Ballerstedt's influential interpretation of the relationship of *culpa in contrahendo* not as a form of legal liability, but as a mode of creating a legal relationship next to the contract that is voluntarily created by the mutual commitments of the negotiating parties to grant each other intensified trust.[287] To Ballerstedt, the institution of *culpa in contrahendo* resembles the creation of legal relationships through contract insofar as it is based on the 'offer' of one party to grant and the 'acceptance' of the other party to demand trust.[288] The most influential and sophisticated theoretical attempt to structure the field of reliance liability next to contract and tort is the study of Canaris.[289] In fact, his ideas became prominent as one of the most far-reaching suggestions to institutionalise reliance as a comprehensive third form of liability that can take two ideal typical forms. Reliance can first be protected positively by giving the parties the remedies to create a situation that corresponds to reliance. Reliance liability can, however, also have the result that the party is only protected to the extent that reliance has resulted in detriment; the relying party

[285] See affirmatively on this distinction Ackermann (2007) 211ff, pointedly at 246: 'Als privatrechtliche Selbstbindungstatbestände, die der Haftung auf das negative Interesse eine Grundlage bieten, kommen auch vor- und außervertragliche Versprechen und sonstige normativitätsstiftende Verhaltensweisen in Betracht.'

[286] eg, BGH NJW 1989, 3095, 1998, 2900, 2901.

[287] Ballerstedt (1950/51) 501ff.

[288] See for this comparison Lüsing (2010) 344.

[289] Canaris (1971).

is therefore put in the position as if he had not been reliant.[290] He interprets the proposed reliance liability as a possibility to create a legal relationship that is complementary to the institution of the contract.[291] It is restricted to situations in which the party causing reliance participates in a context where legal obligations can principally be created by private actors.[292] Moreover, in order to restrict the scope of reliance liability further and not cover all situations in which someone relies, he also argues that the person having relied must bring forward additional reasons why reliance in this particular case was reasonable.[293] In spite of this attempt to restrict the scope of reliance liability with an emphasis on these additional trust criteria (*Vertrauensfaktoren*), his broad understanding of reliance liability was rightly criticised for being too broad and abstract to provide a convincing general justification for why reliance ought to be protected in such a comprehensive way.[294] However, particularly in relation to corporate code promises that are made in order to induce contractual negotiations and further economic activity, a refined justification for a positive reliance liability can be developed with the help of other theoretical contributions.

Here, one can first refer to the initial ideas of Stoll, who argued that reliance liability is a suitable category specifically for unilateral promises to perform an action.[295] This is due to the fact that the particular cause of reliance, ie, the promise, from the perspective of the addressee resembles a contractual offer and there are often severe difficulties involved for the addressee to determine whether or not an intention to be bound is presented and thus whether a contractually binding obligation is created or not.[296] From the perspective of the addressee, it is therefore generally reasonable to rely on the fact that the promise will be fulfilled if the promise was made in a sufficiently serious manner.[297] Using the example of the promise to take over the debts of someone else, Stoll also argues that, as a matter of fact, the courts already partly protect reasonable reliance in a sufficiently serious promise by means of interpreting this relationship as a contract.[298] Recognising reliance in a sufficiently concrete promise as an additional category could, in this context, mainly help to reduce uncertainty in legal transactions.[299] The approach of Köndgen can, in this regard, be read as a first attempt to confine this idea on protecting reliance in the act of promising to specific types of promises. In his theoretical study on self-obligation outside of contract, Köndgen proposes reducing the scope of reliance-based enforcement to promises made in a specific social

[290] ibid 5, 541ff.
[291] ibid 440f.
[292] ibid 442ff ('Vertrauenshaftung als Haftung kraft Teilnahme am rechtgeschäftlichen Verkehr').
[293] ibid 503ff (pointedly at 504: 'daß Vertrauen hier nur innerhalb eines spezifisch *rechtlichen* Zusammenhangs relevant ist und daher für die Begriffsbildung nicht nur psychologische, sondern auch juristisch-normative Kategorien maßgeblich sind' (emphasis in original).
[294] For this critique, see, eg, Stoll (1978) 752; Köndgen (1981) 102f; Picker (1983) 421ff; Bachmann (2006b) 249; Lüsing (2010) 103ff.
[295] Stoll (1978).
[296] ibid 748ff.
[297] ibid 753f.
[298] ibid 758ff. See also Lüsing (2010) 342.
[299] Stoll (1978) 761.

context.[300] He argues that, in the same way as contracts, reliance on promises cannot be protected generally, but only if the particular social system in which the promise is made justifies rendering the promise binding.[301] Focusing on the latter aspect, he argues that reliance liability for promises is particularly valid in the context of a competitive market. This is due to the fact that, pursuant to the functioning of the economic system, promises in the context of the market are an initial step towards conducting a bilateral exchange. Against the background of the general functioning of the market, promises made in the context of the market can be considered as having an inherent seriousness and an implicit reciprocity that renders reliance on them reasonable.[302] Pursuant to this understanding, reliance on a public promise to perform an action can result in possible enforcement in case the promise is made in the course of a deliberate and intentional participation on the market as the social context that is based on the rule of furthering cooperation and ultimately exchange.[303] The basis for allowing the enforcement of promises in this particular context is then to guarantee the functioning of this cooperative order that is dependent on the trust in the seriousness of given promises.[304] In addition, it has also been emphasised in the debate that the enforcement of such promises cannot solely be justified with reference to the expectations of the addressees and the functioning of the market. In order to count as enforceable and voluntarily created obligations, it remains necessary that such reliance-based obligations also be created by an intentional act on the side of the speaker. In particular, Lüsing has proposed here confining the scope of reliance-based enforcement and requiring as an additional criterion the autonomous and deliberate promissory act of the speaker.[305]

With the help of these approaches, one can thus specify the conditions under which positive obligations to perform can be created outside of a contract. The binding obligation would need to be based on an intentional declaration of a party that eventually becomes bound, provided that the declaration is deliberately introduced in a social context, such as the market, that is eventually directed towards

[300] Köndgen (1981) 271ff.

[301] ibid 273: 'Als Ansatzpunkt bieten sich die Bezogenheit vertraglichen Handelns auf je verschiedene soziale (Teil-)Systeme an.'

[302] ibid 275ff.

[303] ibid 277: 'Dem Selbstbestimmungsgrundsatz ist heute dadurch Genüge getan, daß der Eintritt ins Marktsystem in freier Entscheidung und in (gegebenenfalls unterstellter) Kenntnis der—geschriebenen und ungeschriebenen—Spielregeln erfolgt.' See also Lüsing (2010) 396: 'Teilnahme an einer sozialen Interaktion, in Bezug auf die die Rechtsordnung ein Schuldverhältnis begründet.'

[304] Bachmann (2006b) 251.

[305] Lüsing (2010) 384: 'Das Rechtsinstitut der Selbstbindung kraft sozialtypischer Sprechhandlung ist wie das Rechtsinstitut des Rechtsgeschäfts *ein Mechanismus der Selbstbindung, d.h. Erzeugung selbstgestalteter Pflichten*' (emphasis in original). See also Hawickhorst (1987) 127 ('Die Erwartungen des Verkehrs können dem Versprechenden daher persönlich zugerechnet werden, weil er als Autor der Pflichten erscheint') who, however, still seeks to restrict the proposed liability for such promises to the negative reliance interest (at 160ff); and Bachmann (2006b) 297, who distinguishes between promises that are for the promisee of 'existential relevance' where no intentional act of the promisor is required and other types of promises for which an intention to be bound is required. Yet, he seems to leave unanswered the question of what criteria the courts should use in order to determine the 'existential relevance'.

bringing about a legally binding obligation. For these types of declarations, it then becomes possible to justify enforcement based on reliance in relation to those that are induced to benefit the promisor. Translated concretely into the constellation of corporate codes, this would have the result that the codes would qualify as enforceable promises that companies strategically place on the market with the attempt to influence potential contracting partners. Once such a declaration is typically perceived as binding and relied upon according to the institutional rules of the market, it follows that such promises also bind the speaker towards participants on the market and that the company cannot get off by seeking first to obtain a benefit by triggering reliance and later on denying the reliability of this deliberate behaviour. In contrast to the above-mentioned contract enforcement, first, this has the result that the promissory enforcement becomes possible in line with the specific characteristics of the corporate code. The binding effect, as deliberately created by the publishing companies, becomes an enforceable declaration only in the context in which they are introduced in order to induce exchange. In addition, this reliance-based promissory enforcement also gives companies the right to destroy the binding effect more easily. Based on the contractual perspective, the options to revoke the codes and make changes would not be decided by the rules applicable to the termination of long-term contracts. In contrast, the reliance-based promissory enforcement could be terminated in the same way in which reliance has been established, eg, by undertaking active and explicit efforts to destroy reliance in the seriousness of their promise.[306]

As a result, the concept in the literature to create binding enforceable obligations to perform by an intentional promise to the public with the objective of causing others to induce a contract can provide a suitable starting point to enforce the corporate codes as autonomous relied-upon promises. As will be further specified in the concluding chapter nine, this suggested enforcement outside of contract could particularly be linked to the existing forms in the civil code. It is in particular the emerging provisions that deal with the enforcement of the pre-contractual persuasive behaviour of traders, specifically § 661a BGB, that will be of value in this respect.

7.3.2.3.2. The English Debate: Between a Bargain and Non-contractual Liability?

After having intensively analysed the possibilities in German law for promissory enforcement outside of the rules on contract formation, this section discusses whether a comparable proposal is conceivable in English law. Yet, already the starting point for such an undertaking must be significantly different. Due to the

306 Concrete indications on how companies can prevent or cease to be subject to reliance liability could be taken from the rules that determine how pre-contractual public statements can be retracted in order not to become relevant in sales contracts. Pursuant to § 434 I 3 BGB, this is the case if the statement is 'it had been corrected in an equivalent manner' (translation taken from Kornet and Hardt (2013) 309). See also Bachmann (2006b) 298, who suggests developing the rules on termination for publicly declared codes with the help of an analogous application of § 658 BGB.

strong reluctance of English law to interfere at all in the pre-contractual stage and the strict distinction between a binding contract and non-contractual legal liability in tort without a third category, any reasoning for a promissory enforcement outside of a contract is obviously more difficult. The reluctance to impose liability outside a contractual agreement can, in this regard, be related to the prevailing understanding in English law to intervene as little as possible prior to the conclusion of a contract and to protect the parties' freedom to choose whether or not to contract.[307] Accordingly, before suggesting far-reaching changes in the English rules on pre-contractual liability by proposing reliance-based enforcement comparable to German law, it is necessary to deal more intensively with the internal justification for this narrow approach.

When analysing the common law discussion on declarations in the pre-contractual phase, one can identify several considerations that influence the narrow approach. In general, in regulating the pre-contractual phase, the freedom of contract and the distribution of risk are relevant factors to be considered.[308] Most importantly, the reluctance to interfere in the phase prior to the conclusion of the contract is explained by the strong influence of the principle of the freedom of contract in English law and again is based on a particular perception of the contracting process. It is the main understanding that freedom of contract has to be respected by allowing the parties to reach their agreements as they so wish. If the law were to impose obligations prior to the contract, it would effectively imply that the parties would have obligations towards each other without necessarily intending to do so.[309] The reason why the law does interfere in the pre-contractual phase is, in this context, not only explained by referring to the fundamental principle of the freedom of contract; it again follows from a particular understanding of contractual relationships and the negotiation process. In this regard, English law derives from the main assumption that parties negotiating a deal behave antagonistically whereby each party seeks to conclude a contract that is in his respective self-interest.[310] Thus, if in the phase prior to the contract, each party is cautious only to do what is in its interests, there may indeed not be any need to protect the parties from reliance to their detriment.[311] This understanding is equally reflected in the considerations as to the distribution of risk in the pre-contractual phase. If parties are considered to pursue their own interest, one may also require them to allocate their risks and not make the law decide upon a risk distribution.[312] However, in a similar way, as was already discussed when focusing on contract interpretation and supplementation, English courts do, in fact, deviate from this

[307] Collins (2003b) 180.

[308] These three underlying components of pre-contractual liability have been identified by Giliker (2002) 169ff.

[309] Collins (2003b) 180.

[310] See Giliker (2002) 169, referring to the clear statement of Lord Ackner in *Walford v Miles* [1992] 2 AC 128, 138 that liability is 'inherently repugnant to the adverserial position of the parties when involved in negotiations'.

[311] This argument is of course based on the underlying assumption that there is equal bargaining power of both sides and, if not, that interference is at least justified to establish the equality.

[312] Giliker (2002) 170.

general approach.[313] In regulating the pre-contractual phase, the courts are also guided by policy considerations based on the need to achieve justice, including the readiness to establish legal consequences for a pre-contractual declaration, and this is done in particular by invoking the existing narrowly confined doctrines of misrepresentation, collateral or unilateral contracts and equitable estoppel.[314] In this context, it is recognised that such fairness considerations discussed in the application of these concepts play a role in a more ad hoc way, eg, if the particular factual constellation so requires.[315] Thus, with regard to the possibility of transforming the code declarations to the public into binding obligations, one can rely on these specific doctrines and argue that the particular situation on codes of conduct requires intervention. For the particular constellation of corporate codes, the core conceptually suitable device is the doctrine on equitable estoppel. This is due to the fact that this doctrine focuses particularly on the possibility of rendering a deliberate promise subject to legal consequences if it was reasonably relied on by another party. Equitable estoppel embraces the principle that a claim for enforcement cannot only be based on a bargained contract, but also on deliberately creating a belief in an addressee that a bilateral exchange will be conducted.[316] It is thus in particular suitable to accommodate the corporate codes that deliberately create an expectation on the side of the addressees that should induce them to intensify further contractual cooperation. Equitable estoppel, in its application to corporate codes, was envisaged in the first place as a doctrine that makes it possible to enforce deliberate and persuading promises that cause reliance in a relationship that should ultimately result in a contract.[317]

Precisely in relation to the concept of equitable estoppel, it has already been emphasised in the legal analysis in chapter three that this doctrine is, in its current form, unsuitable, as it is restricted in its scope. As a cause of action, it only applies to specific types of promises, eg, to promises concerning land rights.[318] This implies that the question of whether or not this doctrine is suitable depends

[313] Collins (2003b) 213: 'In stark opposition to the traditional view that during the negotiations for a contract no binding obligations may arise, it is possible for the courts to infer implied contractual undertakings from conduct and statements made during the negotiations.'

[314] Giliker (2002) 171; Collins (2003b) 181. See also from the case law Lord Bingham in *Interfoto Picture Library Ltd v Stiletto Visual Programmes Ltd* [1989] QB 433, 439: 'English law has, characteristically, committed itself to no such overriding principle [of fair dealing] but has developed piecemeal solutions in response to demonstrated problems of fairness.'

[315] Giliker (2002) 171.

[316] ibid. See also from the case law Lord Denning in *Combe v Combe* [1951] 2 KB 215, 220: 'The principle, as I understand it, is that, where one party has, by his words or conduct, made to the other a promise or assurance which was intended to affect the legal relations between them and to be acted on accordingly, then, once the other party has taken him at his word and acted on it, the one who gave the promise or assurance cannot afterwards be allowed to revert to the previous legal relations as if no such promise or assurance had been made by him.'

[317] This understanding of using equitable estoppel resembles proposals in the US context on promissory estoppel made by Farber and Matheson (1985) 929ff. They suggest treating promissory estoppel as a doctrine next to ordinary contract formation that makes it possible to enforce the specific types of promises that are made to promote economic activity even without a clear bargain. More precisely, it is proposed to incorporate a rule in the Restatement of Contracts that reads: 'A promise is enforceable when made in furtherance of an economic activity' (at 930).

[318] See section 3.1.4.2.1. (p 100), text and accompanying footnotes.

eventually on whether there are valid justifications for this narrow scope. The main reason in English law for not expanding the scope of this doctrine is, in this context, not difficult to point out. The scope of the doctrine is not broadened due to the concern that such a development would effectively subvert the orthodox understanding that enforceable obligations can only be created by a contract that is supported by consideration.[319] The consideration requirement is also identified as the underlying reason that, in contractual negotiations, even firm and explicit promises are not treated as giving rise to liability.[320] However, in relation to the corporate codes, it was already argued that this specific restriction is not convincing and should be subject to relaxation. As I sought to show above, the internal reasons for sticking to a requirement of consideration, while perfectly relevant for other constellations, in particular, gratuitous gift making, do not fit with respect to the corporate codes.[321] It is thus in this particular constellation that the restrictions inherent in the doctrine of consideration do not qualify as a valid argument against using promissory estoppel as a cause of action.

In addition, one can, as support for a further development of equitable estoppel, refer to different scholarly contributions which argue that a broader scope of equitable estoppel is an emerging and desired development in English law. In fact, contract law scholars already dealt with the question of whether equitable estoppel could eventually serve as a second enforcement model that makes it possible to enforce promises in addition to the enforcement of bargained contractual agreements.[322] The reasons for suggesting such a further development relate first to the potential adaptation of English common law to the developments in other jurisdictions. Partly, this refers to the development on a European level, such as the Principles of European Contract Law or the UNIDROIT Principles, in which the option to enforce contracts and partly even unilateral promises without the requirement of consideration is already laid down.[323] In addition, a development that is considered to be very important for English common law is the recognition of promissory estoppel as a cause of action within other common law jurisdictions. This refers to the situation in the US where promissory estoppel has for a long time already been recognised as cause of action, but, more importantly, to developments in another country with a common law system in the Commonwealth tradition. In particular, the High Court of Australia in *Walton Stores (Interstate) Ltd v Maher* is referred to as an important instance in which pre-contractual promissory liability was recognised.[324] The rationale that underlies this argument is then to

[319] See most explicitly Lord Denning in *Combe v Combe* (n 316) 220: 'Seeing that the principle never stands alone as giving a cause of action in itself, it can never do away with the necessity of consideration when that is an essential part of the cause of action. The doctrine of consideration is too firmly fixed to be overthrown by a side-wind.'

[320] Smith (2004) 195f.

[321] See arguments developed above in section 7.3.2.1.1. (p 270), text and accompanying footnotes.

[322] See, eg, Beatson, Burrows and Cartwright (2010) 129ff; Peel (2011) 169f; McKendrick (2013) 100ff.

[323] This is emphasised by McKendrick (2013) 103f, who refers specifically to art 2:101 of the Principles of European Contract Law (the contract is concluded by the intention to be legally bound without any further requirements) and art 3.1.2 of the UNIDROIT Principles (a contract is concluded by agreement without further requirements).

[324] *Walton Stores (Interstate) Ltd v Maher* (1988) 164 CLR 387.

treat the strict distinction between the bargained contract and non-contract as less fundamental, as it appears as if other legal systems, including those that belong to the same legal family, have already relaxed this distinction considerably. Against the background of a strong mutual influence between legal systems in today's globalised world, it can indeed be convincing to argue that developments in one legal system ought to be followed in another, in particular if they both have a similar legal tradition.

That being said, one might counter this argument by considering that there might still be reasons not to follow the developments in other legal systems due to particular national specific practices and the institutional path-dependencies. For instance, a specific practice that is used in a particular national context could provide a valid justification for a country's own path-dependency and thus imply a rejection of taking over foreign concepts.[325] However, in order to counter this argument, one can again refer to the fact that not only in other common law systems, but also explicitly in English law, the enforcement of promises outside of contract is recognised, namely in the confined boundaries of land rights in the form of proprietary estoppel. Proposing a broader scope for this already existing doctrine in English law, with due respect to its own path-dependent logic, then rests ultimately on the validity of confining the scope of this doctrine to promises concerning land rights. It seems, however, that there is no general reason for this distinction.[326] On the contrary, an explanation for the confined scope of property law in promissory estoppel has, in the academic debate, merely been viewed as having to do particularly with the specific way in which the common law develops. As Collins states:

> The distinction seems highly improbable. No reason other than the certainty achieved by following scrupulously the limits of precedent decisions is given for treating the general grounds for enforceability of promises connected with interests in land any differently from those concerning goods and services.[327]

Hence, the constraint in English law to allow the enforcement of pre-contractual promises only in relation to land can also be explained by the fact that the courts were so far primarily called upon to decide cases in which promises regarding land provided sufficient grounds to establish a promissory enforcement or, to put it the other way around, the restriction is based on the fact that a suitable case has not yet been presented concerning other types of promises. Thus, the existing restriction of equitable estoppel to serve as a cause of action only for pre-contractual promises concerning land rights can be read merely as a coincidental development and not as a conscious decision to determine reliance in promises relating to land

[325] Collins (1999) 190f discusses this argument in relation to promissory estoppel in particular. His main point is that, in constellations of fixed price bids the doctrine of promissory estoppel was deliberately not applied in England as a cause of action because it would have conflicted with the established expectations and conventions of business in England.

[326] Collins (2003b) 87f. See similarly explicitly McKendrick (2013) 98: 'Why is it that detrimental reliance upon a promise to create an interest in property can create a cause of action, but that detrimental reliance upon any other promise cannot do so? No convincing answer has ever been provided to this question.'

[327] Collins (2003b) 87.

as worth being protected while refusing to grant this protection to other types of promises. Following this understanding, the doctrine of equitable estoppel can represent a viable device to translate the binding effect of the particular types of promises present in the corporate policies into legally binding obligations.

7.3.2.4. Conclusion: Enforcement of Publicly Declared Codes in Market Relations

The previous sections sought to identify, from the perspective of private law, the suitable concepts and doctrines to transform the binding effect that companies create with their codes into legally enforceable obligations insofar as the binding effect is related to the social context of contracting on the market. In so doing, it was argued that their enforcement as contracts could be a possibility, but then, from the conceptual perspective, such an interpretation does not quite fit with the reality of the codes. However, to the extent that a contract is eventually concluded, it was presented as a viable option to enforce the corporate codes as contractual terms with the help of the rules of contextual contract interpretation and implication. Finally, it was argued that, based on the current proposals to enforce deliberate relied-upon promises declared in the market context towards potential contractual partners with the aim of inducing a contract, a separate promissory enforcement is also appropriate.

7.3.3. Public Trust in Code Promises

Up to this point, the transformation of the binding character of the corporate codes into private law obligations was scrutinised with regard to actors towards whom the codes are deliberately introduced to further and intensify cooperation and in order to receive ultimately an indirect benefit from them. This section now seeks to focus on how the binding effect of the corporate codes can be accommodated in private law as far as the global public and the protection of trust in the regulatory role of corporate actors is concerned. It is, for this undertaking, equally useful to recall the different options that were identified in the course of the legal analysis to protect this public trust in private law. One can distinguish here on a general level between two different ways in which this trust could become relevant. One could also propose, comparable to the situation above, contractual enforcement based on public trust and reliance, and treat the code as global offers towards the beneficiaries that the latter are deemed to have accepted by continuing to work or by not taking precautionary measures.[328] Alternatively, the binding effect in the form of intensified trust in the promised behaviour could also be accommodated by means of allowing non-contractual liability for non-compliance with the codes

[328] For this suggestion, see the sources referred to in section 3.1.4.1. (p 84), n 166. Alternatively, it is of course also possible to suggest in this context a promissory reliance-based enforcement for the global public including the beneficiaries. This is mainly envisaged by Phillips and Lim (2009) 375.

in the form of a voluntary assumption of responsibility that causes reliance.[329] The core difference between these two options is the legal consequence that the binding effect might have. While the first treatment would allow detrimentally affected beneficiaries to enforce the promised actions as obligations or recover their expectation interest, the latter only provides for compensation of the reliance interest or, to the extent the general rules on tort law apply, even only the integrity interest.

By emphasising in the following section the necessity of maintaining an internal distinction in private law between rights and obligations within cooperative relationships that parties have entered into (contracts) and coincidental relationships between strangers (non-contractual liability), the following section advocates applying the rules on tort rather than contract to constellations of disappointed public trust. On this basis, the second section will then discuss more concretely which of the previously identified concepts in the field of non-contractual liability and unfair commercial practices law is suitable to protect reliance of members of the public, in particular of those specified in the codes as beneficiaries.

7.3.3.1. Protecting Public Trust in Promises by Enforcement?

Considering that the published promise deriving from the corporate code has been considered the cause for both the expectations of parties negotiating a deal and the creation of public trust, one could, at first sight, argue that the legal protection of both of the created expectations would also have to be treated similarly. On this basis, one could in principle argue for comprehensive contractual or promissory reliance-based enforcement of the corporate code towards the parties that the company addresses with the objective of entering into a cooperative relationship, as well as with the members of the global public, in particular the beneficiaries of the code. Pursuant to this understanding, the beneficiaries could enforce the codes based on their reliance on the good corporate behaviour in the future. The contractual offer here could be the global distribution of the corporate code not only in the form of the website, but also in the form of posters that are distributed in factories all over the world.[330] However, while such an interpretation is conceivable, legal intuition would tell us to be very cautious with such an interpretation, as it would put the company under a contractual obligation towards the global public and would thus expose it to a far-reaching risk. It is therefore no coincidence that the sceptical voices against a potential global contractual enforcement prevail. Yet, intuition, although certainly often giving valuable guidance, cannot provide a justification. Once it is assumed that a binding obligation can be created by an intentional public promise, a difference cannot be justified by referring to the lack

[329] See the options presented in section 4.1.2. (p 156), text and accompanying footnotes.

[330] The former option is envisaged, but critically evaluated, by Bachmann (2006b) 297. The latter option is the main link for a potential contract between the publishing companies and the employees of suppliers as beneficiaries in Kenny (2007) 463f: 'Wal-Mart's own "Supplier's Responsibilities" make clear that Wal-Mart requires that a poster version of the Suppliers Standards in the local language and English be placed in each production facility serving Wal-Mart … Therefore, it seems likely that the requirement for contract formation was satisfied.'

of an intention to be bound.[331] It also cannot be a reference to the vague content[332] if it has been concluded that the public declaration is sufficiently concrete in order to represent a successfully performed promise. Yet, there is in fact an important justification for distinguishing between the binding effects in the relations considered above that have been claimed to lead to positive enforcement and the binding effect towards the public where reliance on the commitment must only be protected negatively in the form of non-contractual liability. It is the core internal distinction within private law between the regulation of relations that entail voluntary cooperation between private actors based on their free choice, on the one hand, and the liability of private actors in coincidental relations between strangers, on the other hand, that comes into play.[333] This distinction is based on the underlying and valid rationale that these two forms of social interaction are generally characterised by different degrees of responsibility. The fact that the binding effect of the corporate codes is important in both types of social relations must then not be misinterpreted as a justification to equalise the different degrees of legal responsibility. The corporate codes do not explicitly qualify as a general category of 'contorts';[334] instead, with respect to their transformation into private law duties, it is considered necessary to distinguish between the duties derived from them within a social relation that is ultimately directed towards a voluntary agreement and the relationship between strangers. This internal distinction between a quasi-contractual enforcement of the codes in the companies' cooperative relations and a quasi-tort liability is, from the theoretical perspective, based on the idea of maintaining an internal distinction between contract and tort also within the broad field of reliance liability to which the corporate codes relate.[335]

As a result, the suggestion to enforce the corporate codes as promissory self-commitments must be limited towards those relationships in which the corporate code is included with the deliberate objective of preparing and inducing a transaction to intensify further cooperation for the benefit of the company. However, as far as its general relevance with respect to public trust in the institution of the competitive market and the trust of the global public including the specified beneficiaries is concerned, the intended binding effect remains, from the perspective of the company, an undertaking to induce the reliance of remotely located strangers for merely altruistic reasons. In these relationships between strangers,

[331] But see Bachmann (2006b) 297: 'Wer etwa im Internet die Einhaltung eines globalen Verhaltenskodex verspricht, wird damit kaum jedem Erdenbürger einen einklagbaren Erfüllungsanspruch gewähren wollen.'

[332] But see Kenny (2007) 467: 'Ultimately, because the wording in Wal-Mart's Code of Conduct is too vague ... Wal-Mart's Code of Conduct for foreign suppliers does not create a contractual obligation with the employees of Wal-Mart's foreign suppliers.'

[333] See in this direction Köndgen (1999a) 19f.

[334] Gilmore (1974) 90.

[335] In particular Köndgen (1999a) 20f ('Ein anderes ist es freilich, ob man wirklich die Summe dieser neuen Haftungsfiguren systematisch in einer neuen sogenannten, "dritten Spur" zusammen fassen will ... Die besseren Argumente sprechen nach alledem immer noch dafür, die sogenannte dritte Spur als Systemkategorien wieder aufzulösen und ihre Bestandteile den etablierten rechtsfunktionalen Haftungsgründen Vertrag und Delikt zuzuweisen'); and Köndgen (1999b) 91: 'Wenn schon eine Erweiterung des dualistischen Systems, dann nicht in drei sondern in vier Spuren.'

reliance on the commitments is protected only to the extent that measurable individual damage occurs or, in the case of the collective interest to maintain a fair market, to the extent that the institution of the market is detrimentally affected. It is thus primarily the tools of non-contractual liability that are considered suitable to accommodate the binding effect in the relationship of the company with the global public, including the beneficiaries of the codes and the effects on the institution of the fair market.

7.3.3.2. Reliance Liability in Tort and Unfair Commercial Practices Law

The arguments presented above thus propose using the field of non-contractual liability for the obligations on the side of the publishing company towards the general public and, in relation to the codes, two areas are particularly suitable. Insofar as disappointed trust in relation to the corporate codes occurs in the form of measurable damage on the side of an individual who relies on the promises made in the corporate code concerning its good behaviour, it is particularly the general rules on non-contractual liability that are applicable. Concerning the disappointed trust in the institution of the competitive and fair market that is dependent on the reputation and good behaviour of companies as its main actors, the area of unfair commercial practices law is applicable. Hence, with respect to the disappointed trust of individuals as part of the global public, liability is dependent on the criterion of detriment in the form of measurable damage and it is here that the general restrictions in non-contractual liability as to the kinds of damage have to be respected.[336] Concerning the relationship between the corporate codes and unfair commercial practices law, it is important to also insist on the fact that the regulation of the promises is integrated into an area of law that focuses on the disappointed trust of consumers and is therefore only capable of regulating the corporate codes insofar as they have direct effects on the consumer market.

With regard to the concrete concepts within the rules on non-contractual liability and unfair commercial practices law, a second aspect needs to be addressed. This is due to the fact that there are, in principle, two distinctly different concepts that were, in chapter four, considered to be principally suitable. In the course of general non-contractual liability, it was argued that one could conceive linking liability to the act of making the declaration towards those that detrimentally rely on it in the form of establishing liability for negligent misstatement. Alternatively, it was also considered a viable option to interpret the corporate code as evidence for an existing duty of care based on a voluntary assumption of responsibility towards

[336] Herberg (2007) 115 pointedly observes that the criterion of measurable reliance damage in the public promise can take the form of active investments that were made in the expectation that the commitment will be fulfilled or an omission to take precautionary measures that could have avoided or mitigated the damage. It has to be added here that given the integration into the general rules on tort law, these damages need to be restricted to the kind of damages that this area is prepared to compensate, eg, mainly damages to bodily integrity, health and safety and property, and not automatically pure economic losses that are recoverable only in relationships akin to contract. See section 4.2.2. (p 182), text and accompanying footnotes.

the beneficiaries.[337] A similar distinction could be observed in the different options of regulating corporate codes by unfair commercial practices law. Here, it could be the publication of the corporate code that amounts to an unfair commercial practice in the form of providing misleading information, which is also the current focus in this field; however, it could also be an option to focus on the non-complying behaviour to the extent that it has effects on the market, eg, the distribution and selling of products that were produced in violation of the corporate code.[338] Thus, the relationship between the codes and non-contractual liability mainly depends on whether liability should be related to the act of making the corporate code publicly available or for the non-complying behaviour. The decision for one direction or the other depends mainly on how they protect reliance with respect to public statements and what form is effectively more suitable with respect to the codes. Although both forms do similarly relate reasonable reliance to the declaration and the created trust, there is one crucial difference between them. Liability for false or misleading declarations can be read as a tool that recognises liability for declarations that someone makes dishonestly or at least carelessly.[339] The proposal to focus on the non-complying behaviour instead and use the declaration as mere evidence of an existing duty of care or an aspect influencing the fairness standard views the ultimate ground for liability differently. One can describe this form of liability as sanctioning the careless or dishonest behaviour *after* having created trust by means of a public declaration. What is the most appropriate way forward to deal with the corporate codes against the background of the two different underlying rationales? An answer to this question can be found in the theoretical analysis above. One has to have in mind here first the fact that the analysis on the corporate code declaration could reveal their character as successful and not misleading promises.[340] Second, from the sociological perspective, it has also been demonstrated that such principally successful promises are generally capable of resulting in intensified social trust in relations of anonymity. This already renders it more appropriate to sanction an abuse of trust that is intentionally created by the promise on the side of the company rather than the fact that the company creates trust dishonestly. This also makes sense if one considers the suggested role of the legal system in relation to the protection of public trust. Under conditions of strong distrust, social trust-building in the form of promises is mainly endangered by subsequent untrustworthy conduct, which is why the legal system needs to

[337] See text and accompanying footnotes in section 4.1.2.1. (p 157) and section 4.1.2.2. (p 167) respectively.

[338] See text and accompanying footnotes in section 5.3.1. (p 196) and 5.3.2. (p 201) respectively.

[339] See from the German literature Canaris (1971) 532: 'Der tragende Grund der Einstandspflicht liegt hier ersichtlich darin, *daß jemand für die Folgen einer von ihm abgegebenen fehlerhaften Erklärung aufzukommen hat*' (emphasis in original); and Bachmann (2006b) 241: 'Wer sich an private Regeln nicht binden will, muss es nicht tun; er darf aber *nicht der Wahrheit zuwider die eigene Regelbindung behaupten*, wenn Dritte dadurch Schaden erleiden' (emphasis added). From the perspective of English law, see Collins (2003b) 182f: 'The law imposes a duty of care on parties … when they make statements to each other. The duty requires that statements of fact are made with reasonable care in light of the specialised knowledge and expertise of the representor. The duty is broken by making a statement which is *false* or *misleading* because insufficient care was taken' (emphasis added).

[340] See for this argument above, section 7.2.1.2.2. (p 239), text and accompanying footnotes.

primarily sanction such trust-abusing behaviour. Conversely, the initial attempt of trust-building, the public declaration, needs to be furthered.[341] Against this background, it is fair to say that it is not primarily the dishonest code declaration that currently jeopardises the creation of social trust, but rather the dishonest behaviour following such statements. Translated into the regulation of the corporate codes by means of non-contractual liability and unfair commercial practices law, it is then more appropriate not to hold the company liable for its attempt to regain public trust by means of a public declaration. Companies that publicly declare compliance with their code need instead to be sanctioned for any subsequently disappointed trust that had, at least initially with good reason, sought to be established.

As a result, in order to further the public trust in the institution of good corporate behaviour, it is suggested that corporate codes be related to the rules on non-contractual liability in the form of recognising the code as giving rise to a duty of care in the form of a voluntary assumption of responsibility that gives rise to reliance in a manner that is foreseeable for the company. Concerning the specific discussion on corporate codes in unfair commercial practices law, this implies mainly shifting the regulatory focus from regulating the use of the corporate codes to behaviour that amounts to a breach of the corporate code, to the extent that this behaviour would qualify as a commercial practice.

7.3.4. Towards Conceptualising Publicly Declared Codes in Private Law

After having described the corporate codes theoretically as intentional declarations with binding effect, the analysis proceeded by identifying the appropriate concepts in private law to accommodate this binding effect based on the normative criteria of the law. To that end, a distinction was made between cooperative relationships with business partners and consumers, and possibly also governments when the company uses the promise and its binding effect deliberately in order to further cooperation, and the relationship between the global public when the promise remains part of relationships between strangers. Concerning the former relationship, a transformation of the codes into enforceable obligations was seen as appropriate, first, in the form of interpreting the corporate codes as enforceable terms in subsequently concluded contracts by making use of the rules on contract interpretation (Germany) and supplementation (England). In addition, a specific reliance-based promissory enforcement was also proposed on the ground that this binding promise influences the cooperative relations of companies and other market actors which aim at concluding contractual relations. To that end, developments within legal scholarship towards positive reliance liability deriving from a unilateral public promise made on the market (Germany) and proposals towards broadening the doctrine of equitable estoppel (England) were discussed and considered appropriate. As far as the protection of public trust in the promise

[341] See for this argument, section 7.2.3.2.2.2. (p 262), text and accompanying footnotes.

is concerned, the appropriate way forward was identified in the field of tort law liability in the form of interpreting the public declaration to comply with a code of voluntary assumption of responsibility and as a voluntary commitment that is capable of specifying the fairness standard in unfair commercial practices law. It is these normative claims that chapter nine in this book seeks to work out as more specific proposals for legal reform.

8

Corporate Efforts to Do Just Business

Theorising Public/Private Regulation in Private Law

> The multinational enterprise stands at the center of the system. Through its elaboration of a tightly controlled supplier system, for example, the multinational corporation can serve as the system legislator … Enforcement is through extensive monitoring programs, which are as intrusive as any created by governments. These sanctions are not the stuff of contract breach. They resemble more the form of legislative or administrative management under public law codes.[1]

THE PRECEDING CHAPTER focused particularly on the problem of how publicly declared corporate codes could become relevant for determining the private law obligations of the issuing company. Based on the insight that corporate codes are capable of creating a private law obligation in the form of a public self-commitment as well as by directly integrating it into the contract, the follow-up question arises as to the particular character of this obligation and the precise way in which it can be enforced. In the legal analysis, several proposals were presented that are currently discussed in the legal literature. With regard to the contractual obligations of the company, the current most prominent suggestions are to interpret the codes either as an integral part of the bilateral agreement on the sale of goods or as agreements that specify a benefit for third parties that are enforceable by the contracting parties as well as the third party. In addition, there are also contributions in the corporate codes literature that describe the corporate codes as new self-regulatory standards that, by means of incorporation, introduce a new regulatory dimension into the contracting process. A similar interpretation can be observed in the course of the tort law analysis in which the corporate codes as well as the public codes of conduct are discussed from the perspective of whether they represent self-regulatory standards that are capable of specifying negligent behaviour. Finally, when scrutinising unfair commercial practices law, it was revealed that corporate codes could possibly qualify as codes of conduct in the sense of unfair commercial practices law. Against the background of these different options, the following analysis will be devoted to examining, from a theoretical perspective, the specific character of these corporate policies. In so doing, the first section seeks again to identify a suitable starting point that is developed

[1] Backer (2008) 518.

from the underlying normative controversy (section 8.1), which is followed by an analysis of the codes in light of this framework (section 8.2). Based on the theoretical perspective, the focus will be reversed with regard to the legal perspective, with the objective of identifying the appropriate rules and concepts in order to make visible the specific character of the codes in the course of determining the private law obligations (section 8.3).

8.1. CORPORATE CODES AS REGULATORY CONTRACTS AND COMMITMENTS

In order to identify a feasible link for discussing the codes' content and enforcement structure from the theoretical perspective, it is again considered a fruitful start to reveal the underlying perceptions in the current legal debate and identify their differences.

Focusing first on the interpretation of the corporate codes in contract law, one can identify at least a common denominator among the interpretation of the codes as sales law agreements and third party rights. The main starting point of both these suggestions is that the interpretation of the corporate codes has to take place in light of the intentions and expectations of the contracting parties. Scholars arguing for a product-related interpretation of the corporate codes refer to the autonomy of the parties to create their obligations as they wish and the changing intentions of consumers.[2] In a similar vein, proponents of an interpretation of the code as a third party contract approach the corporate codes in contracts from the intention of the parties.[3] Both thus discuss the corporate codes merely as an agreement between the contracting parties; however, their interpretation differs concerning the content of this agreement and thus the purpose that the contracting parties pursued with integrating the code. With regard to the interpretation of the corporate codes as part of the product specification, the corporate codes are interpreted as tools that relate to the characteristics and quality of the goods; the codes are thus frameworks that concretise the business deal between the company and its respective contracting partner and have merely the function of increasing the market value of the goods for sale. The proposal to interpret the corporate codes as terms that

[2] Wilhelmsson (2002/2003) 89: '[It is] obvious that parties can also *agree* on terms regarding the environmental properties' (emphasis added); Glinski (2007) 124: 'Contract law is based on the principle of party autonomy that allows the contracting parties to determine freely their mutual obligations according to their own needs.'

[3] See explicitly Heijden (2011b) 171: 'The consent and intention of the Transnational Corporation is therefore important as is the consent, i.e. the acceptance of the third person.' See also Vytopil (2012) 161f. The critical perspective on an interpretation of the codes as contractual third party rights refers in parts also to the intention of the contracting parties or better the lack thereof; see especially Estlund (2012) 255: 'The existing corporate codes were not *intended* to give rise to judicially enforceable duties' (emphasis added). That the third party right depends on the agreement seems to underlie the suggestion of Geis (2012) 1178: 'A firm could sign an agreement with B Lab, for example, committing to certain environmental standards (above legal minimums)—and designating that any adversely affected party (perhaps defined by some objective criteria) within say twenty miles of their facility could sue for breach as third party beneficiary … It remains debatable whether a firm is better off committing to a CSR policy, but the tools for a binding multilateral commitment are available.'

constitute a third party benefit for the affected beneficiaries interprets this purpose of the contracting parties differently. Here, the main question is whether the parties had the intention to benefit a large number of parties that are strangers to the contract. In one way or the other, however, it remains the underlying perception that the corporate codes in contracts remain mere bilateral agreements between two parties to which, comparable to other terms in the contracts, mandatory and default rules in contract law apply.

However, it is this understanding that currently seems to be challenged by a perspective on the codes that defines them as regulatory terms in contracts. Pursuant to this understanding, the corporate codes represent more than an orthodox contractual agreement that is interpreted with the help of the default rules on sales contracts or third party rights. Instead, the corporate policy and references to public codes of conduct introduce an entirely new dimension into the contract that signals the role of the contracting parties as regulators.[4] The corporate code, as introduced in contracts, then represents not merely an agreement to which the general rules on contract interpretation and the private law remedies apply, but rather points towards a new form of rights and duties that have the function of fulfilling this political role. In fact, this underlying objective of treating the corporate codes' terms in contracts as fulfilling the function of regulating and realising the companies' role as a political actor seems in part to be also implicitly shared by scholars who suggest an interpretation of corporate codes as contractual third party rights. In the course of discussing the potential interpretation of the corporate codes as agreed third party clauses, it is equally stated that the main consideration behind applying the rules on contractual third party rights is to give effect to another purpose. The interpretation of the codes as contractual third party rights is also explicitly assessed in light of the objective to further general human rights protection against global corporations,[5] to provide a new set of 'default rules for governing corporate activity'[6] or to create 'private causes of action in the same class of individuals who would gain protection under [a] statute'.[7] What can thus be observed is a tendency, in private law scholarship, to view the corporate codes not as ordinary contractual terms, but rather as novel agreements that fulfil a broader regulatory purpose. This regulatory purpose is identified here in the fact that companies specify as an obligation their globally applicable regulatory corporate codes that deal with public (social and environmental) standards;[8] the regulatory aspect is partly identified in the increasing reference to national labour law or

[4] See explicitly Cafaggi (2013) 1559: 'Transnational contracts are used to import and export regulations across countries, sometimes complementing, and in other times, replacing modes of implementation defined by international public regimes'; and Backer (2008) 512: An 'overarching set of regulatory norms is imposed uniformly as the foundation on which traditional individual contracts are entered into for the delivery of goods.'

[5] Heijden (2011b) 183: 'where human rights are integrated into a contract through the code, private contracting dodges the dominant view of international human rights law … International human rights law can be directly applied in horizontal relations through private contracting.'

[6] Geis (2012) 1777.

[7] Ayres and Brown (2006) 1641.

[8] Cafaggi (2013) 1559f: 'Public, private and regulatory regimes as they relate to social, environmental, and safety standards incorporated by reference into transnational contracts.'

environmental law, international public codes of conduct or even international law within the contractual agreement.[9] Hence, the current most pressing underlying debate concerning the interpretation of the corporate codes in contracts appears to be the character of this regulatory objective pursued by the contracting parties and the consequences for contract law enforcement based on the rules of contract law that require further scrutiny. The question on the character of the corporate codes as attempts to regulate proved to be important, though less prominently debated, when analysing non-contractual liability. In the context of tort law, their suggested regulatory character becomes apparent in the proposal to treat the corporate codes or public codes of conduct as regulatory standards that could assist when specifying negligent behaviour. In this sense, they could be interpreted as comparable to private regulatory standards in the area of technical standardisation. Moreover, in the analysis on unfair commercial practices law, the corporate codes and the public codes were discussed as potential regulatory standards that specify fair trading behaviour. In this context, the debate on their regulatory character was in particular subject to controversy in the German debate. In fact, within the debate, some contributions even discussed their proximity to an emerging international political consensus or a legal norm.[10] Here again, the tendencies are to view the corporate codes and the linking with public codes of conduct as elements of an emerging private regulation that fulfils functions similar to those of statutory regulation of states or international law.

Against this background, the following theoretical analysis will focus more in detail on the characteristics of this regulatory function that the companies fulfil with their codes and how they interact with the public codes of international politics. As a suitable theoretical framework to shed light onto this new regulatory role of private actors, the study will engage in a social theory analysis with a particular view to the recent contributions that focus on whether and, if so, how private actors are capable of fulfilling a genuine regulatory role in society comparable to political regulations. In the following theoretical analysis, this private form of political regulation will be described as an emerging substantive political objective that is made part of economic relations. To that end, based on an account of the political in society as presented in postmodern and post-foundational social theory, it is argued that this form of regulation needs to be conceptualised differently from the orthodox regulation by institutionalised politics. It is then this new form of political regulation that needs to be made a visible system of private law, in particular within the debate on public interests in private law, and subsequently translated into appropriate concepts in contract law and the rules on non-contractual liability.

8.2. POLITICAL REGULATION BY ECONOMIC RELATIONS

Due to their substantive focus on social and environmental standards, the corporate codes are an illustrative example of where an interest that is generally deemed

[9] Heijden (2011b) 183f.

[10] See especially Kocher (2005) 648ff.

to be public begins to influence private relations, thereby revealing that '"private" or "technical" initiatives can have "public" or "political" implications'.[11] Consequently, it comes as no surprise that in the social and political science literature, corporate codes are increasingly described as partaking in a general tendency by which private actors begin to take over the substantive responsibilities of the state and thus effectively qualify as political actors[12] or bring forward the claim that the codes are instances that are akin to political constitutions.[13] Using this general perception as a starting point, the following analysis will focus more specifically on this emerging orientation of private economic relations on political objectives in order to identify the specific regulatory role of companies and its relationship to state regulation. This will be done by analysing, from the perspective of economic sociology, how and under what conditions economic relations are capable of becoming oriented to objectives that are in the general interest of society, even if this contradicts their intrinsic motivation as economic actors and the functioning of the economy as based on self-interest (section 8.2.1). Subsequently, based on recent political theory in the tradition of social differentiation, the second section of the analysis seeks to shed light on the characteristics and functioning of this novel political objective. In so doing, the perception of self-committing companies and private contracting as political instances that are comparable to states or international politics is emphatically rejected. Instead, a different tendency towards politicisation is identified in the codes in the form of two novel political objectives that increasingly govern private relations (section 8.2.2).[14] Consequently, from the sociological perspective, a description of the corporate codes evolves, which views them as formally related to a private economic relationship, but substantively adding a double political structure to these relationships. They are, as suggested by the chapter heading, attempts by private actors to stabilise the institution of 'just business' in its truly double sense.[15]

8.2.1. Economic Sociology: Corporate Codes as Re-embedding Economic Relations

Focusing first on the question of how economic relations are, pursuant to the functioning of society, capable of fulfilling a political objective, it is particularly the area of economic sociology that is considered able to provide valuable inspiration.[16] This is due to the fact that this strand focuses specifically on the functioning of

[11] Wood (2005) 268.

[12] See undamentally Cutler, Haufler and Porter (1999); Haufler (2001); Ruggie (2004).

[13] See especially Backer (2007); Backer (2008); Anderson (2010); Anderson (2013); Teubner (2011); Teubner (2012). *cf* also the contributions in Teubner and Beckers (2013b).

[14] For a similar understanding of theorising particularly corporate codes of conduct as an autonomous form of public regulation rather than a substitute for state-based regulation, see Bartley (2005) 232: 'avoid the assumption that private regulation is a substitute for public regulation and instead theorize the more complex emerging combinations of public and private accountability'.

[15] Inspired by the astute title of Ruggie (2013).

[16] For the use of Polanyi's theory when debating the evolving political role of private actors, see Levy and Kaplan (2008); Anderson (2010); Teubner (2012) 27, 78ff with further references.

economic relations, but nevertheless attempts to relate the functioning and objectives of these relations to society at large. In particular, the notion of the 'embeddedness of markets' can be read as an attempt to describe the economy as a sphere of society that never actually functioned entirely autonomously, but at all times remained linked to a broader societal objective. In this regard, specific use can be made of the seminal work of Polanyi, who provided a core theoretical framework for analysing the changing relationship between markets and society in the course of modernisation. To Polanyi, the process of modernisation has led to an increasing disintegration of the economy from society, which, due to its instability, is however likely to produce a counter-movement that leads to a re-embedding of the highly disintegrated market into social relations. Applying this idea to the corporate codes may help in understanding their substance more accurately. They may be the result of a particular counter-movement that rests mainly on civil society and internal market pressures and, as such, becomes a way whereby the market economy is re-embedded within the overall society. The following section seeks to analyse this development of embedding social relations, with respect to the corporate codes, by first introducing the key theoretical terms and concepts of how economic relations can be embedded, which is followed by a discussion on how the process of embedding economic relations took place with regard to the codes and finishing with the discussion of whether, against the background of still important economic objectives underlying the codes, an embeddedness could be successful.

8.2.1.1. The 'Embeddedness' of Markets in Society

When applying the theory of the embeddedness of economic relations to the corporate codes, it is first of all necessary to understand the notion of the embeddedness of markets. The sociological notion of 'embeddedness' can be read as an account criticising the underlying assumption in neoclassical economics that markets are per se and exclusively determined by economic mechanisms (price, demand and supply). On the contrary, Polanyi argued that markets and market behaviour were always embedded in a broader society that profoundly shaped these very economic practices. That being said, the degree of embeddedness is considered to have changed quite remarkably in the course of modernisation. Within pre-modern societies, the social bonds determining market behaviour were remarkably strong, eg:

> [M]an's economy, as a rule, is submerged in his social relationships. He does not so as to safeguard his individual interest in the possession of material goods; he acts so as to safeguard his social standing, his social claims, his social assets. He values material goods only in so far as they serve this end ... These interests will be very different in a small hunting or fishing community from those in a vast despotic society, but in either case the economic system will run on noneconomic motives.[17]

[17] Polanyi (2001 [1944]) 48.

Thus, it is the neoliberal idea of economy as a system functioning entirely autonomously on the basis of the medium of money and with the mechanism of price that is ridiculed by instead showing 'how sharply this concept differs from the reality of human societies throughout recorded human history. Before the nineteenth century … the human economy was always embedded in society'.[18] Accordingly, markets and market relations could be read as implicitly containing broader social objectives and, to use Polanyi's expression, 'the self-regulating market was unknown'.[19] Yet, in the transformation process from a pre-modern to a modern society, Polanyi postulates that this relationship between the economy and society changed quite profoundly. The strong social bonds were softened with the eventual result of a highly disembedded economy in the form of the self-regulatory capital market. Polanyi identifies this fundamental change within the transformation of productive organisation, nature and man as former parts of society into the fictitious commodities of money, land and labour, which became subordinated under the laws of the market.[20] With respect to this observation, his analysis still seems to coincide with other theoretical accounts in general sociology that describe the process of modernisation as a development towards the differentiation of social life into different rationalities and thus the evolution of an autonomous economic system that operates autonomously and self-referentially. It equally reveals itself in the famous description of modernity as a process of rationalisation in which social communities transformed into rational societies[21] and the functional differentiation of society.[22]

Despite this ever-increasing tendency towards a self-regulatory market functioning exclusively along autonomous patterns, Polanyi also emphasised that there is no way for this disintegration to be maintained stably. On the contrary, such a self-regulatory market 'is a dangerous utopian myth' that results in immense costs for society and the environment.[23] As two observers frame it: 'According to Polanyi, economic actions become destructive when they are "disembedded", or not governed by social or noneconomic authorities.'[24] The modern capitalist system of the self-governing market, oriented on self-interest, is consequently unstable and highly unnatural.[25] In fact, markets never worked stably without an overarching social structure[26] and thus this social structure may produce a counter-movement,

[18] ibid, Introduction by Fred Block, xxiii.

[19] ibid 71.

[20] ibid 71ff.

[21] Weber (1968).

[22] See fundamentally Durkheim (1964); and Luhmann (1982). The similarities between Luhmann and Polanyi in relation to their analysis of the self-regulating market are also emphasised by Joerges (2011) 470f, who mentions in this context also the similarities to Juergen Habermas' distinction between system and lifeworld.

[23] Levy and Kaplan (2008) 443.

[24] Swedberg and Smelser (2005) 13.

[25] Polanyi (2001 [1944]) 257: 'The true criticism of market society is not that it was based on economics … but that its economy was based on self-interest. Such an organization of economic life is entirely unnatural, in the strictly empirical sense of *exceptional*' (emphasis in original).

[26] On social relationships as a structure that constantly influences economic relationships, see fundamentally Granovetter (1985).

which, in the end, may result in the re-embedding of markets into society.[27] Thus, according to Polanyi, the relationship between the economy and society has to be described as 'a dynamic process between embedding, disembedding and reembedding'.[28] Assuming that is possible, if not even likely, that the self-regulatory market becomes re-embedded into society by integrating broader non-economic objectives, it remains to be discussed when and how such a process of re-embedding may occur. How, under the conditions of a global and fragmented society, can such a counter-movement take place? Who can initiate this movement? And what could be the results? Polanyi, given the historical setting of his writings, has left open the exact form and drivers of this re-embedding,[29] which gave rise to manifold possible interpretations about the counter-movement and the eventual re-embedding. While there clearly seems to be no realistic possibility of returning to a pre-modern society with strong interpersonal social bonds,[30] one often-discussed driver for the re-embedding is the state in the form of political intervention.[31] When it comes to the corporate codes as a potential element of re-embedded markets, however, this state-centred focus seems not to fit entirely. Taking into consideration the role of the state as a driver towards deregulation and liberalisation, and its strategy of facilitating and incentivising private initiatives towards CSR rather than regulating the responsibilities of companies, it can be questioned whether the state does in fact represent the central component in the counter-movement with regard to CSR aspects. As Levy and Kaplan put it: 'Where CSR differs most sharply from historical efforts to restrain markets is in its reliance on the private realm rather than the state.'[32]

Against this background, it is worth transcending the debate on what contributions the state can make externally in order for a re-embedding of markets to occur and focus on the manifold other social practices that could be relevant as a productive counter-movement. With regard to the corporate codes, particular attention needs to be paid to consumers, investors, competitors and civil society as the driving force. Accordingly, it needs to be discussed whether and, if so, how these social pressures are actually capable of initiating a counter-movement and, if

[27] Polanyi (2001 [1944]) 136: 'Yet simultaneously a countermovement was on foot.' And later at 257: 'After a century of blind "improvement" man is restoring his "habitation". If industrialism is not to extinguish the race, it must be subordinated to the requirements of man's nature.'

[28] Beckert (2007) 19.

[29] Polanyi (2001 [1944]) 259: 'Within the nations we are witnessing a development under which the economic system ceases to lay down the law to society and the primacy of society over that system is secured. This may happen in a great variety of ways, democratic and aristocratic, constitutionalist and authoritarian, perhaps even in a fashion yet utterly unforeseen.'

[30] See pointedly Joerges (2011) 472: 'How likely is it, however, that the *émigré* Polanyi, writing after the breakdown of the liberal world economy and confronted with the rise of Fascism, National Socialism and Bolshevism, should have envisaged a return to some cosy pre-modern world.' See also Stehr (2007) 64: 'Allerdings ist kaum zu erwarten, dass alle von Polanyi beschriebenen Merkmale vormarktlicher Sozialbeziehungen eine Neuauflage in modernen Gesellschaften erfahren warden.'

[31] Beckert (2007) 17: 'The "double movement" is not an automatic response to the devastating effects of self-regulating markets but rather the result of political intervention in markets in the light of their social consequences. The "re-embedding" advocated by Polanyi implied a substantial political authority over the economy as a result of political and social engagement.'

[32] Levy and Kaplan (2008) 444.

so, whether the corporate codes can, against this background, be described as the consequence of such a counter-movement in the form of a genuine re-orientation of the economy towards non-economic objectives.

8.2.1.2. Civil Society and Market Pressure as Counter-movements

Could the external pressure of civil society and the internal pressure from the market have amounted to a productive counter-movement that is sufficiently strong to further a re-embedding of the markets? As far as the role of civil society is concerned, it is possible to make use of the rich theoretical debate on the influence of social movements and NGOs. The literature has already provided manifold evidence on their role as instances that were at the forefront when it came to criticising the self-regulating market and revealing its destructive tendencies.[33] Against this background, it is no coincidence that the notion of the counter-movement has become particularly attractive for describing global protest movements and NGOs in their attempts to contest the current globalised as a liberalised and self-regulating market. Although civil society in the form of NGOs and protest movements does indeed represent an important aspect, it is certainly not the only relevant component.

In addition, an emphasis in the literature is also put on the role of the market as a potential factor in the counter-movement, particularly the role of consumers and investors.[34] The potential of market actors to become a collective counter-movement that contests the self-regulating market is, however, more difficult to conceive, against the background that market actors are perceived to act as self-interested individuals rather than an organised movement with a common objective. Therefore, this part of the counter-movement deserves further scrutiny. Among the theories grasping these new market pressures equally as a counter-movement, one sophisticated attempt can be found in the theory of 'moralised markets'.[35] The theoretical description is based on the observation that, on the self-regulating market, a novel development currently takes place. Consumers and investors, formerly characterised as profit-seeking actors, begin to use 'moral', eg, non-economic objectives as a benchmark.[36] Among the many different

[33] See, among others, Backer (2007) 1756ff; Levy and Kaplan (2008) 443ff; Amstutz (2009) 27; Anderson (2010); Anderson (2013); See also Munck (2006) 176: 'It is not some far-out adventure, tilting at windmills as it were, but "swimming with the current" when the various elements of the counter-globalization movement engage in its contestation. Protests against environmental degradation, the hypocrisy of "free-trade" policies, or workplace closures may find a unifying thread in Polanyi's "double movement", whereby society resists its dissolution by a self-regulating market.'

[34] See, eg, Levy and Kaplan (2008) 444; Amstutz (2009) 26f; Teubner (2012) 95f; and recently Collins (2014) 628f.

[35] Stehr, Henning and Weiler (2006b); Stehr (2007).

[36] In the theoretical account of moralised markets, one important explanation of this shift is seen in the change of the structure of consumption in Western countries where 'pure needs', such as food, clothing or shelter, are easily accessible and more affordable, which allows consumers to also pay attention to 'cultural needs'; see Stehr, Henning and Weiler (2006a) 10f. For empirical evidence on this increasing relevance of non-economic objectives in consumer purchase decisions with differentiated perspectives on how far they actually crowd out the criterion of price, see Schoenheit (2014) 43ff and the references provided by Collins (2014) 629.

non-economic values, it is particularly the natural environment that obtains a place within the economy beyond being merely a production factor or a fictitious commodity. It is the natural environment as such that seems to count on the market.[37] But the debate on Genetically Modified Products or the social standards of those producing the goods also seems to become important for consumers and investors in their purchasing decisions. This change has been brought about by the transformation of the demand structure based on the assumption that production and consumption are not merely economic transactions, but are also culturally shaped practices.[38]

Concerning the potential of this cultural practice of consumption to become a collective counter-movement, it is held that these novel consumer movements in fact indicate a new form of collectivism. They by no means represent a genuine collective cooperation between market actors; instead, they are based on what Granovetter once described as the strengths of weak ties.[39] Because boycotts against corporations are not built around common and stable membership, they are more easily accessible and thus provide a mechanism in line with the 'ethos of individualism' in modern (market) societies.[40] Despite the large number of self-interested consumers that are still considered to orientate their decision on price and quality, this counter-movement is interpreted as being led by a small group of conscious consumers and investors that understand their daily choices as broader political choices and that are often engaged in alternative forms of trading.[41] Once, however, these very few conscious consumers have become a critical mass, options for socially or environmentally friendly consumption become available on a broader scale. Removing the barriers can then induce a broader range of other consumers to choose socially responsible products, with the eventual result that this form of consumerism may become part of the mainstream and thus shape the general expectations on the market.[42] This emphasises that the internal pressure based on consumption does not even necessarily need to evolve as an explicit collective political objective. It merely requires environmental and social consumption patterns to have become sufficiently institutionalised on the market. Following these insights, it can indeed become possible that, even within the market, and although based on individual interests, a counter-movement can evolve once a sufficiently critical mass has engaged in such social and environmental consumption patterns. Notwithstanding its importance, it is, however, also important to note the inherent limits of this form of counter-movement. Since this form of counter-movement

[37] Stehr (2007) 164f.

[38] ibid 66ff. *cf* also the illustration on consumption as cultural practice in Everson and Joerges (2006) 1: 'A simple "buy British campaign", for example, entails a complex combination of social, political and economic impulses: an appeal (successful or otherwise) to sentiments of "national community", a political desire to maintain the national manufacturing base, as well as a co-ordinated economic effort to satisfy "national" consumption demands within "national" production and marketing systems.'

[39] Granovetter (1973).

[40] Stehr, Henning and Weiler (2006a) 9f.

[41] See especially Stehr (2007) 64ff, who describes this small number of market actors, such as producers, consumers and investors within specific sectors or classes, as 'agents' for a moralisation of markets. See also, but with a more critical view, Wheeler (2012) 6f.

[42] The importance of this distinction is highlighted by Wheeler (2012) 7.

employs the market transaction as a way of contesting the market logic, it is primarily effective towards companies and sectors that produce in particular for the end-user and consumer market. Accordingly, any potential re-embedding of economic relations is prone to suffer from an uneven participation across sectors. Depending on the brand vulnerability of the companies, the process of re-embedding might, at least at an initial stage, be limited to specific industry sectors within the economy.[43]

Finally, in addition to the external pressures by civil society and the internal pressures from consumers and investors with their purchase decisions, one can also mention other elements in the literature that have been analysed as putting pressure on companies. In this context, one can mention the works of Gunningham who investigates the importance of the pressure from other actors in the same industry.[44] Noteworthy is also the threat by the political system to impose regulation and the threat of legal liability.[45] In this regard, legal liability can again be traced back to the role of NGOs and social movements, which do not only use the form of protest and campaign but also seek to employ the pressure of the law in the form of initiating lawsuits for socially irresponsible behaviour and in the form of campaigning for stronger regulation.[46]

8.2.1.3. The Process of Re-embedding

Following the understanding of civil society and different forms of market pressure as aspects of a broader counter-movement, is it accordingly possible to describe the corporate codes not only as a response to these pressures, but to go further and define them also as a development in which the broader social orientation of economic relations becomes effectively institutionalised? In the CSR literature, this is one of the possible interpretations. As Teubner puts it: 'Corporate codes partake in this second wave when they restrict corporate activities in the name of public responsibility. They try both to overcome the primacy of shareholder value in favour of a stakeholder-orientation as well as to realise self-restraint in the areas of labour, product quality, environment, and human rights.'[47] Having said that, one could also take a more critical perspective; rather than being a successful result of this counter-movement that furthers re-embedding, the corporate codes could also be read as a strategy of companies to avoid a re-embedding by designing the private codes merely as a means to their profitability. As Levi and Kaplan frame the core critique: 'Crucially, CSR does not compromise the fundamentals of the market

43 Jenkins (2001) 28; McBarnet and Kurkchiyan (2007) 83.

44 Gunningham and Rees (1997) 376ff, 391. In later works, this important form of internal pressure is framed as a collective licence to operate; see Gunningham (2007) 487ff.

45 Teubner (2012) 93 and Teubner and Beckers (2013a) 531ff.

46 On this relationship between social movements and legal liability in relation particularly to CSR, see extensively Rodríguez-Garavito (2005) (instructively at 67: 'Transnational Advocacy Networks simultaneously engage in efforts to bolster national states' regulatory capacity, create effective global corporate codes of conduct for labor and promote direct action campaigns to boycott the products of targeted TNCs at the regional level'); McBarnet (2007) 38f.

47 Teubner (2011) 23.

system; indeed, it proclaims harmony of financial and social interests.'[48] The criticism is closely related here to the debate in microeconomics on voluntary CSR efforts of companies, which partly suggests that including non-economic public objectives into economic relations is not a genuine matter of pursuing social interests, but remains primarily a tool to serve the long-term profitability of a company.[49] This understanding of the corporate codes would imply that the efforts of companies to be socially responsible would be approached in the first place as an attempt to be profitable and economically sustainable rather than truly an attempt to become oriented to a social objective. If, consequently, a code of conduct is considered solely as a tool to increase profits, how is it possible at all to understand the corporate codes as a serious attempt of a company to incorporate a non-economic logic and become oriented to social rather than economic objectives? Is it not, conversely, more appropriate against this background to see the corporate codes as additional proof that 'instead of the economy being embedded in social relations, social relations are embedded in the economic system'?[50] Do these novel non-economic objectives as pursued by companies, from the perspective of economic sociology, remain entirely subordinated under the rationality of the market?

A closer look at the underlying economic argument seems, however, to question this radical perception. Although strategic and financial motivations are indeed among the core internal motives that induce companies to adopt a corporate code and shape the content of the code,[51] one can also identify in the debate evidence suggesting that profitability arguments can, in part but not entirely, explain why these codes have become such a far-reaching development in different sectors. It is also partly doubted in economics whether there is in fact a positive correlation between social and financial performance.[52] In this regard, one can refer to the works of Vogel, who can be considered one of the most influential scholars investigating the 'business case' of CSR. In his investigations, Vogel emphasises that, despite potential economic benefits of adapting voluntary CSR policies, there are limits to the economic argument.[53] The actual demand of market actors can only be used as an economic argument in narrow and niche segments where the social and environmental performance can amount to a monetary value. Yet, in the form of an all-encompassing general observation, the economic argument does not always function.[54] This, however, does not imply that corporate codes would qualify as a

[48] Levy and Kaplan (2008) 444.

[49] For the debate in microeconomics on the profitability of CSR and the discussion on a 'business case' for CSR, *cf* prominently Vogel (2005); Carroll and Shabana (2010); Porter and Kramer (2011). The understanding of CSR as creating value in terms of profits as well as social goals also seems inherent in the definition of the EU Commission in its newest strategy. See European Commission, A Renewed EU Strategy 2011–14 for Corporate Social Responsibility, COM(2011) 681 final 6: CSR is about 'maximizing the creation of shared value for their owners/shareholders and for their other stakeholders and society at large'.

[50] Polanyi (2001 [1944]) 57.

[51] See section 7.2.2.1. (p 248), text and accompanying footnotes.

[52] For an overview of the debate with further references to various studies that emphasise a positive correlation between social and financial performance as well as those identifying no relationship or even a negative relationship, see Griffin and Mahon (1997) 5ff. See on this point also Jackson (2014) 25ff.

[53] Vogel (2005) 45: 'little support for the claim that more responsible firms are more profitable'.

[54] ibid, ch 4.

new morality on the market that companies adopt. A description of the corporate strategies in the field of CSR that is considered more appropriate is, in fact, offered from the sociological perspective that describes voluntary corporate codes as strategic responses of companies between narrow profitability and broader morality.[55] Corporate codes have to be interpreted accordingly as strategic reactions to internalise the institutionalised social expectations,[56] a strategy that is important for companies in order to legitimise themselves within the broader society.[57] Such strategies become particularly important in situations of uncertainty, as is the case in relation to the new expectations concerning adherence to social and environmental standards.[58] It is this partial weakness of the profitability argument and the sociological understanding of corporate codes as a strategic orientation of companies towards institutionalised social expectations in situations of uncertainty that makes it possible to describe the corporate codes as an evolving orientation of economic relations on a social objective and not merely as a means whereby broader social objectives are instrumentalised for economic purposes.

8.2.1.4. Conclusion

Based on this description, it can already be concluded that the corporate codes remain *formally* linked to economic relations, but they represent attempts to connect these economic relations *substantively* with social objectives. That being said, the notion of the embeddedness of markets has one central limit. By describing the process of re-embedding as the connection between economic relations and social objectives, it was not yet possible to describe accurately the actual content of this 'other' normative frame of reference as genuinely political. More specifically, what makes this new embedding of markets akin to the regulation by politics? In order to be able to answer this question, the following section will consult social and political theory that describes the characteristics and functioning of the politics within society under the conditions of a differentiated world society and, on this basis, attempts to explain the understanding of the corporate codes as two autonomous forms in which political rationality is integrated into economic relations.

8.2.2. Social Differentiation: The Political Difference in Corporate Codes

In order to identify more accurately the substance of this newly introduced non-economic objective within the context of economic practices, the concept of economic

[55] Hiß (2005) 94ff.

[56] ibid 16f, 125ff.

[57] ibid 17: 'Organisationen legitimieren sich, indem sie die von der gesellschaftlichen Umwelt an sie herangetragenen institutionalisierten Regeln, die die Funktion von Mythen übernehmen, in ihre Formalstrukturen integrieren.' And at 139: 'Unternehmen implementieren dieser Logik folgend freiwillig Sozialstandards in ihre Wertschöpfungskette, erlegen sich Verhaltenskodizes auf oder schaffen Öffentlichkeitsarbeitsabteilung nur für das Thema CSR, um sich gegenüber ihrer institutionellen Umwelt beziehungsweise ihrem organisatorischen Feld legitimieren zu können und damit einen Ressourcenfluus zu generieren.'

[58] ibid 18, 196ff, 308f.

sociology has to be related to the insights deriving from a general theory of society. In line with the general assumption that characterises this theoretical inquiry, the process of embedding will be discussed from the theoretical perspective on society as a functionally differentiated society.

8.2.2.1. Political Regulation Under Conditions of Social Differentiation

From the perspective of the organisation of society at large that has a tendency towards functional differentiation, this process of 're-embedding economic relations into society' has to be understood as a difficult process given that there is no uniform and overarching societal objective within society. Systems Theory, as an influential description of a differentiated society, identifies as a core aspect of modern societies that they consist of operationally closed systems that have each evolved due to the need to fulfil a specific function.[59] Thus, 'the key attribute of modern society is its composition through the differentiation of social functions'.[60] A core reason for the evolution of differentiation is the ever-increasing complexity within modern society. As modern society has increased in complexity and thus has become increasingly confusing (*unübersichtlich*), a societal need has evolved to develop mechanisms that are capable of reducing this complexity. As pointedly phrased by an observer, 'the world is too complicated for people to understand. Therefore, they must establish collective sense-orientation through which they interpret and simplify the world'.[61] These 'collective sense-orientations' are the evolved 'codes' that each system has established in the course of beginning to fulfil a specific social function that society is in need of. By means of establishing a code through which each system observes its social environment, the system reduces social complexity; it 'simplifies' the world. In the course of this process, however, each system creates and maintains internal complexity. Having the aim of providing a general theory of society, Systems Theory, as developed by Luhmann, has conducted manifold studies on the various systems within modern society about their evolution, their internal organisation, code-orientation and social function. The law, politics, economy, science, morals or arts are different examples of evolved social systems in a functionally differentiated society.

In light of the impossibility of reversing this functional differentiation of society into autonomous sub-systems once it has commenced, a process of re-embedding can explicitly not be thought of as a process whereby economic relations apply system rationality in a different way from economic rationality. The economy, like other social systems, has rather become irrevocably differentiated and thus has been organised around its own code, and has developed money as its core medium.[62] Under these conditions, the corporate codes can only be thought of as an instance by which the economy as a closed system establishes a stable connection

[59] Luhmann (1977) 36ff.
[60] Thornhill (2000) 175.
[61] ibid 177.
[62] Luhmann (1988a) 52ff (focusing on the process of differentiation of the economy) and 344 (emphasising the irrevocability of this differentiation).

to another social system, which allows the different rationality to be reflected within its own rationality.[63] As has become apparent above, the corporate codes have been described as a reaction of companies to accommodate the claims by various social forces and, for that matter, reflect the values that have been put on the agenda as being in the interests of society at large. In the understanding of a socially differentiated system, the communication on matters that are deemed to be of common interest has been described as an elementary part of the political system. The political system has evolved as a reaction to the need within society to produce collectively binding decisions in the public interest.[64] The political system fulfils this function by internally anticipating and reflecting upon those problems that are presented by the social environment as being of general social interest and transforming them into collectively binding decisions.[65] The main factor that legitimises the decisions of the political system as collectively binding is the formalised procedure.[66] Hence, when an interest is 'put on the agenda', the political system is able to transform it within a formalised procedure in a decision that is accepted as collectively binding and, in so doing, stabilises what is considered to be in the public interest. The fact that the corporate codes reflect values that external pressures have put on the agenda as being in the collective interest suggests characterising the corporate codes of conduct as instances that link the economy with politics. More concretely, by means of including the corporate codes in economic relations and rendering them binding in the form of contracts or self-commitments, it can be argued that corporations translate what social pressures have expressed as being of general social relevance into a collectively binding decision.

That being said, this interpretation is based on one assumption that deserves further scrutiny. The corporate codes can only represent a connection to the political system under the condition that the interaction of these social pressures with corporations can be described as part of the political system. The following section will discuss this aspect in more detail (section 8.2.2.2.1), but it will eventually argue that there still remain crucial differences between the functioning of politics and the social pressures to which the corporate codes are reactions. Instead, an evolving connection within the corporate codes to the political system is primarily identified in the tendency of companies to integrate and render binding the political objectives offered by the institutionalised national and international political system by means of reference (section 8.2.2.2.2). With regard to the character of the corporate codes as direct responses to social pressures, it will be argued that these social pressures and their interaction with the corporate codes represent the result

[63] In Systems Theory terms, these connections are described as 'structural couplings': Luhmann (2004) 381ff.

[64] Luhmann (2000) 84: 'dann bleibt die Möglichkeit, auf das *Bereithalten der Kapazität zu kollektiv bindendem Entscheiden* abzustellen' (emphasis in original).

[65] Luhmann (1982) 14: 'by this process of differentiation and the conditions favouring high autonomy within the system, the political system is put in the position of *being able to make decisions*. The specific function of politics is fulfilled at the level of concrete interaction because these decisions are made *binding*'. And later at 146: 'A political system that has been differentiated from the rest of society can no longer bind itself in those areas. It must be able to vary the issues it decides upon, depending on which problems the society places on the political agenda' (emphasis in original).

[66] Luhmann (1983) 137ff.

of a different form of the political as the ultimate basis of society that functions differently from politics (section 8.2.2.3).

8.2.2.2. Corporate Codes and Politics

8.2.2.2.1. Linking the Economy and Politics Through Corporate Codes?

In the literature on the corporate codes, the understanding of the actors drafting the codes as being new political actors has, in this regard, become quite a prominent discussion in the debate. With regard to the supporting arguments, several aspects can be pointed out. First, one can refer to the fact that the interactions between social pressures and corporations are characterised by an *application of the code* and the use of the *medium* of politics. Following this idea, it is mainly the use of power against large companies with the claims for social responsibility, as well as the large power of companies to implement these claims within their global operation and to influence local communities that are referred to. A second argument relates to the *function* that is fulfilled by this interaction between companies and social pressures. If 'transnational political processes are *functionally-delineated* processes'[67] that maintain a sufficient internal complexity, it is in principle possible that this function is equally fulfilled by actors other than the state or an international political organisation.

As to the first aspect, one can argue that the corporate codes represent a form of political regulation due to the factual power present in the interaction of social pressures and the companies that have brought them about. In so doing, this social interaction is effectively characterised by the use of the core medium of the political system. Here, it is mainly the combination of the factual power of large corporations that puts them in the position of making collectively binding decisions and the counter-power of civil society actors, eg, NGOs, consumer pressure and the media, that is relevant.[68] Concerning the latter, NGOs can primarily help to shape 'community consensus on appropriate corporate behaviour' through 'persuasion, lobbying and litigation'.[69] Consumers, investors and the financial market can determine the access to and success on the financial market, which gives them a powerful rule to influence corporate strategies profoundly towards a political objective. Consumers have the 'global power of refusal'.[70] However, while the factual power of companies is certainly an important criterion to bring about these new social and environmental objectives and make them work, it is considered an incomplete criterion to assign private actors a role comparable to the political system. The main reason is that the sheer existence of power is not capable of rendering a social structure a part of the political system. There remains a crucial

[67] Kjaer (2011) 315 (emphasis added). See also Beck (2005) 75: 'Consequently, transnational companies become private sector quasi-states, which on the one hand make collectively binding decisions, and on the other mutate into fictitious decision-makers and virtual organizations.'

[68] Backer (2007) 1751ff.

[69] ibid 1756f.

[70] Beck (2005) 237.

difference between power as a social phenomenon and the specific power as a medium of the political system.[71] Power is only the medium of the political system in case it becomes the system-building instance, eg, when power is institutionalised and differentiated as a politically legitimised power,[72] which does not seem to be the case yet with respect to the private actors at stake.[73] Consequently, the use of the medium of power alone does not seem to be a sufficient reason for assigning these social pressures the role of the political system in society, but additional reasons are required. This leads to the political function as the second criterion that is currently discussed. Does the interaction between companies, consumers, investors and civil society represent the new political actors on the ground making this interaction already fulfil the function of politics?

Focusing on the criterion of the function of the system of politics, Kjaer has argued that non-state actors can indeed take over the function of politics.[74] More concretely, he identifies three constellations already today in which the political function is fulfilled by non-state institutions. While the first constellation relates to international political organisations, such as the IMF or the WTO, the two other categories are of importance here. To him, global political processes may occur within the private sphere when private organisations begin to incorporate public and private elements. As an example, he refers to complex supply chains, which are, as such, economic relations that are firmly embedded in the economic system, but, nevertheless, increasingly include elements of collective self-regulation, such as certification programmes and the programmes of private standardisation bodies that also include public actors. It is this latter constellation that indicates an evolving, yet still subordinated, 'political quality to the extent that the social orders that they constitute remain contested'.[75] Finally, Kjaer defines CSR as such as an 'in-between' structure between functionally differentiated spheres that are influenced by private and public actors and that 'tend to act as the no-man's land in which different normative orders collide because different spheres of meaning (*Sinnwelten*) are colliding'.[76] Although, within this approach, the political function in the private sphere is mainly discussed here in relation to collective certification programmes rather than unilateral codes of conduct of companies,[77] one could also

[71] Luhmann (2000) 69: 'Erst durch Ausdifferenzierung eines politischen Systems wird Macht politische Macht. Macht kann sehr wohl parasitär durch Ausnutzung von Drohchancen in wohl allen sozialen Systemen von einiger Dauer gebildet und genutzt werden. Aber das geschieht dann nur okkasionell und gebunden an das Interesse an Fortsetzung des Systems.'

[72] ibid 73: 'Die Ausdifferenzierung eines machtbasierten, zentralisierten, hierarchiebildenden, politischen Systems setzt voraus, daß Macht selbst zum Fokus der Systembildung wird. Das geschieht im Prinzip durch die Einrichtung von politischen Ämtern mit der Folge daß politischer Machtgebrauch von anderen Formen sozialer Pression und stillschweigender Rücksichtnahme unterschieden werden kann.'

[73] Concerning the political character of NGOs, Beck (2005) 240ff therefore pointedly describes NGOs as having the capital of potential legitimacy as credible institutions, but he seems reluctant to describe them as the legitimised representatives of the private sphere.

[74] Kjaer (2011) 313 phrases this as 'the immanent existence of regulatory structures which produce functional equivalents to political decision-making in the nation-state.'

[75] ibid 315.

[76] ibid.

[77] Kjaer (2013) 799ff.

apply this concept to the corporate codes. Accordingly, corporate codes could be interpreted as such as a 'no-man's land' where the economic system, in the form of a binding contract or a commitment to the market, is linked to the political system in the form of subjecting it to a political objective. The main argument in favour of treating private regulation as genuinely political represents here the reliance of private arrangements on structures that are functionally equivalent to the political system. It is the 'nation', 'public sphere', 'representation' and 'delegation', as the infrastructure of the political system that now appear in the form of functional equivalents, such as the 'stakeholder', 'transparency', 'self-representation' and 'accountability'.[78] This theoretical description of the private sphere as functionally equivalent to politics is, albeit with conceptual differences, shared by other scholars. Smits, for instance, states that since the core functions of democratic politics, namely participation, accountability and transparency, cannot be fulfilled on a global level by parliaments, elections and governmental transparency, private actors may become important in filling this gap.[79] In the course of analysing the equivalents of this privately created system of politics, he also refers to the corporate codes of companies as one potential component that functions comparably to politics.[80] To him, this political component rests upon whether the main functions of political democracy—participation, accountability and transparency—are fulfilled within the private sphere.[81] Following this understanding, the corporate codes could become a new form of political regulation if they are based on the sufficient participation of the affected groups, if they safeguard a certain form of accountability and if they have in place sufficient transparency mechanisms. A functional understanding of political rationality also transpires from the approach taken by MacDonald and MacDonald, who postulate an emerging form of non-electoral accountability in global politics as functional substitutes for democratic elections with particular respect to the consumers and NGO pressures against the corporate practices in the garment industry that bring about corporate codes.[82] The corporate codes, as results of this pressure, are described as formalised frameworks that delineate the roles, identities and responsibilities of the corporations as global political actors.[83] The main conditions for treating corporate codes as a result of a genuine political processes are again transparency in terms of actual factory operations and the internal decision making with respect to the content of the codes, monitoring and remedies, in order to reveal to affected stakeholders the identity of the holders of power and the characteristics of the political action,[84]

[78] Kjaer (2011) 316ff. In a similar direction, see MacDonald and MacDonald (2006) 94: 'We can thus conceptualize the principals in democratic accountability relationships as "stakeholder" communities, whereby democratic "stakeholders" are defined as those individuals affected (in ways that implicate democratic values of autonomy and equality) by the responsible exercise of political power.'

[79] Smits (2008) 30ff.

[80] ibid 29.

[81] ibid 32ff.

[82] MacDonald and MacDonald (2006).

[83] ibid 107.

[84] MacDonald and MacDonald (ibid 105ff) define this as the 'Transparent Political Role Delineation' and the 'Transparent Public Political Action'.

and to allow the possibility of a 'delegitimisation' of these power holders, which is currently most viable in the form of consumer and NGO pressure.[85]

Despite the differences in detail, one can thus identify a common thread in different contributions on the corporate codes that describe them as a substitute for political decision making based on the presence of an infrastructure that is functionally equivalent to the infrastructure in politics. As a result, it is to the extent that the drafting and publication of the corporate codes follow these criteria that these private regulatory initiatives become comparable to the functioning of politics and thus akin to political regulation.

8.2.2.2.2. Against the Functional Understanding of Politics

Such far-reaching suggestions on a fundamental transformation of the system of politics on a global level naturally did not remain uncontested within the debate. On the contrary, in the theoretical debate, one can also identify critical voices that question the possibility of reducing the complex organisation of the system of politics into a small set of functions and thereby ignore the national and historical embedding of the system in the nation state. To quote just one pointed critique:

> Politics applied at the national or at a local level may refer to common historical, social, normative and cultural frameworks. This may not always produce rational or coherent decisions, but there will be a common notion of the pre-conditions for the decision-making which may contribute to a conceived legitimacy. At the international and transnational levels, political communication will have to deal with a qualitatively more heterogeneous social and communicative context … Formulating legal norms and political treaties or decisions in such highly heterogeneous environments is extremely risky both in terms of being correctly understood and in terms of legitimacy and acceptance. The question is whether politics is possible under highly-heterogeneous conditions, or whether a new type of the political emerges.[86]

To my understanding, there are indeed convincing arguments against reducing the understanding of politics to a focus on its function, as the criterion of function seems to be at the same time over- and under-inclusive.[87] It is over-inclusive insofar as it would include many institutions that fulfil functions similar to politics, but they would not qualify as political because they do not deal with interests deemed to be collective. At the same time and more importantly, the strict functional approach seems under-inclusive as it characterises politics solely along a small set of functions and ignores the fact that, after having evolved around fulfilling this specific function, the political system, like all other systems, has produced an immense internal complexity with different components that are relevant in

[85] ibid 112ff. With respect to this aspect, the authors, however, still argue that a more convincing and effective form of delegitimisation would be to allow the directly affected stakeholders to hold the companies accountable for damages suffered on the basis of tort, contract and liability law (at 117).

[86] Sand (2011) 326.

[87] *cf* for this critique on the functional perspective, yet with a view not to politics but to law, Ellis (2012) 316.

order to fulfil this function; the political system consists of political programmes, parties, elections, legislation and administration. It is this immense complexity of politics as an evolved social system that also led Luhmann to the prediction that aspects of democratic consent and majority/minority distinctions as elements of the political processes are difficult to translate to the global level and thus 'the segmentary differentiation of the global political system in states reduces the chance that other function systems become "politicised"'.[88] It is specifically in relation to the globally operating companies and the drafting processes of their corporate codes contested that these genuine private institutions managed to create a similar complexity, including a comparable formalised legitimacy structure, to the institutionalised political system; in fact, the general tendency in the process of functional differentiation has been to depoliticise companies and safeguard their autonomy from the political system.[89]

In addition, it is also challenged that the 'constitutive infrastructure' of private forms of regulation could qualify as such functional equivalents to the infrastructure within the political system. Can concepts such as 'stakeholder', 'transparency', 'self-representation' and 'accountability' substitute for the importance of 'nation', 'public sphere', 'representation' and delegation'?[90] Is it possible that 'networks of relationships replace the political community; interest replaces territory'?[91] With a particular view to the corporate codes, a reluctant attitude is taken towards this possibility. It remains a highly ambivalent undertaking to translate the concepts that characterise the political system into the functioning of economic relations without inevitably losing some of its core characteristics.[92] A closer look, for instance, at the development of the concept 'stakeholder' and a comparison with the concept of 'nation' shows that there still seems to be considerable differences between how the private sphere organises participation and the system of formal politics. The stakeholder concept with respect to companies, for instance, has its origin in corporate theory, where it encompasses quite broadly those affecting or being affected by the corporate organisation.[93] It has thus mainly evolved as a highly fluid concept that covers a wide range of actors depending on the rather vague notion of 'being affected' and 'having an interest'. It is clear that the concept of the 'nation' is subject to a profound change due to migration and the dissolving of territory, and thus is equally in a state of flux, but there is one significant difference: the 'nation', although becoming increasingly fluid, nevertheless uses

[88] Luhmann (1977) 41: 'Even the global system of world society has, so far, not changed the fact that the political function needs a territorial basis for its decision making, and this so much more if it is supposed to maximize consensus and to optimize democratic rule. Thus, the political system of the world society is divided into political states not only in the sense of a more or less obsolete "survival" of history but apparently as a requisite of functional specification.' Luhmann (2000) 223: 'Die Segmentierung des weltpolitischen Systems in Staaten verringert die Wahrscheinlichkeit, daß andere Funktionssysteme "politisiert" werden.'

[89] Willke and Willke (2008) 32ff.

[90] Kjaer (2011) 316. In a similar direction, see MacDonald and MacDonald (2006) 94ff.

[91] Backer (2008) 523.

[92] Sand (2011) 330: 'the main problem with this discussion is that some of the vital qualities of democracy are not included'.

[93] Freeman (2010 [1984]) 24ff.

formalised criteria of territory and citizenship as its core parameters. In contrast to these parameters, the criterion of 'interest' can easily be adapted depending on who the corporate organisation considers relevant.[94] Similar problems concerning a perceived functional equivalence can be identified in other components that are mentioned in relation to the political infrastructure of the private sphere.[95] Against the background of these observations, it is argued that the observable tendency towards re-embedding markets cannot be described as an 'increasing interlocking of society's subsystems',[96] in which the rationality of institutionalised politics appears to be taken over by economic actors and can have the result that privately negotiated rules are functionally equivalent to political regulation by the state.

8.2.2.2.3. Reference to Public Codes of Conduct and National Laws

This sceptical perspective on the interaction between social pressures and companies as part of the political system mainly has the result that the corporate codes could either not be interpreted as a form of political regulation or, alternatively, that the element of political regulation must be identified elsewhere. In this context, a preference is expressed for the latter position, which is based on the consideration that genuine political regulation can also occur on the basis of an increasing network of cooperation between the systems of politics and economy.[97] More concretely, economic relations can exhibit a tendency towards political regulation when they directly cooperate with politics and, in so doing, transform political objectives into economic relations. With respect to the corporate codes, such an interaction between economic relations and political objectives can be identified in the increasing integration of political guidelines and recommendations that the corporate codes make use of. The main result of such increasing reference is accordingly the transformation of politically desired recommendations or aspirations that have been developed by an authority that is generally accepted as politically legitimate into a political objective that is accepted in the context of private economic relations.[98] The increasing integration is thus a way in which political standards adopted in the international arena that are considered to be legitimate

[94] The difficulty of this fluid criterion of interest that determines the relevant 'stakeholders' becomes particularly apparent in the debate of multi-stakeholder initiatives. *cf* Fransen and Kolk (2007) 674ff (at 678: 'expectations about interaction between companies and stakeholders, which is as yet too little specific on what constitutes a "good" or "appropriate" stakeholder and what "good" or "appropriate" stakeholder involvement actually entails').

[95] See in this context in particular the provocative critique of Christodoulidis (2013) 659: 'The political actor is emphatically *not* the conscientious consumer; if activist shopping is the "economic expression" of the "political" then there is something fundamentally wrong with these "re-entries". For one, flip "activist shopping" onto the negative: opposition to consumerism is evidently not the same, it is not equivalent, and it is not even symmetrical to, political apathy' (emphasis in original). *cf* also the observations of Lamla (2013) 450.

[96] For this description in relation to the purported 'moralisation of markets', see Stehr, Henning and Weiler (2006a) 2.

[97] See instructively on this possible linking between economy and politics based on cooperation Abbegg (2009).

[98] Abbott and Snidal (2009) 558ff; Cafaggi (2010) 38: 'strong public institutions are needed for private regulation to operate effectively'; Cafaggi (2013) 1565.

'become the basis of binding regulations in a context in which supranational harmonising legislation is impossible in a political context'.[99] A similar development can be observed when corporate codes include adherence to national law in their codes. This can be described as an integration of an objective into private relations that has been politically developed; it can even be framed as transplanting a particular nationally coined political objective into a global one that subsequently becomes part of the global system of private contracting.[100]

However, it needs to be clear that this form of political regulation nevertheless differs from the traditional regulation of the state; it is emphatically not even remotely similar to the traditional regulation in which politics intervene in economic relations with the tools of regulatory law. Instead, economic relations and political objectives are linked by the choice of the individual company to accept and actively pursue the political objective.[101] It is thus a novel form of political regulation that takes, as its starting point, the internal decision of companies to further the global dissemination of politically legitimised objectives and makes them applicable in the form of a contract or self-commitment. Hence, one can identify regulatory forms akin to political regulation in the corporate codes at the very moment that such codes not only incorporate the substantive claims of civil society and market pressures, but whenever they also specifically respond to such claims by means of integrating the standards that have been developed by national or international political systems. With regard to the corporate codes in their current state, such a connection between the system of the economy and international institutionalised politics is already present with respect to some frameworks. Currently, in particular, the use of the ILO core labour rights conventions is an important political framework by choice. Yet it is conceivable, if not probable, that the UN Guiding Principles, and more precisely the corporate responsibility to respect, will become such an additional framework in the future.

Consequently, when H&M, for instance, explicitly declares that 'We base our requirements mainly on internationally agreed standards such as the Universal Declaration of Human Rights, The UN Convention on the Rights of the Child and applicable ILO Conventions, as well as national legislation' and subsequently in each section refers to the specifically applicable provisions,[102] one can indeed interpret this as a way by which a politically accepted objective of the ILO is subjected to private regulation by contract. In addition, the national rules on workplace standards are in particular part of this new form of political regulation by contract, as well as specific environmental rules on waste management or emissions.[103] This political

[99] Backer (2008) 522.

[100] See pointedly Lin (2009), who describes this reference to national political standards within global supplier codes of conduct as being comparable to 'legal transplants': 'Through the channel of contracting, private transactors have been 'smuggling' tons of regulatory law across borders' (at 713f).

[101] Abbott and Snidal (2009) 560; Teubner (2011) 33ff.

[102] H&M Code of conduct 1, available at: http://sustainability.hm.com/en/sustainability/commitments/choose-and-reward-responsible-partners/code-of-conduct.html.

[103] See Lin (2009) 720ff, who mentions particularly the example of the European Management System and the EU Management and Audit Scheme that is frequently referred to (at 721) and the reference in the codes of US companies to the standards of the United States Occupational Safety and Health Administration (at 722).

regulation by choice also became relevant in the *Adidas* case between Adidas and the University of Wisconsin,[104] in which regulatory labour law in the country of manufacturing effectively became applicable to suppliers in the form of mandatory regulation as well as to the lead company in the form of a regulatory framework by choice in contract. Hence, the interventionist rules on labour law represent not only political regulation in a particular territory but also, from the perspective of lead companies in other countries, a political objective that can become an integral part of economic relations by means of choice and, as a result, can be rendered applicable even outside the sphere of influence of a national political authority.

To conclude, the previous sections have taken a critical attitude on the possibility of describing the interaction between social pressures and corporations that give rise to the corporate codes as a functional equivalent to the global system of politics. However, it has been held that a connection to the system of politics can be observed when an interlinking occurs between the corporate codes and international or national frameworks, guidelines and policies that were developed in the system of politics.

8.2.2.3. A New Understanding of the Political

This conclusion, however, does not give any indication as to the political character of the corporate codes insofar as they do not integrate the political decisions that reveal themselves in international political frameworks, public codes of conduct or national law. As already mentioned in the introduction, the respective codes of conduct by no means only refer to existing guidelines that are adapted in political institutions and national laws. On the contrary, the reference to these public standards seems to be rather the exception that applies predominantly with respect to the ILO core labour rights; major parts of the commitments in corporate codes are still substantive norms that have been developed as a reaction to the contestation of society and consumers without the necessary reference to frameworks developed by national or international politics.[105] How can these substantive claims of civil society and market actors and their incorporation into corporate codes be described as a form of political regulation if the comparison to the characteristics of the political system remains conceptually a contested suggestion?

A constructive way forward has already been inferred by one of the critics of a functional understanding of politics. 'The question', Sand states, 'is whether politics is possible under highly-heterogeneous conditions or whether a new type of political emerges.'[106] Such an attempt has recently been made in the social theory debate by scholars who seek to transcend the economic/political distinction by shaping a new category of the political, which is distinctly different from the system

[104] See the case discussion in section 3.2.1. (p 108), text and accompanying footnotes.
[105] See the evidence provided in section 1.2.3.2.1. (p 21), text and accompanying footnotes.
[106] Sand (2011) 326.

of politics.[107] In particular, the theory of societal constitutionalism has taken up the idea of a new form of the political and described it as an '"internal" politicisation of the economy itself', where 'social systems are dealing with their own founding and decision-making paradoxes'.[108] It also reveals itself in the peculiar notion of 'subpolitics'.[109] The important difference deriving from this understanding, as opposed to the above-discussed description of an evolving functional equivalent to institutionalised political regulation in private relations, is that it explicitly rejects the comparison of these new forms of the political with the system of politics; instead, these claims and their incorporation into the corporate codes are viewed as having a political character on their own. Yet, how can such an understanding of the political be perceived within a theory of society when the system of politics prevents other systems from becoming politicised?[110]

In order to unpack the argument and understand the emerging difference between two forms of the political within society, it is considered fruitful to make use of the concept as suggested in recent political theory that employs ideas of political thought in the tradition of Schmitt[111] and Arendt.[112] One can mention here, amongst others, Lefort, who has advocated a new distinction within political thought between the system of politics as a contingent evolutionary social practice and the political as a distinctly different category that is fundamental to society and that reveals itself in the moment of contestation.[113] A brief explanation of the idea of the political difference will be given below, followed by an analysis of the political character of the social pressures and a discussion on how, against the background of this understanding, the corporate codes can be perceived in terms of their political objective.

8.2.2.3.1. Post-foundational Thought and the Concept of Contingency

In order to understand the character and the functioning of this instance of the political, two fundamental theoretical concepts deserve further explanation: first,

[107] In the following, 'the political' will be used to describe this new category and juxtapose it to 'politics', which refers to the political system as social system. This use of the terms 'politics'/'the political' follows the terminology of scholars that discuss the political difference, eg, Marchart (2007) 1: 'a curious difference, which has assumed some currency in recent continental and Anglo-American political thought: the difference between *politics* and *the political* or, in French, between *la politique* and *le politique*, or again, in German, between *Politik* and *das Politische*' (emphasis in original).

[108] Teubner (2012) 114.

[109] Beck (1997) 62f (using the example of the protests against Shell for the attempt to dispose its oil platform Brent Spar): 'In this sense, the anti-Shell coalition brought about a chance in the political scenery: the politics of the first, industrial modernity made way for the new politics of the second, reflexive modernity. The nation state governments sat on the spectator gallery while unauthorized actors of the second modernity called the tune according to their own rules.'

[110] On this again: Luhmann, above n 88.

[111] Schmitt (1996).

[112] Arendt (2003 [1993]).

[113] For the description of the political in Lefort, see, among others, Lefort (1990). Other important scholars in this tradition include Nancy, Badiou, Ranciere, Laclau, Mouffe and Agamben. The following analysis will primarily be based on the systematic study on the different accounts of the political difference conducted by Marchart. It is emphasised that, in this context, reference will be made to both the German and the English versions of the study; see, eg, Marchart (2007); Marchart (2010). This is due to the fact that the German version is not merely a translation, but a revised and expanded version that contains additional arguments.

the idea of post-foundational political thought,[114] which can be seen as a further development and re-orientation of the theories of social differentiation; and, second, the concept of 'contingency' as the important driver behind social evolution.

The political difference is a concept that is closely connected to post-foundational thought, which is slightly different from the evolutionary account as brought forward by Systems Theory. While the former is limited to the description of society without having the aim of explaining why things have evolved the way they did, the focus of post-foundational thought is to focus on the foundation of and the drivers behind this evolutionary social development. It is, however, *post*-foundational in the sense that the idea of an ultimate foundation, of a normative grounding of society in an overall idea, is explicitly rejected because any conceivable ultimate foundation is inevitably exclusionary and thus ignores other equally possible foundations.[115] Against this background, the idea of the social as something given becomes increasingly contested. Instead, the new postulate is the idea of the absent fundament of society.[116] The evolution of society in the form of increasing differentiation and the evolved system/environment distinction, the codes, programmes and semantic traditions are consequently not a development that is in any way determined, but rather is a *contingent* development. Social evolution thus has no safe backing in the past, but is temporally contingent. It is objectively contingent because it could always have evolved differently, and it is socially contingent because it has no backing in a social consensus.[117] This implies that, for instance, the economic system as a system consisting of monetary transactions oriented on price as the central value is not an absolute, but is rather a social evolution with an inherent possibility of being different. In the course of triggering the further evolution of society, however, the origin of and the specific determinants facilitating the contingent development become concealed. In this theoretical account, the political is considered the absent fundament that brings about the contingent developments within society. As Lefort puts it, 'the fact that something as politics has evolved and has been separated from social life in a given era has precisely a political meaning, which is not particular as such, but general'.[118] However, since the political relates to the absent fundament, it can only

[114] This term is used by Marchart (2007).

[115] See Butler (1992) 7: 'It seems that theory posits foundations incessantly, and forms implicit metaphysical commitments as a matter of course, even when it seeks to guard against it; foundations function as the unquestioned and the unquestionable within any theory. And yet, are these foundations, that is, those premises that function as authorizing grounds, are they themselves not constituted through exclusions, which … expose the foundational premise as a contingent and contestable presumption … How is it that we might ground a theory or politics in a speech situation or a subject position which is "universal", when the very category of the universal has only begun to be exposed for its own ethnocentric biases?'

[116] Marchart (2007) 1 pointedly phrases this as the 'absent ground of the Social'.

[117] Luhmann (1996a) 64; and Luhmann (1995) 106: 'Something is contingent insofar as it is neither necessary nor impossible; it is just what it is (or was or will be), though it could also be otherwise. The concept thus describes something given (something experienced, expected, remembered, fantasized) in the light of its possibility of being otherwise; it describes objects within the horizon of possible variations.'

[118] Lefort (1990) 284. (my translation: 'die Tatsache, dass sich etwas wie die Politik in einer bestimmten Epoche im gesellschaftlichen Leben abzugrenzen begann, hat gerade eine politische Bedeutung, die als solche nicht partikular, sondern allgemein ist').

be thought of as *antagonistic*. As a consequence, the political not only triggers but is equally capable of questioning the contingent evolution and insisting on the ever-inherent 'possibility of being different'.[119] The political is thus the starting point for any evolution in society with the result that it becomes concealed in social contingency in the course of social evolution. Being antagonistic, it is simultaneously the moment of contestation, when the contingent evolution is questioned and excluded possibilities of an alternative social organisation become visible. This antagonistic character frees the political from any fixed political agenda and from the power structures that characterise the operation of the system of politics. The political is thus what Arendt has framed as the innovative moment at which the given order is interrupted in exchange for radical freedom and an antagonistic competition between the manifold possibilities.[120]

Against the background of this particular understanding of the political, can social pressures be considered an instance of the political? And, consequently, can the corporate codes be conceptualised as being linked to the political if they accommodate and institutionalise their claims?

8.2.2.3.2. Corporate Codes and the Political

Following the idea of political difference, the political reveals itself particularly whenever the contingent operation of society is questioned, when there is contestation of the status quo and the 'possibility of being different' is expressed. Since there is no need for this contestation to have in place a comprehensive political agenda, nor does this contestation require a particular set of rules concerning participation, accountability or transparency, civil society movements in particular are viable candidates to initiate such visible moments of politicised societal pressures.[121] Yet, not only can the collective efforts of civil society become expressions of the political, it is equally possible to identify the political in everyday practices, such as the act of buying and consumption. De Certau argues in this direction when he defines the everyday practices as practices with a tactic character that can be used to emancipate and allow individuals to escape from the disciplinary practices of society.[122] It goes without saying that not all everyday practices can be considered instances in which political content is expressed. A criterion to distinguish between the processes of consumption as a political statement and as a private undertaking could be whether the everyday practice that is under scrutiny in fact connects to a broader political project.[123] Hence, consumer

[119] ibid 284.

[120] Arendt (2003 [1993]). A brief and concise analysis of these aspects of Arendt's account of the political can be found in Jaeggi (2008) 9ff.

[121] See intensively on this aspect Fischer-Lescano (2005) 67ff; Möller (2011).

[122] Certau (1984) xiv–xv: 'clandestine forms taken by the dispersed, tactical and make-shift creativity of groups or individuals already caught in the nets of "discipline". Pushed to their ideal limits, these procedures and ruses of consumers compose the network of an anti-discipline'.

[123] Marchart (2010) 300ff 306: 'Trifft dieses Kriterium der Universalisierung zu, dann ist keine Praxis zu armselig, keine Aktion zu ineffektiv, kein Häufchen von Demonstranten zu klein für Politik, da nichts erreicht werden kann ohne jene minimalen, alltäglichen Aktionen, aus denen sich hegemoniale Kämpfe molekular zusammensetzen.'

and investor pressure may only be considered an expression of the political under the condition that they can be interpreted as individual articulations of a larger project that deals with the concerns of society as such.[124]

Based on this perception of civil society and market pressure as a moment of political contestation, what does this mean for the corporate codes? Are they instances in which the political manifests itself or, conversely, are they attempts to render invisible the efforts of political forces by means of subjecting them to a new contingency? In the following, I seek to describe them as both, eg, as a form where the political is accommodated as well as a way to conceal the political. This double function of accommodating and concealing is considered to render it possible to define the corporate code as establishing a stable connection with these political pressures. As regards the function of accommodating the pressures, it can be argued that the corporate codes are pivotal instances for political contestation to realise their objectives. This relates to the character of the political as a form of contestation that can exist without necessarily having a political programme. Protest in its social form can always protest against something; there is no necessity to propose alternatives. As a consequence, once it becomes socially visible, the protest inevitably requires the social system addressed to recognise its claims as valid and offer the structures of realising it. Protest functions in society as 'one half of itself—and on the other side there are those that, seemingly unaffected or at best marginally irritated, do what they would do anyway. Protest negates, in a structural sense, general responsibility for its claims. It presupposes others that execute the claims'.[125] With respect to the corporate codes, this has rather drastic consequences. Provided that in order to become visible and successful, the protest movement is *in need* of the social system, then the codes of the companies become pivotal means to render the political protest successful. Only if companies sense and reflect the political claims by the various protest movements is it possible for the political claims to become realised within the operation of society. Against this background, the corporate codes can be considered important as a way of translating the protest into the communication of the economic system. From the perspective of the protest, this translation must nonetheless remain a Pyrrhic victory only, since reflecting political claims is also a way for the social system to conceal partly the political nature and render it subject to economic organisation. It is no coincidence that criticism is also raised against the corporate codes that they as 'relatively vague voluntary commitments are a way to become immune to far-reaching

[124] See for a similar conclusion on the potential of consumers Beck (1997) 64; Beck (2005) 7f. On the necessity as well as the immense difficulties that are involved in this project of collective political consumerism, see Lamla (2013) 168ff.

[125] Luhmann (1996b) 205 (my translation: 'Protest negiert, schon strukturell, die Gesamtverantwortung. Er muss andere voraussetzen, die das, was verlangt wird, ausführen'). See further: 'Es fehlt, anders gesagt, die Reflexion-in-sich, die für die Codes der Funktionssysteme typisch ist … Man kann von Protestbewegungen also keine Reflexion zweiter Stufe, keine Reflexion der Reflexion der Funktionssysteme erwarten. Sie halten sich *statt dessen* an die Form des Protests' (emphasis in original). See also Anderson (2013) 903: 'The modus operandi of social movements … is not geared towards reordering the established institutional framework of power … they seek to transcend, not capture, the container of institutional power.'

standards for democratic corporate constitutions'.[126] This is due to the fact that the very process of accommodating pressure in the form of a corporate code inevitably makes the political claim part of the social operation. It is transformed into merely a social contingency within the economic system. As such, the political element is concealed with the result that, eventually, pressures against corporations and their attitude to translating the corporate code into an instance that is connected to economic rationality is likely to arise.

One may, however, counter the sceptical position. This process of concealing can be considered a way of establishing a connection to the political forces. This is due to the fact that this very process of concealing is often only the starting point for new pressures.[127] Provided this is the case, the fact that the process of concealing may give rise to protest can then equally be seen as a productive way by which the political in fact becomes institutionalised and signposts a genuine 'politicisation' of the economy. It is then the interaction between both antagonistic perspectives, between constant contestation in civil society and the respective responses of corporations that may be fruitful rather than a threat for institutionalising the political in society.[128] Against this background, it can also be argued with good reason to understand this process of politicisation as a fluid and dynamic process, in which corporate codes always represent a preliminary form of reflecting the political contestation that may subsequently be subject to further struggles over the content, functioning and consequences of the codes. On the concrete example, Backer has pointedly described the functioning of this process. In so doing, he argues that the corporation, when developing and improving its social and environmental standards, was in fact dependent on constant, but also constantly changing, external input from various sources, ranging from international politics and institutionalised multi-stakeholder initiatives to spontaneous protests and boycotts. The example of Apple shows how the company's social responsibility policy and its supplier code of conduct can only develop with the 'assistance' of claims raised by NGOs and consumers and the multi-stakeholder certification programmes with which Apple collaborated.[129] Corporate codes are then as much a means to 'dampen pressures for changes' as to also 'prepare the stage for a new round of struggle in which NGOs build on their successes to demand effective monitoring and enforcement'.[130] Against this background, a theoretical description of the corporate codes becomes viable that interprets them as instances in which the political struggle is fluidly institutionalised.

[126] Möller (2011) 328. In a similar direction, see Shamir (2004).
[127] See with empirical evidence from the apparel industry Bartley (2005) 233ff.
[128] This understanding also underlies the description of Levy and Kaplan (2008), who state that: 'The meaning of CSR itself is a key point of political struggle' (at 442) and conclude by stating that: 'Rather than view the current status of CSR as a disappointing endpoint, CSR can be viewed as a long-term strategy that challenges corporate power on numerous fronts' (at 446).
[129] Backer (2013) 830ff.
[130] Levy and Kaplan (2008) 446.

8.2.3. Conclusion

This sociological analysis has focused on the analysis of the corporate codes as a new form of political regulation. In so doing, it has sought inspiration from the idea of re-embedding economic relations under the conditions of a functionally differentiated society and it has attempted to make these ideas fruitful for the corporate codes. Based on this theoretical framework, it has been argued that the corporate codes indeed represent a politicisation of the economy whereby private regulation by contracting and commitments becomes linked to the genuine political objectives. These are the legitimate objectives in the system of politics, on the one hand, and the objectives expressed by societal, yet genuine political, pressure, on the other hand. There is accordingly a need to differentiate between these two forms of political regulation in the private sphere when seeking to relate the corporate codes to the legal system. As a reason for the need of the legal system to recognise the political objectives pursued in corporate codes, one can refer to the fragility of this evolving political regulation in economic relations. Since these economic relations remain in the first place governed by market rationality, an inherent risk remains that this novel political regulation becomes eventually subordinated under economic rationality and hence marginalised.[131] From this, it follows that the inherent conflict between the market and political rationality as complementary governing elements of economic relations with a dominance of the former eventually call upon the law to institutionalise and thus stabilise this novel double politicisation of markets. Or, as Joerges pointedly puts it:

> The conceptualisation of the economy as polity brings one additional aspect to the fore, namely, the exposure of economic activities to divergent, and often conflicting, concerns, and the ongoing management of these tensions. Law production, *Recht-Fertigung*, has to be accomplished in de-centralised arenas—and the legal system and its courts are required to exercise mediating and co-ordinating functions in such complex conflict constellations.[132]

[131] See generally for this observation on the basis of experimental research the recent noteworthy study of Falk and Szech (2013) 710: 'market interaction displays a tendency to lower moral values, relative to individually stated preferences … For example, anti-child-labor or environmental protection campaigns may not be that effective because markets for goods undermine the relevant social values'. From the perspective of social theory (with a sceptical tone as to whether such an identified political rationality would at all be able to resist market logic), see Christodoulidis (2013) 659: 'The problem is that with the "re-entry" into the other system's rationality, the political ceases to impact, underdetermined to the point at which it is in all cases productive to the receiving system and realigned to its functional imperatives.'

[132] Joerges (2011) 475 (emphasis in original) and later at 499: 'Conflicts within the economy cannot be settled by experts, and will certainly not be settled spontaneously. The elaboration of regimes which strike a fair balance between the concerned economic interests, and mediate between the diverging political orientations will be dependent on the power of states to impose discipline on transnational norm-generation and to defend exit options. This power is by no means negligible.'

8.3. PRIVATE LAW ENFORCEMENT OF POLITICAL REGULATION BY CORPORATE CODES

After having described the new form of political regulation apparent in the corporate codes from the perspective of social theory, this section will reverse the perspective on the legal debates with the aim of identifying the appropriate angles on how this new double form of political regulation by private actors can be integrated into the system of private law. In the first place, the theoretical debate on public interests in private law will serve as a starting point to discuss how this new form of political regulation challenges the general perceptions on public interests in private law and calls for recognising a new dimension (section 8.3.1). Subsequently, the implications of this new dimension will be further specified with respect to the appropriate links in contract law and the enforceable obligation that private actors incur by means of corporate codes (section 8.3.2), as well as its implications for the non-contractual legal liability of regulatory actors (section 8.3.3).

8.3.1. Re-conceptualising the Public/Private Divide

When approaching this specific new form of political regulation from the perspective of private law, it becomes immediately apparent that it challenges the clear-cut distinction between public law and private law and calls for accepting this form of political regulation as a new way in which public interests become integrated into private law. Based on a brief presentation of the influential positions in this debate, it will be analysed whether and how the specific public interests visible in the corporate codes could become relevant.

8.3.1.1. The 'Traditional' Autonomy of Private Law

When revisiting the debate on public interests in private law, one important and, in fact, historically prevailing understanding in the legal debate has been to understand the system of private law as an entirely autonomous system in which public interests should not play a role at all.

In the German debate, this understanding of an autonomous private law is closely connected to the analytical distinction within the law between public and private law, for which the historical school, most prominently Savigny, provided the intellectual and ideological background. Savigny strictly distinguished between two different areas of law, namely public law and private law. Separating these two areas and establishing an *internal* divide within the legal system, he also postulated that both areas had two distinctly separate objectives. Whereas the area of public law was located in the sphere of the state with the aim of reflecting the spirit of the people (*Volksgeist*), it was particularly private law that, by means of regulating the private relations between individuals, had to reflect solely the particular interests of private parties.[133] Despite alternative claims that sought to frame private law as a field that comprised private as well as public elements,[134] this distinction between public and private law and the idea of private law as being formal and oriented on the will of private parties remained influential for the codification of the civil code.[135] In the civil code, political objectives, such as social justice,[136] did not play a significant role. Subsequently, in particular the ordoliberalist school of thought promoted the idea of distinguishing between private law as an apolitical area and public law as a political area. In this context, the concept of the 'private law society' (*Privatrechtsgesellschaft*) was coined, which was understood as a society that would be constituted and governed by private law based only on private autonomy.[137] Civil society, as the object of private law, was thus understood as an apolitical sphere of society that functioned with the institutions of private property and private autonomy. Pursuant to this idea, private law as governing the market society could, however, only remain apolitical because its fundamental political institutions, eg, party autonomy and private property, were institutionalised and protected by the overarching political constitution.[138] Hence, with the help of the political constitution, which constituted freedom of contract and private property as public values, private law, in building on these institutions, could remain free from being oriented on political considerations. In the English debate, to which this strong internal legal distinction between public law and private law is unknown, a comparable historical understanding of the autonomy and apolitical and formal nature of private law reasoning exists. Yet, it was conceptualised differently. Here, it was rather the separation between public

[133] Savigny (1840) vol I 22: 'Übersehen wir von dem nun gewonnenen Standpunkt aus das Recht, so unterscheiden wir in demselben zwei Gebiete, das Staatsrecht und das Privatrecht. Das erste hat zum Gegenstand den Staat, das heißt die organische Erscheinung des Volks: das zweite die Gesamtheit der Rechtsverhältnisse, welche den Einzelnen umgeben, damit er in ihnen sein inneres Leben führe und zu einer bestimmten Gestalt bilde.'

[134] See most prominently Ehrlich (1899), who describes the public/private divide as the distinction between dispositive and mandatory rules, which both have their place in private law, pointedly at 10: 'So aufgefaßt gehört aber die Erörterung des Gegensatzes des zwingenden und nichtzwingenden Rechts nicht in den "Allgemeinen Teil", nicht in die wage Rubrik "Gegensätze im Recht", sondern in die Lehre vom Rechtsgeschäft.' See also Gierke (1889) 13 (who uses the famous expression of the 'little drop of social oil').

[135] For the background of the drafting process of the BGB and the influence of the historical school, see generally Wieacker (1995) 371ff.

[136] See Micklitz (2011) 20, who also observes that in the German context, public policy issues found their way into private relationships by public laws, such as social security laws.

[137] Böhm (1966) 109: 'es sollte künftig im Bereich der Gesellschaft nur noch einen einzigen, für alle gleichen *rechtlichen Status*, nur eine einzige, für alle gleiche Zuständigkeit des Planens und Handelns geben, nämlich die *Privatautonomie*' (emphasis in original).

[138] ibid 109, 115: 'Ohne Obrigkeit kann auch die Privatrechtsgesellschaft nicht auskommen, selbst wenn sie sich nicht gegen äußere und innere Gefahren zu behaupten hätte. Die Privatrechtsgesellschaft bedarf … einer Mitwirkung politischer Herrschaftsfunktionen, wenn auch nur in bescheidenem Umfang und wenn auch bloß pflegegärtnerischen Charakters; im Übrigen aber werden die Pläne ihrer Mitglieder mit Hilfe des Privatrechts geräuschlos, automatisch und mit einem erstaunlichen Minimum von Reibungs- und Ungehorsamswiderstand gelenkt.'

law as an area of public policy intervention and the rules on contracts, torts and property as primarily facilitative rules of rights and entitlements that represented a relevant narrative.[139] In this regard, it should be noted that the English system contains a notion of pragmatism and is primarily oriented towards the concrete problem posed by the particular case, which already influenced the way in which legal reasoning takes place.[140] This sense of pragmatism provided the basis for the understanding that rules dealing with the conduct of private parties had to be interpreted on the particular and concrete needs and interests of the parties involved and not explicitly on abstract political objectives or principles. Nevertheless, the idea that the law of torts, contracts and property had to remain unaffected by public policy objectives also had, besides the sense of pragmatism, influential intellectual roots. Here, on the one hand, the seminal work of Jeremy Bentham and the philosophical ideas of utilitarianism and, on the other hand, the political philosophy of liberalism paved the way for an understanding of private relations as intrinsically connected to the idea of the freedom of contract.[141]

This formal and apolitical approach to private law has been, as will be subsequently analysed, severely criticised and, in the course of the late nineteenth and twentieth centuries has been generally replaced by more public policy-oriented approaches. Nonetheless, it remains vital in the current debate. Particularly in the works of Weinrib and Simmonds, one can still find a strong defence for the autonomy of private law and the argument that private law has to remain free from public policy objectives and focus instead on the interests of the parties in a dispute. Pursuant to this understanding, private law ought to be solely concerned with the bipolar relationship between two private parties, between the claimant and the defendant, and the need to do justice within this very relationship.[142] Legal reasoning dealing with private relations has accordingly to be exclusively oriented to this bipolar relationship and to set aside any broader economic, moral, political or social consequences.[143] Accordingly, the reasoning in private law to accept a right of the claimant has to correspond directly to the reasoning concerning the duty of the defendant, which implies, for instance, granting compensation only for tortuous conduct in case the damage received by the claimant directly corresponds to a wrong committed by the defendant towards the claimant and may not be informed by additional public interests. As Simmonds concludes concerning the tendency towards referring increasingly to public interests in private law

[139] Collins (2007) 3ff.

[140] Micklitz (2011) 8ff.

[141] For the influence of Bentham and utilitarianism on the idea of the freedom of contract, see Atiyah (1979) 324ff; for the influence of political philosophy in the tradition of Locke, see Collins (2007) 3ff.

[142] Weinrib (1995); Weinrib (2000); Simmonds (1984) 120ff.

[143] Weinrib (2000) 37: 'Through its institutions and central doctrines, private law directly connects the parties and attempts a coherent elaboration of the juridical norms applicable to their norms … With this understanding … comes a repudiation of the notion that restitutionary damages are occasions for the promotion of social purposes extrinsic to the relationship between the parties.'

reasoning: 'The distinction between public and private law was and is of great importance for the existence of doctrinal legal science.'[144]

Against the background of this understanding of private law, the substantive interest that is relevant in private law reasoning remains restricted to the respective interest of private parties without broader policy considerations. These policy considerations should instead remain in the realm of public law.

8.3.1.2. Public Policy in Private Law

Although this idea of an autonomous, formal and entirely apolitical private law has influential historical roots and remains one of the central positions in the current debate, it has been strongly criticised in the course of the nineteenth century and later in the twentieth century, and subsequently an alternative understanding of private law reasoning has evolved. This paradigm shift from a formal towards a policy-oriented notion of private law is rooted in initial criticism of the perceived formal and apolitical nature of judicial reasoning in private law decisions as expressed in the common law by the legal realism movement[145] and critical legal studies,[146] and in the continental debate in the form of the evolving understanding of private law as partly functionally public.[147] Scholars began to reveal the inherent public policy orientations behind the perceived apolitical and formal private law reasoning and to unmask the very idea of an apolitical private law as essentially politically motivated. Not intervening in private relations and insisting on the freedom of contract was criticised as 'a socially constructed, historically variable and inevitably political decision' where: 'The state defines "private" as those aspects of life into which it will not intervene, and then, paradoxically, uses this privacy as the justification for its non-intervention.'[148] This strong critique on the (political) premises behind the public/private divide resulted in a shift in the understanding of private law. Having formerly been described as a system

[144] See Simmonds (1984) 120, who proceeds by arguing that 'whether we retain the distinction between public and private law must therefore depend on how we can best interpret the values embodied in the modern legal order. In fact, we are presented with two options, which we may call the options of *resistance* and *revision*' (at 121, emphasis in original) and holds that 'my sympathies are with the resistance option, but … I fear that revision is more likely' (at 131).

[145] See in particular Cohen (1933) 586 ('The law of contract, then, through judges, sheriffs, or marshals puts the sovereign power of the state at the disposal of one party to be exercised over the other party. It thus grants a limited sovereignty to the former … the law of contract may be viewed as a subsidiary branch of public law, as a body of rules according to which the sovereign power of the state will be exercised as between the parties to a more or less voluntary transaction'); and Horwitz (1982).

[146] See fundamentally Kennedy (1982); and more recently Kennedy (2001).

[147] See especially Raiser (1971) 29f: 'Mein Vorschlag geht also dahin, daß Privatrecht nach Funktionsbereichen zu gliedern, die typischen Lebensbereichen unserer Gesellschaft entsprechen, und als Kriterium der Unterscheidung den Grad der Privatheit oder Öffentlichkeit dieser Bereiche zu verwenden. Je stärker der Öffentlichkeitsgehalt in den Vordergrund tritt, desto stärker werden sich bei der Handhabung der Normen und Rechtsinstitute des Privatrechts neben oder anstelle von "klassischen", auf die Einzelpersonen und ihren Handlungs- und Gestaltungswillen bezogenen Rechtsprinzipien die … vom Gedanken der sozialen Verantwortlichkeit bestimmten Grundsätze zur Geltung bringen.' See also Kübler (1974); Wiethölter (1968) 165ff, 246ff.

[148] Rose (1987) 64f.

of facilitative rules that governed the relations of private parties with a view to their individual needs and interests, private law was increasingly understood as a regulatory technique that, like public law, is guided by political objectives and perceptions.[149] This tendency within the academic debate towards a regulatory notion of private law was also influenced by the legislative efforts in the early and mid-twentieth century that introduced structural protection for weaker parties, particularly in the fields of tenancy, consumer and labour law.

After having extensively revealed these ever-inherent public dimensions in private law, the theoretical debate became devoted to debating the valid direction of this specific public policy objective. Among the different suggestions, there are three important approaches that proved to be particularly influential in the debate and that will therefore be highlighted.

First, the claims for public interests informing private law were closely connected to the increasing demands raised against the protective welfare state, which required an active intervention in private relations for the sake of providing social justice. Although there are differences as to how social justice as an ultimate objective became relevant in the different countries, the private law models in Europe seem to have pointed in a similar direction. As an observer states: 'During the 20th century, the Member States of the European Union developed their own models of social justice in private law … All models have a common thread, which is the use of the law by the (social welfare) state as a means to protect the weaker party against the stronger party, the employee against the employer, the tenant against the landlord and the consumer against the supplier.'[150] More recently, this claim for social justice as a relevant public interest in private law was also introduced in the debate on European private law. In this context, pleas have been made to re-introduce a public policy objective particularly into European contract law that is oriented on social justice. The most prominent voice in this regard has been the so-called *Study Group on Social Justice in European Contract Law*, which strongly criticises how, within the field of European contract law, public policy has been equalised with the completion of the internal market and other political objectives, such as aspects of social justice, have been largely ignored in the past.[151] Such social justice perspectives have also been developed concerning general social or environmental standards within private contractual relations. Pursuant to this understanding, these novel social and environmental objectives introduce a substantive dichotomy within the social justice intervention. In contrast to the protection of one of the parties to a contract, these objectives suggest that the protection of those parties that are external to the relationship and—concerning environmental standards—future generations is an integral aspect of social justice.[152] A core

[149] See explicitly on the regulatory character of private law with respect to contract law Collins (1999) 56ff; and, with respect to tort law, Green (1959).

[150] Micklitz (2011) 3.

[151] For claims in the context of European contract law, see the manifesto of the Study Group on Social Justice in European Contract Law (2004).

[152] Wilhelmsson (2004b) 723.

argument from the social justice strand on the regulation of contracts here is that contracts that violate fundamental social standards need to result in the refusal of contract law to enforce such contractual transactions on the transfer of 'contaminated' products.[153] Pursuant to this understanding, mainly the mandatory rules on validity of contracts accommodate the aim for social justice and realise this substantive political objective within private relations.[154]

A second strand in the debate that is closely linked to social justice conceptions on private law[155] is a debate in constitutional law scholarship about the question of a 'constitutionalisation of private law'. Proponents of this approach hold that private law ought to be informed by the substantive values laid down in the constitution. Pursuant to this understanding, judges, when deciding private law cases, would have to apply the constitution as the determining or at least pervasive interpretative framework.[156] The most prominent aspect of this debate is the question on the horizontal effect of fundamental rights, eg, the question whether the rights constituted in the political constitution do not only bind the state but also become relevant in the relationship between private actors. A strong understanding of a constitutionalisation of private law would then be to view the dispute that is decided by private law not as a dispute between two private parties, between the litigant and the defendant, but in essence as 'litigation between competing constitutional rights'.[157] The essential claim within the constitutionalisation of private law is consequently to advocate that the values of the political constitution represent valid public interests that can inform private law reasoning. With regard to social standards and environmental protection in private relations, one can also, within this strand, identify the tendency to argue in favour of giving effect to the constitutional values expressed therein in the form of specific mandatory rules that render contracts void that violate such fundamental rights. More precisely, it is already an argument in the debate that constitutional rights, such as the rights of the child or the freedom of association, should be considered as hindering the legal enforcement of contracts in which such fundamental rights are not respected.[158]

A third influential, but conceptually different, strand concerning public interest reasoning in private law can be derived from the law and economics' perspective

[153] For a monograph treatment of this idea on the example of contracts on goods exchange produced under sweatshop conditions, see Tjon Soei Len (2013). See in a similar direction with respect to environmental aspects Wilhelmsson (2004b) 723.

[154] See Tjon Soei Len (2013) 91ff, who focuses, as angles in private law, mainly on the mandatory rules concerning the invalidity of contracts for breach of good morals and public policy.

[155] For the connection between the constitutionalisation and social justice, see Ciacchi (2006) 177ff.

[156] See, eg, Cherednychenko (2004); Barkhuysen and Lindenbergh (2006); Ciacchi (2006); Kumm (2006); Mak (2008).

[157] Kumm (2006) 359.

[158] See in this direction Study Group on Social Justice in European Contract Law (2004) 667f, where it is argued that in the context of European contract law, the Nice Charter on Fundamental Rights in the European Union is a framework that ought to inform private law: 'Although freedom is a fundamental value and supports private autonomy in contract law, it must be balanced against other values proclaimed in the Charter such as respect for equality, diversity, social inclusion, access to services of general economic interest, a high level of environmental protection and consumer protection, and fair and just working conditions … Similarly, the Charter prohibits child labour, which suggests that products made using child labour should not be placed on the market or at least that consumers should have the right to rescind purchases of such products.'

on private law.[159] While law and economics scholarship has, in the first place, been primarily devoted to analysing the legal system with a view to its efficiency in terms of reducing transaction costs, there is also a normative direction that argues for an orientation on legal rules and reasoning by the courts on the interest of economic efficiency.[160] An important direction deriving from the criterion of economic efficiency is here to focus in private law primarily on the relationship between the private parties, their self-regulatory contract, as well as the productive potential of social norms.[161] In this respect, the perspective of law and economics seems to be similar to the traditional understanding of private law that focused on the private interest. However, law and economics differs from an autonomous understanding in the sense that it views the core of private law not in the individual interests of the parties to a dispute, but it presumes that the interest of such a private and economic relationship is to reduce transaction costs and further economic efficiency.

8.3.1.3. Corporate Codes: Neither Intervention nor Autonomy

Certainly, the analysis has ignored strands that place themselves in between the presented strands and that argue for a combination of different substantive interests that should inform private law[162] and it has also not taken a critical perspective against each of the different positions.[163] Yet, since this study is not concerned with a general discussion on the public/private divide, but rather with the objective of identifying a place for the public interests that are introduced by the corporate codes, the question is not merely the validity of the criteria as such, but rather to what extent they are relevant with respect to the public interest introduced by the corporate codes. How can the substantive public interest that is introduced in the form of a corporate code be integrated into an understanding of private law between autonomy and public policies? Can it be related to one of the sides or is it, conversely, a new form of public interest that has so far not been considered in the debate? This will be discussed below.

The interests that are represented within the corporate codes would, at first sight, fit quite neatly with the understanding of the autonomy of private law given

159 See fundamentally Posner (2003).

160 For the distinction between positive and normative approaches within law and economics and the normative objectives within law and economics scholarship, see Posner (2003) 24ff; Parisi (2004).

161 *cf* for this aspect with further references to the debate Zumbansen (2007) 213: 'Law and Economics scholars seem clearly to favour social norms to govern cooperative behaviour among social actors, while attributing at best an ambivalent role to the state not only in channelling these private norms, but also in effectively intervening into problematic social relations.'

162 See, eg, Collins (2007) 18, who suggests translating the constitutional values into the 'concepts and principles' of private law instead of incorporating constitutional reasoning via direct or indirect horizontal effect; see also Dagan (2010), who combines the perspective of the autonomy of private law and the need for private law to be informed by other social values by arguing that private law needs to be responsive to both the bipolar relationship that it regulates as well as broader social values.

163 For a detailed critique on the social justice positions, see, eg, Kornet (2006) 321ff. For a critique on the constitutionalisation approach, see, eg, Smits (2006). For an overview of the most frequently raised criticisms against efficiency-based law and economics approaches, see, eg, Smith (2004) 119ff.

the origin of this interest in the individual private parties and their private choices. The codes represent policies that are autonomously introduced by private actors without being externally imposed for a public policy reason. Nevertheless, their specific character as policies that include an interest deemed to be public renders it difficult to understand them as being substantively related to the interests of the private parties. On the contrary, the corporate codes instead introduce an additional different interest into the bipolar relationship by referring to parties outside these bipolar relationships that could be affected with the objective of protecting these against the negative effects of the private relations. In this respect, they fulfil a core distributive objective. Against the background of this explicit integration of such an interest external to the private relationship, the corporate codes do not fit with a focus of private law that narrowly focuses on an atomistic view of the interests of the private relationship and it seems here no coincidence that specifically in the debate on CSR, the traditional understanding of the public/private divide is effectively rejected as an under-complex understanding for these new forms of private regulation.[164]

This puts the corporate codes in close proximity to the current positions that accept the influence of public interests within the realm of private law. However, while in the following several similarities are indeed identified, it will also be emphasised that there are differences between the public interest furthered by the codes and the existing positions concerning public interests in private law. The claims for a social justice approach to private law fit, in substance, quite well with the codes insofar as the corporate codes also deal with aspects of distributive justice; the integration of fundamental workplace standards can here be considered a prime example. However, there is one important formal difference between the idea of social justice as envisaged in the debate and the social justice element as introduced by the codes. As has been indicated above, the current position on social justice argues for the requirement for social justice as a political or moral claim that needs to be imposed on private actors by translating it into a mandatory rule in private law. The suggestions to let the substantive interest of prohibiting child labour influence private law, for instance, appears in private law primarily in the form of a mandatory intervention into private relations. For the substantive social justice component introduced by corporate codes, this formal perspective does not fit. The social justice elements included in the corporate code is not based on universal morality or developed in a political decision-making process. Instead, it follows the claim of society to realise this objective in economic relations. Within their codes, companies autonomously codify the prohibition of child labour on the grounds that it is a topic that is widely criticised by, among others, civil society actors and as laid down in the ILO convention, and thereby they fulfil the objective of furthering social justice. However, this distributive

[164] See with particular regard to corporate codes and CSR, among others, Wood (2005) 268ff; Enneking (2012) 497ff. On a similar perception with respect to private regulation in general, see the contributions in Cafaggi (2012); and, in particular, Cassese, D'Alterio and De Bellis (2012) 331f: 'The public-private distinction derives from categories traditional to State regulation of business, while Transnational Private Regulation is mixed … It is not entirely private and can be better defined as hybrid regulation.'

element is not translated into a mandatory rule, but rather represents an immediate choice of the private actor. A similar argument can be made with respect to the relationship between the corporate codes and the idea of a 'constitutionalisation' of private law. Here again, substantive overlaps can be identified when companies integrate into their codes fundamental rights as expressed in national constitutions or international declarations, but the formal validity of these rights differs. In the debate on the constitutionalisation of private law, fundamental rights are considered applicable in private law primarily on the grounds that the political constitution is considered the overarching and hierarchically superior framework that informs private law. In the corporate codes, conversely, the included rights and obligations receive their validity from decisions of the corporate entity, eg, from the self-determination of private parties to make it an obligation. To the extent that corporate codes deal with human rights aspects, it is a different form from the traditional top-down approach. It is a way whereby 'human rights … acquire a contractual dimension' and become in any case, irrespective of the direct or indirect horizontal effect of fundamental human rights, directly integrated in private relations.[165] The corporate codes thus share the substance with respect to the constitutionalist and social justice approach, but differ concerning the form. The emphasis on economic relations as the ultimate formal basis of these new public interests does in fact put them in close proximity to the perspective taken in law and economics scholarship. Here, it is particularly emphasised in private law to focus on the productive potential of the economic relations and the choice of private parties that renders this approach towards public interests valuable. However, in spite of the common focus on the origin of public interests within private law as embedded in private relations, the law and economics perspective and the public interest introduced by the codes nevertheless differ here in terms of the substance. From the law and economics perspective, private law ought to regulate the private relations with a view to the interest of efficiency. Yet, the reduction of public interests to the criterion of efficiency seems to be too narrow. In fact, within the theoretical analysis above, one main point has been to reveal that within the codes, an orientation of the private parties on broader political objectives that exceed the economic interest of an efficient market transaction is present.[166] As is emphasised in the sociological literature, it is difficult to treat fully the voluntary social efforts of companies as being based on the interest to further economic efficiency, as they partly produce highly inefficient market outcomes.[167]

Against this background, it is indeed difficult to relate the interest that the corporate codes introduce, ie, autonomously created public interests, to the existing perspectives on public interests in private law. The strands that have considerable

[165] Marrella (2007) 303; Heijden (2011b) 183.

[166] See above, section 8.2.1.3. (p 316), text and accompanying footnotes.

[167] See Beckert (2006) 121f, who argues that the voluntary socially responsible behaviour of companies (altruism) leads to a shift in the allocation of investment capital towards those actors that are favoured by these social values and simultaneously discriminates against economic actors that do not fulfil these values. From a macro-economic perspective, this shift may eventually lead to a particularisation of exchange with the eventual result that competition is undermined and transaction costs rise.

substantive overlaps with the corporate codes—social justice and constitutionalisation—fall short because they translate this interest mainly into mandatory rules and disregard the potential contributions to this substantive objective from private relations. Conversely, the law and economics strand that argues for a stronger focus on the productive potential of economic relations for overall welfare, as relevant in private law, falls short when it comes to recognising a substantive interest that goes beyond and could even contradict the interest of economic efficiency. What is then needed in order to reflect the corporate codes is an approach towards public interests that takes into consideration the autonomous contributions of private actors to produce public interests that are relevant for private law within the economic relations.

8.3.1.4. A New 'Publicness' in Private Law

8.3.1.4.1. The Formal Distinction between Public and Private Law

Taking into consideration the theoretical description of the corporate codes, it has become clear that the corporate codes indeed contain a mixture of public and private components. Yet, little evidence could be found that the corporate codes represent an entirely novel category in which public and private elements become interwoven in a way that a distinction between the public and the private is impossible. On the contrary, it has been argued that, within the codes, the distinction between private and public elements does in fact re-appear in a different way. The corporate codes remain formally embedded in private economic relations—in either a private contract or a binding public declaration on the market, as discussed in chapter seven—but create in substance public interests in the form of accommodating political pressure from society or by choosing to include the public interests established in the system of politics. Against this background, there is no need to abolish the formal distinction between the public and the private sphere.[168] Instead, the corporate codes render it possible to further differentiate and introduce a position that recognises a formal divide between the public and the private sphere, but recognises that also within the private sphere, substantive public interests are created. Accordingly, as a formal distinction between the two social spheres of politics and economy, the public/private divide remains viable considering that the codes are firmly embedded in the formal context of the economy; they are emphatically not part of the political system and thus are not capable of producing public policies comparable to those created in the institutionalised political process. However, insofar as in private law a substantive distinction is made to allocate to the private sphere only the interests of the parties and a wider economic interest and treat public interests as a matter of the formal public sphere, it begins to become blurred. What it has to be replaced with is a perspective where in the private sphere, both private and public interests are furthered and have

[168] For a similar suggestion, see Teubner (1999) 397: 'neither is there a new fusion of private and public law as suggested by such seductive slogans as "private life is public" or "everything is politics"'.

to be distinguished.[169] This suggestion of formally maintaining and substantively deconstructing and reconstructing the public/private divide will be explained in the following discussion.

With regard to the formal layer of the public/private divide, it is particularly Collins who discusses the public/private divide as an essential formal differentiation within the legal system into two different branches of law that indicate the social sphere to which the respective area of law connects.[170] As Collins pointedly states, public and private law:

> [H]ave co-evolved with their respective spheres of social life—civil society with private law, and relations between citizen and the state with public law. The separation of the subsystems of public and private law evolved in response to the correct perception that they were handling different kinds of conflicts and co-ordination problems.[171]

This evolutionary development has had the consequence that different particular connections between the legal system and the system of the economy and politics were created. Private law established connections to the economy in the form of the institutions of property, contract and competition,[172] and translated these into self-created legal obligations, whereas in public law, the input primarily derived from politics in the form of the constitution and statutes.[173] Although in the evolution of the legal system, exchanges occurred in the form of mandatory rules in private law or the use of contracts in the relations between the state and its citizens, the formal distinction still remained viable. Since the corporate codes are in fact formally related to private relations without being related to the formal arena of political decision making, the corporate codes in fact do not sidestep this formal distinction, but are, within the internal differentiation of the legal system, firmly embedded in the system of private law that regulates the relations between private actors based on contracts and commitments. It remains thus private law that is called upon to regulate this substantive public interest.

8.3.1.4.2. Different Substantive 'Publics' in Private Law

That being said, the public/private divide indeed becomes problematic when substantively assessing the corporate codes in the formal context of private law. While remaining closely connected to the private sphere, it has to be equally emphasised that corporate codes introduce self-imposed obligations that transcend the private interest and even resist an economic logic. Consequently, a clear-cut substantive distinction within legal reasoning between the substantive interests introduced by politics and those introduced by private actors need to be abolished.

169 This comes very close to the understanding of private law as being oriented on 'polycontextuality' of Teubner (1999) 395f; Teubner (2008) 837.
170 Collins (2007).
171 ibid 17. In a similar direction, see Teubner (1999) 396: 'public law, as the law of the political process ... private law, as the law of the economic process'.
172 Luhmann (2004) 390ff (property), 393ff (contract), 400 (competition).
173 For the constitution as a structural coupling between politics and law, see Luhmann (1990).

Concerning the possibility of such different forms of public interest reasoning in law, one can take inspiration from the debate on global administrative law and, more specifically, the notion of 'publicness'. In the course of the debate about an evolving global administrative law, Kingsbury has developed the notion of the 'publicness' of law. Acknowledging that traditionally the main 'publics' have been states, eg, institutionalised politics, he argues that the publics on a global level have expanded. Now, not only states, but also other actors may take over genuine regulatory functions and thus become autonomous publics. These publics may range from self-regulatory bodies over hybrid public/private regulation to network governance arrangements. As a result of these multiple publics, Kingsbury postulates that international law has to transform into an inter-public law, which accommodates the various 'publics' as an *ius gentium* instead of being limited to the bilateral logic of a law in between states (*ius inter gentes*).[174] 'Publics' in this regard not only refers to the state as a regulatory entity but also to 'certain other public entities',[175] which equally fulfil the requirement of publicness when they develop standards that are being 'wrought by the whole society, by the public' and 'address matters of concern to the society as such'.[176] As Kuo puts it: 'Notably, on this view, publicness is rooted in, not imposed on, the various "publics" that produce the nascent global administrative law through regulatory practices.'[177] By postulating this form of publicness for the area of global administrative law, Kingsbury suggests understanding the regulatory practices developed outside state consent as being equally legitimate and as being substantively in the public interest. It is noteworthy that he already accepts as such a form of publicness the global practices of private actors, at least insofar as they engage with the regulative activities of public institutions.[178]

Making this idea of publicness fruitful within private law, it can be posited that by means of the corporate code, a new 'public' dimension is effectively introduced that governs economic relations with the consequence that also in private law, a 'pluralism of publics' begins to come into being. Such a postulated pluralism of publics does have certain consequences. It first implies that the corporate codes do not replace the established categories of public interests that already govern private law. State intervention in the form of mandatory rules is explicitly understood as continuing to play an important role. Private law continues to remain regulatory law and instrumentalises the private relationship in order to pursue particular public policy objectives. This form of public is mainly reflected within private law in the form of mandatory rules and public policy-oriented reasoning by the courts that govern private relations. It is effectively also in the global operations and contracting of companies that these mandatory rules continue to play a role. However, with the integration of corporate codes into private relations of contracting, one can identify how, in a different form, private relations are governed

174 Kingsbury (2006); Kingsbury (2009).
175 Kingsbury (2006) 29.
176 Kingsbury (2009) 31.
177 Kuo (2009) 999.
178 Kingsbury (2009) 57.

by public interests, which have their origin in the regulatory practices of private actors when these develop rules that 'address matters of concern to the society as such' or when they begin to choose such rules that have been developed by international political institutions. On this basis, one can distinguish between three different regulatory layers that influence private relations based on public interests.

First, the political system continues to play a vital role as a regulatory entity that translates political objectives, including requests for social justice or constitutional values, into private law by means of mandatory rules. Second, however, the corporate codes introduce an additional public interest in the form of a corporate response to political pressures from society. In this regard, the substantive interest has been considered public due to the fact that the particular topic—be it workplace standards or particular aspects of environmental protection—has been claimed by societal pressures as an interest that concerns society at large. In the context of private law, this form of public interest derives from the autonomous interaction between different private entities and their own regulatory capacity to produce public standards even if they do not have a global consensus in institutionalised politics. A public interest eventually becomes visible as, so to speak, a result of 'negotiation' between the societal but genuine political, pressures and companies. Thus, for this political substance of the corporate codes, the starting point remains the developed corporate policy referred to or incorporated in the contract as revealed in the public self-commitment. The contract and self-commitments are equally core rules that govern private relations and consequently specify their rights and obligations.[179] Third, the theoretical debate has also indicated a difference within the codes between two types of political regulation. Next to the integration of public interests brought up by social pressures, there is also a public interest introduced by means of reference to international policy frameworks, in particular the ILO core labour rights, and national (mostly labour) laws. It is here that autonomous political regulation is linked to the public interests that are expressed by states and international politics in the form of legislation and international recommendations. Yet, this public interest is introduced into private law differently from political regulation in the form of intervention by mandatory law. It is not based on the category of mandatory rules, but it would equally be too narrow to treat these constant references as effectively the same as the autonomously created public interest that is productively created by contract and commitment. Here the choice of the companies to subject the private relations to a political objective represents the decisive link.[180] Given this understanding, this dimension could probably fit best with the recent private law debate to deem the choice of private actors for a particular type of political regulation as an additional dimension in private law that governs private relations.[181] One could then

[179] This comes very close to what Zumbansen (2007) describes as the new governance by contract that needs to be made visible in the private law rules that govern contracts in the form of translating 'the conflicting, overlapping, and diverging social rationalities [apparent in governance by contract] into its own legal language' (at 233). See also on this point very recently Podszun (2014) 73.

[180] See the arguments presented above, section 8.2.2.2.3. (p 326), text and accompanying footnotes.

[181] See in particular Smits (2010b) 10; Smits (2011) 333. *cf* also in this context Bachmann (2008) 13, who emphasises the advantages of choice for substantive rules in private law as an intermediate form between intervention by mandatory rules and self-regulation by party autonomy.

interpret the choice of corporations in their codes to apply particular national provisions on workplace standards provided they do not qualify as mandatory rules as well as the increasing incorporation of frameworks as the ILO core labour rights as a choice for a particular set of regulatory norms developed by politics to govern their private relations. Interpreted in this way, these political guidelines and statutes become applicable and binding norms governing private relations. The chosen rules deriving from national legislation and international politics would then represent a regulatory tool that is similar to what has in the recent private law debate been discussed as optional law.[182] The international policy frameworks and the national statutory rules certainly do not qualify formally as an optional legal framework comparable to, for instance, the Common European Sales Law.[183] They have not been intentionally designed by politics as such as an optional system and have rather been framed as providing 'authoritative guidance'[184] on what the formal political system deems socially responsible behaviour. However, from the perspective of corporations, these guiding international political frameworks and the national laws that companies voluntarily integrate in their codes effectively fulfil a similar function to optional rules. They represent specific rules developed within politics that, instead of being imposed on private actors in the form of a mandatory rule, are offered to them with the urge to be applied as 'the evolving and recently strengthened global for CSR'[185] that should govern the transnational operations of companies.

As a result, primarily the autonomous political regulation in the corporate policies and the chosen frameworks represent the governing rules for private relations in which these frameworks are included.

8.3.2. Consequences for Contractual and Promissory Enforcement

After having discussed the corporate codes as a new type of political regulation by private actors in light of how it could become a valid public interest debate in private law that governs their relationships, the following section will focus more specifically on the implications that this may have for private law when regulating contractual relations in which this new form of political regulation is integrated. To that end, in particular the character and content of the obligation as specified in contract law, the appropriate remedies and contract law enforcement and the possibility of third party rights require further scrutiny.

8.3.2.1. Towards a Duty to Regulate

Following the understanding provided above, the terms of contracts that integrate the corporate policy need to be viewed in light of the underlying self-regulatory

[182] Smits (2010a).

[183] European Commission, Proposal for a Regulation of the European Parliament and the Council on a Common European Sales Law, COM(2011) 635 final.

[184] European Commission (n 49).

[185] ibid 6f.

policies and the specific rules, ie, ILO labour rights and particular national rules, that have been opted for. Thus, it is not considered suitable to rely on the existing set of default rules within contract law, be they the sale of goods or on third party rights, when specifying the obligation deriving from the contractual term or a public declaration that refers to a corporate code; instead, the autonomous corporate policies and the international guidelines themselves specify the obligations. But what substantive obligation can be derived from these rules or, conversely, what could be taken as a starting point in order to determine the substantive private law obligations between the contracting parties?

A theoretical foundation to discuss this question can be developed when relating the corporate codes to the discussion in contract theory on the different social dimensions or logics that govern contracts.[186] In this context, it has been emphasised that market transactions remain important, but are only one of the core aspects of the contracting which contract law needs to take into consideration when regulating the relations.[187] Instead, one core insight of the theoretical analysis is that the corporate codes productively partake in the objective of regulating social and environmental standards on a global scale. To that end, the corporate codes are not (or at least not only) included in contractual agreements or publicly declared in order to enhance the value of the goods that are subject to an economic transaction. Even more far-reaching, the role of the corporate code is to specify the role of the contracting parties as regulators. As Backer observes with respect to the large retailer Gap Inc:

> In a traditional business environment, Gap Inc. would endeavour to enter into fairly straightforward agreements with its suppliers. In return for the production of a certain amount of products (to be described in the contract), the supplier would be expected to be paid a certain amount. The rest of the terms of such a contract would also be fairly straightforward: quality, place of delivery, inspection of goods and quality control, payment holdbacks and the like. But [by means of including a corporate code] Gap Inc. has entered into a different form of contractual arrangement with its suppliers. These contracts have a substantial social and regulatory dimension.[188]

This additional regulatory purpose behind the codes brings them into close proximity to what has been described in contract theory as the productive dimension of contracting. The productive dimension of contracting refers to the contribution that the contractual agreement makes in relation to a particular social system.[189] Understood from the productive perspective, the manufacturing of a product is not simply an economic transaction, but links this transaction with the productive logic of a technological project; medical treatment is not only a paid-for service but also a piece of medical art that productively contributes to the functioning and further development of the system of medicine.[190] In the context of this study, the productive system that the corporate codes relate to and that they make part

[186] See especially Collins (1999) 129ff; Teubner (2000a); Zumbansen (2007) 222ff; Cafaggi (2013).
[187] Collins (1999) 129f; Teubner (2000a) 404.
[188] Backer (2008) 510. For similar observations, see recently Podszun (2014) 73f.
[189] Teubner (2000a) 400, 407f.
[190] ibid 409.

of the contract essentially represents the two different forms of political regulation. By means of linking the contract or a public self-commitment to a political project, the corporate codes productively partake in the development of political standards. By means of incorporating political guidelines, they contribute to the development in politics that has the objective of realising global adherence to specific fundamental workplace standards (the ILO core labour rights) or human rights (the UN Guiding Principles); whenever they accommodate the global political pressures of society, the codes partake in the expressed political projects in global society. This long-term project has to be translated into the regulation of such contracts within contract law. The obligations of the contracting parties thus need to be specified in light of this political logic of an ongoing project rather than the logic of an economic transaction. The practical consequences of this political logic in contracts as to the substantive obligations of the parties have, so far, been most comprehensively discussed by Cafaggi. Focusing on the integration of social and environmental standards in contracts that refer to corporate policies, private certification or international policy frameworks, he observes how this effectively broadens the scope of substantive contractual obligations between the contracting parties towards regulatory duties.[191] This emerging regulatory logic within contracting mainly has the effect that the content of the contract is enhanced by an obligation to comply with a public standard as specified in an external corporate policy, certification or an international political framework, and, importantly, the obligation to comply is integrated as a process standard that was previously subject to administrative and tort law.[192] Particularly concerning social standards, the substantive obligation of the code is then not merely a specification of the product exchange, but a new requirement to perform actual modifications of working conditions at the factory site.[193] Thus, 'the integration of regulatory provisions in commercial contracts expands the scope of contract law to ensure compliance with process in addition to product standards'.[194]

With respect to the regulation and enforcement of contracts by contract law, this mainly implies that the courts, when determining the contractual obligation created by the corporate code, would primarily need to consult the corporate policy and any chosen international framework in order to identify the substantive standard that serves as the benchmark. The contractual term also needs to be read as a contractual obligation to safeguard and further compliance with this substantive standard on a continuous basis. It is thus, despite having as a principal contract an agreement on a sale of goods or provision of services, an additional and separate substantive obligation in the contract to safeguard compliance with the standard on a constant basis. This regulatory dimension could even be further specified by the principles of global administrative law that specify the duties of regulators.

[191] In fact, Cafaggi (2013) also focuses on the effects of such regulatory provisions on the entire supply chain, including subcontractors, but this aspect will be ignored due to the focus of this study on the effect of corporate codes on the direct relations between the company and other parties (consumer, supplier and beneficiaries).

[192] ibid 1596.

[193] ibid 1597.

[194] ibid.

This would imply recognising not only a general duty to regulate but also ancillary duties relating to transparency, participation, review and accountability.[195]

8.3.2.2. Enforcement Architecture

This regulatory perspective on the substantive contractual obligation also provides a basis for determining the appropriate remedial regime that contract law ought to render applicable when the obligation is breached. The political logic of this contractual obligation must then be equally reflected in the course of choosing the appropriate contractual remedy.

The substantive obligation to regulate public standards effectively puts the contracting parties under the obligation to further the constant improvement of public standards; it assigns them the role as regulators. Thus, one can interpret the role of the contracting parties as enforcing the agreed standard not primarily for their own benefit, but rather to further the protection of the public standards as such. What is therefore required is an enforcement structure that safeguards the ongoing fulfilment of this role. Such an understanding of contract law enforcement can take inspiration from the tradition in legal theory that deems the core function of private law enforcement to be the protection of social institutions. This idea can already be identified in the works of Jhering, who held that enforcing contractual rights with the help of contract law is not only a matter of the parties pursuing their own interests. In addition, by means of enforcing rights granted by the law, every individual is also called upon to enforce and defend the validity of the law as such.[196] From the more recent theoretical literature, this idea of private law enforcement as institutional protection is influenced particularly by the work of Raiser, who argues for a twofold understanding of private law enforcement.[197] To him, private law enforcement is not only in place to provide private parties with a legal right to pursue their own interests; in addition, it comprises a second equally important dimension, which is to protect public institutions by means of giving parties specific private rights of action. Allowing parties to enforce private rights is then not only a way to allow the enforcement of individual subjective rights, but the enforcement of rights is also granted to private parties 'as a means' to serve institutional protection.[198] In short, the private actor is deemed to serve 'as administrator of the overall legal system'.[199] The proposed contract law enforcement of this regulatory duty in contracts is, in this way, closely related to the dimension of private law enforcement that is directed towards furthering the protection of institutions, in

[195] See fundamentally: www.iilj.org/GAL/default.asp; and Kingsbury et al (2005) 5.

[196] Jhering (1989 [1872]) 26f: 'Im Privatrecht ist jeder an seiner Stelle berufen, das Gesetz zu verteidigen, Wächter und Vollstrecker des Gesetzes innerhalb seiner Sphäre zu sein. Das konkrete Recht, das ihm zusteht, läßt sich als eine ihm vom Staate erteilte Ermächtigung auffassen, innerhalb seines Interessenkreises für das Gesetz in die Schranken zu treten und dem Unrecht zu wehren, eine bedingte und spezielle Aufforderung im Gegensatz zu der unbedingten und allgemeinen, die an den Beamten geht. Wer *sein* Recht behauptet, verteidigt innerhalb des engen Raumes desselben auch *das* Recht' (emphasis in original).

[197] Raiser (1963).

[198] Raiser (1963) 159.

[199] Teubner (2006b) 50.

this case the effective private regulatory behaviour. It then views the enforcement position of the contracting parties as an *actio pro institutione*, a fiduciary entitlement.[200] The role of the contracting parties to further institutional protection then also needs to be reflected when specifying the remedy that contract law makes the parties available to enforce the institutional breach. In constellations of an *actio pro institutione*, the appropriate remedy must be directed towards seeking an injunction against the institutional breach, requiring performance of obligations or claiming restitution of adverse effects.[201] It is thus a remedy that is directed towards seeking performance of the public standards and injunctions against breaches. In fact, a remedial scheme of safeguarding performance and seeking corrective action can also be identified as one of the core remedies that the corporate codes specify for breach of regulatory provisions. As Cafaggi observes: 'The primary objective of regulatory remedies is to re-establish the correct functioning of the regulatory process and to correct regulatory failures, rather than to compensate the [individual] victims of the breach.'[202] From the remedies of contract law, this comes the closest to the remedy of specific performance or, in the case of regulatory obligations that concern omissions, an injunction order, and it is consequently this remedy that is suggested as the core remedy to be applicable for breach of corporate codes.

That being said, it is equally recognised that this proposed direction of enforcement has its limits, as contract law enforcement that is directed towards protecting institutions can also conflict with the individual enforcement dimension. Contract law enforcement in the hands of the contracting parties can be a feasible mechanism to the extent that the contracting parties generally fulfil the objective of furthering public interests, eg, with respect to contracting public bodies in procurement contracts.[203] However, with respect to private actors in general, this form of institutional protection by contract law enforcement remains considerably more difficult to realise. Important reasons for this difficulty are certainly several practical obstacles that are associated with such proposals for contract law enforcement.[204] Yet, the proposed institutional contract law enforcement is problematic in a more fundamental way, as it exposes private actors to two contradicting roles that they need to take.[205] In relation to consumers as the entitled parties, this conflict

200 Fikentscher (1983) § 27 V, 527ff.

201 In this direction, see ibid 529: 'handelt es sich um das Eintreten eines einzelnen für den Schutz eines sozialen Werts, dessen Verletzung sonst nicht geahndet würde. Die materiellen Voraussetzungen dieser Klage sind also, daß ein ausreichender Rechtsschutz des sozialen Werts … nicht zur Verfügung steht … Das Ziel der Klage ist … die Beseitigung des durch die Verletzungshandlung herbeigeführten Eingriffs, im Falle des Besorgens der Wiederholung Unterlassung künftiger Verletzungen und die Herausgabe des durch die Zuwiderhandlung erzielten Gewinnes, allerdings nicht an den Kläger allein, sondern an diejenigen Träger privater oder öffentlicher Interessen, denen das verletzte soziale Gut von Rechts wegen zu Nutzung zugedacht ist'.

202 Cafaggi (2013) 1614.

203 On this category see section 3.1.1.2. (p 49), text and accompanying footnotes.

204 Webb and Morrison (2004) 123f mention several practical obstacles in relation to contract enforcement of voluntary codes, such as the missing evidence about whether a breach has occurred, the practical and financial obstacles for individuals to initiate lawsuits, and their minimal individual damage.

205 Wiethölter (1974) 689: 'Begriff des autonomen Individuums entspricht als Abstraktion nicht Handlungszusammenhängen in Beziehungsgruppen, die—"nach eigenen, habituell ausgerichteten Regeln" strukturiert—Institutionen sind. Individualschutz und Institutionenschutz in "polarer Spannung"'. For this conflict between the protection of individual rights and institutions, *cf* also Teubner (2006b) 50f.

becomes visible in the inherent contradiction between the act of consumption that is beneficial to them, and also protected and furthered by consumer sales law and the protection of environmental and social values against the destructive tendencies of consumption to society at large that the proposed institutional contract law enforcement targets.[206] More precisely, based on the individual dimension of consumer sales law, consumers are encouraged to consume and are given rights when this act of consumption fails; however, the institutional dimension of protecting public interests requires them to remedy this protected act of individual consumption. Effectively, the proposed contract law enforcement requires nothing more than remedying and thus undoing a successful market transaction and sanctioning consumption. A similar conflict occurs in relation to enforcement by commercial parties; it is here in particular the contradiction between the necessary contract law enforcement to safeguard the regulation of public standards and the simultaneous embedding of this relationship in a business community that views contract law enforcement sceptically and partly even sanctions it.[207] With respect to the corporate codes, this has the paradoxical result that the contract represents as much the core and serious basis for the code enforcement as it hinders the enforcement due to the reluctance of the contracting parties to bring it to court.[208] It is then not only the possibility of having a contract law enforcement structure in place but also the problems as to its actual use that need to be addressed. It would certainly be an option to conclude with an emphasis on the general limits of contract law to accommodate these new public interests and the limited role of contract law enforcement as opposed to public law regulation,[209] and insist on the benefits of non-judicial enforcement.[210] If, however, the underlying objective remains to open formal private law truly to this new form of political regulation that complements state regulation, it is inevitable and thus a matter of necessity to open up the private law enforcement structure to further this objective effectively. Or, as one observer puts it:

> For the future of private law it is crucial that not just its [private law's] doctrinal-conceptual structures are prepared … Also different litigation procedures, among other rules of

[206] See instructively on this conflict between environmental protection and consumption Wilhelmsson (1998) 66; Wilhelmsson (2002/2003) 99, who sees the possibility of overcoming this conflict with a 'utopian' vision that is based on 'the idea that the concept of the consumer in the long run could be replaced by that of the "citizen"'.

[207] See generally Collins (1999) 128ff, who distinguishes between three different normative frameworks that guide the contracting parties' behaviour: the business relationship that is oriented on the objective of building trust, the economic deal that is oriented on rational self-interest and the self-enforcing contract that specifies the legal rights and obligations. With reference to sociological studies on contracting, he observes that 'the frames of reference provided by the relation and the deal are likely to carry greater weight than the strict contractual point of view' and 'becomes reversed … once the parties perceive that the business relation itself has broken down and that the deal cannot be retrieved by compromise of interests' (at 136).

[208] This paradox of corporate code enforcement in contracts can be empirically observed; see the observations of McBarnet and Kurkchiyan (2007) at 79: 'Despite the insistence by one interviewee that contractual obligation is important to get the issues taken seriously, he was quick to add "even though it is highly unlikely we would ever go to court".'

[209] Wilhelmsson (1998) 59; Wilhelmsson (2004a) 224, 237 ('Admittedly, the practical role of contract law remedies in this context cannot be very important').

[210] See Estlund (2012) 256f, who takes a sceptical perspective of judicial contract law enforcement of both companies against their suppliers and suppliers against companies.

> standing for groups, collective representation, multilateralization of the adverse two-party process, and elements of public interest litigation, would need to be introduced to make private law responsive to the new conflictuality caused by privatization itself.[211]

Admittedly, such a conceptualisation demands a quite far-reaching change within the structure of contract law enforcement. It cannot even be solved within contract law by an internal development, but requires adjustments within other domains, in particular civil procedure in the form of statutory reform. It would go beyond the scope of a study that is concerned with the integration of the codes into private law to discuss all these aspects in general. Therefore, the following analysis will rather discuss and evaluate two more general options that are currently discussed in the corporate codes literature as possible directions in which an effective contract law enforcement of corporate codes could evolve in the future.

On the one hand, one could enhance the possibilities of contract law enforcement by means of instrumentalising the private interests of the parties for public purposes. This could be envisaged as providing incentives for private actors to make use of their entitlement by allowing them to claim punitive damages.[212] On the other hand, one could, as is more frequently indicated in contributions in the corporate code debate, strengthen the collective dimension of the enforcement structure of private law.[213] One could here in particular connect to the collective enforcement in the form of a distinct role of organisations to act in the collective interest of consumers and thereby further the institution of consumer law.[214] There are arguably two strong points to support the latter rather than the former direction. Already from the very idea of interpreting contract law enforcement of the corporate codes as a matter of protecting the institution of effective regulatory behaviour, a choice for incentivising measures that target the private interest seems questionable. Once the emphasis is placed on the enforcement role of private actors as a fiduciary entitlement, it must inevitably be interpreted as a contradiction if mechanisms are proposed that effectively further the private interest and thereby push the fiduciary role to the background. Furthermore, a development towards the latter seems more feasible against the background of the current restrictions in private law. One can refer here to the prominent strong reservations in European legal systems, including England and Germany, against awarding damages beyond compensating the entitled party.[215] This general reluctance seems in line with the general scepticism in the EU. One can refer here only to the sceptical position in the Commission's recent recommendation for the Member States on collective redress, in which it is clearly stated that punitive damages

211 Teubner (1999) 423f.

212 For the general discussion on punitive damages in EU Member States, *cf* the contributions in Meurkens and Nordin (2012). The idea of using punitive damages in consumer law to enforce matters of environmental concern is also indicated in Wilhelmsson (1998) 65.

213 A collective enforcement by NGOs in relation to workplace standards is discussed by Estlund (2012) 253f and by environmental NGOs in relation to environmental standards by Glinski (2011) 172f. A stronger role of consumer associations in the enforcement of environmental and social commitments is mentioned by Wilhelmsson (2002/2003) 101; Webb and Morrison (2004) 124; and Glinski (2011) 193.

214 *cf* the contributions in Boom and Loos (2007).

215 See the evidence provided in section 3.2.2.2. (p 123), in particular n 341.

'should be avoided as a general rule'.[216] Conversely, with regard to rights of organisations, there are already several collective enforcement mechanisms in private law that, in their current form, complement the orthodox private enforcement. This is not only present in relation to unfair commercial practices, where a two-fold individual and collective enforcement structure already exists, which specifically allows designated organisations to seek injunctions in the collective interest of consumers.[217] Collective enforcement has also become a matter in the area of contract law in the form of giving designated organisations the right to take action against traders against standard contract terms in consumer contracts that were included to the detriment of the consumer.[218] Initially, this collective enforcement mechanism was particularly viewed with scepticism because, by giving a party who is a stranger to the contract a contractual remedy, it effectively contradicts the fundamental principle of the privity of contracts.[219] The scepticism concerning this conceptual breach of one of the fundamental principles of contract law notwithstanding, this enforcement mechanism prevailed. This collective enforcement already opens up the possibilities for specifically designated collectives to intervene in the bilateral agreements and thus could be used as a starting point for the enforcement of regulatory norms. Certainly, in its current state, this form of collective enforcement is not suitable and could not be directly used to enforce the regulatory terms. However, one could rather rely on this initial attempt as an existing category in which the strict bilateral enforcement in contract law is opened up towards recognising a legitimate role of organisations. Interpreted this way, one could at least consider, in the long run, pushing this development one step further towards a narrowly confined enforcement of terms in contracts that have been included in contracts for the very sake of furthering and regulating public interests. Admittedly, in the specific form of unfair contract terms already present, this requires a significant shift from understanding collective enforcement not only as a tool to protect the general interest of one contracting party that is deemed to be in a structurally weaker position, but also as a device which furthers the effective enforcement of terms as agreed upon by the contracting parties. Yet, such a development fits with the general attempt to integrate the corporate codes into private law that, rather than focusing on prevention and sanctions, furthers a perspective that recognises the codes' regulatory potential by means of rendering it subject to enforcement. In relation to the existing mechanisms on collective enforcement, it would entail more precisely a transformation of collective enforcement from a

[216] European Commission, Recommendation on common principles for injunctive and compensatory redress mechanisms in the Member States concerning violations of rights granted under Union Law, C(2013) 3539, recital 15 and Principle 31.

[217] See in detail on this type of enforcement, section 5.4.1. (p 208), text and accompanying footnotes.

[218] See Directive 93/13/EEC on unfair contract terms in consumer contracts [1993] OJ L95/29, art 7, para 2, as implemented in the UK by the Unfair Terms in Consumer Contracts Regulation 1994, SI 1994/3159 and replaced by the Unfair Terms in Consumer Contracts Regulations 1999, SI 1999/2083, and in Germany by the *Unterlassensklagegesetz* (UKlG).

[219] For this issue, see especially the initial UK response to art 7, para 2 of the Unfair Contract Terms Directive that 'UK law at present contains no general provision for representative actions; only a party to a contract may sue under a contract. Thus according to the national law concerned this provision can have no effect' (quote taken from Howells and Weatherill (2005) 293).

device to realise liability claims, to prevent the contractual enforcement of unfair terms, or to seek an injunction order against particular trading behaviour into a device that is equipped to safeguard positive enforcement of a narrow set of valid contract terms to the extent that they bring about a regulatory duty.

8.3.2.3. Third Party Rights

The perspective on the codes as a tool that gives rise to substantive regulatory duties concerning public social and environmental standards is finally also important for determining the existence of third party rights. In the course of the contractual analysis, it was emphasised that this is a possible option, but, considering the default rules on third party rights, the existence depends primarily on what is deemed to be the purpose of the particular obligation, as is made apparent in the wording of the contract or in the contextual circumstances.[220] Following this theoretical analysis, with respect to this purpose of the corporate codes, it is considered fruitful to consult the public standards that the parties have committed themselves to or have chosen as the guiding framework. From this perspective, one needs to decide whether the regulatory purpose is connected to a third party right for the beneficiaries of the regulatory undertaking or only an incidental third party benefit. This could be determined in the form of drawing parallels to the question of whether a comparable statutory regulation of these aspects would create only an objective obligation to regulate or would treat the individuals affected by the statutory regulation as rights holders.[221]

One can then translate the question of third party rights in contracts into the question of whether statutory regulation would grant subjective rights or whether improvements of regulation remain only factual reflexes of the objective obligation deriving from the statute.[222] In the common law debate, this could be translated into a question of whether a particular statutory obligation grants individuals a remedy. This has the effect that the existence of a contractual third party right is not only a question of identifying the underlying purpose of the contracting parties, eg, whether they intended to grant a third party right with their regulatory

[220] See the conclusion drawn in section 3.2.3.1.3. (p 141).

[221] This proposal comes very close to the idea of Ayres and Brown (2006) 1641, who envisage the rules on contractual third party rights as an effective tool to replicate the enforcement mechanism of a statute on anti-discrimination by means of a private contractual agreement. To that end, they propose to explicitly incorporate in the contract a clause that 'Licensee and Licensor agree to designate as express third-party beneficiaries of this agreement all persons and entities that would be entitled to sue if [the statute] were in effect' (at 1645). For a similar proposal in the field of environmental standards, *cf* Geis (2012) 1176ff. However, the proposal made here differs insofar as it is not directed towards designing contracts in a manner that they constitute third party rights, but instead suggests interpreting from the perspective of private law existing contracts with such regulatory clauses in light of the equivalent statutory protection.

[222] This distinction between subjective rights and so-called *Reflexrechte* in public law has been developed by Jellinek (1964) 67ff, who distinguishes between regulation that creates subjective rights and objective regulation that serves the public interest with only factual reflexes on individuals (*Reflexrechte*). The notion of subjective rights and factual reflexes has also been used in relation to contractual third party rights; for an overview of the debate concerning inter-banking agreements, *cf* Schäfer (1990) 75ff.

undertaking, nor is it entirely a matter of the phrasing of the codes. Instead, to the extent that the corporate codes provide sufficient evidence for the purpose of the contracting parties to regulate public standards, the rights for affected third parties result mainly from taking this very regulatory purpose seriously.

Although much here will depend on the specific substantive obligation and regulatory objective that the code lays down, one can still draw, at least on a general level, a distinction between the regulation of workplace standards on the one hand and environmental standards on the other. In the area of workplace standards, the existence of third party rights is arguably significantly easier to establish considering that statutory regulation of labour standards ought to not only objectively protect but also empower employees by providing them with remedies for violations of labour law. In anti-discrimination cases, this right is partly even expanded to job applicants.[223] Thus, regulation in labour law on aspects of minimum remuneration, health and safety standards or working time generally gives the employee the remedy to enforce breaches. This, as a result, suggests treating alike the regulation of these standards by contract and interpreting the regulatory dimension of such standards as having the purpose of conferring direct benefits upon employees and, to the extent applicable for the particular regulatory provision, also job applicants. In addition to these individual rights, here one could also refer to collective dimensions in labour law where rights are not only created for individuals to form trade unions, but also for trade unions to represent employees in matters of employment.[224] To the extent that such rights are recognised within the context of labour law, a similar interpretation of rights of union representation can be established whenever they are made part of a regulation by contract. This applies in particular if the applicable ILO convention is referred to. However, as far as environmental protection is concerned, the situation of rights for an individual or groups presents itself quite differently. With respect to environmental matters, it represents, with specific exceptions, at least the traditional understanding that the general public interest of a clean natural environment and public law obligations to further environmental protection do not confer such rights on individuals or groups to enforce these obligations.[225] There still remains, in this area, the inherent scepticism not to open the 'floodgates' for claims of an unforeseeable number of potential litigants and the development towards general public interest litigation. Although there are recent noteworthy developments in this area towards increasing private enforcement, in particular the tendencies to grant environmental NGOs participation rights in administrative procedures and access to

[223] Ayres and Brown (2006) 1646.

[224] See Kocher (2009) 421ff, who criticises that corporate codes are not specified in light of the content of the ILO declarations on employee representation.

[225] From the perspective of European environmental law with further references to the debate, *cf* on this question Eliantonio (2011). The restrictive focus of rights in environmental matters characterises German law in particular, where it remains the understanding that environmental goods (clean air, water or ground) do not confer subjective rights upon individuals; see fundamentally BGHZ 102, 350 (dealing liability of the Federal Republic of Germany for forest damages); and with further references, Palandt-Sprau § 823, para 22; MüKo-Wagner § 823, paras 237, 238; Westermann (2008) 146.

courts in order to remedy administrative decisions,[226] this development is still too recent and contested even in the domain of public law in order to serve as a viable analogy for third party beneficiary recognition in contract law. The recognition of party rights depends, in relation to the area of environmental standards, on the further developments in the area of environmental law.

In spite of this general proposal to draw parallels in contract interpretation between contractual third party rights and rights for individuals or groups in statutory regulation, there is one important difference between the two that needs to be emphasised. Notwithstanding the similarities between statutory and contractual regulations, the regulatory role constituted by the corporate codes remains based on contract and not statute. This makes a difference insofar as the contractual basis allows the regulating private actors to explicitly exclude the suggested third party enforcement. If parties make the effort to include a sufficiently concrete disclaimer, it is difficult from the perspective of contract law to interpret this regulatory obligation as creating third party rights. The general possibility of including disclaimers then raises the question of whether and how such autonomous restrictions in the regulatory role ought to be treated from the perspective of contract law enforcement of the corporate code. Does private law, due to its underlying principle towards party autonomy, fully accept the possibility for the contracting parties to exclude this right? Or does the interpretation of the regulatory dimension need to be given an interpretation whereby the possibility for parties to exclude the third party right becomes restricted? It is again here that the limits of a contractual regulation as a complement to political regulation become apparent and it is—as mentioned already in relation to collective enforcement—again a decision between accepting existing limits within contract law and requiring a necessary adaption of private law to these new developments even at the expense of abandoning some of its core principles.

It is certainly one of the fundamental principles of contract law to respect the autonomy of private parties to preserve their freedom to create but also exclude rights. On the other hand, it is equally true that contract law generally does not only have the function of enforcing the autonomously created obligations by private parties, but also needs to regulate contractual agreements, thereby imposing restraints on how parties can use the contract.[227] An important reason for restricting, in the particular case of the corporate codes, the option for parties to exclude third party rights is here the fact that contract law needs not only to enforce the autonomously created regulatory undertaking, but, in addition, contract law also needs to preserve the general function of regulation by rejecting attempts to regulate 'in an incomplete manner', eg, by pursuing a regulatory objective without sufficiently accompanying accountability towards the regulated collectives. It is with respect to this aspect that the conflict within contract law comes to the fore

[226] See in particular Directive 2003/35/EC [2003] OJ L156/17, which implements the United Nations Economic Commission for Europe Convention on access to information, public participation in decision making and access to justice in environmental matters, 25 June 1998 (Aarhus Convention).

[227] The perspective on contract law as having the role of regulating and not only enforcing the contractual agreements between parties is particularly expressed by Collins (1999) 56ff.

between the objective of effectuating the new productive potential of the corporate codes and the contradicting requirement within private law to retain internal coherence.[228] It is then again a decision between these two conflicting needs, namely to preserve the internal coherence within contract law and the need to react appropriately to this particular new regulatory role of private actors, that is required. A strong argument in favour of the latter position is certainly the underlying justification behind restricting the scope of third party rights. The strategy of contract law to avoid broadening the scope of third party beneficiaries too far and allowing parties to mitigate and exclude the risk of third party liability is based on the justified concern that allowing too significant of an expansion of third party liability effectively results in a situation in which 'worthwhile transactions will be discouraged by the threat of liability to a wide range of persons'.[229] This is particularly an underlying concern in relation to the corporate codes, considering that the likely reaction of companies to extensive recognition of third party rights, without a clear possibility of excluding this consequence, is a more reluctant strategy towards introducing a regulatory dimension in contracts altogether. While it is recognised that social pressures and the fear of negative reputation render this option currently unattractive, this situation may change once the fear of unavoidable liability is recognised.[230] From the perspective of contract law, a strict intervention with regard to the autonomy of the private relations could then eventually turn out to be only a Pyrrhic victory. As a practical example, one can mention the recent experience in English law with setting up presumption in the Contracts (Rights of Third Parties) Act. After the introduction of the presumption, it could be observed that, rather than accepting the consequence of a third party right, the presumption seems instead to have triggered an attitude of putting more effort into the phrasing of disclaimers.[231] It is then against the background of not providing disincentives for companies to use this form of political regulation altogether that a reluctant attitude would essentially be called for.

But at what price does this come? It is equally true that a reluctant attitude in contract law towards intervening in the form of refraining from regulating the use of disclaimers reinforces one of the core critiques against the corporate codes, eg, their character as an ineffective, incomplete and thus unacceptable tool of political regulation that lacks accountability. The effectiveness of the corporate codes and thus their long-term success as an accepted complementary form of political regulation eventually depends on the innovative potential of contract law to prevent

[228] See on this problem of regulatory private law in general ibid 69.

[229] Collins (2003b) 217.

[230] For a similar prediction, see Phillips and Lim (2009) 374: 'While suing on the promise is the easiest way for workers to prevent rescission, the procedure may become useless once buyers-suppliers recognise that they face liability in these situations. Disclaiming language could then become commonplace in their agreements, pre-empting lawsuits.' See also Estlund (2012) 255: 'The existing corporate codes were not intended to give rise to judicially enforceable duties on the part of lead firms to the workers of supplier firms, and are unlikely to do so. Nor would it clearly speed the progress of the CSR movement if firms learned that adopting a code of conduct for their overseas supplier could *inadvertently* expose them to costly litigation and substantial liabilities' (emphasis in original).

[231] On this development, see generally McKnight (2004) 170f.

a form of biased regulation that lacks accountability.[232] Effectively, contract law is faced with a dilemma. It is caught between, on the one side, claims for reconciling the evolving regulatory role in contracting with the general functioning of regulation by setting comparable and reliable standards concerning accountability and, on the other side, the need to pay due respect to the fact that this form of regulation remains based on a voluntary agreement or commitment in the private sphere. There is probably no right answer to solve this dilemma, as suggestions in both directions would do injustice to one side or the other. Accepting the possibility of having different standards for statutory and contractual regulation by allowing private actors to exclude liability for their regulatory duties would significantly reduce the strengths of the identified regulatory function and reduce the trust in corporations as regulators. It would mean giving up and accepting that the regulated entities remain 'the groups that seem to be cut out of the process', that 'things are done on their behalf' and that 'there is little expectation that the objects of all these activities will actually participate actively in the formation and elaboration of standards and enforcement norms'.[233] Conversely, suggesting the same standards for statutory and contract regulation, while furthering accountability in this type of regulation and while at least meeting the criticism of an insufficient accountability, equally jeopardises the success of the codes and the use of the very instrument of regulation by contract and commitment. A conceivable compromise to this dilemma that is worth considering here could be to preserve the option of the parties to use disclaimers in order to exclude third party rights, but nevertheless impose certain threshold requirements in order for such disclaimers not to be unfair in light of the regulatory role. The possibility of parties to exclude the possibility of a third party to enforce the regulatory term could particularly be made dependent on the fact that other forms, such as third party complaint procedures, are made available that safeguard accountability in a comparable manner for the regulatory efforts.

8.3.2.4. Conclusion

The previous section focused on the implications on contract law enforcement that derive from this new form of political regulation by private actors in the form of self-regulatory corporate policies and as an autonomous choice to further particular public standards. In so doing, it was argued that an appropriate way to determine the substantive obligation for contracts, where these forms of political regulation play a role, is not to focus on default rules in sales contracts or third party rights. Instead, the obligation needs to be developed with a view to the substantive commitments in the self-regulatory policies and the chosen political rules and in light of the role of the company as a global regulator. Based on this perspective,

[232] *cf* also MacDonald and MacDonald (2006) 117, who argue that corporate codes require 'significant new forms of legal innovation', in particular by adapting 'instruments in tort law, contract law and liability law to empower stakeholders'.

[233] Backer (2008) 522.

the substantive enforceable obligation was specified as a duty to regulate the autonomously developed and chosen standards on a continuous basis. This regulatory duty then also influences the remedial scheme that contract law ought to offer and the recognition of third party rights. In this context, it was argued that, in general, the appropriate remedy available to the contracting parties must be directed towards safeguarding this private regulatory role. This, as a result, leads to applying the remedial scheme in contract law to the corporate codes that is directed towards safeguarding performance and deterring future violations, eg, performance and injunctions. In this context, a possible further development within contract law was indicated to link the remedial scheme to collective enforcement. Finally, in relation to third party rights, it was proposed to draw analogies to public standards that the corporate codes refer to and discuss whether they treat individuals affected by regulation as objects or rights holders. In relation to the possibility for contracting parties to exclude third party rights, it was argued that a possible further direction could be to make the option of excluding third party liability dependent on the existence of an internal complaint mechanism that safeguards accountability.

8.3.3. Consequences for Legal Liability

After a detailed analysis has been conducted on the way in which the self-regulatory policies and the chosen political standards could influence contract law and the undertaking of specifying the contractual obligations and remedies, this section will briefly consider the potential influence of this new form of regulation on the two other areas that are discussed in the context of this study. With regard to the rules on general non-contractual liability, regulatory private standards are primarily of importance when concretising the open-ended concept of negligence and, more precisely, the applicable standard of due care. With respect to this aspect, the legal analysis already specified two different options in which the corporate codes, and potentially also the public codes, become relevant. It concerned, on the one hand, the existing use of self-regulatory standards to specify the standard of reasonable care.[234] On the other hand, the self-regulatory codes of conduct could serve as a potential standard in unfair commercial practices law for specifying what is considered fair trading behaviour.[235]

Based on the theoretical observations, it is argued that these novel forms of regulation could indeed be accepted as private standards that can represent one of the factors that specify the standard of due care. That being said, keeping in mind the origin of these standards, it equally has to be clear that the corporate codes cannot, at least not based on the theoretical observations of this study, be proposed as constituting the standard of due care on a general level for outsiders. Instead, the codes remain regulatory standards that derive their validity from an autonomous

[234] See text and accompanying footnotes in section 4.2.1.2. (p 179) and 4.2.1.3. (p 180) respectively.
[235] See section 5.3.2. (p 201), text and accompanying footnotes.

commitment or agreement or the choice of the particular company for a public framework. This puts these self-regulatory codes, in their current form, in proximity to an individual standard of reasonable care rather than an accepted practice that reveals a general industry practice. Hence, the codes do not, at least not yet, fall into the same category as technical standards or standards for professions, where the standard setting has been delegated to private bodies or the presumed specific expertise on the side of the standard-setting institution to develop generally accepted standards for an entire industry.[236] Instead, the corporate codes mainly remain standards that represent individually shaped reactions to political pressure and, to the extent that public codes are concerned, a deliberate choice by the company. Based on this qualification, the codes need to be viewed as part of the individual criteria that can influence the open-ended standard of due care.[237]

An argument in favour of the relevance of chosen and autonomously developed self-regulatory codes of conduct when specifying open-ended concepts can, in a similar vein, be envisaged in relation to unfair commercial practices law. Concerning this area, the legal analysis has already focused on the specific provision in the Unfair Commercial Practices Directive that makes it possible to specify fair trading behaviour on the basis of a trader's commitment to comply with a self-regulatory code of conduct, eg, Article 6(2)(b) UCPD. Thus, an appropriate proposal to make use of self-regulatory codes in relation to the standard of fair trading is to consider them to be codes of conduct that specify the fairness standards for a trader to the extent that he has committed to comply with it. This suggestion fits quite neatly with the position of the Office of Fair Trading.[238] However, with respect to the German rules on unfair commercial practices, this proposal seems more difficult in light of the intense and controversial debate on the self-regulatory codes of conduct in relation to fair trading behaviour.[239] This implies that in this national context, the proposal needs to be accompanied by a claim to give this provision a broad interpretation and there are two main arguments that can be raised in support of this. First, the main rationale behind referring to self-regulatory codes of conduct in the UCPD has been to promote and give more weight to self-regulation in this particular field.[240] In this context, it can also be emphasised that the EU sticks to a broad approach concerning the admission of self-regulatory codes. It treats as the admissible codes not only those that deal exclusively with fair trading behaviour, but more broadly those codes that traders employ in their marketing practices.[241] To give greater weight to self-regulatory codes thus does not mean to

[236] *cf* for these categories extensively Schepel (2005); Köndgen (2006) 481ff.

[237] This position thus effectively supports the proposals of Glinski (2007) 135; Glinski (2008) 47ff; and Herberg (2007) 218ff concerning the influence of corporate codes on the individual standard of due care for a particular company, but—based on the theoretical analysis conducted—does not yet share the further interpretation of corporate codes or public codes as an already general standard of due care that also applies to non-committing companies through an interpretation as accepted industry practice.

[238] See section 5.3.2.3. (p 205), text and accompanying footnotes.

[239] See section 5.3.2.2. (p 202), text and accompanying footnotes.

[240] See, eg, Howells (2006) 199; Cafaggi (2011) 119f.

[241] See explicitly Cafaggi (2011) 121: 'The principle does not concern exclusively codes of conduct regulating fair trade but all codes of conduct employed by traders in their marketing and selling practices. It solves the open issue of giving binding nature to codes of conduct that were considered part of social norms enforceable only through non-legal instruments.'

fundamentally reinterpret the German rules on unfair commercial practices, but merely requiring an interpretation of the German provisions in conformity with the EU Directive. In addition, the claim to give greater weight to self-regulation in specifying the fairness standard in fact does not represent a significant breach of the existing principles in German private law, if one considers the long-standing tradition in German law to make use of private standards when specifying open-ended concepts.[242] The claim to recognise self-regulatory standards as specifying the fairness standard can then also be read as an attempt to reconcile the area with the general German approach in private law towards relying on self-regulation when specifying indefinite terms. Yet, eventually, the proposal to treat the corporate codes as self-regulatory standards does not even require a strong re-orientation in unfair commercial practices law towards generally more weight for self-regulation. While it recognises that there might be a general reluctance to use self-regulatory codes in the course of specifying the general fair trading standard, the idea with respect to the corporate codes is only to embrace the specific principle laid down in Article 6 UCPD to specify the standard of fair trading with the individual traders' commitments to comply with a self-regulatory code.

[242] This astonishing difference between the general approach in German private law towards self-regulation and the treatment in specifically unfair commercial practices law is observed by Howells (2006) 197.

9

Conclusion

The Prospects and Limits of Enforcing Corporate Social Responsibility Codes

> There are few bases for being able to radically change whatever society one is living in. There are many bases for making better use of its possibilities.[1]

9.1. REALISING PRIVATE LAW ENFORCEMENT

How can the proposals on the private law enforcement of corporate codes be realised within the existing system of private law? After having developed the foundations with the help of the theoretical framework of sociological jurisprudence, this final chapter seeks to address this question and, to that end, develop recommendations as to how the theoretical claims could be realised on a practical level and how they could function in a broader context. One core objective of this final chapter is thus in the first place to present my own perspective on how private law should deal with the corporate codes phenomenon. The second important objective of this chapter is to present ideas on how the envisaged private law enforcement could work in a broader regulatory and social context, in particular the conditions that I consider crucial for its success. This also includes indicating follow-up questions that the here-presented perspective on corporate codes raises and that future research will have to address.

Translating the theoretical claims into concrete proposals for private law is by no means understood as an easy undertaking. It requires the difficult undertaking of letting the legal system be inspired by the insights of social sciences and the respective understanding of this particular social phenomenon, even though their descriptions differ quite considerably from legal categories. As revealed in the theoretical analysis, corporate codes sidestep existing distinctions that lie at the core of private law and therefore require nothing more than changes in the very fundaments of private law. As declarations to the public, corporate codes are located in a peculiar manner between the formal contract and wrongful behaviour, and thus call for a third source of private law obligations between contract and tort. As private regulatory undertakings on matters of public interest, they

[1] Luhmann (1992) 182 (emphasis added).

resist a clear classification as either public or private and thus would effectively be reflected as a new category of public interest obligations for private actors. Given the difficulties involved in such an undertaking, one may take the easy way out and merely conclude that 'corporate codes are not a legal concept!'.[2] However, this study is based on the firm conviction that the legal system, including private law, plays a vital role in furthering the potential inherent to new social phenomena for society at large and to assist in dealing with the conflicts that such phenomena pose. Therefore, despite the difficulties involved, it is considered a necessity to reconcile the legal concepts with changes in society[3] and thus to attempt, however difficult it may be to do so, to integrate such new phenomena into the private law concepts. In this context, it is also submitted that several of the rules and concepts in private law that are pointed out as appropriate to underpin the private law enforcement of corporate codes already exhibit a high degree of flexibility in their current form and thus make it possible to process societal changes without fundamental conceptual changes. Moreover, there are other concepts and rules in private law that, although in their current form are too narrowly confined, can still become the basis for the proposed private law enforcement if the perspective is broadened to the principle that the specific private law concept or rule is based on, which the courts could embrace in their legal reasoning. Hence, for the most part, the proposed private law enforcement remains possible in the form of an evolutionary development rather than a legal revolution. In other words, private law enforcement of corporate codes is in major parts not a matter of a far-reaching statutory reform. Instead, it merely requires an internal development within the legal system that would be initiated by the courts when they, in the course of legal reasoning, would start to interpret existing legal concepts in a different way or take the legal category gradually, but constantly, further on the basis of the underlying principles.[4] This of course requires as a prerequisite an attitude among social actors to insist on the law and legal precedent as an ordering instance, and bring to court their conflicts on the socially irresponsible conduct of companies that have corporate codes in place. It is furthermore based on the assumption that in a global society, it is also (in fact, in particular) domestic courts that play an important role in developing appropriate rules for global phenomena[5] and it follows incidentally

[2] Inspired by the famous one-sentence conclusion of Buxbaum (1993) 704: '5. Conclusion: Network is not a legal concept!'

[3] See in this direction Wielsch (2009), pointedly at 413: 'lenkt auch für die soziologische Jurisprudenz nicht mehr das Rechtsinstitut als Typus die Suche nach der Regel, die sich ihm einzupassen hätte. Vielmehr sind umgekehrt die privatrechtlichen Grundbegriffe so zu reformulieren und gegebenenfalls um neue Schlüsselbegriffe zu ergänzen, dass sie einen gesellschaftlichen Konstitutionalismus tragen können'.

[4] For the understanding of courts as the core actors to initiate legal change, see Esser (1990) 52f: 'kann der Richterspruch, der einzelne, wie auch die Masse einer ständigen Praxis, Transformator von vorpositiven Prinzipien in positive Rechtssätze und Institutionen werden'. See also Amstutz (2011) 403: 'At issue is the role of socio-legal findings in the normative discourse', which requires 'a reconsideration of the rules of legal reasoning that is, of the rules to be applied when subsuming the facts of a case (the legal "is") under the law in force (the normative "ought")'.

[5] See Michaels (2011).

the understanding that the legal reasoning of courts should be and in fact is greatly influenced by social perceptions.[6] That being said, it is also accepted that there are some theoretical claims for which flexibility of legal concepts and rules are not sufficient and where, accordingly, more profound and far-reaching change is required. Private law enforcement of the codes is thus in some aspects inevitably dependent on statutory reform. Finally, it is clear that private law enforcement does not operate in a vacuum. It needs a specific social and legal environment to be effective and successful in the long run, and it should by all means be read as a starting point rather than as the end of the debate on how to regulate corporate conduct.

The following analysis thus seeks, on the basis of these perceptions, first to tie together the arguments developed in this book and indicate how private law enforcement of corporate codes can be legally conceptualised. To that end, the existing suitable legal rules and concepts are indicated, proposals for their refinement by courts are spelled out, and, if necessary, directions for statutory reform are pointed out. Based on this analysis, the second section attempts to relate the proposals for the broader context in which companies with corporate codes operate and to contemplate other social and legal conditions for their success and the questions that it leaves for future research.

9.2. TOWARDS PRIVATE LAW ENFORCEMENT OF CORPORATE CODES: LEGAL POLICY PROPOSALS

9.2.1. Contract Law

9.2.1.1. Towards the Enforcement of Publicly Declared Corporate Codes

The starting point of this book marked the question about the existing options within private law to enforce the corporate codes. To that end, it could be observed that, to the extent that companies deliberately include the corporate codes in contracts or its ancillary documents, the corporate code is already sufficiently formalised in order to be legally enforceable pursuant to the rules on contract law.[7] The theoretical analysis has also drawn attention to the less formalised unilateral declaration of companies to comply with their corporate codes and has revealed their character as genuine self-commitments that create a legally binding effect.[8] With regard to translating this binding effect into the categories of legal enforcement, two main angles were pointed out in contract law. Corporate codes can first be interpreted as evidence that is consulted by the courts to determine the enforceable terms in subsequently concluded contracts and, second, they are even open to enforcement as relied-upon promises.

[6] See fundamentally Esser (1970) 21ff. See also Amstutz (2011) 405: courts (in particular the European Court of Justice) have 'demonstrated openness to legal arguments that are based in part on social realities external to the legal system itself'.

[7] See text and accompanying footnotes in section 3.1.1. (p 48) and 3.1.2. (p 52) respectively.

[8] See the arguments developed in section 7.2.3.2.2.1. (p 257) and 7.3.1. (p 266).

9.2.1.1.1. Contract Interpretation and Supplementation

Concerning the suggestion to read the publicly declared corporate codes into subsequently concluded contracts, one can take advantage of the fact that the recognition of specifically public declarations is already explicitly laid down as a rule in contract interpretation. Since the implementation of the Consumer Sales Directive into national sales laws, the courts are obliged to construct the terms of a sale contract on product delivery with a view to the public commitments of traders. One option is thus to expand the scope of this very specific provision and develop it into a general principle of contract interpretation.[9] However, it would equally be possible for the courts to rely on the existing rules on contract interpretation and supplementation, and on the flexibility of this approach, although it is emphasised that there are differences between English and German law, which originate from the institutional path dependencies. The English capitalist system is strongly linked to the competitive market, reliance on discrete arm's-length negotiation and formal contracting, consequently producing a system of contract law that focuses on the formal agreement, which, as a result, renders it more difficult to incorporate these less formalised corporate code declarations. The proposal can, in contrast, be realised with relative ease in German contract law, which has evolved in a capitalist organisation that is characterised by long-term cooperation and extensive reliance on incomplete relational contracting, and is thus more prone to recognising informal agreements as part of the agreement.[10]

As regards English law, the analysis must thus begin with an emphasis on the strict focus on express terms and the inherent reluctance to construct the contract in light of the context. It is recognised here that the confined and narrow scope of contract interpretation on the express terms of the agreement remains a vital and stable element that greatly influences English contract law. It is due to this firm embedding in the overall structure of contract law that it remains unlikely that the courts will use the occasion of the corporate codes for the sake of significantly revising this principle. However, as was pointed out in the previous section, English law still has in place specific rules to supplement the express terms that are laid down in the contractual document in the light of pre-contractual declarations. These are, first, the admission of evidence extrinsic to the contract for the sake of rebutting the presumption that the agreement was the entire contract and for identifying additional orally agreed terms that were agreed upon by the parties, second, the interpretation of a pre-contractual statement as a collateral contract or warranty and, finally, the consideration of extrinsic evidence in the course of implying terms.[11] In light of the character of English law to have in place rules for specific factual constellations, these three options are all considered to play a role in relation to publicly declared corporate codes depending on the particular

[9] See the different options presented in 3.1.3.2.1. (p 64), in particular nn 72, 73 and 77.

[10] See again on this important difference between the organisation of contractual relations in liberal and coordinated market economies Hall and Soskice (2001) 8f.

[11] See for these options, section 3.1.3.2.2.1. (p 68), text and accompanying footnotes.

facts. Reliance on the publicly declared corporate code as evidence for additional express terms seems particularly suitable in relation to carefully negotiated supplier contracts in which the corporate code remained not only a public commitment but was also intensively discussed between the contracting parties. One may refer here to the empirical observations concerning company–supplier contracts in which the written agreement remains very brief and the concrete obligations, in particular the obligations relating to the corporate code, are mainly agreed upon orally and informally.[12] In constellations in which there is no evidence of such a clear agreement, but where negotiations nevertheless took place concerning the code obligations and the commitments in the publicly declared code proved to be important for the addressed supplier in its decision as to whether or not to contract, the appropriate device would be probably the collateral contract.[13] To the extent that the corporate code remains merely a public declaration that is not subject to negotiation and is perceived as one component upon which the contractual agreement is built, one needs to revert to the option of implying terms in fact. Publicly declared corporate codes would then be understood as 'background parameters'[14] that spell out the expectations of the parties to the subsequently concluded contract and thus represent an underlying implicit dimension of the contract. This treatment is of course based on the more recent development in the rules on implying terms in fact as such towards refining as the threshold for implication the reasonable expectations of the contracting parties. Thus, the proposal takes account of particularly Lord Steyn's understanding on implied terms brought forward in *Equitable Life Insurance* that 'the implication is essential to give effect to the reasonable expectations of the parties'[15] and, most recently, Lord Hoffmann's re-statement that the underlying objective of the existing tests on implying terms in fact is to 'spell out what the contract actually means'.[16]

With respect to German law, the proposal to treat publicly declared corporate codes as enforceable contract terms is envisaged as a matter of the recognised broad approach of contract interpretation. The legal analysis could reveal that the German approach of contextual contract interpretation exhibits an inherent flexibility and, already in its current form, explicitly makes it possible to read into the contract pre-contractual statements. In this context, one need only refer to the fact that German courts can also consult, as evidence for the agreed contractual terms, public advertisements as admissible material for determining an agreement.[17] This general admissibility of corporate codes for the interpretation of the contract notwithstanding, the courts will still need to be given arguments that these declarations should be given great weight. If the contract at stake is not concluded in a written form, as is mostly the case in mass consumer contracts, the argument for giving the corporate code great weight is the fact that this publicly available

[12] McBarnet and Kurkchiyan (2007) 68ff.
[13] Phillips and Lim (2009) 341ff.
[14] Barron (2007) 19.
[15] *Equitable Life Insurance v Hyman* [2002] 1 AC 408, 459.
[16] Lord Hoffmann in *Belize v Belize* [2009] 1 WLR 1988, 1995.
[17] See on this possibility section 3.1.3.2.2.2. (p 77), text and accompanying footnotes.

material in fact represents the only material available in order for parties to introduce a regulatory dimension in the contract. If consumers increasingly attempt to pursue a transaction not only for the sake of purchasing a product, but also for the sake of furthering a particular social or environmental objective, the public material provided by the trader seems necessary in order to identify a suitable trader to pursue this objective. If, against this background, the public self-commitment were not to be given weight in the interpretation of this contract, the inevitable consequence would be that the regulatory function of the contract, as intended by the consumers and as also offered by the trader, is entirely ignored. Insofar as the relevance of publicly declared codes for written contracts is concerned, the persuasive argument relates to the fact that the regulatory dimension introduced by the corporate code, even if appearing in the form of a written term, ultimately originates from the corporate policy as is publicly declared. It is the terms in the contracts that need to be viewed as one component of the regulatory purpose that is laid down in the publicly declared corporate code rather than vice versa.

The legal consequence of this proposal is thus that the publicly declared corporate codes would be treated as valid and enforceable contractual terms within subsequently concluded contracts. This would mean, more precisely, that companies would become obliged towards individual purchasing consumers or their customers to comply with their corporate codes as publicly declared. In relation to their suppliers, incorporation of the public declaration would mainly have the effect that a duty to cooperate with their suppliers is established in order to further code compliance on the side of the supplier in accordance with what has been publicly declared.[18] A breach of this duty to cooperate could be seen in the failure of companies to realise or to realise properly the promised collaborative undertaking, such as monitoring, corrective action plans, training and advice, in behaviour that is counterproductive for the promised cooperation on achieving greater code compliance, such as tight delivery periods or excessive production loads, or for the failure to assist suppliers organisationally and financially in realising compliance. In relation to the initially presented *Wal-Mart* case, on the basis of which this has been discussed, this proposal would thus mean concretely that the court would be advised to look beyond the 'language and structure of the agreement'[19] and consider, when specifying the CSR obligations in the contract, the broader context in which this agreement has been reached.

9.2.1.1.2. Enforcing Promises

Next to the proposal to translate the publicly declared corporate codes into enforceable contract terms within subsequently concluded contracts with consumers and suppliers, a second important component in the enforcement architecture for corporate codes is their separate enforcement as promises that create 'obligations to

[18] In the corporate code debate, this proposal resembles what Phillips and Lim (2009) 371ff have in mind in relation to supplier contracts, but it goes beyond their proposal by suggesting a similar interpretation of other contracts, including consumer contracts.

[19] See section 3.1.3.2.2.1.1. (p 68), n 81.

perform prior to contract'.[20] These enforceable obligations to perform arise in this respect in relation to the actors that the company addresses with the code, with the objective of inducing cooperation and, possibly, achieving the conclusion of a contract that is beneficial for a company. It is thus an obligation that arises particularly towards potential business partners, suppliers as well as customers, and individual consumers who rely on the code in their decision as to whether or not to intensify further cooperation. Promissory enforcement could possibly also be recognised towards regulators, yet in this relation only if a clear link can be identified between the publicly declared code and a particular policy debate that suggests that the corporate code implicitly sought to influence the policy process. For this proposal, it is accepted that private law in its current form is too narrow to accommodate this proposal, which is why a careful further development of the legal rules and concepts as such becomes necessary. In this context, two different possible directions in relation to promissory enforcement are considered viable. First, the enforcement of publicly declared corporate codes could be based on the existing options of a reliance-based enforcement of pre-contractual promises if the scope of the existing rules is broadened. In fact, this proposal is, from a conceptually perspective, considered the most viable option and is thus preferable because it would mean applying a legal concept to the publicly declared codes that is based on reasonable reliance. Second, the enforcement of publicly declared corporate codes could also be achieved on the basis of the existing categories in contract law that provide for the enforcement of unilateral public promises as a specific form of contracting in which the requirement of acceptance is waived. However, a crucial prerequisite for the success of this proposal remains that the courts are prepared to soften the requirement of reciprocity towards more implicit and indirect forms of benefits for these types of contracts. This option is emphatically not perceived as the conceptually appropriate solution as it does not entirely fit with the reality of the corporate codes as relied-upon promises that prepare a contract.[21] Yet, taking the perspective of a legal realist, it is nonetheless deemed practically feasible given that courts, when being called upon so far to enforce unilateral promises that other market actors rely upon, exhibit a tendency to interpret these declarations in the light of the rules on contract formation as a specific form of remotely concluded contracts rather than making the effort to base the enforcement on a new category of reliance-based enforcement.

In order to realise the suggestion for promissory reliance-based enforcement in English law, a core suggestion is to rely on the doctrine of equitable estoppel. The doctrine in principle already allows the enforcement of clear and unequivocal unilateral promises that cause reliance on the side of the addressee in the form of proprietary estoppel if it is inequitable to permit the promisor to avoid the legal consequences of his promise by insisting on his original legal rights. Hence, the doctrine already embraces for specific types of promises the general principle that someone who deliberately induces an assumption by means of a promise is estopped from insisting on his strict legal rights, which is effectively also the

[20] Lüsing (2010) 341ff (*Leistungspflichten vor Vertrag*).
[21] See on this categorisation section 7.3.2.1.4. (p 280), text and accompanying footnotes.

underlying justification for the enforcement of the corporate codes. In order to use it as a basis for the promissory enforcement of publicly declared corporate codes, it is merely necessary to broaden its currently narrow scope of application from promises related to land rights to other types of promises. This suggestion for a broader scope should, however, not be interpreted as a proposal to open the floodgates to enforce all types of promises and effectively establish promissory estoppel as an encompassing cause of action that becomes a second comprehensive enforcement mode for bargained-for contracts.[22] Instead, its proposed use with respect to publicly declared codes could be envisaged as a refinement of the doctrine of equitable estoppel that remains based on equity considerations[23] that are relevant specifically for corporate codes and may be different for other types of promises. On a practical level, this differentiation mainly has the consequence that the suggested reliance-based enforcement of corporate codes is not conceptually envisaged as giving rise to a remedy for breach of contract. The remedy to enforce corporate codes remains rather specific and narrowly confined according to what is equitable in the particular circumstances in which an institutional rather than individual protection is necessary to regulate the breach of the corporate promises.

That being said, it is accepted that this proposed reliance on the doctrine of equitable estoppel of course requires quite significant changes of the rules on estoppel in English law, which the courts might be reluctant to initiate. In fact, when looking at the decisions specifically on public declarations made in advertisements, there seems to be instead a preference for interpreting such unilateral declarations as a unilateral contract that is concluded by a public offer that an addressee relies on.[24] Against this background, the interpretation of publicly declared corporate codes becomes at least a practically more feasible alternative in this legal system.[25] Comparable to *Bowerman v ABTA*, for instance, in which the court effectively recognised that a declaration made in an advertisement could principally become enforceable as a unilateral contract once the language used therein is sufficiently specific, even if mental reservations not to be bound were present,[26] the courts

[22] This is the interpretation of Collins (2003b) 74.

[23] See Lord Denning in *Crabb v Arun District Council* [1976] 1 Ch 179, 188, who clarifies that 'The basis of this proprietary estoppel—as indeed promissory estoppel—is the interposition of equity' and proceeds by emphasising that the 'early cases did not speak of it as "estoppel". They spoke of it as "raising the equity"'.

[24] The parallels between enforcement based on reliance and the courts' use of the unilateral contract are in particular emphasised by Collins (2003b) 80: 'The absence of a developed reliance model as a test of enforceability in the classical law indubitably led to the practice of the courts becoming ever more ingenious in discovering implied requests to perform actions, in order to bring a deserving case within the exchange model of consideration.'

[25] See pointedly McKendrick (2013) 88f, who argues that the enforcement of relied-upon promises could principally be based either on the argumentative strategy to show that reliance has in fact been sufficient consideration or to challenge the rule that promises not supported by consideration are generally not enforceable and concludes that: 'It may seem rather odd to canvass the first argument when purporting to discuss reliance upon promises which are unsupported by consideration. But claimants do, as a matter of practice, attempt to bring themselves within the fold of the doctrine of consideration before embarking upon the more hazardous task of seeking to persuade a court to enforce a promise which is unsupported by consideration.'

[26] See for this case and the arguments extensively section 3.1.4.1.1. (p 85), text and accompanying footnotes.

could also treat publicly declared corporate codes in a comparable manner, ie, as sufficiently specific offers to perform an action that becomes binding once reasonably perceived as such by the members of the public. Yet, in order to be able to interpret the corporate codes as unilateral contracts based on such precedent, it is of course necessary to propose a slight relaxation of the formal requirement of consideration to also cover promises in which no directly requested benefit is specified, but where only an 'implicit request' and the expectation of receiving an indirect benefit for making a promise is present. In this context, one must of course again note the difficulty for English law to cease from insisting on a formal and explicit dimension of reciprocity for the creation of obligations and treat as sufficient merely an implicit reciprocity as a background parameter if the entire system has evolved around discrete and formal contracting as the main form through which private actors create enforceable obligations on the market.

With regard to the German legal system, the already less strict focus on reciprocity in contract law might provide again at least at first sight an easier starting point for the enforcement of unilateral promises. One may refer here to existing cases in which the courts, and more precisely the lower courts of Bremen and Berlin, have already treated promises as enforceable by constructing them as remotely concluded agreements between the company and the government that constituted a unilateral obligation for the promising company.[27] Yet, this interpretation remains based on the identified characteristics of the corporate codes as unilateral promises and the underlying reasons for enforcing them merely as a compromise solution that stretches the rules on contract formation quite far[28] and conceals the fact that the underlying reason for enforcement is explicitly not a bilateral agreement that is concluded by remote offer and acceptance, but rather a reasonable and institutional reliance in a deliberately declared strategic promise. Thus, instead of forcing such public declarations into the rules on contract formation, it is deemed more appropriate to base the enforcement on the categories in the civil code that already provide for the enforcement of promises to the public. This applies, on the one hand, to § 657, which is so far the core legal basis in the civil code to enforce unilateral promises[29] and, on the other hand, to the recently adapted § 661a BGB, which provides for a right to enforce specific promises by traders that were deliberately made with the subtle expectation that this would cause them to place orders. This provision, notwithstanding its currently narrow scope of application, is suitable because, as will be argued below, it embraces the underlying principle of *venire contra factum proprium* that is already fundamental to private law.

Pursuant to § 657 BGB, a promise is binding if it is intentionally declared to the public with the objective of inducing a party to rely on it and perform a particular action. As a legal basis for the enforcement of relied-upon promises, it is particularly suitable to effectuate the promissory enforcement of corporate codes. Yet, comparable to the category of the unilateral contract in English law that is

[27] See on this option extensively section 3.1.4.1. (p 82), text and accompanying footnotes.

[28] See Bachmann (2006b) 279.

[29] Wennberg (1966) 57 ('Paradepferd der Versprechenslehre'); Bachmann (2006b) 280 ('bekannteste Ausnahme vom Vertragsprinzip').

concluded by an offer to the public, the provision is currently only applicable for promises to pay a particular sum in exchange for performing a required act. Consequently, in order to use § 657 BGB as a legal basis for the enforcement of publicly declared corporate codes, the provision would have to be given a broad interpretation. The request required under § 657 BGB would not necessarily need to be expressed in a public promise. Instead, an informal request read into the promise through implication would need to be considered sufficient.

An alternative and in fact a preferable option is to base the enforcement on an analogous application of the novel provision of § 661a BGB that was introduced fairly recently in the BGB. The provision was initially adopted as a piecemeal form of legislation for the specific problem of prize notifications that traders send to consumers in order to induce them to purchase products.[30] However, as has been discussed already in chapter three, the provision effectively introduces in a similar vein as § 241a BGB (unsolicited performance by traders) and § 434 I 3 BGB a category of legal obligations that are not yet of a contractual nature, but that equally resist a classification as tort liability.[31] While § 434 I 3 BGB views these pre-contractual enforcement obligations retrospectively after a contract is concluded and § 241a BGB clarifies that such pre-contractual performances do not create a bilateral contract with obligations for the addressee, § 661a BGB also contains a legal decision on whether these specific types of deliberately created pre-contractual performance obligations are actually enforceable by the addressees. In fact, a closer look at the debate on this specific provision reveals that this provision is based essentially on the recognised principle of *venire contra factum proprium* and seeks to relate it to behaviour in the pre-contractual phase. First, in the debate on the provision, it is already emphasised that § 661a BGB does not aim to hold the trader liable to pay compensation; instead, the provision seeks to prevent the misuse of public declarations sent to consumers by means of only taking the word of the trader seriously.[32] Second, notwithstanding the fact that § 661a BGB does not require an intention to be legally bound, as would be required for contract formation,[33] it is still an obligation that is not imposed, but rather is based on an autonomous and intentional act of the trader.[34] Third, it is also indicated that the

[30] The suggestion to make use of the principles underlying § 661a BGB in order to enforce public self-commitments is also proposed by Bachmann (2006b) 298: 'Nach dem Gedanken der §§ 116, 661a BGB darf sich der Versprechende dann nicht im Nachhinein darauf berufen, es gar nicht so gemeint zu haben.'

[31] On this debate see extensively section 3.1.4.2.2. (p 102), text and accompanying footnotes.

[32] BT-Drucksachen 14/2658 48; BGH NJW 2003, 3620: 'der Unternehmer sollte beim Wort genommen werden, um Missbrauch abzustellen'; Mankowski (2002) 874 'nimmt die Anbieter beim lauten Wort und schlägt ihnen die Hintertür der leisen Rücknahme zu'; Häcker (2004) 479: 'Man braucht hierfür nur ernst zunehmen, worauf auch die zitierte Gesetzesbegründung im Kern abstellt—nämlich das "Wort" des Unternehmers.'

[33] That these prize notifications do not require a clear intention to be legally bound seems to be broadly accepted in the literature; see, eg, MüKo-Seiler § 661a, para 4 ('Mitteilung des Unternehmers keine Willenserklärung').

[34] Mankowski (2002) 874: 'knüpft an einen privatautonomen Akt des Verpflichteten an'; Prütting/Wegen/Weinreich-Mörsdorf-Schulte § 661a BGB, para 3: 'Inhalt … nach der vom Unternehmer (Ob, Höhe, Art des Preises) *völlig frei gestalteten und gegebenen Zusage* oder Mitteilung' (emphasis added).

provision needed to be incorporated by means of statutory reform in order to be able to overcome restrictions for contract formation, in particular the requirement of form or reciprocity in constellations in which the protective purpose of these restrictions (doubts as to the seriousness or protection of the speaker from creating an obligation over-hastily) does not fit because the declarations are used for the strategic purpose of encouraging consumers to purchase products.[35] Thus, § 661a BGB justifies the enforcement of these particular types of promises by referring to the deliberate and specific promise of a trader and the strategic objective to induce a contract, which would make it unfair to allow the trader to first benefit from the induced assumptions and subsequently insist on his lack of intention to create a legally binding obligation. The novelty of this provision is the fact that it takes this principle further from being a general private law principle that derives from § 242 BGB (good faith) to a specific legal basis for the enforcement of deliberate promises in a market context. Once understood as such, the provision becomes a viable basis for the enforcement of publicly declared corporate codes in their character as publicly declared promises that are strategically placed on the market. This proposal, for an analogous application of § 661a BGB, is based on two assumptions. First, it takes account of § 661a BGB as a broader provision than a specific piecemeal legislation for consumer protection, as it was initially envisaged. It is understood as a provision that, together with § 434 I 3 BGB and § 241a BGB, represents first regulatory attempts in private law to regulate the specific aspects concerning performance obligations that are created in the phase prior to the contract. Second, the provision has to be treated as not having the function of sanctioning the trader and preventing such declarations, but as merely taking the intentional promissory behaviour of traders on the market and the reliance that it creates seriously. If this proposal is realised in private law, it becomes possible to enforce corporate codes on the basis of the contract as well as the public declaration. By means of translating these public declarations into enforceable obligations, private law could demonstrate a high degree of sensitivity for these in modern forms of marketing more frequently used informal forms of creating obligations. Using again as an illustration the initially described *Wal-Mart* case, this suggestion could thus be more precisely framed as criticising the applied legal reasoning by the court and encouraging future courts that ought to decide about breaches of corporate codes to consider not only the contract in which a code might be incorporated, but also the public declaration as a form through which enforceable obligations can be created.

9.2.1.2. Corporate Regulation in Contract Law Doctrine

Next to proposals on how the courts can transform the corporate codes into enforceable obligations, this study has also sought to provide answers on how private law should conceptualise the actual content of the code obligation, the

[35] Schröder and Thiessen (2004) 721: 'dass der Gesetzgeber für Gewinnzusagen lediglich einige Steine aus dem Weg geräumt hat, die er aus ganz anderen Gründen aufgeschichtet hatte'. See also Häcker (2004) 480ff.

remedies that should be available in case of code breaches and the actors that are entitled to exercise this remedy.

9.2.1.2.1. Rules for Regulatory Contracts and Commitments

Concerning the content of the code obligation, initially, three proposals were introduced for how the code obligations can be conceptualised: as obligations that relate to the main performance obligation in sales contracts; as terms that create third party rights; or as a novel duty that is specified by the autonomous regulatory framework as laid down in the code.[36] After having described the corporate codes theoretically as constituting a regulatory duty for the corporate entity, the appropriate direction is viewed in their interpretation as novel contract duties that are specified by three frameworks.

As regulatory duties that are ultimately based on contract or public self-commitment, the first source to specify the duties of the company as a regulator has to be the corporate code that constitutes the regulatory framework.[37] This proposal still fits quite neatly into the existing rules, as it merely requires that the courts interpret the enforceable code obligation in light of the agreement that the contracting parties reached with respect to the actual substantive commitment that has been publicly declared. Second, to the extent that references to public codes of conduct or to particular national legal standards are incorporated, the interpretation would have to take place with a view to the characteristics of these recommendations and frameworks.[38] This proposal could still be realised on the basis of the existing rules by interpreting the chosen frameworks as a specific form of expressly incorporated terms or as a specific legal framework that parties have chosen to apply. Yet, this interpretation already represents a first conceptual novelty for the contract law dispute, as it requires considering in the course of interpreting declarations of intent and contracts not only the rules that generally govern commercial or consumer contracting, but also the rules in the field of labour rights, human rights or environmental protection, and related international political recommendations and their respective interpretation. Incidentally, since this privately agreed or unilaterally committed role is effectively not part of the contracting parties' role as a seller or buyer, but as a regulator, the regulatory duty needs finally to be viewed in light of the duties of administrative regulators under global administrative law, which ought to be treated as ancillary contract duties. From the contract law perspective, this suggestion eventually implies that corporate codes would need to be defined as enforceable performance obligations *sui generis*, a 'CSR contract' or a 'CSR promise' that has as its content a long-term

[36] See extensively on these options, subsections to 3.2. (p 107), text and accompanying footnotes.

[37] This suggestion in the corporate codes debate so far has most explicitly been spelled out by Backer (2008) and Cafaggi (2013), and it is thus their suggested interpretation to which these proposals are linked.

[38] This suggestions resembles what is already suggested as an interpretative strategy with respect to the contract law enforcement of International Framework Agreements; see especially Coleman (2009) 623f, 632.

obligation to regulate the promised public interest aspect, which also comprises ancillary duties that resemble the duties of public administration.

To illustrate this proposal, the two cases that served at the beginning of this study as an introduction to the current legal debate will be focused on. With regard to the dispute over the code of conduct included in the contract between Adidas and the University of Wisconsin, the legal analysis demonstrated that the obligation of the company to comply with the labour code[39] was envisaged in the lawsuit in two different ways: as a positive obligation to pay the legally mandated benefits of suppliers, eg, to benefit the third parties,[40] or as a duty to cease sourcing products that were made in violation of the standards.[41] Based on the above understanding, the code obligation would have to be constructed differently; considering the broader purpose of the contractually included code, it would amount to an obligation on the side of Adidas to adhere to labour standards and—as a private regulator—to ensure that these standards are also followed within the contracting factories. Thus, a breach of the legal duty would occur if the company failed to undertake measures to ensure suppliers' compliance to provide legally mandated benefits after violations were identified and to ensure that these payments were made. With respect to the case *Doe v Wal-Mart*, the contractual obligation created by the code, ie, the regulatory duty, occurred on the side of the supplier and was thus also breached by him when failing to adhere to the required standards. Yet, to the extent that in this supplier contract the publicly declared corporate code is implied as a duty to cooperate[42] and this contract is embedded in the overall regulatory role of the lead firm as spelled out in the corporate policy, one can also identify a breach of the code obligation on the side of the company. This could take the form of a failure to fulfil the role as a regulator and safeguard code compliance in its supply chain and the promised cooperation by not conducting proper monitoring, failing to address events of non-compliance, and organisationally and financially assisting in achieving further code compliance. The courts could then determine the exact content of the rather vague voluntary commitment to 'improve workplace standards' by reference to the actually specified labour rights as laid down in the corporate code, any ILO declarations that are referred to and incidentally on the basis of the general principles on global administrative law.

[39] The exact phrasing (based on the publicly available response of Adidas on www.business-humanrights.org/Links/Repository/1013752) of the code obligation is: 'Standards: Licensees agree to operate work places and contract with companies whose work places adhere to the standards and practices described below' and further that 'Licensees must comply with all applicable legal requirements of the country(ies) of manufacture in conducting business related to or involving the production or sale of Licensed Articles' and 'shall provide legally mandated benefits'.

[40] Statement of Complaint (available at: www.business-humanrights.org/Links/Repository/1013752), para 24: 'The Board of Regents asserts that the Contract obliges Adidas to pay the legally mandated benefits owed to the PT Kizone workers.'

[41] Response of Adidas (www.business-humanrights.org/Links/Repository/1013752) 2: 'The sole legal requirement imposed by the language of the Labor Code is to cease doing business with the offending company.'

[42] See on this suggestion above section 9.2.1.1.1. (p 367), text and accompanying footnotes.

9.2.1.2.2. Performance and Injunction Orders as Remedies

Next to specifying the actual character and substantive content of the duty, the courts would also specify the remedy that is appropriate to deal with breaches of corporate codes. In discussing the enforcement structure, the theoretical analysis has already suggested that the enforcement of the codes needs to be viewed in light of the codes' regulatory character and their objective to protect public institution rather than individuals. This suggests that the appropriate remedy must be directed towards ending the institutional breach by means of requiring the obliged to perform the required action and, in case the obligation comprised an omission, to seek an injunction against harmful conduct.[43]

To justify this remedy is considered not to be particularly difficult in the context of German law, in which specific performance represents the main remedy for the enforcement of contractual obligations[44] and would also apply in relation to the enforcement of the public declaration on the basis of § 657 or 661a BGB.[45] However, it remains more difficult to realise in common law, which envisages duties to perform a contract as a 'prediction that you must pay damages if you do not keep it, and nothing else'.[46] It is thus mainly the attempt to justify this remedy within English law that is at stake.

In English law, an order for specific performance or an injunction order for negative obligations cannot simply be chosen for by the parties and its recognition as an appropriate remedy is severely restricted.[47] As arguments that would support its use in relation to corporate codes, one can bring forward the following. In the first place, specific performance in the particular case of breaches of corporate codes already seems appropriate because this remedy has been stipulated by the parties in their codes.[48] With a view to corporate codes and their integration in the contract, one can mention here the fact that the actions specified in the code in the event of non-compliance are by the choice of the private actors directed towards correcting regulatory failures and thus safeguarding further compliance.[49] An order for specific performance or injunction is also considered preferable as

[43] For this argument see section 8.3.2.2. (p 351), text and accompanying footnotes.

[44] See Faust and Wiese (2008), pointedly at 50: 'Specific performance is the rule; damages are the exception.'

[45] See explicitly BGH NJW 2003, 3620, 3621: 'Die Vorschrift gibt dem Verbraucher *nicht* einen Schadensersatzanspruch, sondern einen *Erfüllungsanspruch* auf den Preis' (emphasis added).

[46] Holmes (1897) 462.

[47] See pointedly Burrows (1987) ch 8, 295: 'specific performance is best approached negatively, that is by examining the numerous restrictions on its availability. Positively, it then follows that if the remedy is not barred by such restrictions, a plaintiff who applies for it will succeed'.

[48] More extensively on the respect for agreed remedies with an affirmative answer as to whether such an agreement is generally to be respected (to the extent that it is valid and not unfair), see, eg, Burrows (1987) ch 8, 338; and Collins (2003b) 364ff.

[49] See, based on empirical evidence of code provisions, Cafaggi (2013) 1614: 'The objectives of the remedial system within private regulatory regimes are multiple but often do not focus on compensation. Sanctions for regulatory breaches are primarily directed at ensuring compliance with the regulatory provisions, and in the case of infringement, at adopting corrective measures to pursue the regulatory objectives, such as safety for consumer protection, lower pollution for environmental protection, and fair labor conditions for employees.'

the appropriate judicial remedy on the ground that damage compensation seems inadequate in this particular constellation. The breach of a regulatory duty prior to an actual accidental event merely affects the institution of socially responsible corporate behaviour and thus resembles a non-pecuniary loss.[50] Effectively in some cases, breach may not even cause a measurable loss at all. Moreover, like the contractual duty to benefit third parties, the corporate code breach is directed towards improving the situation outside the bilateral contractual relationship. As English courts have recognised specific performance for breaches of contract duties that confer benefits upon third parties,[51] a similar treatment could be suggested for other types of breaches with external effects. Finally, while it is accepted that English courts since *Co-operative Insurance Society Ltd v Argyll Stores Holding*[52] significantly narrowed the scope of awarding specific performance as the judicial remedy for contracts on the continuous performance of a service, the arguments raised against its use in this case equally do not to fit in relation to the codes. The reason to deny specific performance because of the requirement of constant supervision by the court[53] is arguably not convincing as far as breaches of corporate codes are concerned. In fact, the task and related costs of supervision could be mitigated by appointing agents,[54] which would, given the global setting of this regulatory duty, be preferable and could significantly result in the avoidance of follow-up litigation. As can be taken from the existing codes, the appointment of third parties, such as NGOs or professional auditors, to monitor code compliance already seems today to be common practice among the parties in order to ensure that the regulatory duty is fulfilled.[55] Incidentally, concerning the remedy for the suggested promissory enforcement of the codes, the claim for specific performance is easier as estoppel gives 'the court the power to do what is equitable in all the circumstances' and, in so doing, it remains 'extremely flexible'.[56] One can here link the suggested use of specific performance to other cases dealing with

[50] For the use of specific performance in case of remote, non-pecuniary and avoidable losses, see Burrows (1987) ch 8, 306ff; Collins (2003b) 428.

[51] See for evidence, section 3.2.3.2. (p 142), text and accompanying footnotes.

[52] *Co-operative Insurance Society Ltd v Argyll Stores Holding* [1998] AC 1.

[53] This is an established rule in which the main authority is *Ryan v Mutual Tontine Westminster Chambers Association* [1893] 1 Ch 116 and *C Williamson Ltd v Lukey and Mulholland* (1931) 45 CLR 282, 297–98 (per Dixon J), but it has been viewed (partly in a similar factual situation as *Ryan*) critically in recent cases and thus relaxed. See, eg, *Posner v Scott-Lewis* [1987] Ch 5; and *Rainbow Estates v Tokenhold Ltd* [1999] Ch 64. See also already the famous statements of Megarry VC in *Giles and Co Ltd v Morris* [1972] 1 WLR 307, 318: 'nor do I think that it can be based on any narrow consideration such as difficulties of constant superintendence by the court. Mandatory injunctions are by no means unknown, and there is normally no question of the court having to send its officers to supervise the performance of the order of the court'. See also Lord Wilberforce in *Shiloh Spinners Ltd v Harding* [1973] AC 691, 724: 'Where it is necessary, and in my opinion right, to move away from some nineteenth century authorities, is to reject as a reason against granting some relief, the impossibility for the courts to supervise the doing of work.'

[54] For this argument, see especially Burrows (1987) 316.

[55] As an illustrative example, one can refer to the contractually binding code between the University of Wisconsin and Adidas where the NGO Worker's Rights Consortium was appointed to monitor code compliance and report breaches; *cf* Statement of claim, para 17 and response by Adidas, Annex at 2 (both available on www.business-humanrights.org/Links/Repository/1013752). For this third party monitoring in regulatory contracts, *cf* also Cafaggi (2013) 1601ff.

[56] *Roebuck v Mungovin* [1994] 2 AC 224, 235 (per Lord Browne-Wilkinson).

equitable estoppel in which the remedy of enforcing the promise by requiring performance has already been awarded.[57]

9.2.1.2.3. Understanding Regulatory Contracts and Third Party Rights

From the proposals developed so far, it follows that the enforcement of the codes by means of claiming specific performance or seeking an injunction order is at its core a matter for the parties to the contract and those that are addressed by the public declaration with the objective of inducing a contract. Yet, the theoretical analysis has suggested that regulatory duties also need to come with an entitlement of the regulated actors and entities to the extent that public law would do so.[58]

Translated into the regulation of contracts, this implies that a strong contextual interpretation of the particular regulatory term is required that, also in relation to the question of third party rights, does not look primarily at the specific wording of the code,[59] but at the character of the frameworks and statutes that seek to administer and regulate. For courts that are called upon to decide about whether a code could be enforced by those it seeks to regulate to their benefit, this means more precisely an urge to construct terms in contracts in light of the background material, which in relation to both legal systems is an available approach for third party rights in contracts.[60] In this context, however, it needs to be emphasised that the possibility of third party enforcement remains, pursuant to the existing rules on third party rights, a proposal that is currently only conceivable for corporate codes that are interpreted as contractual obligations. Insofar as the obligations derive from the above-proposed enforcement of the publicly declared corporate code on the basis of equitable estoppel or an analogy to §§ 657 and 661a BGB, the possibility of creating third party rights for beneficiaries remains quite a far-reaching proposal. It is by no means inconceivable and could be a future development.[61]

[57] See especially *Crabb v Arun District Council* (n 23) and explicitly in *Pascoe v Turner* [1979] 1 WLR 431, 439: 'Weighing such considerations this court concludes that the equity to which the facts in this case give rise can only be satisfied by compelling the plaintiff *to give effect to his promise* and her expectations. He has so acted that *he must now perfect the gift*' (emphasis added).

[58] See the arguments developed in section 8.3.2.3. (p 356).

[59] This is, however, the understanding of Heijden (2011a); Estlund (2012) 254f; and Cafaggi (2013) 1592.

[60] In the context of German law, one can refer here to the accepted rule of broad contextual and supplementary interpretation of third party contracts (§§ 328 II, 133, 157 BGB). But also concerning the English rules for constructing contract terms (including those concerning third party rights; see, eg, Burrows (2000) 545) since Lord Hoffmann's re-statement in *Investors Compensation Scheme* [1998] 1 WLR 896, it has evolved as a rule of contract interpretation to consider the background, which can include 'absolutely anything which would have affected the way in which the language of the document would have been understood by a reasonable man' (at 913).

[61] See especially the analysis of Metzger and Phillips (1983) 543f, who discuss the possibility of promissory estoppel liability towards third party beneficiaries based on the commentary on s 90 of the Restatement (Second) of Contracts. In relation to corporate codes, one may refer here to Phillips and Lim (2009) 376, who deem it to be at least conceivable that employees could invoke a third party beneficiary estoppel claim against companies based on the latter's promises towards suppliers and the doctrinal construction in German law of publicly declared codes as binding unilateral self-commitments with third party effects based on §§ 780, 328 BGB. See the discussion in section 3.1.4.1. (p 82).

Nonetheless, it is from the perspective of an evolutionary development of legal concepts and rules merely a proposal that becomes feasible as an internal development that is initiated by the courts only after the category of unilateral relied-upon promises as such is firmly established in private law.

A similarly cautious position is taken here as to the possibility for the parties to exclude third party rights. Certainly, there are several tools available in contract law that impose constraints on the contracting parties to limit their risk of liability and that could be applicable. One need only refer to the tools of the courts to render invalid particular exclusion clauses and unfair contract terms. In addition, one can refer to the critical voices concerning disclaimers for contractual third party rights that urge the restriction of the 'contractors' exclusionary powers' to veto an enforcement right when their intention had effectively been to benefit third parties.[62] Yet, the ultimate answer to the question of whether excluding the right of third parties would be unfair is closely linked to the more fundamental question on how strongly private law is prepared to limit the freedom of the parties in favour of safeguarding the integrity of their chosen regulatory role. If the regulatory role is truly taken seriously, it has to be clear that private law will sooner or later have to develop constraints for private actors that seek to escape accountability as a regulator through the backdoor. That being said, it remains equally recognised that this requirement becomes a difficult task for private law. Private law is in this regard captured in between its constituting pillar of private autonomy and the equally important objective of regulating the inherent conflicts associated with these new forms of regulation. A proposal for a long-term solution to this conflict would be to encourage the courts to develop specific responses to such disclaimers that derive in the first place from a restrictive position towards excluding accountability for regulatory obligations, but that nonetheless recognise the potential of private regulators to develop autonomous mechanisms that could sufficiently safeguard the requirement of accountability for the regulator.[63] The criteria for acceptable internal accountability mechanisms could possibly be developed here with a view to the rules on effective grievance mechanisms as laid down in the UN Guiding Principles.[64]

9.2.1.2.4. A Collective Enforcement Architecture

In the course of this book, a plea was made to also strengthen the collective enforcement dimension in relation to corporate codes.[65] This proposal, in the corporate

[62] See for the English rules on third party rights Adams, Beyleveld and Brownsword (1997) 240ff, who propose that 'respect for the contracting parties' intentions entails not only that the party has a presumptive right to enforce but also that that right cannot be excluded where the contract would otherwise be unenforceable' (at 242, quote in text also on this page).

[63] A viable candidate as a substitute accountability mechanism that could make it possible to exclude the third party right could here be the third party complaint procedures that some multi-stakeholder initiatives have in place. Companies affiliated with such multi-stakeholder initiatives must participate in a complaints procedure that can be initiated by affected third parties and groups to report breaches of the code; the results of the procedure that is directed towards identifying and remedying the breach are made publicly available. See, eg, the Fair Labor Association's Third Party Complaint, available at: www.fairlabor.org/third-party-complaint-process.

[64] UN Guiding Principles, Principle 31.

[65] See for arguments section 8.3.2.2. (p 351), text and accompanying footnotes.

codes debate, can connect to other contributions that already indicate the necessity of having collective enforcement, although so far a reluctant attitude can be observed towards explicitly spelling out the necessity of having in place collective enforcement not only for affected individuals to obtain damages or for organisations to seek injunctions against the use of codes, but also for the enforcement of the codes.[66] However, it is this form of collective enforcement that is considered crucial for the further debate on an effective private law enforcement of corporate codes and that accordingly would deserve more attention in the further debate.

In this context, it is accepted that on this point the limits are reached for the suggested undertaking to realise private law enforcement for corporate codes in the form of an evolutionary development that can be initiated by the courts. Instead, the proposal requires statutory reform. Given the complexity of the topic of collective enforcement and the many different areas that would be affected in this respect, this study certainly cannot present already comprehensive and precise proposals as to what this collective enforcement could look like. What can be done here is to indicate a direction for this collective enforcement mechanism and point out the main points for further discussion, which would then need to be subject to future research. In general, the envisaged collective enforcement mechanism that would come closest to the proposed collective enforcement for corporate codes is seen in the collective enforcement concerning unfair contract terms, which already introduced a collective enforcement dimension in relation to bilateral contractual relations. Yet, in the further discussion on this collective remedy, two points require further scrutiny. The first aspect that requires further attention is the necessity to focus in the debate on collective enforcement on the potential to transform collective enforcement from a mechanism that focuses merely on injunctions and damage compensation into a tool that organisations can use to also claim positive performance of particular obligations if these seek to protect institutions. In the recent debate on collective enforcement at the EU level, a possibility of using collective enforcement in this way has at least so far not been explored in detail.[67] Second, in the course of developing a specific collective enforcement mechanism with respect to corporate codes, further considerations would need to be given to the organisations that should be entitled to enforce breaches. There are in principle two different angles from which this question can be approached. There are, on the one hand, of course good reasons for developing this collective enforcement mechanism from existing collective enforcement structures, in particular in relation to enforcement for consumer law. This not only makes sense from a practical perspective given that this form of collective enforcement is already established, but could also be justified by the theoretical understanding of the codes as declarations to regulate

[66] The affirmative contributions on the collective enforcement of corporate codes that this proposal builds upon are, in particular, Wilhelmsson (2002/2003) 101 ('to consider that the emergence of various new types of collective procedure for promoting mass interests of this nature can bring with it substantial new possibilities for private law strategies'); and Glinski (2011) 173.

[67] See only European Commission, Recommendation on common principles for injunctive and compensatory redress mechanisms in the Member States concerning violations of rights granted under Union Law, C(2013) 3539, which focuses on common principles only for *injunctive* and *compensatory* redress mechanisms in the Member States.

that are at least in the first place deliberately addressed to the market public and seek to create an enforceable obligation towards them. In relation to the two legal systems chosen as examples, this would have the result that the enforcement is put in the hands of consumers and trader organisations that could bring claims to civil courts (Germany) and as an administrative procedure to the Office of Fair Trading (England). On the other hand, there are equally good reasons to argue that the character of the codes as obligations that ultimately affect the regulated individuals and communities requires enforcement on their side. Pursuant to this understanding, it would be important to provide a collective enforcement right for organisations that represent the affected collectives, eg, human rights organisations, environmental NGOs or trade unions. While this would certainly be favourable in terms of the representation of the affected collectives, it is equally true that this would require significant effort in terms of setting up quite a new procedure. Yet, on this point, the optimal solution might also be found in a compromise in the form of a combination of both collectives. One could develop the collective enforcement as a mechanism that relies on an existing structure within consumer law enforcement, but imposes as an additional requirement for the right to enforcement the necessity of cooperating with the regulated communities.[68] This would make it possible to modify only the existing structures and, simultaneously, would pay due respect to the fact that the codes are, from the perspective of the companies, addressed to persuade other market actors, but mainly affect third parties that thus require legal protection. Concerning this latter proposal, it can even be the organisation of litigation on corporate codes in the past that could point to a way forward. In relation to the litigation on corporate codes in the German *Lidl* case, for instance, the lawsuit was already a product of intense cooperation. The consumer association that was entitled, as the collective organisation, to seek the injunction order closely cooperated with two organisations specialised in human rights (the European Centre for Constitutional and Human Rights) and workplace standards in textile factories (the Clean Clothes Campaign). It might eventually turn out that these cooperative undertakings point to the future for the collective enforcement of corporate codes.

These so far broad suggestions of course require more concretisation, which has to be left to future studies. Yet, once such a procedure is successfully framed and adopted, this additional collective remedy can assist with stabilising the new regulatory role of companies.

9.2.2. Civil Liability Rules

9.2.2.1. Reliance Liability

In the enforcement architecture, the contractual and promissory liability is understood as the core element of the proposed private law enforcement. Nonetheless,

[68] This proposal of a cooperation between consumer associations as those entitled to file claims and the affected communities is made in the context of disputes concerning online privacy rights by Gruber (2013) 196ff.

in relation to beneficiaries that act to their detriment in relying on corporate codes and thus the companies' performance of its promised regulatory role, a reliance-based form of non-contractual liability is still considered a complementary pillar that needs to be taken further. The precise legal basis for this specific reliance-based tort liability depends here mainly on whether the corporate code becomes enforceable by contract or as a public declaration.

To the extent that the corporate code is treated as a contractual obligation, the specific rules in tort law or quasi-contractual liability concerning the negligent performance of services (England) and the contract with protective effect (Germany), respectively, seem particularly suitable. The detrimentally affected beneficiaries could in any case be qualified incidentally as beneficiaries that are affected by the performance of the contractual regulatory duties. Concerning the question of whether establishing such a duty of care of the contracting parties towards the beneficiaries would be 'fair, just and reasonable' (England) or in the reasonable interests of the contracting parties (Germany), respectively, the courts can refer to the need to preserve the evolving regulatory role of companies to pursue political objectives as a normative justification. From a practical perspective, however, this proposal must remain supplementary and would only come into play to the extent that the above construction of corporate codes as third party rights is not feasible.[69] In relation to liability for publicly declared codes, the proposed reliance-based category of legal liability is suggested as a development that needs to be related to the general rules on tort law. Here, it is emphatically not the category of already existing reliance-based liability for negligent statements that is appropriate, as this would conceptually not appropriately consider the dishonest publication of a corporate code as the unlawful act rather than the event that renders reliance reasonable.[70] The proposal envisages reliance-based liability rather as a specific form in which the public declaration is legally treated as the ground to establish reliance-based liability in principle and deems non-complying behaviour as the wrongful act that gives rise to liability. It is thus not, as is currently suggested with respect to the commitments to comply with corporate governance codes, the tort of negligent misstatement that is the appropriate category, but rather the interpretation of the public declaration as a voluntary assumption of responsibility to protect the beneficiaries as spelled out in the code. In the current debate, this proposal comes close to the interpretation of the corporate codes as tort law 'Good Samaritan' duties.[71] For this proposal, however, it has to be clear that in legal reasoning, the courts are not able to establish liability in tort solely on the ground that a publicly declared code has been breached. This follows, first, from the general understanding of tort liability that it is difficult to establish liability on

[69] In this context, it could become particularly attractive in English common law where a statutory requirement for creating third party rights remains the requirement that the third party needs to be expressly named (Contracts (Rights of Third Parties Act) 1999, s 1(3)). Hence, to the extent that the beneficiaries are not named and establishing a third party right would be considered *contra legem*, the negligent performance of services could become a viable alternative.

[70] On this point in detail, section 7.3.3.2. (p 302), text and accompanying footnotes.

[71] See section 4.1.2.2. (p 167), in particular n 69.

the basis of mere words and commitments; instead, it is effectively only the overall behaviour that needs to be taken into consideration. Yet, the focus on the publicly declaring company's overall behaviour is, second, also a matter of paying due respect to the way in which the social trust between the company and the globally spread remote beneficiaries is created by means of a promise. Here, it is not the act of promising only, but rather the promise *in conjunction with* the attempts to fulfil the promise that represents the trust-building behaviour[72] that the law needs to protect by rendering reliance reasonable. In relation to the corporate codes, this means, more precisely, that legal liability for corporate codes is established only to the extent that the company not only publicly declares code compliance, but also engages in the serious undertaking of fulfilling the promises made in the codes, in particular in the form of auditing or intervening in the practice of foreign factories.

With respect to the English system on tort liability, the suggested reliance-based liability for corporate codes could be realised by taking the recent developments in *Chandler v Cape* further, in which the liability of a company towards the employees of its subsidiary for violations of health and safety standards was justified on the ground of superior knowledge as expressed in the corporate group health and safety policy that was organised at the level of the parent and a practice of intervention in the operations of the subsidiary. On the basis of these requirements, it could be possible to treat voluntary corporate policies of a company and its actual monitoring practice as a comparable form of assuming responsibility towards those specified in the code. This interpretation in relation to the code obligation seems here in its current form a feasible rule for commitments in codes that deal specifically with health and safety standards for employees. Yet, this specific category could serve as a starting point for gradually opening up the range of recognised beneficiaries that could hold a company liable for its breaches of code promises if they have relied on the promise to their detriment. It is clear that this proposed linking of the corporate codes with the *Chandler* criteria relies on an interpretation of this specific decision as an evolving form of corporate liability that could mark the starting point for potential future developments of a new category of reliance-based liability and emphatically not a narrowly confined exception that is not to be taken further. As such, it would, to borrow the famous words of Lord Macmillan in *Donoghue v Stevenson*, become an example where 'the conception of legal responsibility may develop in adaptation to altering social conditions and standards'[73] on the ground that the trust-building behaviour of companies in their regulatory role requires adaption of the rules on negligence.

In the context of German tort law, the general proposal to translate the corporate codes into a duty of care is envisaged as an interpretation as *Verkehrspflicht*. In this context, the suggested underlying reason for translating the corporate codes into a *Verkehrspflicht* is proposed as a combination of the principles that underlie the

[72] See pointedly Kimel (2003) 31: 'By the very act of putting the practice of promising into use—I by making the promise, inviting trust, suggesting respect; the promisee by taking the promise as a source of confidence, by trusting—we emulate the behaviour of people in a relationship. The *keeping of the promise* then closes a circle through which we establish a bond of trust and respect' (emphasis added).

[73] *Donoghue v Stevenson* [1932] AC 562, 619.

Verkehrssicherungspflichten and *Fürsorgepflichten*, which were presented as potentially applicable in relation to the codes.[74] From their substantive content, the corporate codes represent self-commitments and observable undertakings to protect specific beneficiaries. In so doing, the codes resemble mainly *Fürsorgepflichten* that can be created by factually assuming responsibility for particular parties. In relation to the corporate codes, this factual undertaking would be derived from the public declaration as such. That being said, it is, on the other hand, also recognised that an interpretation of the corporate codes as genuine forms of *Fürsorgepflichten* would broaden the scope of liability too much for the publicly declaring company and would ignore the exceptional character of these particular types of duties. Certainly, the undertaking of proposing an interpretation of the corporate codes as a *Fürsorgepflicht* cannot have the result that companies are in every respect legally responsible to prevent harm to all beneficiaries even if they are spatially remote. It is at this point that, as a restricting factor, the principle underlying the *Verkehrssicherungspflichten* comes into play that conversely would require limiting the scope of liability to harm that derives from a source that the tortfeasor has control over. In relation to the codes, this element comes into play in the form of the ongoing practice of greatly influencing the operations of subsidiaries and suppliers by means of conducting audits and requiring them to remedy failures as an additional requirement to establish legal liability. The actual practice of already practically intervening in the autonomous sphere of another entity effectively prevents the publishing company from claiming that the obligation to prevent harm would oblige it in an undue manner to intervene in the operations of an autonomously operating subsidiary or supplier.[75]

The proposal to interpret the corporate code as a basis for legal liability would have, in the specific example of the *Wal-Mart* case, the effect that a court could allow a claim for compensation to the extent that the company failed to protect the employees of suppliers from harm as it promised. Yet, this liability would only arise under the condition that the company actively and over a period of time engaged in monitoring activities and consequently conveyed the impression towards beneficiaries that it seriously fulfils its promises.

9.2.2.2. *Individual Standards of Reasonable Care*

In the context of tort law, the corporate codes could, as previously suggested, play a role as an instance that specifies the standard of due care, either as an

[74] For this category see extensively section 4.1.2.2.2. (p 171), text and accompanying footnotes.

[75] One can, for this proposal, also draw analogies to the accepted category of previous dangerous behaviour that gives rise to a *Verkehrspflicht* (see on this category MüKo-Wagner § 823, para 326) if one considers that the practice of intervening in subsidiaries' or suppliers' operations can result in the dangerous situation that, in reliance on further intervention and advice, autonomous precautionary protective measures are not undertaken by suppliers, the employees or the local administration. See for this argument Phillips and Lim (2009) 358f, who argue that the monitoring has the result that employees at suppliers' sites tend to ignore risks involved in reliance on the monitoring of buyers; and Herberg (2007) 115ff.

individual standard for the publishing company[76] or as a general self-regulatory standard.[77] While it has to be emphasised that the codes can only represent but one element that the courts have at their disposal to specify this standard, it is proposed that the courts should consider them. The idea here is to understand them as specific individual aspects that play a role when specifying the standard of due care for a company that has in place a corporate code that contains operational components. A core justification for the courts to consider such individual components when specifying the generally perceived objective standard relates here to the fact that, in the particular field of social and environmental standards, the general industry practice remains quite significantly influenced by the individual efforts and best practices of specific corporations. The proposal in the legal debate to interpret corporate codes with common substantive standards as an evolving general practice that applies not only to the individual companies with codes but also outsiders and their capability to establish a 'safe harbour' could then point to a potential future development that would stabilise corporate codes more firmly as a legal standard. Yet, for such a proposal, more detailed research is required on the private standards of particular sectors and their similarities and, insofar as public codes of conduct are concerned, a more detailed analysis of the underlying political process that brought these codes about and their similarities with other accepted private standards that shape industry practice.

9.2.3. Unfair Commercial Practices Law

Finally, attention needs to be drawn to the area of unfair commercial practices law and its role in the overall enforcement architecture. Concerning corporate codes in unfair commercial practices law, one core proposal following from the analysis so far is to assign this area a narrowly confined rather than a prominent role in the overall enforcement structure and understanding the claims as being again merely supplementary to the contractual and promissory enforcement as specified above. This is due to the fact that the main regulatory focus of this field on the prohibition of misleading and false information provided to consumers is, with respect to the corporate codes, contradictory to the theoretical finding that the codes are successful and intentional promises that should be enforceable by private law. The use of this regulatory field would thus need to be reduced in favour of the enforcement of the codes in contract and tort law. Yet, despite this less prominent role, there are two important constellations in which this regulatory field can play a role.

9.2.3.1. Regulating Corporate Code Marketing

The interpretation of corporate codes as a form of misleading information, as currently frequently discussed in the debate, needs to be confined to what in this

[76] For this possibility see extensively section 4.2.1.2. (p 179), text and accompanying footnotes.
[77] For this possibility see extensively section 4.2.1.3. (p 180), text and accompanying footnotes.

area would be defined as rough traders that use their corporate codes with the apparent objective of misleading the public[78] and that clearly exaggerate their environmental and social credentials.[79] Guiding criteria for the application of unfair commercial practices law here can be the criteria for successful promises that have been spelled out in the theoretical analysis. The public declaration to comply with a corporate code could then amount to an unfair commercial practice in the form of misleading advertisements if the commitment cannot be fulfilled by the company, if it does not contain any meaningful content or contains obvious and irreconcilable contradictions. However, in this context, a particularly sensitive attitude is called for considering that the codes, in order to be convincing, need to exhibit a necessary degree of abstraction.

9.2.3.2. Regulating Non-complying Behaviour

Based on the arguments developed in this book, the regulation of corporate codes through unfair commercial practices law needs to be conceptualised differently. To that end, it is proposed to shift the focus from the interpretation of these codes as potentially misleading advertisements to the non-complying behaviour as a commercial practice that could be unfair. In this context, Article 6 UCPD in its implementation in the national laws on unfair trading plays a crucial role. The envisaged way of dealing with corporate codes in unfair commercial practices law inherently requires a broad understanding of what qualifies as 'codes of conduct' in unfair trading laws and needs to cover self-regulatory codes that specify obligations concerning socially responsible corporate behaviour, including those that specify rules for the production phase. The proposed broad interpretation needs to be particularly emphasised with a view to the German debate in which the category of self-regulatory codes is so far interpreted restrictively.

In accordance with this interpretation of the requirement of a 'code of conduct', it becomes possible to base a claim for an unfair commercial practice on the provisions that have implemented Article 6(2b) UCPD and sanction a companies' non-complying behaviour as an unfair commercial practice if it had previously undertaken to be bound by its code. In this context, a final remark needs to be made concerning the relevance of this proposed interpretation. Given that the non-complying behaviour, in order to qualify as a commercial practice, would have to influence the purchase decision of consumers, it also has to be clear that the use of this provision in the overall enforcement structure of the codes remains limited in its scope. It is here considered only viable to the extent that the non-complying

[78] For such a suggestion with a view to the regulatory focus for statements in advertisements in general, see Köndgen (1981) 304: 'Werbung ist … Qualitätsversprechen und/oder Verleitung zum Vertragsschluß. In ihrer ersten Funktion führt sie zwangslos zur vertraglichen Versprechenshaftung … Culpa bleibt ein geeigneter Anknüpfungspunkt für die Haftung aus Werbung in jenen Fällen, wo es an einer ernstgemeinten—und vom Adressaten auch so verstandenen—Werbeaussage gerade fehlt.'

[79] See on this point the European Commission, A renewed EU Strategy 2011–14 for Corporate Social Responsibility, COM (2011) 681 final 9, in which it is suggested to apply the rules on misleading marketing particularly to companies 'exaggerating their environmental or social credentials'.

behaviour in the production phase has a direct effect on the consumer market, eg, when violations of social and environmental standards have effects on the distribution of the goods, in particular on price calculation or as resulting in a competitive advantage due to lower production costs. Yet, in light of this possibility, it is recognised that violations of social and environmental standards by companies can only in a restricted and incomplete manner be regulated and thus be prevented by this particular area of law. Unfair commercial practices law is, as phrased by an observer, 'not the appropriate place to enforce "good governance" of companies'[80] and thus should only reluctantly be used to the extent that the other enforcement mechanisms, as developed above, fail to address the conflict about the corporate code in a sufficiently comprehensive manner.

9.3. ENFORCEMENT OF CORPORATE CODES IN PERSPECTIVE

Having set out the core recommendations to effectuate the private law enforcement of corporate codes as argued for in this study, some concluding remarks will be made as to the broader social and regulatory context, including some of the core prerequisites for its success and the fundamental questions that it leaves for future research and debate.

The study began with a general analysis of the relationship between the corporate codes of conduct in the field of social and environmental standards and the area of private law, and concluded on the basis of a theoretical fundament on the crucial role of private law in taking corporate codes seriously as voluntarily and autonomously created obligations of private actors to take over the role of an administrative regulator. To that end, it could be revealed that, despite the often-expressed criticism of the corporate codes in the debate, the interpretation of the codes as smokescreens or public relations exercises that seek to mislead the public is by no means a given fact; instead, they can be quite appropriately framed as serious attempts of companies to transform the evolving social expectations directed towards a more active engagement of companies into concrete rules that guide their behaviour. In so understanding, the role of private law in regulating these corporate codes is also claimed to be quite different from what critics of the codes discuss. The role of the law in this study is not seen as 'questioning the seriousness of the codes', demystifying the project of CSR and revealing the inherent dishonesty of corporate CSR policies,[81] but rather is encouraging and translating their inherent potential to serve as a basis for the companies' obligations under private law. However, to proponents of corporate codes that consider their potential in the voluntary self-regulation of CSR and call for a more facilitative and encouraging role, this study also sought to emphasise that in order to become stable and reliable

[80] Henning-Bodewig (2010) 1105 (my translation).

[81] Kocher (2011) 35: 'indem sie die Versprechen ernst nehmen, stellen sie gleichzeitig deren Seriosität in Frage. Es geht um Entmystifizierung und Aufdeckung der Täuschungseignung, die CSR-Politiken inhärent ist'.

instances to specify this regulatory role, corporate codes cannot remain in the realm of pure voluntariness, but require legal regulation and enforcement. This study should thus be read as an attempt to focus on the potential of corporate codes for a fragmented world society in which the regulatory capability of states diminishes and an active role of private actors is required, as much as a plea for a continuing role of the legal system with regard to stabilising the social expectations towards this new regulatory phenomenon even in the case of the occasional disappointment of companies. On a more abstract level, this study takes account of the value of the interaction between privately created norms and formal law as a promising path to make use of the productive aspects of self-regulating corporate behaviour.

9.3.1. Social and Legal Prerequisites

Private law enforcement of corporate codes is, however, not a panacea and it is a development that requires a broader social and legal context in order to become effective and successful. It would certainly be naïve to assume that it will come with no resistance from the side of companies. On the contrary, it will most likely come at the price of more frequent efforts by companies to circumvent this development and an attitude of companies to avoid having their codes legally enforced.[82] This implies that the suggested private law enforcement of the codes, if successfully implemented, will certainly not put an end to the debate on the codes; instead, to the extent that private law succeeds in rendering corporate codes binding, it will trigger new strategies of companies that will, in turn, again require new debates in private law on how to deal with such attempts at evasion. The merits of the proposed private law enforcement thus also lie in its contribution to the evolutionary development of the law where 'new rules produce new circumventions, but also new circumventions produce new rules'[83] in an ongoing learning process. Moreover, although it can be predicted that companies will become more careful to avoid the proposed private law enforcement, the corporate strategy of evading legal liability should also not be overestimated. In fact, based on past experience in particular in relation to liability concerning corporate codes, the mere threat of liability could turn out not to be as strong as would intuitively be assumed to be the case. An apparent example remains here the often-mentioned *Kasky v Nike* case, in which the company was held liable for its statements regarding workplace standards in its supplier factories and eventually agreed to a far-reaching out-of-court settlement. Although it initially represented a major concern in the debate that this signal would deter companies from publishing their corporate codes, the situation over 10 years after *Kasky v Nike* suggests differently. A restrictive attitude

[82] As pointedly observed by Arthurs (2005) 59: 'If corporate codes were to become more closely entangled with state law, they would inevitably lose their distinctive "corporate" or voluntary character. This is likely to make them less attractive to key actors.' See also McBarnet (2007) 47: 'Business is extremely adept at managing law to circumvent and pre-empt legal control, through the art of "creative compliance".'

[83] Teubner (2012) 11.

on the side of companies did not prevail. On the contrary, even Nike, the company that was exposed to the public, resumed its transparency on CSR efforts and also, on a general level, disclosure on social and environmental policies and engagement continues to be important for companies.[84] It is thus not only the threat of liability that influences companies but also the remaining expectations of society that companies need to increase their transparency rather than reduce it. Constant social pressure on companies to take over the regulatory role and be transparent thus plays a crucial role in effectuating private law enforcement. In order to increase the use of corporate codes and mitigate the attitude of companies to prevent legal enforcement by refraining from publicly declaring code compliance, an additional option could also be to link the proposed development towards enforcing corporate codes to another tendency in private law and view it in light of increasing mandatory transparency rules for companies. This could take the form of mandatory rules in the field of disclosure laws, as spelled out in a recent proposal of the Commission on amending the rules on disclosure of non-financial information for particular companies.[85] It could also appear in the form of information duties in unfair commercial practices laws, as is currently discussed in the literature.[86] For private law enforcement of voluntary CSR commitments to be furthered, one could finally also view WTO law as playing a vital role.[87] Thus, from the perspective of the broader regulatory context, private law enforcement might be suitable to be developed in conjunction with such information duties.

Finally, private law enforcement remains ultimately based on an attitude among actors to require a decision from the legal institutions on conflicts that involve corporate codes. This prerequisite may of course be compromised by the fact that, in relation to commercial disputes in particular, it is often not in front of a court, but rather in private arbitration proceedings that the conflict is solved. For the private law enforcement of corporate codes to become truly effective, it is therefore also necessary to focus more in detail on the conditions under which an arbitral award that took a decision as to the binding effect of corporate codes would be officially recognised. In addition, as research on the

[84] See on this development with further references McBarnet (2007) 40ff; Wouters and Chanet (2008) 286.

[85] European Commission, Proposal for Directive amending Council Directive 78/660/EEC and 83/439/EEC as regards disclosure of non-financial and diversity information by certain large companies and groups, COM (2013) 207 final, which (after amendment by the European Parliament) contains in art 1(1) an obligation for companies to publish 'a description of the policy pursued by the undertaking in relation to these matters [ie, environmental, social and employee matters, respect for human rights, anti-corruption and bribery matters] including due diligence processes implemented', adopted by the European Council on 29 September 2014.

[86] See Henning-Bodewig and Liebenau (2013) with further references and the references in section 5.3. (p 194) n 41.

[87] See on this possibility in particular Cottier and Wermelinger (2014) 91ff, pointedly at 94: 'WTO law obliges Members, equal to the Paris Convention, to implement principles and rules of unfair competition law in domestic legislation. A WTO Member that is not providing principles and rules suitable to enforce CSR commitments made by private companies may be challenged and called upon to defend its legislation before a panel and the Appellate body, both of which are mandated to assess compatibility of domestic legislation with obligations under WTO law.' And at 95: 'WTO law, in other words, will enhance the role of courts in enforcing CSR commitments.'

functioning of private arbitration reveals, these tribunals themselves also seem to become gradually more legalised and oriented towards public interest matters,[88] which could consequently render these private forms of dispute solving at least in the long run a possible forum in which the private law enforcement of corporate codes becomes conceivable with due respect to the public interest considerations that were addressed in this study.

9.3.2. Global Self-regulation and Fragmented National Legal Systems

The scrutinised interaction of the corporate codes with private law has also sought to provide inspiration on how a legal solution can be developed for a common global phenomenon in spite of the still-remaining fragmentation of national law. In this context, this study has sought to employ comparative law to develop uniform solutions for this new social phenomenon in light of functional equivalence. Yet, it also remains true that taking the national specifics of legal systems and their evolutionary path-dependency seriously might deem this perception of achieving functional equivalent solutions a pipe dream that might be desirable, but that remains impossible in light of national political, social and economic institutions. This study could, on this particular aspect, only occasionally provide hints as to where remaining fundamental differences exist between, in particular, the German and the English legal systems. An important institutional path-dependency that influences in particular the contractual interpretation of corporate codes was identified in contract law and its development in light of the different forms of contracting between liberal market economies and coordinated market economies. The German coordinated market economy and its reliance on incomplete and informal forms of contracting and cooperative industrial relations seem here to have led to a comparative advantage in dealing with the highly informal corporate codes in comparison to the UK's liberal market economy. A potential way of theorising on these differences could be to describe the corporate codes as specific social arrangements that fit as to their intention neatly into liberal market economies and remain in this context informal arrangements, but, at the same time, amount to 'irritants'[89] that currently undergo a transformation of meaning after being integrated in the national institutional context of coordinated market economies.

It would, in this respect, be very interesting to see whether there are other institutional parameters that determine the feasibility of private law enforcement and whether this so far mainly implicitly indicated stronger conceptual readiness of the Continental coordinated market economies remains a valid conclusion on an overall

[88] *cf* Renner (2011).

[89] For this concept, *cf* Teubner (1998), who, however, focuses mainly on 'legal irritants', ie, legal concepts that are transplanted from one context to another (using the example of 'good faith' in English law). Nevertheless, irritants in the context of this study refer to corporate codes as social irritants, eg, as social arrangements that are embedded in a specific national context and once transplanted into a different one may exhibit a different form.

scale. One could anticipate that the stronger institutions of work councils and trade unions in the German Rhineland capitalism effectively result in a more intense recognition of corporate codes as a way of creating legal rights for individual employees and trade unions as opposed to, for instance, the US, where such institutions are not equally strong. That being said, it is also possible that the comparison between a better or less well-prepared socio-political and economic institutional arrangement for dealing with corporate codes is as such the wrong approach. It is equally conceivable that corporate codes, after undergoing the transformation within a coordinated market economy from voluntary arrangements to legal obligations, re-irritate their functioning within the national context where they have been initially perceived as voluntary. In fact, the proposal of legal enforcement of corporate codes is already today not an anomaly that characterises Continental European debate in the form of a merely hypothetical possibility that is discussed by legal academics. Interestingly, it is actually furthered specifically in the US and the UK in the form of civil litigation that is initiated by victims of corporate human rights abuses or in the form of public interest litigation in the field of consumer law. This at least indicates that the legal enforcement appears to be an option in these national contexts as well, but it might be the case that the characteristics of legal enforcement will differ considerably from the Continental European version. One can, for instance, with good reason predict that the enforcement of corporate codes for the benefit of workers is not equally furthered by the institutional arrangement of liberal market economies, in particular the US, and thus remains less likely. Yet, the strategy of enforcing corporate codes for the benefit of consumers and investors may even be more feasible in this variant of capitalism given the institutional emphasis on the protection of the competitive market and consumers and investors as its main actors. In this context, it is also possible that the institutional preference for formal and complete contracting renders it difficult for courts to enforce codes by means of completing contracts with good faith obligations, but that the legal enforcement is still furthered due to the tendency amongst social actors to develop ex ante more formalised corporate codes. The fact that large universities in the US, as the frequently mentioned throughout this study University of Wisconsin, insist on including corporate codes into contracts may here serve as one of the indicative examples for this trend. It is then not enforcement by means of a court's discretion to complete contracts with a view to informal codes, but rather enforcement in the form of a tendency towards creating complete contracts that contain explicit and formalised codes that could be the future for private law enforcement in liberal market economies.

That being said, it is clear that this comparison must at this point remain at the stage of an uncertain prediction that is developed on the basis of the findings in this study. The necessary evidence in favour or against such a prediction needs to be reserved for future research.

9.3.3. Future Challenges

Finally, on a more fundamental level, the proposed private law enforcement also certainly raises questions on legitimacy that the future debate would need to embrace. It is clear that once the private regulatory role of companies, as created by corporate codes, becomes recognised and legally institutionalised as suggested in this study, the created legal obligations may also collide with the regulatory efforts of institutionalised politics. To the extent that the political system adopts mandatory rules that conflict with the obligations created by corporate codes, private law would then need to develop general criteria on when to recognise these private orders as legitimate. This would require further scrutiny as to the possible legitimacy of private orders in their relationship with formal political processes, which political and legal theory is called upon to discuss.

Private law enforcement of voluntary CSR codes, as developed in this study, is by no means a general choice for self-regulation by private actors over interventionist regulation by the political system. It can instead be read as an encouragement to take the first step towards assigning the legal system again with the role of regulating companies that the law lost in an era of globalisation and major transformations of the corporate entity, but also recognising the role that private actors now play in the regulation process. The enforcement of private self-regulation on CSR matters could be a promising direction in light of the fragmentation of world society in which the search for an effective global uniform legal solution for regulating transnational corporations developed by international politics in the form of an international treaty and its enforcement by a 'world court for multinationals' might turn out to be in vain, but where, simultaneously, social sanctions by the global public may not (or at least not yet) be strong enough to steer alone corporate behaviour on a continuous basis. For CSR matters, the interaction between the formal legal system and the productive potential of the private sphere remains in my view a regulatory form that is at least worth considering.

Bibliography

Abbegg, A (2009) 'Regulation of Hybrid Networks at the Intersection between Governmental Administration and Economic Self-Organisation' in M Amstutz and G Teubner (eds), *Networks. Legal Issues of Multilateral Co-operation* (Oxford, Hart Publishing) 255–89.

Abbott, K and Snidal, D (2009) 'Strengthening International Regulation through Transnational New Governance: Overcoming the Orchestration Deficit' 42 *Vanderbilt Journal of Transnational Law* 501–71.

Abelshauser, W (2003) *Kulturkampf. Der deutsche Weg in die Neue Wirtschaft und die amerikanische Herausforderung* (Berlin, Kadmos Kulturverlag).

Ackermann, T (2007) *Der Schutz des negativen Interesses. Zur Verknüpfung von Selbstbindung und Sanktion im Privatrecht* (Tübingen, Mohr Siebeck).

—— (2014) 'Corporate Social Responsibility und Kartellrecht' in R Hilty and F Henning-Bodewig (eds), *Corporate Social Responsibility—Verbindliche Standards des Wettbewerbsrechts?* (Berlin/Heidelberg, Springer) 147–157.

Adams, JN, Beyleveld, D and Brownsword, R (1997) 'Privity of Contracts—The Benefits and the Burdens of Law Reform' 60 *Modern Law Review* 238–64.

Adams, JN and MacQueen, H (2010) *Atiyah's Sale of Goods* 12th edn (Harlow, Pearson).

Albert, M (1992) *Capitalism against Capitalism* (London, Wiley-Blackwell).

Alexander, C (2002) *Vertrag und unlauterer Wettbewerb. Eine Untersuchung der wechselseitigen Beziehungen von Vertragsrecht und Wettbewerbsrecht zueinander* (Berlin, Duncker & Humblot).

—— (2010) *Schadensersatz und Abschöpfung im Lauterkeits- und Kartellrecht* (Tübingen, Mohr Siebeck).

Alexy, R (1978) *Theorie der juristischen Argumentation. Die Theorie des rationalen Diskurses als Theorie der juristischen Begründung* (Frankfurt am Main, Suhrkamp).

Alston, P (2004) 'Core Labor Standards and the Transformation of International Labor Standards' 15 *European Journal of International Law* 457–521.

—— (2005) 'Facing Up to the Complexities of the ILO's Core Labour Standards Agenda' 16 *European Journal of International Law* 467–80.

Amstutz, M (2009) *Die soziale Verantwortung von Unternehmen im Europäischen Recht* (Bonn, Zentrum für Europäisches Wirtschaftsrecht—Vorträge und Berichte).

—— (2011), 'Mechanisms of Evolution for a Law of the Future' in S Muller, S Zouridis, M Frishman and L Kistemaker (eds), *The Law of the Future and the Future of Law* (Oslo, Torkel Opsahl Academic EPublisher, 2011) 395–405.

Amstutz, M and Teubner, G (eds) (2008) *Networks: Legal Issues of Multilateral Co-operation* (Oxford, Hart Publishing).

Anderson, GW (2010) Corporate Constitutionalism: From Above and Below (But Mostly Below), *Paper for 'The Constitutionalization of the Global Corporate Sphere' Conference* (Copenhagen Business School, 17–18 September).

—— (2013) 'Societal Constitutionalism, Social Movements, and Constitutionalism from Below' 20 *Indiana Journal of Global Legal Studies* 881–906.

Anderson, JC (1999) 'Respecting Human Rights: Multinational Corporations Strike out' 2 *University of Pennsylvania Labor and Employment Law* 463–506.

Andrews, N (2001) 'Strangers to Justice No Longer: The Reversal of the Privity Rule under the Contracts (Rights of Third Parties) Act 1999' 60 *Cambridge Law Journal* 353–81.

Anson, WH and Gwyer M, (1923), *Principles of the English Law of Contract* 16 (Oxford, Clarendon Press).
Arendt, H (2003 [1993]) *Was ist Politik? Fragmente aus dem Nachlass* (Munich, Piper Verlag).
Arthurs, H (2005) 'Corporate Codes of Conduct: Profit, Power and Law in the Global Economy' in W Cragg (ed), *Ethic Codes, Corporations and the Challenge of Globalization* (Cheltenham, Edward Elgar) 51–71.
Atiyah, PS (1979) *The Rise and Fall of the Freedom of Contract* (Oxford, Clarendon Press).
—— (1981), *Promises, Morals, and Law* (Oxford, Clarendon Press).
—— (1986), 'Consideration. A Restatement' in PS Atiyah (ed), *Essays on Contract* (Oxford, Clarendon Press) 179–243.
Augenstein, D (2010) *Study of the Legal Framework on Human Rights and the Environment Applicable to European Enterprises Operating Outside the European Union* (Edinburgh, Study submitted by the University of Edinburgh for the European Commission).
Augenstein, D and Kinley, D (2013) 'When Human Rights "Responsibilities" Become "Duties": The Extra-territorial Obligations of States that Bind Corporations' in S Deva and D Bilchitz (eds), *Human Rights Obligations for Business. Beyond the Corporate Responsibility to Respect?* (Cambridge, Cambridge University Press) 271–94.
Austin, JL (1976 [1962]) *How to do Things with Words* (Cambridge, MA, Harvard University Press).
Ayres, I and Brown, JG (2006) 'Mark(et)ing Nondiscrimination: Privatizing ENDA with a Certification Mark' 104 *Michigan Law Review* 1639–712.
Baade, HW (1980) 'The Legal Effects of Codes of Conduct for MNEs' in N Horn (ed), *Legal Problems of Codes of Conduct for Multinational Enterprises* (Deventer, Kluwer) 3–38.
Bachmann, G (2006a), 'Kontrahierungspflichten im privaten Bankrecht' 18 *Zeitschrift für Bankrecht und Bankwirtschaft* 257–269.
—— (2006b) *Private Ordnung* (Tübingen, Mohr Siebeck).
—— (2008) 'Optionsmodelle im Privatrecht' 63 *Juristenzeitung* 11–20.
Backer, LC (2007) 'Economic Globalization and the Rise of Efficient Systems of Global Private Law Making: Wal-Mart as Global Legislator' 39 *Connecticut Law Review* 1739–84.
—— (2008) 'Multinational Corporations as Objects and Sources of Transnational Regulation' 14 *ILSA Journal for International & Comparative Law* 499–523.
—— (2009) 'Rights and Accountability in Development. ("Raid") v. Das Air and Global Witness v. Afrimex' 10 *Melbourne Journal of International Law* 258–307.
—— (2013) '"Transnational Corporations" Outward Expression of Inward Self-Constitution: The Enforcement of Human Rights by Apple, Inc.' 20 *Indiana Journal of Global Legal Studies* 805–79.
Baeter, A (2011) *Unlauterer Wettbewerb* (Tübingen, Mohr Siebeck).
Baker, MB (1993) 'Private Codes of Conduct: Should the Fox Guard the Henhouse?' 24 *University of Miami Inter-American Law Review* 399–433.
Ballerstedt, K (1950/51) 'Zur Haftung für culpa in contrahendo bei Geschäftsabschluß durch Stellvertreter' 151 *Archiv für die civilistische Praxis* 501–531.
Bar, C von (1980) *Verkehrspflichten. Richterliche Gefahrsteuerungsgebote im deutschen Deliktsrecht* (Cologne/Berlin, Carl Heymanns Verlag).
Baram, MS (1994) 'Multinational Corporations, Private Codes, and Technology Transfer for Sustainable Development' 24 *Environmental Law* 33–65.
Barkhuysen, T and Lindenbergh, S (eds) (2006), *The Constitutionalization of Private Law* (Leiden/Boston, Brill Publishers).
Barnett, RE (1986) 'A Consent Theory of Contract' 86 *Columbia Law Review* 269–321.
Barron, A (2007) 'Reasonable Expectations, Good Faith and Self-Regulatory Codes' in G Howells, A Nordhausen, D Parry and C Twigg-Flesner (eds), *The Yearbook of Consumer Law 2007* (Aldershot, Ashgate Publishing) 3–30.

Bartley, T (2005) 'Corporate Accountability and the Privatization of Labor Standards: Struggles over Codes of Conduct in the Apparel Industry' 14 *Politics and the Corporation. Research in Political Sociology* 211–244.

Bayer, W (1995) *Der Vertrag zugunsten Dritter* (Tübingen, Mohr Siebeck).

Beale, H (2010) 'A Review of the Contracts (Rights of Third Parties) Act 1999' in A Burrows and E Peel (eds), *Contract Formation and Parties* (Oxford, Oxford University Press) 224–50.

—— (2012) *Chitty on Contracts. Volume I. General Principles* 31 (London, Sweet & Maxwell).

Beatson, J, Burrows, A and Cartwright, J (2010) *Anson's Law of Contract* 29th edn (Oxford, Oxford University Press).

Beaucamp, B (2003) 'Das Bewerbungsschuldverhältnis nach § 311 II BGB als rechtlicher Kernbereich des Wettbewerbs' *Neue Juristische Wochenschrift* 3096–97.

Beck, U (1997) 'Subpolitics. Ecology and the Disintegration of Institutional Power' 10 *Organization and Environment* 52–65.

—— (2005) *Power in the Global Age. A New Global Political Economy* (Cambridge, Polity Press).

Beckert, J (2006) 'The Ambivalent Role of Morality on Markets' in N Stehr, C Henning and B Weiler (eds), *The Moralization of Markets* (New Brunswick, Transaction Publishers), 109–28.

—— (2007) 'The Great Transformation of Embeddedness. Karl Polanyi and the New Economic Sociology' 07/01 *MPIfG Discussion Paper*.

Berger, C (2004) 'Der Beschaffenheitsbegriff des § 434 Abs. 1 BGB' 59 *Juristenzeitung* 276–83.

Berle, AA (1931) 'Corporate Powers as Powers in Trust' 44 *Harvard Law Review* 1049–74.

—— (1932) 'For Whom are Managers Trustees: A Note' 45 *Harvard Law Review* 1365–72.

Berle, AA and Means, G (1933) *The Modern Corporation and Private Property* (New York, Macmillan Company).

Berresheim, D (2005) 'Kontrahierungszwang der Kreditwirtschaft für Girokonten aufgrund von Selbstverpflichtungserklärungen?' 17 *Zeitschrift für Bankrecht und Bankwirtschaft* 420–426.

Bertrams, H (2004) *Die Haftung des Aufsichtsrats im Zusammenhang mit dem Deutschen Corporate Governance Kodex und § 161 AktG* (Berlin, Duncker & Humblot).

Birk, A (2011) 'Corporate Responsibility, unternehmerische Selbstverpflichtungen und unlauterer Wettbewerb' *Gewerblicher Rechtsschutz und Urheberrecht* 196–203.

—— (2014) 'Irreführung über CSR—Informationspflichten über CSR?' in R Hilty and F Henning-Bodewig (eds), *Corporate Social Responsibility—Verbindliche Standards des Wettbewerbsrechts?* (Berlin/Heidelberg, Springer) 169–86.

Blackett, A (2000) 'Global Governance: Legal Pluralism and the Decentered State: A Labor Law Critique of Codes of Conduct' 8 *Indiana Journal of Global Legal Studies* 401–47.

Böhm, F (1966) 'Privatrechtsgesellschaft und Marktwirtschaft' in F Böhm (ed), *Freiheit und Ordnung in der Marktwirtschaft* (Baden-Baden, Nomos) 105–68.

Bondy, K, Matten, D and Moon, J (2004) 'The Adoption of Voluntary Codes in MNCs: A Three-Country Comparative Study' 109 *Business and Society Review* 449–77.

Boom, W van and Loos, M (eds) (2007) *Collective Enforcement of Consumer Law: Securing Compliance in Europe through Private Group Action and Public Authority Intervention* (Groningen, Europa Law Publishing).

Bridge, M (2001) 'The Contracts (Rights of Third Parties) Act 1999' 5 *Edinburgh Law Review* 85–102.

Brownlie, I (2008) *Principles of Public International Law* 7th edn (Oxford, Oxford University Press).

Buckel, S, Christensen, R and Fischer-Lescano, A (eds) (2006) *Neue Theorien des Rechts* 1st edn (Stuttgart, Lucius&Lucius).

Burrows A, (1987) *Remedies for Torts and Breach of Contract* (London, Butterworth).

—— (1998), *Understanding the Law of Obligations* (Oxford, Hart Publishing).

—— (2000), 'The Contracts (Rights of Third Parties) Act 1999 and its Implication for Commercial Contracts' *Lloyd's Maritime and Commercial Law Quarterly* 540–54.
—— (ed) (2007), *English Private Law* 2 (Oxford, Oxford University Press).
Butler, J (1992) 'Contingent Foundations: Feminism and the Question of "Postmodernism"' in J Butler and JW Scott (eds), *Feminists Theorize the Political* (New York/London, Routledge) 3–21.
Buxbaum, RM (1993) 'Is "Network" a Legal Concept?' 149 *Journal of Institutional and Theoretical Economics* 698–705.
Bydlinski, F (1967) *Privatautonomie und objektive Grundlagen des verpflichtenden Rechtsgeschäfts* (Vienna/New York, Springer Verlag).
Cafaggi, F (2008) 'Contractual Networks and the Small Business Act: Towards European Principles?' 2008/15 *EUI Working Papers, Department of Law.*
—— (2010) 'New Foundations of Transnational Private Regulation' 2010/53 *EUI Working Papers, Robert Schumann Centre for Advanced Studies.*
—— (2011) 'Self-regulation in European Private Law' in AS Hartkamp, MW Hesselink, EH Houndius, C Mak and CE du Perron (eds), *Towards a European Civil Code* 4 (Alphen aan den Rijn, Kluwer Law International) 91–126.
—— (ed) (2012) *Enforcement of Transnational Regulation: Ensuring Compliance in a Global World* (Cheltenham, Edward Elgar).
—— (2013) 'The Regulatory Functions of Transnational Commercial Contracts: New Architectures' 36 *Fordham International Law Journal* 1557–618.
Cafaggi, F and Randa, A (2012) 'Public and Private Regulation: Mapping the Labyrinth' 1 *The Dovenschmidt Quarterly* 16–33.
Calliess, G-P and Renner, M (2009) 'Between Law and Social Norms: The Evolution of Global Governance' 22 *Ratio Juris* 260–280.
Calliess, G-P and Zumbansen, P (2010) *Rough Consensus and Running Code: A Theory of Transnational Law* (Oxford, Hart Publishing).
Campbell, D and Collins, H (2003) 'Discovering the Implicit Dimensions of Contracts' in D Campbell, H Collins and J Wightman (eds), *Implicit Dimensions of Contract: Discrete, Relational, and Network Contracts* (Oxford, Hart Publishing) 25–49.
Campbell, D, Collins, H and Wightman, J (eds) (2003) *Implicit Dimensions of Contract. Discrete, Relational and Network Contracts* (Oxford, Hart Publishing).
Campbell, K and Vick, D (2007) 'Disclosure Law and the Market for Corporate Social Responsibility' in D McBarnet, A Voiculescu and T Campbell (eds), *The New Corporate Accountability. Corporate Social Responsibility and the Law* (Cambridge, MA, Cambridge University Press) 241–78.
Canaris, C-W (1971) *Die Vertrauenshaftung im Deutschen Privatrecht* (Munich, C.H. Beck).
Carroll, A and Shabana, K (2010) 'The Business Case for Corporate Social Responsibility: A Review of Concepts, Research and Practice' *International Journal of Management Reviews* 85–105.
Casper (2001) 'The Legal Framework for Corporate Governance: The Influence of Contract Law on Company Strategies in Germany and the United States' in PA Hall and D Soskice (eds), *Varieties of Capitalism: The Institutional Foundations of Comparative Advantage* (Oxford, Oxford University Press) 387–416.
Cassese, S, D'Alterio, E and De Bellis, M (2012) 'The Enforcement of Transnational Private Regulation: A Fictitious Oxymoron' in F Cafaggi (ed), *Enforcement of Transnational Regulation. Ensuring Compliance in a Global World* (Cheltenham, Edward Elgar) 331–71.
Castermans, AG (2009) *De burger in het burgerlijk recht of De eigenschappen van perensap* (The Hague, Boom Uitgevers).

Cauffman, C and Olaerts, M (2011) 'Quimica: Further Developing the Rules on Parent Company Liability' 32 *European Competition Law Review* 431–41.
Certau, M de (1984) *The Practice of Everyday Life* (Berkeley, University of California Press).
Cherednychenko, O (2004) 'The Constitutionalization of Contract Law: Something New under the Sun' 8 *Electronic Journal of Comparative Law* 1–17.
Cherry, MA and Sneirson, JF (2011) 'Beyond Profit: Rethinking Corporate Social Responsibility and Greenwashing after the BP Oil Disaster' 85 *Tulane Law Review* 983–1038.
—— (2012) 'Chevron, Greenwashing, and the Myth of "Green Oil Companies"' 3 *Washington & Lee Journal of Energy, Climate and the Environment* 133–54.
Christodoulidis, E (2013) 'On the Politics of Societal Constitutionalism' 20 *Indiana Journal of Global Legal Studies* 629–63.
Ciacchi, AC (2006) 'The Constitutionalization of European Contract Law: Judicial Convergence and Social Justice' 2 *European Review of Contract Law* 167–80.
Coase, R (1937) 'The Nature of the Firm' 4 *Economica* 386–405.
Cohen, M (1933) 'The Basis of Contract' 46 *Harvard Law Review* 553–92.
Coleman, S (2009) 'Enforcing International Framework Agreements in U.S. Courts: A Contract Analysis' 41 *Columbia Human Rights Review* 601–34.
Collins, H (1986) 'Contract and Legal Theory' in W Twining (ed), *Legal Theory and Common Law* (Oxford, Basil Blackwell) 136–54.
—— (1990) 'Ascription of Legal Responsibility to Groups in Complex Patterns of Economic Integration' 53 *Modern Law Review* 731–744.
—— (1999) *Regulating Contracts* (Oxford, Oxford University Press).
—— (2003a) 'Introduction: The Research Agenda of Implicit Dimensions of Contracts' in D Campbell, H Collins and J Wightman (eds), *Implicit Dimensions of Contract. Discrete, Relational and Network Contracts* (Oxford, Hart Publishing) 1–24.
—— (2003b) *The Law of Contract* (Cambridge, Cambridge University Press).
—— (2005) 'The Unfair Commercial Practices Directive' 1 *European Review of Contract Law* 417–41.
—— (2007) 'Utility and Rights in Common Law Reasoning: Rebalancing Private Law Through Constitutionalization' 6/2007 *LSE Law, Society and Economy Working Papers*.
—— (2008) 'Networks and Comparative Sociological Jurisprudence' in G-P Calliess, A Fischer-Lescano, D Wielsch and P Zumbansen (eds), *Soziologische Jurisprudenz—Festschrift für Gunther Teubner zum 65. Geburtstag* (Berlin, De Gruyter) 249–59.
—— (2009) 'The Weakest Link: Legal Aspects of Network Architecture of Supply Chains' in M Amstutz and G Teubner (eds), *Networks: Legal Issues of Multilateral Co-operation* (Oxford, Hart Publishing) 187–210.
—— (2010) 'Harmonisation by Example: European Laws against Unfair Commercial Practices' 73 *Modern Law Review* 89–118.
—— (2014) 'Conformity of Goods, the Network Society, and the Ethical Consumer' 22 *European Review of Private Law* 619–40.
Cooke, E (1997) 'Estoppel and the Protection of Expectations' 17 *Legal Studies* 258–85.
Cottier, T and Wermelinger, G (2014) 'Implementing and Enforcing Corporate Social Responsibility: The Potential of Unfair Competition Rules in International Law' in R Hilty and F Henning-Bodewig (eds), *Corporate Social Responsibility—Verbindliche Standards des Wettbewerbsrechts?* (Berlin/Heidelberg, Springer) 81–97.
Crawley, AT (1993) 'Environmental Auditing and the "Good Samaritan" Doctrine: Implications for Parent Corporations' 28 *Georgia Law Review* 223–68.
Cutler, C, Haufler, V and Porter, T (eds) (1999) *Private Authority and International Affairs* (Albany: State University of New York Press).

Dagan, H (2010) 'The Limited Autonomy of Private Law' 56 *American Journal of Comparative Law* 809–34.
Dam, C van (2008) *Onderneming en mensenrechten. Zorgvuldigheidsnormen voor ondernemingen ter voorkoming van betrokkenheid bij schending van mensenrechten* (The Hague, Boom Juridische uitgevers).
Deakin, S, Johnston, A and Markesinis, BS (2007) *Markesinis and Deakin's Tort Law* 7th edn (Oxford, Oxford University Press).
Derleder, P (2003) 'Kurzkommentar zu LG Berlin Urteil v. 24.4.2003 -21 S 1/03' 19 *Entscheidungen zum Wirtschaftsrecht* 963–64.
Deva, S and Bilchitz, D (eds) (2013) *Human Rights Obligations for Business. Beyond the Corporate Responsibility to Respect?* (Cambridge, Cambridge University Press).
Di Fabio, U (1997) 'Selbstverpflichtung der Wirtschaft—Grenzgänger zwischen Freiheit und Zwang' 52 *Juristenzeitung* 969–1020.
Diller, J (1999) 'A Social Conscience in the Global Marketplace? Labour Dimensions of Codes of Conduct, Social Labelling and Investor Initiatives' 138 *International Labour Review* 99–129.
Dilling, O (2005) 'Die Produktionsbedingung als Produkteigenschaft—Ein Fallbeispiel für die Haftung bei Werbung mit ethischen Produktionsstandards nach der Schuldrechtsreform' in G Winter (ed), *Die Umweltverantwortung multinationaler Unternehmen. Selbststeuerung und Recht bei Auslandsinvestitionen* (Baden-Baden, Nomos) 283–313.
Dilling, O, Herberg, M and Winter, G (2008a) 'Introduction: Private Accountability in a Globalising World' in O Dilling, M Herberg and G Winter (eds), *Responsible Business: Self-governance and Law in Transnational Economic Transactions* (Oxford, Hart Publishing) 1–13.
—— (eds) (2008b) *Responsible Business: Self-governance and Law in Transnational Economic Transactions* (Oxford, Hart Publishing).
Doane, D (2005) 'The Myth of CSR: The Problem with Assuming that Companies Can Do Well While also Doing Good is that Markets Really Don't Work that Way' *Stanford Social Innovation Review*, www.ssireview.org/articles/entry/the_myth_of_csr.
Dodd, EM (1932) 'For Whom are Corporate Mangers Trustees?' 45 *Harvard Law Review* 1145–63.
Dreyer, G (2007) 'Verhaltenskodizes im Referentenentwurf eines Ersten Gesetzes zur Änderung des Gesetzes gegen unlauteren Wettbewerb' *Wettbewerb in Recht und Praxis* 1294–1303.
Dubbink, W and Putten, FP van der (2008) 'Is Competition Law an Impediment to CSR?' 83 *Journal of Business Ethics* 381–95.
Durkheim, E (1964) *The Division of Labor in Society* (New York, Free Press).
Dustmann, C, Fitzenberger, B, Schönberg, U and Spitz-Oener, A (2014) 'From Sick Man of Europe to Economic Superstar: Germany's Resurgent Economy' 28 *Journal of Economic Perspectives* 167–88.
Ehrlich, E (1899) *Das zwingende und nichtzwingende Recht im Bürgerlichen Gesetzbuch für das Deutsche Reich* (Jena, G. Fischer).
Eijsbouts, J (2011) *Corporate Responsibility, beyond Voluntarism. Regulatory Options to Reinforce the License to Operate* (Maastricht, Inaugural Lecture, Maastricht University).
Eisenberg, MA (1982) 'The Principles of Consideration' 67 *Cornell Law Review* 640–65.
—— (2001) 'The Theory of Contracts' in P Benson (ed), *The Theory of Contract Law: New Essays* (Cambridge, Cambridge University Press) 206–64.
Eliantonio, M (2011) 'Towards an Ever Dirtier Europe? The Restrictive Standing of Environmental NGOs before the European Courts and the Aarhus Convention' 7 *Croation Yearbook of European Law and Policy* 69–85.
Elkington, J (1997) *Cannibals with Forks* (Oxford, Capstone Publishers).

Ellis, J (2010) 'Sustainable Development and Fragmentation in International Society' in D French (ed), *Global Justice and Sustainable Development* (Leiden, Martinus Nijhoff) 57–74.
—— (2012) 'Shades of Grey: Soft Law and the Validity of Public International Law' 25 *Leiden Journal of International Law* 313–34.
—— (2013) 'Constitutionalization of Non-governmental Certification Programmes' 21 *Indiana Journal of Global Legal Studies* 1035–59.
Enneking, L (2008) 'Dutch Case Note—Sutradhar (fc) v. Natural Environment Research Council' 16 *European Review of Private Law* 499–511.
—— (2012) *Foreign Direct Liability and Beyond: Exploring the Role of Tort Law in Promoting International Corporate Social Responsibility and Accountability* (The Hague, Eleven International Publishing).
Ernst, S (2010) 'Corporate Social Responsibility (CSR) und das Wettbewerbsrecht' *Wettbewerb in Recht und Praxis* 1304–14.
Esser, J (1970) *Vorverständnis und Methodenwahl in der Rechtsfindung. Rationalitätsgarantien der richterlichen Entscheidungspraxis* (Frankfurt am Main, Athenäum).
—— (1990) *Grundsatz und Norm in der richterlichen Fortbildung des Privatrechts* (Tübingen, Mohr Siebeck).
Estlund, C (2012) 'Enforcement of Transnational Labor Regulation: A New Frontier in the Anti-sweatshop Movement?' in F Cafaggi (ed), *Enforcement of Transnational Regulation: Ensuring Compliance in a Global World* (Cheltenham, Edward Elgar) 237–62.
Everson, M and Joerges, C (2006) 'Consumer Citizenship in Postnational Constellations?' 2006/47 *EUI Working Papers, Department of Law.*
Fabricius, F (1970) 'Anmerkung zu BGH Urteil vom 16 April 1969, VIII ZR 176/66' 25 *Juristenzeitung* 28–31.
Falk, A and Szech, N (2013) 'Morals and Markets' 340 *Science* 707–11.
Farber, DA and Matheson, JH (1985) 'Beyond Promissory Estoppel: Contract Law and the "Invisible Handshake"' 52 *University of Chicago Law Review* 903–47.
Faust, F and Wiese, V (2008) 'Specific Performance—A German Perspective' in J Smits, D Haas and G Hesen (eds), *Specific Performance in Contract Law: National and Other Perspectives* (Antwerp, Intersentia) 47–64.
Fikentscher, W (1983) *Wirtschaftsrecht. Band II* (Munich, C.H. Beck).
Fischer-Lescano, A (2005) *Globalverfassung. Die Geltungsbegründung der Menschenrechte* (Weilerswist, Velbrück).
—— (2012) 'Critical Systems Theory' 38 *Philosophy & Social Criticism* 3–23.
Fischer-Lescano, A and Teubner, G (2004) 'Regime-Collisions: The Vain Search for Legal Unity in the Fragmentation of Global Law' 25 *Michigan Law Journal of International Law* 999–1045.
Flume, W (1979) *Allgemeiner Teil des Bürgerlichen Rechts. Zweiter Band: Das Rechtsgeschäft* 3rd edn (Berlin/Heidelberg/New York, Springer).
Francot-Timmermans, L and Christodoulidis, E (2011) 'The Normative Turn in Teubner's Systems Theory of Law' 40 *Rechtsfilosofie & Rechtstheorie* 187–90.
Fransen, LW and Kolk, A (2007) 'Global Rule-Setting for Business: A Critical Analysis of Multi-Stakeholder Standards' 14 *Organisations* 667–84.
Freeman, E (2010 [1984]) *Strategic Management: A Stakeholder Approach* (Cambridge, Cambridge University Press).
Frenkel, S and Seongsu, K (2004) 'Corporate Codes of Labour Practice and Employment Relations in Sports Shoe Factories in South Korea' 42 *Asia Pacific Journal of Human Resources* 6–31.
Frenz, W (2001) *Selbstverpflichtungen der Wirtschaft* (Tübingen, Mohr Siebeck).

Fried, C (1981) *Contract as Promise: A Theory of Contractual Obligation* (Cambridge, MA, Havard University Press).
Friedman, LM (1975) *The Legal System—A Social Science Perspective* (New York, Russell Sage Foundation).
—— (1999) 'Taking Law and Society Seriously' 74 *Chicago-Kent Law Review* 529–542.
Frynas, JG (1999) 'Legal Change in Africa: Evidence from Oil-Related Litigation in Nigeria' 43 *Journal of African Law* 121–50.
Fuller, LL (1941) 'Consideration and Form' 41 *Columbia Law Review* 799–824.
Fuller, LL and Perdue, WR (1936) 'The Reliance Interest in Contract Damages' 46 *Yale Law Journal* 52–96.
Gambetta, D (ed) (1990) *Trust: Making and Breaking Cooperative Relations* (Oxford/New York, Blackwell Publishers).
Geis, GS (2012) 'Broadcast Contracting' 106 *Northwestern University Law Review* 1153–200.
Gelter, M (2011) 'Taming or Protecting the Corporation? Shareholder-Stakeholder Debates in a Comparative Light' 7 *NYU Journal of Law & Business* 641–730.
Genugten, W van and Bijsterveld, S van (1998) 'Codes of Conduct for Multinational Enterprises: Useful Instruments or a Shield against Binding Liability' 7 *Tilburg Foreign Law Review* 161–77.
Gereffi, G, Humphrey, J and Sturgeon, T (2005) 'The Governance of Global Value Chains' 12 *Review of International Political Economy* 78–104.
Gierke, O von (1887) *Die Genossenschaftstheorie und die deutsche Rechtsprechung* (Berlin, Weidmann).
—— (1889) *Die soziale Aufgabe des Privatrechts: Vortrag gehalten am 5. April 1889 in der juristischen Gesellschaft zu Wien* (Berlin, Verlag Julius von Springer).
Giliker, P (2002) *Pre-contractual Liability in English and French Law* (The Hague, Kluwer Law International).
Gilmore, G (1974) *The Death of Contract* (Columbus, OH, Ohio State University Press).
Glinski, C (2007) 'Corporate Codes of Conduct: Moral or Legal Obligation?' in D McBarnet, A Voiculescu and T Campbell (eds), *The New Corporate Accountability. Corporate Social Responsibility and the Law* (Cambridge, Cambridge University Press) 119–47.
—— (2008) 'Bridging the Gap: The Legal Potential of Private Regulation' in O Dilling, M Herberg and G Winter (eds), *Responsible Business. Self-governance and Law in Transnational Economic Transactions* (Oxford, Hart Publishing, 2008) 41–66.
—— (2011) *Die rechtliche Bedeutung der privaten Regulierung globaler Produktionsstandards* (Baden-Baden, Nomos).
—— (2014) 'Competing Transnational Regimes under WTO Law' (2014) 30 *Utrecht Journal of International and European Law* 44–67.
Glinski, C and Rott, P (2003) 'Umweltfreundliches und ethisches Konsumverhalten im harmonisierten Kaufrecht' 14 *Europäische Zeitschrift für Wirtschaftsrecht* 649–54.
Goffman, E (1959) *The Presentation of Self in Everyday Life* (New York, Anchor Books).
Good, D (1988) 'Individuals, Interpersonal Relations, and Trust' in D Gambetta (ed), *Trust. Making and Breaking Cooperative Relations* (New York/Oxford, Basil Blackwell) 31–48.
Gordley, J (1991) *The Philosophical Origins of Modern Contract Doctrine* (Oxford, Clarendon Press).
Gordon, RW (1990) 'A Dialogue about the Doctrine of Consideration' 75 *Cornell Law Review* 987–1006.
Grabosch, R (2011) 'Prospects of Legal Redress for Victims of Corporate Human Rights Violations in a Globalised World' in L Boulle (ed), *Globalisation and Governance* (Westlaken, Siber Ink Publishers) 158–73.
Granovetter, M (1973) 'The Strength of Weak Ties' 78 *American Journal of Sociology* 1360–80.

—— (1985) 'Economic Action and Social Structure: The Problem of Embeddedness' 91 *American Journal of Sociology* 481–510.
Green, L (1959) 'Tort Law Public Law in Disguise' 38 *Texas Law Review* 257–69.
Greenwald, R (2005) *The Triangle Fire, Protocols of Peace, and Industrial Democracy in Progressive Era of New York* (Philadelophia, Temple University Press).
Griffin, JJ and Mahon, J (1997) 'The Corporate Social Performance and Corporate Financial Performance: Twenty-Five Years of Incomparable Research' 36 *Business and Society* 5–31.
Grigoleit, HC and Herresthal, C (2003) 'Grundlagen der Sachmängelhaftung im Kaufrecht' 58 *Juristenzeitung* 118–127.
Gruber, M (2013) *Bioinformationsrecht* (Frankfurt am Main, Habilitationsschrift).
Grundmann, S (2007) 'Die Dogmatik der Vertragsnetze' 207 *Archiv für die civilistische Praxis* 718–67.
Grundmann, S and Renner, M (2013) 'Vertrag und Dritter—Zwischen Privatrecht und Regulierung' 68 *Juristenzeitung* 379–89.
Guest, AG (2006) *Benjamin's Sale of Goods* 7 (London, Sweet & Maxwell).
Gunningham, N (2007) 'Corporate Environmental Responsibility: Law and the Limits of Voluntarism' in D McBarnet, A Voiculescu and T Campbell (eds), *The New Corporate Accountability: Corporate Responsibility and the Law* (Cambridge, Cambridge University Press) 476–500.
Gunningham, N and Rees J, (1997) 'Industry Self-regulation: An Institutional Perspective' 19 *Law & Policy* 363–414.
Häcker, R (2004) 'Europäisch-zivilverfahrensrechtliche und international-privatrechtliche Probleme grenzüberschreitender Gewinnzusagen—zugleich zu einem europa-rechtlichen Begriff der unerlaubten Handlung' 103 *Zeitschrift für vergleichende Rechtswissenschaft* 464–500.
Hall, P and Soskice, D (2001) 'An Introduction to Varieties of Capitalism' in P Hall and D Soskice (eds), *Varieties of Capitalism: The Institutional Foundations of Comparative Advantage* (Oxford, Oxford University Press) 1–68.
Hansjürgens, B and Lübbe-Wolff, G (eds) (2000) *Symbolische Umweltpolitik* (Frankfurt am Main, Suhrkamp).
Hansmann, H and Kraakman, R (2001) 'The End of History in Corporate Law' 89 *Georgetown Law Journal* 439–68.
Haufler, V (2001) *A Public Role for the Private Sector: Industry Self-regulation in a Global Economy* (Washington DC, Carnegie Endowement for International Peace).
Hawickhorst, H (1987) *Quasi-vertragliche Haftung aufgrund von Versprechensakten* (Berlin, Dissertation Freie Universität Berlin).
Heijden, M-J van der (2011a) 'Supplier codes of conduct en mensenrechten in een keten van contracten' *Contracteren* 3–11.
—— (2011b) *Transnational Corporations and Human Rights Liabilities: Linking Standards of International Public Law to Dutch Civil Litigation Proceedings* (Tilburg, Proefschrift Universiteit Tilburg).
Henning-Bodewig, F (2010) 'UWG und Geschäftsethik' *Wettbewerb in Recht und Praxis* 1094–1105.
—— (2011) 'Der "ehrbare Kaufmann", Corporate Social Responsibility und das Lauterkeitsrecht' *Wettbewerb in Recht und Praxis* 1014–23.
Henning-Bodewig, F and Liebenau, D (2013) 'Corporate Social Responsibility (CSR)—verbindliche Standards des Wettbewerbsrechts?' *Gewerblicher Rechtsschutz und Urheberrecht—Internationaler Teil* 753–57.
Hepple, B (2000) 'The Importance of Law, Guidelines and Codes of Conduct in Monitoring Corporate Behaviour' in R Blanpain (ed), *Multinational Enterprises and the Social Challenges of the XXIst Century* (The Hague, Kluwer Law International) 3–8.

Herberg, M (2001) 'Codes of Conduct und kommunikative Vernunft. Rechtssoziologische Überlegungen zu den umweltbezogenen Selbstverpflichtungen transnationaler Chemiekonzerne' 22 *Zeitschrift für Rechtssoziologie* 25–52.

—— (2005) 'Erzeugen Multinationale Unternehmen ihr eigenes Umweltrecht? Bausteine zu einer Theorie transnationaler Regulative' in G Winter (ed), *Die Umweltverantwortung multinationaler Unternehmen. Selbststeuerung und Recht bei Auslandsdirektinvestitionen* (Baden-Baden, Nomos) 73–113.

—— (2007) *Globalisierung und private Selbstregulierung. Umweltschutz in multinationalen Unternehmen* (Frankfurt am Main, Campus).

—— (2008) 'Global Legal Pluralism and Interlegality: Environmental Self-Regulation in Multinational Enterprises as Global Law-Making' in O Dilling, M Herberg and G Winter (eds), *Responsible Business: Self-Governance and Law in Transnational Economic Transactions* (Oxford, Hart Publishing) 17–40.

Hilty, R and Henning-Bodewig, F (eds) (2014) *Corporate Social Responsibility—Verbindliche Standards des Wettbewerbsrechts?* (Berlin/Heidelberg, Springer).

Hiß, S (2005) *Warum übernehmen Unternehmen gesellschaftliche Verantwortung?* (Frankfurt/New York, Campus).

Hoffmann, J (2004) 'Co-ordinated Continental European Market Economies Under Pressure From Globalisation: Germany's Rhineland Capitalism' 5 *German Law Journal* 985–1002.

Holmes, OW (1897) 'The Path of the Law' 10 *Harvard Law Review* 457–78.

Hong, JC (2000) 'Enforcement of Corporate Codes of Conduct: Finding a Private Right of Action for International Laborers against MNCs for Labor Rights Violations' 19 *Wisconsin International Law Journal* 41–70.

Höpner, M (2003) *Wer beherrscht die Unternehmen? Shareholder Value, Managerherrschaft und Mitbestimmung in Deutschland* (Frankfurt am Main, Campus Verlag).

Hopt, K (1997) 'Europäisches und deutsches Übernahmerecht' 161 *Zeitschrift für das gesamte Handelsrecht und Wirtschaftsrecht* 368–420.

Horwitz, MJ (1982) 'The History of the Public/Private Distinction' 130 *University of Pennsylvania Law Review* 1423–28.

Howells, G (2006) ''Codes of Conduct' in G Howells, H Micklitz and T Wilhelmsson (eds), *European Fair Trading Law: The Unfair Commercial Practices Directive* (Aldershot, Ashgate) 195–215.

Howells, G and Weatherill, S (2005) *Consumer Protection Law* 2nd edn (Aldershot, Ashgate).

Jackson, G (2014) 'A Socio-political Perspective on Corporate Social Responsibility: Understanding Regulatory Substitution and the Persistence of Irresponsibility' in R Hilty and F Henning-Bodewig (eds), *Corporate Social Responsibility—Verbindliche Standards des Wettbewerbsrechts?* (Berlin/Heidelberg, Springer) 19–31.

Jaeggi, R (2008) 'Wie weiter mit Hannah Arendt?' in HIf Sozialforschung (ed), *Wie weiter mit …?* (Hamburg, Edition HIS) 1–47.

Jäger, N and Heijden, M-J van der (2008) 'Corporate Human Rights Violations: The Feasability of Civil Recourse in the Netherlands' 33 *Brooklyn Journal for International Law* 833–70.

Jellinek, G (1964) *System der subjektiven öffentlichen Rechte* (Aalen, Scientia Verlag).

Jenkins, R (2001) 'Corporate Codes of Conduct. Self-regulation in a Global Economy' 2/2001 *United Nations Research Institute for Social Development. Technology, Business and Society Programme Paper*.

Jensen, MC and Meckling, WH (1976) 'Theory of the Firm: Managerial Behaviour, Agency Costs and Ownership Structure' 3 *Journal of Financial Economics* 305–60.

Jhering, R von (1861) 'Culpa in Contrahendo oder Schadensersatz bei nichtigen oder nicht zur Perfection gelangten Verträgen' in CF von Gerber and R von Jhering (eds), *Jahrbücher für die Dogmatik des heutigen römischen und deutschen Zivilrechts* (Jena, Friedrich Mauke) 1–112.

—— (1989 [1872]) *Der Kampf ums Recht* (Frankfurt am Main, Vitario Klostermann).

Joerges, C (2011) 'A New Type of Conflicts Law as the Legal Paradigm of the Postnational Constellation' in J Falke and C Joerges (eds), *Karl Polanyi, Globalisation and the Potential of Law in Transnational Markets* (Oxford, Hart Publishing) 465–501.

Joerges, C and Rödl, F (2008) 'Zum Funktionswandel des Kollisionsrechts II: Die kollisionsrechtliche Form einer legitimen Verfassung der post-nationalen Konstellation' in G-P Calliess, A Fischer-Lescano, D Wielsch and P Zumbansen (eds), *Soziologische Jurisprudenz. Festschrift für Gunther Teubner zum 65. Geburtstag* (Berlin, De Gruyter) 765–78.

Joseph, S (2004) *Corporations and Transnational Human Rights Litigation* (Oxford, Hart Publishing).

Kegel, G (2002) *Vertrag und Delikt* (Cologne, Heymanns).

Keirsbilck, B (2011) *The New European Law on Unfair Commercial Practices and Competition Law* (Oxford, Hart Publishing).

Kennedy, D (1982) 'Distributive and Paternalist Motives in Contract and Tort Law, with Special Reference to Compulsory Terms and Unequal Bargaining Power' 41 *Maryland Law Review* 563–658.

—— (2001) 'The Political Stakes in "Merely Technical" Issues of Contract Law' 10 *European Review of Private Law* 7–28.

Kenny, KE (2007) 'Code or Conduct: Whether Wal-Mart's Code of Conduct Creates a Contractual Obligation Between Wal-Mart and the Employees of its Foreign Suppliers' 27 *Northwestern Journal of International Law and Business* 453–74.

Kerr, M, Janda, R and Pitts, C (2009) *Corporate Social Responsibility: A Legal Analysis* (Markham, LexisNexis Canada).

Kewenig, W (1965) 'Zur Rechtsproblematik der Koalitionsvereinbarungen' 90 *Archiv des öffentlichen Rechts* 182–204.

Kimel, D (2003) *From Promise to Contract: Towards a Liberal Theory of Contract* (Oxford, Hart Publishing).

Kingsbury, B (2006) 'Global Regulation, Jus Gentium and Inter-Public Law' 2 *Papers*, available at: www.iilj.org/courses/documents/Kingsbury.NewJusGentium.pdf.

—— (2009) 'The Concept of "Law" in Global Administrative Law' 20 *European Journal of International Law* 23–57.

Kingsbury, B, Krisch, N, Stewart, RB and Viennaer, JB (2005) 'Global Governance as Administration—National and Transnational Approaches to Global Administrative Law' 68 *Law and Contemporary Problems* 1–13.

Kinley, D, Nolan, J and Zerial, N (2007) 'The Norms are Dead! Long live the Norms! The Politics behind the UN Human Rights Norms for Corporations' in D McBarnet, A Voiculescu and T Campbell (eds), *The New Corporate Accountability. Corporate Social Responsibility and the Law* (Cambridge, Cambridge University Press) 459–75.

Kjaer, PF (2011) 'The Concept of the Political in the Concept of Transnational Constitutionalism' in C Joerges and R Tommi (eds), *After Globalization—New Patterns of Conflict and their Sociological and Legal Reconstruction* (Oslo, Arena Report Series) 285–321.

—— (2013) 'The Constitutionalism of Intra- and Trans-Normative Orders' 20 *Indiana Journal of Global Legal Studies* 777–803.

Kleinschmidt, J (2009) 'Anmerkung zu BGH, Urteil vom 28.5.2009—Xa ZR 9/08' 64 *Juristenzeitung* 1121–24.

Klösel, D (2012) *Compliance-Richtlinien. Zum Funktionswandel des Zivilrechts im Gewährleistungsstaat* (Baden-Baden, Nomos).

Knops, K-O and Bamberger, HG (2009) *Handbuch zum deutschen und europäischen Bankrecht* 2 (Berlin/Heidelberg, Springer).
Koch, J (2006) 'Das Girokonto für jedermann—ein altes Problem in neuem Licht' 60 *Zeitschrift für Wirtschafts- und Bankrecht* 2242–49.
Kocher, E (2002) 'Private Standards between Soft Law and Hard Law: The German Case' 18 *International Journal of Comparative Labour Law and Industrial Relations* 265–80.
—— (2005) 'Unternehmerische Selbstverpflichtungen im Wettbewerb—Die Transformation von "soft law" in "hard law" durch das Wettbewerbsrecht' *Gewerblicher Rechtsschutz und Urheberrecht* 647–52.
—— (2008) 'Codes of Conduct and Framework Agreements on Social Minimum Standards—Private Regulation?' in O Dilling, M Herberg and G Winter (eds), *Responsible Business: Self-governance and Law in Transnational Economic Transactions* (Oxford, Hart Publishing) 67–86.
—— (2009) 'Private Standards for the North—Effective norms for the South' in A Peters, L Koechlin, T Förster and G Fenner Zinkernagel (eds), *Non-state Actors as Standard Setters* (Cambridge, Cambridge University Press) 409–30.
—— (2011) 'Freiwillig, aber nicht beliebig' in G Burckhardt (ed), *Mythos CSR—Unternehmensverantwortung und Regulierungslücken* (Bonn, Horlemann Verlag) 32–36.
—— (2012) 'Verbandsklagen' in M Tamm and K Tonner (eds), *Verbraucherrecht. Rechtliches Umfeld, Vertragstypen, Rechtsdurchsetzung* (Baden-Baden, Nomos) 1384–410.
Köhler, H (2014) 'Mitteilungen über Corporate Social Responsibility—eine geschäftliche Handlung?' in R Hilty and F Henning-Bodewig (eds), *Corporate Social Responsibility—Verbindliche Standards des Wettbewerbsrechts?* (Berlin/Heidelberg, Springer) 161–67.
Köhler, H and Lettl, T (2003) 'Das geltende europäische Lauterkeitsrecht, der Vorschlag für eine EG-Richtlinie über unlautere Geschäftspraktiken und die UWG-Reform' *Wettbewerb in Recht und Praxis* 1019–57.
Kohte, W (2005a) 'Anmerkung zu LG Bremen, Urteil vom 16.6.2005' 20 *Verbraucher und Recht* 352–54.
—— (2005b) 'Das Girokonto für jedermann im Licht der Rechtsgeschäftslehre' in W-R Bub, R Knieper, R Metz and G Winter (eds), *Zivilrecht im Sozialstaat* (Baden-Baden, Nomos) 405–20.
Kolk, A and Tulder, R van (2005) 'Setting New Global Rules? TNCs and Codes of Conduct' 14 *Transnational Corporations* 1–27.
Kollhosser, H (1966) 'Lohnfortzahlung, Schadensersatz und Regreßinteressen beim Unfall eines Angestellten' 166 *Archiv für die civilistische Praxis* 277–310.
Köndgen, J (1981) *Selbstbindung ohne Vertrag: Zur Haftung aus geschäftsbezogenem Handeln* (Tübingen, Mohr Siebeck).
—— (1983) 'Zur Theorie der Prospekthaftung' 28 *Die Aktiengesellschaft* 85–99.
—— (1999a), 'Die Einbeziehung Dritter in den Vertrag' in E Lorenz (ed), *Einbeziehung Dritter in den Vertrag. Karlsruher Forum 1998* (Karlsruhe, Verlag Versicherungswirtschaft GmbH) 3–49.
—— (1999b) 'Diskussionsbeitrag' in E Lorenz (ed), *Einbeziehung Dritter in den Vertrag. Karlsruher Forum 1998* (Karlsruhe, Verlag Versicherungswirtschaft GmbH) 91–93.
—— (2001) 'Die Positivierung der culpa in contrahendo als Frage der Gesetzgebungsmethodik' in R Schulze and H Schulte-Nölke (eds), *Die Schuldrechtsreform vor dem Hintergrund des Gemeinschaftsrechts* (Tübingen, Mohr Siebeck) 233–42.
—— (2006) 'Privatisierung des Rechts. Private Governance zwischen Deregulierung und Rekonstitutionalisierung' 206 *Archiv für die civilistische Praxis* 477–525.
Kopp, R and Klostermann, EA (2009) 'Vorsicht Falle: Verhaltenskodizes im reformierten Lauterkeitsrecht des UWG' 2 *Corporate Compliance Zeitschrift* 155–59.

Kornet, N (2006) *Contract Interpretation and Gap Filling: Comparative and Theoretical Perspectives* (Antwerp, Intersentia).
—— (2009) 'The Doctrine of Privity, Exemption Clauses and Third Parties—A Common Law Perspective' in I Samoy (ed), *Derden in het contractenrecht* (Antwerp, Intersentia) 129–62.
Kornet, N and Hardt, S (2013) *The Maastricht Collection: Selected National, European and International Provisions from Public and Private Law* 3rd edn (Groningen, Europa Law Publishing).
Koster, P de and Eynde, P van den (2009) 'International Framework Agreements on Corporate Social Responsibility: Conflict of Laws and Enforcement' 10 *Business Law International* 128–55.
Krebber, S (2008) 'Globalisierungsbedingter Verlust der Bindungswirkung staatlicher Regulierung und die sich entwickelnden Alternativen' in J Schwarze (ed), *Globalisierung und Entstaatlichung des Rechts* (Tübingen, Mohr Siebeck) 143–89.
Kübler, F (1974) 'Privatrecht und Demokratie. Zur Aktualität gesellschaftstheoretischer Vorstellungen in der Jurisprudenz' in F Baur, J Esser, F Kübler and E Steindorff (eds), *Funktionswandel der Privatrechtsinstitutionen. Festschrift für Ludwig Raiser zum 70. Geburtstag* (Tübingen, Mohr Siebeck) 694–725.
Kübler, F and Kübler, J (2003) 'Werbefreiheit nach Benetton"' in M Habersack, P Hommelhoff, U Hüffer and K Schmidt (eds), *Festschrift für Peter Ulmer zum 70. Geburtstag* (Berlin, De Gruyter) 907–27.
Kumm, M (2006) 'Who is Afraid of the Total Constitution? Constitutional Rights as Principles and the Constitutionalization of Private Law' 7 *German Law Journal* 341–70.
Kuo, M-S (2009) 'The Concept of "Law" in Global Administrative Law—A Reply to Benedict Kingsbury' 20 *European Journal of International Law* 997–1004.
Ladeur, K-H (1995) *Das Umweltrecht in der Wissensgesellschaft. Von der Gefahrenabwehr zum Risikomanagement* (Berlin, Duncker & Humblot).
Lamla, J (2013) *Verbraucherdemokratie. Politische Soziologie in der Konsumgesellschaft* (Berlin, Suhrkamp).
Lando, O and Beale, H (2000) *Principles of European Contract Law* (The Hague, Kluwer Law International).
Langille, B (2004) 'Core Labor Rights—The True Story' 16 *European Journal of International Law* 409–37.
Larenz, K (1956) 'Anmerkung zu BGH NJW 1956, 1193' *Neue Juristische Wochenschrift* 1194–1194.
—— (1966) *Die Methode der Auslegung des Rechtsgeschäfts—Zugleich ein Beitrag zur Theorie der Willenserklärung* (Frankfurt am Main, Alfred Metzner Verlag).
Larenz, K, Wolf, M and Neuner, J (2012) *Allgemeiner Teil des Bürgerlichen Rechts* 10th edn (Munich, C.H. Beck).
Lefort, C (1990) 'Die Frage der Demokratie' in U Rödel (ed), *Autonome Gesellschaft und libertäre Demokratie* (Frankfurt am Main, Suhrkamp) 281–97.
Levy, DL and Kaplan, R (2008) 'Corporate Social Responsibility and Theories of Global Governance: Strategic Contestation in Global Issue Arenas' in A Crane, A McWilliams, D Matten, J Moon and DS Siegel (eds), *The Oxford Handbook of Corporate Social Responsibility* (Oxford, Oxford University Press) 432–51.
Lin, L-W (2007) 'Corporate Social Accountability Standards in the Global Supply Chain: Resistance, Reconsideration and Resolution in China' 15 *Cardozo Journal of International and Comparative Law* 321370.
—— (2009) 'Legal Transplants through Private Contracting: Codes of Vendor Conduct in Global Supply Chains as an Example' 57 *American Journal of Comparative Law* 711–44.

Lindner, A (2006) *Irreführende Gewinnzusagen nach § 661a BGB* (Berlin, Berliner Wissenschafts-verlag).
Lobinger, T (1999) *Rechtsgeschäftliche Verpflichtung und autonome Bindung* (Tübingen, Mohr Siebeck).
Locke, R, Qin, F and Brause, A (2006) 'Does Monitoring Improve Labour Standards? Lessons from Nike' 4612 *MIT Sloan School of Management Working Paper*.
Lorenz, S (2000) 'Gewinnmitteilungen aus dem Ausland: internationalzivilprozessuale Aspekte von §661a BGB' *Neue Juristische Wochenschrift* 3305–09.
Lu, S-P (2000) 'Corporate Codes of Conduct and the FTC: Advancing Human Rights through Deceptive Advertising Law' 38 *Columbia Journal of Transnational Law* 603–629.
Luckmann, T (1986) 'Kommunikative Gattungen' in F Neidhardt, R Lepsius and J Weiss (eds), *Kultur und Gesellschaft. Sonderheft der Kölner Zeitschrift für Soziologie und Sozialpsychologie 27* (Opladen, Westdeutscher Verlag) 191–211.
Luhmann, N (1977) 'Differentiation of Society' 2 *Canadian Journal of Sociology* 29–53.
—— (1979) *Trust and Power: Two Works by Niklas Luhmann* (New York, John Wiley).
—— (1982) *The Differentiation of Society* (New York, Columbia University Press).
—— (1983) *Legitimation durch Verfahren* (Frankfurt am Main, Suhrkamp).
—— (1988a) *Die Wirtschaft der Gesellschaft* (Frankfurt, Suhrkamp/Wissenschaftliche Buchgesellschaft).
—— (1988b) 'Familiarity, Confidence, Trust: Problems and Alternatives' in D Gambetta (ed), *Trust. Making and Breaking Cooperative Relations* (Oxford, Basil Blackwell) 95–107.
—— (1990) 'Verfassung als evolutionäre Errungenschaft' 9 *Rechtshistorisches Journal* 176–220.
—— (1992) 'The Coding of the Legal System' in G Teubner and A Febbrajo (eds), *State, Law and Economy as Autopoietic Systems: Regulation and Autonomy in a New Perspective* (Milan, Giuffrè) 145–86.
—— (1995) *Social Systems* (Stanford, Stanford University Press).
—— (1996a) 'Complexity, Structural Contingencies and Value Conflicts' in P Heelas, S Lash and P Morris (eds), *DeTraditionalization* (Oxford, Blackwell Publishers) 59–71.
—— (1996b) 'Protestbewegungen' in K-U Hellmann (ed), *Niklas Luhmann. Protest. Systemtheorie und soziale Bewegungen* (Frankfurt am Main, Suhrkamp) 201–15.
—— (2000) *Die Politik der Gesellschaft* (Frankfurt am Main, Suhrkamp).
—— (2004) *Law as a Social System* (Oxford, Oxford University Press).
Lüsing, J (2010) *Die Pflichten aus culpa in contrahendo und positiver Vertragsverletzung. Über die Rechtsnatur von Schutzpflichten und die Begründung von Leistungspflichten vor Vertrag* (Baden-Baden, Nomos).
—— (2012) *Selbstbindung durch sprachliches Handeln* (Berlin, Duncker & Humblot).
Lutter, M (2002) 'Kodex guter Unternehmensführung und Vertrauenshaftung' in R Schweizer, H Burkert and U Gasser (eds), *Festschrift für Jean Nicolas Druey zum 65. Geburtstag* (Zürich, Schulthess) 463–78.
Macaulay, S (1963) 'Non-Contractual Relations in Business: A Preliminary Study' 28 *American Sociological Review* 55–67.
—— (2003) 'The Real and the Paper Deal: Empirical Pictures of Relationships, Complexity and the Urge for Transparent Simple Rules' in D Campbell, H Collins and J Wightman (eds), *Implicit Dimensions of Contract: Discrete, Relational and Network Contracts* (Oxford, Hart Publishing) 51–102.
MacDonald, T and MacDonald, K (2006) 'Non-Electoral Accountability in Global Politics: Strenghtening Democratic Control within the Global Garment Industry' 17 *European Journal of International Law* 89–119.
MacMillan, C (2000) 'A Birthday Present for Lord Denning: The Contracts (Rights of Third Parties) Act 1999' 63 *Modern Law Review* 721–38.

MacNeil, IR (1978) 'Contracts: Adjustment of Long-Term Economic Relations under Classical, Neoclassical and Relational Contract Law' 72 *Northwestern University Law Review* 854–905.

—— (2000) 'Contracting Worlds and Essential Contract Theory' 9 *Social and Legal Studies* 431–438.

—— (2003) 'Reflections on Relational Contract Theory after a Neo-classical Seminar' in D Campbell, H Collins and J Wightman (eds), *Implicit Dimensions of Contract. Discrete, Relational and Network Contracts* (Oxford, Hart Publishing) 207–17.

Mak, C (2008) *Fundamental Rights in European Contract Law: A Comparison of the Impact of Fundamental Rights on Contractual Relationships in Germany, the Netherlands, Italy and England* (Alphen aan den Rijn, Wolters Kluwer International).

Maley, K (2009) 'The Limits of the Conformity of Goods in the United Nations Convention on Contracts for the International Sale of Goods (CISG)' 12 *International Trade & Business Law Review* 82–126.

Mankowski, P (2002) 'Urteilsanmerkung EuGH C-96/00' 18 *Entscheidungen zum Wirtschaftsrecht* 873–74.

—— (2003) 'Kurzkommentar zu LG Köln, Urteil vom 16.4.2003—9 S 289/02' 19 *Entscheidungen zum Wirtschaftsrecht* 853–54.

Marchart, O (2007) *Post-foundational Political Thought: Political Difference in Nancy, Lefort, Badiou and Laclau* (Edinburgh, Edinburgh University Press).

—— (2010) *Die Politische Differenz—Zum Denken des Politischen bei Nancy, Lefort, Badiou, Laclau und Agamben* (Berlin, Suhrkamp).

Mares, R (2010) 'Global Corporate Social Responsibility, Human Rights and Law: An Interactive Regulatory Perspective on the Voluntary-Mandatory Dichotomy' 1 *Transnational Legal Theory* 221–85.

Markesinis, BS (1987) 'An Expanding Tort Law—The Price of a Rigid Contract Law' 103 *Law Quarterly Review* 354–97.

Markesinis, BS and Unberath, H (2002) *The German Law of Torts: A Comparative Treatise* 4th edn (Oxford, Hart Publishing).

Markesinis, BS, Unberath, H and Johnston, A (2006) *The German Law of Contract: A Comparative Treatise* 2nd edn (Oxford, Hart Publishing).

Marrella, F (2007) 'Human Rights, Arbitration, and Corporate Social Responsibility in the Law of International Trade' in W Benedek, K de Feyter and F Marrella (eds), *Economic Globalisation and Human Rights* (Cambridge, Cambridge University Press) 266–310.

Massoud, S (2013) 'Die Guiding Principles on Business and Human Rights—eine absehbar begrenzte Agenda' 46 *Kritische Justiz* 9–17.

Matten, D (2003) 'Symbolic Politics in Environmental Regulation: Corporate Strategic Responses' 12 *Business Strategy and the Environment* 215–26.

Mayer, C (2013) *Firm Commitment: Why the Corporation is Failing Us and How to Restore Trust in it* (Oxford, Oxford University Press).

Mayer-Maly, T (1965) 'Vertrag und Einigung' in R Dietz and H Hübner (eds), *Festschrift für Hans Carl Nipperdey zum 70. Geburtstag* (Munich, C.H. Beck) 509–22.

McBarnet, D (2007) 'Corporate Social Responsibility beyond Law, through Law, for Law: The New Corporate Accountability' in D McBarnet, A Voiculescu and T Campbell (eds), *The New Corporate Accountability: Corporate Social Responsibility and the Law* (Cambridge, Cambridge University Press) 9–58.

McBarnet, D and Kurkchiyan, M (2007) 'Corporate Social Responsibility through Contractual Control? Global Supply Chains and "Other Regulation"' in D McBarnet, A Voiculescu and T Campbell (eds), *The New Corporate Accountability: Corporate Social Responsibility and the Law* (Cambridge, Cambridge University Press) 59–92.

McCaughran, J (2011) 'Implied Terms: The Journey of the Man on Clapham Omnibus' 70 *Cambridge Law Journal* 607–22.
McCrudden, C (2004) 'Using Public Procurement to Achieve Social Outcomes' (2004) 28 *Natural Resources Forum* 257–67.
—— (2007) 'Corporate Social Responsibility and Public Procurement' in D McBarnet, A Voiculescu and D Campbell (eds), *The New Corporate Accountability: Corporate Social Responsibility and the Law* (Cambridge, Cambridge University Press) 93–118.
McIntyre, V (2004) 'Note: Nike v. Kasky: Leaving Corporate America Speechless' 30 *William Mitchell Law Review* 1531–69.
McKague, K and Cragg, W (2007) *Compendium of Ethics Codes and Instruments of Corporate Responsibility* (Toronto, York University).
McKendrick, E (2013) *Contract Law* 10th edn (Oxford, Oxford University Press).
McKnight, A (2004) 'A Review of Developments in English Law during 2003: Part 2' 19 *Journal of International Banking Law and Regulation* 151–71.
Medicus, D (2010) *Allgemeiner Teil des BGB* 10th edn (Heidelberg, C.F. Müller).
Meeran, R (2011) 'Tort Litigation against Multinational Corporations for Violations of Human Rights: An Overview of the Position Outside the United States' 3 *City University of Hong Kong Law Review* 1–41.
Meessen, KM (1981) 'Internationale Verhaltenskodizes und Sittenwidrigkeitsklauseln' *Neue Juristische Wochenschrift* 1131–32.
Metzger, M and Phillips, M (1983) 'The Emergence of Promissory Estoppel as an Independent Theory of Recovery' 35 *Rutgers Law Review* 472–557.
Meurkens, L and Nordin, E (eds.) (2012) *The Power of Punitive Damages—Is Europe Missing out?* (Antwerp, Intersentia).
Michaels, R (2005) 'The Re-state-ment of Non-state Law: The State, Choice of Law, and the Challenge from Global Legal Pluralism' 51 *Wayne Law Review* 1209–59.
—— (2006) 'The Functional Method of Comparative Law' in M Reimann and R Zimmermann (eds), *The Oxford Handbook of Comparative Law* (Oxford, Oxford University Press) 339–82.
—— (2011) 'Global Problems in Domestic Courts' in S Muller, S Zouridis, M Frishman and L Kistemaker (eds), *The Law of the Future and the Future of Law* (Oslo, Torkel Opsahl Academic EPublisher) 165–75.
Micklitz, H (2006a) 'The General Clause on Unfair Practices' in G Howells, H Micklitz and T Wilhelmsson (eds), *European Fair Trading Law: The Unfair Commercial Practices Directive* (Aldershot, Ashgate) 83–122.
—— (2006b) 'Legal Redress' in G Howells, H Micklitz and T Wilhelmsson (eds), *European Fair Trading Law: The Unfair Commercial Practices Directive* (Aldershot, Ashgate) 217–40.
—— (2011) 'Introduction' in H Micklitz (ed), *The Many Concepts of Social Justice in European Private Law* (Cheltenham, Edward Elgar) 3–60.
Micklitz, H and Stadler, A (2003a) 'Der Reformvorschlag der UWG-Novelle für eine Verbandsklage auf Gewinnabschöpfung' *Wettbewerb in Recht und Praxis* 559–562.
—— (2003b) *Unrechtsgewinnabschöpfung. Möglichkeiten und Perspektiven eines kollektiven Schadenersatzanspruches im UWG* (Baden-Baden, Nomos).
Millon, D (1990) 'Theories of the Corporation' *Duke Law Journal* 201–62.
Möller, K (2011) 'Struggles for Law: Global Social Rights as an Alternative to Financial Market Capitalism' in PF Kjaer, G Teubner and A Febbrajo (eds), *Financial Crisis in Constitutional Perspective: The Dark Side of Functional Differentiation* (Oxford, Hart Publishing) 305–32.
Mouzas, S (2009) 'The Weakest Link: Legal Aspects of Network Architecture of Supply Chains' in M Amstutz and G Teubner (eds), *Networks: Legal Issues of Multilateral Co-operation* (Oxford, Hart Publishing) 211–24.

Mouzas, S and Furmston, M (2008) 'From Contract to Umbrella Agreement' 67 *Cambridge Law Journal* 37–50.
Muchlinski, PT (2007a) 'Corporate Social Responsibility and International Law: The Case of Human Rights and Multinational Enterprises' in D McBarnet, A Voiculescu and T Campbell (eds), *The New Corporate Accountability: Corporate Social Responsibility and the Law* (Cambridge, Cambridge University Press) 431–58.
—— (2007b) *Multinational Enterprises and the Law* 2nd edn (Oxford, Oxford University Press).
Muir Watt, H (2007) 'Globalization and Comparative Law' in M Reimann and R Zimmermann (eds), *The Oxford Handbook of Comparative Law* (Oxford, Oxford University Press) 579–607.
Müller, H-F (2003) 'Die Einführung des Vertrages zugunsten Dritter in das englische Recht. Eine vergleichende Betrachtung aus deutscher und gemeineuropäischer Perspektive' 67 *Rabels Zeitschrift für ausländisches und internationales Privatrecht* 140–65.
Munck, R (2006) 'Globalization and Contestation: A Polanyian Problematic' 3 *Globalizations* 175–86.
Murphy, SD (2005) 'Taking Multinational Corporate Codes of Conduct to the Next Level' 43 *Columbia Journal of Transnational Law* 389–433.
Natale, AJ (1988) 'Expansion of Parent Corporate Shareholder Liability through the Good Samaritan Doctrine—A Parent Corporation's Duty to Provide a Safe Workplace for Employees of its Subsidiary' 57 *University of Cincinnati Law Review* 717–37.
Nolan, J (2013) 'The Corporate Responsibility to Respect Human Rights: Soft Law or not Law?' in S Deva and D Bilchitz (eds), *Human Rights Obligations for Business. Beyond the Corporate Responsibility to Respect?* (Cambridge, Cambridge University Press) 138–61.
—— (2014) 'Refining the Rules of the Game: The Corporate Social Responsibility to Respect Human Rights' 30 *Utrecht Journal of International and European Law* 7–23.
Nonet, P and Selznick, P (1978) *Law and Society in Transition: Toward Responsive Law* (New York, Harper Torchbooks).
Norberg, J (2003) *In Defense of Global Capitalism* (Washington DC, CATO Institute).
Nowrot, K (2006) *Normative Ordnungsstruktur und private Wirkungsmacht: Konsequenzen einer Beteiligung transnationaler Unternehmen an den Rechtsetzungsprozessen im internationalen Wirtschaftssystem* (Berlin, Berliner Wissenschaftsverlag).
O'Rourke, D (2003) 'Outsourcing Regulation: Analyzing Nongovernmental Systems of Labor Standards and Monitoring' 31 *Policy Studies Journal* 1–29.
Office of Fair Trading (2008) *Guidance on the UK Regulations Implementing the Unfair Commercial Practices Directive* (London, Department for Bsuiness Enterprise & Regulatory Reform).
Organisation for Economic Co-operation and Development (2001) 'Codes of Conduct: Expanded Review of their Contents' 6 *OECD Working Paper Series on International Investment* 1–32.
Osieka, G (2014) *Zivilrechtliche Haftung deutscher Unternehmen für menschenrechtsbeeinträchtigende Handlungen ihrer Zulieferer* (Frankfurt am Main, Peter Lang).
Ostendorf, P (2011) 'Die Grenzlinien des Mangelbegriffs vor dem Hintergrund der Voraussetzungen und Rechtsfolgen des gesetzlichen Mängelhaftungssystems' 66 *Juristenzeitung* 822–26.
Parisi, F (2004) 'Positive, Normative and Functional Schools in Law and Economics' 18 *European Journal of Law and Economics* 259–72.
Parkinson, JE (1993) *Corporate Power and Responsibility* (Oxford, Clarendon Press).
Parry, D (2000) 'The Future of Voluntary Regulation of Advertising' 8 *Consumer Law Journal* 137–59.

Parry, R (2005) 'Directors' Duties within the United Kingdom' in S Tully (ed), *Research Handbook on Corporate Legal Responsibility* (Cheltenham, Edward Elgar) 73–87.

Paton, B (2002) 'Voluntary Environmental Initiatives and Sustainable Industry' in P ten Brink (ed), *Voluntary Environmental Agreements: Process, Practice and Future Use* (Sheffield, Greenleaf Publishing) 37–49.

Peel, E (2011) *Treitel: The Law of Contract* 13th edn (London, Sweet & Maxwell).

Petrin, M (2013) 'Assumption of Responsibility in Corporate Groups: Chandler v. Cape plc' 76 *Modern Law Review* 589–619.

Peukert, A (2014) 'Die Rechtsrelevanz der Sittlichkeit der Wirtschaft—am Beispiel der Corporate Social Responsibility im US.Recht' in R Hilty and F Henning-Bodewig (eds), *Corporate Social Responsibility—Verbindliche Standards des Wettbewerbsrechts?* (Berlin/Heidelberg, Springer) 233–57.

Phillips, J and Lim, S-J (2009) 'Their Brothers' Keeper: Global Buyers and the Legal Duty to Protect Suppliers' Employees' 61 *Rutgers Law Review* 333–79.

Picciotto, S (2003) 'Rights, Responsibilities and Regulation of International Business' 42 *Columbia Journal of Transnational Law* 131–52.

Picker, E (1983) 'Positive Forderungsverletzung und culpa in contrahendo—Zur Problematik der Haftungen "zwischen" Vertrag und Delikt' 183 *Archiv für die civilistische Praxis* 369–520.

Peterkova Mitkidis, K (2014a) 'Sustainability Clauses in International Supply Chain Contracts: Regulation, Enforceability and Effects of Ethical Requirements' *Nordic Journal of Commercial Law* 1–30.

—— (2014b) 'Using Private Contracts for Climate Change Mitigation' 2 *Groningen Journal of International Law* 52–77.

Podszun, R (2014) 'Corporate Social Responsibility-Standards: Rechtstheoretische Aspekte und die Frage, was den "Markenkern" der Rechtswissenschaft ausmacht' in R Hilty and F Henning-Bodewig (eds), *Corporate Social Responsibility—Verbindliche Standards des Wettbewerbsrechts?* (Berlin/Heidelberg, Springer) 51–79.

Polanyi, K (2001 [1944]) *The Great Transformation: The Political and Economic Origins of Our Time* (Boston, MA, Beacon Press).

Porter, ME and Kramer, MR (2011) 'Creating Shared Value—How to Reinvent Capitalism—and Unleash a Wave of Innovation and Growth' *Harvard Business Review* 1–17.

Posner, RA (2003) *Economic Analysis of Law* 6th edn (New York, Aspen Publishers).

Pound, R (1959) 'Promise or Bargain' 33 *Tulane Law Review* 455–72.

Powell, WW (1990) 'Neither Market nor Hierarchy: Network Forms of Organization' 12 *Research in Organizational Behavior* 295–336.

Raiser, L (1963) 'Rechtsschutz und Institutionenschutz im Privatrecht' Ringvorlesung gehalten von Mitgliedern der Tübinger Juristenfakultät im Rahmen des Dies academicus Wintersemester 1962/63 (ed), *Summum Ius Summa Iniuria. Individualgerechtigkeit und der Schutz allgemeiner Werte im Rechtsleben* (Tübingen, Mohr Siebeck) 145–67.

—— (1971) *Die Zukunft des Privatrechts* (Berlin, Walter de Gruyter).

Raiser, T (1988) 'The Theory of Enterprise Law in Germany in the Federal Republic of Germany' 36 *American Journal of Comparative Law* 111–129.

Rathenau, W (1922) *Vom Aktienwesen: Eine geschäftliche Betrachtung* (Berlin, Fischer).

Ratner, S (2008) 'Business' in D Bodansky, J Brunnée and E Hey (eds), *The Oxford Handbook of International Environmental Law* (Oxford, Oxford University Press) 807–28.

Raz, J (1981) 'Book Review: Promises in Morality and Law' 95 *Harvard Law Review* 916–38.

Renner, M (2011) *Zwingendes transnationales Recht. Gemeinwohlinteressen im Recht jenseits des Staates* (Baden-Baden, Nomos).

Revak, H (2012) 'Corporate Codes of Conduct: Binding Contract or Ideal Publicity' 63 *Hastings Law Journal* 1645–70.

Robertson, A (1998) 'Reliance and Expectation in Estoppel Remedies' 18 *Legal Studies* 360–68.
Rodrik, D (2011) *The Globalization Paradox: Democracy and the Future of the World Economy* (New York, W.W. Norton).
Rodríguez-Garavito, CA (2005) 'Nike's Law: The Anti-sweatship Movement, Transnational Corporations, and the Struggle over International Labor Rights in the Americas' in B de Sousa Santos and CA Rodríguez-Garavito (eds), *Law and Globalization from Below: Towards a Cosmopolitan Legality* (Cambridge, Cambridge University Press) 64–91.
Roe, T (2000) 'Contractual Intention under Section 1(1)(b) and 1(2) of the Contracts (Rights of Third Parties) Act 1999' 63 *Modern Law Review* 887–94.
Rogers, WVH (2006) *Winfield and Jolowicz on Tort* 17th edn (London, Sweet & Maxwell).
Ronneberger, F and Rühl, M (1992) *Theorie der Public Relations. Ein Entwurf* (Opladen, Westdeutscher Verlag).
Rösch, F (2006) *Vertragliche Ansprüche Dritter in England und Deutschland. Ein rechtsvergleichender Überblick unter besonderer Berücksichtigung des Contracts (Right of Third Parties) Act 1999* (Baden-Baden, Nomos).
Rose, N (1987) 'Beyond the Public/Private Division: Law, Power and Family' 14 *Journal of Law and Society* 61–76.
Ruggie, JG (2004) 'Reconstituting the Global Public Domain—Issues, Actors, and Practices' 10 *European Journal of International Relations* 499–531.
—— (2007) 'Business and Human Rights: The Evolving International Agenda' 101 *American Journal of International Law* 819–40.
—— (2013) *Just Business: Multinational Corporations and Human Rights* (New York, W.W. Norton).
—— (2014) 'Global Governance and "New Governance Theory": Lessons from Business and Human Rights' 20 *Global Governance* 5–17.
Saage-Maaß, M (2011) *Labour Conditions in the Global Supply Chain. What is the Extent and Implications of German Corporate Responsibility?* (Berlin, Friedrich Ebert Stiftung—International Policy Analysis).
Sack, R (2004) 'Folgeverträge unlauteren Wettbewerbs' *Gewerblicher Rechtsschutz und Urheberrecht* 625–35.
Sand, I-J (2011) 'A Comment on Kjaer' in C Joerges and T Ralli (eds), *After Globalization—New Patterns of Conflict and their Sociological and Legal Reconstruction* (Oslo, Arena Report Series) 323–32.
Savigny, FC von (1840) *System des heutigen römischen Rechts* (Berlin, Bei Veit und Comp).
Schäfer, C (2005) 'Lässt sich die Gewinnzusage nach §661a BGB in das System des Bürgerlichen Rechts einordnen?' 60 *Juristenzeitung* 981–87.
Schäfer, J (1990) *Die zivilrechtliche Qualifizierung der Interbankenabkommen* (Berlin, Duncker & Humblot).
Schapp, J (1986) *Grundfragen der Rechtsgeschäftslehre* (Tübingen, Mohr Siebeck).
Scheltema, M (2014) 'An Assessment of the Effectiveness of International Private Regulation in the Corporate Social Responsibility Arena' 21 *Maastricht Journal of European and Comparative Law* 383–405.
Schepel, H (2005) *The Constitution of Private Governance: Product Standards in the Regulation of Integrating Markets* (Oxford, Hart Publishing).
Scherer, A and Palazzo, G (2008) 'Globalization and Corporate Social Responsibility' in A Crane, D McWilliams, J Moon and D Siegel (eds), *The Oxford Handbook of Corporate Social Responsibility* (Oxford, Oxford University Press) 413–31.
Schiemann, G (2010) 'Das Rechtsgeschäft' in J Staudinger (ed), *Bürgerliches Gesetzbuch—Eckpfeiler des Zivilrechts 2011* (Berlin, Sellier/De Gruyter) 101–79.

Schlechtriem, P (1999) 'Kollidierende Geschäftsbedingungen im internationalen Vertragsrecht' in K-H Thume (ed), *Transport- und Vertriebsrecht 2000. Festgabe für Professor Dr. Rolf Herber* (Neuwied, Luchterhand) 36–49.

—— (2007) 'Non-material Damages—Recovery under the CISG' 89 *Pace International Law Review* 89–102.

Schlieffen, KG von (2005) 'Koalitionsvereinbarungen und Koalitionsgremien' in J Isensee and P Kirchhof (eds), *Handbuch des Staatsrechts der Bundesrepublik Deutschland. Band III: Demokratie—Bundesorgane* (Heidelberg, C.F. Müller), 683–708.

Schmitt, C (1996) *The Concept of the Political* (Chicago, University of Chicago Press).

Schoenheit, I (2014) 'Corporate Social Responsibility und die Konsumenten' in R Hilty and F Henning-Bodewig (eds), *Corporate Social Responsibility—Verbindliche Standards des Wettbewerbsrechts?* (Berlin/Heidelberg, Springer), 41–48.

Schröder, R and Thiessen, J (2004) 'Gewinnzusagen beim Wort genommen—zur Verfassungsmäßigkeit von §661a BGB' *Neue Juristische Wochenschrift* 719–722.

Schwenzer, I (2010) *Commentary on the UN Convention on the International Sale of Goods* (Oxford, Oxford University Press).

Schwenzer, I, Hachem, P and Kee, C (2012) *Global Sales and Contract Law* (Oxford, Oxford University Press).

Schwenzer, I and Leisinger, B (2007) 'Ethical Values and International Sales Contracts' in R Cranston, J Ramberg and J Ziegel (eds), *Commercial Law Challenges in the 21st Century: Jan Hellner in Memorium* (Stockholm, Stockholm Centre for Commercial Law Juridiska Institutionen) 249–75.

Searle, JR (1971) 'What is a Speech Act?' in JR Searle (ed), *The Philosophy of Language* (Oxford, Oxford University Press) 39–53.

—— (2010) *Making the Social World: The Structure of Human Civilization* (Oxford, Oxford University Press).

Segna, U (2006) 'Anspruch auf Einrichtung eines Girokontos aufgrund der ZKA-Empfehlung "Girokonto für jedermann"' 2006/49 *Institute for Law and Finance Working Paper*.

Shamir, R (2004) 'The De-radicalization of Corporate Social Responsibility' 30 *Critical Sociology* 669–689.

Simmonds, N (1984) *The Decline of Juridical Reason: Doctrine and Theory in the Legal Order* (Manchester, Manchester University Press).

Singer, R (1993) *Das Verbot widersprüchlichen Verhaltens* (Munich, C.H. Beck).

Sjåfjell, B (2011a) 'Regulating Companies as if the World Matters: Reflections on the Ongoing Sustainable Companies Project' 47 *Wake Forest Law Review* 113–34.

—— (2011b) 'Why Law Matters: Corporate Social Irresponsibility and the Futility of Voluntary Climate Exchange' 8 *European Company Law* 56–64.

Smith, SA (2004) *Contract Theory* (Oxford, Oxford University Press).

Smits, J (2006) 'Private Law and Fundamental Rights: A Sceptical View' in T Barkhuysen and S Lindenbergh (eds), *Constitutionalisation of Private Law* (Leiden/Boston, Brill Publishers) 9–22.

—— (2008) 'European Private Law and Democracy: A Functional Approach' *European Journal of Legal Studies* 26–40.

—— (2009) 'Redefining Normative Legal Science: Towards an Argumentative Discipline' in F Coomans, F Grünfeld and M Kamminga (eds), *Methods of Human Rights Research* (Antwerp, Intersentia) 45–58.

—— (2010a) 'Optional Law: A Plea for Multiple Choice in Private Law' 17 *Maastricht Journal of European and Comparative Law* 347–52.

—— (2010b) *Private Law 2.0. On the Role of Private Actors in a Post-national Society* (The Hague, Eleven International Publishing).
—— (2011) 'Plurality of Sources in European Private Law, or: How to Live with Legal Diversity?' in R Brownsword, H Micklitz, L Niglia and S Weatherill (eds), *The Foundations of European Private Law* (Oxford, Hart Publishing) 323–35.
—— (2014) 'Law and Interdisciplinarity: On the Inevitable Normativity of Legal Studies' 1 *Critical Analysis of Law* 75–86.
Sobczak, A (2006) 'Are Codes of Conduct in Global Supply Chains Really Voluntary? From Soft Law Regulation of Labour Relations to Consumer Law' 16 *Business Ethics Quarterly* 167–84.
de Sousa Santos, B (1995) *Toward a New Common Sense: Law, Science and Politics in the Paradigmatic Transition* (New York, Routledge).
Spence, M (1999) *Protecting Reliance: The Emergent Doctrine of Equitable Estoppel* (Oxford, Hart Publishing).
Spießhofer, B (2014) 'Wirtschaft und Menschenrechte—rechtliche Aspekte der Corporate Social Responsibility' *Neue Juristische Wochenschrift* 2473–79.
Staudenmeyer, D (2000) 'The Directive on the Sale of Consumer Goods and Associated Guarantees—A Milestone in the European Consumer and Private Law' 9 *European Review of Private Law* 547–63.
Stehr, N (2007) *Die Moralisierung der Märkte* (Frankfurt am Main, Suhrkamp).
Stehr, N, Henning, C and Weiler, B (2006a) 'Introduction' in N Stehr, C Henning and B Weiler (eds), *The Moralization of Markets* (New Brunswick, Transaction Publishers) 1–19.
—— (eds) (2006b) *The Moralization of Markets* (New Brunswick, Transaction Publishers).
Steyn, J (1991) 'The Role of Good Faith and Fair Dealing in Contract Law: A Hair-Shirt Philosophy?' 6 *Denning Law Journal* 131–41.
—— (1996) 'Does Legal Formalism Hold Sway in England?' 49 *Common Legal Problems* 43–58.
—— (1997) 'Contract Law: Fulfilling the Reasonable Expectations of Honest Men' (1997) 113 *Law Quarterly Review* 433–42.
Stoll, H (1978) 'Vertrauensschutz bei einseitigen Leistungsversprechen' in HH Jakobs, B Knoobe-Keuk, E Picker and J Wilhelm (eds), *Festschrift für Werner Flume zum 70. Geburtstag* (Cologne, Otto Schmidt) 741–73.
Streeck, W (2009) *Re-Forming Capitalism: Institutional Change in the German Political Economy* (Oxford, Oxford University Press).
Streinz, R (2014) 'Europäisches und deutsches Verfassungsrecht: Erfassung von geschäftlicher Werbung ("commercial speech")' in R Hilty and F Henning-Bodewig (eds), *Corporate Social Responsibility—Verbindliche Standards des Wettbewerbsrechts?* (Berlin/Heidelberg, Springer) 99–125.
Study Group on Social Justice in European Contract Law (2004) 'Social Justice in European Contract Law: A Manifesto' 10 *European Law Journal* 653–74.
Sutton, M (2004) 'Between a Rock and a Judicial Hard Place: Corporate Social Responsibility Reporting and Potential Legal Liability Under Kasky v. Nike' 72 *University of Missouri Kansas City School of Law Review* 1159–85.
Swedberg, R and Smelser, NJ (2005) 'Introducing Economic Sociology' in NJ Smelser and R Swedberg (eds), *The Handbook of Economic Sociology* 2nd edn (Princeton/Oxford, Princeton University Press), 3–25.
Sztompka, P (1999) *Trust. A Sociological Theory* (Cambridge, Cambridge University Press).
Teubner, G (1983) 'Substantive and Reflexive Elements in Modern Law' 17 *Law and Society Review* 239–85.
—— (1998) 'Legal Irritants: Good Faith in English Law or How Unifying Law Ends Up in New Divergences' 61 *Modern Law Review* 11–32.

—— (1999) 'After Privatisation? The Many Autonomies of Private Law' 51 *Current Legal Problems* 393–424.
—— (2000a) 'Contracting Worlds: The Many Autonomies of Private Law' 9 *Social and Legal Studies* 399–417.
—— (2000b) 'Ein Fall von struktureller Korruption? Die Familienbürgschaft in der Kollision unverträglicher Handlungslogiken' 83 *Kritische Vierteljahresschrift für Gesetzgebung und Rechtswissenschaften* 388–404.
—— (2003) 'Expertise as Social Institution: Internalising Third Parties into the Contract' in D Campbell, H Collins and J Wightman (eds), *Implicit Dimensions of Contract. Discrete, Relational, and Network Contracts* (Oxford, Hart Publishing) 333–63.
—— (2006a) 'Coincidentia oppositorium: Hybrid Networks beyond Contract and Organization' in M Amstutz and G Teubner (eds), *Networks: Legal Issues of Multilateral Cooperation* (Oxford, Hart Publishing) 3–30.
—— (2006b) 'Dealing with Paradoxes of Law: Derrida, Luhmann, Wiethoelter' in O Perez and G Teubner (eds), *On Paradoxes and Inconsistencies in Law* (Oxford, Hart Publishing) 41–64.
—— (2008) 'State Policies in Private Law? A Comment on Hanoch Dagan' 56 *American Journal of Comparative Law* 835–44.
—— (2009) 'The Corporate Codes of Multinationals: Company Constitutions Beyond Corporate Governance and Co-determintion' in R Nickel (ed), *Conflict of Laws and Laws of Conflict in Europe and Beyond: Patterns of Supranational and Transnational Juridification* (Oslo, Arena Report Series) 261–76.
—— (2011) 'Self-constitutionalizing Transnational Corporations? On the Linkage of "Private" and "Public" Corporate Codes of Conduct' 18 *Indiana Journal of Global Legal Studies* 17–38.
—— (2012) *Constitutional Fragments: Societal Constitutionalism in the Globalization* (Oxford, Oxford University Press).
—— (2014) 'Law and Social Theory: Three Problems' *Ancilla Juris* 182–221.
Teubner, G and Beckers, A (2013a) 'Expanding Constitutionalism' 20 *Indiana Journal of Global Legal Studies* 523–50.
—— (eds) (2013b) 'Transnational Societal Constitutionalism' 20 *Indiana Journal of Global Legal Studies* 521–1060.
Teubner, G and Collins, H (2011) *Networks as Connected Contracts. With an Introduction by Hugh Collins* (Oxford, Hart Publishing).
Thornhill, C (2000) *Political Theory in Modern Germany* (Cambridge, Polity Press).
Tjon Soei Len, LKL (2013) *The Effects of Contracts beyond Frontiers: A Capabilities Perspective on Externalities and Contract Law in Europe* (Amsterdam, Proefschrift Universiteit van Amsterdam).
Toftoy, R (1998) 'Now Playing: Corporate Codes in the Global Theater. Is Nike Just Doing it?' 15 *Arizona Journal of International and Comparative Law* 905–29.
Torrance, M (2011) 'Persuasive Authority beyond the State: A Theoretical Analysis of Transnational Corporate Social Responsibility Norms as Legal Reasons within Positive Legal Systems' 12 *German Law Journal* 1573–636.
Tuori, K (2002) *Critical Legal Positivism* (Aldershot, Ashgate).
—— (2006) 'Self-Description and External Description of the Law' 2 *NoFo—No Foundations: An Interdisciplinary Journal of Law and Justice* 27–43.
Ulmer, P (2002a) 'Aktienrecht im Wandel'202 *Archiv für die civilistische Praxis* 143–78.
—— (2002b) 'Der Deutsche Corporate Governance Kodex—ein neues Regulierungsinstrument für börsennotierte Aktiengesellschaften' 166 *Zeitschrift für das gesamte Handelsrecht und Wirtschaftsrecht* 150–81.

Verbruggen, P (2014a) *Enforcing Transnational Private Regulation: A Comparative Analysis of Advertising and Food Safety* (Cheltenham, Edward Elgar).
—— (2014b) 'Regulatory Governance by Contract: The Rise of Regulatory Standards in Commercial Contracts' 35 *Recht der Werkelijkheid. Special Issue Contextualizing regulatory governance* 79–100.
Vesting, T (2007) *Rechtstheorie* (Frankfurt am Main, C.H. Beck).
Vogel, D (2005) *The Market for Virtue* (Washington DC, The Brookings Institution).
Vogenauer, S (2007) 'Interpretation of Contracts: Concluding Comparative Observations' in A Burrows and E Peel (eds), *Contract Terms* (Oxford, Oxford University Press) 123–50.
Voss, E, Wilke, P, Sobczak, A and Schönmann, I (2008) *Codes of Conduct and International Framework Agreements: New Forms of Governance at Company Level* (Loughlinstown, European Foundation for the Improvement of Living and Working Conditions).
Vytopil, L (2012) 'Contractual Control and Labour-Related CSR Norms in the Supply Chain: Dutch Best Practices' 8 *Utrecht Law Review* 155–69.
Walle, JS van de (2009) 'Doe v. Wal-Mart: Revisiting the Scope of Joint Employment' 30 *Berkeley Journal of Employment and Labor Law* 589–601.
Walton, DN and Krabbe, ECW (1995) *Commitment in Dialogue: Basic Concepts of Interpersonal Reasoning* (Albany, State University of New York Press).
Watterson, S (2001) 'Consumer Sales Directive 1999/44/EC—The Impact on English Law' 10 *European Review of Private Law* 197–221.
Webb, K and Morrison A, (2004) 'The Law and Voluntary Codes: Exploring the "Tangled Web"' in K Webb (ed), *Voluntary Codes, Private Governance, the Public Interest and Innovation* (Ottawa, Carleton University Research Unit for Innovation, Science and the Environment) 97–174.
Weber, M (1968) *Economy and Society: An Outline of Interpretive Sociology*. Edited by Guenther Roth and Claus Wittich (New York, Bedminster Press).
Weinrib, EJ (1995) *The Idea of Private Law* (Cambridge, MA, Harvard University Press, 1995).
—— (2000) 'Restitutionary Damages as Corrective Justice' 1 *Theoretical Inquiries in Law* 1–37.
Weller, M-P (2009) *Die Vertragstreue* (Tübingen, Mohr Siebeck).
Wennberg, K (1966) *Die skandinavische Löftetheorie. Das einseitig verpflichtende Versprechen. Seine Bedeutung für die Lehre von der culpa in contrahendo* (Tübingen, Dissertation gedruckt von PAUL JLLG Stuttgart).
Weschka, M (2006) 'Human Rights and Multinational Enterprises: How Can Multinational Enterprises Be Held Responsible for Human Rights Violations Committed Abroad?' 66 *Zeitschrift für ausländisches öffentliches Recht und Völkerrecht* 625–61.
Westermann, HP (2008) 'Drittinteressen und öffentliches Wohl als Elemente der Bewertung privater Rechtsverhältnisse' 208 *Archiv für die civilistische Praxis* 141–81.
Wheeler, K (2012) *Fair Trade and the Consumer Citizen* (Basingstoke, Palgrave Macmillan).
Wieacker, F (1995) *A History of Private Law in Europe with Particular Reference to Germany* (Oxford, Oxford University Press).
Wielsch, D (2009) 'Iustitia Mediatrix: Zur Methode einer soziologischen Jurisprudenz' in G-P Calliess, A Fischer-Lescano, D Wielsch and P Zumbansen (eds), *Soziologische Jurisprudenz. Festschrift für Gunther Teubner zum 65. Geburtstag* (Berlin, De Gruyter) 395–414.
Wiethölter, R (1968) *Rechtswissenschaft* (Frankfurt am Main, Helbig & Lichtenhahn).
—— (1974) 'Privatrecht als Gesellschaftstheorie?' in F Baur, J Esser, F Kübler and E Steindorff (eds), *Funktionswandel der Privatrechtsinstitutionen. Festschrift für Ludwig Raiser zum 70. Geburtstag* (Tübingen, Mohr Siebeck) 645–95.
—— (2005) 'Just-ifications of a Law of Society' in O Perez and G Teubner (eds), *Paradoxes and Inconsistencies in the Law* (Oxford, Hart Publishing) 65–77.

Wilhelmsson, T (1998) 'Consumer Law and the Environment: From Consumer to Citizen' 21 *Journal of Consumer Policy* 45–70.
—— (2002/2003) 'A Green Sales Law?' 6 *Yearbook of New Zealand Jurisprudence* 83–102.
—— (2004a) 'Contract Law Enforcement of Provisions on Marketing: The Solution of the Consumer Sales Directive' in H Collins (ed), *The Forthcoming EC Directive on Unfair Commercial Practices* (The Hague, Kluwer International) 223–37.
—— (2004b) 'Varieties of Welfarism in European Contract Law' 10 *European Law Journal* 712–33.
—— (2006) 'Scope of the Directive' in G Howells, H Micklitz and T Wilhelmsson (eds), *European Fair Trading Law: The Unfair Commercial Practices Directive* (Aldershot, Ashgate) 49–81.
Williams, C and Aguilera, R (2008) 'Corporate Social Responsibility in a Comparative Perspective' in A Crane, A McWilliams, D Matten, J Moon and DS Siegel (eds), *The Oxford Handbook of Corporate Social Responsibility* (Oxford, Oxford University Press) 452–72.
Williamson, O (1985) *The Economic Institutions of Capitalism* (New York, Free Press Mac Millan Publishers).
Willke, H and Willke, G (2008) 'Corporate Moral Legitimacy and the Legitimacy of Morals: A Critique of Palazzo/Scherer's Communicative Framework' 81 *Journal of Business Ethics* 27–38.
Wittgenstein, L (1968) *Philosophical Investigations*. Translated by GEM Anscombe (Oxford, Basil Blackwell).
Wood, S (2005) 'Three Questions about Corporate Codes: Problematizations, Authorizations, and the Public/Private Divide' in W Cragg (ed), *Ethics Codes, Corporations and the Challenge of Globalization* (Cheltenham, Edward Elgar) 245–89.
World Bank Group (2003) *Company Codes of Conduct and International Standards: An Analytical Comparison*, available at: http://documents.worldbank.org/curated/en/docsearch/report/34662.
Wouters, J and Chanet, L (2008) 'Corporate Human Rights Responsibility: A European Perspective' 6 *Northwestern Journal of International Law and Business* 262–303.
Wunderlich, N-C (2002) 'Die kaufrechtliche Haftung beim asset deal nach dem SchuldRModG' *Wertpapiermitteilungen* 981–90.
Yee, WP (2001) 'Protecting Parties' Reasonable Expectations: A General Principle of Good Faith' 1 *Oxford University Commonwealth Law Journal* 195–229.
Yorio, E and Thel, S (1991) 'The Promissory Basis of s 90' 101 *Yale Law Journal* 111–67.
Zenner, A (2009) 'Der Vertrag mit Schutzwirkung zu Gunsten Dritter—Ein Institut im Lichte seiner Rechtsgrundlage' *Neue Juristische Wochenschrift* 1030–34.
Zerk, J (2006) *Multinationals and Corporate Social Responsibility. Limitations and Opportunities in International Law* (Cambridge, Cambridge University Press).
Zumbansen, P (2007) 'The Law of Society: Governance through Contract' 14 *Indiana Journal of Global Legal Studies* 191–233.
Zweigert, K and Kötz, H (1998) *Introduction to Comparative Law* 3rd edn (Oxford, Clarendon Press).

Cited Commentaries to Laws:
AK-BGB-Author: R Wassermann (ed) (1980/1987), *Kommentar zum Bürgerlichen Gesetzbuch, Reihe Alternativkommentare* 1st edn (Neuwied, Luchterhand).
Erman-Author: HP Westermann, B Grunewald and G Maier-Reimer (eds) (2011) *Erman Bürgerliches Gesetzbuch, Handkommentar* 13th edn (Cologne, Verlag Otto Schmidt).
Fezer-UWG: KH Fezer (ed) (2010), *Lauterkeitsrecht, Kommentar zum Gesetz gegen den unlauteren Wettbewerb* 2nd edn (Munich, C.H. Beck).

Götting/Nordemann-UWG: HP Götting and A Nordemann (eds) (2013) *UWG Handkommentar* 2nd edn (Nomos, Baden-Baden).
Halsbury's Laws: Lord Mackay of Clashfern, E Cooke, A Doobay and M Spurrier (eds), *Halsbury's Laws of England* 5th edn, Vol 47: *Estoppel* (2014) and Vol 91: *Sale of Good and Supply of Services* (2012) (Lexis Library).
Harte-Bavendamm/Henning-Bodewig-UWG: H Harte-Bavendamm and F Henning-Bodewig (eds) (2013) *Gesetz gegen den unlauteren Wettbewerb, Kommentar* 3rd edn (Munich, C.H. Beck).
Köhler/Bornkamm-UWG: H Köhler and J Bornkamm (eds) (2013) *Gesetz gegen den unlauteren Wettbewerb, Kommentar* 31st edn (Munich, C.H. Beck).
MüKo-Author: J Säcker and R Rixecker (eds) (2012/2013) *Münchener Kommentar zum Bürgerlichen Gesetzbuch* 6th edn (Munich, C.H. Beck).
MüKo-AktG-Author: W Goette and M Habersack (eds) (2013) *Münchener Kommentar zum Aktiengesetz* 3rd edn (Munich, C.H. Beck).
MüKo-UWG-Author: P Heermann and G Hirsch (eds) (2006) *Münchener Kommentar zum Lauterkeitsrecht* 1st edn (Munich, C.H. Beck).
Palandt-Author: P Bassenge, G Brudermüller, J Ellenberger (eds) (2014) *Palandt. Bürgerliches Gesetzbuch* 73rd edn (Munich, C.H. Beck).
Prütting/Wegen/Weinrich-Author: H Prütting G Wegen, G Weinrich, Gerd (eds) (2009) *BGB Kommentar* 4th edn (Cologne, Wolters Kluwer/Luchterhand).
Schmidt/Lutter-AktG-Author: K Schmidt and M Lutter (eds) (2010) *Aktiengesetz Kommentar*, 2nd edn (Cologne, Verlag Dr. Otto Schmidt)
Soergel-Author: HT Soergel (ed) (2000-2010) *Bürgerliches Gesetzbuch* 13th edn (Berlin, Verlag Kohlhammer).
Staudinger-Author: J v Staudinger (ed), *Staudingers Kommentar zum Bürgerlichen Gesetzbuch mit Einführungsgesetz und Nebengesetzen, Volumes §§ 134–163 (2003), Einleitung zu §§ 241ff, §§ 255–304 (2009) §§ 433–480 (2014); §§ 657–704 (2009)* (Berlin, Sellier/De Gruyter).

Index

www.ingramcontent.com/pod-product-compliance
Ingram Content Group UK Ltd.
Pitfield, Milton Keynes, MK11 3LW, UK
UKHW051416150926
475561UK00005B/197

9 781509 92007